# STUDY GUIDE

# STUDY GUIDE

to accompany

# Macroeconomics

## in Modules Third Edition

### Krugman | Wells

**Elizabeth Sawyer Kelly**
*University of Wisconsin-Madison*

**WORTH PUBLISHERS**
**Macmillan Education**

**Study Guide**
by Elizabeth Sawyer Kelly
to accompany
**Krugman/Wells: Macroeconomics in Modules, Third Edition**

ISBN 10: 1-4641-4344-7
ISBN 13: 978-1-4641-4344-1

Printed in the United States of America

**Worth Publishers**
41 Madison Avenue
New York, NY 10010
www.wortheconomics.com

# Contents

# Key to Corresponding Modules Numbers

| Module Title | Macroeconomics in Modules | Economics in Modules | Microeconomics in Modules |
|---|---|---|---|
| The Study of Economics | 1 | 1 | 1 |
| The Production Possibility Frontier Model | 2 | 3 | 3 |
| Comparative Advantage and Trade | 3 (modified) | 4 | 4 |
| Demand | 4 | 5 | |
| Supply and Equilibrium | 5 | 6 | |
| Changes in Equilibrium | 6 | 7 | |
| Price Controls and Quantity Controls | 7 | — | |
| International Trade | 8 | — | |
| Introduction to Macroeconomics | 9 | 45 | |
| The Circular-Flow Diagram and the National Accounts | 10 | 46 | |
| Gross Domestic Product (GDP) | 11 | 47 | |
| Interpreting Real Gross Domestic Product | 12 | 48 | |
| Defining Unemployment | 13 | 49 | |
| Categories of Unemployment | 14 | 50 | |
| The Costs of Inflation | 15 | 51 | |
| Measuring Inflation | 16 | 52 | |
| Sources of Long-Run Economic Growth | 17 | 53 | |
| Productivity and Growth | 18 | 54 | |
| Long-Run Growth Policy | 19 | 55 | |
| Savings and Investment Spending | 20 | 56 | |
| The Market for Loanable Funds | 21 | 57 | |
| The Time Value of Money | 22 | 58 | 44 |
| The Financial System | 23 | 59 | |
| The Multiplier | 24 | 60 | |
| Consumption and Investment Spending | 25 | 61 | |
| The Income–Expenditure Model | 26 | 62 | |
| Aggregate Demand | 27 | 63 | |
| Aggregate Supply | 28 | 64 | |

| Module Title | Macroeconomics in Modules | Economics in Modules | Microeconomics in Modules |
|---|---|---|---|
| The AD-AS Model | 29 | 65 | |
| Fiscal Policy Basics | 30 | 66 | |
| Fiscal Policy and the Multiplier | 31 | 67 | |
| Budget Deficits and Public Debt | 32 | 68 | |
| Defining and Measuring Money | 33 | 69 | |
| Banking and Money Creation | 34 | 70 | |
| The Federal Reserve System | 35 | 71 | |
| The Federal Reserve and Monetary Policy | 36 | 72 | |
| The Money Market | 37 | 73 | |
| Monetary Policy and the Interest Rate | 38 | 74 | |
| Money, Output, and Prices in the Long Run | 39 | 75 | |
| Inflation, Disinflation, and Deflation | 40 | 76 | |
| The Phillips Curve | 41 | 77 | |
| Crises and Consequences | 42 | 78 | |
| Capital Flows and the Balance of Payments | 43 | 79 | |
| The Foreign Exchange Market | 44 | 80 | |
| Exchange Rate Policy | 45 | 81 | |
| Exchange Rates and Macroeconomic Policy | 46 | 82 | |
| History and Alternative Views of Macroeconomics | 47 | 83 | |
| The Modern Macroeconomic Consensus | 48 | 84 | |

# Preface

This Study Guide is designed for use with **Macroeconomics in Modules, Third Edition** by Paul Krugman and Robin Wells. It is intended to help you evaluate your understanding of the material covered in the textbook and thereby reinforce the key concepts you need to learn.

For each module, the Study Guide is organized as follows:

*Before You Read the Module*
- Summary: an opening paragraph that provides a brief overview of the module.
- Objectives: a numbered list outlining and describing the material that you should have learned in the module. These objectives can be easily used as a study tool.
- Key Terms: a list of bold key terms with their definitions. This section includes room for note-taking.

*After You Read the Module*
- Tips: a numbered list of learning tips with graphical analysis.
- Worked Problems: a set of worked-out problems that take the student step-by-step through a particular problem/exercise.
- Problems and Exercises: a set of comprehensive problems.

*Before You Take the Test*
- Module Review Questions: a set of multiple-choice questions that focus on the key concepts from the text that you should grasp after reading the module. These questions are designed for quick exam preparation.

*Answer Key*
- Answers to Problems and Exercises: detailed solutions to the Problems and Exercises in the Study Guide.
- Answers to Module Review Questions: solutions to the multiple-choice questions in the Study Guide—along with thorough explanations.

Answers as well as explanatory solutions can be found at the end of each module. Students often use an answer section to simply check if they have gotten the "right" answer. I caution you to use the answer section accompanying each module with an eye to getting the highest possible value from the exercises provided. In economics, the reasoning used in coming to conclusions and correctly modeling the problems are as important as coming to an accurate answer. Explanations for each problem have been provided in order for you to check that your understanding of the concepts has been appropriately applied.

The study of economics has the potential of altering the way you evaluate and understand the world. I hope that your use of this guide will help you in your study of basic microeconomics principles and will provide a jumping-off point for further study in the economics field.

Elizabeth Sawyer Kelly

# STUDY GUIDE

# The Study of Economics

## Summary

This module introduces and discusses the concepts of scarcity, choice, opportunity cost, positive and normative economics, and the distinction between microeconomics and macroeconomics. The module also discusses agreement as well as disagreement among economists.

## Module Objectives

This module introduces a set of principles that will guide your study of economics.

**Objective #1.**  Resources—land, labor, physical capital, and human capital—are scarce, so individuals as well as societies must make choices about how to use these resources.

**Objective #2.**  A market economy determines both production and consumption decisions for an economy through the decentralized decisions that are made by individual producers and consumers.

**Objective #3.**  Societies must make decisions about how to allocate their scarce resources. These resource allocation decisions are sometimes the result of many individual choices but sometimes they are the result of decisions made at a higher, community-wide level.

**Objective #4.**  The opportunity cost, or the real cost of something, is what you must give up to get it.

**Objective #5.**  Microeconomics studies the choices that are made by individuals, households, or firms while macroeconomics studies the overall performance of the economy.

**Objective #6.** Macroeconomics focuses on the aggregate economy, or the economy as a whole. Macroeconomics considers how individual and firm behavior in the aggregate interact to produce a particular level of economic performance in the economy. Central topics in macroeconomics include the determination of the overall level of output, the overall level of prices, and the overall level of employment in the economy.

**Objective #7.** Positive economics is factual and descriptive, whereas normative economics is about what ought to be or what should be. Positive economics is objective and can be tested for accuracy, and often involves forecasting. Normative economics is subjective and prescriptive, and it is value based. However, it is possible to rank normative policies designed to achieve a certain prescription on the basis of the efficiency of each policy.

**Objective #8.** Economists may come to different conclusions because they have different values or because they use different economic models.

## Key Terms

**economics** the study of scarcity and choice.

**individual choice** the decision by an individual of what to do, which necessarily involves a decision of what not to do.

**economy** a system for coordinating a society's productive and consumptive activities.

**market economy** an *economy* in which decisions of individual producers and consumers largely determine what, how, and for whom to produce, with little government involvement in the decisions.

**resource** anything, such as land, labor, and capital, that can be used to produce something else; includes natural resources (from the physical environment) and human resources (labor, skill, intelligence).

**land** all resources that come from nature, such as minerals, timber, and petroleum.

**labor** the effort of workers.

**physical capital** manufactured goods used to make other goods and services.

**human capital** the educational achievements and skills of the labor force, which enhance its productivity.

**scarce** in short supply; a *resource* is scarce when there is not enough of the resources available to satisfy all the various ways a society wants to use them.

**opportunity cost** the real cost of an item: what you must give up in order to get it.

**microeconomics** the branch of *economics* that studies how people make decisions and how those decisions interact.

**macroeconomics** the branch of *economics* that is concerned with the overall ups and downs in the *economy*.

*Notes*

## Key Terms *(continued)*

**economic aggregates** economic measures that summarize data across different markets for goods, services, workers, and assets.

**positive economics** the branch of economic analysis that describes the way the *economy* actually works.

**normative economics** the branch of economic analysis that makes prescriptions about the way the *economy* should work.

## AFTER YOU READ THE MODULE

# Tips

**Tip #1.** The study of economics is cumulative. You should master each topic as it is presented since later topics build on earlier topics.

**Tip #2.** Pay attention to new vocabulary and make sure you know, understand, and can apply these terms. Your instructor will expect you to do more than just define the terms: you must also be able to indicate through your work an ability to apply these terms in a meaningful manner.

**Tip #3.** Plan to spend time every day studying economics. Review your lecture notes, review the vocabulary, work on the practice questions, and identify what questions you have about the material. Once you formulate your questions, seek out answers by returning to your text, your lecture notes, your classmates, or your professor.

**Tip #4.** Think about the topics that might be on an exam and the kinds of questions that might be asked about these topics—questions that are strictly definitional, questions that apply the definitions in a problem-solving setting, and questions that force you to really think about the material and apply your knowledge. Most college-level exams include questions designed to make you think about the material.

**Tip #5.** Studying economics requires learning both new vocabulary and a new way of thinking. You will need to familiarize yourself with this information and vocabulary. You may find it helpful to make a set of flash cards for all the vocabulary you learn while studying economics. For each flash card you will find it helpful to write the term on one side of the card and its definition on the other side of the card. You might also find it helpful to identify on the first side of the card the module number where the term is first introduced. After you make a set of flash cards for the module, review these flash cards until you are thoroughly familiar and comfortable with each term.

**Tip #6.** Macroeconomics focuses on the economic behavior of the overall economy, while microeconomics focuses on the economic behavior of individuals, firms, and specific markets. Macroeconomics studies topics like the determination of the aggregate level of output, the aggregate price level, the level of employment, short-run economic fluctuations, and long-run economic growth. Microeconomics considers topics like supply and demand in particular markets, profit maximization by firms, and utility maximization by individuals.

# WORKED PROBLEMS

1. This module defines and describes four types of resources: land, labor, physical capital, and human capital. For each of the following items identify the type of resource and explain why you chose this answer.

   a. Frank is an experienced heart surgeon.

   b. Mary works at an assembly line job that does not require any particular training or educational background.

   c. A large moving truck is used to haul people's furniture across country.

   d. A machine molds plastic into car doors.

   e. A coal seam is still in the ground.

   f. Water flows in a river.

   **STEP 1:** Start by reviewing the four types of resources and their definitions.

   There are four types of resources: land, labor, physical capital, and human capital. Land includes all resources that come from nature, such as minerals, timber, and petroleum. Labor is the effort of workers. Physical capital is manufactured goods used to make other goods and services. Human capital is the educational achievements and skills of the labor force, which enhance its productivity.

   **STEP 2:** Classify each of the examples as one of the four types of resources, and explain why you chose this classification.

   a. Frank is a worker, but he also possesses a high degree of training and education that is required for this work. This is an example of human capital.

   b. Mary is a worker, but the work she does on the assembly line does not require any special training or education: this is labor.

   c. A moving truck is physical capital, since it is a manufactured good that is used to provide moving services.

   d. The machine that molds plastic into car doors is physical capital, since it is used to provide another good: car doors.

   e. The coal seam in the ground is a land resource, since coal comes from nature.

   f. Water in a river is a land resource.

2. For each of the following scenarios identify the opportunity costs of the decision.

   a. Mary needs to study for her economics exam tonight, but she is also considering going to the band concert this evening. The band concert will last for two hours and requires her to purchase a ticket for $10. What is Mary's opportunity cost of going to the band concert?

   b. Joe is considering studying in Mexico next semester rather than attending the university where he is enrolled. The cost of studying abroad is equal to his current tuition payment plus $1,000. His room and board would cost the same with either choice. What is Joe's opportunity cost of studying abroad?

   c. Chen is debating going to the hockey game Friday night or joining a group of friends to see a movie. The hockey game will last three hours and cost $15, while the movie will last three hours and cost $5. What is Chen's opportunity cost of going to the hockey game?

**STEP 1:** Review the concept of opportunity cost.

The opportunity cost of an item is what you must give up to get that item. So for each of the scenarios it will be important to figure out what the individual must give up when choosing a particular activity.

**STEP 2:** For each scenario, identify the opportunity costs of the choices that are being considered.

a. The opportunity cost to Mary of attending the band concert includes the two hours of studying for economics that she must give up as well as the $10 she must pay for the ticket to attend the concert. If she did not attend the concert, she would be able to spend this $10 on some other item or activity.

b. The opportunity cost to Joe of studying abroad includes the extra $1,000 he must pay for this experience. The opportunity cost of studying abroad would not include his regular tuition or his fees for room and board, since no matter where he chooses to study (at home or abroad) he would have these costs. However, if the question had included the possibility that Joe might choose to work (or travel, for example) rather than attend college, then his opportunity costs of studying abroad would have included the $1,000 plus his tuition, since he is choosing between studying and doing something else that does not include enrollment at an institution. No matter what Joe's choices are, the room and board are not a part of his opportunity costs, since he will have living costs no matter what he chooses to do.

c. The opportunity cost to Chen of attending the hockey game includes the $10 difference between the price of the ticket to the hockey game and the cost of the movie. The opportunity cost also includes the movie that she will not be able to see because of this choice.

# Problems and Exercises

1. For each of the following situations describe the opportunity costs of each decision.

   a. Sarah considers two options for Saturday night: she can attend a concert that costs $10 per ticket or she can go to the free movie offered at the student union. She decides to attend the concert.

   b. A new business in town debates paying $20,000 for a prime location versus $10,000 for a less perfect location. The business estimates that it will eventually serve the same number of customers in either location, but that it will take 6 months before the suboptimal location provides the same outcome as the prime location. The business decides to purchase the $10,000 property.

**c.** Jamie is given a choice for his next holiday from school: he can be an unpaid intern at a company or he can earn $2,000 working as a camp counselor. He decides to take the internship.

**d.** Roberto is studying for two midterms this week. He figures he has 20 available hours to study for both midterms. If he studies all 20 hours for the economics exam he will undoubtedly get an A on the exam, but he will at best earn a C on his organic chemistry test. If he studies all 20 hours for the organic chemistry test he will get an A on the organic chemistry exam, but he will likely earn a D on his economics test. Roberto decides to devote all of his available time to economics since he has determined that he does not wish to pursue a premed major.

**2.** The following table presents the possible combinations of study time available to Roberto this week as he prepares for his two midterms (one in economics and the other in organic chemistry). Assume Roberto has 20 hours available to study and that he will use all 20 hours studying economics and chemistry.

| Hours of study time spent on economics | Hours of study time spent on organic chemistry | Grade in economics | Grade in organic chemistry |
|---|---|---|---|
| 0 | 20 | 60 | 90 |
| 5 | 15 | 70 | 85 |
| 10 | 10 | 80 | 75 |
| 15 | 5 | 86 | 73 |
| 20 | 0 | 90 | 70 |

Roberto currently plans to study 10 hours for economics and 10 hours for organic chemistry.

**a.** If he alters his plan and studies 15 hours for economics, what is the opportunity cost of that decision?

**b.** If he alters his plan and studies 15 hours for organic chemistry, what is the opportunity cost of that decision?

**c.** If he alters his plan and studies 20 hours for economics, what is the opportunity cost of that decision?

    **d.** If he alters his plan and studies 20 hours for organic chemistry, what is the opportunity cost of that decision?

**3.** Decide whether each of the following statements is a normative statement or a positive statement, then explain your answer.

    **a.** The gasoline tax is projected to yield $10 million in tax revenue next year.

    **b.** If the gasoline tax was raised by 10 cents per gallon, the tax revenue from this tax would increase by 4%.

    **c.** The state should raise the gasoline tax for the coming year. An increase in the tax will reduce congestion and smog, which is more important than the cost to commuters if they shift from private car transportation to public transportation.

    **d.** Mandatory school enhances the work skills of students.

    **e.** The age of mandatory school attendance should be extended, since this will provide greater benefits to our economy.

    **f.** An extension of mandatory school attendance will increase government education costs by $2 million for the state.

4. Economists sometimes disagree about positive economics, but more often they disagree about normative economics. Briefly define both of these terms and then explain why economists do not always agree.

5. For each of the following questions identify whether the question is more appropriate for the study of microeconomics or macroeconomics, and why.

   a. What will happen to the wages in our community if corporation X, an employer of 1,000 people (that's 40% of our workforce), decides to relocate its plant to a different state?

   b. What will happen to the level of overall economic production in our economy if the federal government continues to run record levels of government deficit?

   c. If the government engages in monetary policy and increases the money supply, what will happen to the interest rate in our economy?

   d. How has the recent increase in the price of a barrel of oil affected the prices of bicycles, cars, and airplane fares?

   e. What will the effect of recent tropical storms be on the price of bananas?

## BEFORE YOU TAKE THE TEST

## Module Review Questions

1. Camillo is offered two jobs: one pays a salary of $30,000 per year and offers four weeks of vacation, and the other job pays a salary of $32,000 per year and offers two weeks of vacation. What is the opportunity cost for Camillo of taking the job offering $32,000 per year?

   a. $2,000 plus two weeks of vacation per year
   b. $2,000 per year
   c. two weeks of vacation per year
   d. $30,000 plus two weeks of vacation per year

2. Ning decides to attend a special speaker presentation tonight at her college instead of staying in her dorm and listening to her music collection. Which of the following statements is true?

   a. Ning faces no opportunity cost with regard to her decision since listening to music or attending the speaker are both free events.

   b. The opportunity cost of Ning's decision is so small that it is not worth calculating.

   c. The opportunity cost of Ning's decision is the loss of her evening of music listening.

   d. The opportunity cost of Ning's decision includes the cost associated with hearing the speaker.

3. Scarcity of resources implies that

   a. people can do whatever they want and do not need to worry about making choices.

   b. life involves making choices about how to best use these scarce resources.

   c. societies need to invest time and money to discover more resources.

   d. only very wealthy individuals are not constrained by their resources.

4. Each day people make decisions about what to wear, what to eat, or where to work,

   a. since they all face constraints that mean they cannot do everything they would like to do.

   b. without regard to the level of resources that are available to them.

5. The university in Smart, USA, has a parking problem and is looking into programs to alleviate the parking shortage. Which of the following ideas is likely to decrease the number of cars parking on campus each day by the greatest amount?

   a. Faculty and staff at the university all receive free parking permits.

   b. Faculty and staff at the university all pay a set fee per year for parking permits.

   c. Faculty and staff at the university must pay an hourly fee for each hour that they park on campus.

   d. Faculty and staff are exempt from any parking policies at the university since they need to be able to come to campus to do their jobs.

6. Salespeople working at Department Store of Suburbia are offered two compensation plans. Plan A pays the worker $4 per hour plus a 5% sales commission on the total dollar value of sales that this worker makes. Plan B pays the worker $6 per hour and does not include a sales commission. Total sales per hour per salesperson averages $100. Which of the following statements is true?

   a. Plan A will result in the salespeople being less helpful to customers than does plan B.

   b. Plan A will result in the salespeople being more helpful to customers than does plan B.

7. Which of the following statements is true about positive economics?

   I. Positive economics is about how the world should work.

   II. Positive economics is about how the world works.

   III. Positive economics is descriptive.

   a. Statements I, II, and III are all true.

   b. Statements I and III are true.

   c. Statements II and III are true.

   d. Statement II is true.

**8.** Which of the following statements is an example of normative economics?

   I. The United States should pass a value-added tax, since this is a tax that will work best for the country.

   II. A value-added tax will add $10 billion to the administrative costs of the U.S. tax system.

   III. A value-added tax will increase the economic burden of taxes on poor people by 15%.

   a. Statements I, II, and III are all examples of normative economics.
   b. Statements I and III are examples of normative economics.
   c. Statements I and II are examples of normative economics.
   d. Statement I is an example of normative economics.

**9.** Macroeconomics, unlike microeconomics,

   a. considers the behavior of individual firms and markets.
   b. focuses on the production and consumption of particular goods.
   c. tries to explain increases in living standards over time.
   d. finds that the behavior of individuals is more important in determining economic activity than is the aggregate summation of this behavior.

**10.** Macroeconomics

   a. focuses on how the behavior of individuals and firms in the aggregate economy interact to produce a market price for each good and service offered in the economy.
   b. focuses on how the actions of individuals and firms in the economy interact to produce a particular economy-wide level of economic performance.
   c. considers how specific markets for goods and services determine their equilibrium prices and quantities.
   d. Answers (a), (b), and (c) are all correct.

## ANSWER KEY

# Answers to Problems and Exercises

1.  **a.** Sarah's decision to attend the concert has two opportunity costs: attending the concert means that she will be unable to attend the movie, and in addition, to attend the concert she must pay $10 for a ticket. Her decision to attend the concert means that she is giving up whatever she could have purchased with the $10.

    **b.** The business gives up $10,000 to get the property, but this is not an opportunity cost since the business must have a business location to exist. However, there is an opportunity cost to this decision: the business gives up the additional business it would have gotten at the prime location during the first six months.

    **c.** When he decides to take the internship, Jamie incurs an opportunity cost of $2,000, since he is giving up this income to work in the intern position.

    **d.** Roberto's opportunity cost with regard to his studying is his diminished grade in organic chemistry. (Obviously Roberto might want to consider some combination of studying that allows him to prepare for both exams, but this question did not offer that possibility.)

2.  Remember that opportunity cost measures what is given up, so when Roberto studies more for his economics exam, he is giving up time he could devote to his organic chemistry exam. This decision will therefore affect his organic chemistry grade. Similarly, if Roberto devotes more time to studying for his organic chemistry exam, then he will be giving up points on his economics exam.

    **a.** The opportunity cost of studying 15 hours for the economics exam instead of 10 hours is two points on the organic chemistry exam.

    **b.** The opportunity cost of studying 15 hours for the organic chemistry exam instead of 10 hours is ten points on the economics exam.

    **c.** The opportunity cost of studying 20 hours for the economics exam instead of 10 hours is five points on the organic chemistry exam.

    **d.** The opportunity cost of studying 20 hours for the organic chemistry exam instead of 10 hours is twenty points on the economics exam.

3.  **a.** Positive: this statement is a forecast of the tax revenue from the gasoline tax. It is verifiable and hence positive.

    **b.** Positive: this is also a forecast, and although it may be wrong, it can be verified through the data once the data are available.

    **c.** Normative: this is a value statement that reflects one person's viewpoint of the way the world should work. It is not refutable since it reflects a person's opinion and not a set of facts.

    **d.** Positive: this statement can be tested for its accuracy.

    **e.** Normative: this statement reflects the opinions of the speaker.

    **f.** Positive: this is a forecast.

4.  Positive economics is descriptive, whereas normative economics is prescriptive—that is, positive economics is objective and expresses how the world works, while normative economics is subjective and expresses how the world should work. Economists may differ because of positive economics: they may use different models with different assumptions

that lead to different conclusions. Economists may also disagree over normative economics: economists may not share the same values and will therefore reach different conclusions about how the world should work. Economists can evaluate alternative policies in terms of their efficiency at reaching stated goals.

5.   **a.** Microeconomics: this question is directed at understanding the local effect of this corporation's move instead of its total effect across the aggregate economy.

**b.** Macroeconomics: this question focuses on the aggregate performance of the economy.

**c.** Macroeconomics: this question considers the impact of monetary policy on the aggregate economy.

**d.** Microeconomics: this question addresses the effect of a change in the price of a barrel of oil on specific markets like the market for bicycles or cars.

**e.** Microeconomics: this question considers the price of a specific good rather than the overall price level in the economy.

## Answers to Module Review Questions

1.   **Answer c.** The opportunity cost of taking the job includes what must be given up. In this case, Camillo is giving up two weeks of vacation since the other job offers four weeks of vacation instead of two weeks. He is not giving up any salary when he selects the job paying $32,000.

2.   **Answer c.** Ning's opportunity cost is measured by what she must give up when she chooses to do something else. In this case, when Ning decides to attend the lecture she is giving up a night of listening to music in her dorm room.

3.   **Answer b.** When resources are scarce, this implies that people and societies must make decisions about how to use those scarce resources since the scarcity of resources is a constraint on production and consumption.

4.   **Answer a.** People must make decisions every day because they do not have an infinite amount of time, income, or resources that would allow them to do everything they might want to do.

5.   **Answer c.** To get the university community to curtail their parking on campus by the greatest amount, the university should adopt a program that makes drivers aware of the cost of bringing a car on campus every time they drive on campus. Thus, charging an hourly parking fee is the best choice offered, since this fee will serve to remind drivers that it will cost them something each time they drive on campus and park. In contrast, a single annual fee does not reward the purchaser for reducing the number of times they park on campus during the year; free parking indicates that parking on campus does not cost anything and will result in people parking on campus more often; and exempting the staff from parking fees eliminates incentives to get staff to think about alternatives to driving on campus and parking.

6.   **Answer b.** When salespeople are awarded the base salary plus a commission, they are encouraged to be helpful to shoppers in the hope of boosting their sales figures. When offered a flat hourly rate, they have no incentive to provide helpful service beyond the minimum required by the store, since their compensation will not be impacted by their extra effort.

7.   **Answer c.** Positive economics is objective, factual, and can be subject to proof. In contrast, normative economics is subjective and expresses what ought to happen or what should happen. Statements II and III are both statements that describe positive economics, since positive economics describes and analyzes how the world works.

8. **Answer d.** Normative economics is subjective and value oriented. Both statements II and III are positive statements that can be evaluated as to their factual accuracy. Statement I is a normative statement since it expresses someone's subjective opinion and therefore cannot be proven true or false.

9. **Answer c.** Macroeconomics studies the aggregate economy, not individual action; in studying the aggregate economy, macroeconomics seeks to explain the factors that determine a country's standard of living. In macroeconomics we are reminded that the aggregation of individual behavior often has a larger impact than just the sum of these individual behaviors.

10. **Answer b.** Macroeconomics is focused on the aggregate economy and its overall performance. Microeconomics focuses on specific markets and how the behavior of firms and individuals interact to determine the prices in those markets as well as the quantities in those markets.

# module **2**

# The Production Possibility Frontier Model

## Summary

This module develops a simple model of the production possibility frontier in order to more fully examine the idea of trade-offs. The module uses this model to explore the concepts of efficiency, opportunity cost, and economic growth. The module discusses two sources of economic growth: increases in the amount of resources available and improvements in technology.

## Module Objectives

**Objective #1.**   The production possibility frontier is a model that represents the production possibilities available to an individual or to an economy. The production possibility frontier model assumes that the individual (or country) has a set amount of resources, a set level of technology, and a set amount of time. Then the production possibility frontier delineates a set of points that indicates the maximum amount of two goods that can be produced by this individual (or country) given their resources, technology, and available time. For simplicity, this Study Guide refers to production possibility frontiers in terms of production by countries rather than individuals, but the arguments made from the perspective of countries also hold for individuals. Figure 2.1 illustrates a linear production possibility frontier for a country, where the frontier indicates the maximum amount of goods X and Y that can be produced from the available resources and technology. Points A and B are points that lie on the production possibility frontier and are feasible production points for this country. Points C and D are points that lie inside the production possibility frontier: this country can produce these points—they are feasible—but the country is not using its available resources fully. Points C and D are therefore feasible points, but not efficient points. Points E and F lie outside the production possibility frontier and are therefore not feasible points of production for this country.

14

**Figure 2.1**

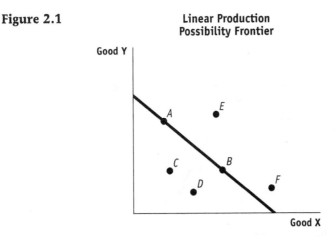

**Objective #2.**  The simplest version of this production possibility frontier model assumes that the frontier is linear and thus has a constant slope. This implies that the opportunity cost of producing another unit of the good measured on the x-axis stays the same as you move along the production possibility frontier. In Figure 2.2 the opportunity cost of moving from point A to point B and the opportunity cost of moving from point C to point D are illustrated. Remember that opportunity cost measures what you give up to get something: thus, when moving from point A to point B, opportunity cost is measured in terms of good Y, the good you give up to get more of good X; whereas, when moving from point C to point D, opportunity cost is measured in terms of good X, the good you give up to get more of good Y. The lines that are bold in Figure 2.2 indicate the opportunity cost of moving from point A to point B or from point C to point D.

**Figure 2.2**

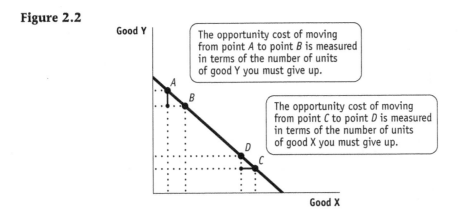

**Objective #3.**  A more realistic production possibility frontier is one that is bowed out from the origin: this implies that as the country produces more and more of one of the goods, the opportunity cost of producing this good increases. The production possibility frontier has this shape due to specialization of resources: some of the resources available to the country are more suited to produce good X than they are good Y. When the country decides to increase the production of one type of good, the first few units can be produced at relatively low opportunity cost since resources can be shifted from the production of one good to the production of the other good that are not particularly well suited to the production of the first good. However, the opportunity cost eventually will rise since the increased production of this good eventually will require the use of resources that are ill-suited to produce this good. Figure 2.3 illustrates a bowed-out production possibility frontier and the opportunity cost of getting one more unit of the good measured on the x-axis. Notice that as we get more and more units of good X, the opportunity cost of each additional unit of X is larger than the opportunity cost of the preceding unit.

**Figure 2.3**

**Objective #4.** There are two types of efficiency to discuss with respect to production possibility frontiers: productive efficiency and allocative efficiency. Productive efficiency refers to producing at a point that lies on the production possibility frontier. Points that lie inside the frontier are inefficient, since it is possible to increase the level of production from the given set of resources. Allocative efficiency refers to producing the right mix of goods from the available resources. For an economy to be allocatively efficient it must allocate its resources in such a way as to make consumers as well off as possible. Another way of saying this is that an allocatively efficient economy produces the mix of goods that people want.

**Objective #5.** For an economy to be efficient it must achieve productive and allocative efficiency: it must not waste resources and it must produce the right mix of goods.

**Objective #6.** The production possibility frontier illustrates scarcity in that there are points of production that cannot be produced because the level of resources and/or technology constrain production. The production possibility frontier illustrates trade-offs: getting more of good X requires giving up some of good Y.

**Objective #7.** Economic growth can be illustrated with the production possibility frontier model. When the frontier shifts away from the origin, this means that the represented economy can now produce more of good X and good Y. The production possibility frontier shifts out when there are increases in resources or increases in the available level of technology.

# Key Terms

**trade-off** when you give up something in order to have something else.

**production possibility frontier** illustrates the trade-offs facing an economy that produces only two goods. It shows the maximum quantity of one good that can be produced for any given quantity produced of the other.

**efficient** describes a market or economy that takes all opportunities to make some people better off without making other people worse off.

**factors of production** resources used to produce goods and services.

**technology** the technical means for producing goods and services.

*Notes*

## AFTER YOU READ THE MODULE

## Tips

**Tip #1.** Economic models can be described verbally, but they can also be represented by graphs or equations. You will want to be comfortable working with all three types of representations.

**Tip #2.** Throughout the course you will find it helpful to be able to sketch graphs to illustrate the ideas you are analyzing. You should practice making precise, numerically significant graphs, but you also should practice less formal graphs that sketch the nature of the relationship rather than the precise mathematical relationship.

**Tip #3.** Opportunity cost can be measured using the production possibility frontier model. To do this calculation pick a point on the production possibility frontier and identify how much of each good is being produced. Then pick a second point on the production possibility frontier and identify the new levels of production. The opportunity cost is measured as the number of units of the good you must give up to get more of the other good. Note that both points must be on the production possibility frontier. Figure 2.4 illustrates the measurement of opportunity cost when moving from point $A$ to point $B$. In this example, the opportunity cost is measured as the amount of good Y, $Y_1 - Y_2$, that must be given up to increase the production of good X from its initial value of $X_1$ to the new level $X_2$. The bold line indicates the amount of good Y that is given up to increase the production of good X from $X_1$ to $X_2$.

**Figure 2.4**

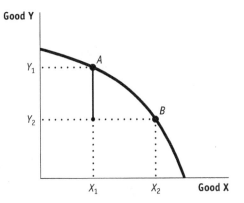

**Tip #4.** If you are using flash cards, make sure you include the following cards: (a) a linear production possibility frontier indicating feasible and infeasible points as well as efficient and inefficient points, and (b) a production possibility frontier bowed out from the origin showing these same concepts. Also, don't forget to include a card for each new vocabulary word as well as the module heading on each card.

**Tip #5.** Calculating opportunity cost in a problem is often challenging for students initially. Let's explore a fail-safe method for this calculation based on a linear production possibility frontier (this is the type of production possibility frontier that we will use in the comparative advantage model). First, construct the production possibility frontier and, since it is linear, calculate the slope of the frontier. Then use this slope measure to generate the opportunity costs you want: the opportunity cost of producing one more unit of the good measured on the x-axis is given by the slope, since the slope tells us the change in the y-variable divided by the change in the x-variable. Thus, if the slope of the production possibility frontier is −2, then the opportunity cost of producing an additional unit of good X is 2 units of good Y. To find the opportunity cost of the good produced on the y-axis, we simply need to use the reciprocal of the slope. Thus, if the slope of the linear production possibility frontier is −2, then the opportunity cost of producing one more unit of good Y is ½ unit of good X, since this is the amount of good X we must give up to get one more unit of good Y. The problems in this module will give you a chance to practice this reasoning and this technique.

# WORKED PROBLEMS

1.  People often face trade-offs about the use of their resources. In this problem, Joe can produce either bicycles or sweaters. The following points lie on Joe's production possibility frontier and represent points where Joe is maximizing his production of the two goods given his available resources, technology, and time. Assume that Joe's production possibility frontier for these two goods is linear.

| Production point | Bicycles per year | Sweaters per year |
|:---:|:---:|:---:|
| A | 160 | 20 |
| B | 120 | 40 |
| C | 60 | 70 |
| D | 40 | 80 |

a.  Draw a graph of Joe's production possibility frontier. In your graph measure bicycles on the y-axis and sweaters on the x-axis.

**STEP 1:** Draw a graph of Joe's production possibility frontier using the given points in the table. The following figure provides a graph of the Joe's production possibility frontier based upon the points given in the provided table.

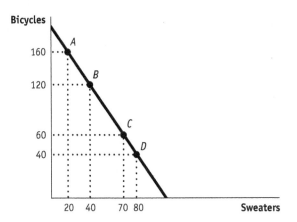

**b.** Write an equation for Joe's production possibility frontier.

**STEP 2:** Use the slope-intercept form to write an equation for Joe's production possibility frontier. The slope-intercept form is given as $y = mx + b$, where $y$ is the variable measured on the vertical axis (in this case bicycles, $B$), $x$ is the variable measured on the horizontal axis (in this case sweaters, $S$), $m$ is the slope of the equation, and $b$ is the $y$-intercept.

To write the equation for Joe's production possibility frontier, you will need to know the slope of the frontier as well as the $y$-intercept for the frontier. Since the frontier is linear, the slope will be constant and equal to the change in the bicycles divided by the change in sweaters. Thus, moving from point $A$ to point $B$, the slope is equal to $(160 - 120)/(20 - 40) = -2$. To find the $y$-intercept, you can use the general formula for a linear equation, $y = mx + b$, and substitute in the slope measure you just computed for $m$, and replace the $y$ and $x$ with $B$ and $S$ (where $B$ is the number of bicycles and $S$ is the number of sweaters). Thus, $y = mx + b$ is now $B = -2S + b$. To find the $y$-intercept, $b$, you need to replace $(S,B)$ with values that you know are on the line. For example, you know that point $A$ is on the line and that point $A$ consists of 20 sweaters and 160 bicycles. Thus, $B = -2S + b$ can be written as $160 = -2(20) + b$. Solving for $b$, you will find that $b = 200$. You can use any of the points you are given in the table to find this $y$-intercept: the only requirement is that the point must lie on the production possibility frontier. The following figure illustrates Joe's production possibility frontier while identifying both the $y$-intercept and the $x$-intercept (to find the $x$-intercept, use the basic formula $B = -2S + 200$ and substitute $B = 0$ into this equation: thus, $S = 100$).

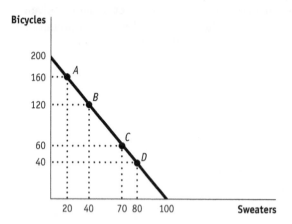

c. Consider each of the following production points and determine whether the production point is (1) feasible and efficient; (2) feasible and inefficient; or (3) infeasible (that is, the point lies beyond the production possibility frontier). Hint: You may find the equation you wrote in part (b) helpful in determining the attributes of these production points.

    **i.** 30 sweaters and 150 bicycles

    **ii.** 15 sweaters and 170 bicycles

    **iii.** 90 sweaters and 15 bicycles

    **iv.** 75 sweaters and 55 bicycles

**STEP 3:** Using the equation for Joe's production possibility frontier you found in part (b), check each of the previously mentioned points to see if they lie on his production possibility frontier, lie beyond his production possibility frontier, or lie inside his production possibility frontier.

**i.** This point is infeasible. To see this, use the equation you found in part (b) and plug in the value for S. Thus, $B = -2S + 200$ and you are told that sweater production is 30. So, $B = -2(30) + 200 = 140$. The maximum number of bicycles that can be produced when 30 sweaters are produced is 140 and not 150. The point (30, 150) lies beyond Joe's production possibility frontier and therefore is not feasible.

**ii.** This point is feasible and efficient. To see this, use the equation from part (b) and this point. Thus, $B = -2(15) + 200 = 170$. The point (15, 170) lies on Joe's production possibility frontier: it is both feasible and efficient.

**iii.** This point is feasible but inefficient. To see this, use the equation from part (b) and this point. Thus, $B = -2(90) + 200 = 20$. The point (90, 15) lies inside Joe's production possibility frontier since the point (90, 20) lies on his frontier. This point is therefore feasible but inefficient.

**iv.** This point is infeasible. To see this, use the equation from part (b) and this point. Thus, $B = -2(75) + 200 = 50$. The point (75, 55) lies outside Joe's production possibility frontier since the point (75, 50) lies on his frontier. This point is therefore not feasible.

d. Suppose that Joe experiences an improvement in his sweater-making technology so that he can now produce twice as many sweaters as he could initially. Assume that his ability to produce bicycles has not changed. Draw this new production possibility frontier for Joe and then write an equation for this new production possibility frontier.

**STEP 4:** Draw Joe's new production possibility frontier and compare it with his original production possibility frontier.

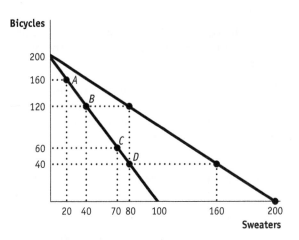

The equation for this new production possibility frontier is $B = -S + 200$.

2.   The following graph depicts Susie's production possibility frontier for producing widgets and gadgets. In this problem assume that Susie is initially producing only widgets and no gadgets.

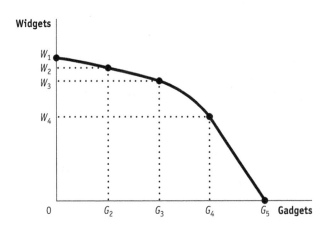

Use this graph to evaluate Susie's opportunity cost of moving from one point of her production possibility frontier to another point on her production possibility frontier.

   **a.** What is Susie's opportunity cost of producing $G_2$ units of gadgets if she is currently producing zero gadgets?

**STEP 1:** For questions (a), (b), and (c), refer to the previous graph and measure Susie's opportunity cost by what she must give up when moving from one point on her production possibility frontier to another point on her production possibility frontier.

The opportunity cost of producing $G_2$ units of gadgets is the number of widgets that must be given up. Initially Susie is producing $W_1$ widgets and 0 gadgets. When Susie moves along her production possibility frontier to produce $G_2$ units of gadgets, she finds that she must decrease her widget production to $W_2$. The opportunity cost of this gadget production is therefore equal to $(W_1 - W_2)$ units of widgets.

**b.** Suppose that Susie is now producing $G_2$ units of gadgets and that she is producing at a point on her production possibility frontier. What is the opportunity cost of producing $G_3$ units of gadgets?

The opportunity cost of producing $G_3$ units of gadgets is the number of widgets that must be given up. Using the same logic as in the answer to part (a), this opportunity cost can be calculated as the distance $(W_2 - W_3)$ since this distance measures the number of widgets that Susie must give up in order to increase her gadget production from $G_2$ units to $G_3$ units.

**c.** Suppose that Susie is now producing $G_3$ units of gadgets and that she is producing at a point on her production possibility frontier. What is the opportunity cost of producing $G_4$ units of gadgets?

The opportunity cost of producing $G_4$ units of gadgets is the number of widgets that must be given up. Using the same logic as in the answer to part (a), this opportunity cost can be calculated as the distance $(W_3 - W_4)$ since this distance measures the number of widgets that Susie must give up in order to increase her gadget production from $G_3$ to $G_4$ units.

**d.** What happens to Susie's opportunity cost of producing gadgets as she decides to produce increasing amounts of gadgets? Provide a verbal explanation and then use the preceding graph to illustrate what happens to Susie's opportunity cost as she produces more and more gadgets.

**STEP 2:** Refer to the graph and use it to see what happens to Susie's opportunity cost as she increases her production of gadgets by one unit at a time starting with zero units of gadgets. Remember that her opportunity cost of producing a gadget is measured by the number of widgets she must give up.

As Susie produces more and more gadgets, her opportunity cost increases. Since her production possibility frontier is bowed outward from the origin, this indicates that Susie's available resources are specialized, with some of those resources being more suited to widget production while others are more suited to gadget production. This idea of increasing opportunity cost is illustrated on the following graph.

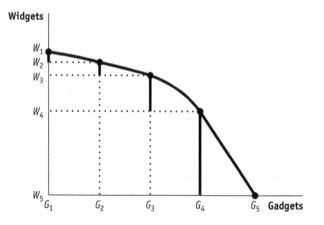

Notice that the bold vertical lines get longer and longer as we move from 0 units of gadgets to a larger level of gadget production (e.g., $G_4$). The length of the bold vertical lines measures the opportunity cost of that level of gadget production: for example, the opportunity cost of moving from 0 units of gadgets to $G_2$ units of gadgets is given by the vertical distance $(W_1 - W_2)$.

 e. Suppose that Susie had initially produced only gadgets and no widgets. Does the opportunity cost of producing widgets increase as Susie increases her widget production by one unit at a time from 0 units of widgets to $W_1$ units of widgets? Use a graph to illustrate your answer.

**STEP 3:** Now, you want to use the graph to think about moving from the point that corresponds to $G_5$ units of gadgets and 0 units of widgets to the point that corresponds to 0 units of gadgets and $W_1$ units of widgets. As you move upward along the curve increasing widget production by one unit at a time, remember that the opportunity cost of this increased widget production will be measured by the number of gadgets that must be given up.

The law of increasing opportunity cost holds if Susie moves from producing only gadgets to producing a mix of gadgets and widgets. The following graph illustrates this idea by considering changing the production of widgets by one unit at a time. Notice that in this case the opportunity cost is measured as a horizontal distance since increasing widget production implies giving up gadget production: thus, the opportunity cost of producing widgets is measured by the number of gadgets that must be given up.

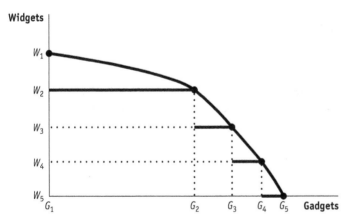

3. All countries face scarcity of resources and must therefore make tough decisions about what they should produce. Consider the following example about the allocation of resources toward health care. Suppose that a kidney transplant costs $50,000, while immunizations against major childhood diseases cost $500 per child. Assume that a country has a total of $10 million available for these two programs and that there is no issue with regard to procuring the necessary kidneys for transplants. Use the provided information to construct the country's production possibility frontier, placing childhood immunizations on the horizontal axis and kidney transplants on the vertical axis. Use your graph to measure the opportunity cost of producing an additional kidney transplant as well as the opportunity cost of producing an additional childhood immunization. Use this example to discuss the trade-offs that an economy faces with regard to the production of these two goods.

**STEP 1:** Use the given information to construct a production possibility frontier for these two goods. Then use this figure to measure the opportunity cost of producing an additional unit of either good.

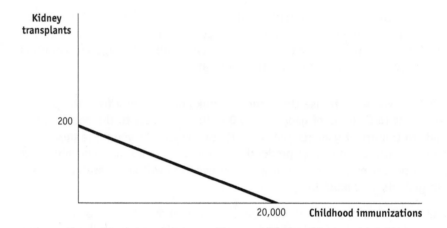

The opportunity cost of a kidney transplant is 100 immunizations. The opportunity cost of an immunization is (1/100) of a kidney transplant.

**STEP 2:** Use this example to discuss the trade-offs an economy faces with regard to the production of these two goods.

If a country is faced with a limited amount of resources, it cannot produce an unlimited amount of goods and services. In this example, the country has only so many financial resources available for the production of kidney transplants and immunizations: the country will have to decide how to allocate these scarce resources, and in allocating these scarce resources it will face a trade-off where the decision to produce more kidney transplants implies a decision to provide fewer immunizations and vice versa.

## Problems and Exercises

1.  The production possibilities frontier model holds resources, technology, and the time period constant in order to construct a path of points that represents the maximum amount of two goods an economy can produce given the constraints of their resources and technology during the given time period. This model allows us to consider the effect of an increase in resources while holding everything else constant. In this example, what is it that we are holding constant? Describe the effect of this change in resources on this economy's production possibility frontier.

2.  Suppose you are stranded on an island by yourself and must therefore produce all the goods you consume. You consume clams and mangos exclusively. If you devote all your available time to harvesting clams, you can harvest 100 clams in a week. If you devote all your available time to collecting mangos, you can find 200 mangos in a week.

  a.  Imagine it is possible for you to divide your time between harvesting clams and collecting mangos and that you can even find fractional amounts of both goods. Draw a sketch of your production possibility frontier for a week, placing mangos on the x-axis and clams on the y-axis.

Clams per week

Mangos per week

  b.  Now, sketch your production possibility frontier for a two-week period. Describe what happens to your production possibility frontier when you increase the amount of time available for production.

Clams per two-week period

Mangos per two-week period

**c.** Now, imagine you invent a clam rake that enhances your ability to harvest clams. With this invention you are able to increase your clam harvest to a maximum of 200 clams per week if you spend all your time on clams. Your invention has no effect on your ability to collect mangos. Sketch your new production possibility frontier. Describe in words the effect of a change in technology that affects the ability to produce one of the goods, but not both of the goods.

**Clams per week**

**Mangos per week**

**d.** Suppose you have your clam rake and, in addition, you procure knowledge over time that enhances your ability to collect mangos. Your ability to gather mangos increases to 300 mangos per week because of this knowledge. Sketch your new production possibility frontier based on this knowledge and your use of the clam rake. In effect you have experienced a change in technology that has a positive effect on the production of both goods. Describe in words the effect of this change on the production possibility frontier.

**Clams per week**

**Mangos per week**

3. Let's return to the example given in problem 2.

   a. What is the opportunity cost of harvesting a clam given the original information in problem 2?

   b. What is the opportunity cost of collecting a mango given the original information in problem 2?

   c. What is the slope of the production possibility frontier that you sketched in your answer to problem 2a? How does this slope measure relate to the answers you provide in parts (a) and (b) of this question?

   d. What happened to the slope of the production possibility frontier once you invent the clam rake (problem 2c)? What happens to the opportunity cost of harvesting clams once you invent the clam rake? What happens to the opportunity cost of collecting mangos once you invent the clam rake?

4. The country of Orange manufactures sofas and lamps. With its available resources and technology, Orange can manufacture in a year 1,000 sofas and 0 lamps or 0 sofas and 250 lamps. It can also manufacture any combination of sofas and lamps that lie on the straight line connecting these two points.

   a. Sketch Orange's production possibility frontier, placing sofas on the y-axis and lamps on the x-axis.

Sofas per year

Lamps per year

**b.** Fill in the following table by listing some of the feasible and efficient combinations of production available to Orange each year given its resources and technology.

| Combination | Number of lamps possible | Number of sofas possible |
|:---:|:---:|:---:|
| A | 0 | |
| B | 50 | |
| C | | 500 |
| D | | 200 |
| E | 225 | |
| F | 250 | |

**c.** What is the slope of the production possibility frontier for Orange?

**d.** What is the opportunity cost of producing one additional sofa for Orange?

**e.** What is the opportunity cost of producing one additional lamp for Orange?

**f.** What is the value of the y-intercept for Orange? (Hint: In this example, the y-intercept is the number of sofas Orange can produce if it does not produce anything else.)

**g.** Write an equation for the production possibility frontier for Orange using S to stand for sofas and L to stand for lamps. Write this equation in y-intercept form. (Hint: This means that the equation will be written with S on the left-hand side of the equation, where the S stands for the value of the variable measured on the vertical axis of your sketch.) Verify that each of the combinations you found in part (b) of this problem are true in the equation you wrote.

5.  The country of Utopia produces two goods from its available resources and technology. The only resource that Utopia has is labor. It takes 3 hours of labor to produce 2 widgets and 4 hours of labor to produce 1 gadget. For this question assume that the production possibility frontier for Utopia is a straight line.

a.  Sketch the production possibility frontier for the country of Utopia. (Hint: To do this, you must first decide on a relevant period. You might pick 120 hours, or 1,200 hours, or 1.2 million hours as your labor constraint, for example, and then you would sketch your production possibility frontier based on this amount of available time and labor.) Draw your production possibility frontier with widgets on the y-axis and gadgets on the x-axis.

b.  What is the slope of your production possibility frontier?

c.  What is the opportunity cost of producing an additional widget in Utopia?

d.  What is the opportunity cost of producing an additional gadget in Utopia?

**6.** The country of Jonesville produces two goods from its available resources and technology. The only resource that Jonesville has is labor. The following table gives the amount of labor necessary to produce a widget or a gadget. For this question assume that the production possibility frontier for Jonesville is a straight line.

|  | Number of hours of labor needed to produce a gadget | Number of hours of labor needed to produce a widget |
| --- | --- | --- |
| Jonesville | 2 | 5 |

**a.** Suppose that you want to draw a production possibility frontier for Jonesville. What must you do first to draw your sketch?

**b.** Sketch the production possibility frontier for Jonesville assuming that Jonesville has 120 hours of labor available. Place gadgets on the *x*-axis and widgets on the *y*-axis.

**c.** What is the slope of the production possibility frontier?

**d.** What is the opportunity cost of producing an additional gadget?

**e.** What is the opportunity cost of producing an additional widget?

**f.** Suppose that Jonesville has 240 hours of labor instead of 120 hours of labor. Does this affect the opportunity cost of producing widgets or gadgets? Explain your answer.

7.  The following table provides six possible production combinations that Smithtown can produce from their available resources and technology during this year. Assume that Smithtown only produces bicycles and tents from their available resources.

| Combination | Bicycles | Tents |
|:---:|:---:|:---:|
| A | 100 | 0 |
| B | 90 | 10 |
| C | 70 | 25 |
| D | 40 | 36 |
| E | 10 | 42 |
| F | 0 | 44 |

**a.** Sketch Smithtown's production possibility frontier. Measure bicycles along the x-axis and tents along the y-axis.

Tents per year

Bicycles per year

**b.** Suppose Smithtown is currently producing at combination C. If Smithtown chooses to produce at combination B, what is the opportunity cost of moving from combination C to combination B?

**c.** Suppose Smithtown is currently producing at combination C. If Smithtown chooses to produce at combination D, what is the opportunity cost of moving from combination C to combination D?

    **d.** Smithtown's production possibility frontier is not linear. Provide an explanation for why the production possibility frontier is not linear.

**8.** Suppose an economy produces two goods in a year using its available resources and technology. This economy's resources are specialized.

    **a.** Describe the general shape of this economy's production possibility frontier.

    **b.** If this economy currently produces only one of these two goods, what do you know must be true about the opportunity cost of producing more and more units of the good that is not being currently produced?

    **c.** If this economy is to be productively efficient, what must be true about its production of these two goods?

    **d.** If this economy is to be allocatively efficient, what must be true about its production of these two goods?

    **e.** Suppose this economy is deemed to be efficient. What must occur for this statement to be true?

# BEFORE YOU TAKE THE TEST

## Module Review Questions

1.  Suppose Mike has a linear production possibility frontier in the production of potatoes and tomatoes. If Mike devotes all his time to the production of potatoes, he can produce 1,000 pounds of potatoes a year; if he devotes all his time to the production of tomatoes, he can produce 2,000 pounds of tomatoes a year. Which of the following combinations of potatoes and tomatoes are not feasible for Mike?
    a.  1,000 pounds of potatoes and 2,000 pounds of tomatoes per year
    b.  1,000 pounds of potatoes and 0 pounds of tomatoes per year
    c.  0 pounds of potatoes and 2,000 pounds of tomatoes per year
    d.  500 pounds of potatoes and 1,000 pounds of tomatoes per year

2.  Suppose Mike has a linear production possibility frontier in the production of potatoes and tomatoes. If Mike devotes all his time to the production of potatoes, he can produce 1,000 pounds of potatoes a year; if he devotes all his time to the production of tomatoes, he can produce 2,000 pounds of tomatoes a year. Which of the following combinations of potatoes and tomatoes are not efficient for Mike?
    a.  500 pounds of potatoes and 500 pounds of tomatoes per year
    b.  500 pounds of potatoes and 1,000 pounds of tomatoes per year
    c.  750 pounds of potatoes and 500 pounds of tomatoes per year
    d.  250 pounds of potatoes and 1,500 pounds of tomatoes per year

3.  Utopia has a linear production possibility frontier in the production of widgets and gadgets. It can produce three gadgets per hour of labor time or four widgets per hour of labor time. What is the opportunity cost of producing one widget in Utopia?
    a.  3 gadgets          c.  0.75 gadget
    b.  4 widgets          d.  1.33 gadgets

4.  Jonesville produces widgets and gadgets and its production possibility frontier is linear. The following table provides the number of units of labor necessary to produce 1 gadget or 1 widget in Jonesville.

| | Number of hours of labor needed to produce a gadget | Number of hours of labor needed to produce a widget |
|---|---|---|
| Jonesville | 5 | 10 |

    Suppose that Jonesville has 100 hours of labor. What is the maximum number of widgets it can produce?
    a.  10 widgets          c.  1 widget
    b.  20 widgets          d.  100 widgets

5. Jonesville produces widgets and gadgets and its production possibility frontier is linear. The following table provides the number of units of labor necessary to produce 1 gadget or 1 widget in Jonesville.

| | Number of hours of labor needed to produce a gadget | Number of hours of labor needed to produce a widget |
|---|---|---|
| Jonesville | 5 | 10 |

Suppose that Jonesville has 100 hours of labor. What is the maximum number of widgets and gadgets it can produce if it devotes half of its labor time to the production of gadgets and half of its labor time to the production of widgets?
a. 20 gadgets and 5 widgets
b. 10 gadgets and 5 widgets
c. 5 gadgets and 20 widgets
d. 5 gadgets and 10 widgets

6. Jonesville produces widgets and gadgets and its production possibility frontier is linear. The following table provides the number of units of labor necessary to produce 1 gadget or 1 widget in Jonesville.

| | Number of hours of labor needed to produce a gadget | Number of hours of labor needed to produce a widget |
|---|---|---|
| Jonesville | 5 | 10 |

Suppose that Jonesville initially has 100 hours of labor. What happens to the opportunity cost of producing a widget if Jonesville's labor resource increases to 200 hours of labor?

a. The opportunity cost of producing a widget decreases.
b. The opportunity cost of producing a widget increases.
c. The opportunity cost of producing a widget does not change.
d. The opportunity cost of producing a widget may increase, decrease, or remain unchanged depending on the number of gadgets that are produced in Jonesville.

7. Jonesville produces widgets and gadgets and its production possibility frontier is linear. The following table provides the number of units of labor necessary to produce 1 gadget or 1 widget in Jonesville.

| | Number of hours of labor needed to produce a gadget | Number of hours of labor needed to produce a widget |
|---|---|---|
| Jonesville | 5 | 10 |

Suppose that Jonesville has 100 hours of labor. Which of the following combinations of gadgets and widgets is not feasible for Jonesville to produce?
a. 4 gadgets and 8 widgets
b. 7 gadgets and 7 widgets
c. 8 gadgets and 6 widgets
d. 0 gadgets and 10 widgets

8.  Utopia has a linear production possibility frontier in the production of widgets and gadgets. It can produce 3 gadgets per hour of labor time or 4 widgets per hour of labor time. Suppose that Utopia has 120 hours of labor time and that it chooses to divide its labor time equally between the production of widgets and gadgets. What is the maximum number of widgets Utopia can produce given this decision?

a. 480 widgets    c. 60 widgets

b. 240 widgets    d. 15 widgets

9.  Suburbia has a production possibility frontier bowed out from the origin for the two goods, guns and butter, that Suburbia produces from its available resources and technology. The following table describes six points that lie on Suburbia's production possibility frontier.

| Combination | Number of guns | Pounds of butter |
|---|---|---|
| A | 0 | 80 |
| B | 10 | 75 |
| C | 20 | 65 |
| D | 30 | 50 |
| E | 40 | 30 |
| F | 50 | 0 |

Suppose Suburbia is initially producing at point D. What is the opportunity cost of moving to point E?

a. 10 guns

b. 40 guns

c. 20 pounds of butter

d. 30 pounds of butter

10. Suburbia has a production possibility frontier bowed out from the origin for the two goods, guns and butter, that Suburbia produces from its available resources and technology. The following table describes six points that lie on Suburbia's production possibility frontier.

| Combination | Number of guns | Pounds of butter |
|---|---|---|
| A | 0 | 80 |
| B | 10 | 75 |
| C | 20 | 65 |
| D | 30 | 50 |
| E | 40 | 30 |
| F | 50 | 0 |

Suppose Suburbia is initially producing at point D. What is the opportunity cost of moving to point B?

a. 25 pounds of butter

b. 20 guns

c. 10 guns

d. 75 pounds of butter

11. Suburbia has a production possibility frontier bowed out from the origin for the two goods, guns and butter, that Suburbia produces from its available resources and technology. The following table describes six points that lie on Suburbia's production possibility frontier.

| Combination | Number of guns | Pounds of butter |
|:-----------:|:--------------:|:----------------:|
| A | 0 | 80 |
| B | 10 | 75 |
| C | 20 | 65 |
| D | 30 | 50 |
| E | 40 | 30 |
| F | 50 | 0 |

Suburbia is currently producing 50 pounds of butter and 20 guns. This combination is
a. allocatively efficient, since butter is tastier than guns.
b. productively efficient, since it is a feasible point for Suburbia to produce.
c. infeasible, because Suburbia cannot produce this combination given its resources and technology.
d. feasible but inefficient, since it is a combination that lies inside the production possibility frontier.

12. Which of the following statements is true?
   I. Points that lie on the production possibility frontier are allocatively efficient.
   II. Points that lie on the production possibility frontier are productively efficient.
a. Statement I is true.
b. Statement II is true.
c. Statements I and II are true.
d. Statements I and II are false.

13. An economy is allocatively efficient provided that
a. it produces at any point along its production possibility frontier.
b. it produces the right mix of goods from its available resources.
c. no resources are wasted.
d. All of the statements are true about allocative efficiency.

## ■ ANSWER KEY

# Answers to Problems and Exercises

1.  Technology and the time period are being held constant so that we can focus on the effect of a change in the level of resources on this economy's production possibility frontier. If resources increase, we would expect the production possibility frontier to shift out because the economy should be able to produce more of both goods now that there are more resources to work with.

2.  **a.**

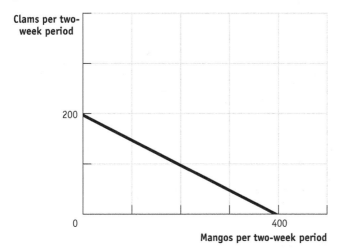

**b.** An increase in the time period, holding everything else constant, increases the level of production.

**c.** The invention of the clam rake shifts the production possibilities frontier out along the clam axis since it is now possible to produce more clams in the same time period.

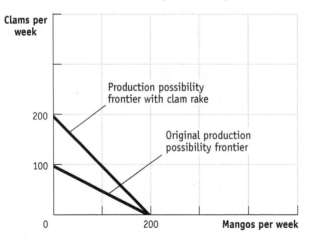

**d.** Technological change shifts the production possibility frontier away from the origin and therefore results in the possibility of greater production of both goods.

**3. a.** The opportunity cost of harvesting a clam is measured in terms of the number of mangos you must give up when you harvest a clam. In the original example, you must give up 2 mangos for every clam you harvest.

**b.** The opportunity cost of collecting a mango is measured in terms of the number of clams you must give up when you collect a mango. In the original example, you must give up ½ of a clam for every mango you collect.

**c.** The slope of the production possibility frontier is –½ (remember, you calculate this as the rise/run, or the change in the y-variable divided by the change in the x-variable). The slope tells us what the change in the y-variable is for a 1-unit change in the x-variable. In this case, the slope tells us what the change in the number of clams is for a 1-unit change in mangos: when mango collection increases by 1 unit, then clam harvesting decreases by ½ unit; when mango collection decreases by 1 unit, then clam harvesting increases by ½ unit. The negative sign of the slope tells us that these two variables move in opposite directions: an increase in mangos requires a decrease in clams, or a decrease in mangos requires an increase in clams. The slope measure tells us what the opportunity cost of one more mango is, since mangos are measured on the horizontal axis in this example. If we take the reciprocal of the slope (in this case, –2), it would give us the opportunity cost of producing one more unit of the good on the y-axis. In this case, harvesting one more clam has an opportunity cost of 2 mangos since that is the number of mangos we must give up to get one more clam.

**d.** The invention of the clam rake changed the slope of the production possibility frontier from –½ to –1 and therefore changed the opportunity cost of producing both goods. The opportunity cost of collecting a mango is now 1 clam and the opportunity cost of harvesting one clam is 1 mango.

**4.  a.**

**b.**

| Combination | Number of lamps possible | Number of sofas possible |
|---|---|---|
| A | 0 | 1,000 |
| B | 50 | 800 |
| C | 125 | 500 |
| D | 200 | 200 |
| E | 225 | 100 |
| F | 250 | 0 |

**c.** The slope of the production possibility frontier is –4 (you can find this by looking at the rise/run, or in this case, –1,000/250).

**d.** The opportunity cost of producing one more sofa is ¼ lamp. (Hint: Remember that because sofas are measured on the y-axis, you can find the opportunity cost by taking the reciprocal of the slope measure.)

**e.** The opportunity cost of producing one more lamp is 4 sofas. (Hint: Remember that because lamps are measured on the x-axis, you can find the opportunity cost by using the slope measure.)

**f.** The y-intercept is 1,000, since if Orange uses all of its resources and technology to produce sofas, this is the maximum number of sofas it can produce in a year.

**g.** The equation for Orange's production possibility frontier is $S = 1,000 - 4L$. You can verify that all the combinations work in this equation by substituting the value of the number of lamps in one of the combinations and verifying that the equation generates the number of sofas you found in the table. For example, if $L$ equals 225, then $S = 1,000 - 4(225)$ or $S = 100$ (the value you found in the table).

**5. a.** To draw the production possibility frontier, you first need to identify the number of hours of labor that Utopia has available. Since it takes 3 hours of labor to produce 2 widgets (or 1.5 hours of labor to produce 1 widget) and 4 hours of labor to produce 1 gadget, you will find it helpful to select an amount of time that is divisible by both three and four. So, for instance, 12 hours would work, as would 120 hours, or 240 hours, or an infinite number of other numbers that are divisible by both three and four. For our sketch let's suppose that there are 120 hours of labor available to Utopia and that its citizens can produce either widgets or gadgets or some combination of the two goods. If they devote all of their labor time to widget production, they can produce 80 widgets since (120 hours of labor/3 hours of labor) × (2 widgets) = 80 widgets. If they devote all of their labor time to gadget production, they can produce 30 gadgets since (120 hours of labor/4 hours of labor) × (1 gadget) = 30 gadgets. The graph below illustrates Utopia's production possibility frontier.

**Utopia's Production Possibility Frontier Based on 120 Hours of Labor**

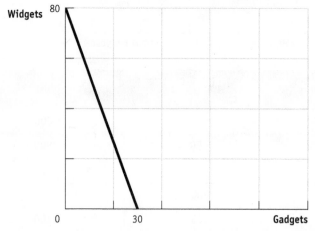

The values of your intercepts will be different depending on the number of hours of labor you assume Utopia has, but the slope of the production possibility frontier should be the same as the one drawn above.

**b.** The slope of the production possibility frontier is −8/3.

**c.** The opportunity cost of producing an additional widget in Utopia is 3/8 gadget.

**d.** The opportunity cost of producing an additional gadget in Utopia is 8/3 widget.

**6. a.** You must first decide how much labor Jonesville has so that you can calculate the maximum amount of widgets and gadgets Jonesville can produce. Since you know gadgets take 2 hours of labor and widgets take 5 hours of labor, you will want to pick a number of hours that is divisible by both two and five. For example, 10 hours would work, or 100 hours, or 20 hours, or 2,000 hours—there is an infinite number of labor quantities that would work in constructing this production possibility frontier.

**b.**

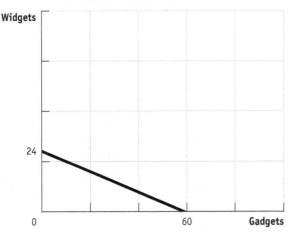

Production Possibility Frontier for
Jonesville Based on 120 Hours of Labor

**c.** The slope of the production possibility frontier is –24/60, or –4/10, or –0.4.

**d.** Recall that you can use the slope measure to quickly find the opportunity cost of producing one more unit of the good measured on the x-axis. To produce one more gadget, you must give up 0.4 widget, therefore the opportunity cost of an additional gadget is 0.4 widget.

**e.** Recall that you can use the reciprocal of the slope measure to quickly find the opportunity cost of producing one more unit of the good measured on the y-axis. To produce one more widget, you must give up 1/0.4 gadgets, therefore the opportunity cost of an additional widget is 2.5 gadgets.

**f.** If Jonesville has an increase in the amount of labor available to use in producing gadgets and widgets, it can produce more gadgets and more widgets. That is, Jonesville's production possibility frontier will shift out from the origin. But the slope of the new production possibility frontier will be the same as the one drawn based upon 120 hours of labor, thus the opportunity cost of producing widgets or gadgets will not change for Jonesville.

**7. a.**

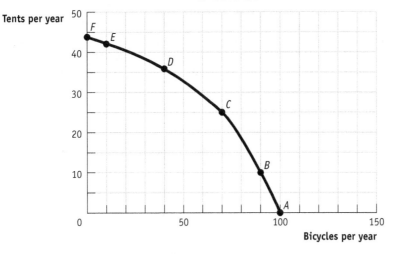

Production Possibility Frontier
for Smithtown

**b.** The opportunity cost of moving from point C to point B is measured in terms of the number of units of production you give up. In this case you give up 15 tents, so this is the opportunity cost.

**c.** The opportunity cost of moving from point C to point D is 30 bicycles.

**d.** Smithtown's resources are not equally well suited to produce bicycles and tents. If Smithtown initially devotes all of its resources to producing bicycles, then some of its resources that are currently going into the production of bicycles are not particularly productive at producing bicycles. Smithtown can move some of these resources away from bicycle production and into tent production without decreasing its bicycle production significantly. However, as Smithtown decides to produce more and more tents, this will eventually require moving resources that are well suited to bicycle production into tent production where they are less productive. This specialization of resources results in a production possibility frontier that is bowed out from the origin.

**8.** **a.** This economy's production possibility frontier must be bowed out from the origin if the economy's resources are specialized: this implies that the opportunity cost of producing more and more units of one of the goods increases because increased production of this good requires the economy to use resources that would be more productive producing the other good.

**b.** The opportunity cost of producing more and more units of the good will increase due to the shape of the production possibility frontier, which is bowed out from the origin.

**c.** To be productively efficient, this economy must be producing at a point that is located on the production possibility frontier.

**d.** To be allocatively efficient, this economy must be producing at a point that represents the optimal mix of these two goods for the economy.

**e.** To be efficient, the economy must be both productively and allocatively efficient—that is, it must produce not only on the production possibility frontier, but it must also produce the right mix of goods.

# Answers to Module Review Questions

**1.** **Answer a.** Mike can produce 1,000 pounds of potatoes and 0 pounds of tomatoes a year or he can produce 2,000 pounds of tomatoes and 0 pounds of potatoes a year. His resources do not allow him to produce a combination of 1,000 pounds of potatoes and 2,000 pounds of tomatoes in a year. Thus, answer (a) is not feasible, while answers (b) and (c) are feasible. Answer (d) is also feasible since if Mike devotes half of his resources this year to producing potatoes and half of his resources this year to producing tomatoes, he will be able to produce 500 pounds of potatoes and 1,000 pounds of tomatoes this year.

**2.** **Answer a.** Any combination of production of potatoes and tomatoes that lies on Mike's linear production possibility frontier is an efficient combination. An inefficient combination must lie inside his production possibility frontier. His linear production possibility frontier includes the two points (1,000 pounds of potatoes, 0 pounds of tomatoes) and (0 pounds of potatoes, 2,000 pounds of tomatoes), and we can use these two points to write an equation for his production possibility frontier. If potatoes are measured on the y-axis and are denoted by P, and tomatoes are measured on the x-axis and denoted by T, then Mike's production possibility frontier is $P = 1,000 - \frac{1}{2}T$. Substitute the number of tomatoes provided in each answer into this equation to calculate the number of potatoes Mike can produce when he produces that level of tomatoes. Thus, for answer (b), when Mike produces 1,000 pounds of tomatoes, the equation states that he will be able to produce 500 pounds of potatoes, which is the number of potatoes given in answer (b). Answers (c) and (d) also fit the equation. Thus, answers (b), (c), and (d) all identify production combinations that are on the production possibility frontier. But answer (a) does not fit the equation: when Mike produces 500 pounds of tomatoes, the equation says that he will be able to produce 750 pounds of potatoes, while answer (a) says that he will produce 500 pounds of potatoes. The combination in answer (a) is a combination that lies inside Mike's production possibility frontier.

3.  **Answer c.** Since 4 widgets can be produced in the same amount of labor time as 3 gadgets in Utopia, then 1 widget can be produced in the same amount of labor time as ¾ of a gadget. Thus, the opportunity cost of producing 1 widget is measured by the number of gadgets that must be given up. In this case, ¾ of a gadget.

4.  **Answer a.** Jonesville uses all of its labor to produce widgets. With 100 hours of labor, it can produce 10 widgets since the production of each widget takes 10 hours of labor.

5.  **Answer b.** When Jonesville devotes 50 hours of labor to widget production, it can produce 5 widgets. When Jonesville devotes 50 hours of labor to gadget production, it can produce 10 gadgets. Thus, when Jonesville divides its labor equally between widget and gadget production, the maximum number of gadgets it can produce is 10 while the maximum number of widgets it can produce is 5.

6.  **Answer c.** Since the number of hours needed to produce each widget and each gadget has not changed in Jonesville, the opportunity cost of producing these goods does not change. Jonesville does see its linear production possibility frontier shift out due to the increase in the amount of available labor, but the new production possibility frontier has the same slope as the original production possibility frontier.

7.  **Answer b.** A combination of gadgets and widgets is not feasible for Jonesville if that combination lies outside of its production possibility frontier. If gadgets are measured on the vertical axis and widgets are measured on the horizontal axis, then the production possibility frontier can be written as $G = 20 - 2W$, where $G$ is the symbol for gadgets and $W$ is the symbol for widgets. Answer (a) lies on the production possibility frontier since $G = 20 - 2(8) = 4$. Answer (c) lies on the production possibility frontier since $G = 20 - 2(6) = 8$. Answer (d) lies on the production possibility frontier since $G = 20 - 2(10) = 0$. Answer (b) does not lie on the production possibility frontier nor does it lie inside the production possibility frontier: $G = 20 - 2(7) = 6$, but the answer in (b) has gadgets equal to 7 and not 6. The combination of 7 widgets and 7 gadgets lies beyond the production possibility frontier for Jonestown.

8.  **Answer b.** Utopia plans to devote 60 hours of labor to the production of widgets. If the production of 4 widgets takes 1 hour of labor time, then 60 hours of labor is enough labor to produce 240 widgets.

9.  **Answer c.** The opportunity cost of moving from point $D$ to point $E$ is measured by what Suburbia must give up when it makes this move. At point $D$, Suburbia has 50 pounds of butter, while at point $E$ Suburbia has only 30 pounds of butter; thus, when moving from point $D$ to point $E$, Suburbia must give up 20 pounds of butter. Notice that when measuring the opportunity cost of moving from one point of a production possibility frontier to another point on the production possibility frontier, it is important to provide the unit of measurement as well as the numerical value.

10. **Answer b.** The opportunity cost of moving from point $D$ to point $B$ is measured by what Suburbia must give up when it makes this move. In this case, Suburbia is giving up guns to get more butter. Moving from point $D$ to point $B$, Suburbia gives up 20 guns.

11. **Answer d.** From the table, we know that Suburbia can produce 50 pounds of butter and 30 guns (point $D$ on the production possibility frontier). When Suburbia produces 50 pounds of butter and 20 guns, it is producing at a point that is inside its production possibility frontier and hence it is producing at a feasible but inefficient point, since the point does not lie on the production possibility frontier. Alternatively,

Suburbia could produce 20 guns and 65 pounds of butter (point C) according to the table. Its choice of 20 guns and 50 pounds of butter is also not efficient from this perspective.

12. **Answer b.** Allocative efficiency focuses on producing the right mix of goods and services. Without additional information, we cannot identify which point is the allocatively efficient point on the production possibility frontier. Productively efficient refers to the maximum production feasible from the available resources. All points on the production possibility frontier are productively efficient.

13. **Answer b.** This is true by definition.

# Comparative Advantage and Trade

## ██ BEFORE YOU READ THE MODULE

## Summary

This module explores trade and how trade between individuals or between economies can lead to gains. The module also discusses the distinction between absolute and comparative advantage and then uses the production possibility frontier model to illustrate how comparative advantage leads to gains from trade in the global marketplace.

## Module Objectives

**Objective #1.** Specialization and trade is beneficial for individuals as well as societies since it allows a higher standard of living than is possible without specialization and trade.

**Objective #2.** An individual has a comparative advantage in the production of a good or service if they can produce that good or service at a lower opportunity cost than can another individual. A society has a comparative advantage in the production of a good or service if they can produce that good or service at a lower opportunity cost than can another society.

**Objective #3.** Absolute advantage refers to the ability to produce more of a good or service from a given amount of resources than anyone else can produce. Absolute advantage is not the same as comparative advantage.

**Objective #4.** Trade among individuals or among economies is beneficial when it is based upon comparative advantage since it allows the individuals or the economies to consume a greater amount of goods and services than would be possible if there was not trade.

**Objective #5.** The model of production possibility frontiers can also be used to illustrate the gains from trade, which is referred to as the model of comparative advantage. This model assumes that there are two countries, that there are two goods that the countries produce, and that each country has a set amount of resources, technology, and time available to them. Furthermore, this model assumes that the two countries have different opportunity costs of production. In this model, countries benefit from specializing in the production of that good for which they have the comparative advantage, or lower opportunity cost of production, and then trade with each other. Countries do not have to have absolute advantage in production to benefit from trade: the benefits from trade only require that countries have different opportunity costs of production for the two goods and that each country specialize in producing the good that it can produce at a lower opportunity cost relative to the other country.

## Key Terms

*Notes*

**trade** when individuals provide goods and services to others and receive goods and services in return.

**gains from trade** an economic principle that states that by dividing tasks and trading, people can get more of what they want through *trade* than they could if they tried to be self-sufficient.

**specialization** a situation in which different people each engage in the different task that he or she is good at performing.

**comparative advantage** the advantage conferred on an individual or nation in producing a good or service if the *opportunity cost* of producing the good or service is lower for that individual or nation than for other producers.

**absolute advantage** the advantage conferred by the ability to produce more of a good or service with a given amount of time and resources; not the same thing as comparative advantage.

## ▮ AFTER YOU READ THE MODULE

## Tips

**Tip #1.** In the previous module you practiced finding the opportunity cost of producing a good or service using the production possibility frontier. In this module you continue with that concept but now you compare the opportunity cost of producing the good for one country or individual with the opportunity cost of producing the good by another country or individual.

**Tip #2.** The comparative advantage in the production of the good or service belongs to that individual or country that can produce the good or service at lowest opportunity cost. Specialization based upon comparative advantage leads to a higher standard of living than would otherwise be possible.

**Tip #3.**   Once you can calculate the opportunity cost of producing good X or good Y, then you can compare the opportunity costs faced by two countries. The model of comparative advantage illustrates that countries will benefit from trade when they specialize and produce the good that has the lowest opportunity cost of production relative to the other country.

# WORKED PROBLEMS

1.   The following provides a numerical example of how trade is advantageous to two countries that decide to trade with each other. Suppose there are two countries, Arcadia and Supreme, that produce bricks and windows. Arcadia and Supreme use only labor to produce these two goods, and each country has 200 units of available labor. The following table provides information about the number of hours of labor needed in each country to produce one unit of bricks or one unit of windows.

|  | Hours of labor to produce one brick | Hours of labor to produce one window |
|---|---|---|
| Arcadia | 2 | 4 |
| Supreme | 5 | 2 |

Use the table's information to draw production possibility frontiers for Arcadia and for Supreme. In your graph, measure bricks on the *x*-axis and windows on the *y*-axis. Then use your graph to find each country's opportunity cost of producing one brick. Identify each country's comparative advantage. Finally, calculate a range of prices for one brick in terms of windows.

**STEP 1:** Draw and label the production possibility frontiers for Arcadia and Supreme.

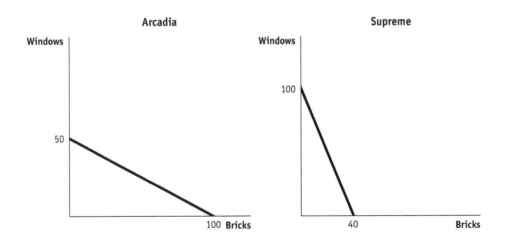

**STEP 2:** Find each country's opportunity cost of producing one brick, as measured by the number of windows that must be given up when the country produces one additional brick.

The opportunity cost of producing one brick for Arcadia is ½ of a window. To see this, remember that the slope of the production possibility frontier tells you how many units of the good on the y-axis must be given up in order to get one more unit of the good on the x-axis. Since the slope of Arcadia's production possibility frontier is equal to –1/2, we know that the opportunity cost of one more brick is equal to ½ of a window. The opportunity cost of producing one brick for Supreme is 2.5 windows.

**STEP 3:** Identify each country's comparative advantage by comparing their opportunity cost of production for each good: a country has the comparative advantage in producing the good when its opportunity cost of producing the good is lower than the other country's opportunity cost of producing the good.

Arcadia has the comparative advantage in producing bricks since Arcadia can produce an additional brick at lower opportunity cost than can Supreme. One additional brick costs Arcadia ½ of a window, while it costs Supreme 2.5 windows: Arcadia can produce bricks at lower opportunity cost and therefore has a comparative advantage in brick production.

**STEP 4:** Find the range of prices for one brick in terms of windows.

Arcadia is willing to produce bricks for any price equal to or greater than ½ of a window. Supreme is willing to purchase one brick for any price equal to or less than 2.5 windows. The range of prices for one brick will therefore fall between ½ window and 2.5 windows.

## Problems and Exercises

1.  Economists believe that specialization and trade are beneficial when they are based on comparative advantage. Briefly explain why economists believe this to be true.

**2.** There are two islands in the middle of the ocean and these two islands produce fish and baskets. Big Island can produce either 100 fish per day and 0 baskets per day or 0 fish per day and 200 baskets per day. Big Island can also produce any combination of fish and baskets that lies on their linear production possibility frontier. Small Island can produce either 80 fish per day and 0 baskets per day or 0 fish per day and 80 baskets per day. Like Big Island, Small Island has a linear production possibility frontier.

**a.** Sketch two graphs. Sketch Big Island's production possibility frontier on the first graph and sketch Small Island's production possibility frontier on the second graph. Place fish/day on the *y*-axis and baskets/day on the *x*-axis.

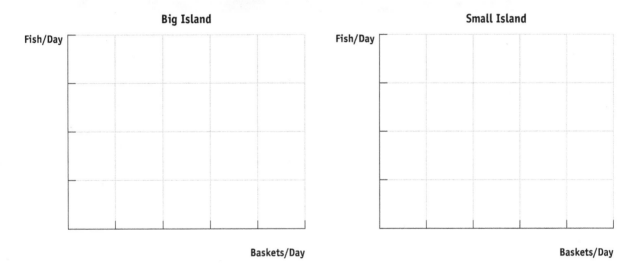

**b.** What is the slope of Big Island's production possibility frontier?

**c.** What is the slope of Small Island's production possibility frontier?

**d.** What is the opportunity cost of producing an additional basket on Big Island? What is the opportunity cost of producing an additional basket on Small Island? Which island can produce baskets at a lower opportunity cost?

**e.** What is the opportunity cost of producing an additional fish on Big Island? What is the opportunity cost of producing an additional fish on Small Island? Which island can produce fish at a lower opportunity cost?

**f.** What good should Big Island specialize in producing?

**g.** What good should Small Island specialize in producing?

3. There are two islands in the middle of the ocean, and these two islands produce fish and baskets. Big Island can produce either 100 fish per day and 0 baskets per day or 0 fish per day and 200 baskets per day. Big Island can also produce any combination of fish and baskets that includes these two combinations and lies on their linear production possibility frontier. Small Island can produce either 80 fish per day and 0 baskets per day or 0 fish per day and 80 baskets per day. Like Big Island, Small Island has a linear production possibility frontier. Currently there is no trade between the two islands. The current production for both islands is given in the table below.

| Initial production | Fish | Baskets |
|---|---|---|
| Big Island | 80 | 40 |
| Small Island | 30 | 50 |
| Total production | 110 | 90 |

a. Is Big Island producing at a productively efficient point? Explain your answer.

b. Is Small Island producing at a productively efficient point? Explain your answer.

Referring back to problem 2, let's analyze what happens to total production if these countries decide to specialize and trade according to their comparative advantage.

c. Suppose that Big Island decides to produce 50 baskets instead of 40 baskets. How many fish will Big Island be able to produce if its basket production is increased to 50 baskets?

d. Suppose that Small Island decides to produce 40 fish instead of 30 fish. How many baskets will Small Island be able to produce if its fish production is increased to 40 fish?

e. Fill in the table below showing the new levels of production given the information in parts (c) and (d).

| New production | Fish | Baskets |
|---|---|---|
| Big Island | | 50 |
| Small Island | 40 | |
| Total production | | |

f. Do specialization and trade benefit both islands in this example? Explain your answer.

Referring back to problem 2, let's analyze what happens to total production if these countries decide to specialize and trade without regard to their comparative advantage.

g. Suppose that Big Island decides to produce 30 baskets instead of 40 baskets. How many fish will Big Island be able to produce if its basket production is increased to 30 baskets?

h. Suppose that Small Island decides to produce 20 fish instead of 30 fish. How many baskets will Small Island be able to produce if its fish production is increased to 20 fish?

i. Fill in the table below showing the new levels of production given the information in parts (g) and (h).

| New production | Fish | Baskets |
| --- | --- | --- |
| Big Island | | 30 |
| Small Island | 20 | |
| Total production | | |

j. Do specialization and trade benefit both islands in this example? Explain your answer.

k. What must be true for specialization and trade to be beneficial? (Hint: Think about the two examples in this problem and how they differ before you write your answer.)

4. Suppose that Jane and Bob live on an island far away from any other countries. Jane and Bob both produce widgets and gadgets from their available resources, but they do not currently trade with one another. The table below gives the number of hours of labor needed to produce one widget or one gadget for Bob and Jane. For this example let's assume that Jane and Bob each have 120 hours of labor time.

| | Hours of labor needed to produce a widget | Hours of labor needed to produce a gadget |
|---|---|---|
| Bob | 2 | 4 |
| Jane | 3 | 1.5 |

**a.** Sketch two graphs: on the first graph draw Bob's production possibility frontier and on the second graph draw Jane's production possibility frontier. Place widgets on the y-axis and gadgets on the x-axis. Label both graphs carefully.

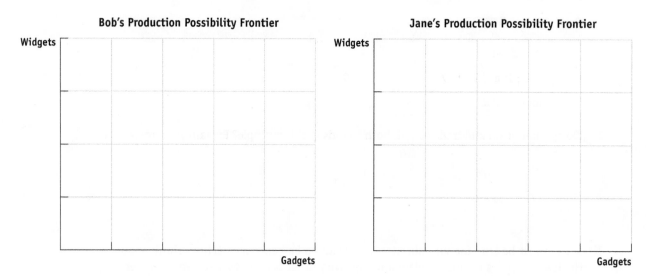

**b.** Suppose that Bob and Jane devote half of their labor time to producing gadgets and half to producing widgets. Fill in the following table based on this allocation of labor.

| Initial production | Widgets | Gadgets |
|---|---|---|
| Bob | | |
| Jane | | |
| Total production | | |

**c.** What is Bob's opportunity cost of producing an additional gadget? What is Jane's opportunity cost of producing an additional gadget? Who can produce gadgets at a lower opportunity cost?

**d.** What is Bob's opportunity cost of producing an additional widget? What is Jane's opportunity cost of producing an additional widget? Who can produce widgets at a lower opportunity cost?

**e.** Bob and Jane decide to specialize and trade. What good should Bob specialize in producing?

**f.** Bob and Jane decide to specialize and trade. What good should Jane specialize in producing?

**g.** Bob and Jane specialize according to their comparative advantage and give us this partially filled-in table that provides some information about their production. Fill in the missing information on the table assuming that Bob and Jane are both productively efficient.

| New production | Widgets | Gadgets |
|---|---|---|
| Bob | 46 | |
| Jane | | 60 |
| Total production | | |

## BEFORE YOU TAKE THE TEST

## Module Review Questions

1. Suppose there are two countries, Texia and Urbania, that produce food and clothing and currently do not trade. Both countries have linear production possibility frontiers. Texia, if it devotes all of its resources to food production, can produce 1,000 units of food this year and 0 units of clothing. If Texia devotes all of its resources to clothing production this year, it can produce 500 units of clothing and 0 units of food. Urbania can either produce 500 units of food this year and 0 units of clothing, or it can produce 200 units of clothing this year and 0 units of food. _____ has the absolute advantage in the production of clothing and _____ has the absolute advantage in the production of food.

   a. Texia; Texia      c. Urbania; Texia

   b. Texia; Urbania      d. Urbania; Urbania

2. Suppose there are two countries, Texia and Urbania, that produce food and clothing and currently do not trade. Both countries have linear production possibility frontiers. Texia, if it devotes all of its resources to food production, can produce 1,000 units of food this year and 0 units of clothing. If Texia devotes all of its resources to clothing production this year, it can produce 500 units of clothing and 0 units of food. Urbania can either produce 500 units of food this year and 0 units of clothing, or it can produce 200 units of clothing this year and 0 units of food. _____ has the comparative advantage in the production of clothing and _____ has the comparative advantage in the production of food.

   a. Texia; Texia      c. Urbania; Texia

   b. Texia; Urbania      d. Urbania; Urbania

3. Suppose there are two countries, Texia and Urbania, that produce food and clothing and currently do not trade. Both countries have linear production possibility frontiers. Texia, if it devotes all of its resources to food production, can produce 1,000 units of food this year and 0 units of clothing. If Texia devotes all of its resources to clothing production this year, it can produce 500 units of clothing and 0 units of food. Urbania can either produce 500 units of food this year and 0 units of clothing, or it can produce 200 units of clothing this year and 0 units of food. Each country devotes half of its resources to the production of food and half of its resources to the production of clothing. Total clothing production is equal to _____ and total food production is equal to _____.

   a. 600; 500      c. 100; 250

   b. 250; 500      d. 350; 750

4. Suppose there are two countries, Texia and Urbania, that produce food and clothing and initially do not trade. Both countries have linear production possibility frontiers. Texia, if it devotes all of its resources to food production, can produce 1,000 units of food this year, and 0 units of clothing. If Texia devotes all of its resources to clothing production this year, it can produce 500 units of clothing and 0 units of food. Urbania can either produce 500 units of food this year and 0 units of clothing, or it can produce 200 units of clothing this year and 0 units of food. Suppose that Texia and Urbania decide to specialize and trade. If Texia increases its clothing production to a total of 400 units, how many units of food will Texia be able to produce if it is productively efficient?

   a. 100 units      c. 300 units

   b. 200 units      d. 400 units

**5.** Specialization and trade benefit
   a. usually only one of the trading partners.
   b. the wealthier country more than the poorer country.
   c. the poorer country more than the wealthier country.
   d. both countries if they specialize according to their comparative advantage.

**6.** True or False: "Provided that their opportunity costs of production are not equal, two countries will find that specialization of production and trade according to their comparative advantage with one another increases the overall level of production."
   a. True                 b. False

*Use the following information to answer the next two questions.*

Each time country A decides to produce 1 bicycle it must give up 2 radios. Each time country B decides to produce 1 radio it must give up 3 bicycles.

**7.** If the two countries specialize according to their comparative advantage, then country B should produce
   a. radios.            b. bicycles.

**8.** If the two countries specialize according to their comparative advantage, then country A should produce
   a. radios.            b. bicycles.

**9.** Suppose that both Tom and Sue each have 100 hours of labor available to them. Tom needs 10 hours of labor to produce a table and 4 hours of labor to produce a chair. Sue needs 5 hours of labor to produce a table and 2 hours of labor to produce a chair. Assuming that labor is the only resource that constrains Tom or Sue, what is the maximum amount of tables that the two of them can produce?
   a. 30 tables
   b. 20 tables
   c. 10 tables
   d. 15 tables

**10.** Suppose that both Tom and Sue each have 100 hours of labor available to them. Tom needs 10 hours of labor to produce a table and 4 hours of labor to produce a chair. Sue needs 5 hours of labor to produce a table and 2 hours of labor to produce a chair. Assuming that labor is the only resource that constrains Tom or Sue, who has the comparative advantage in the production of chairs?
   a. Tom
   b. Sue
   c. Tom and Sue have the same opportunity cost of producing a chair: thus, neither Tom nor Sue has the comparative advantage in the production of chairs.
   d. Tom and Sue both have the comparative advantage in the production of chairs.

**11.** Suppose that both Tom and Sue each have 100 hours of labor available to them. Tom needs 10 hours of labor to produce a table and 4 hours of labor to produce a chair. Sue needs 5 hours of labor to produce a table and 2 hours of labor to produce a chair. Assuming that labor is the only resource that constrains Tom or Sue, who has the absolute advantage in the production of chairs?

a. Sue                 b. Tom

**12.** Suppose that both Tom and Sue each have 100 hours of labor available to them. Tom needs 10 hours of labor to produce a table and 4 hours of labor to produce a chair. Sue needs 5 hours of labor to produce a table and 2 hours of labor to produce a chair. Assuming that labor is the only resource that constrains Tom or Sue, who has the absolute advantage in the production of tables?

a. Sue                 b. Tom

## ANSWER KEY

# Answers to Problems and Exercises

1. Economists believe that specialization and trade based on comparative advantage result in a greater level of production than is possible without specialization and trade. Economists argue that, so long as opportunity costs differ, specialization in the production of the good that has a lower opportunity cost will enhance the overall level of production available and will therefore be beneficial.

2. **a.**

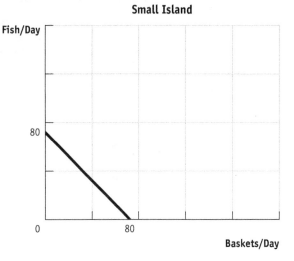

**b.** The slope of Big Island's production possibility frontier is –½.

**c.** The slope of Small Island's production possibility frontier is –1.

**d.** The opportunity cost of producing an additional basket for Big Island is ½ of a fish. The opportunity cost of producing an additional basket for Small Island is 1 fish. Big Island can produce an additional basket at a lower opportunity cost than can Small Island.

**e.** The opportunity cost of producing an additional fish for Big Island is 2 baskets. The opportunity cost of producing an additional fish for Small Island is 1 basket. Small Island can produce an additional fish at a lower opportunity cost than can Big Island.

**f.** Big Island should specialize in producing baskets, since it can produce baskets at a lower opportunity cost than can Small Island.

**g.** Small Island should specialize in producing fish, since it can produce fish at a lower opportunity cost than can Big Island.

3. **a.** Big Island is producing at a productively efficient point because 80 fish and 40 baskets lies on its linear production possibility frontier.

**b.** Small Island is producing at a productively efficient point because 30 fish and 50 baskets lies on its linear production possibility frontier.

**c.** Big Island will be able to produce 75 fish. The easiest way to calculate this answer is to write an equation for Big Island's production possibility frontier: $F = (-½)B + 100$, where $F$ is the symbol for fish and $B$ is the symbol for baskets. Thus, if $B = 50$ then $F$ must equal 75 according to this equation.

**d.** Small Island will be able to produce 40 baskets. The easiest way to calculate this answer is to write an equation for Small Island's production possibility frontier: $F = (-1)B + 80$, where $F$ stands for fish and $B$ stands for baskets. Thus, if $F = 40$ then $B$ must equal 40.

e.

| New production | Fish | Baskets |
|---|---|---|
| Big Island | 75 | 50 |
| Small Island | 40 | 40 |
| Total production | 115 | 90 |

f. Specialization and trade are beneficial to both islands since the total production of fish is increased to 115 fish instead of the original 110. This change in fish production does not change the level of basket production. Thus, the two islands can increase the amount of goods available to them if they specialize according to their comparative advantage and then trade with one another.

g. Big Island will be able to produce 85 fish. One way to calculate this answer is to write an equation for Big Island's production possibility frontier: $F = (-\frac{1}{2})B + 100$, where $F$ is the symbol for fish and $B$ is the symbol for baskets. Thus, if $B = 30$ then $F$ must equal 85 according to this equation.

h. Small Island will be able to produce 60 baskets. One way to calculate this answer is to write an equation for Small Island's production possibility frontier: $F = (-1)B + 80$, where $F$ stands for fish and $B$ stands for baskets. Thus, if $F = 20$ then $B$ must equal 60.

i.

| New production | Fish | Baskets |
|---|---|---|
| Big Island | 85 | 30 |
| Small Island | 20 | 60 |
| Total production | 105 | 90 |

j. Specialization and trade are not beneficial to both islands in this example since the total production of fish decreased to 105 fish instead of the original 110. This change in fish production does not change the level of basket production. Thus, the two islands decrease the amount of goods available to them when they specialize and trade with one another without paying attention to their comparative advantage.

k. For specialization and trade to be beneficial for two countries, they must have different opportunity costs of production, and they must also specialize according to their comparative advantage.

4.   a.

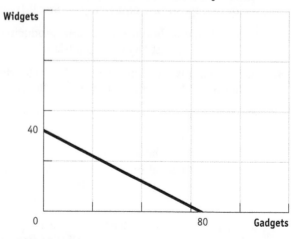

Bob's Production Possibility Frontier

Jane's Production Possibility Frontier

b.

| Initial production | Widgets | Gadgets |
| --- | --- | --- |
| Bob | 30 | 15 |
| Jane | 20 | 40 |
| Total production | 50 | 55 |

c. Bob's opportunity cost of producing an additional gadget is 2 widgets, whereas Jane's opportunity cost of producing an additional gadget is ½ of a widget. Jane can produce gadgets at a lower opportunity cost than can Bob.

d. Bob's opportunity cost of producing an additional widget is ½ of a gadget, whereas Jane's opportunity cost of producing an additional widget is 2 gadgets. Bob can produce widgets at a lower opportunity cost than can Jane.

e. Bob should specialize in producing widgets.

f. Jane should specialize in producing gadgets.

g.

| Initial production | Widgets | Gadgets |
| --- | --- | --- |
| Bob | 46 | 7 |
| Jane | 10 | 60 |
| Total production | 56 | 67 |

# Answers to Module Review Questions

1.  **Answer a.** Given the resources that Texia and Urbania have this year, Texia is able to produce more food and more clothing than Urbania this year.

2.  **Answer b.** For every unit of clothing that Texia produces it must give up 2 units of food, while for Urbania the opportunity cost of producing 1 unit of clothing is 2.5 units of food. Thus, the opportunity cost of producing clothing is lower for Texia than it is for Urbania. Texia therefore has the comparative advantage in producing clothing while Urbania has the comparative advantage in producing food.

3.  **Answer d.** When Texia devotes half of its resources to food production and half of its resources to clothing production, it can produce 500 units of food and 250 units of clothing. When Urbania devotes half of its resources to food production and half of its resources to clothing production, it can produce 250 units of food and 100 units of clothing. Thus, under this arrangement, total food production is 750 units and total clothing production is 350 units.

4.  **Answer b.** Texia's production possibility frontier can be written as $F = 1,000 - 2C$, where $F$ is the number of units of food and $C$ is the number of units of clothing. When Texia produces 400 units of clothing, the maximum amount of food it can produce is 200 units: $F = 1,000 - 2(400) = 200$.

5.  **Answer d.** The logic of comparative advantage is that both trading parties benefit through specialization and trade based on their comparative advantage.

6.  **Answer a.** When two countries have different opportunity costs of production then the two countries will benefit from trading with one another provided that they specialize in producing the good that they can produce at lower opportunity cost than can the other country.

7.  **Answer b.** Country B must give up 3 bicycles to produce one radio while country A only gives up ½ of a bicycle to produce one radio. country B's opportunity cost of producing one radio is greater than country A's opportunity cost of producing one radio. Country B should produce bicycles while country A produces radios.

8.  **Answer a.** See answer to previous question.

9.  **Answer a.** If both Tom and Sue devote all of their labor to the production of tables, Tom will be able to produce 10 tables while Sue will be able to produce 20 tables. Together they will be able to produce 30 tables.

10. **Answer c.** If you draw Tom's production possibility frontier you will see that he can produce a maximum of 10 tables and 0 chairs or 25 chairs and 0 tables. From this information you can construct Tom's linear production possibility frontier and see that the slope of this production possibility frontier is equal to $-\frac{2}{5}$ if chairs are measured on the horizontal axis. If you draw Sue's production possibility frontier you will see that she can produce a maximum of 20 tables and 0 chairs or 50 chairs and 0 tables. From this information you can construct Sue's linear production possibility frontier and see that the slope of this production possibility frontier is equal to $-\frac{2}{5}$ if chairs are measured on the horizontal axis. Thus, the opportunity cost of producing one chair is equal to $\frac{2}{5}$ of a table for both Tom and Sue. There is no comparative advantage in this example.

11. **Answer a.** With 100 hours of labor Sue can produce a maximum of 50 chairs while Tom can only produce a maximum of 25 chairs. Sue can absolutely produce more chairs than can Tom from the same amount of resources (in this case, 100 hours of labor).

12. **Answer a.** With 100 hours of labor Sue can produce a maximum of 20 tables while Tom can only produce a maximum of 10 tables. Sue can absolutely produce more tables than can Tom from the same amount of resources (in this case, 100 hours of labor).

# module 4

# Demand

## Summary

This module introduces the model of supply and demand in the context of a competitive market and discusses the demand for a good or service. It develops the concept of the demand curve and then discusses what causes a movement along the demand curve and what factors cause a shift in the demand curve.

## Module Objectives

**Objective #1.** A competitive market is a market that has many buyers and many sellers of the same good or service. No buyer or seller can affect the price of the good or service in a competitive market.

**Objective #2.** A demand schedule shows the relationship between possible prices of the good or service and the quantity of that good or service demanded at those different prices. As the price increases, the quantity demanded decreases: price and quantity demanded are inversely related to one another. A demand curve is the graphical representation of the demand schedule. The demand curve is drawn with the price of the good on the vertical axis and the quantity demanded on the horizontal axis. Demand curves usually slope downward: this is referred to as the "law of demand." Demand refers to the entire demand curve, while quantity demanded refers to a specific quantity demanded at a specific price.

**Objective #3.** The quantity demanded depends on many factors, but the primary determinants of the quantity demanded are the price of the good, the changes in the price of related goods, and changes in income, tastes, expectations, and the number of consumers. A change in the price of the good, all other things being equal, will cause a movement along the curve and a change in the quantity demanded. A change in any other determinant of demand, all other things being equal, will cause a shift in the demand curve. At any given price, the quantity demanded will increase when demand shifts to the right and decrease when demand shifts to the left.

**Objective #4.**    The module discusses several kinds of specific types of goods.

- Two goods are substitutes if a decrease in the price of one of the goods causes a decrease in the demand for the other good. As the price of the first good decreases, people increase the quantity of this good they demand, which results in a reduction in the overall demand for the other, substitute good. Two goods are complements if a decrease in the price of one of the goods causes an increase in the demand for the other good. As the price of the first good decreases, people increase the quantity of this good they demand, which results in an increase in the overall demand for the other, complementary, good.

- A good is a normal good if a decrease in income causes a decrease in the demand for the good. A good is an inferior good if a decrease in income causes an increase in the demand for the good.

**Objective #5.**    A market demand curve illustrates the combined quantity demanded by all consumers in the market. The market demand curve is found by horizontally adding the individual demand curves. At each price the quantity demanded by each individual is added to give the total quantity demanded at that price.

# Key Terms

**competitive market** a market in which there are many buyers and sellers of the same good or service, none of whom can influence the price at which the good or service is sold.

**supply and demand model** a model of how a *competitive market* works.

**demand schedule** a list or table showing how much of a good or service consumers will want to buy at different prices.

**quantity demanded** the actual amount of a good or service consumers are willing to buy at some specific price.

**demand curve** a graphical representation of the *demand schedule*, showing the relationship between quantity demanded and price.

**law of demand** a higher price for a good or service, other things equal, leads people to demand a smaller quantity of that good or service.

**change in demand** a shift of the demand curve, which changes the quantity demanded at any given price.

**movement along the demand curve** a change in the quantity demanded of a good that is the result of a change in that good's price.

**substitutes** pairs of goods for which a rise in the price of one of the goods leads to an increase in the demand for the other good.

**complements** pairs of goods for which a rise in the price of one good leads to a decrease in the demand for the other good.

**normal good** a good for which a rise in income increases the demand for that good—the "normal" case.

**inferior good** a good for which a rise in income decreases the demand for the good.

**individual demand curve** a graphical representation of the relationship between *quantity demanded* and price for an individual consumer.

*Notes*

## ■ AFTER YOU READ THE MODULE

# Tips

**Tip #1.** A full understanding of this module is critical for your study of economics. The model of supply and demand is used repeatedly in a variety of settings throughout the remainder of this course. You should work with the material in this module until you are confident that you know it well and that you understand the techniques, vocabulary, and information in the module. Pay particular attention to the distinction between demand and the quantity demanded, and shifts of a demand curve versus movements along a demand curve. You also should know the determinants of demand.

**Tip #2.** A demand curve is usually downward sloping. The negative slope of a demand curve implies that the quantity demanded of a good or service is inversely related to its price. Another way to express this idea is that as the price of the good decreases, holding everything else constant, consumers will want to buy more units of the good. Figure 4.1 illustrates this law of demand: at $P_1$, $Q_1$ units of the good are demanded; as the price of the good falls from $P_1$ to $P_2$, the quantity demanded of the good increases from $Q_1$ to $Q_2$.

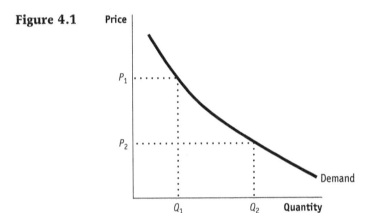

**Figure 4.1**

**Tip #3.** A demand curve illustrates the relationship between the price of the good and the quantity demanded at each specific price. In drawing the demand curve, the other determinants of demand are held constant; this constancy is referred to as the other-things-equal assumption. This assumption allows economists to consider a change in a single variable while holding all other potentially important variables constant. In the examples throughout the remainder of the course,[i] we typically consider a single change in a situation while holding the other variables constant. Students often struggle with this concept and have trouble working with the model of supply and demand because they do not limit themselves to considering a single change at a time.

**Tip #4.** Besides the price of the good, the quantity demanded of a good is affected by the following variables: changes in the price of related goods, changes in income, changes in tastes and preferences, changes in expectations, and changes in the number of consumers. You will need to know this list of variables as well as how each of these variables affects the demand curve.

**Tip #5.** Economists make a distinction between demand and the quantity demanded. The quantity demanded refers to a specific quantity associated with a specific price (as in Figure

4.1, where $Q_1$ is associated with $P_1$ and $Q_2$ is associated with $P_2$). Demand refers to the entire demand curve. Although this may sound like a matter of semantics, economists view this distinction as highly important.

**Tip #6.**   Economists also make a distinction between a movement along a demand curve and a shift of the demand curve. A movement along a demand curve is caused by a change in the good's price, while a shift in a curve is caused by a change in some demand determinant other than the price of the good.

- Figure 4.2 illustrates this distinction for a demand curve. There is a movement from point $A$ to point $B$ when the price decreases from $P_1$ to $P_2$, and there is a shift in the demand curve from $D_1$ to $D_2$ due to a change in some other determinant of demand. A shift causes the quantity demanded of the good to change at every price—for example, at $P_1$ in Figure 4.2, the shift causes the quantity demanded to increase from $Q_1$ to $Q_3$ (compare point $A$ to point $C$). Figure 4.2 illustrates an increase in demand when the demand curve shifts to the right from $D_1$ to $D_2$. A decrease in demand would be illustrated by the demand curve shifting to the left (in Figure 4.2 this would be a shift from $D_2$ to $D_1$).

**Figure 4.2**

**Tip #7.**    Students initially find it easier to understand the concepts of substitutes and complements if they think about concrete examples. For example, consider soft drinks and popcorn. Two different brands of soft drinks are substitutes: holding all other demand determinants constant, if the price of one brand increases, then the demand for the other soft drink will increase since it is now relatively cheaper and the two goods can easily serve as substitutes for one another. In contrast, if the price of soft drinks increases, holding everything else constant, then the demand for popcorn will decrease. Popcorn and soft drinks are consumed together: they are complements to one another, which implies that if one of these goods gets more expensive (and therefore, you move upward along that good's demand curve), the quantity demanded of that good decreases. This in turn leads to a decrease in the demand for the complementary good. Questions about substitutes and complements are far easier to interpret if you take the time to think of two specific goods.

**Tip #8.**   You will find it easier to understand questions about normal and inferior goods if you think of specific examples. A normal good is a good that you will choose to increase the quantity demanded at every price as your income increases (demand shifts to the right as income increases). For example, as your income increases you will increase the quantity demanded of vacations, car travel, and recreation. An inferior good is a good that you will choose to decrease the quantity demanded at every price as your income increases (demand shifts to the left as income increases). For example, as your income increases you will likely consume fewer fast-food restaurant meals or generic pasta dinners.

1.  The supply and demand model is often used to analyze the effect of a change in the market on the equilibrium price and quantity of a good. Consider each of the following markets and the given situation to determine whether the demand curve shifts or there is a movement along the demand curve. For any shift in the demand curve, indicate whether the curve shifts to the left or to the right. The examples are given in a table to help you consolidate your answers.

| Market under consideration | Situation | Shift of or movement along the demand curve |
|---|---|---|
| Automobile market | The price of gas, a complement to cars, increases. | |
| Pizza market | The Surgeon General announces that pizza consumption is detrimental to one's health. | |
| Soap market | Health officials release a study showing the advantages of frequent hand washing. | |
| Automobile market | The price of cars increases. | |
| Insulation market | Homeowners are granted a tax credit for installing home insulation. | |

**STEP 1:** Review the determinants of demand that result in the demand curve shifting.

The demand curve will shift when there is a change in the price of a related good, either a substitute or a complement. It will also shift because of a change in the level of income; the good under consideration may be either a normal good or an inferior good. The demand curve will also shift because of a change in tastes and preferences, in expectations about future prices, or in the number of consumers in the market.

**STEP 2:** For each of the markets determine whether the change in the price of the good will cause a movement along the demand curve or a change in some other demand determinant that will shift the demand curve.

For each of the given situations except the increase in the price of automobiles, the change described in the table will cause a shift in the demand curve. A change in the price of gas is a change in the price of a complementary good to automobiles. The Surgeon General's announcement about pizza and the health officials' report on soap will change people's tastes and preferences for eating pizza or washing their hands, respectively. A government program to reduce homeowners' taxes when they install insulation will change homeowners' tastes and preferences for home insulation.

**STEP 3:** For each demand curve that shifts, determine the direction of the shift and record your responses in the provided table.

| Market under consideration | Situation | Shift of or movement along the demand curve |
| --- | --- | --- |
| Automobile market | The price of gas, a complement to cars, increases. | The increase in the price of gas will cause the demand curve for cars to shift to the left: at every price fewer cars will be demanded. |
| Pizza market | The Surgeon General announces that pizza consumption is detrimental to one's health. | The Surgeon General's announcement will cause the demand curve for pizza to shift to the left: at every price fewer units of pizza will be demanded. |
| Soap market | Health officials release a study showing the advantages of frequent hand washing. | The release of this study will cause the demand curve for soap to shift to the right: at every price more units of soap will be demanded. |
| Automobile market | The price of cars increases. | An increase in the price of cars will cause a movement along the demand curve: the quantity of cars demanded will fall. |
| Insulation market | Homeowners are granted a tax credit for installing home insulation. | The tax credit for home insulation will shift the demand curve for home insulation to the right: at every price more home insulation will be demanded. |

2.  Suppose you are told that the initial demand curve for good X is $P = 100 - Q$. You are then told that incomes increase in this economy and that good X is a normal good. If you know that the quantity demanded of good X changes by 5 units at every price, what is the equation for the new demand curve?

**STEP 1:** Start by drawing a graph of the initial demand curve. The figure that follows illustrates this demand curve.

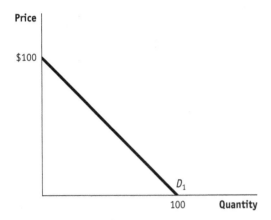

**STEP 2:** You are told that incomes increase in this economy and that this is a normal good. A change in income will cause the demand curve to shift: since incomes increase and the good is a normal good, the demand curve will shift to the right.

**STEP 3:** Calculate the exact location of the new demand curve. You know that, at every price, 5 more units are being demanded than were demanded initially. Thus, if the price was initially $0, the quantity demanded was initially 100 units (use the demand equation to get the quantity demanded when the price is $0). Now, at a price of $0, the original 100 units plus an additional 5 units will be demanded. Thus, you know that the point $(Q,P) = (105,\$0)$ sits on the new demand curve. The new demand curve has the same slope as the original demand curve, so all you need to find is the new $y$-intercept: use the point you know that is on the new demand curve to find this $y$-intercept. Thus, $P = b - Q$, and when $Q = 105$ and $P = \$0$, then $b = 105$. Thus, the new demand equation is $P = 105 - Q$. The figure that follows illustrates the new demand curve, $D_2$, along with the initial demand curve. Alternatively, the initial demand curve can be written as $Q = 100 - P$. The new demand curve has the same slope as the initial demand curve and an x-intercept of 105: thus, the new demand curve can be written as $Q = 105 - P$.

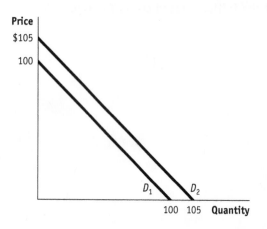

## Problems and Exercises

1.  Why is the assumption that there are many buyers and many sellers in a competitive market important?

2. You are given the following information about demand in the competitive market for bicycles.

| Price per bicycle | Quantity of bicycles demanded per week |
|---|---|
| $100 | 0 |
| 80 | 100 |
| 60 | 200 |
| 40 | 500 |
| 20 | 800 |
| 0 | 1,000 |

**a.** Graph this demand schedule placing price on the vertical axis and quantity on the horizontal axis.

**Demand Curve**

Price

Quantity per week

**b.** Suppose the price is initially $40. If the price rises by $20, what happens to the quantity demanded?

**c.** Suppose the price is initially $40. If the price falls by $40, what happens to the quantity demanded?

3. For each of the following situations in the table below, fill in the missing information. First, determine whether the situation causes a shift or a movement along the demand curve; then, if it causes a shift, determine whether the demand curve shifts to the right or to the left.

| Situation | Specified market | Movement or shift | Rightward or leftward shift in demand |
|-----------|-----------------|-------------------|--------------------------------------|
| People's income increases | Market for exotic vacations | | |
| People's income decreases | Market for goods sold in secondhand shops | | |
| Price of bicycles increases | Market for bicycles | | |
| Price of tennis balls increases | Market for tennis racquets | | |
| Price of movie tickets decreases | Popcorn at movie theaters | | |
| Popularity of music-playing device increases | Market for music-playing device | | |
| Popularity of branded clothing items decreases | Market for brand-name designer clothing | | |
| Winter clothing to go on sale next month | Market for winter clothing | | |
| Increase in urban residents | Market for apartments in urban areas | | |

4. Suppose a market has three consumers (this will simplify the work you need to do!): Joe, Maria, and Chao. Their demand schedules are given in the table below.

| Price | Quantity demanded by Joe | Quantity demanded by Maria | Quantity demanded by Chao |
|-------|-------------------------|---------------------------|--------------------------|
| $0 | 10 | 20 | 5 |
| 1 | 8 | 16 | 4 |
| 2 | 6 | 12 | 3 |
| 3 | 4 | 8 | 2 |
| 4 | 2 | 4 | 1 |

**a.** On the following graphs, sketch a graph of Joe's demand curve, Maria's demand curve, and Chao's demand curve. Then sketch the market demand curve based on the demand of these three individuals.

**Joe's Demand**

**Maria's Demand**

**Chao's Demand**

**Market Demand**

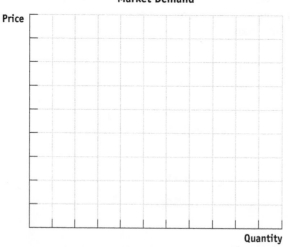

**Price**

**Quantity**

**b.** Summarize the market demand curve you found by filling in the following table.

| Price | Quantity demanded in market |
|-------|------------------------------|
| $0 | |
| 1 | |
| 2 | |
| 3 | |
| 4 | |

## ▊ BEFORE YOU TAKE THE TEST

## Module Review Questions

1. Competitive markets are characterized as having
   a. many buyers and a single seller.
   b. many buyers and a few sellers.
   c. many buyers and many sellers.
   d. a few buyers and many sellers.

2. Sue goes to the store to purchase a bottle of shampoo. When she gets to the store she discovers that her brand of shampoo is on sale for $4 a bottle instead of the usual $5.99 per bottle. According to the law of demand, we can expect that Sue will
   a. purchase one bottle of shampoo.
   b. not purchase the shampoo.
   c. likely purchase more than one bottle of shampoo.
   d. substitute away from her usual brand of shampoo and instead purchase an alternative brand.

**3.** The law of demand states that the quantity demanded is an inverse function of its price. This means that
   a. as price increases, the quantity demanded decreases.
   b. as price increases, the quantity demanded increases.
   c. the demand curve shifts to the left with increases in price.
   d. the demand curve shifts to the right with increases in price.

**4.** Consider the market for mangos. Suppose researchers discover that eating mangos generates large health benefits. Which of the following statements is true?
   a. This discovery will not affect the market for mangos.
   b. This discovery will cause the demand for mangos to shift to the right.
   c. This discovery will cause the price of mangos to decrease due to a movement along the demand curve for mangos.
   d. This discovery will cause a movement along the demand curve for mangos.

**5.** Consider the demand curve for automobiles. An increase in the price of automobiles will
   a. cause a movement along the demand curve for automobiles.
   b. result in an increase in the quantity of automobiles demanded.
   c. have no effect on the quantity of automobiles demanded since the change occurred on the supply side of the model.
   d. Answers (a) and (b) are both true statements.

**6.** The prices of flat-screen TVs are expected to fall next year. Which of the following statements about the market for flat-screen TVs this year are true?
   I. Consumers will decrease their demand for flat-screen TVs at all prices this year in anticipation of the decrease in flat-screen TV prices next year.
   II. Prices today for a given quantity of flat-screen TVs are likely to decrease due to these expectations.
   III. Prices today for a given quantity of flat-screen TVs are likely to increase due to these expectations.
   a. Statement I is true.
   b. Statement II is true.
   c. Statement III is true.
   d. Statements I and II are true.
   e. Statements I and III are true.

**7.** Peanut butter and jelly are considered to be complements in the diet of many people. Holding everything else constant, if the price of peanut butter increases, then the demand for
   a. peanut butter will shift to the left.
   b. peanut butter will shift to the right.
   c. jelly will shift to the left.
   d. jelly will shift to the right.

8. Ham and turkey are considered to be substitutes in the diet of many people. Holding everything else constant, if the price of ham decreases, then the demand for
   a. turkey will shift to the left.
   b. turkey will shift to the right.
   c. ham will shift to the left.
   d. ham will shift to the right.

9. Consider two goods: good X and good Y. Holding everything else constant, the price of good Y increases and the demand for good X decreases. Good X and good Y are
   a. complements.
   b. substitutes.
   c. not related to each other.

10. Consider two goods: good X and good Y. Holding everything else constant, the price of good Y decreases and the demand for good X decreases. Good X and good Y are
    a. complements.
    b. substitutes.
    c. not related to each other.

11. Holding everything else constant, Jon's income increases. If Jon's demand for good X decreases, then it must be the case that good X is a(n)
    a. inferior good.
    b. normal good.
    c. complement.
    d. substitute.

12. Jon's income increases by 10% this year while his purchases of steak increase by 4% this year over last year's purchases of steak. Holding everything else constant, Jon considers steak to be a(n)
    a. inferior good.
    b. normal good.
    c. complement.
    d. substitute.

13. Smalltown experiences an increase in its population due to the economic opportunities available in Smalltown. This event is likely to
    a. cause the demand curve for many products in Smalltown to shift to the right.
    b. cause the demand curve for many products in Smalltown to shift to the left.
    c. have little effect on the demand for products in Smalltown.
    d. cause the supply curve for many products in Smalltown to shift to the left.

14. A market is initially composed of 100 buyers. Holding everything else constant, if an additional 100 buyers join this market, then this will
    a. have no effect on the market demand curve since there is a limit to how many units of the good can be demanded at any price.
    b. cause the market demand curve to shift to the left since the good's price will necessarily increase when there are more buyers.
    c. cause the market demand curve to shift to the right as the additional demand of these new consumers is added to the initial demand curve.
    d. cause a movement along the demand curve as the price of the good rises due to the increase in the number of buyers.

**15.** Consider a market composed of three consumers: Peter, Anya, and Pablo. The market demand schedule is given in the table below. Which of the possible individual demand schedules provided in the answer selection is most likely to correspond to this market demand schedule?

| Price | Market quantity demanded |
|-------|--------------------------|
| $10 | 100 |
| 20 | 75 |
| 30 | 50 |
| 40 | 25 |

a.

| Price | Quantity demanded by Peter | Quantity demanded by Anya | Quantity demanded by Pablo |
|-------|---------|---------|---------|
| $10 | 25 | 25 | 40 |
| 20 | 20 | 20 | 35 |
| 30 | 15 | 14 | 16 |
| 40 | 10 | 10 | 5 |

b.

| Price | Quantity demanded by Peter | Quantity demanded by Anya | Quantity demanded by Pablo |
|-------|---------|---------|---------|
| $10 | 25 | 25 | 50 |
| 20 | 20 | 15 | 35 |
| 30 | 15 | 10 | 25 |
| 40 | 10 | 10 | 5 |

c.

| Price | Quantity demanded by Peter | Quantity demanded by Anya | Quantity demanded by Pablo |
|-------|---------|---------|---------|
| $10 | 25 | 25 | 55 |
| 20 | 15 | 20 | 35 |
| 30 | 10 | 15 | 20 |
| 40 | 5 | 10 | 5 |

d.

| Price | Quantity demanded by Peter | Quantity demanded by Anya | Quantity demanded by Pablo |
|-------|---------|---------|---------|
| $10 | 25 | 25 | 50 |
| 20 | 20 | 20 | 35 |
| 30 | 15 | 15 | 20 |
| 40 | 10 | 10 | 5 |

**16.** The market demand curve for a product is the horizontal summation of the individual demand curves for the product, holding the

a. quantity demanded constant.

b. price constant.

# ANSWER KEY

## Answers to Problems and Exercises

1. This assumption results in a market situation in which no buyer (or group of buyers) and no seller (or group of sellers) can affect the market price. In a competitive market the interaction of demand and supply determines the equilibrium price and the equilibrium quantity rather than the behavior of a particular buyer and/or seller.

2. **a.**

**Demand Curve**

**b.** If the price rises to $60, the quantity demanded will fall by 300 units, from 500 bicycles to 200 bicycles.

**c.** If the price falls to $0, the quantity demanded will increase by 500 units, from 500 bicycles to 1,000 bicycles.

3.

| Situation | Specified market | Movement or shift | Rightward or leftward shift in demand |
|---|---|---|---|
| People's income increases | Market for exotic vacations | Shift | Rightward |
| People's income decreases | Market for goods sold in secondhand shops | Shift | Rightward |
| Price of bicycles increases | Market for bicycles | Movement | |
| Price of tennis balls increases | Market for tennis racquets | Shift | Leftward |
| Price of movie tickets decreases | Popcorn at movie theaters | Shift | Rightward |
| Popularity of music-playing device increases | Market for music-playing device | Shift | Rightward |
| Popularity of branded clothing items decreases | Market for brand-name designer clothing | Shift | Leftward |
| Winter clothing to go on sale next month | Market for winter clothing | Shift | Leftward |
| Increase in urban residents | Market for apartments in urban areas | Shift | Rightward |

4.  **a.** Note: these sketches are not drawn to scale since they are meant to be a guide rather than a perfect mathematical rendering of the data in the table. To find the market demand curve, hold price constant and ask how many units are demanded by all the consumers at this price. For example, at a price of $3, Joe demands 4 units, Maria demands 8 units, and Chao demands 2 units for a total market demand of 14 units at a price of $3. Repeat this for another price (e.g., for a price of $4, Joe demands 2 units, Maria demands 4 units, and Chao demands 1 unit for a total market demand of 7 units).

**Joe's Demand**

**Maria's Demand**

**Chao's Demand**

**Market Demand**

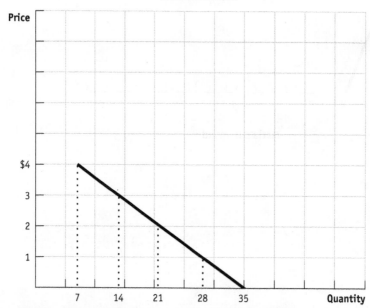

**b.**

| Price | Quantity demanded in market |
|-------|------------------------------|
| $0 | 35 |
| 1 | 28 |
| 2 | 21 |
| 3 | 14 |
| 4 | 7 |

# Answers to Module Review Questions

1.  **Answer c.** This is a definitional statement.

2.  **Answer c.** The law of demand states that as the price of the good decreases, the quantity demanded of the good increases. Since the shampoo is on sale, its price has fallen and the law of demand suggests that the quantity demanded should therefore increase.

3.  **Answer a.** This is a definitional statement. An inverse function of two variables means that an increase in one of the variables will result in a decrease in the other variable, or a decrease in one of the variables will result in an increase in the other variable. The law of demand states that as the price of the good increases, the quantity demanded of the good decreases; thus, price and quantity are inversely related.

4.  **Answer b.** This research finding is likely to result in an increase in tastes and preferences for mangos, which will cause the demand curve for mangos to shift to the right.

5.  **Answer a.** A leftward shift in the supply curve holding everything else constant will cause the price of the good to increase. An increase in price will result in a movement along the demand curve, since as the price increases, the quantity demanded of the good decreases.

6.  **Answer d.** The expected fall in flat-screen TV prices next year will cause the demand curve for flat-screen TVs this year to shift to the left as consumers decrease the quantity of flat-screen TVs they demand at every price. At any given quantity of flat-screen TVs the price demanders are willing to pay will be lower because of the change in expectations.

7.  **Answer c.** Since peanut butter and jelly are considered complements in this example, an increase in the price of peanut butter will cause the demand curve for jelly to shift to the left, since as fewer units of peanut butter are demanded due to the higher price of peanut butter, fewer units of jelly will also be demanded at any given price for jelly.

8.  **Answer a.** Since ham and turkey are substitutes, when the price of ham decreases, this causes the quantity of ham demanded to increase. As more units of ham are demanded, fewer units of turkey are demanded at every price. The demand for turkey therefore shifts to the left.

9.  **Answer a.** As the price of good Y increases, this results in a decrease in the quantity demanded of good Y. Since the demand for good X decreases, this implies that good Y and good X are consumed together; thus good X and good Y are complements.

10. **Answer b.** As the price of good Y decreases, this results in an increase in the quantity demanded of good Y. Since the demand for good X decreases when the quantity demanded of good Y increases, this implies that good X is a substitute for good Y.

11. **Answer a.** When Jon's income increases, the quantity of good X he demands at any given price falls, which implies that good X is an inferior good.

12. **Answer b.** Both Jon's income and the quantity of steak he demands increases; therefore steak is a normal good.

13. **Answer a.** An increase in population shifts the demand curve to the right, as the increase in population implies a larger number of consumers of the product.

14. **Answer c.** An increase in the number of buyers causes the quantity demanded of the good to increase at every price, and the demand curve shifts to the right.

15. **Answer d.** To find the market demand curve, hold price constant and then add the quantity of the good demanded by each of the consumers. Thus, if the price of the good is $10, then the total of Peter's, Anya's, and Pablo's demand must add up to 100 units according to the table provided in the question.

16. **Answer b.** This is a definitional statement. The market demand curve is found by holding price constant and then adding together the quantities demanded by each consumer in the market. This process is repeated for other prices.

# Supply and Equilibrium

| **BEFORE YOU READ THE MODULE** |

## Summary

This module describes the supply curve, explains the distinction between movements along a supply curve versus a shift of the supply curve, and also discusses the primary determinants of supply. The module defines the meaning of equilibrium in the model of demand and supply. The module examines how demand and supply interact to determine a market's equilibrium price and equilibrium quantity. The module also discusses how a market eliminates shortages and surpluses through changes in price and quantity so that the market returns to its equilibrium.

## Module Objectives

**Objective #1.**   The quantity of a good or service supplied by a producer depends on the price producers are offered for their product. The supply schedule illustrates the relationship between various prices and the quantity of the good supplied at each of these prices. Generally speaking, the quantity supplied increases as the price increases, holding everything else constant. A supply curve is the graphical representation of a supply schedule. Usually a supply curve is upward sloping: the quantity supplied increases as the price increases.

**Objective #2.**   The quantity supplied depends on many factors, but the primary determinants of the quantity supplied are the price of the good, the price of its inputs, the price of related goods, and changes in technology, expectations, and the number of producers. A change in the price of the good causes a movement along the supply curve; a change in one of the other supply determinants, other than price, causes a shift in the supply curve. A rightward shift in the supply curve is an increase in supply; a leftward shift in the supply curve is a decrease in supply. An increase in the price of inputs, holding everything else constant, will cause a decrease in supply. This means that the supply curve shifts to the left, and at every price the quantity supplied is now less than it was initially.

**Objective #3.**   Two goods are substitutes in production when an increase in the price of one of these goods results in greater production of this good and reduced production of the other good. Two goods are complements in production when an increase in the price of one of these goods results in greater production of both goods.

80

**Objective #4.** The market supply curve is found by horizontally adding together the individual supply curves. At each price, the quantity supplied by each firm is added together to create the market supply curve. As the number of individual producers increases there is an increase in supply.

**Objective #5.** A competitive market is in equilibrium at the price at which the quantity demanded equals the quantity supplied. This price is called the equilibrium price. The quantity associated with this equilibrium price is called the equilibrium quantity. The equilibrium price is the market-clearing price, since at this price the quantity demanded equals the quantity supplied. The equilibrium in a market occurs at the point of intersection between the demand and supply curves.

**Objective #6.** At a given price, if the quantity supplied of the good is greater than the quantity demanded of the good, there is a surplus, or excess supply, in the market. If there is excess supply, prices will fall until the quantity supplied equals the quantity demanded. At a given price, if the quantity supplied of the good is less than the quantity demanded of the good, there is a shortage, or excess demand, in the market. If there is excess demand, prices will rise until the quantity supplied equals the quantity demanded.

## Key Terms

**quantity supplied** the actual amount of a good or service producers are willing to sell at some specific price.

**supply schedule** a list or table showing how much of a good or service producers will supply at different prices.

**supply curve** a graphical representation of the *supply schedule,* showing the relationship between *quantity supplied* and price.

**law of supply** the general proposition that, all else constant, a higher price leads to higher quantity supplied and a lower price leads to lower quantity supplied.

**change in supply** a shift of the supply curve, which changes the quantity supplied at any given price.

**movement along the supply curve** a change in the *quantity supplied* of a good that results from a change in the price of that good.

**input** a good or service used to produce another good or service.

**individual supply curve** a graphical representation of the relationship between *quantity supplied* and price for an individual producer.

**equilibrium** the state in which no individual would be better off doing something different.

**equilibrium price** the price at which the market is in *equilibrium,* that is, the quantity of a good or service demanded equals the quantity of that good or service supplied; also referred to as the *market-clearing price.*

**equilibrium quantity** the quantity of a good or service bought and sold at the *equilibrium* (or *market-clearing) price.*

**market-clearing price** the price at which the market is in *equilibrium,* that is, the quantity of a good or service demanded equals the quantity of that good or service supplied; also referred to as the *equilibrium price.*

**surplus** the excess of a good or service that occurs when the quantity supplied exceeds the quantity demanded; surpluses occur when the price is above the *equilibrium price.*

**shortage** the insufficiency of a good or service that occurs when the quantity demanded exceeds the quantity supplied; shortages occur when the price is below the *equilibrium price.*

## ■ AFTER YOU READ THE MODULE

## Tips

**Tip #1.** A supply curve is usually upward sloping. The positive slope of a supply curve implies that the quantity supplied of a good or service is directly related to its price. Another way to express this idea is that as the price of the good decreases, holding everything else constant, producers will want to supply fewer units of the good. Figure 5.1 illustrates this idea: at $P_1$, $Q_1$ units of the good are supplied; as the price of the good falls from $P_1$ to $P_2$, the quantity supplied of the good decreases from $Q_1$ to $Q_2$.

**Figure 5.1**

**Tip #2.** A supply curve illustrates the relationship between the price of the good and the quantity supplied at each specific price. In drawing the supply curve, the other determinants of supply are held constant; this constancy is another example of the other-things-equal assumption.

**Tip #3.** Besides the price of the good, the quantity supplied of a good is affected by the following variables: changes in input prices, changes in the price of related goods, and changes in technology, expectations, and the number of producers. You need to know this list of variables as well as how each of these variables affects the supply curve.

**Tip #4.**   Economists make a distinction between supply and the quantity supplied. The quantity supplied refers to a specific quantity associated with a specific price (as in Figure 5.1 where $Q_1$ is associated with $P_1$ and $Q_2$ is associated with $P_2$). Supply refers to the entire supply curve.

**Tip #5.**   Economists also make a distinction between a movement along a supply curve and a shift of the supply curve. A movement is caused by a change in the good's price, while a shift in a supply curve is caused by a change in some supply determinant other than the price of the good.

- Figure 5.2 illustrates this distinction for a supply curve. There is a movement from point A to point B when the price decreases from $P_1$ to $P_2$, and there is a shift in the supply curve from $S_1$ to $S_2$ due to a change in some other determinant of supply. A shift causes the quantity supplied of the good to change at every price—for example, at $P_1$ in Figure 5.2, the shift causes the quantity supplied to increase from $Q_1$ to $Q_3$ (compare point A to point C). Figure 5.2 illustrates an increase in supply when the supply curve shifts to the right from $S_1$ to $S_2$. A decrease in supply would be illustrated by the supply curve shifting to the left (in Figure 5.2 this would be a shift from $S_2$ to $S_1$).

**Figure 5.2**

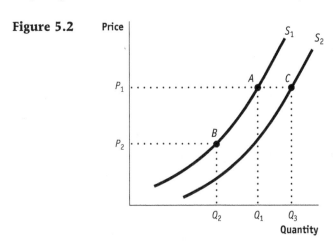

**Tip #6.**   The market equilibrium occurs at the point of intersection of the demand and supply curves. Figure 5.3 indicates that equilibrium at point E, where the equilibrium price is $P_1$ and the equilibrium quantity is $Q_1$. If the price is greater than the equilibrium price, there is excess supply, or a surplus, in the market. Figure 5.3 illustrates a situation of excess supply at the price $P_2$. Note that at price $P_2$ the quantity supplied is $Q_3$, while the quantity demanded is $Q_2$. If the price is less than the equilibrium price, there is excess demand, or a shortage, in the market. Figure 5.3 illustrates a situation of excess demand at the price $P_3$. Note that at price $P_3$ the quantity demanded is $Q_5$, while the quantity supplied is $Q_4$.

**Figure 5.3**

**Tip #7.** If you are given an equation for the demand curve and an equation for the supply curve, you can solve these two equations for the equilibrium price and equilibrium quantity. For example, suppose demand is given by the equation $P = 10 - Q$ and supply is given by the equation $P = Q$. To find the equilibrium, recall that in equilibrium the quantity demanded equals the quantity supplied; thus, $10 - Q = Q$, or the equilibrium quantity equals 5. Replace $Q$ in either equation with 5 and you will find that the equilibrium price is 5.

**Tip #8.** Often a quick sketch of a demand and supply curve is all that you need to answer questions about the effect of a change in the market on the equilibrium price or equilibrium quantity. Practice drawing a quick representation of the demand and supply curves as you do this module's problems, recognizing that you do not always need a precisely plotted graph to find a solution or to guide your solution of a problem.

**Tip #9.** As always, if you are making a set of flash cards, make one for each new definition or concept and then review these cards (as well as the cards from the earlier modules).

# WORKED PROBLEMS

1. The supply and demand model is often used to analyze the effect of a change in the market on the equilibrium price and quantity of a good. Consider each of the following markets and the given situation to determine whether the supply curve shifts or there is a movement along the supply curve. For any shift in the supply curve, indicate whether the curve shifts to the left or to the right. The examples are given in a table to help you consolidate your answers.

| Market under consideration | Situation | Shift of or movement along the demand curve |
|---|---|---|
| Automobile market | The price of steel, a key input in the production of cars, increases. | |
| Pizza market | The number of pizza shops in town doubles. | |
| Shampoo market | The price of plastic used in shampoo bottles decreases. | |
| Automobile market | Manufacturers of cars anticipate that car prices will increase next year. | |
| Leather belt market | The price of leather wallets increases. | |

**STEP 1:** Review the determinants of supply that result in the supply curve shifting.

The supply curve will shift when there is a change in the price of an input, in the price of a substitute in production, in the price of a complement in production, in technology, in expectations about future prices, or in the number of producers in the market.

**STEP 2:** For each of the markets determine whether there is a change in the price of the good, which will cause a movement along the supply curve, or a change in some other supply determinant, which will shift the supply curve.

For each of the given situations the change described in the table will cause a shift in the supply curve. The table in Step 3 summarizes these shifts and their causes.

**STEP 3:** For each supply curve that shifts, determine the direction of the shift and record your responses in the provided table.

| Market under consideration | Situation | Shift of or movement along the demand curve |
|---|---|---|
| Automobile market | The price of steel, a key input in the production of cars, increases. | The supply curve will shift to the left: at every price, the quantity of cars supplied will decrease because of an increase in the price of an input. |
| Pizza market | The number of pizza shops in town doubles. | The supply curve will shift to the right: at every price, the quantity of pizzas supplied will increase because of an increase in the number of producers. |
| Shampoo market | The price of plastic used in shampoo bottles decreases. | The supply curve will shift to the right: at every price, the quantity of shampoo supplied will increase because of a decrease in the price of an input. |
| Automobile market | Manufacturers of cars anticipate that car prices will increase next year. | The supply curve will shift to the left: at every price, the quantity of cars supplied will decrease because of expectations that prices will increase in the future. |
| Leather belt market | The price of leather wallets increases. | The supply curve will shift to the left: at every price, the quantity of leather belts supplied will decrease because of an increase in the price of a substitute in production. |

2. Suppose you are told that each firm in an industry is identical and that there are two firms in the industry. Furthermore, you are told that one firm's supply curve is given by the equation $P = 10 + 2Q$. Find the market supply curve in this industry.

**STEP 1:** To find the market supply curve, you will want to horizontally add all the individual supply curves of the firms in the industry. This will be relatively easy if you draw three horizontally aligned graphs where the first graph illustrates firm 1's supply curve, the second graph illustrates firm 2's supply curve, and the third graph illustrates the market supply curve. The following figure represents this concept.

**STEP 2:** To find the market supply curve, you will want to horizontally add all the individual supply curves of the firms in the industry. Use your sketch to help you write this equation.

From the third graph you can see that the y-intercept is 10. You can also calculate the slope of the market supply curve as the change in price divided by the change in quantity. Using the points (0,10) and (10,20), the slope is equal to 1. The market supply curve can thus be written as $P = Q + 10$.

## Problems and Exercises

1.  The following graph represents the supply curve for the production of widgets in Town Center.

a.  At a price of $20, how many widgets are producers willing to supply?

**b.** At a price of $40, how many widgets are producers willing to supply?

**c.** Suppose there are ten widget producers in Town Center and that the price of widgets is $50. If each widget producer produces exactly the same number of widgets as every other widget producer, how many widgets will each producer produce at this price?

**d.** Suppose the price is initially $30 but then falls to $20. What is the change in the quantity supplied?

**e.** Suppose the price is initially $30 but then increases to $50. What is the change in the quantity supplied?

**f.** What price must suppliers receive in order to be willing to supply 80 widgets?

**g.** What price must suppliers receive in order to be willing to supply 40 widgets?

**h.** What does the slope of a typical supply curve imply about the relationship between price and the quantity supplied?

2. For each of the following situations in the table below, fill in the missing information: first, determine whether the situation causes a shift or a movement along the supply curve; then, if it causes a shift, determine whether the supply curve shifts to the right or to the left.

| Situation | Specified market | Movement or shift | Rightward or leftward shift in supply |
|---|---|---|---|
| Labor costs for air travel and cruise ships increase | Market for exotic vacations | | |
| Prices of office equipment and phone service rise by 40% | Market for call center services | | |
| Price of bicycles increases | Market for bicycles | | |
| Price of leather boots increases | Market for beef products | | |
| Price of leather boots increases | Market for leather belts | | |
| New technology for music-playing device revealed | Market for music-playing devices | | |
| Price of brand-name designer clothing increases | Market for brand-name designer clothing | | |
| Stock market prices expected to fall next quarter | Stock market today | | |
| Increase in number of coffee shop owners in the metro area | Market for coffee shops in the metro area | | |

3. The demand and supply schedules for Healthy Snacks, Inc., is provided in the table below.

| Price | Quantity demanded | Quantity supplied |
|---|---|---|
| $ 0 | 1,000 | 0 |
| 10 | 800 | 125 |
| 20 | 600 | 275 |
| 30 | 400 | 400 |
| 40 | 200 | 550 |
| 50 | 0 | 675 |

**a.** Draw a sketch of the demand and supply curves for Healthy Snacks, Inc. Don't worry about drawing a precise graph but instead focus on drawing a simple rendering of the underlying relationships captured in the table. This drawing should be accurate with regard to x-intercepts and y-intercepts and it should also indicate the point of equilibrium.

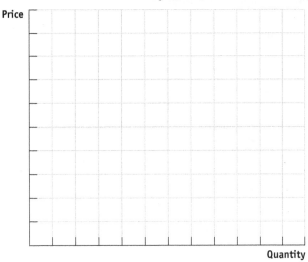

**b.** From the table, what are the equilibrium price and the equilibrium quantity in this market? Indicate these on your graph.

**c.** Fill in the following table based on the data given to you. Assume that for each row in the table, the price is as given and that you are calculating the number of units of excess demand or excess supply. (Hint: Some of the cells in your table will be left empty—for example, if there is excess supply, then there isn't excess demand.)

| Price | Excess demand | Excess supply |
|-------|---------------|---------------|
| $ 0   |               |               |
| 10    |               |               |
| 20    |               |               |
| 30    |               |               |
| 40    |               |               |
| 50    |               |               |

**d.** Why is a situation of excess demand referred to as a shortage? Explain using a simple graph to illustrate your answer.

e. Why is a situation of excess supply referred to as a surplus? Explain using a simple graph to illustrate your answer.

4. Use the following graph to answer this next set of questions. The graph illustrates the competitive market for garbage cans in Cleantopia.

**Market for Garbage Cans in Cleantopia**

a. What is the equilibrium price in this market?

b. What is the equilibrium quantity in this market?

c. Suppose the current price of garbage cans in Cleantopia is $P_2$. Describe this market in detail and explain what you think will happen in this market.

d. Suppose the current price of garbage cans in Cleantopia is $P_4$. Describe this market in detail and explain what you think will happen in this market.

e. Suppose at the current market price the quantity demanded equals $Q_4$. Describe this market and identify the quantity supplied given this information. What do you expect will happen in this market?

f. Suppose at the current market price the quantity supplied equals $Q_5$. Describe this market and identify the quantity demanded given this information. What do you expect will happen in this market?

g. At what price is the quantity demanded equal to zero? What does it mean to have the quantity demanded equal to zero?

h. At what price is the quantity supplied equal to zero? What does it mean to have the quantity supplied equal to zero?

5. The competitive market for bicycles in Pedal City is described by the demand curve $P = 2{,}000 - 2Q$ and the supply curve $P = 6Q$. There are twenty bicycle manufacturers in Pedal City and each of these manufacturers produces the same number of bicycles as every other manufacturer.

a. Using the two equations for the demand and supply curves, fill in the following table describing the demand and supply schedules for bicycles in Pedal City.

| Price | Quantity demanded | Quantity supplied |
|---|---|---|
| $   0 | | |
| 240 | | |
| 480 | | |
| 720 | | |
| 960 | | |
| 1,200 | | |
| 1,440 | | |
| 1,680 | | |
| 1,920 | | |

b. Examine the table you created in (a) and provide a range of prices that you expect the equilibrium price to fall between. Why do you expect the equilibrium price to fall within this range?

    **c.** Sketch a graph of the demand and supply curves for bicycles in Pedal City.

**Market for Bicycles in Pedal City**

Price

Quantity

    **d.** If the current price for bicycles is $240, how many bicycles will be supplied in Pedal City and how many bicycles will a single manufacturer produce? At a price of $240, how many bicycles will be demanded? At a price of $240, is the market in equilibrium? Explain your answer.

    **e.** If the current price for bicycles is $480, how many bicycles will be supplied in Pedal City and how many bicycles will a single manufacturer produce? At a price of $480, how many bicycles will be demanded? At a price of $480, is the market in equilibrium? Explain your answer.

    **f.** If the current price for bicycles is $1,680, how many bicycles will be supplied in Pedal City and how many bicycles will a single manufacturer produce? At a price of $1,680, how many bicycles will be demanded? At a price of $1,680, is the market in equilibrium? Explain your answer.

    **g.** Calculate the equilibrium price and the equilibrium quantity in the market for bicycles in Pedal City.

## BEFORE YOU TAKE THE TEST

# Module Review Questions

1. Consider a supply curve. When the price of the good increases, then this results in a movement along the supply curve resulting in a greater
   a. supply of the good.
   b. quantity supplied.

2. The cost of ground beef used to produce Fast Wally's hamburgers increases. Holding everything else constant, this will result in
   a. the supply curve shifting to the left.
   b. the supply curve shifting to the right.
   c. a movement along the supply curve to a smaller quantity supplied.
   d. a movement along the supply curve to a greater quantity supplied.

3. The cost of raw materials used to produce Ever Strong Batteries decreases. Holding everything else constant, this will result in
   a. the supply curve shifting to the left.
   b. the supply curve shifting to the right.
   c. a movement along the supply curve to a smaller quantity supplied.
   d. a movement along the supply curve to a greater quantity supplied.

4. Input prices decrease for a manufacturer. Holding everything else constant, this implies that at any given price the manufacturer will supply
   a. more of the good.
   b. less of the good.

5. A manufacturer produces two different products from its fixed set of resources. When the manufacturer increases the production of the first good, it must necessarily reduce the level of production of the second good due to these fixed resources. These two goods are
   a. complements in production.
   b. substitutes in production.

6. A sawmill operator produces lumber used in the construction industry as well as sawdust used for pet bedding. An increase in the supply of lumber is likely to
   a. increase the supply of sawdust, since lumber and sawdust are complements in production.
   b. decrease the supply of sawdust, since lumber and sawdust are complements in production.
   c. increase the supply of sawdust, since lumber and sawdust are substitutes in production.
   d. decrease the supply of sawdust, since lumber and sawdust are substitutes in production.

7. Research and development result in the discovery of a new technology for electricity generation. Holding everything else constant, this discovery will
   a. increase the supply of electricity.
   b. increase the quantity supplied of electricity.
   c. decrease the supply of electricity.
   d. decrease the quantity supplied of electricity.

8.  The sawmill industry expects lumber prices to rise next year due to growing demand for the construction of new homes. Holding everything else constant, this expectation will shift

a. the supply curve for lumber this year to the left.

b. the supply curve for lumber this year to the right.

9.  The graph below illustrates the supply curve for the competitive market for widgets. Currently there are sixteen producers in this market and each producer produces exactly the same number of widgets as every other producer. Suppose the price of widgets is $40. If all the producers continue to produce the same number as every other producer, what will be the level of production for each producer?

a. 8 widgets

b. 10 widgets

c. 5 widgets

d. 20 widgets

10. Which of the following statements is true about equilibrium in a competitive market for a good?

   I. In equilibrium, the quantity demanded equals the quantity supplied.

   II. The equilibrium price and the equilibrium quantity correspond to the price and quantity at which the demand curve intersects the supply curve.

   III. In equilibrium, every consumer who wishes to consume the product is satisfied.

a. Statement I is true.

b. Statement II is true.

c. Statement III is true.

d. Statements I and II are true.

e. Statements I, II, and III are true.

**11.** The competitive market for widgets is described by the following table.

| Price | Quantity demanded | Quantity supplied |
|-------|-------------------|-------------------|
| $ 0   | 400               | 0                 |
| 20    | 300               | 100               |
| 40    | 200               | 200               |
| 60    | 100               | 300               |
| 80    | 0                 | 400               |

If the current price is $20, then there is a(n)

a. excess supply of 200 widgets.

b. shortage of 200 widgets.

c. excess demand of 100 widgets.

d. surplus of 100 widgets.

**12.** The competitive market for widgets is described by the following table.

| Price | Quantity demanded | Quantity supplied |
|-------|-------------------|-------------------|
| $ 0   | 400               | 0                 |
| 20    | 300               | 100               |
| 40    | 200               | 200               |
| 60    | 100               | 300               |
| 80    | 0                 | 400               |

If the current price is $60, then there is a(n)

a. excess supply of 200 widgets.

b. excess demand of 200 widgets.

c. shortage of 100 widgets.

d. surplus of 100 widgets.

13. The competitive market for widgets is described by the following table.

| Price | Quantity demanded | Quantity supplied |
|-------|-------------------|-------------------|
| $ 0 | 400 | 0 |
| 20 | 300 | 100 |
| 40 | 200 | 200 |
| 60 | 100 | 300 |
| 80 | 0 | 400 |

The equilibrium quantity in this market is _____ widgets and the equilibrium price is _____.
a. 300; $20
b. 200; $20
c. 200; $40
d. 200; $60

14. The competitive market for widgets is described by the following table. Furthermore, you are told that both the demand curve and the supply curve are linear.

| Price | Quantity demanded | Quantity supplied |
|-------|-------------------|-------------------|
| $ 0 | 400 | 0 |
| 20 | 300 | 100 |
| 40 | 200 | 200 |
| 60 | 100 | 300 |
| 80 | 0 | 400 |

Which of the following equations is the demand equation for widgets?
a. $Q = 80 - 5P$
b. $P = 80 - 5Q$
c. $Q = 400 - 5P$
d. $Q = 1/5P$

15. The competitive market for widgets is described by the following table. Furthermore, you are told that both the demand curve and the supply curve are linear.

| Price | Quantity demanded | Quantity supplied |
|-------|-------------------|-------------------|
| $ 0 | 400 | 0 |
| 20 | 300 | 100 |
| 40 | 200 | 200 |
| 60 | 100 | 300 |
| 80 | 0 | 400 |

Which of the following equations is the supply equation for widgets?

a. $P = 5Q$

b. $P = 1/5Q$

c. $Q = 1/5P$

d. $Q = 100 + 1/5Q$

16. Use the following graph of a competitive market for candles to answer this question.

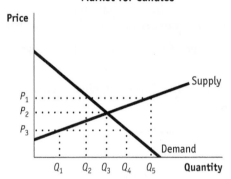

**Market for Candles**

At a price of $P_1$, there is an excess

a. supply of the good equal to $Q_2 - Q_5$.

b. supply of the good equal to $Q_5 - Q_2$.

c. supply of the good equal to $Q_3 - Q_2$.

d. demand for the good equal to $Q_3 - Q_2$.

17. Use the following graph of a competitive market for candles to answer this question.

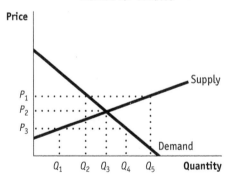

**Market for Candles**

At a price of $P_3$, there is an excess

a. demand for the good of $Q_4 - Q_1$.

b. demand for the good of $Q_1 - Q_4$.

c. demand for the good of $Q_3 - Q_2$.

d. supply of the good of $Q_3 - Q_2$.

### ANSWER KEY

## Answers to Problems and Exercises

1.  **a.** At a price of $20, producers are willing to supply 40 units.

    **b.** At a price of $40, producers are willing to supply 80 units.

    **c.** At a price of $50, 100 widgets are supplied. Thus, if there are ten producers producing exactly the same number of widgets, then each producer must produce 10 widgets.

    **d.** When price falls from $30 to $20, the number of widgets supplied decreases by 20 widgets (from 60 widgets to 40 widgets).

    **e.** When price rises from $30 to $50, the number of widgets supplied increases by 40 widgets (from 60 widgets to 100 widgets).

    **f.** Suppliers are willing to supply 80 widgets if the price is $40.

    **g.** Suppliers are willing to supply 40 widgets if the price is $20.

    **h.** The typical supply curve is upward sloping: its slope is positive. This implies that the quantity supplied increases when price increases and that the quantity supplied decreases when price decreases.

2.

| Situation | Specified market | Movement or shift | Rightward or leftward shift in supply |
|---|---|---|---|
| Labor costs for air travel and cruise ships increase | Market for exotic vacations | Shift | Leftward |
| Prices of office equipment and phone service rise by 40% | Market for call center services | Shift | Leftward |
| Price of bicycles increases | Market for bicycles | Movement | |
| Price of leather boots increases | Market for beef products | Shift | Rightward |
| Price of leather boots increases | Market for leather belts | Shift | Leftward |
| New technology for music-playing device revealed | Market for music-playing devices | Shift | Rightward |
| Price of brand-name designer clothing increases | Market for brand-name designer clothing | Movement | |
| Stock market prices expected to fall next quarter | Stock market today | Shift | Rightward |
| Increase in number of coffee shop owners in the metro area | Market for coffee shops in the metro area | Shift | Rightward |

**3. a.,b.** Equilibrium occurs at the price at which the quantity demanded equals the quantity supplied. From the table we can see that the quantity demanded equals the quantity supplied at a price of $30. The equilibrium price is thus $30 and the equilibrium quantity is 400 units. This point is illustrated in the graph in part (d).

**c.**

| Price | Excess demand | Excess supply |
|---|---|---|
| $ 0 | 1,000 units | |
| 10 | 675 units | |
| 20 | 325 units | |
| 30 | Equilibrium | Equilibrium |
| 40 | | 350 units |
| 50 | | 675 units |

**d.** When there is excess demand this means that the quantity demanded by consumers is greater than the quantity supplied by producers. The market for some reason does not provide an adequate amount of the good, and thus there is a shortage of the good. The figure below illustrates a shortage at a price of $P_1$. Note that at $P_1$, the quantity demanded is $Q_1$, the quantity supplied is $Q_2$, and the excess demand is equal to $Q_1 - Q_2$. When a market has excess demand, this implies that the current price of the good is less than the market-clearing price.

**Illustration of a Situation of
Excess Demand, or a Shortage**

**e.** When there is excess supply this means that the quantity demanded by consumers is less than the quantity supplied by producers. The market for some reason provides too much of the good, and thus there is a surplus of the good. The figure below illustrates a surplus at a price of $P_1$. Note that at $P_1$, the quantity demanded is $Q_1$, the quantity supplied is $Q_2$, and the excess supply is equal to $Q_2 - Q_1$. When a market has excess supply of a good, this implies that the current price in the market is greater than the market-clearing price.

**Illustration of a Situation of Excess Supply, or a Surplus**

**4.   a.** The equilibrium price in this market is $P_3$ since the quantity demanded ($Q_3$) equals the quantity supplied ($Q_3$) at this price.

**b.** $Q_3$.

**c.** At $P_2$ there is an excess supply, or surplus, of the good, since the quantity supplied equals $Q_5$ while the quantity demanded equals $Q_2$. The price should fall toward the equilibrium price. As the price falls, consumers will increase the quantity demanded of the good while producers will decrease the quantity supplied of the good until the price reaches the point where the quantity demanded equals the quantity supplied.

**d.** At $P_4$ there is an excess demand, or shortage, for the good, since the quantity supplied equals $Q_1$ while the quantity demanded equals $Q_4$. The price should rise toward the equilibrium price. As the price increases, consumers will reduce the quantity demanded of the good while producers will increase the quantity supplied of the good until the price reaches the point where the quantity demanded equals the quantity supplied.

**e.** When the quantity demanded is equal to $Q_4$, this implies that the current price in the market is $P_4$, which is the situation of excess demand described in part (d).

**f.** When the quantity supplied is equal to $Q_5$, this implies that the current price in the market is $P_2$, which is the situation of excess supply described in part (c).

**g.** At $P_1$ the quantity demanded is equal to zero. This implies that at a price of $P_1$ the price is too high for consumers to be willing to demand the product.

**h.** At $P_5$ the quantity supplied is equal to zero. This implies that at a price of $P_5$ the price is too low for producers to be willing to supply the good.

**5.** **a.**

| Price | Quantity demanded | Quantity supplied |
|---|---|---|
| $    0 | 1,000 | 0 |
| 240 | 880 | 40 |
| 480 | 760 | 80 |
| 720 | 640 | 120 |
| 960 | 520 | 160 |
| 1,200 | 400 | 200 |
| 1,440 | 280 | 240 |
| 1,680 | 160 | 280 |
| 1,920 | 40 | 320 |

**b.** Examination of the table reveals that prices less than or equal to $1,440 result in a situation of excess demand, while prices greater than or equal to $1,680 result in a situation of excess supply. Thus, the equilibrium price will fall somewhere in the range of $1,440 to $1,680 in this market.

**c.**

**Market for Bicycles in Pedal City**

**d.** At a price of $240, 40 bicycles will be supplied and each manufacturer will produce 2 bicycles. At a price of $240, 880 bicycles will be demanded. The market is not in equilibrium since there is an excess demand for bicycles.

**e.** At a price of $480, 80 bicycles will be supplied and each manufacturer will produce 4 bicycles. At a price of $480, 760 bicycles will be demanded. The market is not in equilibrium since there is an excess demand for bicycles.

**f.** At a price of $1,680, 280 bicycles will be supplied and each manufacturer will produce 14 bicycles. At a price of $1,680, 160 bicycles will be demanded. The market is not in equilibrium since there is an excess supply of bicycles.

**g.** Since $P = 2,000 - 2Q$ and $P = 6Q$, we can use this information to write $2,000 - 2Q = 6Q$. Solving this equation gives us the equilibrium quantity of 250 bicycles. Substituting this quantity into either the demand equation or the supply equation yields the equilibrium price: $P = 2,000 - 2(250) = \$1,500$, or $P = 6(250) = \$1,500$.

# Answers to Module Review Questions

1.  **Answer b.** This question is asking you to recall that a change in the price of the good, holding everything else constant, results in a movement along the curve. This movement along the curve causes a change in the quantity supplied and not a change in the supply curve.

2.  **Answer a.** Ground beef is an input in the production of Fast Wally's hamburgers. When ground beef gets more expensive, this increases the cost of producing hamburgers, which causes the supply curve to shift to the left.

3.  **Answer b.** When the cost of raw materials decreases, more batteries can be produced at any given price. This decrease in the cost of raw materials causes the supply curve for batteries to shift to the right.

4.  **Answer a.** When input prices decrease, producers are willing to supply more units of the good at every price.

5.  **Answer b.** Since an increase in the production of one of the goods results in a decrease in the production of the other good, these two goods must be substitutes in production.

6.  **Answer a.** Sawdust and lumber are complements in production. As the producer increases its production of lumber, the production of sawdust is also increased since sawdust is a by-product of lumber production.

7.  **Answer a.** New technology causes the supply curve to shift to the right, resulting in an increase in the quantity supplied of the good at every price.

8.  **Answer a.** The sawmill industry will want to decrease the supply of lumber it provides to the market this year due to the expectation that next year's lumber prices will be higher. At every price the quantity of lumber supplied this year will be decreased, and the supply curve for lumber this year shifts to the left.

9.  **Answer c.** When the price is $40, 80 widgets are produced. Since there are sixteen producers in this market and each of these producers produce the same number of widgets, this implies that each producer must be producing 5 widgets.

10. **Answer d.** The first two statements are fairly straightforward, but statement III may be somewhat appealing at first glance. At equilibrium, however, even though the quantity demanded equals the quantity supplied, this does not imply that every potential consumer of the good is consuming the good. Those consumers who would like to consume the good, but who are unwilling to pay the equilibrium price, will not consume the good.

11. **Answer b.** At a price of $20, 300 widgets are demanded while 100 widgets are supplied. Thus, at a price of $20 there is an excess demand, or shortage, of 200 widgets.

12. **Answer a.** At a price of $60, 100 widgets are demanded while 300 widgets are supplied. Thus, at a price of $60 there is an excess supply, or surplus, of 200 widgets.

13. **Answer c.** The equilibrium quantity is the quantity at which demand equals the quantity supplied. The equilibrium quantity is 200 widgets, and the equilibrium price is $40.

14. **Answer c.** To find the demand curve, you can either plot the demand curve (although this is time consuming) or you can calculate the slope (rise/run = $-20/100 = -1/5$) and then use the slope-intercept form, $y = mx + b$, to write the equation. Thus, $P = (-1/5)Q + 80$, or solving for Q, $Q = 400 - 5P$.

15. **Answer b.** To find the supply curve, you can either plot the supply curve (although this is time consuming) or you can calculate the slope (rise/run = $20/100 = 1/5$) and then use the slope-intercept form, $y = mx + b$, to write the equation. Thus, $P = (1/5)Q + 0$.

16. **Answer b.** At $P_1$ the quantity demanded is $Q_2$ units while the quantity supplied is $Q_5$ units. The quantity supplied is greater than the quantity demanded at $P_1$: this excess supply is equal to $Q_5 - Q_2$.

17. **Answer a.** At $P_3$ the quantity demanded is $Q_4$ units while the quantity supplied is $Q_1$ units. The quantity demanded is greater than the quantity supplied at $P_3$: this excess demand is equal to $Q_4 - Q_1$.

# Changes in Equilibrium

## Summary

This module describes how the equilibrium price and equilibrium quantity are affected when there is a change in either the supply or demand curves. The module also describes the effect of a simultaneous shift in the demand and supply curves on the equilibrium price and equilibrium quantity.

## Module Objectives

**Objective #1.** A shift in the demand curve, holding everything else constant, causes a change in the equilibrium price and quantity. The shift in the demand curve causes a movement along the supply curve. An increase in demand leads to a rise in both the equilibrium price and equilibrium quantity. A decrease in demand leads to a fall in both the equilibrium price and equilibrium quantity. A shift in the supply curve, holding everything else constant, causes a change in the equilibrium price and quantity. The shift in the supply curve causes a movement along the demand curve. An increase in supply leads to a fall in the equilibrium price and a rise in the equilibrium quantity. A decrease in supply leads to a rise in the equilibrium price and a fall in the equilibrium quantity.

**Objective #2.** If demand and supply both change simultaneously but without specific information about the relative magnitude of these changes, there will be ambiguity about the value of either the new equilibrium price or the new equilibrium quantity. The four possible outcomes of these changes are summarized in Table 6.1.

**Table 6.1**

| Shift in demand | Shift in supply | Effect on equilibrium price | Effect on equilibrium quantity |
|---|---|---|---|
| Right | Left | Increase | Ambiguous |
| Right | Right | Ambiguous | Increase |
| Left | Left | Ambiguous | Decrease |
| Left | Right | Decrease | Ambiguous |

## ■ AFTER YOU READ THE MODULE

## Tips

**Tip #1.** A shift in the demand or supply curve causes a movement along the supply or demand curve. Figure 6.1 illustrates this idea for a demand curve shift. Notice that when demand shifts to the left (a decrease in demand) this causes a movement along the supply curve: the equilibrium price falls from $P_1$ to $P_2$ and the equilibrium quantity falls from $Q_1$ to $Q_2$.

**Figure 6.1**

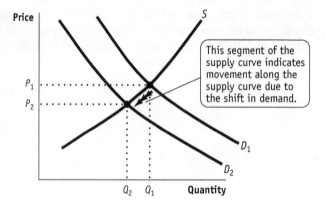

This segment of the supply curve indicates movement along the supply curve due to the shift in demand.

Figure 6.2 illustrates this idea for a supply curve shift. Notice that when supply shifts to the right (an increase in supply) this causes a movement along the demand curve: the equilibrium price falls from $P_1$ to $P_2$ and the equilibrium quantity increases from $Q_1$ to $Q_2$.

**Figure 6.2**

Tip #2. When both supply and demand shift simultaneously it may be impossible to determine what happens to the equilibrium price or the equilibrium quantity unless you are given specific numeric information about the demand curve, the supply curve, and the size of the shifts.

• For example, if demand and supply both shift to the right simultaneously the equilibrium quantity will increase but the equilibrium price will be ambiguous. Figure 6.3 illustrates two possible outcomes for this type of situation.

**Figure 6.3**

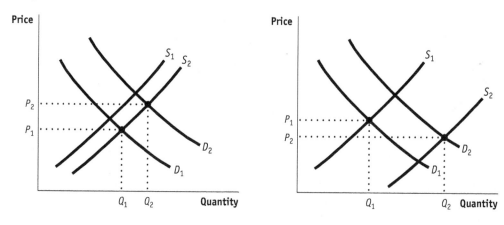

- If demand and supply both shift to the left simultaneously, the equilibrium quantity will decrease but the equilibrium price will be ambiguous. Figure 6.4 illustrates two possible outcomes for this type of situation.

**Figure 6.4**

 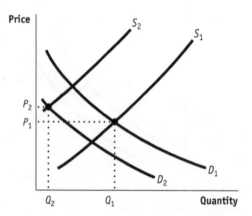

- If demand shifts to the right and supply shifts to the left simultaneously, the equilibrium price will increase but the equilibrium quantity will be ambiguous. Figure 6.5 illustrates two possible outcomes for this type of situation.

**Figure 6.5**

- If demand shifts to the left and supply shifts to the right simultaneously, the equilibrium price will decrease but the equilibrium quantity will be ambiguous. Figure 6.6 illustrates two possible outcomes for this type of situation.

**Figure 6.6**

 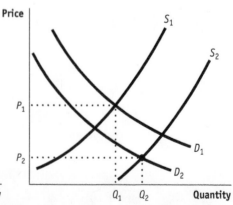

**WORKED PROBLEMS**

1. The supply and demand model is often used to analyze the effect of a change in the market on the equilibrium price and quantity of a good. Consider each of the following markets and the given situation to determine whether the demand and/or supply curve shift(s), and what the impact on the equilibrium price and equilibrium quantity will be relative to the initial equilibrium price and equilibrium quantity. For any shift in the demand or supply curve, indicate whether the curve shifts to the left or to the right. The examples are given in a table to help you consolidate your answers.

| Market under consideration | Situation | Shift or movement along the demand curve | Shift or movement along the supply curve | Effect on equilibrium price | Effect on equilibrium quantity |
|---|---|---|---|---|---|
| Automobile market | War in the Middle East disrupts petroleum exports substantially | | | | |
| Pizza market | Price of cheese increases | | | | |
| Shampoo market | Health advisors release study showing danger of frequent hair washing | | | | |
| Oil market | Oil-producing countries form cartel and agree to restrict output | | | | |
| Insulation market | Homeowners granted tax credit for installing home insulation | | | | |

**STEP 1:** For each of the situations, draw the initial market situation and then label the initial equilibrium price and equilibrium quantity.

**STEP 2:** Next look at the situation and decide whether the situation will cause a movement or a shift of the demand curve, or a movement or a shift of the supply curve. Draw the appropriate shift on your base graph.

**STEP 3:** Mark the new equilibrium price and equilibrium quantity and then compare the new equilibrium to the initial equilibrium. For example, when war in the Middle East disrupts petroleum exports substantially, this will cause the price of gas to rise, and since cars and gas are complements, the demand for cars will shift to the left due to the increase in the price of gas. As demand shifts left, there is a movement along the supply curve resulting in a reduction in the equilibrium quantity and the equilibrium price of cars.

**STEP 4:** Record your answers on the given table.

| Market under consideration | Situation | Shift or movement along the demand curve | Shift or movement along the supply Curve | Effect on equilibrium price | Effect on equilibrium quantity |
|---|---|---|---|---|---|
| Automobile market | War in the Middle East disrupts petroleum exports substantially | Demand shifts left as the price of gas rises: cars and gas are complements | Movement along the supply curve as price falls | Decrease in the price of cars | Decrease in the quantity of cars |
| Pizza market | Price of cheese increases | Movement along the demand curve as price increases | Supply shifts left since cheese is an input in making pizza | Increase in the price of pizza | Decrease in the quantity of pizza |
| Shampoo market | Health advisors release study showing danger of frequent hair washing | Demand shifts left due to change in tastes and preferences for washing hair: people wish to wash their hair less often at any price of shampoo after the study | Movement along the supply curve as the price of shampoo falls | Decrease in the price of shampoo | Decrease in the quantity of shampoo |

| Market under consideration | Situation | Shift or movement along the demand curve | Shift or movement along the supply curve | Effect on equilibrium price | Effect on equilibrium quantity |
|---|---|---|---|---|---|
| Oil market | Oil-producing countries form cartel and agree to restrict output | Movement along the demand curve due to the shift in the supply curve | Supply shifts left due to the cartel restricting output at every price | Increase in the price of oil | Decrease in the quantity of oil |
| Insulation market | Homeowners granted tax credit for installing home insulation | Demand shifts right due to the government subsidizing consumption of home insulation: at every price, the quantity of insulation demanded increases | Movement along the supply curve due to the shift in the demand curve | Increase in the price of home insulation | Increase in the quantity of home insulation |

2.  In the market for corn flakes, the price of cardboard used in packing the cereal has risen at the same time that the Surgeon General releases a report detailing the dangers of a diet high in corn products. What happens to the equilibrium price and equilibrium quantity relative to the equilibrium before these two changes?

**STEP 1:** First identify that there are two different changes occurring in the market for corn flakes: the price of cardboard used in packing the cereal is increasing and the Surgeon General has released a report that reveals the danger of eating corn products. In this question you will want to model each of these changes to see what the overall effect is in the market for corn flakes.

**STEP 2:** Draw the initial market situation and label the initial equilibrium price and equilibrium quantity. The figure that follows illustrates the initial situation.

**STEP 3:** Consider the change in the price of cardboard: this is an input used to produce a box of corn flakes, and thus an increase in the price of cardboard will cause the supply curve for corn flakes to shift to the left. Draw the appropriate shift on your base graph and label it clearly. The figure that follows illustrates this shift.

**STEP 4:** Next, consider the Surgeon General's report: people will decrease the quantity of corn flakes they demand at every price once this report is released. This will cause the demand curve to shift to the left. But we are not told the magnitude of the shift: a small shift will cause the equilibrium price to rise while the equilibrium quantity will fall (the intersection of $D_2$ and $S_2$, with the equilibrium occurring at $Q_2$ and $P_2$); a moderate shift might cause the equilibrium price to remain at its initial level, while the equilibrium quantity falls (the intersection of $D_2'$ and $S_2$, with the equilibrium occurring at $Q_2'$ and $P_2' = P_1$); and a large shift would cause the equilibrium price to fall, while the equilibrium quantity also falls (the intersection of $D_2''$ and $S_2$, with the equilibrium occurring at $Q_2''$ and $P_2''$). Price is therefore indeterminate, while quantity will definitely decrease with these two changes in the market for corn flakes. Study the following figure carefully to see this concept.

**3.** In the market for chocolate, people read that the consumption of chocolate has major health benefits. At the same time, the cost of growing and harvesting cocoa beans increases. What happens to the equilibrium price and equilibrium quantity relative to the equilibrium before these two changes?

**STEP 1:** First, identify that there are two different changes occurring in the market for chocolate: eating chocolate provides health benefits and the cost of growing and harvesting cocoa beans increases. In this question, you will want to model each of these changes to see what the overall effect is in the market for chocolate.

**STEP 2:** Draw the initial market situation and label the initial equilibrium price and equilibrium quantity. The following figure illustrates the initial situation.

**STEP 3:** Consider the change in the cost of growing and harvesting cocoa beans: cocoa beans are an input used to produce chocolate, and thus an increase in the price of cocoa beans will cause the supply curve for chocolate to shift to the left. Draw the appropriate shift on your base graph and label it clearly. The figure that follows illustrates this shift.

**STEP 4:** Next, consider the health benefits from consuming chocolate: this will cause the quantity demanded of chocolate to increase at every price. Thus, the demand curve for chocolate will shift to the right. But we are not told the magnitude of the shift:

- A small shift will cause the equilibrium price to rise while the equilibrium quantity will fall (the intersection of $D_2$ and $S_2$, with the equilibrium occurring at $Q_2$ and $P_2$)

- A moderate shift might cause the equilibrium price to rise while the equilibrium quantity remains at its initial level (the intersection of $D_2'$ and $S_2$, with the equilibrium occurring at $P_2'$ and $Q_2' = Q_1$)

- A large shift would cause the equilibrium price to rise while the equilibrium quantity also rises (the intersection of $D_2''$ and $S_2$, with the equilibrium occurring at $Q_2''$ and $P_2''$).

Price will definitely increase while quantity is indeterminate with these two changes in the market for chocolate.

Study the following figure carefully to see this concept.

# Problems and Exercises

1. For each of the following situations, sketch a graph of the initial market demand ($D_1$) and supply ($S_1$) curves and indicate the initial equilibrium price ($P_1$) and equilibrium quantity ($Q_1$). Then sketch any changes in the market demand ($D_2$) and supply ($S_2$) curves and indicate the new equilibrium price ($P_2$) and equilibrium quantity ($Q_2$). For each situation, identify which curve(s) shift and whether there is a movement along the demand or supply curves.

   a. The price of gasoline increases by 40%. What happens in the market for bicycles?

**Market for Bicycles**

   b. The price of gasoline increases by 40%. What happens in the market for fuel-inefficient SUVs?

**Market for SUVs**

**c.** New technology for music-playing devices is developed. What happens in the market for music-playing devices?

**Market for Music-Playing Devices**

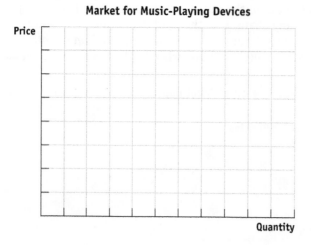

**d.** The price of labor decreases. What happens in the market for fast-food restaurants?

**Market for Fast-Food Restaurants**

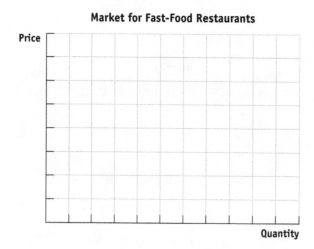

**e.** Income increases and good X is a normal good. What happens in the market for good X?

**Market for Good X**

**f.** Income increases and good X is an inferior good. What happens in the market for good X?

**Market for Good X**

2. You are given the following information about the demand and supply schedules for gadgets in Micro Town. Assume that gadgets in Micro Town are produced in a competitive market.

| Price | Quantity demanded | Quantity supplied |
|-------|-------------------|-------------------|
| $ 0 | 100 | 0 |
| 2 | 80 | 20 |
| 4 | 60 | 40 |
| 6 | 40 | 60 |
| 8 | 20 | 80 |
| 10 | 0 | 100 |

**a.** From the above data, write an equation expressing the demand schedule and an equation expressing the supply schedule.

**b.** Using the equations you wrote in part (a), find the equilibrium price and the equilibrium quantity in this market.

c. Now suppose that the quantity demanded increases by 20 units at every price and that the quantity supplied increases by 40 units at every price. What happens to the equilibrium price and equilibrium quantity in this market relative to the initial levels of the equilibrium price and equilibrium quantity? (Hint: You might find it helpful to draw a sketch of the original demand curve and then the new demand curve to help guide you in your work. Then, once you have the new demand curve equation, you could draw a sketch of the original supply curve and the new supply curve to help you calculate the new supply curve equation.)

d. Now suppose that the quantity demanded increases by the same amount as in part (c), but that the quantity supplied increases by only 10 units at every price. What happens to the equilibrium price and the equilibrium quantity in this market relative to the initial levels of the equilibrium price and equilibrium quantity?

e. In parts (c) and (d), the demand and supply curves shifted to the right. If you knew the direction of these shifts, but did not know the size or magnitude of the shift, what would you know about the new equilibrium price and quantity?

3. Let's generalize the findings of problem 2 for four different situations in which both the demand and supply curves shift at the same time. In each of these situations we assume that we know the direction of the shift but not the size of the shift. Fill in the table below for each of the possible situations. The first situation (the one in problem 2) has already been done for you.

| Situation | Effect on equilibrium price | Effect on equilibrium quantity |
|---|---|---|
| Demand shifts to the right and supply shifts to the right | May increase, decrease, or remain the same | Increases |
| Demand shifts to the left and supply shifts to the left | | |
| Demand shifts to the right and supply shifts to the left | | |
| Demand shifts to the left and supply shifts to the right | | |

## ▌BEFORE YOU TAKE THE TEST

# Module Review Questions

1. In the competitive market for candles, there is an increase in the number of people purchasing candles and a decrease in the cost of beeswax, a major ingredient in the production of candles. Which of the following statements is true?

    a. The equilibrium price and the equilibrium quantity of candles will increase.

    b. The equilibrium price and the equilibrium quantity of candles will decrease.

    c. The equilibrium price may increase, decrease, or remain the same, but the equilibrium quantity will increase.

    d. The equilibrium quantity may increase, decrease, or remain the same, but the equilibrium price will increase.

2. Consumers in Mayville consider houses and apartments to be substitutes. There is an increase in the price of houses in Mayville at the same time three new apartment buildings are opened in Mayville. In the market for apartments in Mayville

    a. the equilibrium price will rise relative to its level before these two events.

    b. the equilibrium price will fall relative to its level before these two events.

    c. the equilibrium quantity will rise relative to its level before these two events.

    d. the equilibrium quantity will fall relative to its level before these two events.

3. The production of good X requires labor inputs and therefore the price of good X is directly affected by labor costs. Suppose that the price of labor increases while simultaneously people's income rises. If good X is a normal good, then we know in the market for good X

    a. the equilibrium price will increase and the equilibrium quantity may increase, decrease, or remain the same relative to their initial levels.

    b. the equilibrium price will decrease and the equilibrium quantity may increase, decrease, or remain the same relative to their initial levels.

    c. the equilibrium quantity will increase and the equilibrium price may increase, decrease, or remain the same relative to their initial levels.

    d. the equilibrium quantity will decrease and the equilibrium price may increase, decrease, or remain the same relative to their initial levels.

4. People's income rises, while simultaneously there is a technological advance in the production of good X. Good X is an inferior good. Given this information we know in the market for good X

    a. the equilibrium price will increase and the equilibrium quantity may increase, decrease, or remain the same relative to their initial levels.

    b. the equilibrium price will decrease and the equilibrium quantity may increase, decrease, or remain the same relative to their initial levels.

    c. the equilibrium quantity will increase and the equilibrium price may increase, decrease, or remain the same relative to their initial levels.

    d. the equilibrium quantity will decrease and the equilibrium price may increase, decrease, or remain the same relative to their initial levels.

5. The price of bubble gum increases at the same time that sugar, a major ingredient in candy, gets more expensive. If candy and bubble gum are substitutes, what happens to the equilibrium price and the equilibrium quantity in the market for candy?

a. The equilibrium price will increase and the equilibrium quantity may increase, decrease, or remain the same relative to their initial levels.

b. The equilibrium price will decrease and the equilibrium quantity may increase, decrease, or remain the same relative to their initial levels.

c. The equilibrium quantity will increase and the equilibrium price may increase, decrease, or remain the same relative to their initial levels.

d. The equilibrium quantity will decrease and the equilibrium price may increase, decrease, or remain the same relative to their initial levels.

## ANSWER KEY

# Answers to Problems and Exercises

1. **a.** Gasoline and bicycles are substitutes for one another. When the price of gasoline rises, people substitute away from gasoline toward bicycle transportation. This is illustrated in the graph below with the demand curve for bicycles shifting to the right, resulting in a higher equilibrium price ($P_2$) and a higher equilibrium quantity ($Q_2$). Note that there is a shift in the demand curve and a movement along the supply curve.

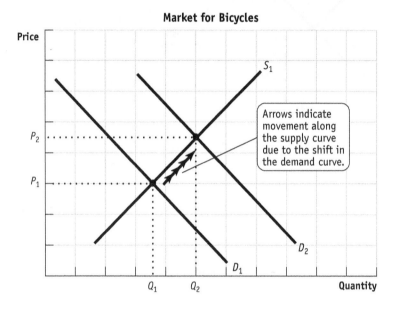

**Market for Bicycles**

**b.** Gasoline and SUVs are complements for one another. When the price of gasoline rises, people find that driving SUVs is relatively more expensive and therefore decrease their demand for SUVs at every price. This is illustrated in the graph below with the demand curve for SUVs shifting to the left, resulting in a lower equilibrium price ($P_2$) and a lower equilibrium quantity ($Q_2$). Note that there is a shift in the demand curve and a movement along the supply curve.

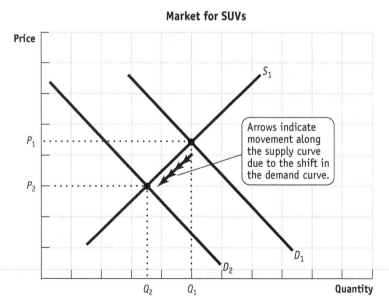

**Market for SUVs**

**c.** New technology shifts the supply curve to the right from $S_1$ to $S_2$. This causes a movement along the demand curve and results in a decrease in the equilibrium price and an increase in the equilibrium quantity. This is illustrated in the figure below.

**Market for Music-Playing Devices**

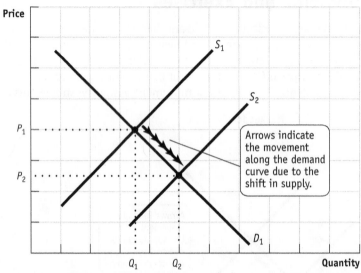

**d.** When the price of labor decreases, this causes the supply of fast food to shift to the right since labor is an input in the production of fast-food meals. This results in a movement along the demand curve and a decrease in the equilibrium price and an increase in the equilibrium quantity.

**Market for Fast-Food Restaurants**

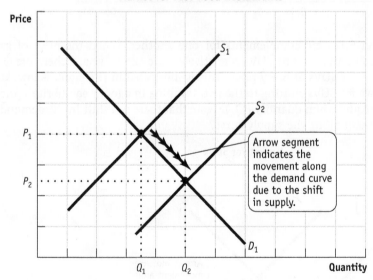

**e.** An increase in income shifts the demand curve to the right if the good is a normal good. This shift in demand causes a movement along the supply curve and an increase in both the equilibrium price and the equilibrium quantity.

**Market for Good X**

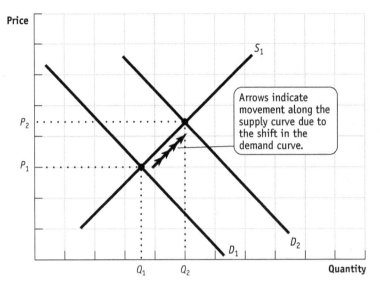

**f.** An increase in income shifts the demand curve to the left if the good is an inferior good. This shift in demand causes a movement along the supply curve and a decrease in both the equilibrium price and the equilibrium quantity. The graph below illustrates this situation.

**Market for Good X**

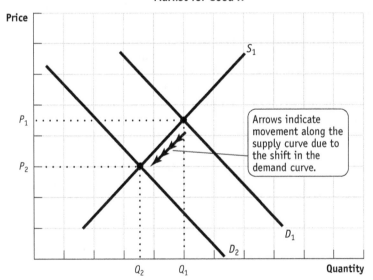

**2.   a.** The demand equation is $P = 10 - (1/10)Q$ and the supply equation is $P = (1/10)Q$.

    **b.** Solving the two equations from part (a), we find that the equilibrium price equals $5 and the equilibrium quantity equals 50.

**c.** To find the new equilibrium price and quantity, we need to know the new demand and supply curves. Draw a sketch of the original demand curve and the new demand curve (shifted to the right at every price by 20 units) to guide you in your calculations. The figure below illustrates this sketch.

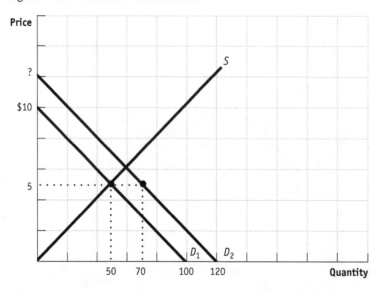

We know from part (b) that the initial equilibrium is at price $5 and the equilibrium quantity is 50, which gives us two points on the new demand curve: (70, 5) and (120, 0). We also know that the new demand curve is parallel to the original demand curve and thus has the same slope as the original demand curve. But we do not know the y-intercept for the new demand curve. To find the equation, let's write the new equation as $P = b - (1/10)Q$. This equation has the same slope as the original demand curve, but has not yet identified the y-intercept. To find the value of $b$, let's substitute the coordinates of one of the points we know is on $D_2$: thus, using (70, 5) yields $5 = b - (1/10)70$, or $b = 12$. So our new demand curve equation is $P = 12 - (1/10)Q$. Use the same technique to find the new supply curve equation. The graph below sketches the original demand and supply curve and also the new supply curve, which illustrates an increase of 40 units in the quantity supplied at every price. We know the coordinates of two points on this new supply curve—(40, 0) and (90, 5)—and we also know that the new supply curve has the same slope as the original supply curve. So we can rewrite the new supply curve as $P = b + (1/10)Q$ and then use one of our known points to solve for $b$, the y-intercept. Thus, using (90, 5) we get $5 = b + (1/10)90$, or $b = -4$, and the new supply curve is $P = (1/10)Q - 4$.

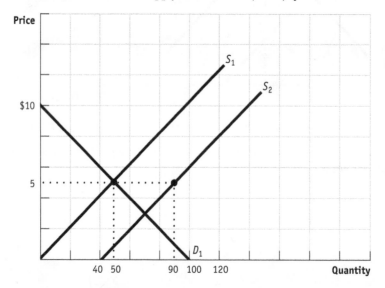

Using the new demand curve and new supply curve, we can easily solve for the equilibrium price and the equilibrium quantity in this market. Since $P = 12 - (1/10)Q$ and $P = (1/10)Q - 4$, we have $12 - (1/10)Q = (1/10)Q - 4$, or the equilibrium quantity ($Q$) equals 80. Then, replacing $Q$ with 80 in either the demand or supply equation, we find that the equilibrium price ($P$) equals 4. In this case, the equilibrium price decreases relative to its initial level, while the equilibrium quantity increases relative to its initial level.

**d.** Since the change in the quantity demanded at each price is the same as in part (c), we know that the new demand curve can be written as $P = 12 - (1/10)Q$. But we need to use the same technique as we employed in part (c) to find the new supply curve. When you do this, you will find that the new supply curve equation is $P = (1/10)Q - 1$. Solving these two equations for the equilibrium price and the equilibrium quantity, we find that the new equilibrium price is 5.5 while the new equilibrium quantity is 65 units. In this case, the equilibrium price and the equilibrium quantity increase relative to their initial quantities.

**e.** You would know with certainty that the equilibrium quantity increased, but you would not know if the equilibrium price increased, decreased, or remained the same, since you do not know the magnitude of the shifts in the demand and supply curves.

**3.**

| Situation | Effect on equilibrium price | Effect on equilibrium quantity |
|---|---|---|
| Demand shifts to the right and supply shifts to the right | May increase, decrease, or remain the same | Increases |
| Demand shifts to the left and supply shifts to the left | May increase, decrease, or remain the same | Decreases |
| Demand shifts to the right and supply shifts to the left | Increases | May increase, decrease, or remain the same |
| Demand shifts to the left and supply shifts to the right | Decreases | May increase, decrease, or remain the same |

## Answers to Module Review Questions

**1.** **Answer c.** Since we do not know the relative magnitude of the shifts in the demand and supply curves, we cannot know for certain what happens to both the equilibrium price and the equilibrium quantity. The demand curve shifts to the right with the increase in the number of people purchasing candles, while the supply curve shifts to the right with the decrease in the price of beeswax. The equilibrium quantity will increase, but the equilibrium price may increase, decrease, or remain the same depending on the relative magnitude of the shifts in the two curves.

**2.** **Answer c.** The demand curve for apartments shifts to the right with the increase in the price of houses (houses and apartments are substitute goods for consumers in Mayville), while the supply curve for apartments also shifts to the right with the opening of the new apartment buildings. Since we do not know the magnitude of the shifts in the demand and supply curves, we know that the equilibrium quantity is now larger, but the equilibrium price may increase, decrease, or remain the same with these shifts in the demand and supply curves.

**3.** **Answer a.** The demand curve for good X shifts to the right since good X is a normal good and income has increased. At the same time, the supply curve for good X shifts to the left since the price of labor has increased. These two shifts result in the equilibrium price increasing while the equilibrium quantity may have increased, decreased, or remained the same depending on the magnitude of the shifts in the demand and supply curves.

4. **Answer b.** Since good X is an inferior good, the increase in income results in the demand curve for good X shifting to the left. At the same time, the technological advance causes the supply curve for good X to shift to the right. The equilibrium price will decrease, but the equilibrium quantity may increase, decrease, or remain the same depending on the magnitude of the shifts in the demand and supply curves.

5. **Answer a.** The supply curve for candy shifts to the left with the increase in the price of sugar, while the demand curve for candy shifts to the right with the increase in the price of bubble gum. The equilibrium price will increase, but the equilibrium quantity may increase, decrease, or remain the same depending on the magnitude of the shifts in the demand and supply curves.

# Price Controls and Quantity Controls

## ■ BEFORE YOU READ THE MODULE

## Summary

This module develops the ideas of price controls and quantity controls in competitive markets and then illustrates how the implementation of these controls reduces the efficiency of a market. In particular, the module discusses effective price ceilings, whereby the government sets the price of the good below the equilibrium price; and effective price floors, whereby the government sets the price of the good above the equilibrium price. The module also discusses the distributional impact of price controls. The module also analyzes quantity controls and their effect on the market: the module discusses how quantity controls create problems and result in less efficient markets.

## Module Objectives

**Objective #1.** Price controls refer to the government's intervention in a market to set the price of the good or service at some level other than the equilibrium price. A price ceiling is the maximum price for a good or service allowed by the government, and a price floor is the minimum price for a good or service allowed by the government.

**Objective #2.** An effective price ceiling in a competitive market creates a situation of excess quantity demanded. If the price ceiling is set above the equilibrium price in the market, the price ceiling will not be effective and therefore will have no effect on the equilibrium price and the equilibrium quantity in the market.

**Objective #3.** An effective price ceiling prevents a market from being efficient because the price ceiling prevents transactions from occurring that would make some people better off without making other people worse off. In particular, an effective price ceiling prevents demanders who are willing to pay more for the good from consuming the good since the good's supply is artificially limited by the imposed price ceiling. Inefficiency arises because the price ceiling:

- reduces the quantity of the good available;

- reduces the value of total surplus;

- misallocates the good or service among consumers;

- wastes resources, as consumers spend resources searching for the good that is artificially scarce due to the price ceiling; and

- reduces the quality of the available units that would have been supplied in the absence of the price ceiling.

**Objective #4.**   Price ceilings provide incentives for illegal activities. Price ceilings are primarily instituted because they benefit some particular group of demanders.

**Objective #5.**   An effective price floor in a competitive market creates a situation of excess quantity supplied. If the price floor is set below the equilibrium price in the market, the price floor will have no effect on the equilibrium price and the equilibrium quantity in the market.

**Objective #6.**   An effective price floor results in market inefficiency because it prevents transactions from occurring that would make some people better off without making other people worse off. In particular, an effective price floor prevents suppliers who are willing to supply the good from selling the good since the good's demand is artificially limited by the imposed price floor. Inefficiency arises because the price floor:

- reduces the quantity of the good demanded;

- reduces the value of total surplus;

- misallocates the provision of the good or service by sellers;

- wastes resources, as suppliers search the market for a potential demander of the good; and

- increases the quality of the available units above the level that would have been demanded in the absence of the price floor.

**Objective #7.**   Price floors provide an incentive for illegal or black market activities, including the bribery and corruption of government officials. Price floors are primarily instituted because they benefit a particular group of sellers.

**Objective #8:**   The government may also implement quantity controls or a quota in a market. In this case the government sets a limit on the total quantity of the good that can be bought and sold in a market. This quantity is usually limited through the selling of licenses that legally grant the holder of the license the right to supply the good. Quantity controls always set a maximum amount allowed. To be binding in the market, the quota must be set below the equilibrium quantity.

**Objective #9:**   A quota or quantity control creates a wedge between the price consumers are willing to pay for the good and the price producers must receive in order to be willing to supply the good. The difference between these two prices is the quota rent, or the income that the license holder receives from their ownership of a valuable commodity (the license).

**Objective #10:** Quantity controls are inefficient because they prevent some mutually beneficial transactions from occurring, since the demand price for a given quantity (the quota amount) is greater than the supply price for that quantity. These missed transactions create an incentive to evade the quota limit, often through illegal activity.

## Key Terms

**price controls** legal restrictions on how high or low a market price may go.

**price ceiling** a maximum price sellers are allowed to charge for a good or service; a form of *price control.*

**price floor** a minimum price buyers are required to pay for a good or service; a form of *price control.*

**quantity control** an upper limit, set by the government, on the quantity of some good that can be bought or sold; also referred to as a *quota.*

**quota** an upper limit, set by the government, on the quantity of some good that can be bought or sold; also referred to as a *quantity control.*

**license** the right, conferred by the government, to supply a good.

**inefficient allocation to consumers** a form of inefficiency in which people who want the good and are willing to pay a high price don't get it, and those who care relatively little about the good and are only willing to pay a low price do get it; often a result of a *price ceiling.*

**wasted resources** a form of inefficiency in which people expend money, effort, and time to cope with the shortages caused by a *price ceiling.*

**inefficiently low quality** a form of inefficiency in which sellers offer low-quality goods at a low price even though buyers would prefer a higher quality at a higher price; often a result of a *price ceiling.*

**black market** a market in which goods or services are bought and sold illegally, either because it is illegal to sell them at all or because the prices charged are legally prohibited by a *price ceiling.*

**minimum wage** a legal floor on the wage rate. The wage rate is the market price of labor.

**inefficient allocation of sales among sellers** a form of inefficiency in which sellers who would be willing to sell a good at the lowest price are not always those who actually manage to sell it; often the result of a *price floor.*

**inefficiently high quality** a form of inefficiency in which sellers offer high-quality goods at a high price even though buyers would prefer a lower quality at a lower price; often the result of a *price floor.*

**demand price** the price of a given quantity at which consumers will demand that quantity.

**supply price** the price of a given quantity at which producers will supply that quantity.

**wedge** the difference between the *demand price* of the quantity transacted and the *supply price* of the quantity transacted for a good when the supply of the good is legally restricted. Often created by a *quantity control,* or *quota.*

## Key Terms *(continued)*

**quota rent** the difference between the *demand price* and the *supply price* at the *quota limit;* this difference, the earnings that accrue to the license-holder, is equal to the market price of the license when the license is traded.

**deadweight loss** the lost gains associated with transactions that do not occur because of market interventions.

## ▌ AFTER YOU READ THE MODULE ▐

## Tips

**Tip #1.**  Students often find it confusing to remember the difference between a price floor and a price ceiling.

- A floor is a surface that you stand on and that is solid. A price floor is the *lowest* price that can be charged for a good. Figure 7.1 illustrates a price floor. To be effective, a price floor must be set at a price that is greater than the equilibrium price. At $P_F$, $Q_1$ units will be supplied and $Q_2$ units will be demanded. An effective price floor always results in a surplus of the good.

**Figure 7.1**

- A ceiling is a surface that you hope is solid and stays above your head. A price ceiling is the *highest* price that can be charged for a good. Figure 7.2 illustrates a price ceiling. To be effective, a price ceiling must be set at a price that is less than the equilibrium price. At $P_C$, $Q_1$ units will be supplied and $Q_2$ units will be demanded. An effective price ceiling always results in a shortage of the good.

**Figure 7.2**

**Tip #2.** A quota, or quantity control, is a policy implemented by the government to set a maximum amount of the good or service that can be sold in a market. A quota has no effect if it is set at a level greater than the equilibrium quantity; to be effective a quota must be set at a level smaller than the equilibrium quantity. Figure 7.3 illustrates an effective quantity control, or quota, where the maximum allowed quantity is set by the government at $Q_1$. At $Q_1$ demanders are willing to pay $P_1$ for each unit of the good they consume, while suppliers are willing to supply the good at price $P_2$. This difference, $P_1 - P_2$, is referred to as a wedge. This wedge corresponds to the quota rent the license-holder of the good receives when the quantity control is imposed in a market. This quota rent represents the additional compensation the license-holder receives from selling the good in a market where the quantity of the good has been artificially restricted.

**Figure 7.3**

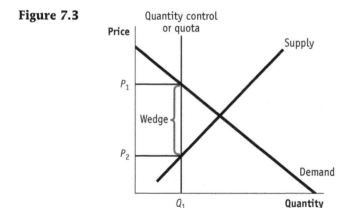

# WORKED PROBLEMS

1. Consider a market for cotton in which the market demand curve is given by the equation $Q = 40,000 - 200P$ and the market supply curve is given by the equation $Q = 200P$, where $Q$ is bales of cotton and $P$ is the price per bale of cotton. Suppose this market is initially in equilibrium and then cotton farmers successfully lobby the legislature to impose a price floor of $150 per bale of cotton. After imposition of this price floor, what will be the price of cotton in this market, and how does this price compare with the initial equilibrium price? Identify the number of bales of cotton consumers will purchase once the price floor is implemented. How does this quantity compare with the initial equilibrium quantity in this market? What will the surplus or shortage of cotton equal with the imposition of this price floor? If the government purchases the surplus cotton, what will be the cost of this purchase to the government?

**STEP 1:** First draw a graph of the market for cotton and find the initial equilibrium price and quantity in this market. Use the two equations to solve for the equilibrium price and quantity.

Thus, $40,000 - 200P = 200P$, or $P = 100$. If $P = 100$, then the quantity demanded at this price can be found using the demand equation: $Q = 40,000 - 200(100)$, or $Q = 20,000$. If $P = 100$, then the quantity supplied at this price can be found using the supply equation: $Q = 200(100) = 20,000$. Since the market is in equilibrium, the quantity demanded is equal to the quantity supplied when the price is equal to 100.

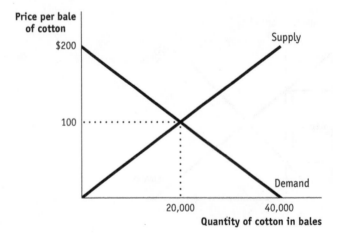

**STEP 2:** Draw the price floor on your graph and determine if the price floor is an effective price floor. Once you have determined if the price floor is effective, you will know whether the price in this market is the price floor price of $150 per bale or the equilibrium price of $100 per bale. Identify the number of bales of cotton that consumers demand by using the demand equation to see how many bales of cotton they are willing to demand at the new price for cotton. The effective price floor raises the price of cotton and this causes consumers to purchase fewer units of cotton.

Since the price floor is greater than the equilibrium price, the price floor is effective in this market. The price of cotton in this market will now be the price floor price of $150 per bale: the price of cotton is now higher than it was before the implementation of the price floor. When the price of cotton is $150 per bale, consumers are willing to purchase 10,000 bales of cotton.

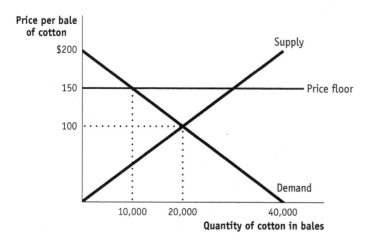

**STEP 3:** Identify the surplus of cotton that will be produced in this market when there is a price floor and then determine what the cost of purchasing this surplus will be for the government.

To find the surplus with the price floor requires identifying how many units of cotton suppliers are willing to supply at a price of $150, then subtracting out the number of units of cotton that demanders are willing to demand at a price of $150. At a price of $150, suppliers are willing to supply 30,000 bales of cotton, but consumers are willing to purchase only 10,000 bales. Thus, the surplus of cotton is equal to 20,000 bales. If the government purchases this amount of cotton at $150 per bale, it will cost the government $4,500,000. The shaded area in the following graph identifies this cost to the government.

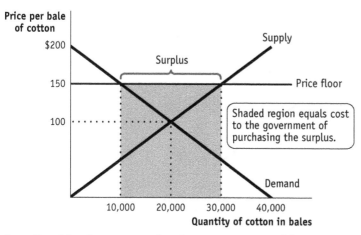

2.  Consider the same market for cotton as in problem 1. Suppose this market is initially in equilibrium and then cotton farmers successfully lobby the legislature to impose a quantity control, or quota, in this market of 10,000 bales of cotton. What will the "wedge" or quota rent be equal to in this market?

**STEP 1:** Start by drawing a graph of the market for cotton, identifying the initial equilibrium price and quantity. From your work in problem 1, you already have identified the equilibrium price as $100 per bale of cotton and the equilibrium quantity as 20,000 bales of cotton. After labeling these points on your graph, draw the quantity control or quota on your graph. The quantity control will be a vertical line where the quantity of bales of cotton is 10,000.

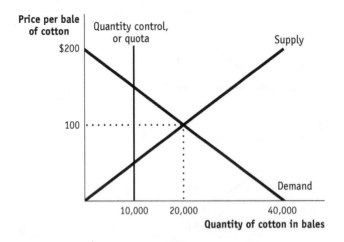

**STEP 2:** To find the "wedge" or quota rent, you will need to see what price consumers are willing to pay for the quota amount and what price producers must receive in order to provide the quota amount. The difference between the price consumers are willing to pay and the price producers must receive is the "wedge."

Consumers are willing to pay $150 per bale of cotton when 10,000 bales of cotton are offered in the market. Producers must receive $50 per bale of cotton if they supply 10,000 bales of cotton. The "wedge" is therefore $100, or the difference between these two prices. The following figure illustrates this wedge.

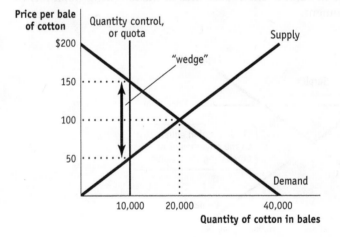

3. The following table describes several interventions in a market. Complete the table.

| Situation | This is an example of a 1) Price Floor, 2) Price Ceiling, or 3) Quantity Control or Quota | What must be true for this intervention in the market to be effective? |
|---|---|---|
| The government decides to limit the number of taxicab licenses in Chicago | | |
| The minimum price that can be charged for a sports car is set at $75,000 by the government | | |
| The minimum wage that can be paid to a worker is set at $10 an hour by the government | | |
| The maximum tuition that can be charged by a public university is set at $5,000 a year by the government | | |

**STEP 1:** To answer this question, you must first have a firm grasp of the differences among a price floor, a price ceiling, and a quantity control or quota. You need to understand what makes each of these interventions effective in the market: this will require that you understand and are comfortable with each type of market intervention.

A price ceiling is a maximum price that can be charged for a good. A price floor is a minimum price that can be charged for a good. A quantity control or quota is a maximum amount of the good that can be provided in the market. This maximum amount is set by the government. To fill in the second column of the table, you will want to consider each situation and determine whether the situation is one in which the government is setting a maximum price, a minimum price, or a maximum quantity.

**STEP 2:** For each type of market intervention by the government, you will want to think about what must be true in order for the intervention to have any impact on the market.

For a price ceiling to be effective, the price ceiling must be set at a price that is less than the market equilibrium amount. For a price floor to be effective, the price floor must be set at a price that is greater than the market equilibrium amount. For a quantity control or quota to have any effect on the market, the quantity control must be set at a quantity that is less than the market equilibrium quantity. The completed table follows.

| Situation | This is an example of a 1) Price Floor, 2) Price Ceiling, or 3) Quantity Control or Quota | What must be true for this intervention in the market to be effective? |
|---|---|---|
| The government decides to limit the number of taxicab licenses in Chicago | Quantity control or quota | Quota amount must be less than the market equilibrium quantity |
| The minimum price that can be charged for a sports car is set at $75,000 by the government | Price floor | Price floor must be set at a price that is greater than the market equilibrium price |
| The minimum wage that can be paid to a worker is set at $10 an hour by the government | Price floor | Price floor must be set at a price that is greater than the market equilibrium price |
| The maximum tuition that can be charged by a public university is set at $5,000 a year by the government | Price ceiling | Price ceiling must be set at a price that is less than the market equilibrium price |

# Problems and Exercises

1. Use the graph below to answer the following questions.

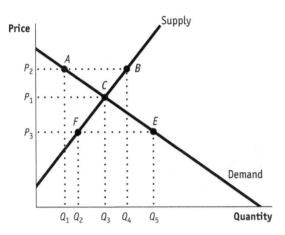

   a. Identify the equilibrium price and the equilibrium quantity.

   b. Suppose a price floor of $P_3$ is implemented by the government in this market. Describe what will happen to the price and quantity once this price floor is implemented.

   c. Suppose a price floor of $P_2$ is implemented by the government in this market. Describe what will happen to the price and quantity once this price floor is implemented.

   d. What must be true about a price floor in a market for a good or service in order for that price floor to be effective?

   e. You are told that an effective price floor has been implemented in this market and that the resultant surplus is greater than $Q_4 - Q_1$. What do you know about the level of this price floor?

**2.** Use the graph below to answer the following questions.

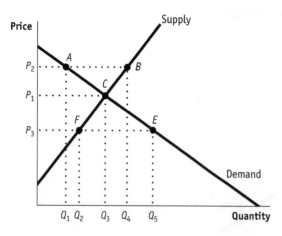

**a.** Identify the equilibrium price and the equilibrium quantity.

**b.** Suppose a price ceiling of $P_2$ is implemented by the government in this market. Describe what will happen to the price and quantity once this price ceiling is implemented.

**c.** Suppose a price ceiling of $P_3$ is implemented by the government in this market. Describe what will happen to the price and quantity once this price ceiling is implemented.

**d.** What must be true about a price ceiling in a market for a good or service in order for that price ceiling to be effective?

**e.** You are told that an effective price ceiling has been implemented in this market and that the resultant shortage is smaller than $Q_5 - Q_2$. What do you know about the level of this price ceiling?

**3.** Consider the market for housing in Metropolitan City, where all housing units are exactly the same. Currently the equilibrium price of housing is $2,000 a month and local residents consume 1,500 units of housing. The local residents argue that housing is too expensive and that an effective price ceiling should be implemented. Once the price ceiling is implemented by the local government council, only 1,200 units of housing are supplied in this market. Is this an efficient level of housing for Metropolitan City? Explain your answer. To support your answer, provide two sketches: in the first sketch indicate the equilibrium quantity, the equilibrium price, and the area of total surplus; in the second sketch indicate the price ceiling, the area of total surplus, and the area that represents the efficiency loss due to the reduction in the quantity of housing units.

**4.** A price ceiling is implemented in the market for housing in Metropolitan City, where all housing units are identical. You know that before the price ceiling is implemented, the demand for housing in Metropolitan City is given by the equation $P = 1,000 - 0.1Q_D$ and the supply of housing is given by the equation $P = 200 + 0.3Q_S$.

**a.** Prior to the implementation of the price ceiling, what is the equilibrium price for housing in Metropolitan City and what is the equilibrium quantity of housing?

**b.** Fill in the following demand and supply schedules for this market given the above equations.

| Price | Quantity demanded | Quantity supplied |
|---|---|---|
| $ 200 | | |
| 400 | | |
| 600 | | |
| 800 | | |
| 1,000 | | |

c. When the price ceiling is implemented, a housing shortage develops. This shortage is equal to 4,000 housing units. Calculate the price ceiling in this market for housing. (Hint: You may find the table from part (b) helpful in thinking about this problem.)

d. Who benefits from the imposition of the price ceiling in the market for housing in Metropolitan City?

e. Who is hurt by the imposition of a price ceiling in the market for housing in Metropolitan City?

f. Why is this price ceiling apt to result in black market activities in the market for housing? Provide at least two examples of potential black market activities.

g. Does an effective price ceiling in this market result in too many or too few resources being allocated to the market for housing in Metropolitan City? Explain your answer.

5. Farmers in Corntopia successfully lobby their government to enact a price floor for their agricultural commodity. The price floor is set at $10 above the equilibrium price. The initial demand and supply curves for agricultural production in Corntopia are as follows: $P = 100 - Q$ and $P = Q$, where price is per bushel and quantity is measured in bushels.

a. What is the level of the price floor in this market?

b. How many units of the agricultural product will be demanded and supplied at this price floor level?

c. Suppose the government purchases the surplus in this market once the price floor is implemented. What will be the cost to the government of buying this surplus?

**d.** Given the price floor, what is the expenditure consumers make when purchasing this commodity? Do not include in your calculation the cost to the government of buying the surplus.

**e.** What is total farm revenue equal to in this market once the price floor is implemented? What is the relationship between total farm revenue, consumer expenditure, and government expenditure on the good, given the price floor? Does total farm revenue increase when the government enacts a price floor? Explain your answer.

**f.** Who benefits from the enactment of a price floor in this market?

**6.** **a.** Draw a graph of the demand and supply curves given to you in problem 5. Label the equilibrium price and the equilibrium quantity on this graph. Shade in the area that corresponds to total farm revenue in this market and label this area clearly.

Price

Quantity

**b.** Redraw the graph of the demand and supply curves given to you in problem 5, and draw in a line indicating the price floor. On the graph, indicate the quantity demanded and the quantity supplied using the values you found in problem 5. Shade in and clearly label the areas that correspond to consumer expenditure on the good and government expenditure on the good, given the price floor.

Price

Quantity

**7.** Consider the labor market in Utopia. You are told that the equilibrium wage in this market is $10 per hour and that the equilibrium amount of labor in this market is 1,000 hours of labor. Furthermore, you know that at a wage of $14 per hour, 600 hours of labor are demanded and 1,400 hours of labor are supplied. The workers in Utopia successfully lobby Utopia's government for the implementation of a price floor. This price floor results in 1,200 hours of labor being supplied and 800 hours of labor being demanded.

**a.** Use the above information to derive the labor demand curve for Utopia. Assume this labor demand curve is linear. In your equation, abbreviate the price of labor, or its hourly wage rate, as $W$, and the quantity of labor demanded, measured as hours of labor, as $L$. (Hint: You may find sketching a graph of the above information helpful.)

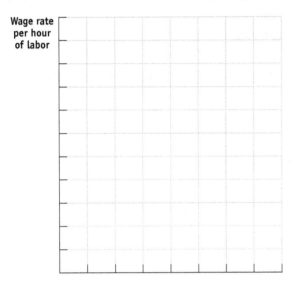

**b.** Use the above information to derive the labor supply curve for Utopia. Assume this labor supply curve is linear. In your equation, abbreviate the hourly wage rate as $W$ and the hours of labor supplied as $L$.

**c.** What wage rate did the government set when it implemented the price floor?

**d.** Describe the effects of this price floor on the labor market in Utopia. Who benefits from the price floor? Who is hurt by the price floor?

## BEFORE YOU TAKE THE TEST

# Module Review Questions

1. The implementation of an effective price ceiling
   a. decreases the area of producer surplus.
   b. increases the area of producer surplus.

2. The implementation of an effective price floor
   a. decreases the area of consumer surplus.
   b. increases the area of consumer surplus.

3. When demanders can make a strong moral or political case for lower prices in a market, the government may decide to enact an effective
   a. price floor.          b. price ceiling.

4. When suppliers can make a strong moral or political case for higher prices in a market, the government may decide to enact an effective
   a. price floor.          b. price ceiling.

5. Consider minimum-wage legislation requiring that all workers receive a wage payment greater than the equilibrium market wage. Which of the following two groups is more likely to have advocated for this legislation?
   a. demanders of labor      b. suppliers of labor

6. Use the information in the table below to answer the following question.

| Price | Quantity demanded | Quantity supplied |
|-------|-------------------|-------------------|
| $ 20  | 200               | 0                 |
| 40    | 150               | 50                |
| 60    | 100               | 100               |
| 80    | 50                | 150               |
| 100   | 0                 | 200               |

If the government mandates that prices in this market can fall no lower than $50, this results in

a. a situation of excess quantity demanded.
b. a situation of excess quantity supplied.
c. fewer than 100 units being supplied in this market.
d. no effect in this market, since the equilibrium price is greater than $50.

7. Use the information in the table below to answer the following question.

| Price | Quantity demanded | Quantity supplied |
|-------|-------------------|-------------------|
| $ 20  | 200               | 0                 |
| 40    | 150               | 50                |
| 60    | 100               | 100               |
| 80    | 50                | 150               |
| 100   | 0                 | 200               |

Suppose a price floor of $40 is implemented in this market. This results in

a. an excess demand of 100 units.

b. an excess supply of 100 units.

c. no effect in this market, since the price floor is set below the equilibrium price.

d. no effect in this market, since the price floor is set above the equilibrium price.

8. Use the information in the table below to answer the following question.

| Price | Quantity demanded | Quantity supplied |
|-------|-------------------|-------------------|
| $ 20  | 200               | 0                 |
| 40    | 150               | 50                |
| 60    | 100               | 100               |
| 80    | 50                | 150               |
| 100   | 0                 | 200               |

Suppose a price ceiling of $40 is implemented in this market. This results in

a. an excess demand of 100 units.

b. an excess supply of 100 units.

c. no effect in this market, since the price ceiling is set below the equilibrium price.

d. a temporary shortage of the good while prices rise, and the quantity demanded and the quantity supplied adjust until they are equal.

9. Use the information in the table below to answer the following question.

| Price | Quantity demanded | Quantity supplied |
|-------|-------------------|-------------------|
| $ 20  | 200               | 0                 |
| 40    | 150               | 50                |
| 60    | 100               | 100               |
| 80    | 50                | 150               |
| 100   | 0                 | 200               |

If the price ceiling is set at $40 in this market, then

a. too few resources are being allocated to the production of this good.

b. too many resources are being allocated to the production of this good.

**10.** Which of the following statements are true?

    I. Price ceilings are inefficient because they result in too much of the good being produced in the market.

    II. Price ceilings are inefficient because they result in the production of goods with too low a level of quality.

    III. Price ceilings are inefficient because they lead to wasted resources since they increase the amount of time consumers must search for the price-controlled good.

    a. Statement I is true.

    b. Statement II is true.

    c. Statements I and II are true.

    d. Statements II and III are true.

**11.** Use the information in the table below to answer the following question.

| Price | Quantity demanded | Quantity supplied |
|---|---|---|
| $ 20 | 200 | 0 |
| 40 | 150 | 50 |
| 60 | 100 | 100 |
| 80 | 50 | 150 |
| 100 | 0 | 200 |

If the price ceiling is set at $40 in this market, the loss in total surplus in this market equals

    a. $2,000.

    b. $1,000.

    c. $500.

    d. $200.

**12.** An effective price ceiling typically causes an inefficient allocation of the good to

    a. consumers of the good.

    b. producers of the good.

**13.** Black market or illegal activities increase with the imposition of price controls in markets. Black markets result in

    a. improving the situation of all participants in the price-controlled market.

    b. worsening the situation for those people who attempt to obey the rules and restrictions imposed by the government in a price-controlled market.

    c. have little or no real impact in price-controlled markets.

    d. the creation of greater respect in society for the need to obey all laws.

**14.** Use the following graph to answer this question.

An effective price floor is implemented in the market depicted in the graph. This price floor generates an excess quantity supplied of 2 units in this market. This price floor must be equal to

a. $10.

b. $7.

**15.** Use the following graph to answer this question.

An effective price floor is enacted in this market, and with this price floor the government promises to purchase any unwanted units produced. If the price floor is set at $10, then the government will spend _____ purchasing the unwanted units of the good.

a. $50

b. $30

c. $21

d. $20

**16.** Use the following graph to answer this question.

An effective price floor is enacted in this market at a price of $10. With this price floor, consumers' expenditure on this good will equal

a. $50.                  c. $21.

b. $30.                  d. $20.

**17.** Which of the following statements is true?

a. An effective price ceiling reduces the quantity of the good available to consumers, while an effective price floor increases the quantity of the good available to consumers.

b. An effective price floor reduces the quantity of the good available to consumers, while an effective price ceiling increases the quantity of the good available to consumers.

c. Government intervention in markets in the form of effective price ceilings or price floors increases the quantity of the good available to consumers.

d. Government intervention in markets in the form of effective price ceilings or price floors decreases the quantity of the good available to consumers.

**18.** When a price is artificially set above the equilibrium price in a market, who determines the quantity of the good bought and sold in the market?

a. demanders            b. suppliers

**19.** When suppliers determine the quantity of the good bought and sold in a market, this must be due to the imposition of an effective

a. price floor.          b. price ceiling.

**20.** An effective price floor prevents suppliers from competing for customers through lower prices, so suppliers compete for customers by offering goods with

a. greater quality than consumers desire.

b. lower quality than consumers desire.

**21.** Which of the following statements is true?

   I. An effective price floor benefits some suppliers.

   II. An effective price floor benefits all demanders.

   III. An effective price floor results in a persistent surplus.

   IV. An effective price floor results in an inefficiently high level of quality in the good offered by suppliers.

a. Statements I and III are true.

b. Statements I, III, and IV are true.

c. Statements III and IV are true.

d. Statements II, III, and IV are true.

## ANSWER KEY

# Answers to Problems and Exercises

1.  **a.** The equilibrium price is $P_1$ and the equilibrium quantity is $Q_3$.

    **b.** This is not an effective price floor since the price floor of $P_3$ is less than the equilibrium price $P_1$. Since it is a nonbinding/ineffective price floor, the equilibrium price and quantity will not change.

    **c.** This is an effective price floor since the price floor of $P_2$ is greater than the equilibrium price $P_1$. At $P_2$, $Q_1$ units of the good will be demanded and $Q_4$ units of the good will be supplied. This excess supply of $Q_4 - Q_1$ will not be eliminated by price decreases since the price is artificially set at $P_2$ by the government and is not allowed to decrease. An effective price floor creates a situation of excess supply, or a surplus, that is not eliminated by changes in the price of the good because the price has been set at a level that is greater than the market-clearing price.

    **d.** For a price floor to have an effect in a market, the price floor must be set at a price that is greater than the equilibrium price.

    **e.** The price floor must be set at a price that is greater than $P_2$ since we know from part (c) that the surplus in the market at $P_2$ equals $Q_4 - Q_1$.

2.  **a.** The equilibrium price is $P_1$ and the equilibrium quantity is $Q_3$.

    **b.** This is not an effective price ceiling since the price ceiling of $P_2$ is greater than the equilibrium price $P_1$. Since it is a nonbinding/ineffective price ceiling, the equilibrium price and quantity will not change.

    **c.** This is an effective price ceiling since the price ceiling of $P_3$ is less than the equilibrium price $P_1$. At $P_3$, $Q_5$ units of the good will be demanded and $Q_2$ units of the good will be supplied. This excess demand of $Q_5 - Q_2$ will not be eliminated by price increases since the price is artificially set at $P_3$ by the government and is not allowed to increase. An effective price ceiling creates a situation of excess demand, or a shortage, that is not eliminated by changes in the price of the good because the price has been set at a level that is less than the market-clearing price.

    **d.** For a price ceiling to have an effect in a market, the price ceiling must be set at a price that is less than the equilibrium price.

    **e.** The price ceiling must be set at a price that is greater than $P_3$ but still less than the equilibrium price of $P_1$. We know this because when the price ceiling is set at $P_3$, the shortage is equal to $Q_5 - Q_2$, and the new price ceiling results in a smaller shortage than the shortage at price $P_3$.

**3.** The market is in equilibrium when there are 1,500 units of housing offered at the price of $2,000 per month, so 1,200 is not an efficient level of housing. The price ceiling forces consumers to reduce their consumption of the good from the efficient level. In the sketch below, the shaded area represents the total surplus received when 1,500 units of housing are supplied at a price of $2,000 per unit.

The second sketch illustrates the area of total surplus once the effective price ceiling is implemented. Notice that the area of total surplus is reduced relative to its initial level. The amount of this loss in total surplus is the measure of the efficiency cost of the reduction in quantity provided in the market due to the imposition of the price ceiling.

**4.    a.** The equilibrium price is $800 per unit of housing and the equilibrium quantity of housing is 2,000 units.

**b.**

| Price | Quantity demanded | Quantity supplied |
|-------|-------------------|-------------------|
| $ 200 | 8,000 | 0 |
| 400 | 6,000 | 666.67 |
| 600 | 4,000 | 1,333.33 |
| 800 | 2,000 | 2,000 |
| 1,000 | 0 | 2,666.67 |

**c.** From the table in part (b), you know that a price ceiling of $400 is too low (the shortage is greater than 4,000 units of housing at this price) while a price ceiling of $600 is too high (the shortage at this price is less than 4,000 units of housing). You could try some prices between $400 and $600 or you could solve this problem algebraically. The shortage of 4,000 units is the difference between the quantity demanded and the quantity supplied at the price ceiling, or in other words, $Q_S + 4,000 = Q_D$. Thus, the demand equation can be rewritten as $P_C = 1,000 - 0.1(Q_S + 4,000)$ and the supply equation is equal to $P_C = 200 + 0.3Q_S$, where $P_C$ is the price ceiling level. Solving this set of equations, we find that the quantity supplied is equal to 1,000 units. Thus, the quantity demanded is equal to 5,000 units while the price ceiling level is $500.

**d.** The people lucky enough to get one of the housing units supplied at the price ceiling price benefit from this government intervention. These individuals pay less than the market-clearing price for their housing unit.

**e.** Consumers who want housing but who cannot find housing due to the price ceiling are hurt by the decision to implement the price ceiling. Additionally, as landlords fail to maintain the housing units in Metropolitan City, the whole community is affected as the general condition of the housing stock deteriorates. And if a black market develops in the housing market, this will erode the general level of lawful behavior in the community.

**f.** Since the quantity demanded of housing exceeds the quantity supplied of housing at the price ceiling, persistent shortages will exist in this market. Consumers eager to find housing will resort to activities that are illegal—for example, subletting housing units at rates higher than the price ceiling rate or making illegal payments to landlords.

**g.** Too few resources are devoted to the housing market. We know this because the effective price ceiling creates a persistent shortage in the market for housing.

**5.  a.** The level of the price floor in this market is $60 per bushel. To find the price floor level, first solve for the equilibrium price in the market: set demand equal to supply. Thus, $100 - Q = Q$, and thus the equilibrium quantity is 50 bushels of the agricultural commodity. We can then substitute this quantity into either the demand or supply equation to find the equilibrium price. The equilibrium price is $50 per bushel. If the price floor is set $10 above the equilibrium price, we know the price floor must be at $60 per bushel.

**b.** At $60 per bushel, demanders demand 40 bushels and suppliers supply 60 bushels. There is an excess supply of 20 bushels.

**c.** If the government buys the surplus 20 bushels at the price floor level of $60 per bushel, it will spend $1,200.

**d.** Consumers demand 40 bushels at the price of $60 per bushel. The expenditure by consumers on the product will equal $2,400.

**e.** Total farm revenue equals the total number of bushels supplied times the price floor, or (60 bushels)($60 per bushel), or $3,600. Total farm revenue equals the sum of consumer expenditure on the good plus government expenditure on the good. Total farm revenue without the price floor is equal to the equilibrium price times the equilibrium quantity, or (50 bushels) ($50 per bushel), or $2,500. Total farm revenue increases with the imposition of an effective price floor.

**f.** The farmers benefit from the imposition of the price floor since it increases total farm revenue.

**6.  a.**

**b. Price**

7.  **a.** The information you are given in this problem can be represented as follows:

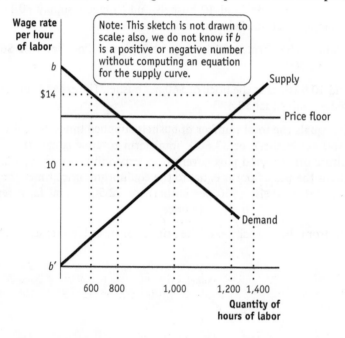

Thus, we know two points of the labor demand curve: (1,000, $10) and (600, $14). Use these two points to compute the slope of the demand curve: slope = rise/run = $(y_1 - y_2)/(x_1 - x_2) = (10 - 14)/(1,000 - 600) = -0.01$. The demand equation can be written as $W = b - 0.01L$. Then, use one of the points that you know is on the demand curve—either (1,000, $10) or (600, $14)—with this equation to solve for $b$. Thus, $W = b - 0.01L$ can be written as $10 = b - 0.01(1,000)$, or $b = 20$. The labor demand curve is therefore $W = 20 - 0.01L$.

**b.** Use a similar procedure to write the supply equation: $W = 0.01L + b'$, where $b'$ is the y-intercept of the labor supply curve. Then use one of the points that you know is on the supply curve—either (1,000, $10) or (1,400, $14)—with this equation to identify the value of $b'$. Thus, $W = 0.01L + b'$ can be rewritten as $10 = 0.01(1,000) + b'$ and $b'$ therefore equals 0. The labor supply equation is thus $W = 0.01L$.

**c.** At the price floor, we know that the quantity of labor demanded is 800 units. Substitute this number for $L$ in the labor demand equation: $W = 20 - 0.01(800)$, or $W = \$12$ per hour of labor. To verify that the price floor has been set at a wage of $12 per hour of labor, check your answer with the labor supply equation. At the price floor, we know the quantity of labor supplied is equal to 1,200 units. Using this number for $L$ in the labor supply equation, we find $W = 0.01(1,200)$, or $W = \$12$ per hour of labor.

**d.** This price floor creates a surplus of labor when the price floor is set at a wage rate of $12 per hour of labor. In a labor market, a surplus of labor implies that there is unemployment: workers who want to work (i.e., they are willing to supply their labor at the prevailing wage rate) cannot find work (i.e., there is insufficient demand for their services at the prevailing wage rate). Workers lucky enough to get a job paying $12 per hour benefit from the price floor while workers who are unable to find work at that wage rate are harmed by the price floor.

## Answers to Module Review Questions

1.  **Answer a.** Since an effective price ceiling reduces the price that producers receive and consumers pay, this results in a decrease in producer surplus.

2.  **Answer a.** Since an effective price floor increases the price that producers receive and consumers pay, this results in a decrease in consumer surplus.

3.  **Answer b.** Demanders desire lower prices for the good and this can be achieved through the enactment of an effective price ceiling, since it reduces the price below the equilibrium price.

4.  **Answer a.** Producers desire higher prices for the good and this can be achieved through the enactment of an effective price floor, since it raises the price above the equilibrium price.

5.  **Answer b.** Suppliers of labor will receive this higher wage and therefore benefit from it. Demanders of labor will find that this higher wage increases the cost of hiring labor, and they will not benefit from it.

6.  **Answer d.** Setting a lower limit on prices of $50 in this market is an example of an ineffective price floor since a price floor of $50 is less than the equilibrium price of $60. This price floor would have no effect on the market.

7.  **Answer c.** Setting a price floor of $40 in this market is an example of an ineffective price floor since a price floor of $40 is less than the equilibrium price of $60. This price floor would have no effect on the market.

8.  **Answer a.** A price ceiling of $40 results in 150 units being demanded and 50 units being supplied. This is therefore a situation of excess demand of 100 units.

9.  **Answer a.** At a price ceiling of $40, consumers wish to consume 150 units of the good while suppliers are only willing to supply 50 units of the good. This indicates that too few resources are being allocated to this market.

10. **Answer d.** Statement I is incorrect because price ceilings result in too little of the good being produced in the market. Statement II is correct because when price is limited to a level below the equilibrium price, producers have an incentive to reduce the quality of the product they provide to the market. Statement III is correct because an effective price ceiling results in greater costs as demanders seek out the artificially scarce good.

11. **Answer b.** The total surplus in the market when there is no price ceiling is equal to $4,000. With the imposition of the effective price ceiling the total surplus equals $3,000. To find these areas of total surplus, sketch a graph and then calculate the relevant areas. The initial total surplus is equal to $(1/2)(\$100/\text{unit} - \$20/\text{unit})(100 \text{ units})$ or $4,000. The total surplus with the effective price ceiling is equal to $(1/2)(\$100/\text{unit} - \$80/\text{unit})(50 \text{ units}) +$

(1/2)($40/unit – $20/unit)(50 units) + ($80/unit – $40/unit)(50 units), or $3,000. The graph below illustrates this.

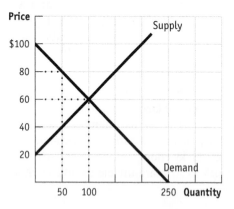

The change in total surplus is $4,000 – $3,000, or $1,000.

12. **Answer a.** An effective price ceiling limits the amount of the good available to consumers in the market by limiting the price to a level that is less than the equilibrium price. Producers produce the amount they are willing to produce at that price, and they do not expand production even though consumers are willing to consume more units of the good.

13. **Answer b.** Answers (a) and (b) are mutually exclusive: if one of these answers is correct, then the other must by necessity be incorrect. Reading answer (b) helps to identify a group that is hurt by black market activities: those individuals who decide not to engage in black market activities are left worse off because of their obedience to the rules imposed by the price-controlled market. Answer (c) is incorrect since price controls do affect markets and do have impacts when they are effective. Answer (d) is also incorrect since price-controlled markets generate black market activities, which are against the law.

14. **Answer a.** An effective price floor is the minimum price that can be charged for a good, and this price must be set above the equilibrium price. At a price of $10, the quantity demanded is 3 units while the quantity supplied is 5 units. At a price floor of $10, there will be excess supply of 2 units. The price floor must equal $10.

15. **Answer d.** At a price floor of $10, the excess supply is 2 units. If the government purchases these 2 units at $10 each, the cost to the government of this purchase is $20.

16. **Answer b.** With a $10 price floor, consumers in this market will demand 3 units of the good. Their expenditure on the good will equal ($10/unit)(3 units), or $30.

17. **Answer d.** Effective price ceilings and price floors both reduce the quantity of the good available to consumers, so answers (a), (b), and (c) are not true.

18. **Answer a.** When the price is artificially set above the equilibrium price, demanders determine the quantity demanded in the market since they select the quantity they are willing to demand based on the price of the good.

19. **Answer b.** A price ceiling is set below the equilibrium price. This limits the price that can be charged for a good in the market. Producers take this price and then determine the number of units of the good they are willing to provide in the market at this price.

20. **Answer a.** When producers cannot compete for customers through prices, they must look for other ways to compete. One way is to offer goods of higher quality, and with an effective price floor producers will compete by offering higher-quality goods.

21. **Answer b.** Statement I is correct because those suppliers who are lucky enough to sell their good at the higher price are benefited. Statement III is also correct since an effective price floor results in excess supply of the good. Statement IV is correct as well because suppliers will compete for customers by offering higher-quality goods since they cannot compete for customers by offering lower prices. Statement II is incorrect: demanders of this good now have to pay a higher price than they would have in a freely functioning market.

# module 8

# International Trade

## Summary

This module discusses the importance of international trade in the world economy today. It also explores the question of who gains and who loses from international trade. The module also analyzes the impact of tariffs and quotas on the level of imports and exports. The module also discusses the challenges created by globalization.

## Module Objectives

**Objective #1.** Trade is beneficial to both parties that engage in the trade, whether they are individuals or countries. Countries that specialize in producing different goods and then trade these goods with other countries benefit from this trade. Goods and services purchased from abroad are called imports, and goods and services sold abroad are called exports. Countries trade goods and services with one another, but they also invest funds: this linking of the markets for goods and services as well as financial assets between different countries is referred to as globalization.

**Objective #2.** A country has the comparative advantage in producing a good or service when that country can produce the good or service at a lower opportunity cost than can other countries.

**Objective #3.** Autarky refers to the situation in which a country does not engage in trade with any other countries.

**Objective #4.** Gains from trade depend on comparative advantage and not absolute advantage. Comparative advantage is based on the opportunity cost of producing the good and not the absolute amount of resources used to produce the good. A country with low wage rates generally reflects low labor productivity, while a country with high wage rates reflects high labor productivity.

**Objective #5.**   The model of demand and supply can be used to analyze the benefits of international trade. Figure 8.1 illustrates a market for a country that does not trade. In this figure, domestic demand represents the total demand for this good from individuals who live in this country, while domestic supply represents the total supply of this good from firms producing this good in this country. In autarky, the equilibrium in this market would be determined by the intersection of the domestic demand curve with the domestic supply curve: $P_A$ is the equilibrium price and $Q_A$ is the equilibrium quantity under autarky. Consumer and producer surplus are indicated in the figure, and total surplus in this market equals the sum of consumer and producer surplus.

**Figure 8.1**

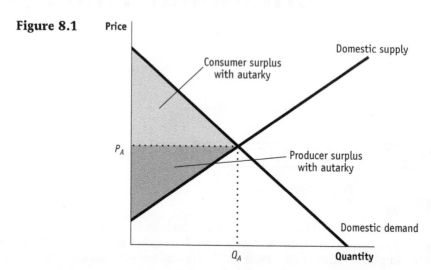

Consider what happens in this market if this country opens to trade. Suppose the world price for this good is lower than the autarky price ($P_A$) for this good. In Figure 8.2, this world price ($P_W$) is drawn on the graph. Notice that if the country opens to trade, the quantity of the good demanded domestically in this country at the world price ($Q_D$) will be greater than the amount of the good supplied domestically at this price ($Q_S$). This excess demand will be satisfied by the country importing ($Q_D - Q_S$) units of the good. Trade will also change the areas of consumer and producer surplus in this country: consumer surplus will increase as consumers get more units of the good at a lower price, while producer surplus decreases as domestic producers sell fewer units of the good at the lower price. Study Figure 8.2 carefully and recall that consumer surplus is the area that is beneath the demand curve but above the equilibrium price, while producer surplus is the area that is above the supply curve but below the equilibrium price. With trade, total surplus increases, but domestic producers of this good see a reduction in their producer surplus while domestic consumers see an increase in their consumer surplus. In the case of an imported good, domestic consumers benefit while domestic producers lose. Trade is beneficial since total surplus increases, but trade has distributional consequences as you can see from what happens to the areas of consumer and producer surplus.

**Figure 8.2**

We can use the same analysis to consider the situation when the world price is greater than the autarky price. Starting from Figure 8.1, a market under autarky, let's consider a situation in which the world price exceeds the autarky price. Figure 8.3 illustrates this example: $P_W$ is the world price and, in this case, when this country opens to trade, it finds that the quantity demanded domestically at the world price ($Q_D$) is less than the amount supplied domestically at this price ($Q_S$). This excess supply of ($Q_S - Q_D$) will be exported to other countries. Figure 8.3 also identifies the areas of consumer surplus and producer surplus once trade is allowed. As in Figure 8.2, we find that the area of total surplus is larger than in autarky. However, the distribution of the surplus has changed: in Figure 8.2, domestic consumers benefited from trade while domestic suppliers were hurt; in Figure 8.3, domestic suppliers benefit from trade while domestic consumers are hurt. In both of these examples we find that trade is beneficial since it increases total surplus, but that trade has distributional consequences.

**Figure 8.3**

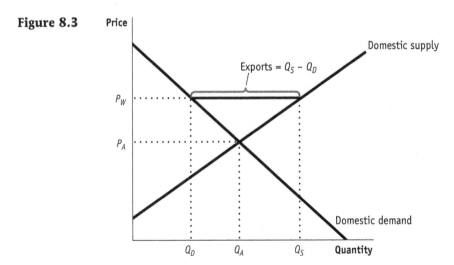

**Objective #6.** A country's industries can be broken down into two broad categories: exporting industries that produce goods and services to be sold abroad, and import-competing industries that produce goods and services also imported from abroad. When a country opens to trade, this leads to higher production in the exporting industries and lower production in the import-competing industries, and these changes affect the demand for factors of production in these two types of industries. International trade increases the demand for those factors of production that are relatively abundant in the country and decreases the demand for those factors of production that are relatively scarce. Thus, the price of abundant factors tends to rise while the price of scarce factors tends to fall. This price movement redistributes income toward a country's abundant factors and away from a country's less abundant factors.

**Objective #7.** Countries engage in trade protection, or protection, to limit the level of imports with the idea of protecting domestic producers in import-competing industries from foreign competition. Tariffs are a form of excise tax levied on the sales of imported goods, while quotas are legal limits on the quantity of a good that can be imported.

- Figure 8.4 illustrates a tariff placed on the good represented in this diagram. The tariff raises the world price of the good and therefore reduces the level of imports while simultaneously reducing the overall domestic demand for the good and increasing the domestic supply of the good. In Figure 8.4, the domestic supply and domestic demand curves are illustrated. $P_W$ is the world price for the good with open trade, and $P_T$ is the price of the good once the tariff is applied. At $P_T$, the quantity supplied domestically is $Q_{ST}$ while the quantity demanded domestically is $Q_{DT}$. Thus, the level of imports with the imposition of the tariff is ($Q_{DT} - Q_{ST}$). The tariff results in a decrease in consumer surplus, an increase in producer surplus, and the capture of some of the consumer surplus as tariff revenue that the government earns. These areas are marked on the graph. In addition, the tariff results in deadweight loss: some mutually beneficial trades fail to occur and the economy wastes some resources on inefficient production since some producers produce the good even though their costs are greater than the world price of $P_W$. These two areas of deadweight loss are also identified on the graph. Study Figure 8.4 carefully and then compare it with Figure 8.2 to see how a tariff changes the outcome in this market. Notice that the tariff redistributes part of the consumer surplus to domestic producers and to the government as well as creates the areas of deadweight loss.

**Figure 8.4**

• Imposition of a quota in a market with free trade creates a limit on the number of units of the good that can be imported into the domestic market. This legal limit is typically administered through a license whereby the license holder purchases the legal right to import a certain number of units of the good into the domestic market. A quota results in a similar outcome as the tariff, but with one crucial difference. With a quota, the area labeled tariff revenue is now license-holder revenue. Instead of the government earning tax revenue from the imposition of the tariff, the quota results in the license holder earning quota rents equal to the area $(P_Q - P_W)(Q_{D\ QUOTA} - Q_{S\ QUOTA})$. The quota results in an increase in the domestic producer surplus and a decrease in the domestic consumer surplus. In addition, the quota results in the same two areas of deadweight loss that occurred with the tariff. Figure 8.5 illustrates the impact of a quota of $(Q_{D\ QUOTA} - Q_{S\ QUOTA})$ units on the market.

**Figure 8.5**

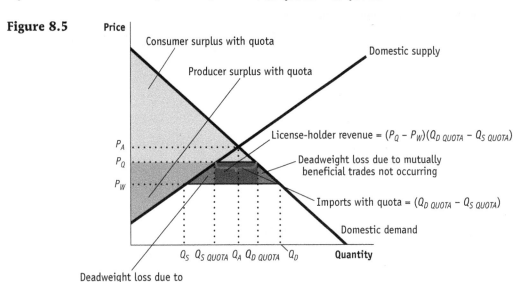

**Objective #8.** Globalization or growing world trade has generally been seen as a positive outcome. However, concerns have arisen over the growing wage gap between more educated and less educated workers. In addition, the growth of offshore outsourcing has generated concerns about increasing economic insecurity.

## Key Terms

**imports** goods and services purchased from other countries.

**exports** goods and services sold to other countries.

**globalization** the phenomenon of growing economic linkages among countries.

**autarky** a situation in which a country does not trade with other countries.

**domestic demand curve** a *demand curve* that shows how the quantity of a good demanded by domestic consumers depends on the price of that good.

**domestic supply curve** a *supply curve* that shows how the quantity of a good supplied by domestic producers depends on the price of that good.

**world price** the price at which a good can be bought or sold abroad.

*Notes*

## Key Terms *(continued)*

**exporting industries** industries that produce goods and services that are sold abroad.

**import-competing industries** industries that produce goods and services that are also imported.

**free trade** *trade* that is unregulated by government *tariffs* or other artificial barriers; the levels of *exports* and *imports* occur naturally, as a result of supply and demand.

**trade protection** policies that limit *imports*.

**protection** an alternative term for *trade protection;* policies that limit *imports*.

**tariff** a tax levied on *imports*.

**import quota** a legal limit on the quantity of a good that can be imported from abroad.

**offshore outsourcing** businesses hiring people in another country to perform various tasks.

## ■ AFTER YOU READ THE MODULE

## Tips

**Tip #1.** Working with quotas is often difficult for students: a quota is a legally established limit to the amount of imports a country allows during a given period. An alternative way of thinking about this legal limit is to recognize that the quota is the amount of imports that leads to the sum of the quantity supplied domestically plus the quota amount equaling the quantity demanded domestically. Thus, if you are told the quantity demanded domestically and the quantity supplied domestically at a given price, you can then calculate what the necessary quota would be in order for the total quantity supplied of the good (both the domestic production plus the world production) to equal the quantity demanded domestically. With this thought in mind, go back and revisit Figure 8.5 to see if you can apply this concept to the graph.

## WORKED PROBLEMS

1. The small economy of Newville produces chocolate, and this market for chocolate is characterized by the following equations:

Domestic Demand for Chocolate: $P = 100 - Q$
Domestic Supply of Chocolate: $P = Q$

You are asked to determine the equilibrium price and quantity in this market if Newville continues to be a closed economy with regard to the chocolate market. You are also asked to provide a measure of the consumer and producer surplus when this market is closed to trade. Newville is considering opening this market to trade and imagines two possible scenarios: in the first scenario, the chocolate market is open to trade and the world price of chocolate is $80 per unit. Newville's government wants you to analyze the effect of opening this market to trade given this price: the government in particular wants to know the impact of opening the market on the level of imports or exports of chocolate it could anticipate as well as on the values of consumer and producer surplus when there is trade. In the second scenario, the chocolate market is open to trade, and the world price of chocolate is $20 per unit. You are also asked to provide an analysis of the impact of opening the market on the level of imports or exports of chocolate as well as on the values of consumer and producer surplus if the world price for chocolate is equal to $20 per unit. For both scenarios, you are asked to illustrate your answer with a graph to help the government officials understand the impact of opening the market to world trade. The government also wishes to understand if opening its market to trade is beneficial whether it is confronted by the first or the second scenario. Who (domestic consumers or domestic producers of chocolate) in Newville is more likely to favor opening the chocolate market to trade if the world price is anticipated to be $80 per unit?

**STEP 1:** Start by drawing a graph of the market for chocolate in Newville when its economy is closed to trade. Use this graph to calculate the levels of consumer and producer surplus if there is no trade.

Graph the two equations and then use these two equations to find the equilibrium price and equilibrium quantity in this market when the market is closed to world competition. Using the demand and supply equations—$P = 100 - Q$ and $P = Q$, respectively—we can solve for the equilibrium quantity and then use this quantity to find the equilibrium price. Thus, $100 - Q = Q$, or $2Q = 100$, and therefore $Q = 50$. Plugging $Q = 50$ back into either the demand or the supply equation, we can find that the equilibrium price is equal to $50.

The value of consumer surplus is equal to $(1/2)(\$100$ per unit $- \$50$ per unit$)(50$ units$)$, or \$1,250. The value of producer surplus is equal to $(1/2)(\$50$ per unit $- \$0$ per unit$)(50$ units$)$, or \$1,250. These areas are marked on the preceding graph.

**STEP 2:** Modify your graph from Step 1 by adding in a line that represents a world price for chocolate of \$80 per unit.

**STEP 3:** Analyze the impact on this market if the world price is equal to \$80 and Newville opens its chocolate market. Be sure to identify whether Newville will export or import chocolate. In addition, determine the impact of this decision on consumer and producer surplus. Finally, analyze whether trade is beneficial if the world price of chocolate is equal to \$80 per unit.

When Newville opens its chocolate market to international trade and the world price of chocolate is \$80 per unit, domestic suppliers will be willing to supply 80 units of the good, while domestic demanders are willing to buy only 20 units of the good. This excess supply of 60 units will therefore be exported into the world market for chocolate.

To find the consumer surplus, first recognize that it is the area that is under the domestic demand curve but above the world price for chocolate. Then, calculate the value of this area: consumer surplus is equal to $(1/2)(\$100$ per unit $- \$80$ per unit$)(20$ units$)$, or \$200.

To find the producer surplus, first recognize that it is the area that is under the world price for chocolate but above the domestic supply curve. Then, calculate the value of this area: producer surplus is equal to $(1/2)(\$80$ per unit $- \$0$ per unit$)(80$ units$)$, or \$3,200.

The following figure illustrates the impact on consumer and producer surplus when the world price is equal to $80 per unit.

Trade is beneficial to Newville when the world price is $80 per unit since the value of total surplus, the sum of consumer and producer surplus in this case, is greater than the value of total surplus when Newville has a closed chocolate market.

**STEP 4:** Redraw your graph from Step 1 and revise it by adding in a line that represents a world price for chocolate of $20 per unit.

**STEP 5:** Analyze the impact on this market if the world price is equal to $20 and Newville opens its chocolate market. Be sure to identify whether Newville will export or import chocolate. In addition, determine the impact of this decision on consumer and producer surplus. Finally, analyze whether trade is beneficial if the world price of chocolate is equal to $20 per unit.

When Newville opens its chocolate market to international trade and the world price of chocolate is $20 per unit, domestic suppliers will only be willing to supply 20 units of the good, while domestic demanders want to buy 80 units of the good. This excess demand of 60 units will be met by Newville's importing 60 units of chocolate from the world market.

To find the consumer surplus, first recognize that it is the area that is under the domestic demand curve but above the world price for chocolate. Then, calculate the value of this area: consumer surplus is equal to (1/2)($100 per unit – $20 per unit)(80 units), or $3,200.

To find the producer surplus, first recognize that it is the area that is under the world price for chocolate but above the domestic supply curve. Then, calculate the value of this area: producer surplus is equal to (1/2)($20 per unit – $0 per unit)(20 units), or $200.

The following figure illustrates the impact on consumer and producer surplus when the world price is equal to $20 per unit.

Trade is beneficial to Newville when the world price is $20 per unit since the value of total surplus, the sum of consumer and producer surplus in this case, is greater than the value of total surplus when Newville has a closed chocolate market.

**STEP 6:** Review your analysis in Step 3 to determine whether domestic demanders or domestic suppliers of chocolate will be more likely to favor opening the chocolate market to trade when the world price is $80 per unit.

Domestic producers will favor opening the chocolate market to trade when the world price is equal to $80 per unit, since they will be able to sell more units at a higher price. We can easily see the benefits to these producers by comparing the area of producer surplus when the economy is closed to trade (see Step 1) with the area of consumer surplus when the economy is open to trade and the world price is $80 (see Step 3). In contrast, domestic consumers of chocolate will be opposed to opening this market to trade, since their consumer surplus will shrink once the market is open to trade.

2. The small economy of Newville produces chocolate, and this market for chocolate is characterized by the following equations:

$$\text{Domestic demand for chocolate: } P = 100 - Q$$
$$\text{Domestic supply of chocolate: } P = Q$$

Furthermore, you know that the world price for chocolate is $20 per unit. Newville has decided to open its market for chocolate, and although recognizing that this will allow domestic consumers to consume more chocolate at lower prices, it has also determined that it will levy a tariff that raises the price of chocolate in Newville to $40 per unit. You are asked to compare the areas of consumer surplus with and without the tariff, the areas of producer surplus with and without the tariff, the amount of tax revenue the government of Newville will earn from this tariff, and the deadweight loss or efficiency cost of this tariff. The government of Newville has asked that you provide them with graphs that depict what happens if the market is opened to trade and what happens if this tariff is imposed.

**STEP 1:** Start by drawing a graph of the market for chocolate in Newville when its economy is closed to trade. Then, use the two equations to solve for the equilibrium price and quantity in this market. Once you have plotted the equilibrium price and quantity in your graph, you will then be able to use this graph to calculate the levels of consumer and producer surplus if there is no trade.

From Step 5 of problem 1, we can review the graph that represents this market if it opens to trade and the world price of chocolate is $20 per unit. In addition, we know from problem 1 that consumer surplus is equal to $3,200 and producer surplus is equal to $200.

**STEP 2:** Draw a graph of the market for chocolate in Newville showing the effect of a tariff that raises the price of chocolate to $40 per unit. In this graph, indicate the areas that represent consumer surplus, producer surplus, tariff revenue for the government, and deadweight loss from the tariff. Calculate the values of these different areas.

The tariff raises the price of chocolate to $40 per unit. This increase in price will reduce the quantity of chocolate demanded by domestic consumers while increasing the quantity of chocolate supplied by domestic producers. When the price of chocolate is $40, domestic consumers demand 60 units while domestic producers are willing to provide 40 units. Newville will import that difference, or 20 units of chocolate. The government of Newville will collect $20 from every unit of chocolate that is imported and will therefore earn $400 in tariff revenue.

The deadweight loss for the tariff will equal $400. To find the area of deadweight loss, you first need to recognize that it is the sum of the areas of two triangles. Then, calculate the area of each triangle. From the following graph, we can see that the area of deadweight loss is equal to (1/2)($40/unit – $20/unit)(20 units) + (1/2)($40/unit – $20/unit)(20 units), or $400.

The graph that follows depicts the impact of this tariff on the market for chocolate in Newville.

3. Suppose that Newville is still considering opening the market for chocolate that was described in problem 1, but is also now considering imposing a quota in the market once it is opened to trade. Suppose the government of Newville wishes to achieve the same outcome that it did with the tariff in problem 2, but now use a quota instead. What limit on imported chocolate would achieve the same outcome as the tariff described in problem 2, and what should the government of Newville charge the importer for the license to bring these imported chocolates into the Newville economy?

**STEP 1:** Review the graph in Step 2 of problem 2 to determine how many units of the chocolate are imported into Newville when there is a tariff that raises the price of chocolate to $40. This amount of imports is the amount that the quota must be set at in order to achieve the same outcome as under the proposed tariff.

From the graph we can see that Newville imports 20 units of chocolate when the price of chocolate is raised to $40 per unit. Thus, if the government of Newville limits imports to 20 units, this will cause the price of chocolate to rise to $40 per unit, since it is only at this price that the difference between the quantity demanded domestically (60 units) and the quantity supplied domestically (40 units) is exactly equal to the amount of allowed imports (20 units).

**STEP 2:** Determine the price of the license for importing the chocolates by looking at the tariff revenue.

The tariff revenue represents the revenue the government receives when it places a tax on the imported good. With the quota, the government places a limit on how many units of the good can be imported, and it limits these imports by selling the right to bring the imports into the market. By selling the rights for the same price as the tariff revenue, the government imposes a quota limit that has exactly the same impact as the proposed tariff. The government of Newville should sell the rights to import chocolate for $20 per unit, or a total of $400 for all the rights.

4.  Consider the market for bananas in Paradise, a small country that grows all the bananas that are eaten in Paradise. Suppose that the market for bananas in Paradise is described by the demand and supply curves that are given in the following graph. You are asked to identify the equilibrium price and quantity in this market as well as the value of consumer surplus, producer surplus, and total surplus. Paradise is considering implementing a price floor of $20 per box of bananas. How will this price floor affect consumer surplus, producer surplus, and total surplus?

**STEP 1:** To find the equilibrium price and quantity in this market, you will need both the equation for the demand curve and the equation for the supply curve.

The demand curve has a $y$-intercept of 50 and a slope equal to $-1/10$. The demand curve can be written as $P = 50 - (1/10)Q$, or $Q = 500 - 10P$. The supply curve has a $y$-intercept of 0 and a slope equal to $1/40$. The supply curve can be written as $P = (1/40)Q$, or $Q = 40P$. Use these two equations to find the equilibrium price and quantity: the equilibrium price is $10 per box of bananas and the equilibrium quantity is 400 boxes of bananas.

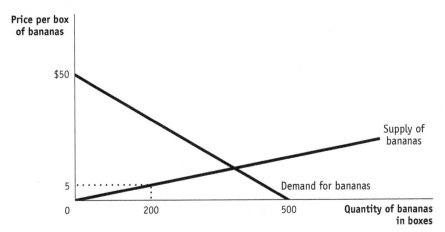

**STEP 2:** Identify the area of consumer surplus and the area of producer surplus, and then calculate the value of these two areas. Sum these two values to find total surplus.

First, identify on the graph the areas that correspond to consumer surplus and producer surplus. Then, use the formula for the area of a triangle to calculate the value of these areas. Remember that the area of a triangle is equal to (1/2) (the base of the triangle)(the height of the triangle). The following graph identifies the areas of con-

sumer surplus and producer surplus. Recall that total surplus is just the sum of consumer and producer surplus.

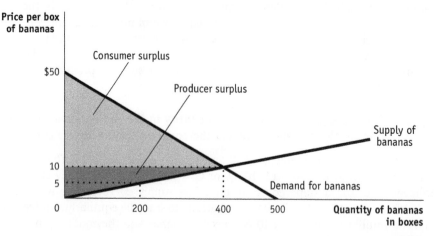

The value of consumer surplus is equal to (1/2)($50 per box of bananas − $10 per
box of bananas)(400 boxes of bananas) = $8,000. The value of producer surplus is
equal to (1/2)($10 per box of bananas − $0 per box of bananas)(400 boxes of
bananas) = $2,000. The value of total surplus is equal to the sum of consumer plus
producer surplus, or $10,000.

**STEP 3:** Analyze the effect of a price floor equal to $20 per box of bananas in
Paradise.

First, check to see if the price floor is effective: recall that a price floor must be set above
the equilibrium price in order for it to impact the market. In this example, the equilibrium price in the market is $10 per box of bananas, so the price floor of $20 per box
of bananas will be effective. Then, determine how many bananas will be demanded at
the price floor price of $20 per box of bananas. To find the number of bananas demand-
ed when the price is $20 per box, use the demand equation. When the price is $20 per
box, demanders will demand 300 boxes of bananas. Notice that suppliers need to
receive a price of only $7.50 in order to be willing to supply 300 boxes of bananas.

Then, determine the new areas that correspond to consumer and producer surplus.
The preceding graph will help you identify these areas.
   The new value for consumer surplus is equal to $4,500. The new value for producer
surplus is a bit more difficult to calculate since it is composed of a rectangle and a triangle. Producer surplus will equal [($20 per box of bananas − $7.50 per box of
bananas)(300 boxes of bananas) + (1/2)($7.50 per box of bananas − $0 per box of
bananas)(300 boxes of bananas)], or $4,875.

# Problems and Exercises

1. Do you agree or disagree with the following statement: "If two workers have different labor productivity, then their wage rates will usually differ from one another, with the worker with greater labor productivity earning a higher wage rate." Explain your answer.

2. Use the following graph to answer this next set of questions. The graph depicts the domestic demand and domestic supply of bicycles in a small closed economy.

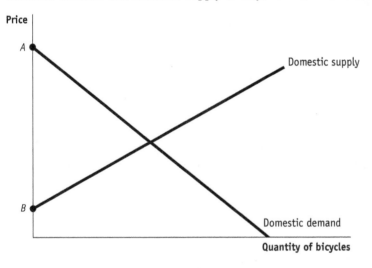

   a. In the preceding graph, label the equilibrium price ($P_e$) and the equilibrium quantity ($Q_e$) for this autarky. Label the areas that correspond to producer surplus and consumer surplus.

   b. Provide a mathematical expression for the areas of producer and consumer surplus based on the symbols and labels in the graph.

**c.** The same graph is replicated here, but this time the world price is also drawn on the graph. Suppose this autarky opens to trade. On the graph, indicate the quantity supplied domestically ($Q_{S_{dom}}$) and the quantity demanded domestically ($Q_{D_{dom}}$) when this country opens to trade. Identify how many bicycles this country will import or export when it opens its economy to trade.

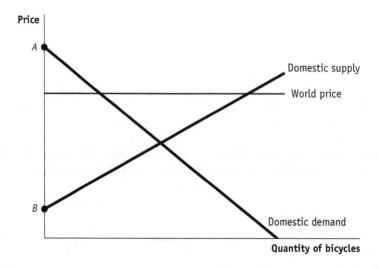

**d.** On the graph in part (c), label the areas that correspond to producer surplus with trade and consumer surplus with trade. Who benefits in this example from trade? Explain your answer.

**e.** The initial graph is replicated here, but this time the world price is also drawn on the graph. Suppose this autarky opens to trade. On the graph, indicate the quantity supplied domestically ($Q_{S_{dom}}$) and the quantity demanded domestically ($Q_{D_{dom}}$) when this country opens to trade. Identify how many bicycles this country will import or export when it opens its economy to trade.

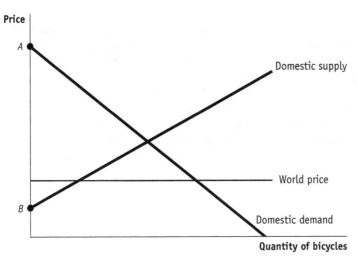

**f.** On the graph in part (e), label the areas that correspond to producer surplus with trade and consumer surplus with trade. Who benefits in this example from trade? Explain your answer.

**3.** Suppose the market for TVs in the small closed economy of Kennet can be described by the following domestic demand curve and domestic supply curve:

$$\text{Domestic demand: } Q = 1{,}000 - (1/2)P$$
$$\text{Domestic supply: } Q = (1/2)P$$

(Hint: For this question you will find it helpful to sketch graphs of the market.)

**a.** What is the equilibrium price and quantity in the market for TVs in Kennet? What is the value of consumer surplus, producer surplus, and total surplus?

**b.** Suppose Kennet opens to trade and the world price for TVs is $1,200. What is the quantity supplied domestically, the quantity demanded domestically, and the number of TVs imported into or exported out of Kennet given this world price? What happens to the value of consumer surplus, producer surplus, and total surplus when Kennet opens to trade?

   **c.** Given the information and the analysis you did in part (b), who benefits from trade in the television market when Kennet opens its economy? Explain your answer.

   **d.** Suppose Kennet's economy is still open to trade, but domestic demand in Kennet has significantly increased so that at every price domestic demand is now 500 units higher than it was initially. Although domestic demand in Kennet has increased, this has not impacted the world price for TVs since Kennet is a small economy. Given this change in demand, how many TVs will be domestically supplied and domestically demanded? Will Kennet import or export TVs? Calculate the numeric value of Kennet's imports or exports. What is the value of consumer surplus, producer surplus, and total surplus given this change in demand? (Hint: You will find it helpful to draw a sketch of these changes in the market for TVs and to calculate the new domestic demand equation.)

**4.** Pepperville is a small economy that currently operates as an autarky. In the market for green peppers, domestic demand and domestic supply can be represented as $P = 5,000 - 0.5Q$ and $P = 1.5Q$, respectively, where $P$ is the price per ton of green peppers and $Q$ is the quantity of green peppers measured in tons.

   **a.** Identify the equilibrium price and quantity of green peppers in Pepperville. What is the value of consumer surplus and producer surplus?

   **b.** The current world price of green peppers is $3,000 per ton, and domestic producers of green peppers are lobbying the government of Pepperville to remain an autarky. Explain why domestic producers of green peppers are not in favor of open trade in the green pepper market.

   **c.** Domestic consumers of green peppers in Pepperville successfully lobby the Pepperville government to open trade in the green pepper market. How many tons of green peppers will be imported into or exported out of Pepperville, given the world price of $3,000 per ton when this market opens to trade? What is the value of consumer surplus and producer surplus with trade?

Domestic producers wage a successful campaign to enact a tariff in the market for green peppers. The tariff effectively raises the price of green peppers to $3,450 per ton. Answer questions (d) through (g) based on this tariff. Assume the world price for green peppers is unchanged and equal to $3,000 per ton.

**d.** How many tons of green peppers will be imported into Pepperville once this tariff is enacted?

**e.** What is the value of consumer surplus and producer surplus once this tariff is implemented?

**f.** What is the tariff revenue the government earns with this tariff?

**g.** What is the deadweight loss associated with this tariff?

**h.** Pepperville is considering replacing the tariff on green peppers with a quota. If consumer surplus and producer surplus are to remain the same under the quota as they are with the tariff, what must the amount of the quota equal?

**i.** From the domestic consumers' perspective, which trade policy—closed economy, open economy, or open economy with a tariff or quota—would they prefer? Explain your answer.

**j.** From the domestic producers' perspective, which trade policy—closed economy, open economy, or open economy with a tariff or quota—would they prefer? Explain your answer.

    **k.** Given your answers in (i) and (j), why do governments frequently adopt tariffs or quotas in particular markets?

**5.** Evansville is a small closed economy. The domestic demand curve for shoes is given by the equation $P = 200 - Q$, where $P$ is the price for a pair of shoes and $Q$ is the quantity of pairs of shoes demanded. The domestic supply curve for shoes is given by the equation $P = 10 + Q$. Currently the world price of shoes is $40 a pair. Evansville is considering opening its economy to trade, and the government is debating three possible trade positions. Option I is to open the economy to trade with no trade protection intervention in the market. Option II is to open the economy to trade but limit the amount of pairs of shoes imported to a quota of 50 pairs of shoes. Option III is to open the economy to trade but impose a tariff on the shoe market that would increase the price of shoes to $80 a pair.

    **a.** Analyze these three policies and enter your findings in the following table.

| | Option I | Option II | Option III |
|---|---|---|---|
| Pairs of shoes imported | | | |
| Consumer surplus | | | |
| Producer surplus | | | |
| Tariff revenue or quota rent | | | |
| Deadweight loss | | | |

    **b.** From the perspective of domestic consumers, which is the best option?

    **c.** From the perspective of domestic producers, which is the best option?

    **d.** Which option results in the greatest efficiency cost? Explain your answer.

# BEFORE YOU TAKE THE TEST

## Module Review Questions

1.  International trade based on comparative advantage is
    a.  beneficial to some of the countries involved in the trade, but not beneficial to other countries.
    b.  beneficial to all of the countries involved in the trade.
    c.  rarely benefits any of the countries involved in the trade.
    d.  only beneficial to relatively rich countries.

2.  Sarah purchases wine from France, cheese from Italy, wheat crackers from Minnesota, potatoes from Idaho, and lamb from Australia. Sarah lives in New York.
    a.  Sarah purchases imports of wine, cheese, and lamb.
    b.  Sarah purchases only domestically produced goods, since she can purchase all of these goods at her local grocery store.
    c.  The wine, cheese, and lamb represent exports from the perspective of the United States.
    d.  Answers (a) and (c) are both true.

3.  Which of the following statements is true?
       I.  Gains from trade depend on absolute advantage.
       II.  Comparative advantage depends on the amount of resources used to produce a good.
       III.  A country's comparative advantage is translated into world markets through its wage rates: a country's wage rate typically reflects that country's labor productivity.
    a.  Statement I is true.
    b.  Statement II is true.
    c.  Statement III is true.
    d.  Statements I, II, and III are true.
    e.  Statements II and III are true.

4.  Which of the following statements is true?
       I.  Countries with highly skilled labor will tend to import goods whose production requires high levels of human capital.
       II.  Countries whose exporting industries focus on using a higher ratio of highly educated workers to other workers are human capital intensive.
       III.  Countries will find that their exporting industries utilize their relatively more abundant factors of production.
    a.  Statement I is true.     d.  Statements I and II are true.
    b.  Statement II is true.    e.  Statements II and III are true.
    c.  Statement III is true.    f.  Statements I, II, and III are true.

Use the following graph to answer the next four questions. The graph shows the market for bicycles for the country of Pedalland. The demand curve indicates the domestic demand for bicycles and the supply curve indicates the domestic supply of bicycles.

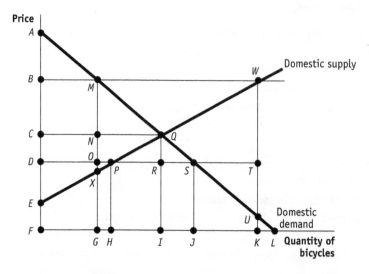

5.  Suppose Pedalland is initially an autarky. In the graph, the area that corresponds to consumer surplus is equal to area _____, and the area that corresponds to producer surplus is equal to area _____.

    a. *ACQ; CQIF*          c. *ACQ; CQE*
    b. *ADS; DPE*           d. *BMNC; CNOD*

6.  Suppose this country opens to trade and that the world price is equal to *B* in the preceding graph. Then we know that Pedalland will
    a. import the number of bicycles represented by the distance between points *M* and *W*.
    b. import the number of bicycles represented by the distance between points *W* and *T*.
    c. export the number of bicycles represented by the distance between points *M* and *W*.
    d. export the number of bicycles represented by the distance between points *W* and *T*.

7.  Suppose this country opens to trade and that the world price is equal to *D* in the preceding graph. Then we know that Pedalland will import the number of bicycles represented by the distance between points
    a. *R* and *S*.          c. *P* and *R*.
    b. *P* and *S*.          d. *P* and *T*.

8.  Suppose this country opens to trade and that the world price is equal to *B* in the preceding graph. Consumer surplus is equal to area _____, and producer surplus is equal to area _____.

    a. *ABM; BWE*           c. *ACNM; CNXE*
    b. *ABM; BMNE*          d. *ABM; BMQE*

Use the following graph to answer the next four questions. The graph shows the market for bicycles for the country of Pedalland. The demand curve indicates the domestic demand for bicycles and the supply curve indicates the domestic supply of bicycles.

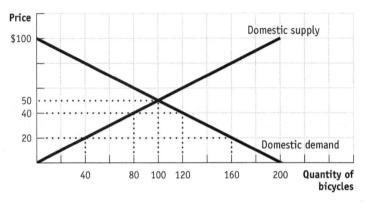

9. The world price in this market equals $20. If the market opens to trade,
   a. Pedalland will import 120 bicycles, and the area of total surplus will increase by $6,800.
   b. Pedalland will export 120 bicycles, and the area of total surplus will increase by $6,800.
   c. Pedalland will import 120 bicycles, and the area of total surplus will increase by $1,800.
   d. Pedalland will export 120 bicycles, and the area of total surplus will increase by $1,800.

10. Suppose the world price for bicycles is $20 and Pedalland opens its bicycle market to trade. Domestic producers successfully lobby the government of Pedalland, and the government imposes a quota on the number of bicycles that can be imported into Pedalland. Suppose license-holder revenue from the quota is equal to $800. Which of the following are possible quota limits that result in this license-holder revenue?
    a. 20 bicycles
    b. 40 bicycles
    c. 60 bicycles
    d. 80 bicycles
    e. Answers (b) and (d) are both possible answers.

11. Suppose the world price of bicycles is $20 and Pedalland opens to trade. Domestic producers of bicycles in Pedalland successfully lobby for a tariff on imported bicycles, which results in the price of bicycles being $40. The deadweight loss associated with this tariff is equal to
    a. $400.
    b. $800.
    c. $1,600.
    d. $2,000.

**12.** The world price of bicycles is $20 and Pedalland opens its economy to trade. A quota of 60 bicycles is imposed in Pedalland. This will result in consumer surplus increasing by _____ relative to the level of consumer surplus when Pedalland was an autarky.

a. $1,725

b. $2,500

c. $4,225

d. $6,725

**13.** A country that engages in international trade will find that this international trade increases the demand for the factors used by the exporting industries and decreases the demand for the factors used in the import-competing industries.

a. True

b. False

## ▮ ANSWER KEY ▮

# Answers to Problems and Exercises

1. Agree. Workers with lower labor productivity will earn a lower wage than workers with higher labor productivity since the competition for less-productive workers is less intense, resulting in a lower wage rate.

2. **a.**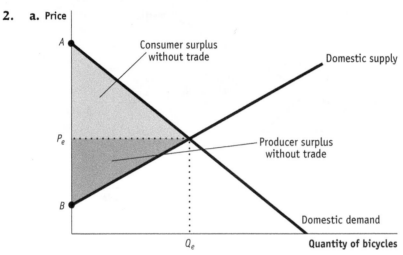

   **b.** Consumer surplus $= (1/2)(A - P_e)(Q_e)$
   Producer surplus $= (1/2)(P_e - B)(Q_e)$

   **c.**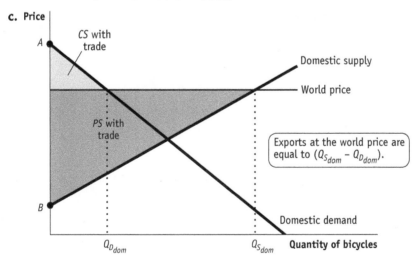

**d.** Domestic producers benefit from this trade because they can produce more units of the good and sell each unit at a higher price relative to the initial autarky equilibrium. Compare the graphs from part (a) and part (c) and note that the area of producer surplus is larger with trade than without trade.

**e.**

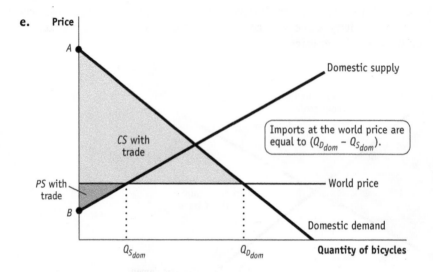

**f.** Domestic consumers benefit from this trade because they can consume more units of the good and purchase the good at a lower price relative to the initial autarky equilibrium. Compare the graphs from part (a) and part (e) and note that the area of consumer surplus is larger with trade than without trade.

**3.** **a.** Here is a sketch of Kennet's market for TVs.

The equilibrium price is $1,000 and the equilibrium quantity is 500 TVs. Consumer surplus is equal to $250,000; producer surplus is equal to $250,000; and total surplus is equal to $500,000.

**b.** When Kennet opens to trade, it will buy and sell TVs at the world price since it is a small economy. Since $1,200 is greater than the domestic equilibrium price when Kennet is a closed economy, the quantity domestically demanded will fall and the quantity domestically supplied will increase. The quantity demanded domestically will equal 400 TVs, and the quantity supplied domestically will equal 600 TVs. Kennet will export the excess supply of 200 TVs. Consumer surplus with trade will decrease to

$160,000 while producer surplus with trade will increase to $360,000; total surplus with trade will increase to $520,000. The following sketch illustrates this answer.

c. Domestic producers of TVs benefit from trade when Kennet opens its economy, because trade increases their producer surplus and decreases consumer surplus. The gain to producers is greater than the loss to consumers, so the net gain from trade is positive.

d. The following sketch provides a helpful guide to solving this problem.

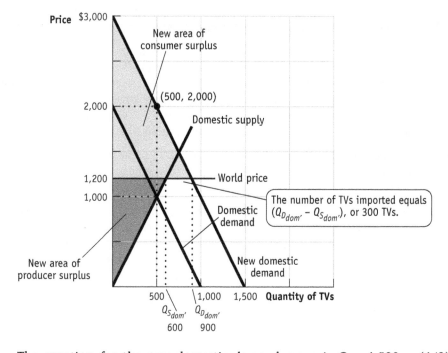

The equation for the new domestic demand curve is $Q = 1,500 - (1/2)P$. The domestic supply curve is still $Q = (1/2)P$. Use these two equations to analyze the effect on this market of the increase in domestic demand for TVs. At a world price of $1,200, the domestic demand for TVs is 900 while the domestic supply of TVs is 600. Kennet will import 300 TVs to meet this excess demand. Consumer surplus will now equal $810,000; producer surplus will equal $360,000; and total surplus will equal $1,170,000.

4.  **a.** The equilibrium price of green peppers is $3,750 per ton, and the equilibrium quantity of green peppers in Pepperville is 2,500 tons. Consumer surplus is equal to $1,562,500 and producer surplus is equal to $4,687,500.

**b.** Domestic producers are currently selling 2,500 tons of green peppers at a price of $3,750 per ton. If the market opens to trade, each ton of peppers will sell for a lower price: domestic producers will sell fewer tons of peppers as the price falls (2,000 tons instead of 2,500 tons), and they will receive a lower price per ton than they do when the green pepper market is closed ($3,000 versus $3,750).

**c.** When the green pepper market is open to trade, the domestic demand for green peppers at $3,000 per ton is equal to 4,000 tons of green peppers. At a price of $3,000 per ton, the domestic quantity supplied is equal to 2,000 tons of green peppers. There is an excess demand for peppers when Pepperville opens to trade, and this excess demand will result in Pepperville importing green peppers to make up the difference between the amount domestically supplied and the amount domestically demanded. Pepperville will import 2,000 tons of green peppers. The value of consumer surplus with trade is equal to $4,000,000 and the value of producer surplus with trade is equal to $3,000,000.

**d.** At a price of $3,450, the quantity of green peppers demanded domestically is equal to 3,100 tons while the quantity supplied domestically is equal to 2,300 tons. Pepperville will import 800 tons of green peppers.

**e.** The value of consumer surplus is equal to (1/2)($5,000 per ton – $3,450 per ton)(3,100 tons), or $2,402,500. The value of producer surplus is equal to (1/2)($3,450 per ton)(2,300 tons), or $3,967,500.

**f.** The government earns the difference between the tariff price per ton of green peppers and the world price of green peppers on every ton of green peppers imported into Pepperville. The tariff revenue is equal to ($3,450 per ton – $3,000 per ton)(800 tons), or $360,000.

**g.** The deadweight loss is the difference between the total surplus with open trade and the sum of consumer surplus + producer surplus + tariff revenue, or $7,000,000 – ($2,402,500 + $3,967,500 + $360,000) = $270,000. Alternatively, the deadweight loss can be calculated as the sum of the areas of two triangles, which is equal to (1/2)($3,450 per ton – $3,000 per ton)(2,300 tons – 2,000 tons) + (1/2)($3,450 per ton – $3,000 per ton)(4,000 tons – 3,100 tons), or $270,000.

**h.** The quota has to equal the number of units Pepperville imports when the tariff raises the price of green peppers to $3,450 per ton. That is, the quota must be 800 tons of green peppers.

**i.** Consumer surplus is greatest when the trade policy is one of an open economy. Consumers rank these choices from best to worst in this order: open economy, open economy with a tariff or quota, closed economy. This ranking occurs whenever the world price is less than the closed economy price for the good.

**j.** Producer surplus is greatest when the trade policy is one of a closed economy. Producers rank these choices from best to worst in this order: closed economy, open economy with a tariff or quota, open economy. This ranking occurs whenever the world price is less than the closed economy price for the good.

**k.** Governments can successfully provide a benefit to both consumers and producers by choosing this option. If you review the consumer and producer surplus under each of these options, you will see that the middle option gives consumers a greater consumer surplus than they would get with a closed economy and it provides producers with a greater producer surplus than they would get with an open economy. It is a compromise position for the government to take between these two constituencies.

**5. a.**

|  | Option I | Option II | Option III |
|---|---|---|---|
| Pairs of shoes imported | 130 pairs | 50 pairs | 50 pairs |
| Consumer surplus | $12,800 | $7,200 | $7,200 |
| Producer surplus | 450 | 2,450 | 2,450 |
| Tariff revenue or quota rent | 0 | 2,000 | 2,000 |
| Deadweight loss | 0 | 1,600 | 1,600 |

**b.** From the perspective of domestic consumers, the best option is the option that results in the greatest value for consumer surplus: option I, the open economy option.

**c.** From the perspective of domestic producers, the best option is the option that results in the greatest value for producer surplus: option II and option III result in equivalent values for producer surplus, with the license holder earning a quota rent for option II and the government earning tariff revenue for option III. If the license holder is a domestic producer, then option II would be the best option from the perspective of domestic producers.

**d.** Options II and III result in the largest, and equivalent, efficiency cost as measured by the deadweight loss that occurs with the imposition of these two trade protectionist policies.

# Answers to Module Review Questions

1. **Answer b.** International trade is a source of mutual benefit to the countries involved in the trade.

2. **Answer a.** The wine, cheese, and lamb are all imported goods into the American economy since these goods are produced elsewhere in the world and then brought into the American market. Exports refers to those goods produced in the domestic economy and sold in a foreign economy.

3. **Answer c.** Gains from trade stem from a country's comparative advantage and not its absolute advantage (statement I is false). Absolute advantage focuses on the amount of resources used to produce a good (for example, the number of hours of labor it takes to produce a shirt) while comparative advantage focuses on the opportunity cost of producing the good—that is, what must be given up to produce a unit of this good (statement II is false). When a country has a comparative advantage in producing a good, this means that its opportunity cost of producing the good is lower than the opportunity cost of producing the same good in some other country: this advantage in terms of opportunity cost is translated into wage rates. When a country has less-productive labor, then the wage rate for this labor is lower than it is for a country that has more-productive labor.

4. **Answer e.** Countries will tend to import those goods that are produced using factors of production which are relatively scarce in the importing country (statement I is therefore false). Countries that utilize a high ratio of highly skilled workers to less skilled workers are countries that tend to produce goods that are intensive in human capital (statement II is true). Countries will export goods whose production takes advantage of the relative abundance of the factor (statement III is true).

5. **Answer c.** The area of consumer surplus is the area beneath the demand curve but above the equilibrium price, or in this example, area *ACQ*. The area of producer surplus is the area above the supply curve but below the equilibrium price, or in this example, area *CQE*.

6.  **Answer c.** When the world price of the good is greater than the autarky price and the country opens to trade, Pedalland will export the good to other countries in order to sell the good at the higher world price. In this case, domestic suppliers are willing to supply the amount represented as the distance between points B and W while domestic consumers are only willing to consume the number of bicycles represented by the distance between B and M. Thus, domestic producers will export the number of bicycles represented by the distance between points M and W.

7.  **Answer b.** When the world price is below the domestic equilibrium price and the country opens to trade, the country will import goods. The country will import the number of goods that represents the difference between the amount domestically supplied at the world price and the amount domestically demanded at the world price. In this case, the country will import the number of goods represented by the distance between points P and S.

8.  **Answer a.** The area of consumer surplus is the area beneath the demand curve and above the equilibrium price, while the area of producer surplus is the area above the supply curve and below the equilibrium price. When this country opens to trade and the world price is equal to B, the country will export the good, which benefits domestic producers who are able to sell more units of the good than they could when the country was closed to trade.

9.  **Answer c.** When the world price of the good is less than the autarky price, the country will import the good if it opens its economy to trade. In this case, the country will import the difference between the quantity demanded domestically at a price of $20 and the quantity supplied domestically at a price of $20, or 120 bicycles. The area of total surplus is initially equal to $5,000, and when the country opens to trade, the area of total surplus has a value of $6,800, so the increase in total surplus is $6,800 − $5,000 or $1,800.

10. **Answer e.** To calculate the license-holder revenue from the quota you first need to rewrite the supply curve taking into account the quota. So, for example, if the supply equation is initially $P = (1/2)(Q)$, then with a quota of 40 units this supply equation will be $P = (1/2)q − 20$. Using this new supply equation and the demand equation, $P = 100 − (1/2)Q$, you can find the new price with a quota of 40 units. The price with this level of quota is $40 per bicycle. The license-holder revenue is equal to the difference between the price with the quota and the world price times the number of bicycles imported with the quota: ($40/bicycle − $20/bicycle), (40 bicycles) or $800. This argument, however, also works for a quota of 80 units: when the quota is 80 bicycles the supply curve can be written as $P = (1/2)Q − 30$ and the new price with this quota limit is $30 per bicycle. The license-holder revenue is equal to the difference between the price with the quota and the world price times the number of bicycles imported with the quota: (30/bicycle − $20/bicycle)(80 bicycles), or $800.

11. **Answer b.** The deadweight loss associated with this tariff is the result of two forces: (a) mutually beneficial trades do not take place because of the imposition of the tariff, and (b) the bicycles sold are produced at a price that exceeds the world price for bicycles. The area of deadweight loss can be calculated as the sum of the area of two triangles: (1/2)($40 per bicycle − $20 per bicycle)(80 bicycles − 40 bicycles) + (1/2)($40 per bicycle − $20 per bicycle)(160 bicycles − 120 bicycles) = $800.

12. **Answer a.** This is a tough problem! You first need to figure out the price with the quota, the quantity supplied domestically with the quota, and the quantity demanded domestically with the quota. From the graph you know that if the quota price was $40, the quota would be equal to 40 units. From the graph you also know that, at the world price, 120 bicycles are imported into Pedalland. So, logically you know that the quota price must be lower than $40 and higher than $20. When the quota price is $35, the quantity demanded domestically is equal to 130 bicycles and the quantity supplied domestically is equal to 70 bicycles, for a difference of 60 bicycles. This difference is the

same as the quota amount given in the question. Now you need only compute the original consumer surplus (equals $2,500) and the consumer surplus with the quota ($4,225) and subtract the original consumer surplus from the new consumer surplus to get the change in the value of consumer surplus that occurs with the imposition of the quota.

13. **Answer a.** When countries engage in trade, they produce those goods and services for which they have a comparative advantage. This specialization results in these countries producing those goods and services for which they have an abundant amount of resources. Thus, the exporting industries in the country will bid up the price of these resources as they increase their production of the good. The country will tend to import goods and services that are intensive in the factors that are scarce in its economy. This effectively decreases the demand for the relatively scarce factors and increases the demand for the relatively abundant factors. Trade will cause the factor price to increase for the relatively abundant factor and to decrease for the relatively scarce factor.

# module 9 (45)

# Introduction to Macroeconomics

## BEFORE YOU READ THE MODULE

## Summary

This module provides an overview of macroeconomics. The module introduces the concepts of business cycles, the management of business cycles through government policies, long-run growth, inflation, deflation, price stability, and the distinction between open economies, where countries trade with one another, and closed economies, where there is no international trade.

## Module Objectives

**Objective #1.** Macroeconomics is the study of the aggregate economy or the economy as a whole. Macroeconomics considers how individual and firm behavior in the aggregate interact to produce a particular level of economic performance in the economy. Central topics in macroeconomics include the determination of the overall level of output, the overall level of prices, and the overall level of employment in the economy. Macroeconomics also considers the impact of the global economy on the behavior of the economy.

- Macroeconomics uses various economic aggregates to study the economy. Economic aggregates are measures of economic variables that summarize data collected from different markets for goods, services, workers, and assets. Examples of economic aggregates include unemployment, aggregate output, investment, and savings.

- Macroeconomics studies long-run economic growth and its causes. Long-run economic growth in the economy is measured as the economy's overall output per person. Long-run growth in an economy raises the level of aggregate income and results in a higher standard of living for people living in that economy. Long-run growth is more important than business cycles in determining a country's standard of living.

**Objective #2.** In the short run, when the economy is in an economic expansion or boom, jobs are plentiful; when the economy is in an economic recession or bust, jobs are difficult to find. A business cycle consists of a period of short-run aggregate economic prosperity and a period of short-run aggregate economic hardship.

185

- Macroeconomics provides a rationale for government intervention to reduce short-run fluctuations in the economy. John Maynard Keynes argued that a government can help a depressed economy through fiscal and/or monetary policy. Fiscal policy refers to government spending and taxation policy, while monetary policy refers to the control of interest rates and the quantity of money in circulation. Both fiscal and monetary policy are useful tools for offsetting the economic effects of short-run fluctuations (recession or expansion) in the aggregate economy.

**Objective #3.** Employment measures the total number of people working in the economy, while unemployment is the total number of people who are actively looking for work but currently not working. The unemployment rate is the most widely used indicator of conditions in the labor market. In a recession, the employment rate decreases while the unemployment rate increases. In an expansion, the employment rate increases while the unemployment rate decreases.

**Objective #4.** The economy's real output level and unemployment rate move in opposite directions: as output increases, unemployment decreases and as real output decreases, unemployment increases. The economy's real aggregate output is the real value of the total production of final goods and services produced during a given time period and is referred to as real gross domestic product or real GDP.

**Objective #5.** Long-run growth occurs when aggregate output per person increases. This growth in the economy occurs over several decades and does not refer to the short-run increase in aggregate output that occurs during an expansion. Long-run economic growth is essential in order for wages and the standard of living in an economy to increase.

**Objective #6.** Inflation refers to a rise in the overall level of prices while deflation refers to a fall in the overall level of prices. In the short run, movements in inflation are closely related to the business cycle. In the long run, movements in inflation are primarily determined by changes in the money supply. Price stability is a desirable macroeconomic goal.

**Objective #7.** An economy that does not engage in international trade is a closed economy. An economy that participates in international trade is an open economy. Countries engage in trade because this trade is mutually beneficial to them. Imports refer to the value of the goods and services a country buys from the rest of the world, and exports refer to the value of the goods and services a country sells to the rest of the world.

**Objective #8.** An open economy runs a trade deficit when the value of its imports is greater than the value of its exports. An open economy runs a trade surplus when the value of its imports is less than the value of its exports. A country's trade surplus or trade deficit ultimately depends on the saving and investment decisions made by that country.

# Key Terms

**recession** a period of economic downturn when output and unemployment are falling; also referred to as a contraction.

**expansion** period of economic upturn in which output and employment are rising; most economic numbers are following their normal upward trend; also referred to as a recovery.

## Key Terms *(continued)*

**business cycle** the short-run alternation between economic downturns, known as *recessions*, and economic upturns, known as *expansions*.

**business-cycle peak** the point in time at which the *economy* shifts from *expansion* to *recession*.

**business-cycle trough** the point in time at which the *economy* shifts from *recession* to *expansion*.

**long-run economic growth** the sustained rise in the quantity of goods and services the *economy* produces.

**inflation** a rise in the overall level of prices.

**deflation** a fall in the overall level of prices.

**price stability** a situation in which the overall cost of living is changing slowly or not at all.

**open economy** an *economy* that trades goods and services with other countries.

**trade deficit** when the value of the goods and services bought from foreigners is more than the value of the goods and services sold to consumers abroad.

**trade surplus** when the value of goods and services bought from foreigners is less than the value of the goods and services sold to them.

## ■ AFTER YOU READ THE MODULE

## Tips

**Tip #1.** Studying economics requires learning both new vocabulary and a new way of thinking. This module provides an overview of macroeconomics, the topics covered in the study of macroeconomics, and general definitions of macroeconomic variables. You will need to familiarize yourself with this information and vocabulary. You may find it helpful to make a set of flash cards for all the vocabulary you learn while studying macroeconomics. For each flash card you will find it helpful to write the term on one side of the card and its definition on the other side of the card. You might also find it helpful to identify on the first side of the card the module number where the term is first introduced. After you make a set of flash cards for the module, review these flash cards until you are thoroughly familiar and comfortable with each term.

**Tip #2.** Macroeconomics focuses on the economic behavior of the overall economy, while microeconomics focuses on the economic behavior of individuals, firms, and specific markets. Macroeconomics studies topics like the determination of the aggregate level of output, the aggregate price level, the level of employment, short-run economic fluctuations, and long-run economic growth.

**Tip #3.** Aggregation of data is at the heart of macroeconomics. This module briefly describes the meaning of aggregation and gives examples of aggregated measures like employment, real GDP, and the overall price level. The concept of aggregation is important to understand as you begin your study of macroeconomics.

# WORKED PROBLEMS

1.  This module introduces the concepts of recession, business cycles, unemployment, and trade deficits. Since 2007, many of these terms have been widely used in media reporting about the U.S. economy. For each term, think about what has been happening in the U.S. economy since 2007 and relate these real-life events to these terms.

    **STEP 1:** In order to answer this question you will first want to make sure you know each of the terms and their definitions.

    **STEP 2:** Once you have the definitions of these terms clearly in mind, then you will want to review what the economic situation in the United States has been since 2007. Then, apply these terms where appropriate.

    Since 2007, the U.S. economy has experienced a serious recession that has resulted in high levels of unemployment. This recession represents a part of the business cycle, since a business cycle is composed of both periods of economic downturn and periods of economic expansion. At the same time that the U.S. economy experienced this recession, it was also running a large trade deficit: the U.S. economy was importing more goods than it was exporting.

2.  The following table includes a number of potential research projects that a group of economists are considering working on during the next few years. Fill in the table to help them identify whether the topic is more likely a microeconomics topic or more likely a macroeconomics topic.

| Research Topic | Macroeconomic or Microeconomic Topic? | Explanation for your answer |
|---|---|---|
| Impact of Gulf of Mexico oil spill on beach tourism in the Gulf states | | |
| Impact of fiscal stimulus spending programs on employment and production in the United States | | |
| The effect of a government program subsidizing investment on the level of aggregate production and aggregate employment in the economy | | |
| Impact of China's allowing its exchange rates to be market-determined on the demand for Chinese textile goods | | |
| Impact of recent monetary policy on inflation in the U.S. economy | | |

**STEP 1:** In order to answer this question, you will obviously need to read the module. But you will also find it helpful to think about what topics macroeconomics addresses and then try to relate these topics to the previous table.

Here is the filled-in table:

| Research topic | Macroeconomic or microeconomic topic? | Explanation for your answer |
|---|---|---|
| Impact of Gulf of Mexico oil spill on beach tourism in the Gulf states | Micro | This topic looks at the impact of an event on a specific market rather than on the aggregate economy |
| Impact of fiscal stimulus spending programs on employment and production in the United States | Macro | This topic looks at the impact of a policy on the entire, or aggregate, economy |
| The effect of a government program subsidizing investment on the level of aggregate production and aggregate employment in the economy | Macro | This topic looks at the impact of a policy on the entire, or aggregate, economy |
| Impact of China's allowing its exchange rates to be market-determined on the demand for Chinese textile goods | Micro | This topic looks at the impact of an event on a specific market rather than on the aggregate economy |
| Impact of recent monetary policy on inflation in the U.S. economy | Macro | This topic looks at the impact of a policy on the entire, or aggregate, economy |

3. On page 101 (Econ page 473) of your text, the authors present Figure 9-5 (45-5) as an illustration of long-run economic growth in America. To get a concrete sense of this economic growth, identify three people you can interview: these three people should be of different ages, and if possible, try to find someone who is at least seventy-five. Do a survey of these three people's memories of what items their family possessed and what items they can remember as new and original: for example, most college students today will list portable computers and cell phones, while someone in the fifty-year-old range may recall the family's first color television, while someone who is eighty may be able to remember the first family car. After completing this survey, decide whether or not it convinces you that there has been significant economic growth over the past eighty years.

**STEP 1:** In order to answer this question, you will first want to think about how you want to collect your data: that is, you will want to think about what questions you will ask the people you have chosen to interview.

Since you are trying to get a sense of how people lived at different times, you will want to compose a set of questions that is designed to get this information. Thoughtful consideration before you start will help you get more and better information. You will want to make sure that some of your questions are specific, while other questions may be more open-ended.

**STEP 2:** Identify several people that you think will make good interview subjects. You might want to identify more than three people, since some of the people you have identified may be unavailable to interview. Contact these people to set up a time to come for the interview.

Make sure you are prepared to take notes on what is said at the interview. As you collect your information, you will want to think about what things you can contrast or compare between the different individuals you are interviewing.

**STEP 3:** Create a summary statement comparing the information you received. Think about how this information helps support the argument that economic growth has occurred during this period.

For example, you might decide to present your information in a table or graph. Review Figure 9-4 (45-4) to see one example of a representation of changes that reflect economic growth over time. Think about and plan a method of presenting your data that makes a strong case in support of your argument.

The answers and presentations with respect to this question will vary with each student: underlying all of the presentations should be a sense of the economic growth and change that have occurred in the last seventy to eighty years.

4.   Suppose Jerry's income was $40,000 last year and this year it is $50,000. But over the course of the year, the price of the food that he purchases has risen from $6,000 per year to $10,000 per year, and the price of the gasoline that he purchases has risen from $2,000 per year to $4,000 per year. All other prices that Jerry faces have remained constant over this period. Is Jerry better off now that his salary has increased to $50,000?

**STEP 1:** To answer this question, you will want to think about what is happening to Jerry's income and what is happening to the prices of gasoline and food. It would be helpful to calculate the percentage change in income, the percentage change in food prices, and the percentage change in gasoline prices in order to see how Jerry is doing.

The percentage change in a variable can be found by calculating [(the new value – the previous value)/(the previous value)] × 100. Thus, the percentage change in Jerry's income is equal to [($50,000 – $40,000)/($40,000)] × 100 = 25%. The percentage change in the price of food and the percentage change in the price of gasoline can be calculated similarly. The percentage change in the price of food is equal to 67%, while the percentage change in the price of gasoline is 100%.

**STEP 2:** Once you have calculated the percentage changes, you will want to think about what this implies about how Jerry is doing.

Jerry's income has increased, but so have the price of food and the price of gasoline; all other prices that Jerry faces have remained constant. Clearly, Jerry's income cannot purchase as much food or gasoline as it could when his income and the prices were at their initial level: Jerry is worse off than he was in the first year.

# Problems and Exercises

1.  For each of the following questions identify whether the question is more appropriate for the study of microeconomics or macroeconomics, and why.

    a.  What will happen to the wages in our community if Corporation X, an employer of 1,000 people (that's 40% of our workforce), decides to relocate its plant to a different state?

    b.  What will happen to the level of overall economic production in our economy if the federal government continues to run record levels of government deficit?

    c.  If the government engages in monetary policy and increases the money supply, what will happen to the interest rate in our economy?

    d.  How has the recent increase in the price of a barrel of oil affected the prices of bicycles, cars, and airplane fares?

    e.  What will the effect of recent tropical storms be on the price of bananas?

2.  Suppose that people anticipate an economic recession and decide to increase their rate of saving so they are better prepared financially for the recession. Explain why this response might actually make the recession worse.

3.  This module distinguishes between an economic expansion as part of the business cycle and long-run economic growth. Concisely explain the difference between these two terms.

## ■ BEFORE YOU TAKE THE TEST

## Module Review Questions

1.  Macroeconomics, unlike microeconomics,
    a. considers the behavior of individual firms and markets.
    b. focuses on the production and consumption of particular goods.
    c. tries to explain increases in living standards over time.
    d. finds that the behavior of individuals is more important in determining economic activity than is the aggregate summation of this behavior.

2.  Which of the following statements is true?
    a. In macroeconomics, there is no role for government intervention in the economy.
    b. In microeconomics, the prices determined in economic models are aggregate price levels for the economy.
    c. Microeconomics studies business cycle fluctuations in the economy.
    d. Fiscal and monetary policy may be helpful in reducing short-term economic fluctuations in the economy due to adverse economic events.

3.  In a recession,
    a. unemployment increases, aggregate output decreases and people enjoy higher living standards.
    b. unemployment increases while aggregate output and aggregate income decrease.
    c. aggregate output and aggregate income decrease, eventually leading, in all cases, to an economic depression.
    d. aggregate output must fall for at least three consecutive quarters.

4.  Macroeconomics
    a. focuses on how the behavior of individuals and firms in the aggregate economy interact to produce a market price for each good and service offered in the economy.
    b. focuses on how the actions of individuals and firms in the economy interact to produce a particular economy-wide level of economic performance.
    c. considers how specific markets for goods and services determine their equilibrium prices and quantities.
    d. Answers (a), (b), and (c) are all correct.

5.  Which of the following statements is true?
    a. An economy in a recession will have a lower unemployment rate than will the same economy operating in an expansion.
    b. In an economic expansion, the unemployment rate decreases while aggregate output increases.
    c. An economy's output level and employment rate move in opposite directions.
    d. Answers (b) and (c) are correct.

6.  Inflation occurs when
    a. the aggregate level of output increases.
    b. the unemployment rate decreases.
    c. the aggregate price level rises over time.
    d. consumers' purchasing power increases over time.

**7.** A country that trades goods and services with another country is known as a(n)

    a. open economy.

    b. real economy.

    c. weak economy.

    d. closed economy.

**8.** Economic recessions and economic expansions are

    a. long run in nature.

    b. short run in nature.

**9.** An economic contraction is

    a. another term for an economic recession.

    b. indicates that the economy is experiencing a decrease in the level of employment.

    c. part of the business cycle.

    d. Answers (a), (b), and (c) are all correct.

**10.** An economic expansion

    a. is another term for an economic recovery.

    b. indicates that the economy is experiencing a decrease in the level of unemployment.

    c. is that part of the business cycle between the business-cycle trough and the business-cycle peak.

    d. Answers (a), (b), and (c) are all correct.

    e. Answers (a) and (c) are both correct.

**11.** Which of the following statements is true?

    I. The 2007–2009 recession in the United States hit the economy much harder than the 2001 recession did.

    II. The Great Depression in the United States lasted from 1929 to 1933, though unemployment continued to be high throughout the 1930s.

    III. The U.S. recession of 2001 lasted only eight months, while the recession of 2007–2009 lasted more than twice as long.

    a. Statements I, II, and III are all true.

    b. Statements II and III are true.

    c. Statements I and III are true.

    d. Statement II is true.

**12.** A sustained rise in the quantity of goods and services a country produces is referred to as

    a. an economic expansion or recovery.

    b. a period of employment.

    c. long-run economic growth.

    d. sound fiscal policy.

**13.** Deflation occurs when

    a. economic production increases in the aggregate economy.

    b. the overall price level decreases in an economy.

    c. the overall level of employment decreases in the aggregate economy.

    d. both the overall price level and the overall level of employment in an economy decrease.

**14.** When the economy is in a recession, jobs are
    a. hard to find and the overall level of prices in the economy tends to rise.
    b. easy to find and the overall level of prices in the economy tends to rise.
    c. hard to find and the overall level of prices in the economy tends to fall.
    d. easy to find and the overall level of prices in the economy tends to fall.

**15.** A country runs a trade deficit when
    a. its level of employment decreases.
    b. its overall price level is falling.
    c. the value of the goods and services it imports exceeds the value of the goods and services it exports.
    d. the value of the goods and services it exports exceeds the value of the goods and services it imports.

**16.** The value of a country's imports is equal to $1.2 billion this year while the value of the country's exports is equal to $1.3 billion this year. This country is running a
    a. trade surplus this year.
    b. trade deficit this year.

**17.** Whether a country runs a trade surplus or a trade deficit depends on
    a. what part of the business cycle the country is currently in.
    b. whether or not the country is experiencing deflation or inflation.
    c. whether the country is employing fiscal or monetary policy.
    d. decisions about saving and investment spending in the country.

**18.** A country's investment spending during the current year is equal to $400 million, while its level of saving for the current year is $350 million. Given this information, this country will likely run a trade
    a. surplus.
    b. deficit.

## ANSWER KEY

## Answers to Problems and Exercises

1.  **a.** Microeconomics: this question is directed at understanding the local effect of this corporation's move instead of its total effect across the aggregate economy.

    **b.** Macroeconomics: this question focuses on the aggregate performance of the economy.

    **c.** Macroeconomics: this question considers the impact of monetary policy on the aggregate economy.

    **d.** Microeconomics: this question addresses the effect of a change in the price of a barrel of oil on specific markets like the market for bicycles, cars, or air travel service.

    **e.** Microeconomics: this question considers the price of a specific good rather than the overall price level in the economy.

2.  Even though the individual's decision is a rational path to follow, the effect of many individuals making this decision is to reduce spending dramatically in the aggregate economy. As spending decreases, producers respond by decreasing their production and reducing their use of labor. This paradox of thrift has the effect of worsening the recessionary tendencies in the economy.

3.  An economic expansion is a short-run increase in the level of aggregate output that may not be sustained indefinitely, while long-run economic growth reflects a sustainable increase in an economy's ability to produce more goods and services.

## Answers to Module Review Questions

1.  **Answer c.** Macroeconomics studies the aggregate economy, not individual action; in studying the aggregate economy, macroeconomics seeks to explain the factors that determine a country's standard of living. In macroeconomics we are reminded that the aggregation of individual behavior often has a larger impact than just the sum of these individual behaviors.

2.  **Answer d.** In the aggregate economy, output and employment fluctuate in the short run. Macroeconomic theory analyzes the effect of fiscal and monetary policy on short-run economic fluctuations and provides a rationale for government intervention to lessen the economic impact of business cycles.

3.  **Answer b.** A recession, by definition, occurs when aggregate output decreases and income decreases. As the economy produces a smaller level of output, employment of labor decreases since less labor is needed to produce the smaller level of output. Not all recessions turn into depressions, and there is no uniform agreement about the length of time aggregate output must decrease for the downturn in economic activity to be viewed as a recession.

4.  **Answer b.** Macroeconomics is focused on the aggregate economy and its overall performance. Microeconomics focuses on specific markets and how the behavior of firms and individuals interact to determine the prices in those markets as well as the quantities in those markets.

5.  **Answer b.** This question centers on the relationship between aggregate output and employment: as aggregate output increases, employment also increases and hence unemployment decreases. An economy can reduce its level of unemployment but cannot eliminate unemployment, since there will always be people newly entering the labor force and searching for their first jobs.

6. **Answer c.** Inflation is defined as the increase in the aggregate price level over time.

7. **Answer a.** A country that engages in international trade is referred to as an open economy, while a country that does not trade is a closed economy.

8. **Answer b.** Business cycle fluctuations in the economy, whether recessions or expansions, are short-run fluctuations.

9. **Answer d.** An economic contraction or recession is that part of the business cycle where output and employment are falling.

10. **Answer d.** An economic expansion or recovery is that part of the business cycle when output and employment are increasing, and therefore unemployment is decreasing. The economic expansion occurs in that part of the business cycle between the business cycle trough and the business cycle peak, since this is the part of the business cycle when output and employment are increasing.

11. **Answer a.** All of these statements are factual statements that are discussed in this chapter.

12. **Answer c.** When the increase in the production of goods and services is sustained, this implies that the economy is experiencing economic growth; an economic expansion or recovery refers to a short-run increase (not sustained) in the level of production of goods and services in an economy.

13. **Answer b.** Deflation refers to a decrease in the overall level of prices in an economy and, although deflation may occur at the same time that employment in the economy decreases, the term only refers to the decrease in the overall price level.

14. **Answer c.** In a recession, production is falling, which implies that fewer units of labor will be employed. This, in turn, implies that jobs will be difficult to find. In addition, as the level of production falls in the economy there is less demand for goods and services, which leads to a general decrease in the overall level of prices in the economy.

15. **Answer c.** Answer (c) is the basic definition of a trade deficit.

16. **Answer a.** When the value of a country's exports is greater than the value of its imports for a given time period, then the country is running a trade surplus during that period of time.

17. **Answer d.** The saving and investment spending decisions made in a country ultimately determine whether or not that country will run a trade deficit or a trade surplus. When a country has high investment spending relative to its level of saving, it will run a trade deficit; when a country has low investment spending relative to its level of saving, it will run a trade surplus.

18. **Answer b.** When a country's level of investment spending is high relative to its saving, then the country will run a trade deficit. Since this country's investment spending exceeds its saving for the period under consideration, this implies that the country will run a trade deficit.

# The Circular Flow Diagram and the National Accounts

█ BEFORE YOU READ THE MODULE

## Summary

This module focuses on the idea of economic aggregation and what aggregation means when measuring the level of aggregate production in an economy. In this module, a circular-flow diagram of the economy is presented. This diagram is a way of illustrating the ideas and concepts provided by the national accounts.

## Module Objectives

**Objective #1.** Good macroeconomic policy depends on good measurement of key economic variables that provide information about how the aggregate economy is performing. These key variables include the level of aggregate income and aggregate output.

**Objective #2.** A simple circular-flow diagram can be used to represent the relationship between households and firms. Households supply factors of production to firms that then use these factors of production to produce goods and services. These goods and services are sold to households. In this simple circular-flow diagram of the economy the sum of the payments made to households for the factors of production equal the sum of spending on goods and services by households. Thus, the two flows of money are equal to one another: the flow of money to households for the use of their resources and the flow of money to firms for the provision of goods and services.

**Objective #3.** The national income and product accounts, or the national accounts, provide a set of numbers that indicate the country's state of economic performance. The Bureau of Economic Analysis calculates the national accounts for the United States.

- An expanded circular-flow diagram of the economy, focusing on money flows, illustrates the key concepts underlying the national accounts. Note that the flow of money into each market or sector must be equal to the flow of money out of each market or sector. For instance, the value of household income, the sum of wages, dividends, interest, and rent equals the sum of the values of household tax payments and government transfer payments, consumer spending, and private saving. Figure 10.1 illustrates the expanded circular-flow diagram.

**Figure 10.1**

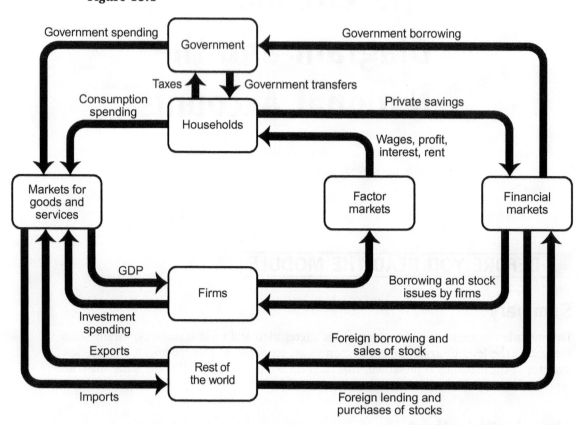

- The circular-flow diagram includes the output market, the factors of production market, and the financial market. The sectors represented in the more complicated circular-flow diagram in this module include households, firms, the government, and the rest of the world.

- Referring to Figure 10.1, note the following observations:

  - GDP is equal to the sum of wages, profit, interest, and rent.

  - GDP is equal to the sum of consumer spending, government spending, investment spending, and net exports (exports minus imports).

  - The flow of funds into the household sector is equal to wages, profits, interest, rent, and transfer payments while the flow of funds out of the household sector is equal to consumer spending, taxes, and private saving. These two flows are equal to one another.

  - The flow of funds into the firm sector is equal to GDP plus the borrowing and stock issues by firms while the flow of funds out of the firm sector is equal to investment spending plus wages, profit, interest, and rent. These two flows are equal to one another.

  - The flow of funds into the government sector is equal to taxes and government borrowing while the flow of funds out of the government sector is equal to government spending and transfer payments. These two flows are equal to one another.

- The flow of funds into the rest of the world is equal to spending on imports plus foreign borrowing and sales of stock while the flow of funds out of the rest of the world is equal to spending on exports plus foreign borrowing and sales of stock. These two flows are equal to one another.

- Referring to Figure 10.1 and focusing on the three markets, note the following observations:

  - The flows into the market for goods and services are equal to the sum of consumer spending, investment spending, government spending, and net exports, and the flow out of the market for goods and services is equal to GDP. These two flows are equal to one another.

  - The flows into the factor market are equal to the flows out of the factor market, and these flows are equal to the sum of wages, interest, profit, and rent.

  - The flows into the financial market are equal to the flows out of the financial markets. The flows into the financial market are equal to the sum of foreign lending and purchases of stock plus private savings while the flows out of the financial markets are equal to the sum of borrowing and stock issues by firms (domestic firms) plus foreign borrowing and the sales of stock.

**Objective #4.**   The circular-flow diagram provides a simplified illustration of national income and national spending. Here is a brief summary of each sector's activity.

- Households receive income from selling factors of production to firms. Households receive income from wages earned by selling their labor; income, in the form of dividends and interest, from their indirect ownership (their stock and bond ownership) of physical capital used by firms; and income, in the form of rent, earned by selling the use of their land. Households gain the income they earn from selling factors of production and then use this income to purchase goods and services, to pay their taxes, and to provide private savings to financial markets. Household income net of taxes and government transfers is called disposable income. Private saving is that part of disposable income that is not spent on goods and services.

- The government collects tax revenue and then returns part of this money as transfer payments. Government transfer payments are payments made by the government to individuals for which no good or service is provided in return; for example, Social Security payments and unemployment insurance payments are government transfer payments. The sum of tax revenue net of transfer payments plus funds the government borrows from the financial markets is then used by the government to purchase goods and services.

- Firms hire factors of production to produce goods and services but they also expend funds to buy goods and services. This investment spending on productive physical capital and on inventories is included in the national accounts as part of total spending on goods and services. Investment spending includes expenditure on inventories, since these inventories will contribute to greater future sales of a firm. Construction of new homes is also included in investment spending since a new home produces a future stream of housing services for the people who live in the house.

- The rest of the world participates in the domestic economy by purchasing goods and services produced in the domestic economy (the domestic economy's exports), by selling goods and services to the domestic economy (the domestic economy's imports), and by making transactions in the domestic economy's financial markets.

**Objective #5.**   The financial markets receive funds from households, as well as from the rest of the world. These funds provide the basis for loans to the government, firms, and the rest of the world.

# Key Terms

**national income and product accounts, or national accounts** method of calculating and keeping track of *consumer spending*, sales of producers, business *investment spending*, government purchases, and a variety of other flows of money among different sectors of the *economy*; also referred to as *national accounts*.

**circular-flow diagram** a diagram that represents the transactions in an economy by two kinds of flows around a circle: flows of physical things such as goods or labor in one direction and flows of money to pay for these physical things in the opposite direction.

**household** a person or group of people who share income.

**firm** an organization that produces goods and services for sale.

**product markets** where goods and services are bought and sold.

**factor markets** where resources, especially capital and labor, are bought and sold.

**consumer spending** *household* spending on goods and services from domestic and foreign *firms*.

**stock** a share in the ownership of a company held by a shareholder.

**bond** a legal document based on borrowing in the form of an IOU that pays interest.

**government transfers** payments by the government to individuals for which no good or service is provided in return.

**disposable income** income plus *government transfers* minus taxes; the total amount of *household* income available to spend on consumption and saving.

**private savings** *disposable income* minus *consumer spending*; disposable income that is not spent on consumption but rather goes into *financial markets*.

**financial markets** the banking, *stock*, and *bond* markets, which channel *private savings* and foreign lending into *investment spending*, *government borrowing*, and foreign borrowing.

**government borrowing** the amount of funds borrowed by the government in *financial markets* to buy goods and services.

**government purchases of goods and services** total purchases by federal, state, and local governments on goods and services.

**exports** goods and services sold to other countries.

**imports** goods and services purchased from other countries.

**inventories** stocks of goods and raw materials held to satisfy future sales.

**investment spending** spending on productive *physical capital*, such as machinery and construction of structures, and on changes to *inventories*.

## ■ AFTER YOU READ THE MODULE

## Tips

**Tip #1.**  It is important that you understand thoroughly the concepts underlying the more complicated circular-flow diagram presented in this module. The circular-flow diagram tracks the flows of money into and out of different markets and sectors in the economy. The flows into a market or sector must equal the flows out of that market or sector. Review this material and practice working with some numerical examples until you are very comfortable with the concepts and relationships.

**Tip #2.**  A primary focus of this module is the topic of economic aggregation. Discussion of macroeconomic issues requires the construction and development of different measures that can be used to describe the macroeconomy. Economic aggregation addresses this issue. In this module, you need to fully understand the process of economic aggregation and how it relates to the measurement of economic production.

**Tip #3.**  The national income accounts provide measures about the aggregate or overall economy; understanding the concept of economic aggregation is essential in the study of macroeconomics. The national income accounts are data collected and provided by the government about aggregate economic performance. The national income accounts break down the components of total spending so the behavior of households, firms, the government, and the foreign sector can be studied. The national income accounts also break down national income into wages, interest, rent, and other factor payments so factor income can be analyzed.

## Problems and Exercises

1.  You are given the following information about Macronesia. During 2014, the government of Macronesia spent $200 million on goods and services as well as $20 million on transfer payments, while collecting $150 million in taxes. During 2014 households paid $150 million in taxes, purchased goods and services worth $400 million, and received $800 million in the form of wages, dividends, interest, and rent. Firms in 2014 had $100 million of investment spending, and they borrowed or had stock issues of $170 million from the financial markets. In 2014, exports to this economy equaled $150 million while imports to this economy equaled $50 million. In the financial markets, there was foreign borrowing of $50 million and foreign lending of $20 million.

    **a.**  Sketch a circular-flow diagram of Macronesia's economy showing the quantitative flows.

    **b.**  What is GDP in 2014 in Macronesia?

c. What is the value of disposable income in Macronesia in 2014?

d. What is the value of household saving in Macronesia in 2014?

e. Is the government running a balanced budget during 2014? Explain your answer.

f. Compute the flows of money into the financial markets and the flows of money out of the financial markets. Are they equal?

g. Compute the flows of money into the market for goods and services and the flows of money out of the market for goods and services. Are they equal?

h. Compute the flows of money into the factor markets and the flows of money out of the factor markets. Are they equal?

2. The diagram below provides a circular-flow diagram for the economy of Littleville.

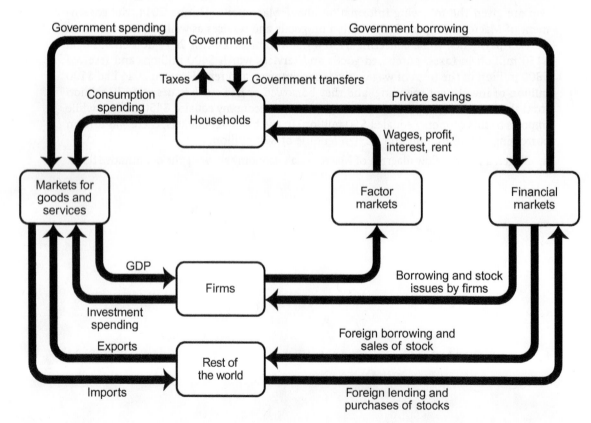

You are also told the following about the economy of Littleville:

> Consumer spending (C) = $200 million
> Investment spending (I) = $50 million
> Spending on exports (X) = $20 million
> Wages + profit + interest + rent = $320 million
> Government borrowing = $60 million
> Taxes = $20 million
> Transfers = $10 million

**a.** What is the GDP in Littleville? Explain how you found this value given the above information.

**b.** What is the value of government spending (G) in Littleville's economy? Explain how you found this value.

**c.** What is the value of imports in Littleville's economy? Explain how you found this value.

**d.** What is the value of private savings in Littleville's economy? Explain how you found this value.

**e.** What is the level of firm borrowing and stock issues in this economy? Explain how you found this value.

**f.** Is the rest of the world a net borrower or a net lender given the above information and your calculations in parts (a) through (e)? Explain your answer.

## ■ BEFORE YOU TAKE THE TEST

## Module Review Questions

1. Which of the following statements is true?
   a. In the circular-flow diagram of the economy, the flow of money into each market or sector is not necessarily equal to the flow of money coming out of each market or sector.
   b. GDP in the United States includes income earned by American citizens living in foreign countries during a given time period.
   c. GDP in the United States is equal to the sum of consumer spending, government spending, investment spending, and export spending.
   d. None of the above statements is true.

2. Households receive income from
   a. wages they earn from selling their labor.
   b. their indirect ownership of the physical capital used by firms.
   c. interest earned from bonds, dividends earned from stock ownership, and rent earned when they sell the use of their land to firms.
   d. All of the above are ways households earn income.

3. After the payment of net taxes (taxes minus transfers) to the government, household income is referred to as
   a. transfer income.
   b. gross income.
   c. net income.
   d. disposable income.

**4.** Households, in the circular-flow diagram of the economy, can use their income to
   a. pay taxes, purchase goods and services, and engage in private saving.
   b. pay taxes and purchase goods and services only.
   c. purchase factors of production, pay taxes, or purchase goods and services.
   d. purchase factors of production, pay taxes, or engage in private saving.

**5.** Government raises funds through
   a. taxation and by borrowing in financial markets.
   b. taxation, purchases of goods and services, and by borrowing in financial markets.
   c. taxation, purchases of goods and services, and revenues received for intermediate goods produced by the government.
   d. taxation and transfer payments.

**6.** Investment spending includes
   a. expenditures on new residential housing.
   b. expenditures on new inventories by businesses.
   c. expenditures by businesses on productive physical capital.
   d. Answers (a), (b), and (c) are included in investment spending.

**7.** Which of the following statements is true?
   I. In the circular-flow diagram the flows into each market or sector must equal the outflow coming from that market or sector.
   II. The flow of money into the household sector includes the value of all the final goods and services that households purchase.
   III. The flow of money into the household sector does not include the value of government transfers.
   a. Statement I is true.
   b. Statements I and II are true.
   c. Statements I, II, and III are true.
   d. Statements I and III are true.
   e. Statements II and III are true.

**8.** From a household's perspective, a bond represents
   a. the indirect ownership of physical capital used by firms.
   b. a loan to the firm that will provide interest to the household.

**9.** From a household's perspective, a share of stock represents
   a. the indirect ownership of physical capital used by firms.
   b. a loan to the firm that will provide interest to the household.

**10.** When households receive income, they can
   a. pay taxes, pay transfer payments, purchase goods and services, and engage in private saving.
   b. pay taxes, receive transfer payments, purchase goods and services, and engage in private saving.
   c. pay taxes, purchase goods and services, and engage in private saving.
   d. pay taxes and receive transfer payments.

11. Disposable income is equal to
    a. total income minus taxes.
    b. total income minus transfer payments.
    c. total income and transfer payments.
    d. total income minus taxes and plus government transfers.

12. The outflow of funds from the financial markets include
    a. funds for private savings to households.
    b. funds to finance government purchases of goods and services.
    c. funds to foreign borrowers.
    d. Answers (a), (b), and (c) are all correct.
    e. Answers (b) and (c) are both correct.

13. When inventories increase, this
    a. leads to an increase in investment spending and an increase in GDP for the time period.
    b. leads to an increase in investment spending but no change in GDP since no one purchased the inventory items.
    c. leads to a decrease in investment spending and no change in GDP since no one purchased the inventory items.
    d. leads to a decrease in consumption spending since households could have bought these items but instead the items were held as inventory.

14. Which of the following is NOT an aggregate macroeconomic variable?
    a. Savings: the sum of household, government, and business savings during a given year
    b. Investment: the addition to the economy's supply of productive physical capital
    c. Bicycle production: the total number of bicycles manufactured in an economy during a given year
    d. Capital account: the total net amount of assets sold to foreigners

# ANSWER KEY

## Answers to Problems and Exercises

1.  **a.**

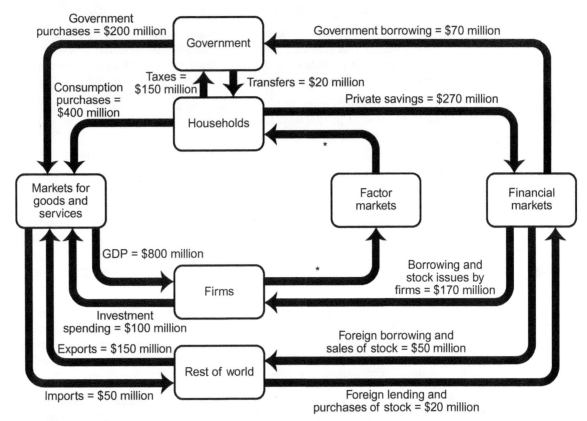

*Wages, dividends, interest, and rent = $800 million

**b.** The value of GDP in 2014 in Macronesia is $800 million: this is equivalent to the sum of factor payments to households in the form of wages, dividends, interest, and rent. It is also equivalent to the sum of consumption spending, government spending, investment spending, and net exports.

**c.** Disposable income is income received by households less taxes plus transfers. In this problem, disposable income equals $670 million.

**d.** Household saving equals household income minus taxes plus transfers minus consumption spending, or $270 million. Household saving is the amount households have left of their income once they pay their taxes and make their consumer purchases.

**e.** No. The government spends $200 million, and its net tax collections equal $130 million. To finance this level of spending without a change in taxes, the government will need to borrow $70 million from the financial markets.

**f.** The flow of money into the financial markets must equal the flow of money out of the financial markets in order for these markets to be in equilibrium. Borrowing in the financial markets equals the sum of government borrowing ($70 million) plus firm borrowing ($170 million) plus foreign borrowing ($50 million); lending in the financial market is equal to the sum of household saving ($270 million) plus foreign lending ($20 million).

**g.** The flow of money into the market for goods and services must equal the flow of money out of the market for goods and services. In this case, these flows equal $800 million. The flow of money into the market for goods and services includes government spending of $200 million, household purchases of $400 million, investment spending by firms of $100 million, and net exports of $100 million for a total of $800 million. The flow of money out of the market for goods and services equals GDP or the sum of wages, dividends, interest, and rent ($800 million).

**h.** The flow of money into the factor markets must equal the flow of money out of the factor markets. In this problem, these flows equal $800 million. The flow of money into the factor markets is equal to GDP ($800 million), while the flow of money out of the factor markets must equal the sum of wages, dividends, interest, and rent ($800 million).

**2.    a.** GDP in Littleville is equal to $320 million and can be found by recognizing that GDP can be expressed in two ways given the above circular-flow diagram: (1) GDP is the sum of all the spending in Littleville's economy or $GDP = C + I + G + X - IM$; and (2) GDP is the sum of the value of factor payments in the economy or GDP = wages + profit + interest + rents. You are given the value of these factor payments in the above information.

**b.** To find government spending ($G$) we can focus on the government sector of the economy and recognize that the flow of funds into that sector must equal the flow of funds out of that sector. This idea can be expressed in equation form as Government borrowing + taxes = government spending + transfer payments. From the given information we know government borrowing, taxes, and transfers. Thus, $60 million + $20 million = G + $10 million or $G = $70 million$.

**c.** The value of imports ($IM$) in Littleville's economy is $20 million. To find this value, first recognize that $GDP = C + I + G + X - IM$. We know the value of GDP from answer (a), as well as the values of $C$, $I$, and $X$ from the given information. In addition, answer (b) generated the value for G. So, $320 million = $200 million + $50 million + $70 million + $20 million - IM$, or $IM = $20 million$.

**d.** To find the value of private savings remember that the inflow of funds into the household sector must equal the outflow of funds from this sector. Households receive funds from their selling of factors of production and these funds are equal to the sum of wages, profit, interest, and rent, or $400 million in this example. In addition, households receive funds from the government in the form of transfer payments; in this example, transfer payments are equal to $10 million. So, the total amount of funds flowing into the household sector is equal to $410 million. The flow of funds out of the household sector is equal to the sum of consumer spending, taxes, and private saving. Since consumer spending and taxes are given in the information ($220 million), this enables us to calculate private savings as $410 million − $220 million, or private savings = $190 million.

**e.** Recall that the flow of funds into the firm sector must equal the flow of funds out of the firm sector, or GDP + (Borrowing and stock issues by firms) = (sum of wages, profits, interest, and rent) + investment spending. Since GDP is equal to the sum of wages, profits, interest, and rent, this implies that borrowing and stock issues by firms must equal investment spending, or $50 million.

**f.** To determine whether or not the rest of the world is a net borrower or a net lender, one needs to focus on the relationship between the flow of funds into and out of the rest of the world sector. The flow of funds into the rest of the world is equal to the sum of imports and foreign borrowing and sales of stock while the flow of funds out of the rest of the world is equal to the sum of exports and foreign lending and purchases of stock. Or, $60 million + foreign borrowing and sales of stock = $20 million

+ foreign lending and purchases of stocks. This can be rewritten as $40 million = foreign lending and purchases of stocks – foreign borrowing and sales of stocks. This implies that the rest of the world in this example is a net lender.

## Answers to Module Review Questions

1.  **Answer d.** An underlying principle of the circular-flow diagram is that the flow of money into a market or sector must equal the flow of money out of that market or sector. GDP measures the value of final production in an economy during a given time period, GDP is the sum of consumer spending, government spending, investment spending, and net export spending.

2.  **Answer d.** All three answers describe different ways households can earn income through their selling of factors of production—land, labor, and capital—to businesses.

3.  **Answer d.** By definition, household income less taxes is referred to as disposable income since this is the income that households are left to "dispose of" once they have paid their tax obligations. Households use this disposable income to make purchases of goods and services and for private saving.

4.  **Answer a.** Households use their income to pay taxes, to purchase goods and services, and to accumulate private saving.

5.  **Answer a.** The sources of funding for the government are tax revenue and the funds the government borrows in the financial markets. Transfer payments are not a source of revenue for the government, since they represent a redistribution of purchasing power from one individual to another individual in the economy. The government purchases goods and services but does not actually manufacture intermediate or final goods.

6.  **Answer d.** Investment spending, by definition, is the sum of expenditure on productive physical capital, inventories, and new residential housing.

7.  **Answer a.** The circular-flow diagram is based upon the principle that all the flows into each sector or market must equal all the outflows out of each sector or market. The flow of funds into the household sector includes the value of wages, interest, rent, and profit. In addition, the flow of funds into the household sector includes the value of government transfer payments. The value of all the final goods and services that households purchase is an outflow from the household sector.

8.  **Answer b.** A bond from a household's perspective represents an IOU that the household has received from a firm. The firm borrows money from the household and provides the household with a bond, which symbolizes the money that the firm owes to the household. The household will receive interest from the firm as long as it holds the bond.

9.  **Answer a.** A share of stock allows the firm to acquire funds to operate its business by selling a fractional ownership of the business to households. When a household purchases a share of stock, it provides funds to the business in exchange for part ownership in the business. This stock ownership therefore represents the household's indirect ownership of the physical capital that the firm uses, since the firm uses the funds it acquires through the sale of stock to acquire the use of physical capital.

10. **Answer b.** Households use their income to pay taxes, purchase goods and services, and set aside funds as private savings. In addition, some households receive transfer payments from the government.

11. **Answer d.** Disposable income is equal to the income households have left over after paying taxes and receiving government transfers.

12. **Answer e.** The outflow of funds from the financial market to households is represented by the loans that households undertake. The flow of private savings is a flow of funds into the financial market and not an outflow of funds from this market. The financial market provides funds to the government through government borrowing to enable the government to purchase more goods and services than is possible from the government's tax revenue. The financial market also lends funds to foreign borrowers.

13. **Answer a.** When a firm increases their inventories, this is a form of investment spending and therefore this increase in inventories increases both investment spending and GDP for the economy during this time period.

14. **Answer c.** Although each of these variables is aggregated to some extent, the bicycle production for the year only aggregates in a market for a single product rather than aggregating over multiple markets.

# Gross Domestic Product (GDP)

## Summary

This module provides a definition of gross domestic product (GDP) and then describes three different methods for calculating GDP. These three methods are: measuring GDP by adding up the value of all the final goods and services produced in an economy during a specified period; measuring GDP as the value of spending on domestically produced goods and services during a specified period; and measuring GDP as the value of factor income earned from firms in the economy during a specified period.

## Module Objectives

**Objective #1.** Gross domestic product, or GDP, is the sum of consumer spending on goods and services, investment spending, government spending, and the difference between spending on exports and imports. GDP is the total value of all final goods and services produced in an economy during a given time period. Final goods and services are goods and services sold to the final user. Intermediate goods and services are those items that are used as inputs for the production of final goods and services.

**Objective #2.** There are different ways to calculate GDP. One method is to add up the total value of final goods and services produced in an economy during a given time period. This method requires that the value of intermediate goods be excluded from the calculation in order to avoid double counting. An alternative method is to add up total spending on domestically produced final goods and services in an economy during a given time period. A third method of computing GDP is to sum the total value of factor income paid by firms in the economy to households. All three of these methods will yield identical values of GDP for an economy during a given time period.

- In calculating GDP, care must be taken to avoid double counting. For example, in measuring GDP as the value of total spending on final goods and services in an economy, we count only each producer's value added in the calculation. Or, if we calculate GDP as the value of total spending on final goods and services on domestically produced final goods and services, we avoid double counting by counting only the value of sales to final purchasers. When estimating GDP using spending data, we omit sales of inputs from one business to another, unless that spending represents investment spending by firms. Investment spending by firms represents a purchase that will last for a considerable time.

- GDP for an economy can be expressed as an equation: $GDP = C + I + G + X - IM$, where $C$ is consumer spending, $I$ is investment spending, $G$ is government spending, $X$ is spending on domestically produced goods and services by foreigners (the domestic economy's exports), and $IM$ is spending on imports, or the spending on goods and services produced by foreign economies. The difference between exports and imports, or $X - IM$, is referred to as net exports.

- GDP can also be measured as the sum of all the income earned by factors of production in the economy: this is the sum of wages, interest, rent, and profit.

## Key Terms

**final goods and services**  goods and services sold to the final, or end, user.

**intermediate goods and services**  goods and services, bought from one *firm* by another firm, that are inputs for production of *final goods and services*.

**gross domestic product (GDP)**  the total value of all *final goods and services* produced in the *economy* during a given period, usually a year.

**aggregate spending**  the total flow of funds into markets for domestically produced *final goods and services*; the sum of *consumer spending*, *investment spending*, *government purchases of goods and services*, and *exports* minus *imports*.

**value added** (of a producer)  the value of a producer's sales minus the value of input purchases.

**net exports**  the difference between the value of *exports* and the value of *imports*. A positive value for net exports indicates that a country is a net exporter of goods and services; a negative value indicates that a country is a net importer of goods and services.

*Notes*

## AFTER YOU READ THE MODULE

## Tips

**Tip #1.**  There are three methods for calculating GDP, but each method yields the same measure of GDP for a given time period. GDP calculation for an economy can be done using three methods: (1) multiply the price of final goods and services produced in an economy during a given time period by the quantities produced in that time period and then sum together these products; (2) add up the total expenditures in the domestic economy on final goods and services during a given time period by the sectors of the economy, or in other words, by households, government, firms, and the rest of the world; and (3) sum the value of factor payments in the domestic economy over the given time period. Each method yields the same value of GDP for a given time period. It is important for you to thoroughly understand the concepts underlying each of these approaches.

1.  You are given the following information about an economy that has three firms: Wisconsin Clothing Ltd., which produces clothing; Georgia Fabric Inc., which produces the various fabrics used in clothing production; and Texas Cotton Co., which grows the cotton needed for the production of fabric. From this set of information, you are asked to determine this economy's GDP. In addition, you are asked to identify what information you would need from the table to measure GDP using the factor payments approach. Finally, you are asked to fill in the missing values in the table.

| | Wisconsin Clothing Ltd. | Georgia Fabric Inc. | Texas Cotton Co. | Total factor income |
|---|---|---|---|---|
| Value of sales | $3,200 | $2,000 | $750 | |
| Intermediate goods | A | B | 0 | |
| Wages | 500 | 1,000 | 400 | C |
| Interest payments | 200 | 25 | 50 | D |
| Rent | 400 | 150 | 200 | E |
| Profit | 100 | 75 | 100 | F |
| Total expenditures by firm | 3,200 | 2,000 | 750 | |
| Value added per firm | G | H | I | |

**STEP 1:** Start by reviewing the information in the table and thinking about the three ways of measuring GDP. Do you have enough information to measure GDP using one of these methods?

There are three ways to measure GDP: (1) survey firms and add up the total value of their production of final goods and services (the value-added approach); (2) add up aggregate spending on domestically produced final goods and services in the economy (the expenditure approach); and (3) sum the total factor income earned by households from firms in the economy (the factor payments approach). Surveying the table, we could measure GDP as the value of the final good being produced: the final good is the clothing that Wisconsin Clothing Ltd. produces. We could also measure GDP using the factor payments approach, since we know the value of payments to households in the form of wages, interest payments, rent, and profits. The value-added approach would take more work, since we would need to calculate the value added at each stage of production.

**STEP 2:** Provide a measure of this economy's GDP.

The value of GDP in this economy is equal to $3,200. We can see that this is the value of sales made by Wisconsin Clothing Ltd. Alternatively, we could sum the wages in this economy ($C = \$1,900$), the interest payments ($D = \$275$), rent ($E = \$750$), and profits ($F = \$275$) to get $3,200, the value of GDP for this economy.

**STEP 3:** Identify what information you would need in order to measure GDP using the factor payments approach.

The factor payments approach to measuring GDP says that the sum of wages, interest payments, rent, and profit is equal to GDP. We would need to have the values for

C, D, E, and F in order to do this calculation. These values have already been found in Step 2.

**STEP 4:** Fill in the missing values in the table.

| | Wisconsin Clothing Ltd. | Georgia Fabric Inc. | Texas Cotton Co. | Total factor income |
|---|---|---|---|---|
| Value of sales | $3,200 | $2,000 | $750 | |
| Intermediate goods | A = 2,000 | B = 750 | 0 | |
| Wages | 500 | 1,000 | 400 | C = $1,900 |
| Interest payments | 200 | 25 | 50 | D = 275 |
| Rent | 400 | 150 | 200 | E = 750 |
| Profit | 100 | 75 | 100 | F = 275 |
| Total expenditures by firm | 3,200 | 2,000 | 750 | |
| Value added per firm | G = 1,200 | H = 1,250 | I = 750 | |

We already know the values for C, D, E, and F from Step 2. The value of B is $750, since this is the value of the cotton that Georgia Fabric Inc. purchases from Texas Cotton Co. The value of A is $2,000, since this is the value of the fabric that Wisconsin Clothing Ltd. purchases from Georgia Fabric Inc. To find the value for I, subtract the value of intermediate goods from the value of sales at Texas Cotton Co. The value of I is thus $750. The value of H is found in the same way: it is the difference between the value of sales and the cost of the intermediate goods at Georgia Fabric Inc. The value of H is $1,250. The value of G is found similarly: it is the difference between the value of sales and the cost of the intermediate goods at Wisconsin Clothing Ltd. The value of G is $1,200. Adding G + H + I together will give us a measure of GDP using the value-added approach: GDP is equal to $3,200, which is exactly the value we found using the other two approaches.

2. Suppose the government of Monrovia reports that during 2014 wages paid by firms in Monrovia equaled $200 million, consumer expenditures equaled $400 million, interest payments received by households equaled $150 million, investment expenditures equaled $50 million, government expenditures equaled $40 million, exports equaled $20 million, rent payments received by households equaled $100 million and profits earned by households equaled $50 million. The government officials of Monrovia have asked you to help them determine what the level of GDP in 2014 was for Monrovia and also what the level of net exports for Monrovia were for 2014. Finally, they have asked you to identify whether Monrovia had a trade surplus or a trade deficit in 2014.

**STEP 1:** First arrange the data you have been given in an organized manner taking into account the different methods you know for calculating GDP.

Organizing data is often critical to answering economic questions and problems. Sometimes it is also helpful to put the data in a table. But, before doing that it is worth considering how the data might be organized with regard to the different methods we have for calculating GDP. One method of measuring GDP focuses on expenditure: here we find that GDP = C + I + G + (X – M). So, we could organize a table that considers C, the level of consumer spending; I, the level of investment spending; G, the level of government spending; and (X – M), the level of net exports. An alternative method for calculating GDP focuses on factor income earned by households: here GDP = wages + rent + interest + profits. So, we could organize the data in terms of these different measures. Here is the data organized so that we can inspect it.

| GDP using expenditure approach | Value provided |
|---|---|
| C | $400 million |
| I | $50 million |
| G | $40 million |
| X – M | We know X = $20 million, but do not know M = $10 million |

| GDP using factor payments approach | Value provided |
|---|---|
| Wages | $200 million |
| Interest | $150 million |
| Rent | $100 million |
| Profits | $50 million |

**STEP 2:** Identify which method of measuring GDP will work given the data you have been provided.

From the table in Step 1 it is easy to see that there is missing information if you want to calculate GDP using the expenditure approach. In contrast, the information that is needed for calculating GDP using the factor payment approach is available.

**STEP 3:** Calculate the value of GDP and then use this information to calculate the value of any missing data.

Using the factor payments approach to measuring GDP and summing wages, interest, rent, and profits we find that GDP equals $500 million in Monrovia in 2014. Since the different methods of measuring GDP yield equivalent values for GDP we can use this value of $500 million to extrapolate what the value of imports into Monrovia must be in 2014. Recall that GDP = C + I + G + (X – M). We now have $500 million = $400 million + $50 million + $40 million + $20 million – I. Solving this equation for the value of I, the imports into Monrovia in 2014, we find that I equals $10 million.

**STEP 4:** Determine the level of net exports and then determine whether Monrovia is running a trade deficit or trade surplus.

The level of net exports is defined as the dollar value of expenditures on exports minus the dollar value of expenditures on imports. In this problem net exports are equal to $20 million minus $10 million or $10 million. Since net exports is a positive number in this problem that tells us that exports for Monrovia are greater than their imports and this implies that Monrovia is running a trade surplus.

# Problems and Exercises

1. For the following list decide how the item affects the calculation of GDP for Macro States in 2014.

   **a.** A new house is constructed in Macro States during 2014.

   **b.** Bruce sells his house in Macro States without the help of a realtor in January 2014.

   **c.** The government purchases new textbooks for the schools of Macro States during 2014.

   **d.** Macro States sells 100,000 pounds of beef to Neverlandia during 2014.

   **e.** Judy tutors Ellen's children in exchange for Ellen's driving the children's carpool three days a week throughout 2014.

   **f.** A candlemaker produces 500 candles during 2014 but only sells 200 candles during 2014; the other 300 candles are added to the candlemaker's inventories.

2. You are given the following information about the small economy of Hyattville.

   Hyattville's economy is composed of three firms: Hyattville Forest, Inc., that harvests trees that are used by Hyattville Lumber Products, Inc., to manufacture various lumber products that are used by Hyattville Houses, Inc., to produce houses. Assume lumber is the only raw material used to produce the houses in Hyattville.

   | | Hyattville Forest, Inc. | Hyattville Lumber Products, Inc. | Hyattville Houses, Inc. | Total factor income |
   |---|---|---|---|---|
   | Value of sales | $15,000 | A | $100,000 | |
   | Intermediate goods | B | $15,000 | 40,000 | |
   | Wages | 6,000 | 15,000 | 35,000 | G |
   | Interest payments | 1,000 | 3,000 | 6,000 | H |
   | Rent | 3,000 | D | 3,000 | I |
   | Profit | 5,000 | 4,000 | F | J |
   | Total expenditures by firm | 15,000 | 40,000 | 100,000 | |
   | Value added per firm | C | E | 60,000 | |

a.  Fill in the missing entries (*A* through *J*) in the above table recalling that GDP can be calculated in three different ways: (1) by measuring GDP as the value of the production of final goods and services in an economy as measured by the value added by each firm; (2) by measuring GDP as the sum of aggregate spending on domestically produced final goods and services in an economy; and (3) by measuring GDP as the sum of factor income earned from firms in the economy.

b.  Using the value added approach, what is the value of GDP? Explain how you found this answer using the above table as a reference.

c.  Using the factor income approach, what is the value of GDP? Explain how you found this answer using the above table as a reference.

d.  Using the aggregate spending on domestically produced final goods and services approach, what is the value of GDP? Explain how you found this answer using the above table as a reference.

## ▮ BEFORE YOU TAKE THE TEST

# Module Review Questions

1.  Suppose Country A sells $100 million worth of goods and services to Country B. Country B sells $50 million worth of goods and services to Country A. These are the only two countries in Macro World. Then,
    a.  net exports in Country B equal –$50 million.
    b.  net exports in Country A equal $150 million.
    c.  net exports in Country B equal $100 million.
    d.  net exports in Country B equal $50 million.

Use the information and the following table to answer the next three questions. The table represents data about an economy's performance during a year. Suppose in the economy represented in the table there are only three firms: American Racquet Co., which produces tennis racquets; American Metal Co., which produces the various metals that go into racquet production; and American Ore Co., which mines the ores needed for the manufacture of the metal. This economy produces 100 racquets that sell for $50 each.

| | American Racquet Co. | American Metal Co. | American Ore Co. | Total factor income |
|---|---|---|---|---|
| Value of sales | $5,000 | $3,000 | $500 | |
| Intermediate goods | A | B | | |
| Wages | 3,000 | 1,000 | 100 | C |
| Interest payments | 100 | 50 | 20 | D |
| Rent | 500 | 100 | 50 | E |
| Profit | 200 | 750 | 130 | F |
| Total expenditures by firm | 5,000 | 3,000 | 500 | |
| Value added per firm | G | H | I | |

2.  GDP for this hypothetical economy is equal to
    a. $5,000 or the value of sales for American Racquet Co.
    b. $8,500 or the sum of the value added for the three firms.
    c. $3,500 or the value of the intermediate goods used by the American Racquet Co.
    d. $980 or the sum of the profits for the three firms.

3.  GDP can be measured using different methods. If you were using the factor payments approach, which entries would you combine to get a measure of GDP?
    a. G, H and I
    b. A and B
    c. A, B, C, and D
    d. C, D, E, and F

4.  GDP can be measured using the value added method. Using this method, which of the following values are correct for the missing entries in the table?
    a. A = $3,000, B = $3,000, G = $2,000, H = $0, I = $500
    b. A = $3,000, B = $500, G = $2,000, H = $2,500, I = $500
    c. A = $3,000, B = $3,000, G = $0, H = $4,500, I = $500
    d. A = $3,000, B = $500, G = $0, H = $4,500, I = $500

5.  Double counting is
    a. the inclusion of the value of goods and services more than once when calculating GDP.
    b. the failure to include the value of intermediate goods in the final calculation of an economy's GDP.
    c. a process that artificially lowers the value of GDP.
    d. avoided if we do not use the value added method in calculating GDP.

6. $C + I + G + X - IM$ is
   a. equal to an economy's GDP for a given period of time.
   b. a measure of the overall market value of the goods and services the economy produces during a given period of time.
   c. the value of all final goods and services produced in an economy during a given time period.
   d. Answers (a), (b), and (c) are all correct.
   e. Answers (a) and (c) are both correct.
   f. Answers (a) and (b) are both correct.

7. Which of the following is *not* included in the calculation of GDP?
   a. Joey's Electronics manufactures CD players that individuals install in cars that do not have CD players.
   b. Susy's Leather Goods manufactures leather pieces that are sold to manufacturers that produce handbags and wallets from these leather pieces.
   c. Harry's Ice Cream Shoppe sells ice cream cones at the beach.
   d. Monica's Hair Salon sells haircuts and manicures to the residents of Marco Island.

8. To avoid double counting when computing GDP for an economy, it is important to
   a. count the total value of each producer's sales in an economy.
   b. only count each producer's value added in the calculation.
   c. include the cost of all inputs at each stage of production.
   d. exclude the cost of all inputs at each stage of production.

9. Income spent on imported goods
   a. represents income that has "leaked" across national borders.
   b. must be subtracted from spending data in order to calculate an accurate value for domestic production.
   c. is income that is not spent on domestically produced goods and services.
   d. Answers (a), (b), and (c) are all correct.

10. The difference between spending on inputs and spending on investment is
    a. spending on inputs is not included in the calculation of GDP.
    b. spending on investment goods is included in the calculation of GDP.
    c. inputs that are purchased by businesses are used up while capital goods that are purchased with business investment are not used up.
    d. Answers (a), (b), and (c) are all correct.
    e. Answers (a) and (c) are both correct.
    f. Answers (b) and (c) are both correct.

## ANSWER KEY

# Answers to Problems and Exercises

1.  **a.** New home construction is included in GDP as investment spending.

    **b.** This is not included in GDP since the value of the house was counted in GDP the year the house was built.

    **c.** Textbook purchases by the government are included in GDP as government spending.

    **d.** Macro States exports beef and the value of these exports are included in the GDP of Macro States.

    **e.** Although there is production occurring, Ellen and Judy do not exchange money, and therefore this transaction does not get included in GDP.

    **f.** This increase in inventory is included in GDP as part of investment, since it represents new production in the economy of Macro States.

2.  **a.**

    |  | Hyattville Forest, Inc. | Hyattville Lumber Products, Inc. | Hyattville Houses, Inc. | Total factor income |
    |---|---|---|---|---|
    | Value of sales | $15,000 | $40,000 | $100,000 | |
    | Intermediate goods | 0 | 15,000 | 40,000 | |
    | Wages | 6,000 | 15,000 | 35,000 | $56,000 |
    | Interest payments | 1,000 | 3,000 | 6,000 | 10,000 |
    | Rent | 3,000 | 3,000 | 3,000 | 9,000 |
    | Profit | 5,000 | 4,000 | 16,000 | 25,000 |
    | Total expenditures by firm | 15,000 | 40,000 | 100,000 | |
    | Value added per firm | 15,000 | 25,000 | 60,000 | |

    **b.** To find GDP using the value added approach requires summing the horizontal entries that are found in the row labeled "Value added per firm" in the above table. From your answer in part (a) the sum of these entries is equal to $15,000 + $25,000 + $60,000, or $100,000.

    **c.** To find GDP using the factor income approach requires first summing horizontally the entries of the amount of wages paid, the amount of interest payments, the amount of rent, and the amount of profit (which corresponds to finding the values of *G, H, I,* and *J* in the above table). Then, once these amounts have been calculated, these four values must be summed to find the total factor income in the economy; thus, from part (a) of this question we have $56,000 (the amount of total wages paid in the economy) + $10,000 (the total amount of interest payments in the economy) + $9,000 (the total amount of rent payments in this economy) + $25,000 (the total amount of profits in this economy) for a total of $100,000 (GDP using the factor payments approach).

    **d.** To find GDP using the aggregate spending on domestically produced final goods and services approach, first recognize that Hyattville only produces one type of final good or service: houses. The value of the houses produced in Hyattville is equal to $100,000.

# Answers to Module Review Questions

1. **Answer a.** Net exports are defined as exports minus imports. Country A's net exports equal ($100 million – $50 million), or $50 million. Country B's net exports equal ($50 million – $100 million), or –$50 million.

2. **Answer a.** Since GDP is equal to the value of all final goods and services produced in an economy during a given time period, GDP for this economy can be found by multiplying the number of racquets produced during the given time period times their price. This yields $5,000. Alternatively, one could add up the total payments to factors of production: wages, interest payments, rent, and profit sum to $5,000.

3. **Answer d.** To get the value of GDP using the factor payments approach, you would need to add up the sum of factor payments: this would be the sum of wages, interest payments, rent, and profit, or cells C, D, E, and F.

4. **Answer b.** The cost of intermediate goods in entry A is equal to the value of metal sales from American Metal Co., or $3,000. The cost of intermediate goods in entry B is equal to the value of ore sales from American Ore Co., or $500. The value added by American Racquet Co., or entry G, is equal to the value of sales by this company minus the value of intermediate goods used by this company ($5,000 – $3,000, or $2,000). The value added by American Metal Co., or entry H, is equal to the value of sales by this company minus the value of intermediate goods used by this company ($3,000 – $500, or $2,500); the value added by American Ore Co., or entry I, is equal to the value of sales by this company minus the value of intermediate goods used by this company ($500 – $0, or $500).

5. **Answer a.** Double counting is when you count the production of an item more than once when calculating the value of GDP. This can arise because the good is used as an intermediate good in the production of a final good. For this reason, intermediate goods are not counted as part of GDP because this would result in an overstatement of the level of production that has occurred in an economy.

6. **Answer d.** The sum of consumer spending, investment spending, government spending, and net exports is equal to GDP. GDP provides a measure of the market value of the goods and services produced in an economy: this is the value of all final goods and services produced in the economy.

7. **Answer b.** Answers (a), (c), and (d) are all included in GDP since they each represent a final good or service. Answer (b) is not included in GDP since the leather pieces are intermediate goods that are used to manufacture the final goods—handbags and wallets—that are included in GDP.

8. **Answer b.** To avoid double counting when calculating GDP, it is important to only count each producer's value added to GDP; alternatively, we can think about avoiding the double counting problem by subtracting out the cost of inputs—the intermediate goods—at each stage of production in order to arrive at the value added at that stage. Then, if the value added at each stage is summed, this will yield the economy's GDP without any double counting.

9. **Answer d.** Income spent on imported goods is by definition income that is not being spent on domestically produced goods and services; this income is leaking out of the domestic economy since it is being spent in a foreign economy. In order to accurately calculate domestic production from spending data, it is necessary to subtract all the spending that occurs on foreign-produced final goods and services.

10. **Answer d.** All of these answers are correct. Spending on inputs represents expenditure by firms on resources that are used up. Spending on investment goods represents the purchase of capital that is not used up, but instead represents the purchase of equipment whose service life will last many years. Spending on inputs is not included in GDP while investment spending is included: inputs get used up while investment spending purchases maintain a useful life for the firm for many years.

# Interpreting
# Real Gross
# Domestic Product

## ▮ BEFORE YOU READ THE MODULE

## Summary

This module discusses the difference between real GDP and nominal GDP, and why real GDP provides a better measure of the actual economic activity that occurs in an economy over time.

## Module Objectives

**Objective #1.** GDP can change over time because the economy is producing more or because the prices of the goods and services it produces have increased. Real GDP calculates the value of aggregate production during a given time period, using prices from some given base year. In effect, real GDP uses constant prices. In contrast, nominal GDP is the calculation of GDP using current prices. Real GDP measures allow one to compare the growth in aggregate production in an economy over time.

**Objective #2.** In comparing GDP across countries or over time, we can eliminate differences in population size by dividing each country's GDP by its population to get GDP per capita, or the average GDP per person. Real GDP per capita is one of many important determinants of human welfare: it measures what a country can do, but it does not address how that country uses that output to affect living standards.

**Objective #3.** Real GDP does not provide a measure of human welfare: real GDP excludes many items that contribute to human happiness such as leisure time, volunteer activities, housework, or natural beauty. Real GDP does, however, include expenditures on some items that make people unhappy, such as disease, divorce, and natural disasters. In other words, real GDP does not provide a measure of the quality of life.

# Key Terms

**aggregate output** the total quantity of *final goods and services* the *economy* produces for a given time period, usually a year. *Real GDP* is the numerical measure of aggregate output typically used by economists.

**real GDP** the total value of all *final goods and services* produced in the *economy* during a given year, calculated using the prices of a selected base year.

**nominal GDP** the value of all *final goods and services* produced in the *economy* during a given year, calculated using the prices current in the year in which the output is produced.

**chained dollars** method of calculating *real GDP* that splits the difference between growth rates calculated using early base years and the growth rates calculated using late base years.

**GDP per capita** GDP divided by the size of the population; equivalent to the average GDP per person.

**real GDP per capita** is real GDP divided by the size of the population; equivalent to the average real GDP per person.

## ■ AFTER YOU READ THE CHAPTER

## Tip

**Tip #1.** To calculate nominal GDP requires that you take the sum of the product of each final good's price measured in current dollars times the quantity of each final good produced during the current period. To calculate real GDP requires that you take the sum of the product of each final good's price measured in constant dollars times the quantity of each final good produced during the current period. Examine these two sentences carefully and you will see the distinction between nominal GDP and real GDP: with nominal GDP the prices you use in the calculation may vary with every period and thus, nominal GDP may be increasing, decreasing, or even remaining the same over time due to changes in both the prices of the goods and the quantities of the goods. In contrast, real GDP changes over time only because the quantities of goods and services being produced over time have changed.

# WORKED PROBLEMS

1. You are given the following information about an economy and you are asked to calculate nominal and real GDP for 2013 and 2014 in this economy. When calculating real GDP for this economy you are asked to use 2013 prices. In addition, you are asked to calculate the growth rate in nominal GDP and real GDP during this period. Finally, you are asked to provide guidance as to which growth rate is the more accurate one to use if you are trying to ascertain how much the economy is growing.

| | 2013 | 2014 |
|---|---|---|
| Quantity of bicycles | 20 | 22 |
| Price of bicycle | $100 | $110 |
| Quantity of sweaters | 10 | 9 |
| Price of sweater | $20 | $30 |
| Quantity of hamburgers | 100 | 140 |
| Price of hamburger | $2 | $3 |

**STEP 1:** Calculate nominal GDP for these two years.

Nominal GDP is found by multiplying the price of the good in the current year times the quantity of the good in the current year and then summing these products for all the goods produced in the economy. Nominal GDP in 2013 is equal to (20 bicycles)($100 per bicycle) + (10 sweaters) ($20 per sweater) + (100 hamburgers)($2 per hamburger) = $2,400. Nominal GDP in 2014 is equal to (22 bicycles)($110 per bicycle) + (9 sweaters)($30 per sweater) + (140 hamburgers)($3 per hamburger) = $3,110.

**STEP 2:** Calculate real GDP for these two years.

Real GDP is found by multiplying the price of the good in the base year times the quantity of the good in the current year and then summing these products for all the goods produced in the economy. Real GDP in 2013 is equal to nominal GDP in 2013, since both measures are using prices from 2013 and quantities from 2013. Real GDP in 2014 is equal to the price of the good in 2013 times the quantity of the good in 2014. Real GDP in 2014 is thus calculated as (22 bicycles)($100 per bicycle) + (9 sweaters)($20 per sweater) + (140 hamburgers)($2 per hamburger) = $2,660.

**STEP 3:** Calculate the growth rate of nominal GDP and real GDP during this period.

To find the growth rate of a variable, use the following formula: [(value of the measure in the current period – value of the measure in the previous period)/(value of the measure in the previous period)] × 100. The rate of change in nominal GDP = [(3,110 – 2,400)/2,400] × 100 = 29.58%. The rate of change in real GDP = [(2,660 – 2,400)/(2,400)] × 100 = 10.83%.

**STEP 4:** Now, you need to provide guidance as to which growth rate measure is the better one if you are trying to decide how much the economy is growing. You will need to explain your answer.

Given the goal of measuring the growth in the economy, the better measure is the growth rate of real GDP. This is because nominal GDP does not distinguish whether the change in nominal GDP is due to changes in production or changes in prices. In contrast, the growth rate of real GDP removes price fluctuation by holding prices constant and then looks at what is happening to aggregate production.

2.  Belgium produces only three goods: chocolate, strawberries, and waffles. The following table gives you information about production and prices for these three goods for 2013 and 2014. You have been asked to calculate real GDP for Belgium using 2013 as the base year. In addition, you have been asked to calculate the growth rate of real GDP during this period and a measure of the GDP deflator for this period.

|  | Quantity in 2013 | Price in 2013 | Quantity in 2014 | Price in 2014 |
|---|---|---|---|---|
| Units of chocolate | 20 | $3 | 30 | $4 |
| Units of strawberries | 75 | 4 | 150 | 2 |
| Units of waffles | 120 | 5 | 110 | 1 |

**STEP 1:** Calculate real GDP for 2013 and 2014 using 2013 as the base year.

Since 2013 is the base year, we know that real GDP in 2013 is the same as nominal GDP in 2013. To find this value, multiply the price of the good in 2013 times the quantity of the good, then sum these products together for all the goods produced in Belgium. Thus, real GDP in 2013 = (price of chocolate in 2013)(quantity of chocolate in 2013) + (price of strawberries in 2013) (quantity of strawberries in 2013) + (price of waffles in 2013)(quantity of waffles in 2013) = $960. Real GDP in 2014 = (price of chocolate in 2013)(quantity of chocolate in 2014) + (price of strawberries in 2013)(quantity of strawberries in 2014) + (price of waffles in 2013)(quantity of waffles in 2014) = $1,240.

**STEP 2:** Calculate the growth rate of real GDP during this period of time.

The growth rate of real GDP during this period = [(real GDP in 2014 – real GDP in 2013)/(real GDP in 2013)] × 100 = 29.17%.

# Problems and Exercises

1. In the beginning of 2011, suppose the population in Neverland was 2 million people and the level of real GDP, or aggregate output, was $40 million. During 2011, population increased by 2%, while real GDP increased by 5%. During this same period, the aggregate price level was constant. Furthermore, suppose these growth rates continued into 2012 and 2013.

   Fill in the following table using the given information. (Make all calculations to two places past the decimal.)

   |                  | Beginning of 2011 | Beginning of 2012 | Beginning of 2013 | Beginning of 2014 |
   |------------------|-------------------|-------------------|-------------------|-------------------|
   | Real GDP         |                   |                   |                   |                   |
   | Population       |                   |                   |                   |                   |
   | Real GDP/person  |                   |                   |                   |                   |

2. In the beginning of 2011, suppose the population in Funland was 2 million people and the level of real GDP, or aggregate output, was $40 million. During 2011, population increased by 3% while real GDP increased by 3%. During 2012, population increased by 4% while real GDP increased by 3%. During 2013, population increased by 5% while real GDP increased by 3%.

   a. Fill in the following table using the given information. (Make all calculations to two places past the decimal.)

   |                  | Beginning of 2011 | Beginning of 2012 | Beginning of 2013 | Beginning of 2014 |
   |------------------|-------------------|-------------------|-------------------|-------------------|
   | Real GDP         |                   |                   |                   |                   |
   | Population       |                   |                   |                   |                   |
   | Real GDP/person  |                   |                   |                   |                   |

   b. What do you know about this country's standard of living between the beginning of 2011 and the beginning of 2014? Explain your answer.

   c. In comparing your answers in problem 1 to your answers in problem 2, what major concept do these problems illustrate?

3. China's economy is growing at a much faster annual rate than the U.S. economy. Does this mean that the standard of living in China is higher than the standard of living in the United States? Explain your answer.

**4.** Suppose you are told that Finlandia produces three goods: tennis shoes, basketballs, and lawn mowers. The following table provides information about the prices and output for these three goods for the years 2010, 2011, and 2012.

| Year | Price of tennis shoes | Quantities of tennis shoes | Price of basketballs | Quantities of basketballs | Price of lawn mowers | Quantities of lawn mowers |
|------|------|------|------|------|------|------|
| 2010 | $50 | 100 | $10 | 200 | $100 | 10 |
| 2011 | 52 | 108 | 10 | 205 | 100 | 12 |
| 2012 | 54 | 115 | 10 | 212 | 110 | 12 |

**a.** Using the previous information, fill in the following table.

| Year | Nominal GDP |
|------|------|
| 2010 | |
| 2011 | |
| 2012 | |

**b.** What was the percentage change in nominal GDP from 2010 to 2011?

**c.** What was the percentage change in nominal GDP from 2011 to 2012?

**d.** Using 2010 as the base year, fill in the following table.

| Year | Real GDP |
|------|------|
| 2010 | |
| 2011 | |
| 2012 | |

**e.** What was the percentage change in real GDP from 2010 to 2011?

**f.** What was the percentage change in real GDP from 2011 to 2012?

## ▉ BEFORE YOU TAKE THE TEST

# Module Review Questions

1. Economic growth
   a. refers to increases in real GDP per capita over the long run.
   b. refers to short-term fluctuations in real GDP per capita.
   c. is best measured using the employment rate.
   d. is of little importance to economists.

2. Long-run growth per capita is
   a. the key to higher wages and a rising standard of living.
   b. a situation that occurs when the economy's overall production grows at a faster rate than the economy's population.
   c. a sustained upward trend in output per person.
   d. Answers (a), (b), and (c) are all correct.

Use the information in the following table to answer the next three questions.

Smallville produces tractors and pizzas. You are given the following information about Smallville's production of these two goods and their prices for three years.

|                      | Year 2010 | Year 2011 | Year 2012 |
|----------------------|-----------|-----------|-----------|
| Quantity of tractors | 5         | 5         | 5         |
| Price of tractors    | $10,000   | $12,000   | $15,000   |
| Quantity of pizzas   | 100       | 80        | 100       |
| Price of pizzas      | $10       | $20       | $20       |

3. Nominal GDP in 2011
   a. is greater than nominal GDP in 2010.
   b. is less than nominal GDP in 2012.
   c  cannot be calculated until a base year is specified.
   d. Answers (a) and (b) are both correct.

4. Suppose the base year is 2010. Real GDP in 2011 using 2010 as the base year
   a. is greater than nominal GDP in 2011.
   b. is less than nominal GDP in 2011.
   c. is equal to nominal GDP in 2011.
   d. may be greater than, less than, or equal to nominal GDP in 2011.

5. Using 2011 as the base year, real GDP is greatest in
   a. 2010.
   b. 2011.
   c. 2012.
   d. 2010 and 2012 since real GDP using 2011 as the base year is the same for these two years.

Answer the next two questions based on the following information.

Littleville is a small economy whose current GDP in 2013 is $10,000 and whose population is 10 people.

6.  GDP per capita in Littleville in 2013 is
    a. $10,000 per person.
    b. $1,000 per person.
    c. $100 per person.
    d. $100,000 per person.

7.  Suppose GDP in Littleville in 2014 increases to $20,000 while the population increases by 50%. Then, GDP per capita in Littleville in 2014
    a. increases, since the percentage change in GDP is greater than the percentage change in population.
    b. equals approximately $1,333 per person.
    c. decreases due to the very large percentage increase in population.
    d. Answers (a) and (b) are correct.

## ANSWER KEY

# Answers to Problems and Exercises

1.

|  | Beginning of 2011 | Beginning of 2012 | Beginning of 2013 | Beginning of 2014 |
|---|---|---|---|---|
| Real GDP | $40 million | $42 million | $44.1 million | $46.31 million |
| Population | 2 million | 2.04 million | 2.08 million | 2.12 million |
| Real GDP/person | $20 | $20.59 | $21.20 | $21.84 |

2.  a.

|  | Beginning of 2011 | Beginning of 2012 | Beginning of 2013 | Beginning of 2014 |
|---|---|---|---|---|
| Real GDP | $40 million | $41.20 million | $42.44 million | $43.71 million |
| Population | 2 million | 2.06 million | 2.14 million | 2.25 million |
| Real GDP/person | $20 | $20 | $19.31 | $19.43 |

**b.** The standard of living in Funland between the beginning of 2011 and the end of 2013 is decreasing, since the rate of population growth exceeds the rate of real GDP growth.

**c.** Problems 1 and 2 illustrate the importance of the growth rates of population and real GDP in determining the standard of living. In problem 1, the standard of living increases, since real GDP grows at a faster rate than the rate of population increase, while in problem 2, the standard of living decreases since the population growth rate is greater than the rate of real GDP growth.

3.   Although China's economy in recent years has grown at a much faster rate than the U.S. economy, this does not necessarily imply that China's standard of living is higher than the standard of living in the United States. Standard of living depends upon both the level of production in an economy and the population in the economy as well as the initial level of standard of living. Ten years ago the output per person in the United States was much larger than the output per person in China. Over the past ten years, even though China's rate of economic growth has surpassed the U.S. rate of economic growth, it has not been sufficiently long enough for the Chinese standard of living to catch up with the U.S. standard of living.

4.  a.

| Year | Nominal GDP |
|---|---|
| 2010 | $8,000 |
| 2011 | 8,866 |
| 2012 | 9,650 |

To calculate nominal GDP, multiply the price of each good times the quantity produced of that good and then sum together these products. For example, nominal GDP in 2010 = (price of tennis shoes) (quantity of tennis shoes) + (price of basketballs)(quantity of basketballs) + (price of lawn mowers)(quantity of lawn mowers) = $8,000.

**b.** The percentage change in nominal GDP from 2010 to 2011 was 10.83%: [(8,866 – 8,000)/8,000] × 10 × 0 = 10.83%.

**c.** The percentage change in nominal GDP from 2011 to 2012 was 8.84%: [(9,650 – 8,866)/8,866]100 = 8.84%.

**d.**

| Year | Real GDP |
|------|----------|
| 2010 | $8,000 |
| 2011 | 8,650 |
| 2012 | 9,070 |

To calculate real GDP, multiply the price of each good in the base year (2010) times the quantity produced of that good in a given year and then sum together these products. The value of real GDP will equal nominal GDP in the base year. In 2011, real GDP can be calculated as the following sum: ($50 per pair of tennis shoes)(108 pairs) + ($10 per basketball)(205 basketballs) + ($100 per lawn mower)(12 lawn mowers).

**e.** The percentage change in real GDP from 2010 to 2011 was 8.13%: [(8,650 – 8,000)/8,000] × 100.

**f.** The percentage change in real GDP from 2011 to 2012 was 4.86%: [(9,070 – 8,650)/8,650] × 100.

# Answers to Module Review Questions

1. **Answer a.** Economic growth is measured as an increase in the level of real GDP in the economy. This increase refers to an increase over the long run, rather than a short-run economic expansion.

2. **Answer d.** For wages and the standard of living to increase in the aggregate in an economy, it is necessary that production increases at a faster rate than the rate of population growth. Answer (b) is just an alternative way of stating long-run growth per capita.

3. **Answer d.** To answer this question, it is helpful to calculate the nominal GDP for each of these years. Nominal GDP in 2010 equals the sum of the product of the prices of the goods produced times the quantity of the goods produced or ($10,000/tractor)(5 tractors) + ($10/pizza)(100 pizzas), or $51,000. Using the same process, nominal GDP in 2011 equals $61,600 and nominal GDP in 2012 equals $77,000. Thus, nominal GDP in 2011 is greater than nominal GDP in 2010 and less than nominal GDP in 2012.

4. **Answer b.** To answer this question, first calculate real GDP in 2011 using 2010 as the base year. Real GDP in 2011 equals the sum of the product of the quantities produced in 2011 times the price of the product in the base year. Thus, real GDP in 2011 using 2010 as the base year equals ($10,000/tractor)(5 tractors) + ($10/pizza)(80 pizzas), or $50,800. Nominal GDP in 2011 equals $61,600 (see previous question), so real GDP in 2011 using 2010 as the base year is less than nominal GDP in 2011.

5. **Answer d.** To answer this question, first compute real GDP for each year using 2011 as the base year. Real GDP in 2011 will equal nominal GDP in 2011 since 2011 has been designated the base year. Thus, real GDP in 2011 equals $61,600. Real GDP in 2010 using 2011 as the base year equals ($12,000/tractor)(5 tractors) + ($20/pizza)(100 pizzas), or $62,000. Real GDP in 2012 using 2011 as the base year equals ($12,000/tractor)(5 tractors) + ($20/pizza)(100 pizzas), or $62,000.

6. **Answer b.** To find GDP per capita, divide the economy's GDP by its population. For Littleville, GDP per capita in 2013 is equal to ($10,000)/(10 people), or $1,000 per person.

7. **Answer d.** Littleville's GDP in 2014 increases by $10,000 (a 100% increase) from its GDP in 2013, while its population increases by 50%. Since the percentage increase in GDP is greater than the percentage increase in population, this implies that GDP per capita has risen in Littleville. To find GDP per person in 2014, we need to first find the level of population in 2014. Since population in 2014 is 50% larger than the population in 2013, this implies population in Littleville is now 15 people. GDP per capita in 2014 in Littleville is thus equal to ($20,000)/(15 people), or approximately $1,333 per person.

# Defining Unemployment

## BEFORE YOU READ THE MODULE

### Summary

This module discusses how unemployment is measured and why the unemployment rate in the economy is significant. The module also discusses the relationship between the unemployment rate and the growth rate of the economy.

### Module Objectives

**Objective #1.** A person is considered to be employed if he or she has a job. To be considered unemployed, an individual must currently not have a job and, in addition, must have actively sought employment during the past four weeks. Individuals who are disabled or retired are not included in the number of unemployed in an economy. The economy's labor force is equal to the sum of the employed and the unemployed in that economy.

- The labor force participation rate is the percentage of the population over 16 years of age that is either employed or unemployed. The labor force participation rate is equal to [(labor force)/(population age 16 and older)] × 100.

- The unemployment rate is equal to [(number of unemployed workers)/(number of unemployed workers + number of employed workers)] × 100.

- Since the number of unemployed workers plus the number of employed workers is equal to the labor force, the unemployment rate is equal to [(number of unemployed workers)/(labor force)] × 100.

**Objective #2.** The unemployment rate provides a good indicator of current conditions in the labor market, but it is not a perfect measure.

- The unemployment rate overstates the difficulty of finding a job since it includes those individuals who are looking for a job and are confident that they will be employed once they identify a suitable position.

- The unemployment rate understates the difficulty of finding a job since it does not include discouraged workers, those jobless individuals who have given up searching for a job because there are no jobs available where they live. The unemployment rate also does not include the marginally attached workers, a group of individuals who are out of work and have recently looked for work, but who are currently not seeking employment. Lastly, the unemployment rate does not include those individuals who are currently working part-time jobs but who want to work full-time; these underemployed workers are counted as employed rather than unemployed even though they are unable to find jobs that are full-time.

- The unemployment rate varies among demographic groups: younger workers and older workers typically experience higher rates of unemployment than do workers between the ages of 25 and 54.

**Objective #3.**   The unemployment rate rises during economic recession and generally falls during economic expansion. Economic data generally indicates that there is a negative relationship between economic growth and the rate of unemployment: when real GDP grows at a high rate, the unemployment rate falls; and when real GDP grows at a low or negative rate, the unemployment rate rises. A falling level of real GDP is always associated with increases in the unemployment rate and its resultant hardship on families.

# Key Terms

**employed**  people currently holding a job in the economy, either full-time or part-time.

**unemployed**  the total number of people who are actively looking for work but aren't currently employed.

**labor force**  the sum of *employment* and *unemployment*; that is, the number of people who are currently working plus the number of people who are currently looking for work.

**labor force participation rate**  the percentage of the population age 16 or older who are in the *labor force*.

**unemployment rate**  the percentage of the total number of people in the *labor force* who are unemployed, calculated as *unemployment/ (unemployment + employment)*.

**discouraged workers**  individuals who want to work but who have stated to government researchers that they aren't currently searching for a job because they see little prospect of finding one given the state of the job market.

**marginally attached workers**  nonworking individuals who say they would like a job and have looked for work in the recent past but are not currently looking for work.

**underemployed**  people who work part time because they cannot find full time jobs.

**jobless recovery**  a period in which the GDP growth rate is positive, but the unemployment rate is still rising.

*Notes*

## AFTER YOU READ THE MODULE

## Tips

**Tip #1.** Students often find it challenging to understand why the unemployment rate understates the unemployment rate for an economy. This understatement is due to the treatment of discouraged workers, marginally attached workers, and underemployed workers. For each of these types of workers the unemployment rate fails to include them as part of the number of unemployed people even though each of these workers either does not have a job or is not satisfied with their working situation.

**Tip #2.** There is a strong negative relationship between the growth of the economy and the unemployment rate. When the economy is growing the unemployment rate is typically falling and when the economy's level of economic growth is below-average the unemployment rate rises.

# WORKED PROBLEMS

1. Consider an economy that has 100,000 people who are 16 years old or older. Of this group, 2,000 are currently in the military, 1,000 are homemakers, 10,000 are retired, and 14,000 are full-time students who are not employed. Further, 10,000 people are currently not working and are actively seeking jobs, 5,000 people are temporarily laid off and anticipate that their jobs will resume within the next two months, and 5,000 people are currently not working and are not actively seeking jobs because they live in a community with a severely depressed economy (like Detroit today). All other adults in this economy can be assumed to be working: in this group, 80% are fully employed and 20% are underemployed. You are asked to identify what the civilian labor force is in this economy, what the number of unemployed people is in this economy, and what the number of employed people is in this economy. You are also asked to calculate the unemployment rate and the civilian labor force participation rate for this economy. The government of this economy is considering changing its definition of *unemployed* so that it includes discouraged workers. If this new policy is implemented, what will the new unemployment rate equal? Suppose the government changes its classification of discouraged workers and, in addition, decides to treat underemployed workers as unemployed workers since this group is not fully utilizing their labor resources. If both of these policy changes are implemented, what will happen to the unemployment rate?

**STEP 1:** Start by identifying all those individuals who would not be in the civilian labor force. Then identify all those who are considered employed and all those who are considered unemployed. Remember that the number of the employed plus the unemployed must sum to the civilian labor force. (*Hint:* Your text refers to the labor force, but this is just the civilian labor force—in this example, we are emphasizing this since we want to make sure you do not include the military in your calculations of the employed and the unemployed.)

The intent of the unemployment rate is to measure that fraction of the labor force that is not employed. The government does not want to include in this measurement individuals who are clearly not interested in working, individuals who clearly cannot work, or individuals who are not part of the adult population. The government also does not want to include military personnel since they are employed by the military. Thus, in this example, the civilian labor force excludes all those under 16, the military, homemakers who are not currently seeking work, the retired, and full-time students who are not currently seeking work. The civilian labor force is equal to 68,000. To find the civilian labor force, start with the initial population of 100,000 and then subtract out those in the military (2,000), full-time students (14,000), those not working and not looking for work (10,000), those that are discouraged workers (5,000), and those who are homemakers (1,000). The 5,000 who are laid off but who expect to be called back are treated as unemployed workers, since they are currently not working. The civilian labor force is equal to the sum of the employed plus the unemployed. We can find the number of unemployed workers: it is the sum of the unemployed plus the laid-off workers, or 10,000 plus 5,000, for a total of 15,000. To find the number of employed people, subtract the unemployed from the civilian labor force: 68,000 – 15,000 = 53,000.

**STEP 2:** Calculate the unemployment rate and the civilian labor force participation rate for this economy.

The unemployment rate is equal to [(number of unemployed)/(civilian labor force)] × 100. Recall that the civilian labor force is just the sum of the unemployed plus the employed. In this example, the civilian labor force is equal to 68,000. The unemployment rate is [(15,000)/(68,000)] × 100, or 22%.

The civilian labor force participation rate is equal to [(civilian labor force)/(civilian population age 16 or older)] × 100 = [(68,000)/(98,000)] × 100, or 69.4%.

**STEP 3:** Recalculate the unemployment rate, but this time treat discouraged workers as part of the group of unemployed workers.

This change in policy will change the number of unemployed from 15,000 to 20,000 and the number of the civilian labor force from 68,000 to 73,000. The new unemployment rate can be calculated as [(20,000)/(73,000)] × 100 = 27.4%. Notice that the treatment of discouraged workers can have a significant impact on the unemployment statistics. Current treatment makes the unemployment rate lower than it would be if discouraged workers were treated as unemployed workers.

**STEP 4:** Recalculate the unemployment rate, but this time treat both discouraged workers and underemployed workers as part of the group of unemployed workers.

Initially, there are 53,000 employed people in this economy. Of that 53,000, we are told that 80% are fully employed and 20% are underemployed. The number of employed people is equal to 0.8(53,000), or 42,400, and the number of unemployed people is equal to 0.2(53,000), or 10,600. If the government changes its policy to include discouraged workers and underemployed workers in the category of unemployed workers, this means that the number of unemployed workers will increase from 15,000 to 30,600. In addition, the civilian labor force will now equal 73,000: the 30,600 who are unemployed and the 42,400 who are employed. To calculate the number of employed people, recall that initially there were 53,000 employed people but that this number included the underemployed. If we categorize the underemployed as unemployed, this will cause the unemployed number to increase by 10,600 and the employed number to decrease by 10,600. The new unemployment rate with these changes in policy will equal [(30,600)/(73,000)] × 100, or 41.92%. Notice that the treatment of discouraged workers and underemployed workers can have a significant impact on the unemployment statistics. Current treatment makes the unemployment rate lower than it would be if discouraged workers and underemployed workers were treated as unemployed workers.

**2.** The following data on the labor market have been provided to you by the U.S. Bureau of Labor Statistics. You are asked to provide the overall unemployment rate for this economy, the unemployment rate for males, and the unemployment rate for females. Furthermore, you are asked to compute the labor force participation rate for this economy as well as the female labor force participation rate and the male labor force participation rate.

| Adult Population | % Female |
|---|---|
| 400 | 52% |
| Labor Force | % Female |
| 310 | 40% |
| Employed | % Female |
| 260 | 45% |

**STEP 1:** **It would be helpful to know the number of men and women in each of the above categories rather than just the percentages that have been provided.**

Take the time to construct a table that provides these data in a straightforward, easy-to-access manner. The following table provides this information.

| Variable | Male | Female |
|---|---|---|
| Adult Population | 192 | 208 |
| Labor Force | 186 | 124 |
| Employed | 143 | 117 |

**STEP 2:** **Find the unemployment rate in general and then find the unemployment rate for men and the unemployment rate for women.**

Recall that the unemployment rate = [(number of unemployed)/(number of unemployed + number of employed)] × 100. To find the number of unemployed, you need to remember that the labor force is the sum of employed plus unemployed. Since the labor force is equal to 310 and the number of employed is equal to 260, the number of unemployed is equal to 50. The unemployment rate is [(50)/(310)] × 100, or approximately 16%.

To find the unemployment rate for males, you will need to find the number of unemployed men and the number of men in the labor force. From the preceding table, we know that there are 186 men in the labor force and 143 of them are employed. That implies that 43 are unemployed. The male unemployment rate is [(43)/(186)] × 100, or approximately 23%.

To find the unemployment rate for females, you will need to find the number of unemployed women and the number of women in the labor force. From the preceding table, we know that there are 124 women in the labor force and 117 of them are employed. That implies that 7 are unemployed. The female unemployment rate is [(7)/(124)] × 100, or approximately 5.6%.

**STEP 3:** **Compute the labor force participation rate for the entire economy and then compute the labor force participation rate for men and the labor force participation rate for women.**

Recall that the labor force participation rate = [(labor force)/(population)] × 100. From the table, we know both the labor force and the population: the labor force participation rate is [(310)/(400)] × 100, or approximately 77.5%.

To find the labor force participation rate for men, you will need to know how many men there are in the labor force and how many men there are in the population. This information is in the table you created in Step 1. The labor force participation rate for men = [(number of men in the labor force)/(number of men in the population)] × 100. The labor force participation rate for men is [(186)/(192)] × 100, or approximately 97%.

To find the labor force participation rate for women, you will need to know how many women there are in the labor force and how many women there are in the population. This information is in the table you created in Step 1. The labor force participation rate for women = [(number of women in the labor force)/(number of women in the population)] × 100. The labor force participation rate for women is [(124)/(208)] × 100, or approximately 60%.

## Problems and Exercises

1. Suppose there are 12,000 people living in Macroland. Of these 12,000 people, 1,000 are either too old to work or too young to work. Of the remaining individuals, 5,000 are employed with full-time jobs; 3,000 are employed part-time, but wish to work full-time; 1,000 are underemployed, but working full-time jobs; 1,000 are currently not working, but are looking for work; and the remainder are discouraged workers.

   **a.** What is the size of the labor force in Macroland?

   **b.** What is the employment rate in Macroland?

   **c.** What is the unemployment rate in Macroland?

   **d.** What percentage of the population are discouraged workers?

   **e.** Suppose you are told that 100 people find jobs for every $10,000 increase in the level of aggregate output in Macroland. If you wanted the unemployment rate to equal 8%, what would the change in output need to be? Assume no changes in the number of young and old in the population or in the number of discouraged workers.

**f.** Suppose the government department in Macroland responsible for compiling unemployment statistics redefines the employed as including only those with full-time jobs. How does this change the unemployment rate, given the initial information?

**2.** Suppose that there are 10,000 adults in Finlandia and that 5,000 of these adults are employed, 2,000 are unemployed, 500 are discouraged workers, and the rest are not currently working and/or not seeking employment.

**a.** What is the labor force equal to in Finlandia?

**b.** What is the unemployment rate in Finlandia?

**c.** What would the unemployment rate equal in Finlandia if discouraged workers were counted as unemployed workers?

**d.** Currently the Bureau of Labor Statistics does not count discouraged workers as unemployed workers. How does this decision affect the calculated value of the unemployment rate?

**e.** Suppose that for every $10,000 increase in GDP in Finlandia, unemployment decreases by 100 people. If GDP increases by $20,000, what will Finlandia's unemployment rate equal? Assume there is no change in the number of discouraged workers and that discouraged workers are not counted as unemployed workers.

**f.** What is the relationship between GDP and unemployment?

3. Currently the United States Bureau of Labor Statistics counts underemployed people as employed. What are the arguments that support this position? What arguments can you offer for why the underemployed might be counted as unemployed? Does it matter how the Bureau of Labor Statistics categorizes this group of workers?

4. Does the unemployment rate for the United States economy provide a good measure of the job situation for different age groups or different racial groups?

5. Suppose an economy enters a recession and real GDP falls. What do you predict will be true about this economy's unemployment rate?

## BEFORE YOU TAKE THE TEST

## Module Review Questions

Use the following information to answer the next two questions.

Suppose the adult population of Macronesia is 100,000 people. Of these 100,000 people, 20,000 are not in the labor force. Of the remaining 80,000 people, 16,000 have given up searching for a job and are not actively seeking work; 4,000 are unemployed and actively seeking work; 14,000 work part-time; and the remainder are fully employed.

1. What is the unemployment rate in Macronesia?
   a. 5%
   b. 6.25%
   c. 8.5%
   d. 10%

2. What would happen to Macronesia's unemployment rate, relative to your answer in the last question, if discouraged workers were counted as unemployed workers?
   a. The unemployment rate would be unchanged.
   b. The unemployment rate would decrease.
   c. The unemployment rate would increase.
   d. The unemployment rate could increase, decrease, or remain the same.

Answer the next three questions based on the following information about a small economy.

An economy is composed of five people: George, Sarah, Mason, Abbot, and Jin. George works for Plastics, Inc., 40 hours a week. Sarah works for Baker's United for 20 hours a week and would like to move from part-time work to full-time work. Mason has been looking for work for the past six months after he completed his high school education. Abbot worked for Baker's United for the first six months of the year before he was fired; for the next four months Abbot sought work, but finally gave up looking for work when he realized that it was unlikely he would be able to find work in this economy. Jin is 70 years old and enjoys reading, needlepoint, and watching movies.

3. In this economy, the employed include
   a. George, Sarah, and Mason.
   b. George and Sarah.
   c. George since he is the only person in this economy who is fully employed.
   d. George, Sarah, Mason, and Jin. (Jin is fully employed with a variety of activities that occupy all her waking moments.)

4. What is the labor force participation rate in this economy?
   a. 40%
   b. 60%
   c. 80%
   d. 100%

5. What is the unemployment rate in this economy?
   a. 20%
   b. 33%
   c. 40%
   d. 50%

6. Which of the following statements is true?
   I. To be considered unemployed, one must simply not have a job.
   II. To be considered unemployed, one must not have a job and must also not be looking for a job.
   III. To be considered unemployed, one must not have a job and must also be looking for a job.
   a. Statement I is true.
   b. Statement II is true.
   c. Statement III is true.
   d. Statements I, II, and III are all false.

7. When the unemployment rate is high, this usually implies that it is
   a. easy to find a job.
   b. difficult to find a job.

8. The Bureau of Labor Statistics' treatment of discouraged workers results in the unemployment rate
   a. overstating the true level of unemployment.
   b. understating the true level of unemployment.

9. Underemployed workers, those workers currently working part-time jobs but wishing to work full-time jobs, are
   a. not included in the calculation of the employment rate.
   b. included in the calculation of the employment rate.

10. Different age groups and different ethnic groups in the economy typically experience
    a. the same unemployment rate.
    b. different unemployment rates.

11. During an economic expansion, the unemployment rate typically
    a. increases.          b. decreases.

12. Historically, the relationship between the change in unemployment and the annual growth rate of real GDP is a
    a. positive relationship.
    b. negative relationship.

# ANSWER KEY

## Answers to Problems and Exercises

1. **a.** The labor force is defined as the number of employed workers plus the number of unemployed workers. The number of employed workers equals the sum of full-time workers, part-time workers, and underemployed workers, or, in this example, 9,000 workers. The number of unemployed workers is equal to the 1,000 workers who are currently not working, but who are actively looking for work. Thus, the labor force equals 10,000 workers.

   **b.** Employment rate = (employed/labor force) × 100 = (9,000/1,000) × 100 = 90%

   **c.** Unemployment rate = (unemployed/labor force) × 100 = (1,000/10,000) × 100 = 10%

   **d.** Percentage of discouraged workers in population = [(discouraged workers)/population] × 100 = (1,000/12,000) × 100 = 8.33%

   **e.** The current unemployment rate is 10%. To reduce the unemployment rate to 8% requires that 200 of the currently unemployed workers find jobs. If output increases by $10,000 for every 100 people who find jobs, then output must increase by $20,000 for 200 people to find employment.

   **f.** Using the new definition of employment, the number of employed now equals 6,000, and the unemployed would increase by 3,000 for a total of 4,000 unemployed. This change in definition results in a much higher unemployment rate (40%) and a much lower employment rate (60%). The definitions underlying calculations do matter.

2. **a.** The labor force is equal to the sum of employed plus unemployed workers. In this case, the labor force is equal to 5,000 + 2,000, or 7,000.

   **b.** To find the unemployment rate, use the formula Unemployment rate = (unemployed/labor force) × 100. In this case, the unemployment rate equals (2,000/7,000) × 100, or 28.57%.

   **c.** If discouraged workers were counted as unemployed workers, the formula for calculating the unemployment rate would change to Unemployment rate = [(unemployed + discouraged workers)/(labor force)] × 100. The unemployment rate would equal (2,500/7,000) × 100, or 33%.

   **d.** The decision by the Bureau of Labor Statistics to exclude discouraged workers from the calculation of the unemployment rate results in an understatement of the unemployment rate in the economy.

   **e.** Since GDP increases by $20,000, we know that unemployment decreases by 200 people (2,000 − 200 = 1,800). Thus, the unemployment rate is now equal to (1,800/7,000) × 100, or 25.72%.

   **f.** As GDP increases, unemployment decreases.

3. When the underemployed are counted as employed workers this reduces the level of the unemployment rate for the economy, other things being equal. Although this group of underemployed workers is working, they are not working as much as they would like. If the Bureau of Labor Statistics categorized underemployed workers as unemployed, the unemployment rate would increase, other things being equal. Workers in this group could argue that their level of employment is less than they desire and they are still looking for full-time employment. How the Bureau of Labor Statistics categorizes different individuals with regard to whether they are considered employed or unemployed matters since this categorization can affect the calculated unemployment rate.

4.  No, the unemployment rate for the United States economy does not provide a good measure of the job situation for different age groups or different racial groups. Unemployment rates vary widely among different demographic groups: older and younger workers find it harder to find work than do workers in their "prime" working years. African-American workers find it far more difficult to find work than the general unemployment rate would suggest: the unemployment rate for African-Americans is considerably higher than the general unemployment rate.

5.  During recessions the unemployment rate rises as the level of real GDP falls. Since the economy's level of aggregate production is falling, fewer people are needed to produce that lower level of output. As the level of employment falls, this implies that the rate of unemployment rises.

## Answers to Module Review Questions

1.  **Answer b.** Calculate the unemployment rate using this formula: Unemployment rate = [(number of unemployed)/(labor force)] × 100, where the labor force is equal to the number of employed workers plus the number of unemployed workers. In this case, the unemployment rate = [(4,000)/(64,000)] × 100 = 6.25%. Note that the labor force does not include discouraged workers (16,000) or the 20,000 people who are not currently in the labor force.

2.  **Answer c.** The unemployment rate now equals [(20,000)/(80,000)] × 100, or 25%. The unemployment rate increases when discouraged workers are counted as unemployed workers.

3.  **Answer b.** To be considered employed, an individual must have a part-time or full-time job. Only George and Sarah satisfy this requirement in the described economy.

4.  **Answer b.** The labor force participation rate is equal to the product of 100 times the sum of the employed plus the unemployed divided by the population over 16 years of age. In this example, the employed is equal to 2 (George and Sarah), the unemployed is equal to 1 (Mason), and the population over 16 years of age is equal to 5. Thus, (3/5) × 100 = 60%.

5.  **Answer b.** The unemployment rate is equal to the product of 100 times the number of unemployed divided by the labor force. There is one unemployed person (Mason) and two employed people (George and Sarah); therefore, the labor force is equal to 3 while the number of unemployed is equal to 1. The unemployment rate equals (1/3) × 100 or 33%.

6.  **Answer c.** To be considered unemployed, a person must not have a job and must, in addition, be actively seeking a job. For example, the retired neither have jobs nor are they seeking employment: they are not part of the unemployed and they are not part of the labor force since they do not intend to work. The discouraged worker, although not working, is not considered unemployed since the discouraged worker has given up looking for a job.

7.  **Answer b.** The unemployment rate is a good indicator of how easy or difficult it is to find a job in the economy. When the economy's unemployment rate is high, this implies that many people are out of work and it will therefore be difficult to find employment. When the economy's unemployment rate is low, this implies that it will be relatively easy to find a job.

8.  **Answer b.** Currently the Bureau of Labor Statistics does not include discouraged workers in the number of unemployed even though these workers are currently not working. This exclusion results in a lower rate of unemployment than would be the case if these discouraged workers were included in the number of unemployed.

9.  **Answer b.** Underemployed workers are included in the number of employed workers even though these workers would like to attain full-time employment.

10. **Answer b.** Unemployment rates in an economy vary widely depending upon the age group and ethnic group; for example, teenagers have much higher rates of unemployment than do adults between the ages of 25 and 54, while African-Americans experience higher unemployment rates than the national average.

11. **Answer b.** When the economy is in an economic expansion, the unemployment rate usually falls as increase in the level of aggregate output usually requires an increase in the level of aggregate employment in the economy.

12. **Answer b.** If the relationship between the change in unemployment and the annual growth rate of real GDP is graphed as a scatter diagram, these points indicate a negative relationship between these two measures.

# Categories of Unemployment

---

■ **BEFORE YOU READ THE MODULE**

## Summary

This module develops the concept of the natural rate of unemployment and the factors that determine the natural rate of unemployment. The module also describes three different types of unemployment: frictional, structural, and cyclical unemployment. The module discusses the causes of each type of unemployment.

## Module Objectives

**Objective #1.** The unemployment rate never falls to zero. This is due to several reasons. First, jobs are constantly being created and eliminated. Jobs are created and eliminated due to structural changes in the economy: these changes reflect new technologies as well as changes in consumers' tastes. In addition, the process of locating a job or the job search can take time. "Frictional unemployment" is the term that describes unemployment that is due to job search, whether this job search is due to the process of job creation and job destruction or the fact that new workers are constantly entering the labor force.

**Objective #2.** Structural unemployment refers to unemployment that occurs when there are more people seeking jobs in a labor market than there are jobs. Structural unemployment may reflect a situation where there are more workers with a particular skill than there are available jobs using that skill, or where there are more workers in a particular geographic area than there are jobs in that area.

**Objective #3.** In a labor market, the demand for labor indicates the amount of labor employers demand at different wage rates while the supply of labor indicates the amount of labor that individuals are willing to supply at different wage rates. The demand for labor is downward sloping: as the wage rate falls, firms demand more labor. The supply of labor is typically upward sloping: as the wage rate falls, individuals supply less labor. The equilibrium wage rate is that wage rate where the quantity demanded of labor is equal to the quantity supplied of labor. However, at that equilibrium wage rate there is still frictional unemployment since there will always be some workers who are searching for a job even if the number of available jobs equals the number of available workers. But, at the equilibrium wage rate, structural unemployment is equal to zero. Whenever the wage rate exceeds the equilibrium wage rate, there is structural unemployment: the primary causes of this structural unemployment are the minimum wage, labor unions, efficiency wages, and the side effects of government policies.

- A minimum wage is a government-imposed floor on the price of labor and, when binding, the minimum wage can lead to structural unemployment since it artificially raises the wage rate above the equilibrium wage rate in the labor market. Although an effective minimum wage helps those who secure employment, it may also eliminate the opportunity to work for some workers who would have been willing to work for lower wages.

- Effective labor unions may also result in structural unemployment if the unions are successful in bargaining for wage contracts that are higher than the equilibrium market wage rate. Through successful collective bargaining, labor unions may raise the wage rate to a level where the number of people willing to work is greater than the number of jobs available at that wage rate.

- Firms that pay efficiency wages as an incentive for better worker performance may also create structural unemployment: the efficiency wage is a wage rate greater than the equilibrium wage rate.

- Public policy may generate unintended side effects that result in structural unemployment. For example, generous unemployment benefits may reduce the incentive of the unemployed to find new jobs.

**Objective #4.**  The natural rate of unemployment is that rate of unemployment that the actual unemployment fluctuates around. This natural rate of unemployment takes into account frictional unemployment as well as structural unemployment. In contrast, cyclical unemployment is the difference between the actual rate of unemployment and the natural rate of unemployment: cyclical unemployment measures the amount of unemployment due to the business cycle. Thus,

Natural unemployment = frictional unemployment + structural unemployment

Actual unemployment = natural unemployment + cyclical unemployment

**Objective #5.**  The natural rate of unemployment is not constant over time and may be affected by economic policies. The natural rate of unemployment changes with changes in the characteristics of the labor force, changes in labor market institutions, changes in government policies, and changes in productivity.

- When the labor force has many inexperienced workers, the result is higher rates of frictional unemployment since these workers are apt to stay in a particular job for a shorter period of time than are experienced workers. In addition, older workers often have family responsibilities that provide a stronger incentive to find and keep jobs.

- Economies with strong labor unions tend to have higher rates of natural unemployment since these labor unions may contribute to higher rates of structural unemployment. Temporary employment agencies and websites listing jobs may reduce the level of frictional unemployment, and therefore the natural rate of unemployment, by helping match unemployed workers to jobs.

- Government policies such as a high minimum wage or generous unemployment benefits can cause structural unemployment and, thus, lead to a higher rate of natural unemployment. Government policies may also reduce the natural rate of unemployment. For example, job training works to provide unemployed workers with skills that will enable them to widen the range of jobs they can do, while employment subsidies provide payments to either workers or firms to create an incentive for these groups to accept or offer jobs.

# Key Terms

**job search** when workers spend time looking for *employment*.

**frictional unemployment** *unemployment* due to time workers spend in *job search*.

**structural unemployment** *unemployment* that results when there are more people seeking jobs in a labor market than there are jobs available at the current wage rate.

**efficiency wages** wages that employers set above the *equilibrium* wage rate as an incentive for workers to deliver better performance.

**natural rate of unemployment** the normal *unemployment rate* around which the actual unemployment rate fluctuates; the unemployment rate that arises from the effects of *frictional* and *structural unemployment*.

**cyclical unemployment** the difference between the actual rate of *unemployment* and the *natural rate of unemployment*.

## ▉ AFTER YOU READ THE MODULE

# Tips

**Tip #1.** The distinction among frictional, structural, and cyclical unemployment is important. All economies experience frictional unemployment. Jobs are created and destroyed and new workers are constantly entering the labor market: these events make some unemployment inevitable. Structural unemployment occurs because there is a mismatch between the supply of labor and the demand for labor: this mismatch is the result of the current wage exceeding the wage rate that would equate the supply of labor to the demand for labor. Cyclical unemployment is the unemployment that occurs due to fluctuations in economic production due to the business cycle.

**Tip #2.** Students often find the concept of the natural rate of unemployment challenging. It is not possible for an economy to achieve and maintain zero unemployment due to the ongoing creation and destruction of jobs as well as the entry of new labor market participants. The natural rate of unemployment is that level of unemployment that the economy can achieve when it is producing with no cyclical unemployment: it is the rate of unemployment achieved when the economy produces at its potential output level.

1. In the library, you read the following newspaper headline from the 2008 archives: "Sharp rise in unemployment rate as global financial crisis hits jobs market." Based on this reading, what do you know about frictional, structural, and cyclical unemployment in this economy? What do you know about the relationship between this economy's current unemployment rate and its natural rate of unemployment?

**STEP 1:** Review the definitions of frictional, structural, and cyclical unemployment and then apply these definitions to this situation.

The headline about the global financial crisis and the rise in unemployment suggests that the world economy is experiencing a deviation from the natural rate of unemployment, the level of unemployment that is the normal unemployment rate around which the actual unemployment rate fluctuates. This deviation is referred to as cyclical unemployment. So, in this economy not only is there frictional and structural unemployment, the kinds of unemployment that occur normally in an economy, but there is also the additional kind of unemployment that refers to the departure of the economy from its normal unemployment rate.

**STEP 2:** Review the definition of the natural unemployment rate and then consider how this economy's current unemployment rate differs from its natural unemployment rate.

This economy is experiencing frictional, structural, and cyclical unemployment: this implies that its current unemployment rate is greater than its natural unemployment rate.

## Problems and Exercises

1. Use the following graph to answer this question.

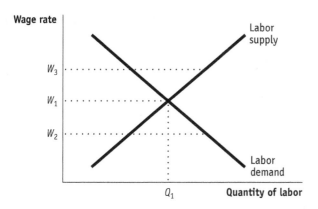

a. What is the equilibrium wage and quantity of labor in this labor market?

b. At the equilibrium wage rate, what is the structural unemployment rate? Explain your answer.

c. If the structural unemployment rate is a positive number, what do you know must be true about the current wage in this labor market? Explain your answer.

d. Suppose the government passes minimum wage legislation setting the minimum wage at $W_2$, where $W_2$ is less than $W_1$. Explain the effect of this legislation on this labor market.

e. Suppose the government passes minimum wage legislation setting the minimum wage at $W_3$, where $W_3$ is greater than $W_1$. Explain the effect of this legislation on this labor market.

2.   Economists believe that the natural rate of unemployment is greater than zero. Assuming structural unemployment and cyclical unemployment are both zero, how do you explain this insistence that the natural rate of unemployment must still be a positive number? Explain your answer fully.

**3.** The text considers the effect of minimum wage legislation and union power on the workings of the labor market. Compare and contrast the effects of minimum wage legislation and union power on the labor market, noting how they are similar in their impact on the labor market as well as how they differ in their impact on the labor market.

**4.** Consider the following simple scenario. A small country has 10 adults of working age. Five of these adults currently are working; two of these adults have recently left college and are seeking full-time employment; one of these adults would like to work but has recently lost his job at a local manufacturing plant because the company has decided to close the plant and open it in another country with lower-cost labor; and two adults would like to work but are not working due to the economy being in a recession.

**a.** Given the above information, what is the unemployment rate in this country?

**b.** What is the structural unemployment rate in this country?

**c.** What is the frictional unemployment rate in this country?

**d.** What is the cyclical unemployment rate in this country?

**e.** What is the natural rate of unemployment in this country?

5.  Consider the following simple scenario. A small country has 10 adults of working age. Six of these adults currently are working: of the six, two are part-time workers, two have full-time jobs, and two are underemployed. Of the remaining four workers, two are actively seeking jobs, one is not working but is not actively applying for jobs because she does not believe there are any jobs available, and the other is out of work due to the economy being in a recession.

   a.  Given the above information, what is the unemployment rate in this country?

   b.  What is the structural unemployment rate in this country?

   c.  What is the frictional unemployment rate in this country?

   d.  What is the cyclical unemployment rate in this country?

   e.  What is the natural rate of unemployment in this country?

## ▌ BEFORE YOU TAKE THE TEST

## Module Review Questions

1.  Which of the following statements is true?
   a.  The natural rate of unemployment equals a country's unemployment rate during a recession.
   b.  The natural rate of unemployment equals a country's unemployment rate during an expansion.
   c.  The natural rate of unemployment is the sum of frictional and structural unemployment.
   d.  The natural rate of unemployment is the sum of frictional and cyclical unemployment.

2. Job creation and job destruction are
   a. a natural occurrence in a labor market.
   b. only a problem during an economic expansion.
   c. a primary reason for why there is unemployment even when the economy is at full employment.
   d. Answers (a), (b), and (c) are all correct.
   e. Answers (a) and (c) are both correct.

3. Which of the following statements is true?
   a. Even small amounts of structural unemployment are harmful to an economy.
   b. There is always frictional unemployment since there are always new workers entering the job market.
   c. Even small amounts of frictional unemployment are harmful to an economy.
   d. Answers (a), (b), and (c) are all correct.
   e. Answers (a) and (b) are both correct.
   f. Answers (b) and (c) are both correct.

4. Which of the following statements is true?
   a. Structural unemployment refers to the unemployment that occurs when there are more employers demanding labor than there are employees supplying labor.
   b. Structural unemployment refers to a situation when the market wage rate is lower than the equilibrium wage rate.
   c. Structural unemployment occurs when there is a surplus of labor at the current wage rate.
   d. When there is structural unemployment, frictional unemployment equals zero.

5. In order to be binding, a minimum wage must be
   a. equal to or less than the equilibrium wage rate.
   b. greater than the equilibrium wage rate.
   c. set so that there is a persistent surplus in the labor market.
   d. set so that there is a persistent shortage in the labor market.
   e. Answers (a) and (d) are both correct.
   f. Answers (b) and (c) are both correct.

6. Which of the following statements is true?
   a. Strong labor unions and an effective minimum wage reduce the level of structural unemployment in an economy.
   b. Strong labor unions and an effective minimum wage benefit all workers equally.
   c. Workers acting collectively through a union may find that they have more power than if they act individually.
   d. Answers (a), (b), and (c) are all correct.
   e. Answers (b) and (c) are both correct.

7. Efficiency wages
   a. are wages negotiated by unions.
   b. are always less than the minimum wage.
   c. are wages paid by employers that exceed the equilibrium wage rate and that are offered as an incentive for better performance.
   d. are a means for employers to retain employees while providing incentives for greater work effort.
   e. Answers (b), (c), and (d) are all correct.
   f. Answers (c) and (d) are both correct.

8. The natural rate of unemployment is
   a. equal to 0% in every economy, since this is the level of unemployment that every economy should naturally want to achieve.
   b. the sum of frictional and cyclical unemployment.
   c. equal to cyclical unemployment when the economy is producing at the full employment level of aggregate output.
   d. Answers (b) and (c) are correct.
   e. None of the above is correct.

9. The natural rate of unemployment
   a. is constant and does not change over time.
   b. changes when there are changes in labor force characteristics.
   c. may change due to changes in labor market institutions like unions, temporary employment agencies, and technological change.
   d. increases with increases in the minimum wage level.
   e. Answers (a), (b), (c), and (d) are all correct.
   f. Answers (b), (c), and (d) are correct.
   g. Answers (b) and (d) are both correct.

10. Which of the following statements is true?
    I. The two principal goals of macroeconomic policy are price stability and low frictional unemployment.
    II. The primary goals of macroeconomic policy are price stability and low unemployment.
    III. In order to achieve the two primary goals of macroeconomic policy of price stability and low unemployment, it is necessary for policy makers to reduce the level of frictional unemployment.
    a. Statements I, II, and III are all true.
    b. Statements I and II are true.
    c. Statements II and III are true.
    d. Statement I is true.
    e. Statement II is true.
    f. Statement III is true.

11. Job search refers to the time that workers spend looking for employment. Job search results in
    a. cyclical unemployment.
    b. structural unemployment.
    c. frictional unemployment.
    d. both structural and frictional unemployment.

**12.** Suppose the demand for labor is given by the equation $W = 15 - (1/200)L$ and the supply of labor is given by the equation $W = 5 + (1/200)L$ where $W$ is the wage rate and $L$ is the quantity of labor. What is the equilibrium wage and quantity of labor in this market?

a. The equilibrium wage is $15 while the equilibrium quantity of labor is 200 workers.

b. The equilibrium wage is $5 while the equilibrium quantity of labor is 100 workers.

c. The equilibrium wage is $10 while the equilibrium quantity of labor is 1,000 workers.

d. The equilibrium wage is $10 while the equilibrium quantity of labor is 200 workers.

**13.** Suppose the demand for labor is given by the equation $W = 15 - (1/200)L$ and the supply of labor is given by the equation $W = 5 + (1/200)L$ where $W$ is the wage rate and $L$ is the quantity of labor. Suppose the government imposes a minimum wage of $12 in this market. What will be the effect of this minimum wage in this market?

a. The minimum wage will not be binding since it is set below the equilibrium wage.

b. The minimum wage will create a situation of excess demand for labor since it is a binding minimum wage.

c. The minimum wage will create a situation of excess supply of labor since it is a binding minimum wage.

d. This minimum wage will benefit all workers in this labor market.

**14.** Binding minimum wages generally lead to

a. cyclical unemployment since not everyone can find a job at the minimum wage rate.

b. frictional unemployment since the binding minimum wage results in longer job search.

c. structural unemployment since more people want to work than can find jobs at the minimum wage.

d. Answers (a), (b), and (c) are all correct.

**15.** Which of the following statements is true?

   I. An employer can encourage its workers to work hard by paying an efficiency wage.

   II. An efficiency wage is equal to the market wage rate.

   III. When many firms pay efficiency wages, this creates structural unemployment.

a. Statement I is true.

b. Statement II is true.

c. Statement III is true.

d. Statements I and II are true.

e. Statements II and III are true.

f. Statements I and III are true.

g. Statements I, II, and III are all true.

## ■ ANSWER KEY

# Answers to Problems and Exercises

1.  **a.** The equilibrium wage rate is $W_1$ and the equilibrium quantity of labor is $Q_1$, where the quantity of labor supplied is equal to the quantity of labor demanded.

    **b.** At the equilibrium wage rate, the structural unemployment rate equals zero since the number of people seeking jobs in the labor market equals the number of jobs available at that equilibrium, or current, wage rate.

    **c.** If the structural unemployment rate is a positive number, then the wage rate must be greater than the equilibrium wage rate, and the supply of labor must exceed the demand for labor, resulting in a surplus of labor.

    **d.** For a minimum wage to have any impact on the market, it must be set above the equilibrium wage rate. The minimum wage rate is just a specific example of a price floor, and price floors only impact markets when they are set above the equilibrium price.

    **e.** When the government sets the minimum wage above the equilibrium wage rate, it affects the market by preventing the wage rate from adjusting to that point where the demand for labor equals the supply of labor. Thus, an effective minimum wage will create a surplus of labor and, hence, a positive structural unemployment rate.

2.  Even when the economy produces at its potential output and the unemployment rate equals the natural rate, there will be people entering the job market as well as workers moving between jobs. This frictional unemployment is a natural part of the working of the labor market; hence, even when the economy is at its natural rate of unemployment, there will still be positive frictional unemployment.

3.  Labor unions and effective minimum wage legislation both affect the labor market by working to raise the current wage above the equilibrium wage rate and by creating barriers to prevent the wage from adjusting back to the equilibrium level. Both labor unions and minimum wage legislation have the potential to create structural unemployment through their ability to create a situation where the supply of labor is greater than the demand for labor. The work of labor unions, through collective bargaining, often results in workers securing higher wages than the market would have provided if workers bargained individually. Labor unions often negotiate for long-term contracts, and these contracts may lead to structural unemployment due to the wage rigidity they introduce into the labor market.

4.  **a.** The unemployment rate is equal to 100 times the number of unemployed workers divided by the sum of the number of employed workers plus the number of unemployed workers. Thus, the unemployment rate is equal to 100(5/10) = 50%.

    **b.** The structural unemployment rate is equal to 100[(number of structurally unemployed workers)/(number of employed plus unemployed workers)] = 100(1/10) = 10%.

    **c.** The frictional unemployment rate is equal to 100[(number of frictionally unemployed workers)/(number of employed plus unemployed workers)] = 100(2/10) = 20%.

    **d.** The cyclical unemployment rate is equal to 100[(number of cyclically unemployed workers)/(number of employed plus unemployed workers)] = 100(2/10) = 20%.

    **e.** The natural rate of unemployment is equal to 100[(frictional unemployed + structurally unemployed)/(number of employed plus unemployed workers)] = 100(3/10) = 30%.

5.  **a.** The first step in answering these five questions is to sort the workers into the appropriate category: six workers are employed even though two of them are part-time and two are underemployed; the two workers actively seeking jobs are frictionally unemployed; the one individual who is not working and not actively seeking a job is a discouraged worker; and the individual who is out of work because of the recession is cyclically unemployed. Thus, the unemployment rate is 33% since there are three unemployed people and the labor force (the sum of employed plus unemployed) is equal to 9.

   **b.** The structural unemployment rate is 0% since there are no structurally unemployed individuals in this country.

   **c.** The frictional unemployment rate is 22% since there are two frictionally unemployed individuals and the labor force is equal to nine individuals. Thus, the frictional unemployment rate is equal to $100(2/9) = 22\%$.

   **d.** The cyclical unemployment rate is equal to $100(1/9) = 11\%$.

   **e.** The natural rate of unemployment is equal to $100(2/9) = 22\%$ since the natural rate of unemployment is equal to the sum of the structural and frictional unemployment rates.

## Answers to Module Review Questions

1.  **Answer c.** The natural unemployment rate is defined as the sum of frictional and structural unemployment. It is the unemployment rate that occurs when there is no cyclical unemployment, which is the unemployment directly tied to economic business cycles.

2.  **Answer e.** Job creation and job destruction naturally occur in an economy, and it is this natural process that leads to economies always having some unemployment even if the economy is producing at full employment. We can think about how there are always people in the economy who are entering the labor force and looking for work, and there are always people whose jobs are ending and are in need of finding new work. This process occurs during both economic expansions and recessions.

3.  **Answer b.** All economies will experience some frictional and structural unemployment as a natural functioning of their labor market. Frictional unemployment occurs because of job creation and job destruction and because there are always new workers entering the job market. Frictional unemployment can be beneficial to an economy, since the economy may be more productive if workers take the time to find jobs that are well matched to their skills. Structural unemployment occurs because of such factors as minimum wages, unions, efficiency wages, and government policies that are designed to help laid-off workers.

4.  **Answer c.** Structural unemployment occurs when there is an excess supply of labor in a labor market. This occurs when the wage rate is greater than the equilibrium wage rate in the market. Every economy has frictional unemployment due to job creation and job destruction as well as the entry of new workers into the economy.

5.  **Answer f.** To be effective and therefore binding, a minimum wage must be set at a level in excess of the equilibrium wage rate. This will result in the supply of labor exceeding the demand for labor and thus a surplus of labor.

6.  **Answer c.** Strong labor unions and an effective minimum wage act to increase the level of structural unemployment in an economy, since they both tend to create a surplus of labor in the labor market. It is true, though, that workers acting collectively may possess greater negotiating power in an industry than would those workers acting individually. Strong unions and an effective minimum wage benefit those people who continue to work, but hurt those who become unemployed when the wage rate rises above the equilibrium wage rate in the labor market.

7.  **Answer f.** Efficiency wages are those paid by employers in excess of the equilibrium wage rate. They are offered to improve employee work effort while also providing an incentive for workers to stay with their current employer. Efficiency wages may be equal to or greater than the minimum wage.

8.  **Answer e.** The natural rate of unemployment is equal to the sum of frictional and structural unemployment. It will always be greater than zero, since there will always be new workers entering the job market and workers moving from one job to another. The cyclical unemployment rate is equal to zero when the economy produces at the full employment level of aggregate output, but at this level of output there is still frictional unemployment.

9.  **Answer f.** The natural rate of unemployment is affected by changes in labor force characteristics and by changes in labor market institutions. In addition, the natural rate of unemployment will increase whenever the government mandates more generous benefits for workers (for example, an increase in the minimum wage rate).

10. **Answer e.** The two primary macroeconomic policy goals are low unemployment and price stability. In order to achieve low unemployment, the economy must produce at or near its potential output level: low unemployment necessitates reducing the level of cyclical unemployment. Economies always have some amount of frictional unemployment and although policymakers can adopt policies that will lower the level of frictional unemployment, they cannot eliminate it.

11. **Answer c.** Frictional unemployment is unemployment due to the time workers spend in job search. Structural unemployment is the unemployment due to the number of people seeking work exceeding the number of available jobs at the current wage rate. Cyclical unemployment is unemployment due to economic recession; cyclical unemployment is a result of business cycle fluctuations.

12. **Answer c.** To find the equilibrium quantity of labor, set the demand equation equal to the supply equation and solve for $L$. $L$ will equal 1,000 workers. Using either the demand equation or the supply equation, substitute 1,000 into the equation for $L$ and then solve for $W$: the equilibrium wage will equal $10.

13. **Answer c.** To find out if $12 is a binding minimum wage requires first solving for the equilibrium wage in this market. From the previous question we know that the equilibrium wage is equal to $10, so $12 is a binding minimum wage. A binding minimum wage will create a situation of excess labor supply since the wage is artificially raised above that level where the quantity demanded of labor equals the quantity supplied of labor. The minimum wage, when binding, does not benefit all workers since some workers would like to work at this higher minimum wage but cannot find jobs.

14. **Answer c.** A binding minimum wage results in the quantity supplied of labor exceeding the quantity demanded of labor; thus, more people want to work at the minimum wage rate than can find jobs. Thus, the binding minimum wage results in structural unemployment.

15. **Answer f.** An efficiency wage is one that is greater than the equilibrium wage rate in the labor market. A firm will pay an efficiency wage for a variety of reasons, including the hope that a wage exceeding the equilibrium wage rate will encourage its employees to put forth greater work effort since the workers do not want to risk losing their relatively high-paying jobs. Payment of an efficiency wage results in excess supply of labor and therefore structural unemployment.

# module 15(51)

# The Costs of Inflation

## Summary

This module considers the costs of inflation and deflation and how inflation and deflation create winners and losers. It defines the meaning of inflation, deflation, and disinflation as well. The module discusses the distinction between nominal and real values of income, wages, and interest rates.

## Module Objectives

**Objective #1.** The level of prices in an economy does not determine how well off people are, but the percentage increase in the overall level of prices per year, or the inflation rate, does matter since a high rate of inflation imposes significant economic costs. The inflation rate for a given year (for example, year 2) can be calculated using the following formula:

$$\text{Inflation rate for year 2} = \{[(\text{price index in year 2}) - (\text{price index in year 1})]/(\text{price index in year 1})\} \times 100$$

High rates of inflation result in shoe-leather costs, menu costs, and unit-of-account costs.

- Shoe-leather costs refer to the effort people expend to reduce their holdings of money during periods of high inflation. The high rate of inflation reduces the purchasing power of money and makes holding money less desirable since the money does not hold its value. The high rate of inflation significantly increases transaction costs as individuals expend valuable resources to reduce their money holdings.

- Menu costs refer to the cost of changing the list price of items that are offered for sale. In periods of high inflation, firms are forced to alter prices often, which results in higher costs for the economy as a whole.

- Unit-of-account costs of inflation refer to the way inflation makes money a less reliable unit of measurement; in particular, in periods of high inflation, contracts that are stated in monetary terms are harder to evaluate due to the changing value of the monetary unit. Tax systems are subject to unit-of-account costs if these tax systems are not adjusted for inflation, since the inflation can distort the measures of income on which taxes are collected.

**Objective #2.**    In addition to the three overall costs on the economy (shoe-leather costs, menu costs, and unit-of-account costs), inflation also produces winners and losers within the economy. This distributional effect of inflation primarily arises because many economic transactions involve contracts that extend over a period of time and these contracts are normally specified in nominal, rather than real, terms. To understand this issue requires understanding the distinction between nominal and real interest rates: the nominal interest rate is the interest rate in dollar terms, while the real interest rate is the nominal interest rate minus the rate of inflation. When the actual inflation rate is greater than the expected inflation rate, borrowers gain at the expense of lenders: borrowers will repay their loans with funds that have a lower real value than had been expected. When the actual inflation rate is lower than the expected inflation rate, lenders gain at the expense of borrowers: borrowers will repay their loans with funds that have a higher real value than had been expected.

- Long-term contracts are adversely affected by uncertainty about the future inflation rate since this uncertainty discourages people from entering into long-term contracts with one another. Thus, high rates of inflation and high levels of uncertainty about future rates of inflation reduce long-term investment in an economy.

- Deflation, an unexpected fall in the price level, also produces winners and losers. In periods of deflation borrowers see a sharp increase in the real value of their debt: deflation redistributes wealth from borrowers to lenders.

**Objective #3.**    Reducing the level of inflation in an economy, a process called disinflation, is difficult and costly once a high rate of inflation is established. To eliminate established inflation in an economy requires policies that temporarily depress the economy—and these policies lead to high levels of unemployment.

# Key Terms

**real wage**  the wage rate divided by the price level.

**real income**  income divided by the price level.

**inflation rate**  the annual percent change in a price index—typically the *consumer price index*.

**shoe-leather costs**  (of inflation) the increased costs of transactions caused by *inflation*.

**menu costs**  the real cost of changing a listed price.

**unit-of-account costs**  (of inflation)  costs arising from the way *inflation* makes money a less reliable unit of measurement.

**nominal interest rate**  the *interest rate* in dollar terms.

**real interest rate**  the *nominal interest rate* minus the *inflation rate*.

**deflation**  a fall in the overall level of prices

**disinflation**  the process of bringing down *inflation* that has become embedded in expectations.

*Notes*

## ▮ AFTER YOU READ THE MODULE

## Tips

**Tip #1.** This module introduces new vocabulary and, as usual, you will want to make sure you learn and understand these new terms. In particular, you will want to be able to define and distinguish between real and nominal interest rates, and deflation and disinflation. The nominal interest rate is the interest rate expressed in money terms, while the real interest rate is the interest rate adjusted for inflation. The real interest rate is equal to the nominal interest rate minus the inflation rate. Deflation refers to a fall in the aggregate price level, and disinflation refers to a decrease in the inflation rate reflecting policy makers' decisions that the economy has built-in inflationary expectations that need to be reduced.

# WORKED PROBLEMS

1.  Croatland has recently experienced very high rates of inflation in their economy. Because of this inflation many people have had to make adjustments in how they perform their daily activities. In the table below are a few examples of these changed behaviors. You have been asked to identify which of these activities represent shoe-leather costs of inflation, menu costs of inflation, and unit-of-account costs of inflation.

| Description of modified activity | Type of inflation represented |
|---|---|
| Home Reconstruction, a firm that provides building materials, has stopped including fliers in their monthly brochures advertising their business: the company finds the cost of updating these brochures has risen dramatically because of the inflation. | |
| Pete's Steakhouse no longer lists prices on its menu after 50 years of including prices with each item on the menu. | |
| Joey has requested that his employer pay him four times a month rather than monthly. In addition, Joey has asked for and gotten permission to leave work on his payday in order to immediately cash his check and use the funds to purchase the items he needs rather than hold on to the cash. | |
| Tony is thinking about purchasing a new car but he is uncertain whether the current price for the model he is considering is a good price. Over the last four months of watching the car's price, it has fluctuated, as have the prices of other similar-style cars. | |
| Michele's business has been quite successful this year in terms of its nominal profit. This means that she will have to pay taxes at a higher rate. The tax system does not consider her real return, only her nominal return, in deciding the tax rate that she must pay. | |
| Susie has stopped carrying any cash and she has reduced her checking account balance to $500. She is doing everything she can to reduce the amount of money she holds. | |

**STEP 1:** Start by reviewing the definitions and descriptions of shoe-leather costs, menu costs, and unit-of-account costs.

Shoe-leather costs of inflation refer to the increased costs of transaction due to the presence of inflation. This cost includes the time spent trying to reduce your holding of cash since the purchasing power of that cash you are holding is being eroded by the inflation.

Menu costs refer to the increased costs of printing new menus or price lists when there is inflation. When there are periods of high inflation, firms are forced to frequently alter the prices they charge, which results in greater costs for the aggregate economy.

Unit-of-account costs refer to the way that inflation erodes the usefulness of money as a unit of measurement: for example, in periods of high inflation, contracts that are written in nominal terms are much harder to evaluate because of the uncertainty created by the inflation and its impact on the value of the monetary unit. Tax systems that are not adjusted for inflation are particularly subject to unit-of-account costs since the assessed tax is based on a distorted measure of income.

**STEP 2:** Apply the definitions of these three types of inflation to the examples in the table. Provide an explanation for your answer.

Here is the completed table with an explanation for each choice.

| Description of modified activity | Type of inflation represented |
|---|---|
| Home Reconstruction, a firm that provides building materials, has stopped including fliers in their monthly brochures advertising their business: the company finds the cost of updating these brochures has risen dramatically because of the inflation. | Menu costs. In this example we have Home Reconstruction opting to not provide printed information about prices because the prices are changing so frequently that printing new fliers is prohibitively expensive. |
| Pete's Steakhouse no longer lists prices on its menu after 50 years of including prices with each item on the menu. | Menu costs. In this example Pete's Steakhouse opts to provide "price-less" menus in order to not have to pay the costs of printing new menus so frequently. |
| Joey has requested that his employer pay him four times a month rather than monthly. In addition, Joey has asked for and gotten permission to leave work on his payday in order to immediately cash his check and use the funds to purchase the items he needs rather than hold on to the cash. | Shoe-leather costs. Joe wants his pay more often and he wants to be able to convert his dollar-denominated pay into an item that is more protected from inflation. He is expending time and energy to reduce his cash holdings: this is referred to as the shoe-leather costs of inflation. |
| Tony is thinking about purchasing a new car but he is uncertain whether the current price for the model he is considering is a good price. Over the last four months of watching the car's price, it has fluctuated, as have the prices of other similar-style cars. | Unit-of-account costs. Tony can no longer be certain that the prices of major purchases reflect an accurate unit of comparison since these prices are changing so frequently due to inflation. The dollar as a unit of account does not work when there are periods of high inflation. |
| Michele's business has been quite successful this year in terms of its nominal profit. This means that she will have to pay taxes at a higher rate. The tax system does not consider her real return, only her nominal return, in deciding the tax rate that she must pay. | Unit-of-account costs. Michele faces potentially higher taxes based upon her nominal profit rather than her real profit. When there are periods of high inflation, a tax system based on nominal values will collect more than it would if the tax system were based on real values. |
| Susie has stopped carrying any cash and she has reduced her checking account balance to $500. She is doing everything she can to reduce the amount of money she holds. | Shoe-leather costs. Susie is using time and energy to reduce her cash holdings because she recognizes that the purchasing power of any cash she holds is eroded by the high inflation she faces. |

2. Wooyoung, Moheb, and Zander all live in New York City and work full-time for three different corporations. Wooyoung earns a salary of $50,000; Moheb earns a salary of $60,000; and Zander earns a salary of $70,000. Suppose that next year each of these individuals expect to receive a salary increase of 10%. But they also expect there to be significant inflation in New York City. Wooyoung expects that prices will rise by 5% next year; Moheb expects prices to rise by 10% next year; and Zander expects prices to rise by 20% next year. Tonight they have met for dinner and they are busy discussing their economic prospects for next year. They have asked you to join them and help them understand how their real incomes will be affected by the scenarios that they imagine. In your analysis make sure you help them see what their real incomes will be under each possibility, as well as help them to identify the possibility that will leave them with the greatest purchasing power.

**STEP 1:** Calculate the nominal income for each individual for next year.

Each of these individuals expects that their nominal income will increase by 10% next year. To find the nominal income for any of these individuals requires only that we multiply their current income by 1.1 in order to find what their new income will be. The table below summarizes these calculations.

| Name | Nominal income this year | Nominal income for next year |
|------|--------------------------|------------------------------|
| Wooyoung | $50,000 | $50,000(1.1) = $55,000 |
| Moheb | 60,000 | 60,000(1.1) = 66,000 |
| Zander | 70,000 | 70,000(1.1) = 77,000 |

**STEP 2:** Review the relationship between the nominal wage and the real wage.

To convert a nominal income into a real income requires that we divide the nominal income by the price level. An easy way to think about this process is to assign the current year a price level of 1. Then if you expect the price level to increase by 5% the next year, or in other words, you expect there to be inflation of 5%, then the price level will be 5% higher or at 1.05. If you expect inflation to be 10%, then the price level will be at 1.10. The following table summarizes this idea.

| Expected inflation for next year | Price level for next year (based on this year's price level equaling 100) |
|----------------------------------|----------------------------------------------------------------------------|
| 5% | 1.05 |
| 10 | 1.10 |
| 20 | 1.20 |

**STEP 3:** Calculate the real wage for each of these individuals if Wooyoung is correct about what the inflation rate will be for next year.

To calculate the real wage for each of these individuals we will take the nominal wage and divide it by the price level. In this case Wooyoung is projecting an inflation rate of 5% for next year, or a price level of 1.05 (see Step 2). Thus, to find the real wage we will take the nominal wage for each of these individuals in year 2 and divide this nominal wage by 1.05. The table below summarizes this calculation.

| Name | Nominal salary for next year | Expected price level for next year | Real salary for next year |
|------|------------------------------|-------------------------------------|----------------------------|
| Wooyoung | $55,000 | 1.05 | $52,381 |
| Moheb | 66,000 | 1.05 | 62,857 |
| Zander | 77,000 | 1.05 | 73,333 |

**STEP 4:** Calculate the real wage for each of these individuals if Moheb is correct about what the inflation rate will be for next year.

To calculate the real wage for each of these individuals we will take the nominal wage and divide it by the price level. In this case Moheb is projecting an inflation rate of 10% for next year, or a price level of 1.10 (see Step 2). Thus, to find the real wage we will take the nominal wage for each of these individuals in year 2 and divide this nominal wage by 1.10. The table below summarizes this calculation.

| Name | Nominal salary for next year | Expected price level for next year | Real salary for next year |
|---|---|---|---|
| Wooyoung | $55,000 | 1.10 | $50,000 |
| Moheb | 66,000 | 1.10 | 60,000 |
| Zander | 77,000 | 1.10 | 70,000 |

**STEP 5:** Calculate the real wage for each of these individuals if Zander is correct about what the inflation rate will be for next year.

To calculate the real wage for each of these individuals we will take the nominal wage and divide it by the price level. In this case Zander is projecting an inflation rate of 20% for next year, or a price level of 1.20 (see Step 2). Thus, to find the real wage we will take the nominal wage for each of these individuals in year 2 and divide this nominal wage by 1.20. The table below summarizes this calculation.

| Name | Nominal salary for next year | Expected price level for next year | Real salary for next year |
|---|---|---|---|
| Wooyoung | $55,000 | 1.20 | $48,833 |
| Moheb | 66,000 | 1.20 | 55,000 |
| Zander | 77,000 | 1.20 | 64,167 |

**STEP 6:** Determine which scenario results in the greatest purchasing power next year for these three individuals.

To answer this question review the results you got in Steps 3, 4, and 5 to see which scenario results in the highest real salary. On inspection we see that Wooyoung's scenario results in the highest real salary: this should not be surprising since a 10% increase in nominal salaries and only a 5% inflation over the same period this indicates that the individual's purchasing power is increasing. However, a 10% increase in nominal salaries and a 10% inflation over the same period would indicate that the individual's purchasing power is staying constant: the individual's nominal income is increasing but their ability to purchase goods and services with this higher nominal income is no greater than what they had before the salary increase and the inflation. Finally Zander's scenario leaves these three in the worse position: yes, they get the 10% increase in salary but the 20% expected inflation exceeds this salary increase and will result in less purchasing power if this scenario comes true.

# Problems and Exercises

1. Macroland decides to join the Central Union, which is a group of countries that have negotiated a trade zone. All members of the Central Union must adopt the CU dollar, the currency of the Central Union. Currently a Macroland dollar purchases three CU dollars.

   **a.** Suppose you live in Macroland and have lent someone 50,000 Macroland dollars. Once Macroland joins the Central Union, how many CU dollars is your loan worth? Has the value of your loan changed with the change from Macroland dollars to CU dollars?

   **b.** You have agreed to lend a friend of yours 10,000 Macroland dollars. Once Macroland joins the Central Union, how many CU dollars will your friend owe you?

   **c.** When you made the loan described in part (b), you negotiated that you would be paid 10% of the value of the loan this year as compensation for the use of your funds. If this payment is made in Macroland dollars, how many Macroland dollars will you receive? If this payment is made in CU dollars, how many CU dollars will you receive? Are you better off being paid in Macroland dollars or CU dollars? Explain your answer.

2. Sarah currently works for a firm in which her union has negotiated a cost-of-living adjustment that automatically adjusts her income to whatever the annual rate of inflation is for her community. Bob works for a firm that routinely grants its employees a 5% annual income increase. Milt is retired and receives two payments: a pension payment from his former employer that is fixed at $2,000 per month and a government-provided retirement payment whose real value is equal to $1,000 per month in the base year. The government-provided retirement payment is indexed to the inflation rate in the community.

   **a.** Suppose the rate of inflation is 8% this year. Describe the effect of this inflation rate on Sarah, Bob, and Milt in terms of their real purchasing power. Who is left in worse shape with this inflation? Does anyone end up better off despite this inflation rate? Explain your answer.

    **b.** Suppose the rate of inflation is 20% this year. Describe the effect of this inflation rate on Sarah, Bob, and Milt.

3. Steve wants to borrow $1,000 from Harry and promises to repay the borrowed money plus interest a year from now. During the course of the year Harry anticipates that inflation will be 15% while Steve anticipates that inflation will be 12%. Use this information to answer this series of questions.

    **a.** Steve is willing to pay a real interest rate of 4% for this loan. If Harry charges Steve a nominal interest rate of 19% will Steve borrow the money?

    **b.** Steve has agreed to pay Harry $1,200 at the end of the year if Harry loans Steve $1,000 at the beginning of the year. If inflation is 15% for the year, what is the real interest rate that Steve will pay for this loan?

    **c.** Steve has agreed to pay Harry $1,200 at the end of the year if Harry loans Steve $1,000 at the beginning of the year. If inflation is 12% for the year, what is the real interest rate that Steve will pay for this loan?

4. Suppose that your country has high inflation for the next five years. Provide a description of shoe-leather costs, menu costs, and unit-of-account costs that might occur with this scenario.

## ▮ BEFORE YOU TAKE THE TEST

# Module Review Questions

1.  Which of the following statements is true?

    a.  Most contracts that extend over a period of time are expressed in real terms so that borrowers and lenders can fully understand the consequences of their economic agreement.

    b.  The nominal interest rate is equal to the real interest rate minus the inflation rate.

    c.  When the actual inflation rate equals the anticipated inflation rate, borrowers are better off.

    d.  Anticipated inflation can inflict real costs on the economy.

2.  Mary expects the inflation rate to be 5%, and she is willing to pay a real interest rate of 3%. Joe expects the inflation rate to be 5%, and he is willing to lend money if he receives a real interest rate of 3%. If the actual inflation rate is 6% and the loan contract specifies a nominal interest rate of 8%, then

    a.  Joe is glad he lent out funds even though his real interest rate has fallen.

    b.  Joe is sorry he lent out funds since his real interest rate is now 9%.

    c.  Mary is glad she borrowed the funds because her real interest rate has fallen.

    d.  Mary is sorry she borrowed funds since her real interest rate is now 9%.

3.  Disinflation in an economy that has grown to expect inflation is

    a.  easy to achieve and does not affect actual output.

    b.  difficult to accomplish and invariably results in an increase in the natural rate of unemployment.

    c.  possible only if policy makers are willing to accept higher rates of unemployment and a lower level of aggregate output.

    d.  Answers (a) and (c) are both correct.

    e.  Answers (b) and (c) are both correct.

4.  In a period of unexpected deflation,

    a.  borrowers find that it is easier for them to make their loan payments, since prices are falling.

    b.  lenders benefit, since there are more people eager to borrow money during a period of deflation.

    c.  lenders benefit, since they are repaid dollars with greater real value than they anticipated when signing the loan contract.

    d.  Answers (a), (b), and (c) are all correct.

5.  Utopia has recently experienced a high rate of inflation and proposes changing its currency from the Utopian dollar to the Utopian mark at an exchange rate of 5.0 Utopian dollars per Utopian mark. Suppose Joe currently has a debt of 100,000 Utopian dollars. Which of the following statements is true?

    a.  The switch to Utopian marks will make Joe better off since the Utopian mark is replacing the Utopian dollar, whose purchasing power has fallen due to the presence of inflation in Utopia.

    b.  The switch to Utopian marks will reduce the real value of Joe's debt.

    c.  Joe's debt will now equal 20,000 Utopian marks.

    d.  Joe's debt will now equal 500,000 Utopian marks.

6.  The extra time and effort expended to make transactions during times of high rates of inflation impose
    a. shoe-leather costs.
    b. menu costs.
    c. unit-of-account costs.

7.  The real wage is
    a. constant over time.
    b. equal to the nominal wage divided by the price level.
    c. increasing over time.
    d. decreasing over time.

8.  Inflation is often associated with increased costs of transactions as people spend time trying to avoid holding money since the value of the money they hold decreases over time when there is inflation. This increased transaction cost is referred to as
    a. shoe-leather costs.
    b. menu costs.
    c. unit-of-account costs.
    d. real costs.

9.  Inflation is often associated with businesses having to issue new price lists for their products. It is costly for firms to have to expend resources to change prices, especially if they must change prices frequently. The term that best represents this type of cost from inflation is
    a. shoe-leather costs.
    b. menu costs.
    c. unit-of-account costs.
    d. real costs.

10. The dollar is used for the basis of contracts and calculation; when its value changes when there is inflation it becomes difficult for individuals to accurately know how to allocate their resources since the value of the dollar is not constant. This reduction in the quality of economic decisions due to the instability of the dollar in inflationary times is referred to as
    a. shoe-leather costs.
    b. menu costs.
    c. unit-of-account costs.
    d. real costs.

11. Joe loans Mary $100 for a year. At the end of the year, Mary pays Joe $110. There is no inflation during the year. The nominal interest rate that Joe charges Mary is equal to
    a. $10.
    b. $110.
    c. 10%.
    d. Cannot be calculated from the given information.

**12.** Joe loans Mary $100 for a year. At the end of the year, Mary pays Joe $110. There is inflation of 5% during the year. The real interest rate that Joe earns from this loan is equal to approximately

    a. 0%.

    b. 5%.

    c. 10%.

    d. 15%.

**13.** Joe loans Mary $100 for a year. At the end of the year, Mary pays Joe $110. Joe and Mary anticipate that the inflation for the year will equal 5%. The actual inflation for the year is 4%. Which of the following statements is true?

    a. Joe earns a higher real rate of interest than he anticipated at the time that he made the loan.

    b. Mary pays a higher real rate of interest than she anticipated at the time that she borrowed the money.

    c. Joe earns a lower real rate of interest than he anticipated at the time that he made the loan.

    d. Mary pays a lower real rate of interest than she anticipated at the time that she borrowed the money.

    e. Answers (a) and (b) are both correct.

    f. Answers (c) and (d) are both correct.

## ANSWER KEY

# Answers to Problems and Exercises

1.  **a.** With the change to CU dollars, your loan will now be valued at 150,000 CU dollars. But, since 3 CU dollars trade for 1 Macroland dollar, the value of the loan has not changed with the switch to the new currency.

    **b.** As in part (a), the change to CU dollars will make your loan value three times larger: your loan value will be 30,000 CU dollars. But, since 3 CU dollars trade for 1 Macroland dollar, the value of the loan has not changed with the switch to the new currency.

    **c.** When the loan is 10,000 Macroland dollars, the interest payment the first year is equal to (0.1)(10,000 Macroland dollars) or 1,000 Macroland dollars. When the loan is denominated in CU dollars, the interest payment the first year is equal to (0.1)(30,000 CU dollars) or 3,000 CU dollars, which has the same value as 1,000 Macroland dollars when 1 Macroland dollar is exchanged for 3 CU dollars. The two payments are equivalent: the switch to the new currency does not change the value of the interest payment or the loan value.

2.  **a.** With an inflation rate of 8% for the year, Sarah finds that her income is automatically adjusted upward by that 8%: Sarah's real income has not changed since prices rose by 8% as did her income. Bob's income will rise by 5% even though the inflation rate was 8%: Bob is worse off since his nominal income rose but by an amount smaller than the amount needed to stay even with the inflation rate. Bob has less purchasing power than he did initially. Milt's situation is complicated: his pension from his former employer is fixed and does not adjust with the inflation rate: this implies that Milt will now have less purchasing power from his fixed pension of $2,000 per month than he did initially. Milt's government-provided retirement payment maintains its real value since it is adjusted with changes in the rate of inflation. Overall Milt has less purchasing power than he did initially. No one in this example ends up better off despite this inflation rate.

    **b.** Again, Sarah's purchasing power is not affected since her nominal income is adjusted each year based upon the rate of inflation. Bob is much worse off this year since the overall price level rose 20% while his nominal income only rose 5%. Milt's fixed pension sees an even bigger erosion in its purchasing power than in part (a), while his government-provided retirement payment maintains its real value.

3.  **a.** No, Steve will not borrow the money. Steve anticipates that inflation will be 12% for the year. Thus, if the nominal interest rate is 19%, then the real interest rate would be 7%, which is higher than Steve is willing to pay.

    **b.** If Steve repays Harry $1,200 at the end of the year he is paying back the $1,000 plus an interest payment of $200. $200 is 20% of the total loan amount. Thus, Steve is paying a nominal interest rate of 20%, and if the inflation rate is 15%, then this results in a real interest rate of 5%.

    **c.** If Steve repays Harry $1,200 at the end of the year he is paying back the $1,000 plus an interest payment of $200. $200 is 20% of the total loan amount. Thus, Steve is paying a nominal interest rate of 20%, and if the inflation rate is 12%, then this results in a real interest rate of 8%.

4.  Answers to this question will vary: each student will have their own examples. Shoe-leather costs refer to the transactions costs associated with inflation. When a country experiences inflation, people are forced to spend more time searching for ways to avoid holding money. For example, if the inflation was high enough, people would want to immediately take their paychecks and go out and spend that money before any time had elapsed, since the value of the paycheck is decreasing with time. Menu costs refer to the

cost of printing new price lists when there is inflation. For example, if there is substantial recurring inflation, then restaurants will find it necessary to print new menus in order to keep up with the price changes. They may eventually find it easier to simply print a menu that does not include any prices. Unit-of-account costs refer to how inflation makes money a less reliable unit of measurement. This is particularly important with regard to contracts and calculations that are stated in monetary terms: if the value of the dollar is not stable, then there is greater uncertainty as to the real value of the contracts and calculations.

## Answers to Module Review Questions

1.  **Answer d.** Most contracts that extend over time are expressed in nominal terms and not real terms. The nominal interest rate equals the real interest rate plus the inflation rate. When the actual inflation rate equals the anticipated inflation rate, the inflation rate does not create winners or losers in loan contracts, since both parties to the contract have used accurate expectations of inflation to anticipate the inflation rate, and they have both agreed to the real rate they actually receive when the contract is honored. Anticipated inflation diverts resources from productive uses to less productive uses: resources are used to avoid the inflation tax.

2.  **Answer c.** Both Mary and Joe would like to negotiate a contract where the real interest rate is 3%, and they both anticipate the expected inflation rate will be 5%. Thus, the nominal rate in the contract will equal the desired real rate of interest plus the expected inflation rate, or 8%. When the actual rate of inflation is 6%, this means that the dollars paid back have less purchasing power than anticipated: Mary will find this beneficial to her as the borrower, while Joe will find this hurts him since the dollars he receives in payment for the loan have less purchasing power than the dollars he loaned out.

3.  **Answer c.** Disinflation in an economy where inflationary expectations are embedded is possible only if policy makers are willing to push the economy into a recession and thereby reduce inflationary expectations. This will necessarily result in an increase in the unemployment rate and a decrease in the level of aggregate output the economy produces. This policy does not affect the natural rate of unemployment.

4.  **Answer c.** In a period of unexpected deflation, borrowers will find that the real value of the loan payments they make have risen in value, so borrowers will be hurt by the unexpected deflation. Lenders will benefit because the loan payments they receive will have greater real value due to the deflation. Borrowers, due to the increased economic burden of their debt, will typically reduce their overall spending and will choose, therefore, to borrow less during a period of deflation.

5.  **Answer c.** To find Joe's debt measured in Utopian marks, multiply Joe's debt in Utopian dollars times the ratio (1 Utopian mark)/(5 Utopian dollars) or (100,000 Utopian dollars)(1 Utopian mark)/(5 Utopian dollars) to get 20,000 Utopian marks. Joe is not better off since he is only changing the unit of measurement of his debt but not his real debt level.

6.  **Answer a.** The transactions costs associated with high rates of inflation are referred to as shoe-leather costs. Menu costs refer to the cost associated with printing new menu and price lists due to the presence of inflation. Unit-of-account costs refer to the costs inflation imposes because of its effects on contracts that are stated in monetary, instead of real, terms.

7.  **Answer b.** The real wage may increase, decrease, or remain constant over time since the real wage is equal to the nominal wage divided by the price level. If the price level increases at a faster rate than the nominal wage increases, then the real wage will fall. If the price level increases at a slower rate than the nominal wage increases, then the real wage will rise. If the price level and the nominal wage increase (or decrease) at the same rate, then the real wage will stay constant.

8.  **Answer a.** The definition of shoe-leather costs is the increased costs of transactions caused by inflation.

9.  **Answer b.** Menu costs are the real costs of changing listed prices.

10. **Answer c.** Unit-of-account costs arise from the way inflation makes money a less reliable unit of measurement. It is hard for individuals to know what the price of a good should be relative to another good's price when prices in an economy are frequently changing.

11. **Answer c.** The nominal interest rate is a percentage: thus, answers (a) and (b) are eliminated since they are in dollar units. Mary pays Joe $110 at the end of the year: $100 is a repayment of the money ($100) that Mary borrowed and $10 is an interest payment. The nominal interest rate in this case is equal to the interest payment divided by the amount of money borrowed: or, $10/$100 = .1 or 10%.

12. **Answer b.** The real interest rate can be approximated as the nominal interest rate minus the inflation rate. Thus, the real interest rate is equal to 10% − 5% or 5%.

13. **Answer e.** Joe and Mary, when they made the contract, anticipated earning/paying a real interest rate of 5%. But, because actual inflation was only 4%, the real interest rate was 6% (real interest rate = nominal interest rate − inflation rate). Joe will earn a higher real interest rate and Mary will pay a higher real interest rate. Joe benefits when the inflation rate is lower than he anticipated while Mary is hurt when the inflation rate is lower than she anticipated.

# Measuring Inflation

## BEFORE YOU READ THE MODULE

## Summary

This module explores the calculation of the inflation rate through the construction of a price index. The module also discusses the importance of the consumer price index as well as describing a variety of other price indices.

## Module Objectives

**Objective #1.** Economists measure changes in the aggregate price level by tracking changes in the cost of buying a given market basket. A price index measures the cost of purchasing a given market basket in a given year, where that cost is normalized so that it is equal to 100 in the base year. To calculate the cost of the market basket, multiply the quantities of each good in the market basket times its price and then sum these products. Then use this information to calculate a price index by dividing the cost of the market basket for a particular time period by the cost of the market basket in the base year and then multiplying this ratio by 100. The price index for the base year is always equal to 100. An example of a price index is the consumer price index, or the CPI. The producer price index (also known as the wholesale price index), or the PPI, is another price index that measures the cost of a basket of goods typically purchased by producers. The inflation rate between two years can be calculated using this formula: Inflation rate = [(price index in year 2) – (price index in year 1)/(price index in year 1)] × 100.

**Objective #2.** Many payments are tied or "indexed" to the CPI: that is, many payments are adjusted up or down when the CPI rises or falls. For example, Social Security checks are indexed to the CPI as are income tax brackets and some wage settlements. Due to this indexing, there is concern as to whether the CPI accurately reflects changes in the aggregate price level. Some economists believe that the CPI overstates the rate of inflation due to the fact that the CPI calculation uses a fixed market basket and does not allow for the fact that consumers substitute away from relatively more expensive goods and toward relatively cheaper goods when prices change. In addition, the CPI may be biased due to the presence of innovation. Innovation, by widening the range of consumer choice, makes a given amount of money worth more and this is like a fall in consumer prices.

**Objective #3.** The GDP deflator is not a price index, but it does provide a measure of prices. The GDP deflator is calculated as the ratio of nominal GDP for that year to real GDP for that year times 100: GDP deflator = [(nominal GDP for year $n$)/(real GDP for year $n$)] × 100. The value of the GDP deflator for the base year is always equal to 100.

## Key Terms

*Notes*

**aggregate price level** a single number that represents the overall price level for *final goods and services* in the *economy*.

**market basket** a hypothetical consumption bundle of consumer purchases of goods and services, used to measure changes in overall price level.

**price index** a measure of the cost of purchasing a given *market basket* in a given year, where that cost is normalized so that it is equal to 100 in the selected base year; a measure of overall price level.

**consumer price index (CPI)** a measure of prices; calculated by surveying market prices for a *market basket* intended to represent the consumption of a typical urban American family of four. The CPI is the most commonly used measure of prices in the United States.

**producer price index (PPI)** a measure of the cost of a typical basket of goods and services purchased by producers. Because these commodity prices respond quickly to changes in demand, the PPI is often regarded as a leading indicator of changes in the *inflation rate*.

**GDP deflator** a price measure for a given year that is equal to 100 times the ratio of *nominal GDP* to *real GDP* in that year.

## ■ AFTER YOU READ THE MODULE

## Tips

**Tip #1.** To create a price index and then use it to find the inflation rate, follow these steps:

- First define the market basket of goods that will be used to create the price index.

- Collect market prices for each of the goods in the market basket over the time period in which you want to create the price index.

- Calculate the cost of the market basket in each time period.

- Define a base year and then calculate the values of the price index for each time period by finding the value of [(the cost of the market basket in the current period)/(cost of the market basket in the base period)] × 100.

- Calculate the inflation rate: the inflation rate = [(price index in current year − price index in previous year)/(price index in previous year)] × 100.

**WORKED PROBLEMS**

1.  Answer the following set of questions using this CPI information for an economy.

| Year | CPI with base year 2005 |
|------|-------------------------|
| 2008 | 100 |
| 2009 | 105 |
| 2010 | 110 |
| 2011 | 115 |

**a.** Joe's nominal income in 2009 is $100,000. What must his nominal income be in 2011 in order for his real income to be unchanged?

**STEP 1:** Examine the given data and determine what the base year is from the information that you are given.

Examination of the data indicates that 2008 is the base year, since the value of the consumer price index in the base year is always equal to 100.

**STEP 2:** Now calculate the rate of inflation between each year.

The rate of inflation can be calculated from the CPI numbers that you are given. Thus, the rate of inflation between 2008 and 2009 is equal to {[(price index for 2009) – (price index for 2008)]/(price index for 2008)} × 100, or 5%. The rate of inflation for the other years can similarly be calculated. The following table provides the inflation rates.

| Year | CPI with base year 2005 | Rate of yearly inflation |
|------|-------------------------|--------------------------|
| 2008 | 100 | |
| 2009 | 105 | 5% |
| 2010 | 110 | 4.76 |
| 2011 | 115 | 4.55 |

**STEP 3:** Calculate how much Joe's nominal income needs to change each year in order for him to have the same real purchasing power that he did in 2009.

If Joe earns $100,000 in 2009, then he will need to earn $100,000(1.0476) in 2010 to maintain the same purchasing power. Thus, in 2010, he needs to earn $104,760. If he earns $104,760 in 2010, then he will need to earn $104,760(1.0455) in 2011 to maintain the same purchasing power. Thus, in 2011, he needs to earn $109,526.

**STEP 4:** Here's an alternative method for figuring out what nominal income Joe must earn in 2011 in order to maintain the same purchasing power that he had in 2009.

Use the following formula to calculate what nominal income Joe must receive in 2011 in order to have the same purchasing power as he has in 2009: the real value of the variable = [(nominal value of the variable)/(price index)] × 100. In this example, the price index is the CPI. So, in 2009, the nominal value of Joe's income is $100,000 and the CPI is 105. We can find the real value of this income for Joe measured in the base year or 2008 dollars as follows: the real value of Joe's income measured in 2008 dollars = [($100,000)/(105)] × 100, or $95,238.

In 2011, Joe wants his real income to have the same purchasing power that he had in 2009. From our calculation, we know that this real income measured in 2008 dollars was equal to $95,238. So, let's use this information and our CPI information to solve for the nominal income Joe must get in 2011 in order to have the same command over goods and services. Thus, (real income in 2008 measured in 2008 dollars) = [(nominal income in 2011)/(CPI for 2011)] × 100, or $95,238 = [(nominal income in 2011)/(115)] × 100. Solving this equation, we get that Joe's nominal income in 2011 must equal $109,524. If you compare this nominal income with the nominal income you found in Step 3, you will see that they are very close to each other: the difference is due to rounding error.

**b.** Mike borrows $1,000 in 2009 and repays this loan in 2011. Mike pays the lender $1,060 in 2011. What is the real value of this payment in 2011 using 2008 as the base year? What nominal interest rate is Mike paying for this loan? What real interest rate is Mike paying for the loan?

**STEP 1:** Start by calculating the nominal interest rate that Mike is paying for the loan.

The nominal interest rate refers to the payment that a borrower makes in excess of the amount of the loan or principal that he or she borrowed. In this example, Mike borrowed $1,000, so he needs to repay this loan amount, or the principal amount. He also needs to compensate his lender for the use of the lender's money. So, when Mike pays the lender $1,060 a year after the loan, he is in effect making two payments: a payment of $1,000 representing the amount he borrowed, and a payment of $60 that represents the interest payment he is making. To find the nominal interest rate, you need to calculate what percentage of the loan amount the interest payment is: thus, the nominal interest rate is equal to [(the amount of money paid back – the principal)/(the principal)] × 100. The nominal interest rate is therefore equal to [(1,060 – 1,000)/1,000] × 100, or 6%.

**STEP 2:** Calculate what the real value of Mike's payment of $1,060 is, given the information you have about the CPI.

Mike's payment of $1,060 is a nominal payment. To convert this payment to a real payment, you need to use the following formula: real payment = [(nominal payment)/(CPI)] × 100. Or, real payment = ($1,060/105) × 100 = $1,009.52.

**STEP 3:** Calculate the real interest rate that Mike is paying for the loan.

The real interest rate is equal to [(the real payment made – the principal)/(the principal)] × 100. In this example, the real interest rate is equal to [(1,009.52 – 1,000)/1,000] × 100, or 0.952%. Alternatively, we can approximate the real interest rate by recalling that the real interest rate is equal to the nominal interest rate minus the rate of inflation. In this case, the rate of inflation is 5%, the nominal interest rate is 6%, and therefore the real interest rate is 1%. If you compare these two answers, you see that the approximation method provides a good estimate of the real interest rate.

**2.** You are given the following information about an economy and you are asked to calculate nominal and real GDP for 2012 and 2013 in this economy. When calculating real GDP for this economy you are asked to use 2012 prices. In addition, you are asked to calculate the growth rate in nominal GDP and real GDP during this period. Finally, you are asked to provide guidance as to which growth rate is the more accurate one to use if you are trying to ascertain how much the economy is growing.

| | 2012 | 2013 |
|---|---|---|
| Quantity of bicycles | 20 | 22 |
| Price of bicycle | $100 | $110 |
| Quantity of sweaters | 10 | 9 |
| Price of sweater | $20 | $30 |
| Quantity of hamburgers | 100 | 140 |
| Price of hamburger | $2 | $3 |

**STEP 1:** Calculate nominal GDP for these two years.

Nominal GDP is found by multiplying the price of the good in the current year times the quantity of the good in the current year and then summing these products for all the goods produced in the economy. Nominal GDP in 2012 is equal to (20 bicycles)($100 per bicycle) + (10 sweaters) ($20 per sweater) + (100 hamburgers)($2 per hamburger) = $2,400. Nominal GDP in 2013 is equal to (22 bicycles)($110 per bicycle) + (9 sweaters)($30 per sweater) + (140 hamburgers)($3 per hamburger) = $3,110.

**STEP 2:** Calculate real GDP for these two years.

Real GDP is found by multiplying the price of the good in the base year times the quantity of the good in the current year and then summing these products for all the goods produced in the economy. Real GDP in 2012 is equal to nominal GDP in 2012, since both measures are using prices from 2012 and quantities from 2012. Real GDP in 2013 is equal to the price of the good in 2012 times the quantity of the good in 2013. Real GDP in 2013 is thus calculated as (22 bicycles)($100 per bicycle) + (9 sweaters)($20 per sweater) + (140 hamburgers)($2 per hamburger) = $2,660.

**STEP 3:** Calculate the growth rate of nominal GDP and real GDP during this period.

To find the growth rate of a variable, use the following formula: [(value of the measure in the current period – value of the measure in the previous period)/(value of the measure in the previous period)] × 100. The rate of change in nominal GDP = [(3,110 – 2,400)/2,400] × 100 = 29.58%. The rate of change in real GDP = [(2,660 – 2,400)/(2,400)] × 100 = 10.83%.

**STEP 4:** Now, you need to provide guidance as to which growth rate measure is the better one if you are trying to decide how much the economy is growing. You will need to explain your answer.

Given the goal of measuring the growth in the economy, the better measure is the growth rate of real GDP. This is because nominal GDP does not distinguish whether the change in nominal GDP is due to changes in production or changes in prices. In contrast, the growth rate of real GDP removes price fluctuation by holding prices constant and then looks at what is happening to aggregate production.

3.   Belgium produces only three goods: chocolate, strawberries, and waffles. The following table gives you information about production and prices for these three goods for 2012 and 2013. You have been asked to calculate real GDP for Belgium using 2012 as the base year. In addition, you have been asked to calculate the growth rate of real GDP during this period and a measure of the GDP deflator for this period.

| | Quantity in 2012 | Price in 2012 | Quantity in 2013 | Price in 2013 |
|---|---|---|---|---|
| Units of chocolate | 20 | $3 | 30 | $4 |
| Units of strawberries | 75 | 4 | 150 | 2 |
| Units of waffles | 120 | 5 | 110 | 1 |

**STEP 1:** Calculate real GDP for 2012 and 2013 using 2012 as the base year.

Since 2012 is the base year, we know that real GDP in 2012 is the same as nominal GDP in 2012. To find this value, multiply the price of the good in 2012 times the quantity of the good, then sum these products together for all the goods produced in Belgium. Thus, real GDP in 2012 = (price of chocolate in 2012)(quantity of chocolate in 2012) + (price of strawberries in 2012) (quantity of strawberries in 2012) + (price of waffles in 2012)(quantity of waffles in 2012) = $960. Real GDP in 2013 = (price of chocolate in 2012)(quantity of chocolate in 2013) + (price of strawberries in 2012)(quantity of strawberries in 2013) + (price of waffles in 2012)(quantity of waffles in 2013) = $1,240.

**STEP 2:** Calculate the growth rate of real GDP during this period of time.

The growth rate of real GDP during this period = [(real GDP in 2013 – real GDP in 2012)/(real GDP in 2012)] × 100 = 29.17%.

**STEP 3:** Calculate the value of the GDP deflator for this period.

The GDP deflator is equal to [(real GDP)/(nominal GDP)] × 100. With 2012 as the base year, real GDP in 2012 is equivalent to nominal GDP and therefore the GDP deflator for 2012 is equal to 100. In 2013, we already know from Step 1 that real GDP is equal to $1,240. To calculate nominal GDP for 2013, multiply the quantities from 2013 by the prices from 2013: thus, nominal GDP in 2013 is equal to $530. Using this information, we can calculate the GDP deflator for 2013 as ($1,240/$530) × 100 = 2.34.

4.  In Belgium the market basket is always equal to 4 units of chocolate, 5 units of strawberries, and 2 waffles. Using the information given in Worked Problem 3, calculate the consumer price index in Belgium for 2012 and 2013 using 2012 as your base year. Use this information to calculate the consumer price index for both years and then find the rate of inflation during this period. You are also asked to provide an interpretation of the inflation rate you calculate.

**STEP 1:** This first step in calculating the consumer price index is to calculate the cost of the market basket for each year.

The cost of the market basket is equal to the sum of the product of the price of each good in the current year times the market basket quantity of each good. The cost of the market basket in 2012 is equal to (price of chocolate in 2012)(4 units of chocolate) + (price of strawberries in 2012)(5 units of strawberries) + (price of waffles in 2012)(2 waffles) = $42. The cost of the market basket in 2013 is equal to (price of chocolate in 2013)(4 units of chocolate) + (price of strawberries in 2013)(5 units of strawberries) + (price of waffles in 2013)(2 waffles) = $28.

**STEP 2:** Now, use the cost of the market baskets you calculated in Step 1 to create the consumer price index.

The consumer price index in any year is calculated as [(cost of the market basket in the current year)/(cost of the market basket in the base year)] × 100. Since 2012 is the base year, the cost of the market basket in the current year is equal to the cost of the market basket in the base year: the consumer price index for 2012 has a value of 100. The consumer price index for 2013 is equal to ($28/$42) × 100 = 67.

**STEP 3:** **Use the consumer price index you calculated in Step 2 to find the rate of inflation between 2012 and 2013. Provide an interpretation of the meaning of the inflation rate you calculate.**

The inflation rate is calculated as [(price index in 2013 − price index in 2012)/(price index in 2012)] × 100 = −33%. The negative percentage tells us that using the consumer price index to measure the inflation rate indicates that the aggregate price level has fallen between 2012 and 2013 by 33%.

# Problems and Exercises

1.  In Macro Space, the price index is based upon a market basket consisting of 10 apples, 2 pizzas, and 5 ice cream cones. You are given prices for these three items for 2011, 2012, and 2013 in the following table.

| Year | Price of apples | Price of pizzas | Price of ice cream cones |
|------|-----------------|-----------------|--------------------------|
| 2011 | $0.50 | $4.00 | $1.00 |
| 2012 | 0.52 | 3.85 | 1.10 |
| 2013 | 0.49 | 3.90 | 1.30 |

a.  Fill in the following table using year 2011 as your base year.

| Year | Cost of market basket | Price index value |
|------|-----------------------|-------------------|
| 2011 |  |  |
| 2012 |  |  |
| 2013 |  |  |

b.  Using the information you computed in part (a), what was the rate of inflation between 2011 and 2012?

c.  Using the information you computed in part (a), what was the rate of inflation between 2012 and 2013?

**d.** Fill in the following table using year 2012 as your base year.

| Year | Cost of market basket | Price index value |
|------|----------------------|-------------------|
| 2011 |                      |                   |
| 2012 |                      |                   |
| 2013 |                      |                   |

**e.** Using the information you computed in part (d), what was the rate of inflation between 2011 and 2012?

**f.** Using the information you computed in part (d), what was the rate of inflation between 2012 and 2013?

**g.** Compare your answers in parts (b) and (c) to your answers in parts (e) and (f).

**2.** Suppose that in Monrovia the consumer market basket is defined as three oranges, 6 cupcakes, and 2 quarts of milk. Furthermore suppose you have the following price information.

| Year | Price of oranges | Price of cupcakes | Price of milk |
|------|------------------|-------------------|---------------|
| 2011 | $1 per orange    | $2 per cupcake    | $2 per quart  |
| 2012 | $1 per orange    | $3 per cupcake    | $1 per quart  |
| 2013 | $2 per orange    | $4 per cupcake    | $1 per quart  |

**a.** Use the above information to complete the following table.

| | |
|------|---|
| Cost of market basket in 2011 | |
| Cost of market basket in 2012 | |
| Cost of market basket in 2013 | |

**b.** Using 2012 as the base year complete the following table. Calculate your answer to one place past the decimal.

| Year | CPI with base year 2012 |
|------|-------------------------|
| 2011 |                         |
| 2012 |                         |
| 2013 |                         |

c. Calculate the rate of inflation using the CPI you calculated in part (b) and fill in your results in the table below. Calculate the inflation rate to the nearest whole percent.

| Year | Annual Inflation Rate |
|------|----------------------|
| 2011 | — |
| 2012 | |
| 2013 | |

d. Now suppose that the base year is 2013. Complete the following table using 2013 as the base year. Calculate your answer to one place past the decimal.

| Year | CPI with base year 2013 |
|------|------------------------|
| 2011 | |
| 2012 | |
| 2013 | |

e. Calculate the rate of inflation using the CPI you calculated in part (d) and fill in your results in the table below. Calculate the inflation rate to the nearest whole percent.

| Year | Annual Inflation Rate |
|------|----------------------|
| 2011 | — |
| 2012 | |
| 2013 | |

f. Compare your results in parts (c) and (e). Does the choice of the base year alter the values you get for the annual inflation rate?

3. Consider computers and how they have changed over the last 10 years. How has innovation in computer technology made a given amount of money worth more?

## ▉ BEFORE YOU TAKE THE TEST

## Module Review Questions

Use the information in the following table to answer the next three questions.

|          | Price in 2012 | Price in 2013 |
|----------|---------------|---------------|
| Oranges  | $0.50         | $0.40         |
| Apples   | 0.25          | 0.40          |
| Bananas  | 0.40          | 0.50          |

Suppose 2012 is the base year and the market basket for purposes of constructing a price index consists of 200 oranges, 100 apples, and 100 bananas.

1.  What is the value of the price index in 2012?
    a.  1.15
    b.  100
    c.  165
    d.  190

2.  What is the value of the price index in 2013, using 2012 as the base year?
    a.  0.97
    b.  1
    c.  100
    d.  103

3.  What is the rate of inflation between 2012 and 2013 in this economy?
    a.  0%
    b.  3%
    c.  103%
    d.  67%, since two of the three prices increased between 2012 and 2013

4.  In Macroland the GDP deflator for 2013 is 105, with 2012 the base year. Real GDP in 2013 equals $210 billion; therefore, nominal GDP in 2013 equals _____ while nominal GDP in 2012 equals _____.
    a.  $220.5 billion; $200 billion
    b.  $220.5 billion; $210 billion
    c.  $200 billion; $210 billion
    d.  $200 billion; $220.5 billion

5.  To create a price index, economists track
    a.  the cost of a consumption bundle or market basket of goods and services over time.
    b.  the change in the price of a particular good that consumers consume on a regular basis.
    c.  the change in the quantity of a particular good produced over time.
    d.  changes in the rate of inflation.

Use the information in the table below to answer the next three questions.

| Year | CPI |
|------|-----|
| 2011 | 80  |
| 2012 | 100 |
| 2013 | 125 |

6.  Given the above information, what year is the base year?
    a. 2011
    b. 2012
    c. 2013
    d. The base year cannot be determined from the above information.

7.  What is the rate of inflation between 2011 and 2012?
    a. 20%
    b. 25%
    c. 80%
    d. 10%

8.  What is the rate of inflation between 2012 and 2013?
    a. 10%
    b. 20%
    c. 25%
    d. 45%

9.  The CPI is based upon
    a. prices in only the 10 largest metropolitan areas in the United States.
    b. prices found only at large box stores.
    c. weighting all goods and services that consumers buy with equal weights.
    d. None of the above statements are true statements.

10. Which of the following statements is true?
    I. The CPI may overstate the rate of inflation since it prices a constant market basket while consumers alter their consumption choices depending upon the relative prices of goods and services.
    II. Innovation makes a given amount of money worth more.
    III. The United States is the only country that calculates a CPI.
    IV. Different countries calculate the CPI but the choice of weight for each item in the CPI varies with the country.
    a. Statements I, II, and III are correct.
    b. Statements I, II, and IV are correct.
    c. Statements I and II are correct.
    d. Statements I and III are correct.
    e. Statements I and IV are correct.
    f. Statements II and III are correct.
    g. Statements II and IV are correct.

## ANSWER KEY

## Answers to Problems and Exercises

**1. a.**

| Year | Cost of market basket | Price index value |
|------|----------------------|-------------------|
| 2011 | (10)(0.5) + (2)(4) + (5)(1) = $18 | (18/18) × 100 = 100 |
| 2012 | (10)(0.52) + (2)(3.85) + (5)(1.1) = $18.4 | (18.4/18) × 100 = 102.22 |
| 2013 | (10)(0.40) + (2)(3.9) + (5)(1.3) = $19.2 | (19.2/18) × 100 = 106.67 |

**b.** The rate of inflation between 2011 and 2012 was 2.22%: [(102.22 − 100)/100] × 100 = 2.22%.

**c.** The rate of inflation between 2012 and 2013 was 4.35%: [(106.67 − 102.22)/102.22] × 100 = 4.35%.

**d.**

| Year | Cost of market basket | Price index value |
|------|----------------------|-------------------|
| 2011 | (10)(0.5) + (2)(4) + (5)(1) = $18 | (18/18.4) × 100 = 97.83 |
| 2012 | (10)(0.52) + (2)(3.85) + (5)(1.1) = 18.4 | (18.4/18.4) × 100 = 100 |
| 2013 | (10)(0.40) + (2)(3.9) + (5)(1.3) = $19.2 | (19.2/18.4) × 100 = 104.35 |

**e.** The rate of inflation between 2011 and 2012 was 2.22%: [(100 − 97.83)/97.83] × 100 = 2.22%.

**f.** The rate of inflation between 2012 and 2013 was 4.35%: [(104.35 − 100)/100] × 100 = 4.35%.

**g.** Answers (b) and (c) are the same as answers (e) and (f). This is not surprising since the choice of a base year will generate different values for the price index, but the rate of change in prices between years should be equivalent, no matter what year is chosen as the base year.

**2. a.**

| | |
|---|---|
| Cost of market basket in 2011 | $19 |
| Cost of market basket in 2012 | 23 |
| Cost of market basket in 2013 | 32 |

**b.**

| Year | CPI with base year 2012 |
|------|------------------------|
| 2011 | 82.6 |
| 2012 | 100 |
| 2013 | 139.1 |

**c.**

| Year | Annual Inflation Rate |
|------|----------------------|
| 2011 | — |
| 2012 | 21% |
| 2013 | 39 |

**d.**

| Year | CPI with base year 2013 |
|------|------------------------|
| 2011 | 59.4 |
| 2012 | 71.9 |
| 2013 | 100 |

**e.**

| Year | Annual Inflation Rate |
|------|----------------------|
| 2011 | — |
| 2012 | 21% |
| 2013 | 39 |

**f.** The annual rate of inflation is the same irrespective of which year is chosen as the base year. The price index allows us to get a consistent measure of inflation based upon comparing the cost of the market basket over time to the price of the market basket in some designated base year.

**3.** Innovation is like a decrease in the price of the good since the innovation results in the consumer getting greater value from the expenditure of a given sum of money. For example, a $1000 computer today is vastly different from a computer that cost $1000 five years ago: the newer computer has greater speed and greater memory and is clearly a much better good than the computer from five years ago even though both computers cost the same.

## Answers to Module Review Questions

**1.   Answer b.** The value of a price index in the base year is always equal to 100. To calculate a price index in general, you need to calculate the ratio of the cost of the market basket in the current year to the cost of the market basket in the base year and then multiply this ratio by 100. In this question, the ratio is equal to 1 since the cost of the two market baskets is the same, and thus the price index equals 100.

**2.   Answer d.** Calculate the value of the market basket in the base year: (200 oranges) ($0.5/orange) + (100 apples)($0.25/apple) + (100 bananas)($0.4/banana) = 165. Calculate the value of the market basket in 2013: (200 oranges)($0.4/orange) + (100 apples)($0.4/apple) + (100 bananas)($0.5/banana) = 170. Then put these two values into the following formula:

Price index = [(cost of market basket in current year)/(cost of market basket in base year)] × 100

Price index = [(170)/(165)] × 100 = 103

Note that the market basket stays fixed when calculating a price index.

**3.   Answer b.** To calculate the inflation rate between two time periods, you need the price index for each time period. Then, use the following formula:

Inflation rate = [(price index in period 2 − price index in period 1)/(price index in period 1)] × 100

In this case,

Inflation rate = [(103 − 100)/100] × 100 = 3%

4.  **Answer a.** To answer this question, it is helpful to first organize the information you are given in a table.

| Year | GDP deflator | Nominal GDP | Real GDP |
|------|-------------|-------------|----------|
| 2012 | 100 | | |
| 2013 | 105 | | $210 billion |

We know that in the base year nominal GDP equals real GDP, but we still need to calculate this value. We can calculate this value using the formula:

Price index in 2013 = [(real GDP in 2013)/(real GDP in base year)] × 100

Or, in this case

105 = [($210 billion)/(real GDP in base year)] × 100

or

Real GDP in base year = $200 billion

To calculate nominal GDP in 2013, we use the formula for the GDP deflator:

Price index in 2013 = [(nominal GDP in 2013)/(real GDP in 2013)] × 100

Rearranging the formula we have

Real GDP in 2013 = [(nominal GDP in 2013)/(price index in 2013)] × 100

or

$210 billion = [(nominal GDP in 2013)/105] × 100

or

Nominal GDP in 2013 = $220.5 billion

Our completed table is

| Year | GDP deflator | Nominal GDP | Real GDP |
|------|-------------|-------------|----------|
| 2012 | 100 | $200 billion | $200 billion |
| 2013 | 105 | 220.5 billion | 210 billion |

5.  **Answer a.** A price index is based upon measuring the cost of a set of goods and then repeatedly measuring the cost of this same set of goods at periodic points in time. A price index uses the price of more than one good and it holds constant the quantities of the goods and services it includes in the market basket or consumption bundle. Once a price index is created, it can be used to calculate the rate of inflation.

6.  **Answer b.** The base year is 2012 since the value of the CPI is equal to 100 in this year. To see this, remember that the price index for a year is equal to [(cost of the market basket in the current year)/(cost of the basket market in the base year)] × 100. For the CPI to be equal to 100, it must be the case that the cost of the market basket in the current year is equal to the cost of the market basket in the base year.

7.  **Answer b.** To find the inflation rate, remember that this is equal to the [(CPI for the current year − CPI for the previous year)/(CPI for the previous year)] × 100. So, [(100 − 80)/80] × 100 = 25%.

8.  **Answer c.** Inflation rate = [(125 − 100)/100] × 100 = 25%.

9.  **Answer d.** The CPI is based upon gathering prices from 23,000 retail outlets in 87 cities. Prices are gathered from all sorts of different kinds of stores and not just from large box stores. Items in the CPI are given different weights: for example, housing accounts for 43% of the CPI market basket while apparel accounts for 4%.

10. **Answer b.** Consumers do substitute away from relatively more expensive goods toward relatively cheaper goods, while the CPI is based upon a constant market basket of goods and services. When there is innovation, this is like a fall in consumer prices since each dollar spent now buys a better product than it did prior to the innovation. Many countries calculate a CPI, but each country assigns different weights to the goods and services they include in their CPI.

# module 17 (53)

# Long-Run Economic Growth

## BEFORE YOU READ THE MODULE

## Summary

This module focuses on long-run economic growth and its sources. Long-run economic growth can be measured as the change in real GDP per capita over time. Comparison of real GDP per capita for different countries reveals different economic growth experiences: some countries have experienced rapid economic growth over time, while other countries have been much less fortunate. Long-run economic growth depends on productivity, which depends on physical capital, human capital, and technological progress.

## Module Objectives

**Objective #1.** Real GDP per capita provides a measure of economic growth. This measure calculates the value of final goods and services produced in an economy in a given time period divided by the population of that economy.

**Objective #2.** When computing how long it takes real GDP per capita, or any other variable that grows slowly over time, the rule of 70 is useful. This rule states that the number of years it takes a variable to double is approximately equal to 70 divided by the annual growth rate of the variable.

**Objective #3.** Long-run economic growth depends almost exclusively on increases in output per worker, or labor productivity. For the aggregate economy, we can measure labor productivity as real GDP divided by the number of people working. Increases in labor productivity are due to increases in physical capital, human capital, or changes in technology.

- Physical capital refers to manmade resources such as buildings and machines.

- Human capital refers to the improvement in labor created by education and knowledge.

- Technology refers to the technical means of producing goods and services.

## Key Terms

**rule of 70** a mathematical formula that states that the time it takes *real GDP* per capita, or any other variable that grows gradually over time, to double is approximately 70 divided by that variable's annual growth rate.

**labor productivity** output per worker; also referred to as simply *productivity*. Increases in labor productivity are the only source of *long-run economic growth*.

**productivity** output per worker; a shortened form of the term *labor productivity*.

**physical capital** manufactured resources, such as buildings and machines.

**human capital** the improvement in labor created by the education and knowledge embodied in the workforce.

**technological progress** an advance in the technical means of the production of goods and services.

## ■ AFTER YOU READ THE MODULE

## Tips

**Tip #1.** Real GDP per capita is a key statistic for measuring economic growth. Real GDP and not nominal GDP is used to measure economic growth since real GDP focuses on the increase in the quantity of goods and services being produced and not on the effects of an increase in the aggregate price level. Real GDP per capita provides a measure of the average standard of living in a country.

**Tip #2.** Familiarize yourself with the rule of 70 and how to apply it. The rule of 70 provides a simple mathematical formula for estimating the amount of time it takes a variable that grows gradually over time to double. The rule of 70 states that the number of years it takes for a variable to approximately double is equal to 70 divided by the annual growth rate of the variable.

**Tip #3.** It is important to understand and know the sources of long-run economic growth. Economic growth arises because of increases in productivity, or output per worker. This increase in productivity is due to increases in human capital per worker, physical capital per worker, and/or technological advance.

# WORKED PROBLEMS

1. Suppose that a country in 2010 has a GDP per capita that is equal to $20,000. Furthermore, suppose that GDP grows by 10% a year and that population holds steady at its current level. Using the rule of 70, in what year will this economy's GDP per capita quadruple? If the country's GDP grew by 5% a year, in what year would this economy's GDP quadruple? Does the growth rate of an economy's GDP matter?

**STEP 1:** Start by reviewing the rule of 70.

The rule of 70 states that the number of years it takes a variable to double is approximately equal to 70 divided by the annual growth rate of the variable. If the growth rate is 10% a year, then it will take approximately 7 years for the variable to double and 14 years for the variable to quadruple. Therefore, GDP per capita in this economy will be approximately $40,000 in 2017 and approximately $80,000 in 2024.

**STEP 2:** Complete a similar calculation, but this time assume that the growth rate of GDP per year is 5%.

When GDP grows by 5% a year, the rule of 70 predicts that it will take approximately 14 years for GDP to double. Thus, GDP per capita in this economy will be approximately $40,000 in 2024 and approximately $80,000 in 2038.

**STEP 3:** Discuss why the growth rate of GDP in an economy matters.

An economy's growth rate of GDP, considered along with its population growth rate, determines the rate of growth in GDP per capita. Holding everything else constant, when an economy grows at a faster rate, the implication is that GDP per capita will increase by a faster rate: on average, living standards will improve.

2. You recently went to a lecture on economic growth where the speaker, a noted expert, stressed the importance of increases in human capital, as well as increases in physical capital. The speaker then asserted that the most important factor determining the rate of economic growth is technological improvement. Comment on how changes in each of these factors improve an economy's ability to produce goods and services.

**STEP 1:** Discuss what improvements in human capital mean and how an improvement in human capital affects an economy's growth rate.

Improvements in human capital refer to changes in the labor force that reflect education and knowledge. The more educated and knowledgeable the workforce is, the greater the ability of this workforce to produce goods and services from a given amount of resources. As human capital increases, labor becomes more productive and real GDP increases.

**STEP 2:** Discuss what improvements in physical capital mean and how an improvement in physical capital affects an economy's growth rate.

Improvements in physical capital refer to increases in manufactured resources such as buildings and machines. When there are improvements in physical capital, workers are more productive, and this enables a given amount of labor to produce a greater amount of output. As physical capital increases, this increases the rate of economic growth possible in an economy.

**STEP 3:** Discuss what improvements in technology mean and how an improvement in technology affects an economy's growth rate.

Improvement in technology is broadly defined as improvement in the technical means for the production of goods and services. When technology improves, this implies that labor is more productive and that the economic growth rate in an economy increases.

3.    You are given the following information about Productiva and Macrostan. You are asked to compute and then compare labor productivity for both countries as well as GDP per capita for both countries.

| Country | Population | Employment | Output (Real GDP) |
|---------|-----------|------------|-------------------|
| Productiva | 80 million | 40 million | $300 billion |
| Macrostan | 60 million | 30 million | 200 billion |

**STEP 1:** Compute labor productivity for both countries.

Labor productivity is defined as output per worker. For this example, output is measured as real GDP and the number of workers is given by the employment figures. Thus, labor productivity in Productiva is equal to ($300 billion)/(40 million workers), or $7,500 per worker. Labor productivity in Macrostan is equal to ($200 billion)/(30 million workers), or $6,667 per worker.

**STEP 2:** Compute GDP per capita for both countries.

GDP per capita in a country is equal to the country's GDP divided by the country's population. Thus, GDP per capita in Productiva is equal to ($300 billion)/(80 million people), or $3,750 per person. GDP per capita in Macrostan is equal to ($200 billion)/(60 million people), or $3,333 per person.

**STEP 3:** Compare the labor productivity and GDP per capita for these two countries.

Productiva has higher labor productivity and higher GDP per capita than does Macrostan.

# Problems and Exercises

1. You are given the following information about the country of Macronesia.

| Year | Nominal GDP | CPI | Real GDP | Population |
|------|-------------|-----|----------|-----------|
| 2011 | $10 billion | 100 | | 1 million |
| 2012 | 10.5 billion | 105 | | 1.05 million |
| 2013 | 11 billion | 108 | | 1.08 million |

a. What is the base year for the economy represented in the previous table? How did you identify the base year?

b. Calculate the missing values in the table. Calculate the missing value and then round to the nearest thousand million: e.g., 14,829,000,000 would be rounded to 14.8 billion.

c. Use the completed table from part (b) to calculate the missing values in the following table. You will find it helpful to define real GDP in millions (for example, 14.8 billion is 14,800 million), since population is expressed in millions.

| Year | Real GDP per capita |
|------|---------------------|
| 2011 | |
| 2012 | |
| 2013 | |

d. Let's compare the percentage changes in some of the variables we are working with in this problem. Use the following table to organize your calculations.

| Year | Percentage change in nominal GDP | Percentage change in real GDP | Percentage change in population | Percentage change in real GDP per capita |
|------|----------------------------------|-------------------------------|---------------------------------|------------------------------------------|
| 2011 | | | | |
| 2012 | | | | |
| 2013 | | | | |

e. In order for real GDP per capita to increase over time, what must be true about the relationship between the percentage change in real GDP and the percentage change in population?

f. Why do we focus on computing real GDP per capita instead of nominal GDP per capita?

2.   Suppose real GDP per capita in Fun Land is $10,000 in 2014. Fun Land economists pre-dict steady increases in real GDP of 7% a year for the foreseeable future.

   a.   According to the rule of 70, how many years will it take for Fun Land's real GDP per capita to double?

   b.   To verify your answer in part (a), compute the values for real GDP per capita in the following table.

| Year | Real GDP per capita |
|------|---------------------|
| 2014 | $10,000 |
| 2015 | |
| 2016 | |
| 2017 | |
| 2018 | |
| 2019 | |
| 2020 | |
| 2021 | |
| 2022 | |
| 2023 | |
| 2024 | |

   c.   Is your value for real GDP per capita for 2024 equal to $20,000? If it differs, does this surprise you? Explain your answer.

3.   Suppose there are two countries, Macroland and Pacifica, that currently have real GDP per capita of $10,000 and $15,000, respectively. Furthermore, suppose Macroland's economy has an average annual growth rate of 2%, while Pacifica has an average annual growth rate of 1.4%.

   a.   Compute real GDP per capita for both Macroland and Pacifica 50 years from now.

   b.   Compute real GDP per capita for both Macroland and Pacifica 100 years from now.

   c.   Initially, Macroland's real GDP per capita is 67% of Pacifica's real GDP per capita. After 50 years, what is the relationship of Macroland's real GDP per capita to Pacifica's real GDP per capita in percentage terms? What is this relationship after 100 years?

## ▊ BEFORE YOU TAKE THE TEST

# Module Review Questions

1.  Real GDP per capita is
    a. the value of real GDP divided by the number of units of capital in an economy in a given time period.
    b. always increasing over time for any given economy.
    c. the value of real GDP divided by population for a given country.
    d. Answers (b) and (c) are both correct.

2.  Suppose real GDP for Macronesia is $200 million in 2008. Furthermore, suppose population in Macronesia is 100,000 in 2008. If population increases to 105,000 in 2009 while GDP increases by 5%, then it must be true that real GDP per capita in Macronesia in 2009
    a. increased.
    b. decreased.
    c. stayed constant.
    d. may have increased, decreased, or remained constant.

3.  Suppose that real GDP per capita grows at 2% per year. How many years will it take for real GDP per capita to approximately double? It will take:
    a. 70 years because of the rule of 70.
    b. 140 years, because the rule of 70 states that a variable will double in 70 years if the variable has an annual growth rate of 1%; therefore, a variable growing at 2% will take twice as long to double.
    c. 35 years, because the rule of 70 states that the number of years it takes for a variable to double is equal to 70 divided by the annual growth rate of the variable.
    d. 50 years, since at 2% per year it takes 50 years to reach 100% more than the initial real GDP per capita.

4.  Which of the following has been most important in driving long-run economic growth?
    a. rising labor productivity or output per worker
    b. putting more people to work
    c. being a relatively rich country initially
    d. the availability of abundant natural resources

5.  Productivity increases can be attributed to
    a. increases in physical capital or the amount of machinery and office space available to workers.
    b. increases in human capital or the level of workers' education.
    c. technological advances.
    d. Answers (a), (b), and (c) are all correct.

6. Suppose that real GDP per capita in an economy doubles in 10 years. Using the rule of 70, the average growth rate of real GDP for this economy is approximately

   a. 70%.

   b. 0.7%.

   c. 7%.

   d. 1.43%.

### ANSWER KEY

## Answers to Problems and Exercises

1. **a.** 2011. The base year is that year with the CPI value of 100.

   **b.**

   | Year | Nominal GDP | CPI | Real GDP | Population |
   |------|-------------|-----|----------|-----------|
   | 2011 | $10 billion | 100 | $10 billion | 1 million |
   | 2012 | 10.5 billion | 105 | 10 billion | 1.05 million |
   | 2013 | 11 billion | 108 | 10.19 billion | 1.08 million |

   **c.**

   | Year | Real GDP per capita |
   |------|---------------------|
   | 2011 | $10,000 |
   | 2012 | 9,524 |
   | 2013 | 9,435 |

   **d.**

   | Year | Percentage change in nominal GDP | Percentage change in real GDP | Percentage change in population | Percentage change in real GDP per capita |
   |------|----------------------------------|-------------------------------|---------------------------------|------------------------------------------|
   | 2011 | — | — | — | — |
   | 2012 | 5% | 0% | 5% | −4.8% |
   | 2013 | 4.8 | 1.9 | 2.9 | −0.93 |

   **e.** The percentage change in real GDP must be greater than the percentage change in population for real GDP per capita to increase over time.

   **f.** Real GDP per capita allows us to track the increase in the quantity of goods and services available in our economy rather than just the effects of a rising price level.

2.   **a.** Ten years, since the rule of 70 says the number of years it takes for a variable to double is approximately equal to 70 divided by the annual growth rate of the variable.

**b.**

| Year | Real GDP per capita |
|------|---------------------|
| 2014 | $10,000 |
| 2015 | 10,700 |
| 2016 | 11,449 |
| 2017 | 12,250 |
| 2018 | 13,108 |
| 2019 | 14,026 |
| 2020 | 15,007 |
| 2021 | 16,058 |
| 2022 | 17,182 |
| 2023 | 18,385 |
| 2024 | 19,672 |

**c.** The value of real GDP per capita for 2014 is $19,672, which is less than the estimated $20,000. This is not surprising since the rule of 70 is an estimation of the number of years it takes a variable to double rather than a numerically precise calculation.

3.   **a.** Real GDP per capita in Macroland in 50 years will equal $(\$10,000)(1 + 0.02)^{50}$, or $26,916. Real GDP per capita in Pacifica in 50 years will equal $(\$15,000)(1 + 0.014)^{50}$, or $30,060.

**b.** Real GDP per capita in Macroland in 100 years will equal $(\$10,000)(1 + 0.02)^{100}$, or $72,446. Real GDP per capita in Pacifica in 100 years will equal $(\$15,000)(1 + 0.014)^{100}$, or $60,240.

**c.** In 50 years, Macroland's real GDP per capita to Pacifica's real GDP per capita in percentage terms is 89.5%, while in 100 years, it is 120.3%.

# Answers to Module Review Questions

1.   **Answer c.** Real GDP per capita is defined as the value of real GDP in a country divided by that country's population. Real GDP per capita may increase, decrease, or remain steady over time.

2.   **Answer c.** In 2009, the population in Macronesia increased by 5% as did real GDP. Since both population and real GDP increased by the same percentage amount, real GDP per capita is unaffected.

3.   **Answer c.** This is a straightforward use of the definition of the rule of 70: this rule states that an estimation of the number of years it takes for a variable to double is equal to 70 divided by the annual growth rate of the variable.

4.   **Answer a.** Sustained economic growth occurs only when an economy steadily increases the amount of output each worker produces: in other words, long-run economic growth depends upon rising labor productivity. Putting more people to work can increase output in the short run, but it does not result in sustained economic growth. Long-run economic growth is possible in relatively poor countries (for example, South Korea before 1970) and countries endowed with low levels of resources (for example, Japan).

5.   **Answer d.** Each of these reasons—physical capital, human capital, and technological advances—contributes to increases in productivity, or the ability to produce more output per worker.

6.   **Answer c.** The rule of 70 says that the number of years for a variable to double is approximately equal to 70 divided by the annual growth rate of that variable. Hence, if the real GDP per capita in an economy doubles in 10 years, then the annual growth rate of that variable must equal 70/10, or 7%.

# module 18 (54)

# Productivity and Growth

## BEFORE YOU READ THE MODULE

## Summary

This module develops the aggregate production function and then uses it to illustrate changes in productivity. The module also discusses the challenges to growth posed by limited natural resources, as well as efforts to make growth sustainable.

## Module Objectives

**Objective #1.** The aggregate production function is a mathematical equation describing the relationship between the level of output per worker (productivity) and the amount of human capital per worker, physical capital per worker, and the state of technology. The aggregate production function exhibits diminishing returns to physical capital: holding the level of human capital per worker and the state of technology constant, increases in physical capital per worker eventually increase output per worker by smaller and smaller amounts. That is, as the quantity of physical capital per worker increases, holding everything else constant, the growth rate of productivity will fall but remain positive. Figure 18.1 illustrates an aggregate production function. This function is drawn with a given amount of labor, human capital per worker, and technology, and it shows the relationship between physical capital per worker and real GDP per worker.

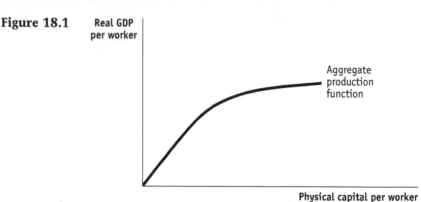

Figure 18.1

Real GDP per worker

Aggregate production function

Physical capital per worker

Notice that real GDP per worker eventually increases at a decreasing rate as physical capital per worker is increased. An increase in technology, the amount of labor, or the level of human capital will cause the aggregate production function to shift upward. Figure 18.2 illustrates the shift that occurs if there is an increase in one of these variables. The aggregate production function shifts upward whenever productivity is raised. This may be due to an increase in technology or an increase in human capital per worker.

**Figure 18.2**

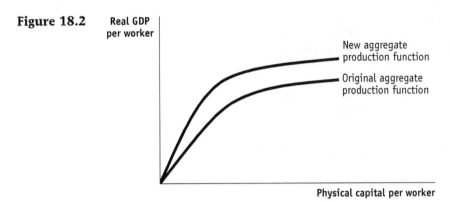

**Objective #2.** Growth accounting estimates the contribution of each major factor—physical capital per worker, human capital per worker, and the state of technology-to-economic growth. Total factor productivity is the amount of output that can be produced from a given set of factor inputs. When total factor productivity increases, the economy can produce a high level of output from a given amount of physical capital, human capital, and labor. Technological change results in increases in total factor productivity: technological change is crucial for economic growth.

**Objective #3.** There is debate about the sustainability of economic growth because of the scarcity of natural resources and the impact of economic growth on the environment. Economists are optimistic about the ability of economies to continue to grow despite resource scarcity because they believe that increases in the price of these resources will provide strong incentives to conserve them, as well as to find alternatives to them. Economists recognize that economic growth may be threatened by environmental damage and that the problem of addressing such damage is a difficult one, since it requires effective political action.

**Objective #4.** Environmental damage from production often represents a negative externality, a situation in which individuals or firms impose costs on others without offering compensation for these costs. Without government intervention, these negative externalities will continue. Effective government intervention is necessary to eliminate or reduce negative externalities. In the case of climate change, the government can implement a set of market-based incentives, like a "carbon tax" or a "cap and trade" system in order to provide incentives for firms to reduce the amount of greenhouse gases they emit into the environment.

## Key Terms

**aggregate production function** a hypothetical function that shows how productivity (*real GDP* per worker) depends on the quantities of *physical capital* per worker and *human capital* per worker as well as the state of technology.

**diminishing returns to physical capital** in an *aggregate production function* when the amount of *human capital* per worker and the state of technology are held fixed, each successive increase in the amount of *physical capital* per worker leads to a smaller increase in productivity.

**growth accounting** estimates the contribution of each of the major factors (physical and human capital, labor, and technology) in the *aggregate production function*.

**total factor productivity** the amount of output that can be produced with a given amount of factor inputs.

**sustainable long-run economic growth** long-run growth that can continue in the face of the limited supply of natural resources and the impact of growth on the environment.

## ▮ AFTER YOU READ THE MODULE

## Tips

**Tip #1.** Productivity increases when physical capital per worker, human capital per worker, or technology increases. Increases in productivity are the primary source of economic growth over time. It is important to understand what productivity is and how an economy's productivity can be improved. You should make sure you understand what an aggregate production function is and how it illustrates the relationship between productivity and the variables that determine productivity.

**Tip #2.** The concept of diminishing returns to physical capital is important. Holding everything else constant, an increase in physical capital per worker will eventually lead to smaller increases in productivity. Adding additional physical capital to a fixed level of labor and technology initially increases output at an increasing rate, but eventually each successive addition to physical capital per worker produces a smaller increase in output per worker.

1. The following graph depicts the aggregate production function for Macroland. This aggregate production function has been drawn holding the level of physical capital and technology in Macroland fixed. Currently, Macroland employs 200 units of labor per year. The graph indicates this level of labor usage and the level of real GDP that can be produced when 200 units of labor are employed. Holding everything else constant, what will happen to real GDP in Macroland if 400 units of labor are employed? What will happen to labor productivity when labor usage increases? Suppose that at the same time that Macroland increases its use of labor to 400 units, it simultaneously experiences a technological advance. How will this alter the following graph, and how will it affect the level of real GDP produced in Macroland and labor productivity?

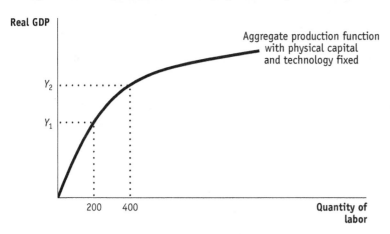

**STEP 1:** First describe the effect on real GDP of increasing the use of labor from 200 units to 400 units.

When this economy increases its employment of labor from 200 units to 400 units, this leads to an increase in real GDP from $Y_1$ to $Y_2$. With more labor employed, the economy can produce more goods and services than it could when it employed a smaller amount of labor.

**STEP 2:** Now think about what happens to labor productivity as the level of labor usage increases, holding everything else constant.

Labor productivity is defined as output per worker. In the graph, we can see that as labor usage increases from 200 units to 400 units, output increases. But from the graph, we can also see that although output increases as labor usage increases, it does so at a diminishing rate. This is due to the fact that capital and technology are being held constant: as more and more units of labor are employed, each additional unit of labor will be less productive due to the growing scarcity of capital for labor to use (since capital is fixed, the amount of capital available is not increasing as the amount of labor is increased). Thus, although both output and labor increase, output increases by a smaller proportion than does labor: labor productivity decreases.

**STEP 3:** Consider the effect of a change in technology holding the use of labor constant at 200 units and the effect of this change on real GDP and labor productivity. Now think about the effect of this change in technology on real GDP and labor productivity if labor simultaneously increases to 400 units.

If technology increases, this will cause the aggregate production function to shift upward at every level of labor usage, since this improvement in technology will allow the economy to produce a larger amount of goods and services (real GDP increases) from the available labor and capital. If technology changes and labor and capital are held constant, this will cause labor productivity to rise since each unit of labor can now produce more than it could before the technological change.

If technology improves and the amount of labor employed simultaneously increases to 400 units, real GDP will increase, but the effect of these two changes on labor productivity is impossible to calculate without quantitative information about the size of the shift in the aggregate production function due to the change in technology. Labor productivity may increase, decrease, or remain the same depending upon whether real GDP increases by a greater proportionate amount than does labor, it increases by a smaller proportionate amount than does labor, or it increases by the same proportionate amount as does labor.

**STEP 4:** Illustrate the changes in the above graph of this increase in technology and labor usage. Discuss the effect of these two changes on real GDP and labor productivity.

From Step 3 we know that an increase in technology will shift the aggregate production function upward. We also know from Step 3 that when technology improves and there is an increase in the amount of labor used, this leads to a situation where labor productivity may increase, decrease, or remain the same. The two graphs provided depict two possible scenarios: the first graph illustrates the case of increasing labor productivity, while the second graph illustrates the case of decreasing labor productivity.

2.  Suppose that a country's aggregate production function can be described by the equation

$$Y = 10K^{1/2} L^{1/2}$$

where $Y$ is real GDP, $K$ is units of capital, and $L$ is units of labor. Furthermore, suppose this economy initially has 100 units of capital. You are asked to describe what happens to the level of real GDP as labor usage increases from 4 units to 100 units. You are also asked to evaluate the impact on this country's real GDP of an increase in the amount of capital available from 100 units to 144 units.

**STEP 1:** **Start by analyzing the impact of a constant amount of capital equal to 100 units on this country's aggregate production function.**

In the equation given for the aggregate production function we see that we are asked to take the square root of capital ($K^{1/2}$): in this example, if capital is equal to 100 units, then the square root of 100 is 10. Thus, the aggregate production function can be rewritten as $Y = 10(10)\ 10L^{1/2}$ or $Y = 100L^{1/2}$. To calculate the level of production of real GDP in this economy we must know the level of labor that is employed: from the equation it is easy to see that $Y$ will get larger as the level of labor usage increases. In our next steps we will analyze this a bit more.

**STEP 2:** **Analyze the impact of using 4 units of labor on this country's aggregate production function. Then analyze the impact of using more units of labor, including a total of 100 units of labor. Describe the relationship between this country's aggregate production or real GDP and its use of labor.**

Building on our work in Step 1 we need only substitute $L = 4$ into our equation to find when labor usage is four units real GDP equals 200. As we increase our use of labor we should find that real GDP increases: thus, when labor is equal to 9 units (this is a number for which it is easy to take the square root) we find that real GDP is 300; when labor is equal to 16 units we find that real GDP is 400; and when labor is equal to 100 units we find that real GDP is equal to 1000. But note that as we use more and more labor real GDP increases, but it increases at a decreasing rate. To see this, think about increasing labor usage from 4 units to 9 units, an increase of 5 units: this results in an increase in real GDP from 200 to 300. But when you increase labor usage from 81 units to 100 units, an increase of 19 units, this results in an increase in real GDP from 900 to 1,000. As this country increases its labor usage, output increases but as it hires more and more labor to work with its fixed level of capital it finds that its real GDP increases at a decreasing rate.

**STEP 3:** **Now, analyze the impact of increasing the amount of capital available in this country from 100 units to 144 units.**

If this country increases its level of capital to 144 units, we can rewrite its aggregate production function as $Y = 120\ L^{1/2}$. At every level of labor usage, this country's real GDP will increase now that it has more capital to employ in producing output. Thus, when the country uses 4 units of labor, its real GDP is now 240; when it uses 9 units of labor, its real GDP is 360; and when it uses 100 units of labor, its real GDP is 1,200.

# Problems and Exercises

1.  The economy of Freeland estimates its aggregate production function as

    $$Y/L = 20(K/L)^{1/2}$$

    where $Y/L$ is real GDP per worker and $K/L$ is physical capital per worker. In Freeland's economy, technology and human capital per worker are held constant. Suppose that Freeland has 100 workers.

    **a.** Calculate real GDP per worker ($Y/L$) and physical capital per worker ($K/L$) of the given levels of physical capital in the following table. Round ($K/L$) to the nearest hundredth and ($Y/L$) to the nearest whole number.

    | K | K/L | Y/L |
    |---|-----|-----|
    | 0 | | |
    | 500 | | |
    | 1,000 | | |
    | 1,500 | | |
    | 2,000 | | |

    **b.** On the graph below draw Freeland's aggregate production function with physical capital per worker measured on the *x*-axis and real GDP per worker measured on the *y*-axis.

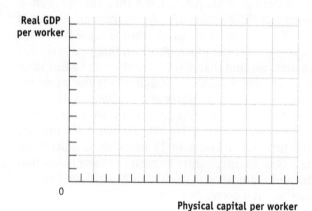

    **c.** Suppose that the aggregate production function changes to

    $$Y/L = 40(K/L)^{1/2}$$

    Describe how this change in the aggregate production function will affect the productivity curve.

2. The economy of Macro States estimates its aggregate production function as

$$Y/L = 50(K/L)^{1/2}$$

when technology and human capital per worker are held constant. In the equation $Y$ is real GDP, $L$ is the number of workers, and $K$ is the quantity of physical capital. Macro States has 500 workers.

a. Calculate real GDP per worker $(Y/L)$ and physical capital per worker $(K/L)$ for the given levels of physical capital in the following table. Round both $(K/L)$ and $(Y/L)$ to the nearest hundredth.

| K | K/L | Y/L |
|-----|-----|-----|
| 0 | | |
| 20 | | |
| 40 | | |
| 60 | | |
| 80 | | |
| 100 | | |
| 200 | | |
| 400 | | |

b. Plot Macro States' aggregate production function on the following graph, where physical capital per worker is measured on the x-axis and real GDP per worker is measured on the y-axis.

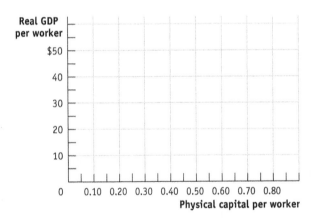

c. As physical capital per worker increases, what happens to real GDP per worker?

3. Suppose that Macro States increases its level of technology and human capital per worker relative to its economic condition in problem 2. Now, Macro States' economists estimate that the aggregate production function for Macro States is given by the equation

$$Y/L = 60(K/L)^{1/2}$$

a. Relative to the aggregate production function you plotted in problem 2b, what do you anticipate will happen to Macro States' aggregate production function because of this increase in human capital per worker and technology?

b. Compare productivity in Macro States in the initial situation to its new situation, assuming that Macro States has $100 worth of physical capital.

c. Why are increases in productivity important?

4. Many people worry that the world may run out of important resources like oil and that this depletion of a vital resource will bring an end to economic growth. Why do many economists *not* believe in this particular perspective?

5. Economists argue that the problems presented by widespread climate destruction can only be resolved through government intervention as well as cooperation among different governments. Why do they hold this view?

## ▮ BEFORE YOU TAKE THE TEST

# Module Review Questions

1. Which of the following statements is true?

    a. An aggregate production function indicates how output per worker depends on the level of physical capital per worker, human capital per worker, and the state of technology.

    b. Holding everything else constant, an increase in human capital per worker reduces the level of output per worker.

    c. Holding everything else constant, a decrease in physical capital per worker increases the level of output per worker.

    d. Answers (a), (b), and (c) are all true.

2. Holding human capital per worker, the number of workers, and the level of technology constant, suppose an economy increases the amount of physical capital per worker. In this economy, output per worker will

    a. initially increase at a diminishing rate but will eventually increase at an increasing rate as the economy uses greater amounts of physical capital per worker.

    b. eventually lead to output per worker increasing at a diminishing rate.

    c. eventually lead to output per worker increasing at an increasing rate.

    d. eventually lead to output per worker staying constant at the potential output level for the economy.

3. Growth accounting

    a. estimates the effect of a change in physical capital per worker on real GDP per worker.

    b. estimates the effect of a change in human capital per worker on real GDP per worker.

    c. estimates the effect of a change in the growth rate of real GDP per worker on a country's average standard of living.

    d. estimates the contribution of each major factor in the aggregate production function to economic growth.

4. Suppose that the amount of human capital per worker grows by 6% a year in Myland. Furthermore, suppose that estimates of the aggregate production function in Myland show that for each 1% increase in human capital per worker, holding physical capital per worker and technology constant, output per worker increases by 0.5 of 1%. What is your estimate of the effect of this growing human capital per worker on the productivity growth per year in Myland? The growth in human capital per worker in Myland accounts for approximately

    a. 6% of productivity growth per year.

    b. 0.5% of productivity growth per year.

    c. 3% of productivity growth per year.

    d. 30% of productivity growth per year.

5. When total factor productivity increases, the implication is that
   a. the economy can produce the same amount of output with a greater quantity of physical capital, human capital, and labor.
   b. the economy can produce the same amount of output with a smaller quantity of physical capital, human capital, and labor.
   c. the economy can produce a greater amount of output with a greater quantity of physical capital, human capital, and labor.
   d. each factor's productivity increases by the same amount.

6. Natural resources in the modern world are
   a. less important in determining productivity than human or physical capital for the majority of countries.
   b. more important in determining productivity than human or physical capital for the majority of countries.

7. Which of the following statements is true?
   a. An aggregate production function indicates how output per worker depends on the level of physical capital per worker, human capital per worker, and the state of technology.
   b. Holding everything else constant, an increase in human capital per worker reduces the level of output per worker.
   c. Holding everything else constant, a decrease in physical capital per worker increases the level of output per worker.
   d. Answers (a), (b), and (c) are all true.

8. Suppose the amount of human capital per worker and the state of technology are held constant. As physical capital per worker increases, each additional increase in physical capital per worker leads to
   a. greater increases in output per worker.
   b. greater decreases in output per worker.
   c. smaller increases in output per worker.
   d. smaller decreases in output per worker.

Use the following information to answer the next two questions.

An economy initially has 100 units of physical capital per worker. Each year it increases the amount of physical capital by 5%. According to the aggregate production function for this economy, each 1% increase in physical capital per worker, holding human capital and technology constant, increases output per worker by 1/5th of 1%, or 0.20%.

9. In two years time, what is the level of physical capital per worker in this economy?
   a. 110 units of physical capital per worker
   b. 105 units of physical capital per worker
   c. 110.25 units of physical capital per worker
   d. 210 units of physical capital per worker

10. Suppose output per worker is initially $1,000. After one year, what does estimated output per worker equal? Assume there is no inflation in this economy: real GDP equals nominal GDP.
    a. $1,000
    b. $1,001
    c. $1,010
    d. $1,100

11. Resource scarcity
    a. is inevitable and will lead to reduced economic growth.
    b. will result in price increases for those scarce resources, and these price increases will provide incentives to conserve them and to find alternatives to them.

12. Environmental damage from economic growth
    a. is of no great consequence and can easily be remedied through market forces.
    b. may lead to climate change, and this environmental damage can only be reduced by concerted government intervention to provide incentives for businesses and individuals to reduce environmentally degrading activities.
    c. can be remedied through the appropriate use of "carbon taxes" or "cap and trade" systems for carbon emissions.
    d. Answers (b) and (c) are both correct.

## ▮ ANSWER KEY

# Answers to Problems and Exercises

**1. a.**

| K | K/L | Y/L |
|---|-----|-----|
| 0 | — | — |
| 500 | 1 | 20 |
| 1,000 | 2 | 28 |
| 1,500 | 3 | 35 |
| 2,000 | 4 | 40 |

**b.**

**c.** The productivity curve will shift up at every level of physical capital/worker. For instance, when physical capital is initially 500 units and labor is 500 units, the physical capital/worker is equal to 1 and the output per worker is equal to 20 units. But, with the new aggregate production function, the same physical capital per worker ratio is now able to produce 40 units of output. This same effect would be true at each physical capital per worker ratio.

**2. a.**

| K | K/L | Y/L |
|---|-----|-----|
| 0 | 0 | 0 |
| 20 | 0.04 | 10.00 |
| 40 | 0.08 | 14.14 |
| 60 | 0.12 | 17.32 |
| 80 | 0.16 | 20.00 |
| 100 | 0.20 | 22.36 |
| 200 | 0.40 | 31.62 |
| 400 | 0.80 | 44.72 |

**b.**

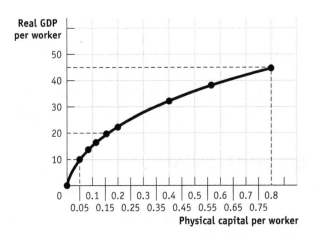

**c.** Real GDP per worker increases as physical capital per worker increases, but it increases at a diminishing rate. For example, if we hold the number of workers and all other variables constant, real GDP per worker increases by $4.14 when physical capital increases from $20 to $40, but real GDP per worker increases by $3.18 when physical capital increases from $40 to $60.

**3.**  **a.** Macro States' aggregate production function will shift up relative to its initial position for every level of physical capital per worker. We can see this by recalculating output per worker given the new aggregate production function.

| K | K/L | Y/L |
|---|---|---|
| 0 | 0 | 0 |
| 20 | 0.04 | 12.00 |
| 40 | 0.08 | 16.97 |
| 60 | 0.12 | 20.78 |
| 80 | 0.16 | 24.00 |
| 100 | 0.20 | 26.83 |

**b.** Productivity is defined as output per worker. When physical capital equals $100, output per worker is initially $22.50, while, after the increase in human capital per worker and technology, output per worker increases to $27.

**c.** Increases in productivity are important because they indicate that each worker on average is now producing a greater level of output. This, in turn, makes it possible for people on average to experience higher standards of living.

**4.** Economists argue that vital resources, as they grow scarce, will command increasing higher prices and that these high prices will cause people to conserve these resources and in addition spur the development of alternatives to replace the scarce, but vital, resources.

5.  Climate destruction arises from widespread economic growth, and this destruction is an example of a negative externality. Negative externalities arise when a market fails to include all the costs of producing a good in the calculation of the good's price. Many goods produced today also produce significant pollution, and the market does not internalize these costs of pollution. Without government intervention, firms and individuals do not have any incentive to reduce negative externalities. Reducing pollution and the climate destruction that accompany this pollution will require the cooperation of governments in the imposition of some form of market-based incentives: for example, a "carbon tax" or a "cap and trade" system both would reduce the amount of carbon emitted into the air.

## Answers to Module Review Questions

1.  **Answer a.** Answer (a) provides a definition of the aggregate production function. In answers (b) and (c), we know there is a relationship between output per worker and the amount of human capital per worker or physical capital per worker: in both cases, an increase in either human or physical capital, holding everything else constant, will lead to an increase in output per worker.

2.  **Answer b.** With fixed technology, labor, and human capital, an increase in physical capital per worker will eventually result in output per worker increasing at a decreasing rate due to diminishing returns to physical capital. The economy, despite its increased physical capital per worker, finds that each additional unit of this physical capital per worker results in smaller and smaller increases to output per worker since the fixed amount of labor cannot fully utilize the increases in physical capital per worker.

3.  **Answer d.** This answer is the definition of growth accounting. Growth accounting seeks to assign the contribution of each major factor—physical capital per worker, human capital per worker, and technology—in the aggregate production function to economic growth.

4.  **Answer c.** To find the productivity growth per year from this growth in human capital per worker, multiply the growth rate of human capital per worker times the effect of a 1 percent change in the human capital per worker on output per worker, or 6%(0.5). The growth in human capital per worker is responsible for 3 percentage points of productivity growth per year.

5.  **Answer b.** When total factor productivity increases, this enables an economy to produce more output from a given set of resources or to produce the same amount of output from fewer resources.

6.  **Answer a.** In the world today, human and physical capital are far more important in determining a country's productivity than are natural resources.

7.  **Answer a.** Answer (a) provides a definition of the aggregate production function. In answers (b) and (c), we know there is a relationship between output per worker and the amount of human capital per worker or physical capital per worker: in both cases, an increase in either human or physical capital, holding everything else constant, will lead to an increase in output per worker.

8.  **Answer c.** This question focuses on the concept of diminishing returns to physical capital: given an aggregate production function with a constant level of human capital per worker and state of technology, an increase in the quantity of physical capital per worker will lead the rate of productivity to fall while remaining positive. Thus, output per worker will increase but by smaller and smaller amounts.

9.  **Answer c.** Physical capital per worker in the first year increases by 5%, or (100)(1.05) = 105 units. In the second year, physical capital per worker increases another 5%, or (105)(1.05) = 110.25 units.

10. **Answer c.** Using growth accounting, we can estimate output per worker as being equal to the percentage change in physical capital per worker times the impact on output per worker. In this case, a 5% increase in physical capital per worker will lead to a 1% increase in output per worker. Since output is initially $1,000, a 1% increase in output will equal $1,010.

11. **Answer b.** Economists believe that resource scarcity will lead to higher prices for those resources. As the prices of these resources rise, people will move to conserve the scarce resources and, in addition, new alternatives to replace these scarce resources will be developed.

12. **Answer d.** Environmental damage from economic growth and, in particular, the use of fossil fuels contributes to climate change and can be remedied by the government imposing "carbon taxes" or "cap and trade" systems for carbon emissions. Government intervention is necessary, since the negative externality of the pollution created by firms and individuals will not be eliminated without government intervention to limit these activities through the appropriate incentive system.

# Long-Run Growth Policy

## BEFORE YOU READ THE MODULE

## Summary

This module focuses on explaining why long-run growth rates differ among countries. Comparison of real GDP per capita for different countries reveals different economic growth experiences: some countries have experienced rapid economic growth over time, while other countries have been much less fortunate. Long-run economic growth depends on productivity, which depends on physical capital, human capital, and technological progress. This module also discusses the convergence hypothesis, which states that relatively poor countries should have higher rates of growth of real GDP per capita than relatively rich countries.

## Module Objectives

**Objective #1.** Growth rates differ across countries and across periods of time. Countries with rapid growth rates tend to be countries that increase their physical capital, human capital, and/or technology. Countries that pursue policies and support institutions that enhance these three factors experience greater economic growth.

- An economy increases its physical capital through investment spending. This type of spending can be funded by domestic savings or by borrowing funds from foreigners.

- A well-functioning banking system is very important for economic growth because this system is a primary means for directing savings into productive business investment. Financial regulation is necessary to ensure a well-functioning banking system.

- A government can adversely affect economic growth if there is political instability, poor enforcement of property rights, government corruption, or excessive government intervention.

- A country's human capital is primarily enhanced through government spending on education. The quality of education in a country has a significant impact on a country's economic growth rate.

- A country's infrastructure, or that part of its physical capital that serves as a foundation of economic activity, is critical. Inadequate infrastructure slows the rate of economic growth. Government plays a critical role in building both physical capital and human capital infrastructure. For example, the government plays a vital role in ensuring clean water and disease control.

**Objective #2.**   Technological improvement is a key force behind economic growth. Technological improvement depends upon scientific advance. Spending on research and development (R&D) enhances the development of new technologies and their practical uses.

**Objective #3.**   The convergence hypothesis says that economic differences between countries, measured as real GDP per capita, tend to narrow over time. That is, the convergence hypothesis suggests that differences in living standards between countries should narrow over time. Countries with relatively low real GDP per capita will tend to have higher growth rates than countries with relatively high real GDP per capita.

**Objective #4.**   Conditional convergence states that countries with relatively low real GDP per capita will tend to have higher rates of growth than countries with relatively high real GDP per capita provided other things are equal. When there are differences in education, infrastructure, and political stability among countries, there is no clear tendency toward convergence in the world economy as a whole.

## Key Terms

**research and development (R&D)**   spending to create new technologies and prepare them for practical use.

**infrastructure**   *physical capital,* such as roads, power lines, ports, information networks, and other parts of an *economy,* that provides the underpinnings, or foundation, for economic activity.

**convergence hypothesis**   according to the convergence hypothesis, the national differences in real GDP per capita tend to narrow over time.

*Notes*

## AFTER YOU READ THE MODULE

## Tips

**Tip #1.**   Investment spending determines the level of physical capital available to workers. Investment spending plays a vital role in determining an economy's rate of economic growth. Investment spending can be funded through domestic saving or through the borrowing of foreign saving.

**Tip #2.** It is important to understand and know the sources of long-run economic growth. Economic growth arises because of increases in productivity, or output per worker. This increase in productivity is due to increases in human capital per worker, physical capital per worker, and/or technological advance. Economic growth is enhanced by high levels of saving and investment spending, a strong educational system, adequate infrastructure, well-supported research and development, political stability, and appropriate levels of government intervention in the economy.

# WORKED PROBLEMS

1.  Carmen has just finished reading a book about economic development that stressed the importance of the level of physical capital, human capital, technological progress, government policies, well-defined property rights, political stability, and good governance in the determination of how fast an economy grows. Carmen is still a bit unclear as to why these elements are so important and has asked you to clarify why each item on her list is important in determining a country's growth rate.

**STEP 1:** **Review the list and the module to get a broad overview of these topics.**

The module provides a careful review of each of these elements that support economic growth. The module also compares and contrasts the economic growth experience of many different countries: in particular, the module discusses the economic development history of South Korea, the countries of Latin America, and the countries of sub-Saharan Africa (in particular, Nigeria). These country-specific descriptions of economic growth and development are worthy of review since each highlights the importance of the elements listed as critical for economic growth.

**STEP 2:** **Briefly discuss why the level of physical capital is important as a factor that helps to determine a country's growth rate.**

Physical capital refers to machinery and equipment that a country possesses that can be used, along with other inputs, to produce goods and services. Countries with low levels of capital will not be able to produce as much output from a given amount of labor as can countries with high levels of capital. Countries that increase their level of physical capital are increasing their capacity to produce higher levels of output.

**STEP 3:** **Briefly discuss why the level of human capital is important as a factor that helps to determine a country's growth rate.**

Human capital refers to the education and skill set that individuals possess. Countries possessing high levels of human capital have more skilled workers, and these skilled workers will be more productive than less-skilled labor. Countries that invest in education help to increase their levels of human capital, which eventually enables these countries to produce higher levels of goods and services than were possible before this investment in human capital.

**STEP 4:** **Briefly discuss why the rate of technological progress is an important factor in determining a country's growth rate.**

For a given set of resources, a country with greater technological progress will be able to produce more goods and services than a country with less technological progress. Technological progress enables a country to take their resources and produce more from these resources than they could prior to this technological progress.

**STEP 5:** Discuss why a country's governmental policies can affect the country's growth rate.

Government policies can hamper economic development or spur economic development. High levels of taxation, unnecessary government regulation, and policies that reduce competition will likely hamper economic development. Policies that promote education, investment in capital, research and development, and competition are likely to spur economic development. The module reviews many examples of government interference with economic development.

**STEP 6:** Explain why a country must have well-defined property rights for economic growth to occur.

Property rights refer to the individual's right to dispose of items that they own as they wish. When well-defined property rights exist, individuals are encouraged to create new products, to provide innovative approaches to current challenges, and to work hard to accumulate wealth. When well-defined property rights do not exist or are not protected by the government, individuals have far less incentive to engage in these activities since they recognize that any effort they expend may not accrue to their own benefit. Economies with poorly defined property rights will find it quite difficult to have ongoing substantial economic growth.

**STEP 7:** Explain why political stability and good governance are important for economic growth.

Political stability and good governance makes it possible for countries to address their infrastructure needs. It is difficult for countries to provide safe, clean drinking water; eliminate diseases; and provide transportation and communication networks if they do not have stable political regimes with good governance. Many of the world's poorest countries are hampered by their ineffectual and/or corrupt governments, which are not willing or able to address these very basic needs necessary for economic growth.

2.  Last week Tony and Marie were discussing economic growth and Tony insisted that the poor countries of the world would never experience the same standard of living as rich countries. Marie told Tony that she thought he was wrong, but she had trouble making a good argument about this. Marie would like you to help her organize an argument that would help her prove to Tony that he is mistaken. She thinks it would be helpful if you could provide her with at least one real example that supports her position.

**STEP 1:** Review the issue of long-run growth and the elements that determine long-run growth.

Long-run growth depends upon many elements, including the country's level of physical capital, its level of human capital, its rate of technological progress, the policies that are enacted by its government, how property rights are defined in the country, its level of political stability, and whether the country has good governance.

**STEP 2:** Provide an example using the rule of 70 to illustrate how two countries with different growth rates may change their relative level of real GDP per capita over time.

Suppose you have two countries, Country A and Country B. Initially, these two countries have real GDP per capita of $50,000 and $10,000, respectively. Country A's economy is growing at a constant annual rate of 2%, while Country B's economy is growing at a constant annual rate of 5%. To simplify matters let's assume that population is unchanged in both Country A and Country B. The rule of 70 tells us that

Country A's real GDP per capita will double in approximately 35 years; Country B's real GDP per capita will double in approximately 14 years. Thus, if we were to approximate Country A's real GDP per capita 70 years from now we would have $200,000 per capita. If we were to approximate Country B's real GDP per capita 70 years from now we would have $320,000 per capita. The critical factor in this example is not that one country is initially rich and the other country is poor; the critical factor is that the two countries do not have the same growth rate of real GDP per capita and that the country with the greater growth rate of real GDP per capita will grow faster than the other country and over time. This implies that the poorer country has the potential to catch up or even surpass the initially richer country.

**STEP 3:** Provide a real-world example of a country that was poor but became rich through development.

In 1820, Mexico had higher real GDP per capita than Japan, but today Japan has higher real GDP per capita than Mexico. South Korea in 1960 had real GDP per capita that was lower than India's real GDP per capita today, and today South Korea is considered a developed country. The module includes other examples.

## Problems and Exercises

1.  Increases in capital, holding everything else constant, will help a country grow faster. Contrast the recent experience of the United States and China with respect to investment spending as a percent of GDP.

2.  Discuss why research and development is important in determining a country's rate of growth. Is research and development strictly undertaken by the government or subsidized by the government?

3.  What is meant by the term *infrastructure*? Provide at least four examples of infrastructure.

# ■ BEFORE YOU TAKE THE TEST

## Module Review Questions

1. An economy increases its level of physical capital per worker by increasing the level of investment spending. This can be achieved by
   a. having domestic residents spend more of their income on consumption spending.
   b. having domestic residents spend less of their income on consumption spending while increasing their domestic saving.
   c. borrowing foreign savings from residents of other countries.
   d. Answers (a) and (c) are both correct.
   e. Answers (b) and (c) are both correct.

2. Suppose real GDP in Macroland was $400 billion in 2007 and $450 billion in 2008. Then the growth rate of real GDP in Macroland between 2007 and 2008 was
   a. 50%.
   b. 5%.
   c. 125%.
   d. 12.5%

3. Which of the following statements is true?
   a. Countries with low levels of infrastructure typically experience low rates of economic growth.
   b. Infrastructure is primarily provided by private companies.
   c. Basic public health measures, like clean water, are not considered part of an economy's infrastructure.
   d. Answers (a), (b), and (c) are all true.

4. Long-run economic growth requires
   a. the imposition of bureaucratic restrictions on business and household activity.
   b. political stability and respect for property rights.
   c. extensive government intervention in markets in the form of import restrictions, government subsidies, and protection of firms from competitive economic pressures.
   d. Answers (a), (b), and (c) are all correct.

5. Sometimes the development of a new technology does not immediately translate into a large increase in productivity because
   a. the new technology provides a new means of producing the good, but the new means may not necessarily enable greater production from a given set of resources.
   b. it may take time for firms to learn how to effectively use the new technology.

6. Fast-growing economies typically spend a
   a. very small share of their GDP on investment goods.
   b. large share of their GDP on government-provided goods and services.
   c. very large share of their GDP on investment goods.
   d. very large share of their GDP on consumer goods.

7. Economic growth can be especially fast
   a. for countries playing catch-up with countries that already have high real GDP per capita.
   b. for relatively poorer countries, if the convergence hypothesis holds true.
   c. if the country is able to benefit from adopting the technological advances already utilized in advanced countries.
   d. Answers (a), (b), and (c) are all true.

## ■ ANSWER KEY

## Answers to Problems and Exercises

1.  China in recent years has invested heavily in their economy. For example, in 2010, China's investment spending represented 38% of its GDP, while in the United States investment spending represented only 16% of its GDP. In addition, the level of saving is greater than the level of investment spending in China, and that has allowed China to lend some of their excess saving to the United States.

2.  Research and development can lead to important technological discoveries, or to the creation of new products or techniques. Although government often subsidizes basic research and development, it is also undertaken by private companies eager to develop new products or new technology. New technology makes it possible to produce more from a given set of resources, since it effectively shifts the country's aggregate production function.

3.  Infrastructure refers to roads, power lines, ports, water and sewer systems, disease prevention, information and communication networks, as well as any other capital-intensive project that helps a country more effectively produce and deliver goods and services. Government often provides the bulk of infrastructure because of its capital intensity.

## Answers to Module Review Questions

1.  **Answer e.** Investment spending depends upon the availability of savings. An increase in investment spending is possible either by increasing the level of domestic savings or by borrowing foreign savings.

2.  **Answer d.** To find the growth rate of real GDP in Macroland between 2007 and 2008, use the following formula:

    Growth rate of real GDP between 2007 and 2008 = {[(real GDP in 2008) − (real GDP in 2007)]/(real GDP in 2007)} × 100 = [(450 − 400)/(400)] × 100 = 12.5%

3.  **Answer a.** Infrastructure includes roads, power lines, ports, information networks, and basic public health measures. Countries lacking this infrastructure find it hard to maintain high rates of economic growth. Infrastructure is primarily provided by government, not private enterprise.

4.  **Answer b.** Long-run economic growth requires political stability and well-defined property rights. Long-run economic growth is hindered by bureaucratic restrictions and excessive government intervention in markets.

5.  **Answer b.** New technology takes time to fully incorporate at the firm level: the new technology may require reconfiguring the physical setup of the firm, or the training of labor in the new technology. In addition, it may take time for firms to learn how to best use the new technology.

6.  **Answer c.** Fast-growing economies grow fast because their capital stock is increasing rapidly. This increase in capital stock can only occur if there is a high level of investment spending. Thus, the share of GDP that reflects investment goods tends to be very large in comparison to countries that have lower economic growth rates.

7.  **Answer d.** The convergence hypothesis says that differences in real GDP per capita among countries tend to narrow over time because countries that start with lower GDP per capita tend to grow at faster rates than countries that start with higher GDP per capita. Answers (a) and (b) express comparable ideas. Relatively poor countries may experience fast economic growth if they implement existing technological advances.

# Savings and Investment Spending

## Summary

This module examines the relationship between saving and investment and how financial markets facilitate economic growth. The module also discusses the savings–investment spending identity and why it is always true that savings equals investment.

## Module Objectives

**Objective #1.** Long-run economic growth depends on a well-functioning financial system that can link savers with excess funds to borrowers in need of funds to finance productive investment activities. The financial system provides the mechanism for increasing physical capital, a critical source of productivity growth.

**Objective #2.** Investment spending refers to spending on physical capital, while investment refers to the purchase of financial assets like stocks, bonds, or existing real estate.

**Objective #3.** Human capital is primarily provided by the government through its support of education, while physical capital, excluding infrastructure, is provided through private investment spending.

**Objective #4.** Recall that the budget balance equals tax revenue minus government spending on both goods and services as well as government transfers. We can write the budget balance, $S_{Government}$, symbolically as $S_{Government} = T - G - TR$.

- A positive budget balance indicates a budget surplus, while a negative budget balance indicates a budget deficit.

- Holding everything else constant, discretionary expansionary fiscal policy reduces the budget balance, while discretionary contractionary policy increases the budget balance.

- Equal-sized changes in government spending or taxes impact the budget balance equally, but have very different impacts on *AD* due to the multiplier effect of a change in government spending being greater than the multiplier effect of an equal-sized change in government taxes or transfers.

- Changes in the budget balance often are the result of economic fluctuations.

**Objective #5.**    The savings–investment spending identity states that saving is always equal to investment whether the economy is a closed economy with no international trade or an open economy with trade.

- In a closed economy, investment spending (*I*) can be written as $I = GDP - C - G$.

- Private savings ($S_{Private}$) in a closed economy can be expressed as total income plus government transfers minus taxes and consumption, or $S_{Private} = GDP + TR - T - C$.

- When the government spends more than it collects in tax revenue, it runs a budget deficit; and when the government spends less than it collects in tax revenue, it runs a budget surplus. A budget surplus is equivalent to savings by the government. The budget balance ($S_{Government}$) is equal to taxes minus government transfers and government spending, or $S_{Government} = T - TR - G$. A positive budget balance indicates the government is saving, while a negative budget balance indicates the government is dissaving.

- National savings ($S_{National}$) is the sum of private savings plus government savings, or $S_{National} = GDP - C - G$.

**Objective #6.**    In an open economy, savings need not be spent on physical capital in the same country where the savings occurred. Countries can receive inflows of savings from other countries, and countries can generate outflows of savings to other countries. We call the net effect of international inflows and outflows of funds on the total savings that is available for investment spending in a country its capital inflow, or *KI* symbolically.

- Capital inflow can be positive or negative. When capital inflow is positive, the inflow of funds into a country exceeds the outflow of funds; and when capital inflow is negative, the inflow of funds into a country is less than the outflow of funds.

- A positive capital inflow represents funds borrowed from foreigners, while a negative capital inflow represents funds lent to foreigners. Capital inflow is related to a country's exports and imports: a country that spends more on imports than it earns from exports must borrow the difference from foreigners. That borrowing is equal to the country's capital inflow. This implies that a country's capital inflow is equal to the difference between imports and exports, or $NCI = IM - X$.

- In an open economy, investment spending equals the sum of national savings and capital inflows, or $I = S_{Private} + S_{Government} + NCI = S_{National} + NCI$.

- We can restate our findings: investment spending equals savings, where savings is defined as national savings plus capital inflow. In an open economy, some of the funds supporting investment spending may be the savings of foreigners.

# Key Terms

**savings–investment spending identity** an accounting fact that states that savings and *investment spending* are always equal for the *economy* as a whole.

*Notes*

## Key Terms *(continued)*

**budget surplus** the difference between tax revenue and government spending when tax revenue exceeds government spending; saving by the government in the form of a budget surplus is a positive contribution to *national savings*.

**budget deficit** the difference between tax revenue and government spending when government spending exceeds tax revenue; dissaving by the government in the form of a budget deficit is a negative contribution to *national savings*.

**budget balance** the difference between tax revenue and government spending. A positive budget balance is referred to as a *budget surplus*; a negative budget balance is referred to as a *budget deficit*.

**national savings** the sum of *private savings* and the government's *budget balance;* the total amount of savings generated within the *economy*.

**net capital inflow** the net inflow of funds into a country; the difference between the total inflow of foreign funds to the home country and the total outflow of domestic funds to other countries. A positive net capital inflow represents funds borrowed from foreigners to finance domestic investment; a negative net capital inflow represents funds lent to foreigners to finance foreign investment.

## AFTER YOU READ THE MODULE

## Tips

**Tip #1.** It is important to understand that savings and investment spending are always equal whether the economy is open or closed. This is an accounting fact and is referred to as the savings–investment spending identity.

**Tip #2.** It is important to review the savings–investment identity. Recall that in a simplified economy:

Total income = Total spending

When people receive income they can spend it on consumption or they can save it:

Total income = Consumer spending + Savings

Total spending in a simplified economy is equal to the consumer spending and investment spending. That is,

Total spending = Consumer spending + Investment spending

Thus,

Consumer spending + Savings = Consumer spending + Investment spending

or

Savings = Investment spending

**Tip #3.**   Remember that governments as well as households can save in an economy. The government running a budget surplus implies that the government is saving. When the government runs a budget deficit the implication is that the government is dissaving. The value of the budget balance tells us whether the government is saving or dissaving. When the budget balance is positive, the government is running a budget surplus and is therefore saving. When the budget balance is negative, the government is running a budget deficit and is therefore dissaving.

**Tip #4.**   Remember that an economy can also use savings from other countries to finance its investment spending. Positive capital inflows implies that savings from other countries are available to finance investment spending in the economy. When capital inflows are negative the implication is that more funds are flowing out of the country than are flowing into the country.

**Tip #5.**   It is important to know and understand the formulas and definitions of investment spending, private savings, the budget balance, national savings, and capital inflow. This module includes a number of equations that provide a mathematical expression of important relationships among variables. Make sure you familiarize yourself thoroughly with these formulas:

$I = GDP - C - G$ in a closed economy

$S_{Private} = GDP + TR - T - C$

$S_{Government} = T - TR - G$

$S_{National} = S_{Private} + S_{Government} = GDP - C - G$ in a closed economy

$NCI = IM - X$ in an open economy

$I = S_{Private} + S_{Government} + (IM - X)$ in an open economy

$I = S_{National} + NCI$

# WORKED PROBLEMS

1.   Suppose that consumption spending in an economy is given by the equation $C = 100 + .8(Y - T)$ where $C$ is consumption spending, $Y$ is real GDP (or aggregate spending), and $T$ is net taxes. In this economy, $T$ is a constant $20 per year. Furthermore, suppose that investment spending, $I$, is also constant and equal to $40 per year. The government in this economy spends a constant $20 per year. This economy is a closed economy. You have been asked to prove to government officials that saving in this economy is equal to investment spending. You have also been asked to identify the level of total income for this economy given the above information.

**STEP 1:** **Write an expression that depicts the relationship between total income and total spending in this economy.**

Recall that the circular flow diagram of the economy tells us that total spending in an economy must equal total income in the economy: that is, one person's spending on goods and services is someone else's income. Thus, if total income is equal to total spending, we can rewrite this as total income is equal to the consumption spending plus investment spending plus government spending, since in this economy spending can only come from households, businesses, and government. Symbolically, we have

$$\text{Total income} = C + I + G$$

**STEP 2:** Use the expression you found in Step 1 to calculate the value of total spending, or real GDP, for this economy.

We can rewrite the expression in Step 1, using the data that was provided, as

$$Y = 100 + .8(Y - T) + 40 + 20$$
$$Y = 160 + .8(Y - 20)$$
$$Y = 144 + .8Y$$
$$.2Y = 144$$
$$Y = 720$$

Real GDP in this economy is equal to $720 per year.

**STEP 3:** Given your work in Steps 1 and 2, determine the level of consumption spending in this economy.

Consumption spending is given as $C = 100 + .8(Y - T)$. Since we now know the value of $Y$ as well as $T$ it is a simple matter to calculate the value of $C$. Thus, $C = 100 + .8(720 - 20) = \$660$.

**STEP 4:** Calculate the value of national savings for this economy.

National savings is equal to the sum of private savings and the budget balance, where private savings is disposable income (income after taxes) minus consumption. The budget balance is the difference between tax revenues and government spending. In this example private savings is equal to $(720 - 20) - 660$ or $40 while the budget balance is equal to $20 - 20$ or $0. National savings is therefore equal to $40 + \$0$ or $40 per year.

**STEP 5:** Compare the value of national savings to investment spending in this economy. Are the two equal?

National savings and investment spending are both equal to $40. The savings–investment identity is true for this economy.

2. Suppose that all of the information you were given in problem 1 is true except that taxes have fallen to $10 per year. You have been asked by the government officials to evaluate the effect of this tax decrease on this economy. In particular you have been asked to calculate the value of real GDP and the value of the budget balance. You have also been asked to explain the significance of the number you have calculated for the budget balance. Finally you have been asked to verify that the savings–investment spending identity is still true for this economy.

**STEP 1:** To address the issues raised by this question you will first want to calculate the value of total spending in this economy for the year.

Total spending for this economy will equal total income in the economy (review Step 1 from the previous question if you are still struggling with this concept). Total spending in this closed economy is equal to $C + I + G$. Or,

$$\text{Total spending} = 100 + .8(Y - T) + 40 + 20$$
$$Y = 160 + .8(Y - 10)$$
$$Y = 152 + .8Y$$
$$.2Y = 152$$
$$Y = \$760$$

Total income (and total spending or real GDP) in this economy will equal $760 per year given the reduction in net taxes and holding everything else constant.

**STEP 2:** Calculate the value of the budget balance for this economy and explain whether the budget balance indicates a budget surplus or a budget deficit.

The budget balance is equal to taxes minus government spending or 10 − 20 in this example. The budget balance is therefore equal to −$10. A negative budget balance indicates that the government is running a budget deficit: the government is spending more than it is receiving in tax revenues. The government will need to borrow in order to finance this expenditure that exceeds its tax revenue.

**STEP 3:** Determine the level of consumption spending in this economy.

Consumption spending is given as $C = 100 + .8(Y − T)$. Since we now know the value of $Y$ as well as $T$, it is a simple matter to calculate the value of $C$. Thus, $C = 100 + .8(760 − 10) = $700$.

**STEP 4:** Calculate the value of national savings for this economy.

National savings is equal to the sum of private savings and the budget balance, where private savings is disposable income (income after taxes) minus consumption. The budget balance is the difference between tax revenues and government spending. In this example private savings is equal to $(760 − 10) − 700$ or $50, while the budget balance is equal to $10 − 20$ or −$10. National savings is therefore equal to $50 + −$10, or $40 per year.

**STEP 5:** Compare the value of national savings to investment spending in this economy. Are the two equal?

National savings and investment spending are both equal to $40. The savings–investment identity is true for this economy.

# Problems and Exercises

1. For each of the following decide whether they represent investment in physical assets, investment in financial assets, or investment in human capital. For each example also decide whether it represents investment spending.

    **a.** The government increases expenditures on education for children and training for post-high school graduates.

    **b.** Michael purchases a $100 bond issued by a local company that provides technical support for computer users.

    **c.** Susan purchases $1,000 worth of filing cabinets and office desks for her business office.

    **d.** A neighboring country purchases $10 million in U.S. government bonds.

    **e.** Mary purchases a newly constructed factory that manufactures auto parts.

2.  You are given the following information about the open economy of Macroland for 2009.

| GDP | $100 billion |
|---|---|
| C | 70 billion |
| T | 15 billion |
| TR | 8 billion |
| G | 20 billion |
| X | 10 billion |
| IM | 12 billion |

In 2009:

a.  What is the level of investment spending in Macroland?

b.  What is the level of capital inflow for Macroland? Is Macroland borrowing from foreigners or lending to foreigners? Explain your answer.

c.  What is private savings equal to in Macroland?

d.  What is the budget balance equal to in Macroland?

e.  Does national savings plus capital inflow equal investment spending for this economy?

f.  Is the government of Macroland saving or borrowing funds? Explain your answer.

3.  Use the following information about the three economies, Funland, Upland, and Downland, to answer the following questions.

|  | Funland | Upland | Downland |
|---|---|---|---|
| GDP | $1,000 | $5,000 | $4,000 |
| C | 800 | 3,500 | 3,000 |
| I |  |  |  |
| G | 100 | 800 | 300 |
| X | 50 | 400 | 400 |
| IM | 30 | 500 | 500 |
| T | 50 | 600 | 600 |
| TR | 20 | 200 | 200 |

a.  Fill in the missing information in this table.

**b.** From the information you are given and your calculations in part (a), fill in the following table.

|  | Funland | Upland | Downland |
|---|---|---|---|
| $S_{Private}$ |  |  |  |
| $S_{Government}$ |  |  |  |
| NCI |  |  |  |

**c.** Now, calculate capital inflow, private saving, and investment spending as a percentage of GDP for each economy. Report your calculations in an organized table.

**d.** What is the budget balance as a percentage of GDP for Funland, Upland, and Downland?

**e.** Are Funland, Upland, and Downland running a budget deficit or a budget surplus? How does your answer relate to the capital inflow each economy experiences?

## BEFORE YOU TAKE THE TEST

## Module Review Questions

**1.** Investment spending includes all of the following *except*
a. the construction of a new residence during the current year.
b. the purchase of a new piece of equipment at a factory during the current year.
c. the purchase of a home, built 20 years ago, during the current year.
d. the acquisition of new computers for a business during the current year.

**2.** Sources of funds for investment spending include
a. domestic savings.
b. foreign savings.
c. expenditures by businesses on plant and equipment.
d. Answers (a), (b), and (c) are all correct.
e. Answers (a) and (b) are both correct.

**3.** Which of the following statements is true?
a. In an open economy, the only source of funds for investment spending is domestic savings.
b. In a closed economy, the only use of savings is to provide funds to finance government deficits.
c. In a closed economy, the only source of funds for investment spending is domestic savings.
d. Statements (a) and (b) are both true.
e. Statements (b) and (c) are both true.

**4.** Which of the following statements is true?

a. $I = GDP - C - G$ in a closed economy

b. $GDP = C + I + G + X - IM$ in an open economy

c. $GDP = S_{Private} + T + C - TR$

d. $S_{Government} = T - TR - G$

e. Answers (a), (b), (c), and (d) are all true.

**5.** When government spending is greater than net taxes,

a. government savings is positive.

b. there is a budget surplus.

c. there is a positive surplus.

d. there is a budget deficit.

**6.** The term *budget balance* can be abbreviated as $S_{Government}$. The value of $S_{Government}$ is

a. positive when the government is running a budget surplus.

b. positive when the government is running a budget deficit.

c. negative when the government is running a budget deficit.

d. zero when the government's expenditure equals its net taxes.

e. Answers (a), (c), and (d) are all correct.

f. Answers (b) and (d) are both correct.

**7.** Which of the following statements is true about national savings in a closed economy?

a. National savings is the sum of private savings plus the budget balance.

b. National savings is GDP minus consumption spending minus government spending.

c. National savings is always equal to investment spending.

d. Answers (a), (b), and (c) are all correct.

**8.** Capital inflow is

a. the net inflow of foreign funds plus domestic savings into an economy.

b. the net inflow of funds into a country, or the total inflow of foreign funds into a country minus the total outflow of domestic funds to other countries.

c. the total outflow of domestic funds to other countries minus the net inflow of foreign funds into a country.

d. the total outflow of domestic funds to other countries plus the net inflow of foreign funds into a country.

**9.** Economists differentiate between these types of capital: physical capital, human capital, and financial capital. Which of the following statements is false?

a. Human capital includes changes in the level of education or training that workers possess.

b. Physical capital includes changes in inventories.

c. Financial capital refers to the funds available in an economy for investment spending.

d. Financial capital refers to expenditures on manufacturing equipment.

10. Suppose a country exports $50 million worth of goods and services, while it imports $60 million worth of goods and services. This country
    a. has a positive capital inflow.
    b. lends funds to foreigners.
    c. has a negative capital inflow.
    d. Answers (a) and (b) are both correct.
    e. Answers (b) and (c) are both correct.

11. In an open economy, investment spending equals
    a. domestic savings.
    b. private savings plus the budget balance.
    c. the sum of private savings, the budget balance, and the difference between imports and exports.
    d. private savings plus capital inflows.

12. In most economies, human capital
    a. is largely provided by the private sector.
    b. is largely provided by the government.

13. When the government runs a budget surplus in an open economy, this implies
    a. that the government is spending more than its tax revenue.
    b. that net exports are positive.
    c. that net exports are negative.
    d. that the government is saving.
    e. Answers (b) and (d) are both correct.
    f. Answers (c) and (d) are both correct.

14. Which of the following statements is true?
    I. A dollar of investment spending financed by a capital inflow results in interest being paid to a foreigner for the use of that dollar.
    II. A dollar of investment spending, no matter how it is financed, results in interest being paid to the lender for the use of that dollar.
    III. No matter the source, a dollar of investment spending results in exactly the same outcome.
    a. Statement I is true.
    b. Statement II is true.
    c. Statement III is true.
    d. Statements I and II are true.
    e. Statements II and III are true.
    f. Statements I and III are true.
    g. Statements I, II, and III are all true.

**15.** Which of the following statements is true?

a. Since the 1980s, the United States has had consistently low levels of savings when compared to other wealthy countries.

b. Over the past 30 years, the difference in the U.S. savings level relative to other wealthy countries is attributable to the large government deficits the U.S. government has run during much of this time period.

c. Investment spending in the United States during 2007 was financed through a combination of private savings and capital inflows while U.S. government savings was negative.

d. Statements (a), (b), and (c) are all true.

e. Statements (a) and (b) are both true.

f. Statements (b) and (c) are both true.

g. Statements (a) and (c) are both true.

## ■ ANSWER KEY

# Answers to Problems and Exercises

1. **a.** Increases in expenditures on education and training represent investment in human capital.

   **b.** Michael's purchase of the bond represents an investment in a financial asset, since Michael will receive a payment in the future as compensation for the use of his money today.

   **c.** Susan's purchases represent investment spending, since they are investments in physical capital.

   **d.** The purchase of government bonds by a country or by an individual represents an investment in a financial asset.

   **e.** Mary's purchase represents investment spending, since it is an investment in physical capital.

2. **a.** The level of investment spending can be calculated using the formula GDP $= C + I + G + (X - IM)$. Using the information in the table and solving for $I$ we find investment spending is equal to $12 billion.

   **b.** Capital inflow equals imports minus exports, or $2 billion. Since capital inflow for Macroland in 2009 is a positive number we know capital is flowing into Macroland from other countries and therefore Macroland is borrowing funds from foreigners.

   **c.** We can calculate private savings, $S_{Private}$, using this formula:

   $$S_{Private} = GDP + TR - T - C$$

   Using the information from the table, $S_{Private}$ equals $23 billion.

   **d.** We can calculate the budget balance, $S_{Government}$, using the following formula:

   $$S_{Government} = T - TR - G$$

   Using the information from the table, $S_{Government}$ equals –$13 billion.

   **e.** Yes, national savings plus capital inflow is equivalent to private savings plus the budget balance plus capital inflow. For Macroland in 2009 this sums to $12 billion, which is equivalent to the level of investment spending.

   **f.** The government of Macroland has a negative budget balance in 2009. This indicates that the government is running a budget deficit and is therefore borrowing funds.

3. **a.** To find investment spending for any of the economies use the formula GDP $= C + I + G + X - IM$. For Funland, investment spending equals $80; in Upland, investment spending equals $800; and in Downland, investment spending equals $800.

   **b.** To find $S_{Private}$, use the formula $S_{Private} = GDP + TR - T - C$. To find $S_{Government}$, use the formula $S_{Government} = T - TR - G$. To find $NCI$ use the formula $NCI = IM - X$. Using the formulas and the given information you can complete the table as follows:

|  | Funland | Upland | Downland |
|---|---|---|---|
| $S_{Private}$ | 170 | 1,100 | 600 |
| $S_{Government}$ | −70 | −400 | 100 |
| $NCI$ | −20 | 100 | 100 |

**c.** Capital inflows as a percentage of GDP can be calculated as $[NCI/GDP] \times 100$. This formula can be modified for all the other percentage calculations by replacing $NCI$ in the numerator with the relevant variable. Here are the calculations organized in a table.

|  | Funland | Upland | Downland |
|---|---|---|---|
| Capital inflow as a percentage of GDP | −2% | 2% | 2.5% |
| Private savings as a percentage of GDP | 17 | 22 | 15 |
| Investment spending as a percentage of GDP | 8 | 16 | 20 |

**d.** We can answer this question using the information we calculated in part (b) or we can use the formula $I = S_{Private} + S_{Government} + NCI$ and solve for $S_{Government}$ while measuring all terms as a percentage of GDP. The first method calculates the budget balance as a percentage of GDP for Funland as $[-70/1,000] \times 100$, or −7%; for Upland as $[-400/5,000] \times 100$, or −8%; and for Downland as $[100/4,000] \times 100$, or 2.5%. Using the equation we get $S_{Government}$ for Funland as −7% (since $S_{Government}$ = 8% − 17% − (−2%); $S_{Government}$ for Upland as −8% (since $S_{Government}$ = 16% − 22% − 2%); and $S_{Government}$ for Downland as 2.5% (since $S_{Government}$ = 20% − 15% − 2.5%).

**e.** Funland is running a government deficit of $70, since Funland collects $50 in taxes and expends $20 on transfers and $100 on government spending. This implies Funland's government is borrowing funds: since private savings in Funland equals $170 and the capital inflow equals −$20; this indicates that Funland is lending funds to foreigners because their level of private savings is sufficient to cover the government's budget deficit as well as its level of investment spending.

Upland is running a government deficit of $400, since Upland collects $600 in taxes and expends $200 on transfers and $800 on government spending. When we look at the relationship among $I$, $S_{Private}$, $S_{Government}$, and $NCI$, we find that Upland's capital inflow is a positive $100; so Upland is borrowing from foreigners. Private savings is equal to $1,100, government savings is −$400, and capital inflow is $100, resulting in investment spending in Upland of $800.

Downland is running a government surplus of $100, since Downland collects $600 in taxes and expends $200 on transfers and $300 on government spending. When we look at the relationship among $I$, $S_{Private}$, $S_{Government}$, and $NCI$, we find that Downland's capital inflow is a positive $100; so Downland is borrowing from foreigners. Private savings is equal to $600, government savings is $100, and capital inflow is $100, resulting in investment spending in Downland of $800.

## Answers to Module Review Questions

1.  **Answer c.** Investment spending refers to spending on the economy's stock of physical capital. It includes spending on physical equipment, inventories, and new construction. It does not include the selling of a preexisting structure since this represents a change of ownership rather than new productive capacity.

2.  **Answer: e.** Expenditures by businesses on plant and equipment is investment spending and not a source of funds for investment spending, while domestic and foreign savings do provide funds for investment spending.

3.  **Answer c.** A closed economy does not have any economic interaction with the rest of the world while an open economy does. A closed economy finances its investment spending solely through domestic savings, while an open economy funds its investment spending through both domestic and foreign savings.

4. **Answer e.** We know that GDP is equal to total spending on goods and services in an open economy (answer b); in a closed economy there are no imports or exports, so GDP is equal to total domestic spending on goods and services (answer a). Private savings plus consumption plus net transfers equals GDP (answer c), and government savings is equal to net taxes minus the level of government spending (answer d).

5. **Answer d.** If the government spends more than its net revenue, it runs a budget deficit or a negative surplus. This implies that government saving is negative.

6. **Answer e.** By definition $S_{Government}$ is equal to government net taxes (taxes minus transfers) minus government spending. When $S_{Government}$ is greater than zero this indicates that net taxes exceed government spending: this is a budget surplus. When $S_{Government}$ is less than zero this indicates that government spending exceeds net taxes: this is a budget deficit.

7. **Answer d.** All of these statements are true by definition.

8. **Answer b.** Capital inflow measures the total level of funds available in a country to finance investment spending. It consists of the inflow of foreign funds into the economy minus the outflow of domestic funds to other economies, or the net inflow of funds into an economy.

9. **Answer d.** Expenditures on manufacturing equipment are considered physical capital and not financial capital.

10. **Answer a.** Capital inflow is defined as imports minus exports: in this case, capital inflow is positive. When capital inflow is positive the country spends more on imports than it earns from exports and must therefore borrow the difference from foreigners.

11. **Answer c.** In any economy, investment spending equals savings. In an open economy, savings is equal to the sum of private saving, the budget balance, and capital inflows. Capital inflow is defined as the difference between imports and exports.

12. **Answer b.** In most economies, human capital is primarily provided by the government through public education.

13. **Answer d.** When the government runs a budget surplus, this means that tax revenue is greater than government spending: the government is saving. It is not possible with the information given to determine whether or not net exports are positive or negative.

14. **Answer d.** A dollar of investment spending financed by national savings or capital inflow results in an additional dollar of investment spending; however, the dollar of investment spending financed by national savings results in interest being paid to someone domestically while a dollar of investment spending financed by capital inflow results in interest being paid to a foreigner. No matter the source of the financing, interest is paid, but the recipient of that interest varies depending upon the source of the financing.

15. **Answer g.** These are statements discussed in the text. The statement in answer (b) is incorrect since the disparity in savings level between the United States and other wealthy countries over the past 30 years is primarily due to low U.S. private savings over this period rather than large budget deficits.

# The Market for Loanable Funds

## BEFORE YOU READ THE MODULE

## Summary

This module discusses how the loanable funds market matches savers and investors. The module then analyzes the determinants of supply and demand in the loanable funds market. The module also discusses how changes in the expected future inflation rate affect the nominal interest rate.

## Module Objectives

**Objective #1.** The loanable funds market is a hypothetical market where savers, or those individuals supplying funds, interact with borrowers, or those individuals demanding funds. The loanable funds market maximizes the gains from trade between lenders and borrowers.

- The equilibrium price or interest rate equates the quantity demanded of funds with the quantity supplied of funds. This interest rate is the return a lender receives for allowing borrowers the use of a dollar for one year.

- The real interest rate is the interest rate adjusted for changes in prices over the length of the loan, while the nominal interest rate is the interest rate unadjusted for changes in prices.

- The relationship between the nominal interest rate and the real interest rate can be expressed as "the real interest rate is equal to the nominal interest rate minus the inflation rate." When there is no inflation, the nominal and real interest rates are equivalent.

- The Fisher effect asserts that the expected real interest rate is unaffected by the change in expected inflation. As long as inflation is expected, the inflation does not affect the equilibrium quantity of loanable funds or the expected real interest rate; the expected inflation only affects the equilibrium nominal interest rate.

**Objective #2.**  The demand for loanable funds curve represents the relationship between the interest rate and the amount of loanable funds that are demanded at each interest rate. The demand for loanable funds curve represents the demand for funds from borrowers. The demand for loanable funds curve is downward sloping: as the interest rate falls, the quantity of loanable funds demanded increases. The demand for loanable funds curve shifts with changes in perceived business opportunities and with changes in the government's borrowing.

- When perceived business opportunities are optimistic the demand for loanable funds curve will shift to the right: at every interest rate the quantity of loanable funds demanded will increase.

- When the government runs a deficit or increases the level of the deficit the demand for loanable funds curve will shift to the right: at every interest rate the quantity of loanable funds demanded will increase.

**Objective #3.**  The supply for loanable funds curve represents the relationship between the interest rate and the amount of loanable funds that are supplied at each interest rate. The supply of loanable funds curve represents the supply of funds from savers. The supply of loanable funds curve is upward sloping: as the interest rate increases, the quantity of loanable funds supplied increases. The supply for loanable funds curve shifts with changes in private savings behavior and with changes in capital inflows.

- When private savers decide to increase their saving at every interest rate it causes the supply of loanable funds curve to shift to the right.

- When capital inflows increase, the supply of loanable funds at every interest rate increases: the supply of loanable funds curve will shift to the right.

**Objective #4.**  Crowding out refers to the negative effect on private investment spending from government budget deficits. If the government's budget deficit results in crowding out, less physical capital is accumulated each year in the economy. Holding everything else constant, this can result in lower long-run economic growth.

**Objective #5.**  Some government spending is essential for long-run economic growth. For example, government expenditure on infrastructure is critical for long-run economic growth. The negative impact of crowding out is based on the other-things-equal assumption that all government spending necessary for the economy's infrastructure has occurred and that any additional government expenditure resulting in a government deficit will reduce the level of private investment spending and therefore the level of economic growth in the economy.

# Key Terms

*Notes*

**loanable funds market** a hypothetical market that brings together those who want to lend money (savers) and those who want to borrow (*firms* with *investment spending* projects).

**crowding out** the negative effect of *budget deficits* on private investment, which occurs because government borrowing drives up *interest rates*.

**Fisher effect** the principle by which an increase in expected future *inflation* drives up the *nominal interest rate*, leaving the expected real interest rate unchanged.

## ■ AFTER YOU READ THE MODULE

## Tips

**Tip #1.** It is important to realize that the market for loanable funds is essentially another application of the model of supply and demand. It will prove extremely helpful to know the factors that shift the demand for loanable funds curve and the supply of loanable funds curve. Without this knowledge it will be difficult to analyze the impact of a specific change on the market for loanable funds.

**Tip #2.** Students often find it challenging to understand the impact of government budget deficits or government budget surpluses on the market for loanable funds. Review this material until you feel confident that you can accurately analyze the impact of a budget deficit or a budget surplus on the equilibrium interest rate in the loanable funds market: when the government runs a budget deficit, holding everything else constant, this results in an increase in the interest rate in the loanable funds market; and when the government runs a budget surplus, holding everything else constant, this results in a decrease in the interest rate in the loanable funds market.

**Tip #3.** Students often find it challenging to understand the impact of net capital inflows on the market for loanable funds. Review this material until you feel confident that you can accurately analyze the impact of an increase or decrease in net capital inflows on the equilibrium interest rate in the loanable funds market: when there is an increase in net capital inflows, holding everything else constant, the equilibrium interest in the loanable funds market decreases; when there is a decrease in net capital inflows, holding everything else constant, the equilibrium interest rate in the loanable funds market increases.

# WORKED PROBLEMS

1. The demand for loanable funds from businesses in an economy is a downward sloping line: as the interest rate decreases, the quantity of loanable funds demanded by businesses increases. In addition, in this economy the government also demands a constant amount of loanable funds due to the government operating with a persistent, but constant, deficit. The supply of loanable funds curve in this economy is upward sloping: as the interest rate increases, the quantity of loanable funds supplied in this economy increases. Initially the level of capital inflows in this economy is equal to zero. Given this information, you have been asked to provide a graph of the loanable funds market that depicts business demand for loanable funds, total demand for loanable funds (this is business demand as well as the government's demand), and the total supply of loanable funds. In this graph you are asked to identify the equilibrium level of loanable funds as well as the equilibrium interest rate. You are also asked to identify the level of investment spending ($I_1$) by businesses. In a second graph you are asked to analyze how an increase in government spending to a new, but constant, level will affect the level of investment spending ($I_2$) by businesses. In this second graph you are also asked to identify the new equilibrium interest rate as well as the new equilibrium level of loanable funds. Indicate the amount of business investment spending that is

crowded out due to the increase in the government spending. Finally, suppose that this second graph is modified one more time. In your third graph analyze the effect of an increase in capital inflows on the interest rate, the level of investment spending by businesses, and the equilibrium level of loanable funds. In this analysis compare your results with the results you had in the second graph.

**STEP 1:** Draw the initial loanable funds situation presented in this question. In your graph note the business demand for loanable funds curve ($I$), the total demand for loanable funds curve ($D_{LF}$), which includes the business demand as well as the government demand for loanable funds, and the total supply of loanable funds curve ($S_{LF}$). In this graph, label the equilibrium interest rate as $r_1$, the equilibrium level of loanable funds as $LF_1$, and the initial level of business investment spending as $I_1$.

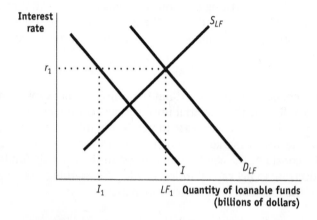

**STEP 2:** Draw a new graph of the loanable funds market illustrating the effect of an increase in the government deficit in this market. In this graph note the business demand for loanable funds curve ($I$), the total demand for loanable funds curve ($D_{LF_2}$), which includes the business demand as well as the new, higher level of government demand for loanable funds, and the total supply of loanable funds curve ($S_{LF}$). In this graph, label the equilibrium interest rate as $r_2$, the equilibrium level of loanable funds as $LF_2$, and the new level of business investment spending as $I_2$. Indicate on this graph, as well as verbally, the amount of business investment spending that is crowded out due to the increase in government spending holding everything else constant.

The demand for loanable funds curve will shift to the right when the government increases its level of spending while holding constant its level of taxation. In the following graph, this shift is illustrated as $D_{LF_2}$. When the demand for loanable funds curve shifts to the right, holding everything else constant, this causes the equilibrium interest rate to increase and the equilibrium quantity of loanable funds to increase. However, the increase in the interest rate will cause the level of business investment spending to fall: note how as the interest rate rises from $r_1$ to $r_2$ there is a movement along the curve labeled $I$ in the following graph. The increase in government expenditure results in crowding out of business investment of $I_1 - I_2$.

Amount of business investment
spending crowded out by increase
in government deficit is $I_1-I_2$

**STEP 3:** Draw a third graph of the loanable funds market illustrating the effect
of an increase in capital inflows on this market. In this graph note the business
demand for loanable funds curve ($I$), the total demand for loanable funds curve
($D_{LF_2}$), which includes the business demand as well as the new, higher level of
government demand for loanable funds, and the new total supply of loanable
funds curve ($S_{LF_2}$), which includes the increase in capital inflows. In this graph
label the equilibrium interest rate as $r_3$, the equilibrium level of loanable funds
as $LF_3$, and the new level of business investment spending as $I_3$.

When capital inflows increase, holding everything else constant, this causes the supply of loanable funds curve to shift to the right. At every interest rate there is a greater
quantity of loanable funds supplied in this market due to the increase in capital
inflows. In the following graph, two potential supply of loanable funds curves have
been drawn. Look closely at each of these. Relative to $r_2$ and $LF_2$, we can see that the
equilibrium interest rate will decrease and the equilibrium quantity of loanable funds
will increase with this increase in capital inflows. But, relative to $r_1$ and $LF_1$, we see
that the equilibrium interest rate may increase, decrease, or equal $r_1$ depending upon
the size of the rightward shift in the supply of loanable funds curve. Relative to $LF_1$
we see that the equilibrium level of loanable funds has increased. Thus, this change
relative to $r_1$ and $LF_1$ results in the equilibrium interest rate being indeterminate,
while the equilibrium quantity of loanable funds increases.

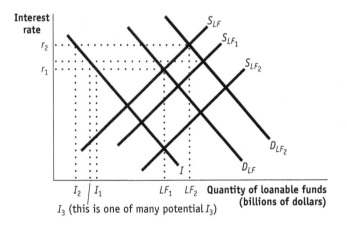

2. The following table describes five situations using the loanable funds market framework. For each of the following situations assume that the loanable funds market is initially in equilibrium and then the described event occurs. Complete the table, which asks you to state the effect on the equilibrium interest rate and the equilibrium quantity of loanable funds. The table also asks you to identify the impact on the demand and supply curves in the loanable funds market. For each situation assume that this is the only change that is occurring and that everything else is being held constant. After you complete the table you are asked to provide a statement that generalizes your reasoning.

| Situation | Impact on the equilibrium interest rate | Impact on the equilibrium quantity of loanable funds | Impact on the demand for loanable funds curve | Impact on the supply of loanable funds curve |
|---|---|---|---|---|
| The expected inflation rate increases | | | | |
| Businesses become more confident about potential business opportunities | | | | |
| The government increases its level of government spending while holding taxes constant | | | | |
| Individuals decide to increase their level of saving at every interest rate | | | | |
| Net capital inflows decrease | | | | |

**STEP 1:** Review the factors that shift the demand for loanable funds curve and the supply of loanable funds curve.

To provide the analysis asked for in this question it is imperative that you have a firm grasp on the factors that shift the demand for loanable funds curve and the factors that shift the supply of loanable funds curve. The demand for loanable funds curve will shift if there are changes in perceived business opportunities or if there are changes in the government's budget balance. The supply of loanable funds curve will shift if there are changes in private saving behavior or if there are changes in net capital inflows. Both curves will shift if there is a change in the expected inflation rate.

**STEP 2:** Using the information you reviewed in Step 1 fill in the missing cells of the table.

To fill in the table you will need the information in Step 1 to identify which curve is shifting, but you will also need to be able to discern the direction of the shift. For example, if there are increased business opportunities, the demand curve for loanable funds will shift and it will shift to the right. At every interest rate, businesses will now demand a greater quantity of loanable funds since there is greater confidence about potential business opportunities.

If there is an increase in the expected inflation rate, this will cause both curves to shift: the demand for loanable funds curve will shift to the right and the supply of loanable funds curve will shift to the left. Suppliers will need to receive a higher nominal interest rate at every quantity of loanable funds in order to be willing to supply the loanable funds, and demanders will find that at every quantity of loanable funds they are willing to pay a higher nominal interest rate due to the increase in the expected inflation rate.

Similar analysis should be done on the other scenarios provided in the table: first, identify which curve or curves are shifting and then identify the direction of the shift. Here is the completed table.

| Situation | Impact on the equilibrium interest rate | Impact on the equilibrium quantity of loanable funds | Impact on the demand for loanable funds curve | Impact on the supply of loanable funds curve |
|---|---|---|---|---|
| The expected inflation rate increases | The nominal interest rate increases | There is no impact on the equilibrium quantity of loanable funds | The demand curve shifts to the right | The supply curve shifts to the left |
| Businesses become more confident about potential business opportunities | The nominal interest rate increases | The equilibrium quantity of loanable funds increases | The demand curve shifts to the right | There is a movement along the supply curve |
| The government increases its level of government spending while holding taxes constant | The nominal interest rate increases | The equilibrium quantity of loanable funds increases | The demand curve shifts to the right | There is a movement along the supply curve |
| Individuals decide to increase their level of saving at every interest rate | The nominal interest rate decreases | The equilibrium quantity of loanable funds increases | There is a movement along the demand curve | The supply curve shifts to the right |
| Net capital inflows decrease | The nominal interest rate increases | The equilibrium quantity of loanable funds decreases | There is a movement along the demand curve | The supply curve shifts to the left |

**STEP 3:** Provide a general explanation of the analysis you have done.

The loanable funds market provides a demand and supply curve framework for analyzing the impact on the equilibrium quantity of loanable funds and the equilibrium nominal interest rate of changes in the government budget balance, private saver behavior, inflationary expectations, net capital inflows, or business opportunities. With this analysis we can make predictions about how specific events will affect the equilibrium nominal interest rate and the equilibrium quantity of loanable funds.

## Problems and Exercises

1. Suppose in a closed economy, the demand for loanable funds can be expressed as $r = 0.1 - .00005Q$ and the supply of loanable funds can be expressed as $r = 0.00005Q$, where $r$ is the real interest rate expressed as a decimal (for example, 8% is expressed as 0.08 in the equation) and $Q$ is the quantity of loanable funds. Assume the government initially has a budget balance of zero.

   a. What is the equilibrium real interest rate and the equilibrium quantity in the loanable funds market?

   b. Suppose the government's budget balance decreases to −$100 at every real interest rate. What will happen to the demand and supply of loanable funds with this change? What do you predict will happen to the equilibrium interest rate and the equilibrium quantity in the loanable funds market?

   c. Does crowding out occur in this economy when the budget balance is −$100? Explain your answer.

2. Suppose that in Macroland the expected inflation rate is 5% for the coming year. Suppose that the nominal interest rate in the loanable funds market is currently 10%.

   a. What do you predict is the value of the real interest rate given this information?

   b. According to the Fisher effect, what would happen to the nominal interest rate if the expected inflation rate for Macroland increased to 7% for the coming year?

3. Suppose the demand for loanable funds from firms is given by the equation $r = 10 - (10/1,000) \times I$, where $r$ is the interest rate in the loanable funds market (expressed as a percentage and not a decimal) and $I$ is the amount of investment spending. Furthermore, suppose that the supply of loanable funds is given by the equation $r = 2 + (3/500) \times S_{Private}$. Assume initially that there are no capital inflows and that the government has a budget balance.

   a. What is the equilibrium interest rate, given the above information, and what is the equilibrium amount of investment spending in this market?

**b.** Suppose that the government runs a budget deficit and that at every interest rate the government now finds that it needs to borrow $200 in loanable funds. How will this budget deficit affect the demand for loanable funds curve and the supply of loanable funds curve? What do you predict will happen to the equilibrium interest rate in this market? (Do not make a calculation here; just simply give an intuitive answer.)

**c.** Given the information in part (b), calculate what the equilibrium interest rate will be with the government running a deficit. In addition, identify the amount of private investment spending that will occur when the government runs a deficit. How does the government deficit affect the level of private investment spending?

**4.** Holding everything else constant: For each of the following situations, state the effect on the equilibrium interest rate and the equilibrium quantity of loanable funds. In your answer make reference to how the demand and supply curves in the loanable funds market are affected.

**a.** There is an increase in capital inflows into a country.

**b.** The government reduces the government deficit.

**c.** There is an increase in the expected inflation rate. Comment on the real interest rate as well as the nominal interest rate in your answer to this question.

   **d.** There is an increase in private savings.

   **e.** There is a decrease in perceived business opportunities.

## BEFORE YOU TAKE THE TEST

## Module Review Questions

1.  The loanable funds market
    a. provides a market where savers and borrowers can make mutually beneficial transactions.
    b. uses supply and demand to determine an equilibrium price or interest rate.
    c. interest rate is the return a lender receives for allowing borrowers the use of a dollar for one year.
    d. Answers (a), (b), and (c) are all correct.

Use the following information to answer the next two questions.

Suppose Joe lends Maxine $100 for the year. At the end of the year, Maxine repays Joe the $100 plus an additional payment of $15 for the use of Joe's money during the year.

2.  Assuming there is no inflation during the year, what is the interest rate Maxine pays Joe?
    a. 0.15%
    b. 1.5%
    c. 15%
    d. 115%

3.  Maxine, when borrowing the funds from Joe, anticipates the inflation rate for the year will be 10%, while Joe expects it to be 7%. Inflation is actually 8% for the year. Which of the following statements is true?
    a. Joe benefits unexpectedly from this higher-than-expected inflation rate.
    b. Maxine benefits unexpectedly from this lower-than-expected inflation rate.
    c. The nominal interest rate for this loan is 7%.
    d. The real interest rate for this loan is 7%.

4.  When the government runs a deficit, this shifts the
    a. supply of loanable funds curve to the right.
    b. supply of loanable funds curve to the left.
    c. demand for loanable funds curve to the right.
    d. demand for loanable funds curve to the left.

5. In the loanable funds market, which of the following statements is true?
   a. Savers are best represented by the demand for loanable funds curve.
   b. Borrowers are best represented by the demand for loanable funds curve.
   c. The equilibrium interest rate equates the quantity of loanable funds supplied to the quantity of loanable funds demanded.
   d. Statements (a), (b), and (c) are all true.
   e. Statements (a) and (b) are both true.
   f. Statements (b) and (c) are both true.
   g. Statements (a) and (c) are both true.

6. Holding everything else constant, when the government runs a deficit this results in
   a. the equilibrium interest rate in the loanable funds market increasing.
   b. the level of private investment spending in the loanable funds market decreasing.
   c. a decrease in capital inflows into this economy.
   d. Answers (a), (b), and (c) are all correct.
   e. Answers (a) and (b) are both correct.

## ■ ANSWER KEY

# Answers to Problems and Exercises

1.  **a.** To find the equilibrium quantity in the loanable funds market, set demand equal to supply, or $0.1 - 0.00005Q = 0.00005Q$. Solving for $Q$, we get $Q$ equals \$1,000. The equilibrium interest rate equals $0.00005Q$, using the supply equation, or $0.1 - 0.00005Q$, using the demand equation. Substituting 1,000 for $Q$, we get the equilibrium real interest rate, $r$, which equals 5%.

    **b.** The government is now running a deficit and must demand funds in the loanable funds market. At every real interest rate, demand for loanable funds has now increased by \$100. Thus, the demand curve shifts to the right. There is no shift in the supply of loanable funds with this change. When the demand curve shifts, there is a movement along the supply curve: we anticipate that the equilibrium real interest rate and quantity of loanable funds will increase when the government runs a negative budget balance.

    **c.** In this economy, there is partial crowding out when the budget balance is −\$100. Investment spending decreases when the government's budget balance is −\$100.

2.  **a.** The real interest rate is equal to the nominal interest rate minus the inflation rate. In this case, the real interest rate is equal to 10% − 5%, or 5%.

    **b.** The nominal interest rate would increase by the amount of the increase in the inflation rate. Thus, if the expected inflation rate increases from 5% to 7%, this implies that the nominal interest rate will need to increase by 2% in order to maintain the same real interest rate of 5%.

3.  **a.** In equilibrium in the loanable funds framework we know that investment spending must equal saving at the equilibrium interest rate. Thus, $2 - (10/1,000) \times I = 2 + (3/500) \times S$, where $I = S$ since the government is running a balanced budget and there are no capital inflows. Solving this equation yields $I = S = 500$, and plugging this value back into either the demand for loanable funds equation or the supply of loanable funds equation, we have that $r = 5\%$.

    **b.** When the government runs a budget deficit, this causes the demand for loanable funds curve to shift to the right since at every interest rate there is now greater demand for loanable funds. This will cause a movement along the supply of loanable funds curve. The new loanable funds demand curve can be written as $r = 12 - (10/1,000) \times I$. When the loanable funds demand curve shifts to the right for a given loanable funds supply curve, this should result in the equilibrium interest rate increasing.

    **c.** The new equilibrium interest rate equals 5.75%. To find this equilibrium interest rate, first solve for the equilibrium quantity of loanable funds: $12 - (10/1,000) \times I = 2 + (3/500) \times S$ since in equilibrium the level of investment spending equals the level of savings. Solving this equation yields $I = S = 625$ and plugging this value back into either the demand for loanable funds equation or the supply of loanable funds equation, we have that $r = 5.75\%$. But remember that now 200 of the investment spending represents the government's demand for loanable funds: this implies that private investment spending is now equal to 625 − 200, or 425. The government deficit results in less private investment spending occurring due to the crowding out effect.

4.  **a.** An increase in capital inflows into a country will shift the supply of loanable funds curve to the right, which will cause the equilibrium interest rate to decrease and the equilibrium quantity of loanable funds to increase.

    **b.** When the government reduces the level of the government deficit, this implies that the demand for loanable funds from the government has diminished. This will cause the demand for loanable funds curve to shift to the left and result in a decrease in the equilibrium interest rate and a decrease in the total equilibrium quantity of loanable funds. But, since the interest rate is now lower, this will cause the quantity of funds for private investment spending to increase.

**c.** Both the demand and the supply curves for loanable funds will shift due to the change in expected inflation. The demand curve will shift to the right reflecting the fact that borrowers are willing to borrow just as much as they did at the original nominal interest rate as they are now willing to borrow at the now-higher nominal interest rate (remember that the real interest rate is equal to the nominal interest rate minus the inflation rate). The supply curve will shift to the left since lenders now are willing to lend the same amount of funds only if the nominal interest rate they receive reflects the new higher expected inflation rate. Both curves shift, resulting in the nominal interest rate rising by the amount of the change in the expected inflation rate; there is no change in the equilibrium quantity of loanable funds.

**d.** An increase in private savings will cause the supply of loanable funds curve to shift to the right resulting in a decrease in the equilibrium interest rate and an increase in the equilibrium quantity of loanable funds.

**e.** When there is a decrease in perceived business opportunities, this causes the demand for loanable funds curve to shift to the left, which will result in both the equilibrium interest rate and the equilibrium quantity of loanable funds decreasing.

## Answers to Module Review Questions

1.   **Answer d.** The loanable funds market is a hypothetical market where savers can lend money or supply funds to borrowers, the demanders of funds. The price for borrowing funds is the interest rate, or the return the lender of funds receives for loaning out a dollar for a year.

2.   **Answer c.** To calculate the interest rate Maxine pays, use the following formula:

Interest rate $= [$(total payment at end of year $-$ amount of loan)$/$(amount of loan)$] \times 100$

which yields the following:

Interest rate $= [115 - 100)/(100)] \times 100 = 15\%$

3.   **Answer d.** When making the loan, Joe, with his expected inflation rate of 7%, anticipates a real interest rate of 8%; when the actual inflation rate is 8% rather than 7%, Joe's real interest rate on the loan falls to 7% and he is worse off than he anticipated. When making the loan, Maxine, with her expected inflation rate of 10%, anticipates a real interest rate of 5%; when the actual inflation rate is 8% rather than 5%, Maxine's real interest rate on the loan rises to 7% and she is worse off than she anticipated. The nominal interest rate is 15%, while the real interest rate is the nominal interest rate minus the inflation rate, or 7%.

4.   **Answer c.** When the government runs a deficit, it becomes a borrower in the loanable funds market and this implies that the demand curve for loanable funds shifts to the right at any given interest rate.

5.   **Answer f.** The demand for loanable funds curve represents borrowers who enter this market in order to demand funds for investment spending. The supply of loanable funds curve represents savers who provide excess funds to this market in order to supply these excess funds to those individuals who want to borrow funds. The equilibrium interest rate equates the supply of funds with the demand for funds.

6.   **Answer e.** When the government runs a deficit, this implies that the government is spending more than its tax revenue. This requires the government to borrow funds to finance the deficit, which results in the demand for loanable funds curve shifting out to the right. Holding everything else constant, this causes the equilibrium interest rate in the loanable funds market to increase. At a higher interest rate, less private investment spending will occur: the government deficit will crowd out private investment spending. There is not enough information to know with certainty what will happen to capital inflows when the government runs a deficit.

# 22(58)

# The Time Value of Money

## BEFORE YOU READ THE MODULE

## Summary

This module discusses the concept of present value and explains why a dollar today is more valuable than a dollar received in the future. The module also explains how the concept of present value can help individuals and firms make decisions when costs or benefits occur in the future.

## Module Objectives

**Objective #1.** The present value calculation is a method for evaluating the value today of a payment to be received or made at some point in the future. This calculation is useful when comparing the benefits and costs from an activity when the benefits and costs arrive at different points in time. By using present values in evaluating a project, you can evaluate the project as if all the costs and benefits from the project were occurring today rather than at different times.

- The present value calculation recognizes that a dollar held today is worth more than a dollar held a year from now. You can use the interest rate to compare the value of a dollar today to a dollar received at some point in the future: the interest rate measures the cost to you of delaying the receipt of a dollar of benefit, or the benefit to you of delaying the payment of a dollar of cost.

- Suppose you lend out $x today with the expectation that you will be repaid a dollar a year from now. The dollar you receive a year from now should be equal to $x plus the interest you receive from the borrower. If interest rate is represented as $r$, then we can express this idea as follows: the payment you receive a year from now ($1) equals $x(1 + r)$. Thus $x is the present value of the $1 you receive a year from now, and the present value of a payment of $1 made a year from now is $x = 1/(1 + r)$. This method converts future dollars into their present values so that the time factor issue can be eliminated when making decisions. The present value concept can be expanded to a number of years. For example, the present value of a payment made $N$ years from now is (future value)$/(1 + r)^N$.

- The net present value is the present value of current and future benefits minus the present value of current and future costs. When comparing potential projects, the project with the highest net present value is financially the most attractive project to undertake.

## Key Terms

**present value** the amount of money needed at the present time to produce, at the prevailing *interest rate,* a given amount of money at a specified future time.

**net present value** the *present value* of current and future benefits minus the present value of current and future costs.

*Notes*

## ◼ AFTER YOU READ THE MODULE

## Tip

The calculation of present value is a calculation that allows you to compare a stream of payments occurring over time to another stream of payments occurring over some other period of time. This calculation is highly useful, and you should practice using it until you are comfortable with the concept as well as the technique.

## WORKED PROBLEMS

1.  Joel starts the year with $0. Each year Joel is able to earn $5,000 during the year so that at the beginning of the next year he has another $5,000. For example, at the beginning of the first year Joel has $0, and at the end of the first year (or the beginning of the second year) he has $5,000 to add to his first $0. Joel is contemplating two options for this money: in the first option, Joel simply places the money in a box under his bed; and in the second option, Joel places the money at the beginning of each year in the bank and earns 5% interest on that money during that year. He does not remove the money, and whatever interest he earns in the first year gets added to his initial deposit for that year. With this second option, he plans to keep the money in for five years. Joel has asked you to provide a numerical calculation of the value of these two options to him at the end of five years.

**STEP 1:** Calculate the value of the first option for Joel.

It is helpful when calculating the value to Joel to think about a number line with each mark on the number line signifying a year. For Joel, we start at the initial point (Year 0) and note that he has $0. At the end of the first year, Joel has this $0 plus an additional $5,000. Look at the following sketch to see how we can illustrate the first option.

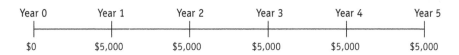

| Year 0 | Year 1 | Year 2 | Year 3 | Year 4 | Year 5 |
|--------|--------|--------|--------|--------|--------|
| $0 | $5,000 | $5,000 | $5,000 | $5,000 | $5,000 |

From the sketch, we can see that Joel has a total of $25,000 if he earns $5,000 per year and saves this amount of money for five years.

**STEP 2:** Calculate the value of the second option for Joel.

In the second option, Joel places the first $5,000 in the bank at the beginning of the second year and earns interest of 5% on this deposit for the year. At the end of the year, Joel will have his initial $5,000 plus his interest payment: we can write this amount as $(5,000)(1 + .05)$. Joel plans to keep all of this in the bank and earn interest of 5% on this total amount for the next year. Thus, for the first $5,000 he deposited, he will earn $(5,000)(1 + .05)(1 + .05)$ after it has been deposited at the bank for two years. Joel will be able to keep this first deposit in the bank for four years, so this first deposit will have a value of $(5,000)(1 + .05)^4$ after five years. But, Joel plans to deposit a second $5,000 at the end of year 2: this second $5,000 will earn interest for three years, and its value to Joel after five years can be written as $(5,000)(1 + .05)^3$. This same reasoning can be used for the $5,000 Joel will deposit at the end of year 3: its value will be $(5,000)(1 + .05)^2$. The $5,000 Joel will deposit at the end of year 4 will have a value of $(5,000)(1 + .05)$. The value of the $5,000 Joel will deposit at the end of year 5 will simply be $5,000. Total value of option 2 for Joel can be written as

Total value = $(5,000)(1 + .05)^4 + (5,000)(1 + .05)^3 + (5,000)(1 + .05)^2 + (5,000)(1 + .05) + 5,000 = \$27,628.16$.

**STEP 3:** Compare the values of the two options for Joel and make a recommendation.

Clearly, option 2 results in Joel having a larger amount of savings after five years.

2. Bernie just won the Wisconsin State Lottery and he can either receive his payout from this win as a single payment of $5,000 in cash now, or he can receive a payment of $2,500 a year for two years starting now. Bernie is confident that the interest rate will be constant throughout the two years at 5% per year. He has asked you to advise him on which payment plan he should take. Provide Bernie with an analysis to help him make his decision.

**STEP 1:** To answer this problem you will need to have a solid grasp of the concept of present value.

Calculating a present value on the payments that Bernie will receive over the two-year period will enable you to then compare the value of the single payment received now with the two payments received over time.

**STEP 2:** Calculate the present value of the payments Bernie could receive over the two-year period of time.

The present value of the payments Bernie will receive if he chooses to receive his winnings over a two-year period can be calculated as:

Present value of payment stream = $2,500 + (2,500)/(1.05) = 2,500 + 2,380.95 = \$4,880.95$

**STEP 3:** Provide Bernie with guidance as to which payment plan he should choose, as well as a reason for your recommendation.

Bernie can either receive $5,000 today or $4,880.95 if he opts to receive his winnings over a two-year period. Clearly his winnings are greater if he elects the single payment today rather than spreading his winnings over a longer period. Bernie should opt for the single payment if his only concern is maximizing the dollar value of his payout.

# Problems and Exercises

1.  Mary offers to pay Joe $1,000 a year from now if he will loan her money today. Suppose Joe wants to earn 10% interest and there is no inflation over this period. What is the maximum amount Joe will lend Mary, given her offer?

2.  Sarah borrows $1,000 from Joe at the beginning of the year and promises to repay him at the end of five years. She also agrees to pay him an annual interest rate of 12%. What is the total amount Joe will receive at the end of the fifth year?

3.  Joe can't decide between two financial options: he can loan Sarah $1,000 as outlined in problem 2, or he can invest the $1,000 in a new venture. He estimates that during the first year the venture will earn 5% interest, during the second and third years it will earn 10% interest, and during the fourth and fifth years it will earn 18% interest. Evaluate these two options for Joe and then make a recommendation based on this evaluation.

4.  You have won the lottery and you can receive your winnings as a single payment of $2 million in cash now or you can receive a payment of $500,000 a year for five years starting now. The interest rate is constant and equal to 10% per year. Which payment plan do you prefer?

5.  Does your decision in problem 4 change if the interest rate is constant and equal to 8% instead of 10%? Explain your answer.

**6.** Does your decision in problem 4 change if the interest rate is constant and equal to 15% instead of 10%? Explain your answer.

## ■ BEFORE YOU TAKE THE TEST

## Module Review Questions

Use the following information to answer the next two questions.

Marty borrows $1,000 from Harry on January 1, 2014, and promises to repay Harry on December 31, 2019, a payment that will result in Harry earning an annual rate of interest of 10%.

**1.** Which of the following expressions correctly states the value of Marty's payment on December 31, 2014?

a. $(\$1,000)(1 + 10)$

b. $(\$1,000)/(1 + 0.10)^5$

c. $(\$1,000)(1 + 0.10) + (\$1,000)(1 + 0.10)^2 + (\$1,000)(1 + 0.10)^3 + (\$1,000)(1 + 0.10)^4 + (\$1,000)(1 + 0.10)^5$

d. $(\$1,000)(1 + 0.10)^5$

**2.** Suppose Harry tells Marty he will lend him the money if he earns an annual rate of interest of 12%. This will result in Marty paying Harry a

a. smaller amount than if the interest rate were 10%.

b. larger amount than if the interest rate were 10%.

**3.** Holding everything else constant, the present value of a future payment increases when the interest rate rises.

a. True

b. False

Use the following information to answer the next three questions.

Courtney's Computers is thinking about whether they should invest in a new software program. Development of this program will require an initial expenditure of $4 million now but will result in annual profits of $2 million for three years.

**4.** No matter what the interest rate, Courtney's Computers should invest in this new software since the profits from the new software far outweigh the costs of developing the software.

a. True

b. False

5.  Given the information and an interest rate of 20%, Courtney's Computers should
    a. invest in the development of the new software.
    b. not invest in the development of the new software.

6.  Given the above information and an interest rate of 20%, the net present value of this new software for Courtney's Computers is equal to
    a. −$2 million.        c. $0.21 million.
    b. $2 million.         d. −$0.21 million.

7.  When considering a new investment project, companies
    a. do not care if the net present value is positive or negative provided the interest rate is at least 10%.
    b. are willing to undertake investment projects only when the interest rate is 5% or lower.
    c. ignore the interest rate.
    d. None of the above answers is correct.

## ANSWER KEY

## Answers to Problems and Exercises

1. To calculate this value, use the present value formula: $PV = \text{(future value)}/(1 + r)$. Thus, $PV = (\$1{,}000)/(1 + 0.10) = \$909.09$. Joe will be willing to lend Mary $909.09 today, given her offer.

2. The future value Joe will receive equals $(\$1{,}000)(1 + 0.12)^5$, or $1,762.34.

3. From problem 2, we know Joe will earn a total of $762.34 if he loans Sarah $1,000 for five years. To evaluate what Joe should do requires a calculation of the value of the second option. This second option is a bit more complicated to calculate than the loan to Sarah. At the end of the first year, this option is worth $(\$1{,}000)(1 + 0.05)$, or $1,050. This amount remains with the venture, and at the end of the second year the value of this option will equal $(\$1{,}050)(1 + 0.10)$. At the end of the third year the value of this option will equal $(\$1{,}050)(1 + 0.10)(1 + 0.10)$, or $1,270.50. At the end of the fourth year the value of this option is $(\$1{,}270.50)(1 + 0.18)$, and at the end of the fifth year the value of this option is $(\$1{,}270.50)(1 + 0.18)(1 + 0.18)$ or $1,769.04. Subtracting out Joe's initial investment of $1,000 yields Joe a net income of $769.04. Since this amount is greater than what he receives from Sarah, Joe should invest in the new venture.

4. To compare these payments requires calculating the present value of the future payments you would receive if you opted for five payments over time instead of a single payment now. The present value of these payments is $\$500{,}000 + (\$500{,}000)/(1.1) + (\$500{,}000)/(1.1)^2 + (\$500{,}000)/(1.1)^3 + (\$500{,}000)/(1.1)^4$, or $2,086,174. You will receive a larger total payment if you choose to receive the lottery winnings over a five-year period.

5. No, the decision does not change, although this change in the interest rate does change the present value of the stream of payments received over five years. The present value of this stream of payments is now equal to $\$500{,}000 + (\$500{,}000)/(1.08) + (\$500{,}000)/(1.08)^2 + (\$500{,}000)/(1.08)^3 + (\$500{,}000)/(1.08)^4$, or $2,154,785. A decrease in the interest rate makes the stream of payments over five years even more attractive to you.

6. Yes, when the interest rate increases to 15%, this makes the single payment option more valuable than the stream of five payments. To see this, compare the single payment of $2 million to the present value of the stream of payments. The present value of the payments over five years is equal to $\$500{,}000 + (\$500{,}000)/(1.15) + (\$500{,}000)/(1.15)^2 + (\$500{,}000)/(1.15)^3 + (\$500{,}000)/(1.15)^4$, or $1,928,232, which is less than $2 million.

## Answers to Module Review Questions

1. **Answer d.** This is a simple illustration of the present value formula.

2. **Answer b.** When the interest rate increases, this means the cost of borrowing money has risen and therefore the amount of money to be paid back will rise.

3. **Answer b.** The present value of a future payment decreases when the interest rate rises, since the higher interest rate means that a smaller amount today will accumulate to a larger amount in the future.

4. **Answer b.** Whether an investment project should be undertaken or not depends on the benefits as well as the costs associated with the investment project. It is possible that even though this project has positive projected profits, the cost of borrowing funds to undertake the project will exceed these projected profits.

5.  **Answer a.** If you compute the net present value for the project, the value is a positive number and therefore the project should be undertaken. This computation is done in the answer to question 6.

6.  **Answer c.** To compute the net present value entails calculating the present value of the benefits and the present value of the costs and then subtracting the present value of the costs from the present value of the benefits. The present value of the benefits is equal to $(2)/(1+0.2) + (2)/(1+0.2)^2 + (2)/(1+0.2)^3$, and the present value of the costs is equal to 4. The difference between these two present values is approximately \$0.21 million.

7.  **Answer d.** None of the answers is true. Companies decide to undertake investment projects when the net present value is a positive number for the given interest rate.

# module 23(59)

# The Financial System

## BEFORE YOU READ THE MODULE

### Summary

This module discusses four principal types of assets: stocks, bonds, loans, and bank deposits. The module examines the role of financial intermediation in the economy and how it enables investors to diversify while simultaneously reducing their exposure to risk, reducing the costs of their financial transactions, and increasing their access to liquidity. The module also discusses how financial fluctuations occur in the financial system.

## Module Objectives

**Objective #1.** Households invest their savings and wealth, or accumulated savings, by purchasing financial assets in financial markets. Financial assets are paper claims that provide the buyer of the claim future income from the seller of the claim. Financial assets represent an asset to the purchaser of the claim and a liability to the seller of the claim. For example, if you borrow funds from a bank, the loan represents an asset to the bank because the bank will receive income in the future from the loan. And the loan represents a liability to you, since you must repay the funds you have borrowed at some point in the future.

**Objective #2.** The financial system provides borrowers and lenders a cost-effective way to reduce transactions costs and risk while enhancing their liquidity.

- Transactions costs are the expenses suppliers and demanders incur when they negotiate and execute a transaction.

- Financial risk refers to the uncertainty about future outcomes that involve financial losses and gains. A risk-averse person views potential losses and gains in an asymmetrical way: the total decrease in the person's welfare from losing a given amount of money is greater than the total increase in the person's welfare from gaining an equivalent amount of money. The risk-averse person is willing to expend a greater amount of resources to avoid losing a dollar than he or she is willing to expend to gain a dollar.

360

- Diversification, or the holding of different types of financial and physical assets, reduces the level of financial risk an individual faces. Investing in several assets with unrelated risks lowers the total risk of loss for the individual.

- *Liquidity* refers to the ease with which an asset can be converted into cash. A liquid asset is easily converted into cash, while an illiquid asset cannot be easily converted into cash.

**Objective #3.** The four primary types of financial assets are loans, bonds, stocks, and bank deposits.

- A loan is an agreement between a particular lender and a particular borrower. Loans are typically tailored to the needs of the borrower. Loans have high transactions costs.

- A bond is a promise to repay the owner of the bond a specific amount at some point in the future plus yearly interest for the life of the bond. Information about the bond issuer is freely available from bond-rating agencies that assess the creditworthiness of the bond issuer. Bonds are easy to resell, which enhances their liquidity.

- A stock is a share in the ownership of a company. Owning a share of stock in a given company is riskier than owning a bond from this same company; stock ownership generally results in a higher return for the investor than a bond, but it also carries higher risk.

**Objective #4.** Financial intermediaries are institutions that transform funds gathered from many individuals into financial assets. Four important financial intermediaries are mutual funds, pension funds, life insurance companies, and banks.

- A mutual fund creates a diversified stock portfolio and then resells shares of the stock portfolio to individual investors. This enables investors with a small amount of money to indirectly invest in a diversified portfolio that yields a better return for any given level of risk than would otherwise be available to the investor.

- Pension funds are nonprofit institutions that collect savings from their members and then invest these funds in a wide variety of assets in order to provide retirement income for their members.

- Life insurance companies collect funds from policyholders in order to guarantee payments to the policyholders' beneficiaries when the policyholders die. Life insurance companies increase individual welfare by reducing risk.

- Banks are institutions that gather funds from depositors and then use these funds to make loans. Banks enhance financial liquidity while serving the financing needs of those borrowers who do not want to use the stock or bond markets.

  - A bank deposit is an asset for the individuals depositing their funds at the bank and a liability for the bank.

  - A bank loan is an asset for the bank and a liability for the individuals who borrow the funds.

  - Bank deposits provide liquid assets to the owners of these deposits while simultaneously providing a source of funds to finance the illiquid investments of borrowers.

# Key Terms

*Notes*

**wealth** (of a *household*) the value of accumulated savings.

**financial asset** a paper claim that entitles the buyer to future income from the seller. *Loans, stocks, bonds,* and *bank deposits* are types of financial assets.

# Key Terms *(continued)*

**physical asset** a claim on a tangible object that gives the owner the right to dispose of the object as he or she wishes.

**liability** a requirement to pay income in the future.

**transaction costs** the expenses of negotiating and executing a deal.

**financial risk** uncertainty about future outcomes that involve financial losses and gains.

**diversification** investment in several different assets with unrelated, or independent, risks, so that the possible losses are independent events.

**liquid** describes an asset that can be quickly converted into cash without much loss of value.

**illiquid** describes an asset that cannot be quickly converted into cash without much loss of value.

**loan** a lending agreement between an individual lender and an individual borrower. Loans are usually tailored to the individual borrower's needs and ability to pay but carry relatively high *transaction costs*.

**default** the risk that the bond issuer fails to make payments as specified by the bond contract.

**loan-backed securities** assets created by pooling individual *loans* and selling shares in that pool.

**financial intermediary** an institution, such as a *mutual fund, pension fund, life insurance company*, or *bank*, that transforms the funds it gathers from many individuals into *financial assets*.

**mutual fund** a *financial intermediary* that creates a *stock* portfolio by buying and holding shares in companies and then selling shares of this portfolio to individual investors.

**pension fund** a type of *mutual fund* that holds assets in order to provide retirement income to its members.

**life insurance company** a *financial intermediary* that sells policies guaranteeing a payment to a policyholder's beneficiaries when the policyholder dies.

**bank deposit** a claim on a *bank* that obliges the bank to give the depositor his or her cash when demanded.

**bank** a *financial intermediary* that provides *liquid* assets in the form of *bank deposits* to lenders and uses those funds to finance the *illiquid* investments or *investment spending* needs of borrowers.

## ▮ AFTER YOU READ THE MODULE

## Tips

**Tip #1.** This module defines several types of financial assets (stocks, bonds, loans, and bank deposits). For some students this may be the first time you have thought about the topic of financial assets: it is important that you understand what each of these terms means and how they all represent a financial asset.

**Tip #2.** This module explains three important tasks that the financial system strives to address: a way to reduce transactions costs, a way to reduce risk, and a way to enhance liquidity. If these are new concepts to you it will be important that you spend time thinking about these ideas and getting more familiar with these concepts.

# WORKED PROBLEMS

1. Susie has been studying the financial system and is still a bit confused about what constitutes a financial asset. She has asked you to help her increase her understanding of this concept. In addition, she would like you to explain what is meant by bonds, loans, stocks, and bank deposits. Susie typically understands best if she is given examples and not just definitions. Help her to understand these concepts.

**STEP 1:** Start by providing Susie with some guidance on the meaning of the term *financial asset.*

A financial asset is a way to transform the cash you currently hold into a claim for a future payment. For example, suppose that Susie is currently holding $1,000 in her wallet. If she does not anticipate needing this money in the near future, she could take these funds and purchase a financial asset that would allow her to claim a future payment. For example, Susie could conclude that it is dangerous to carry so much cash in her wallet (it could be stolen, or tempt her to buy frivolous items), so Susie could take the funds to the bank and deposit them in an account. Her deposit would provide her with a paper claim to those funds in the future. But, depositing these funds in a bank account is not the only option available to Susie. In Step 2, several other options for Susie's funds are described.

**STEP 2:** Now that Susie has a better understanding of what a financial asset is, help her to understand how a stock, bond, loan, and bank deposit all represent examples of financial assets.

If Susie takes her funds and uses them to buy shares of stock, she is essentially trading these cash funds for a share in the ownership of some businesses. In the future if Susie wishes to convert these shares of stock to cash she can sell her shares. Essentially Susie trades her cash today for a paper claim to a future payment when she sells the shares of stock.

Susie could also loan out her funds. If she did that she would give up her funds today for a promise of a future payment from the individual who has borrowed the funds. Once again this transaction represents Susie giving up the use of her cash today for a paper claim to a future payment when the loan is repaid.

Susie could also purchase a bond with her funds: essentially when Susie does this she is buying an IOU, which is a promise by the issuer of the bond (the IOU) to make a future payment to the holder of the bond. Susie is giving up the use of her cash today for a paper claim to a future payment when the bond is repaid.

2.   George has been studying the financial system and is still a bit confused about the functions that a financial system provides to an economy and why these functions are important. He has asked you to help him understand these ideas. George would find it helpful to have some examples to further his understanding.

**STEP 1:** **Review the three functions the financial system addresses.**

A well-developed financial system addresses three primary functions: reduction in transaction costs, reduction in risk, and enhanced liquidity. A reduction in transaction costs essentially means that the financial system reduces the costs associated with negotiating and making a deal. The financial system can reduce transaction costs by providing markets (for example, the bond market) that are able to make these negotiations less costly to execute. A reduction in risk can be accomplished in the financial system through shared ownership: when an individual or business allows others to invest in their business, they effectively increase their diversification and reduce their exposure to risk. Enhanced liquidity is provided by the financial system because the financial system provides a means to quickly convert a financial asset to cash.

**STEP 2:** **Review why these three functions are important for an economy. Provide some examples to help illustrate these points.**

By reducing transactions costs and risk while enhancing liquidity, the financial system allows for lenders and borrowers to make mutually beneficial deals. A well-developed financial system allows for greater investment in the economy, greater specialization and complexity within the economy, and higher economic growth due to the ability to finance and create more capital in the economy.

# Problems and Exercises

1.   Briefly describe three important problems that lenders and borrowers face and how the financial system addresses these three problems.

2. Consider the following three lists of assets.

| List A | List B | List C |
|---|---|---|
| $50 in cash | A car | A boat |
| A six-month CD worth $50,000, redeemable without penalty six months from today's date | A checking account deposit<br><br>A Treasury bond issued by the government of the United States | The coins you collect in a jar<br><br>A savings account deposit |
| A share of stock | | |
| A savings account deposit | | |

a. Rank each of these lists of assets from the most liquid asset to the least liquid asset.

b. Why is money *not* equivalent to wealth?

## BEFORE YOU TAKE THE TEST

## Module Review Questions

1. Financial markets are beneficial
   a. to savers, since they provide interest payments for the use of savers' funds.
   b. to borrowers, since they provide a source of funds for productive investments.
   c. to the government, since they provide both a use for surplus government funds and a source of funds should the government run a deficit.
   d. Answers (a), (b), and (c) are all correct.

2. Which of the following is an asset from a bank's perspective?
   a. Joe's checking account deposit of $500 at the bank
   b. Mike's car loan for $2,000 that he borrowed from the bank
   c. Mary's savings account balance of $325 at the bank
   d. From the bank's perspective, answers (a), (b), and (c) are all assets.

**3.** Financial markets provide a means for
   a. reducing risk for borrowers and lenders.
   b. reducing transaction costs for borrowers and lenders.
   c. enhancing liquidity for borrowers and lenders.
   d. Answers (a), (b), and (c) are all correct.

**4.** Which of the following assets is most liquid?
   a. a home with a market value of $200,000
   b. a checking account balance of $1,000
   c. a three-carat diamond engagement ring
   d. a rare edition of an out-of-print book

**5.** Financial intermediaries
   a. transform funds gathered from many individuals into financial assets.
   b. provide a means of increasing risk for investors as well as business owners.
   c. only invest in bonds.
   d. only invest in stocks.

**6.** Banks
   a. provide liquidity to lenders.
   b. serve the financing needs of borrowers who do not use or cannot be served by the stock and bond markets.
   c. accept deposits from individuals who have excess funds.
   d. Answers (a), (b), and (c) are all correct.

## ◼ ANSWER KEY

# Answers to Problems and Exercises

**1.**  Lenders and borrowers face three broad categories of problems: the problem of transaction costs, the problem of risk, and the problem of achieving the desired level of liquidity.

Transaction costs refer to the costs of making transactions: both borrowers and lenders face transaction costs when they commit to borrowing or lending funds. The financial system reduces transaction costs by making the arrangements between lenders and borrowers more efficient. For example, a business can borrow funds from a bank much more efficiently than it can borrow the same amount of funds from 1,000 potential lenders.

Financial risk, or risk, refers to the uncertainty people face with regard to future outcomes that involve financial gains and losses. The financial system helps borrowers and lenders share the risk they are exposed to through diversification, since this diversification, or investing in assets with unrelated risks, reduces the total risk of loss the individual faces.

The financial system also addresses the need for liquidity for investors. Stocks and bonds as well as banks provide a mechanism for individuals to have liquid assets while also enabling the financing of illiquid investments.

**2.  a.** List A: $50 in cash, a savings account deposit, a share of stock, a six-month CD redeemable without penalty six months from today's date

List B: The checking account deposit, a Treasury bond issued by the government of the United States, a car

List C: The coins you collect in a jar, a savings account deposit, a boat

**b.** Wealth includes all assets, physical or financial, that an individual owns at a particular point in time. Although these assets may be quite valuable, they may not all possess the characteristic of liquidity. Money possesses this characteristic, and thus includes only those items that can easily be used to purchase goods and services. In this question, the bonds, stock, and boat are assets and therefore part of the owner's wealth, but they are not considered money.

# Answers to Module Review Questions

**1.**  **Answer d.** Financial markets provide funds for those who need to borrow funds, as well as a means of earning interest for those with surplus funds.

**2.**  **Answer b.** Joe's checking account balance is an asset from Joe's perspective and a liability from the bank's perspective. Mary's saving account balance is similarly an asset from her perspective and a liability from the bank's perspective. Mike's car loan represents an asset for the bank since Mike is legally obligated to repay the funds he has borrowed; the car loan represents a liability from Mike's perspective.

**3.**  **Answer d.** Answers (a), (b), and (c) focus on three problems that financial markets address for borrowers and lenders.

**4.**  **Answer b.** The checking account balance is the most liquid asset in this list, since it can be effectively used as cash at most business locations. The other three assets must be sold to a buyer in order to convert them into cash: this transaction takes time and reduces the liquidity of these assets.

5.  **Answer a.** Financial intermediaries provide a means for reducing risk for investors and business owners when they gather funds from many individuals and then invest these funds in a diversified portfolio of financial assets that can include stocks as well as bonds.

6.  **Answer d.** Banks do provide liquidity for lenders in the form of deposits that can be accessed easily, while at the same time banks provide funds to finance the illiquid investments of borrowers.

# The Multiplier

## BEFORE YOU READ THE MODULE

### Summary

This module introduces the concept of the marginal propensity to consume (*MPC*) and then discusses its significance. The module also develops the concept of the multiplier: the multiplier describes how an initial change in spending can lead to further changes in spending in the aggregate economy.

### Module Objectives

**Objective #1.** This module makes four simplifying assumptions in building a model of income and expenditure. These assumptions are:

- Producer prices are fixed and therefore any change in aggregate spending results in a change in aggregate output or real GDP. Given this assumption, real GDP and nominal GDP are equivalent since the aggregate price level is fixed and does not change.

- The interest rate is given in this simple model.

- Government spending and taxes are equal to zero.

- Exports and imports are equal to zero.

**Objective #2.** The marginal propensity to consume, or the *MPC*, measures the increase in consumer spending that occurs if current disposable income increases by $1. The *MPC* can be calculated as the change in consumer spending divided by the change in disposable income. The *MPC* is a number between 0 and 1. The marginal propensity to save, or the *MPS*, is the fraction of an additional dollar of disposable income that is saved. The *MPS* is equal to $(1 - MPC)$.

**Objective #3.** An initial rise or fall in aggregate spending at a given level of GDP is an autonomous change in aggregate spending. This change in aggregate spending will result in a multiplier process where the total change in real GDP caused by the initial change in autonomous spending is equal to the multiplier times the initial change in autonomous aggregate spending. The simple multiplier developed in this chapter is equal to $[1/(1 - MPC)]$. Thus, the change in real GDP = $[1/(1 - MPC)] \times$ (change in autonomous aggregate spending).

369

## Key Terms

**marginal propensity to consume (MPC)** the increase in *consumer spending* when *disposable income* rises by $1. Because consumers normally spend part but not all of an additional dollar of disposable income, *MPC* is between 0 and 1.

**marginal propensity to save (MPS)** the fraction of an additional dollar of *disposable income* that is saved; *MPS* is equal to 1 − *MPC*.

**autonomous change in aggregate spending** an initial rise or fall in *aggregate spending* at a given level of *real GDP*.

**multiplier** the ratio of total change in *real GDP* caused by an *autonomous change in aggregate spending* to the size of that autonomous change.

## AFTER YOU READ THE MODULE

## Tips

**Tip #1.** This module develops the concept of the marginal propensity to consume (*MPC*). The *MPC* expresses the ratio of the change in consumer spending to the change in disposable income. For example, if the *MPC* = 0.8 for an economy, this tells us that if disposable income increases by $1 in this economy it will lead to an increase of $0.80 in consumer spending; or, if disposable income increases by $100 in this economy, it will lead to an increase of $80 in consumer spending. In other words, any increase in income will result in consumer spending increasing by 0.8 (the change in income) in this example.

**Tip #2.** The relevance of the multiplier for our understanding of the aggregate economy is that it explains in a simple manner why an increase in spending expands the overall level of spending in an economy beyond this initial increase in spending; or, conversely, why a decrease in spending decreases the overall level of spending in an economy beyond this initial decrease in spending. Review this module and this concept until you feel very comfortable with this idea.

# WORKED PROBLEMS

1. Suppose that the marginal propensity to save in an economy is equal to 0.2. Furthermore, suppose that you are told that the level of investment spending increases by $200 during this year. Trace out the total increase in real GDP showing the increase in consumer spending for at least the second, third, and fourth round of spending. Provide the numeric value of the increase in consumer spending for each of these rounds as well as the total increase in real GDP. Assume that in this economy there is no government sector, no taxes, no transfers, and that the aggregate price level and the interest rate are fixed.

**STEP 1:** Find the marginal propensity to consume from the given information.

We are given information about the marginal propensity to save (*MPS*) but are not given the information about the marginal propensity to consume (*MPC*). Since the

MPS is equal to 1 – MPC, we can easily compute the MPC as equal to 0.8. To see why this is true, recall that disposable income is income minus net taxes. So, if disposable income is equal to consumption spending plus savings, then a change in disposable income must be equal to the change in consumption spending plus the change in savings. Or, symbolically, $\Delta$(Disposable Income) = $\Delta C + \Delta S$, where C is consumption spending and S is savings. Dividing both sides of this equation by $\Delta$(Disposable Income) we get 1 = MPC + MPS, since the MPC = $\Delta C/\Delta$(Disposable Income) and the MPS = $\Delta S/\Delta$(Disposable Income).

**STEP 2:** Create a table to record the change in spending for each round as well as the initial impact of the change in investment spending.

In the table, we will want a column that identifies the change and a column to record its numeric value. Thus,

| | |
|---|---|
| Increase in investment spending | $200 |
| + Second-round increase in consumer spending | = (MPC × $200) = $160 |
| + Third-round increase in consumer spending | = (MPC)(MPC × $200) = $128 |
| + Fourth-round increase in consumer spending | = (MPC)[(MPC)(MPC × $200)] = $102.40 |
| **...Total increase in real GDP** | = [1/(1 – MPC)] × ($200) = $1,000 |

**STEP 3:** Calculate the total increase in real GDP.

Our table in Step 2 already provides the answer to this question, but let's review the process. To find the total increase in real GDP, recall that the change in real GDP will equal the product of [1/(1 – MPC)] × (the initial change in spending). In this case since the MPC is equal to .8, we can calculate the value of [1/(1 – MPC)], or the multiplier, as 5. Since the initial change in spending is equal to $200, we can therefore calculate that the change in real GDP will be equal to 5 × ($200), or $1,000.

2. Suppose that the marginal propensity to consume in an economy is equal to 0.75 and that you are told that investment spending decreases this year by –$50. You are asked to calculate the change in consumer spending for the second round, third round, and fourth round, and in addition, you are asked to calculate the change in real income due to this change in investment spending. Assume that in this economy there is no government sector, no taxes, no transfers, and that the aggregate price level and the interest rate are fixed.

**STEP 1:** Create a table to record the change in spending for each round as well as the initial impact of the change in investment spending.

In the table, we will want a column that identifies the change and a column to record its numeric value. Thus,

| | |
|---|---|
| Increase in investment spending | –$50 |
| + Second-round increase in consumer spending | = [MPC × (–$50)] = –$37.50 |
| + Third-round increase in consumer spending | = (MPC)[(MPC) × (–$50)] = –$28.125 |
| + Fourth-round increase in consumer spending | = MPC(MPC)[(MPC) × (–$50)] = –$21.094 |
| **...Total increase in real GDP** | = [1/(1 – MPC)] × (–$50) = –$200 |

**STEP 2:** Calculate the total increase in real GDP.

The table in Step 2 already provides this answer for us, but let's take a moment to review the process. Since we know the *MPC*, it is easy to calculate the value of the multiplier: the multiplier is equal to $1/(1 - MPC)$, or 4 in this example. Since investment spending has decreased by –$50, then we know the overall change in real GDP must be a decrease of $4 \times (-\$50)$ or –$200.

## Problems and Exercises

1. Suppose the *MPC* in an economy is equal to 0.75. Furthermore, to simplify the analysis assume that there are no taxes in this economy and no international trade. Suppose the initial level of real GDP in this economy is $200 million. Using the table below calculate what the effect on real GDP will be if there is an increase in investment spending of $50 million.

   **a.** Fill in the table below given the above information.

   | Change in spending | Effect on real GDP |
   | --- | --- |
   | Initial increase in investment spending | = $50 million |
   | + Second-round increase in consumer spending | = |
   | + Third-round increase in consumer spending | |
   | + Fourth-round increase in consumer spending | |
   | ....... | |
   | **Total increase in real GDP** | |

   **b.** What is the value of the multiplier in this example?

   **c.** What is the value of real GDP after the economy fully adjusts to this increase in investment spending?

**2.** Suppose the *MPC* in an economy is equal to 0.8. Furthermore, to simplify the analysis assume that there are no taxes in this economy and no international trade. Suppose the initial level of real GDP is $500 million. Using the table below calculate what the effect on real GDP will be if there is a decrease in investment spending of $10 million.

**a.** Fill in the table below given the above information.

| Change in spending | Effect on real GDP |
|---|---|
| Initial increase in investment spending | = –$10 million |
| + Second-round increase in consumer spending | = |
| + Third-round increase in consumer spending | |
| + Fourth-round increase in consumer spending | |
| ....... | |
| **Total increase in real GDP** | |

**b.** What is the value of the multiplier in this example?

**c.** What is the value of real GDP after the economy fully adjusts to this increase in investment spending?

**3.** Suppose that the marginal propensity to save, *MPS*, is equal to .25 in Econoland. If autonomous aggregate spending increases by $100 million what do you predict will be the change in real GDP? Explain how you arrived at your answer.

## ▐ BEFORE YOU TAKE THE TEST

# Module Review Questions

**1.** Which of the following is *not* an assumption underlying the multiplier process for this module?

a. Since this is a short-run process, the aggregate price level is sticky but not fixed.

b. The interest rate is assumed to be fixed and unaffected by the factors analyzed in our model of the multiplier process.

c. The multiplier process assumes a closed economy where government spending, taxes, and transfers equal zero.

d. In the short run, the economy always produces at the full-employment level of output.

2. Holding everything else constant in an economy, the larger the *MPS*, the
   a. smaller the value of the multiplier.
   b. larger the value of the multiplier.

3. Suppose the *MPC* is equal to 0.5. A $100 increase in investment spending will lead to a
   a. $100 increase in spending in the first round, and a total increase in spending of $500.
   b. $50 increase in spending in the first round, and a total increase in spending of $100.
   c. $100 increase in spending in the first round, and a total increase in spending of $200.
   d. total increase in spending of $100 since an increase in investment spending does not create a multiplier effect.

4. The marginal propensity to consume
   a. is the increase in disposable income from a $1 increase in consumer spending.
   b. is the increase in consumer spending from a $1 increase in disposable income.
   c. is usually a number between zero and one, but occasionally is a number greater than one.
   d. can be written as the change in consumer spending divided by the change in disposable income.
   e. Answers (a), (c), and (d) are all correct.
   f. Answers (b), (c), and (d) are all correct.
   g. Answers (b) and (d) are both correct.

5. Joe's disposable income increases by $500, and he finds that he spends $400 of this increase in disposable income. Joe
   a. saves $100 and his *MPS* is equal to 0.8.
   b. saves $100 and his *MPC* is 0.8.
   c. saves 20% of any increase in his disposable income.
   d. Answers (a) and (c) are both correct.
   e. Answers (b) and (c) are both correct.

6. During the multiplier process, the final change in real GDP is limited because
   a. with each round of spending, some disposable income leaks out of the income–expenditure stream as households choose to save some portion of any increase in disposable income.
   b. people reach a point where they have all the goods and services they need and so they stop spending the additional increases in disposable income they receive.

## ANSWER KEY

# Answers to Problems and Exercises

**1.  a.**

| Change in spending | Effect on real GDP |
|---|---|
| Initial increase in investment spending | = $50 million |
| + Second-round increase in consumer spending | = (0.75)($50 million) = $37.5 million |
| + Third-round increase in consumer spending | = (0.75)[(0.75)($50 million)] = $28.125 million |
| + Fourth-round increase in consumer spending | = (0.75)[(0.75)(0.75)($50 million)] = $21.094 million |
| ....... | ....... |
| **Total increase in real GDP** | **= $200 million** |

**b.** The value of the multiplier is $1/(1 - MPC)$ or in this case $1/(1 - 0.75) = 4$.

**c.** Real GDP after full adjustment to this change in investment spending is equal to $400 million.

**2.  a.**

| Change in spending | Effect on real GDP |
|---|---|
| Initial increase in investment spending | = –$10 million |
| + Second-round increase in consumer spending | = –(0.8)($10 million) = –$8 million |
| + Third-round increase in consumer spending | = –(0.8)[(0.8)($10 million)] = –$6.4 million |
| + Fourth-round increase in consumer spending | = –(0.8)[(0.8)(0.8)($10 million)] = –$5.12 million |
| ....... | ....... |
| **Total increase in real GDP** | **= –$50 million** |

**b.** The value of the multiplier in this example is equal to $1/(1 - MPC)$ and since the $MPC$ is equal to 0.8, this implies that the multiplier value is 5.

**c.** After the economy fully adjusts to this decrease in investment spending real GDP will equal $450 million.

**3.** If the $MPS$ is equal to .25, then the $MPC$ must be equal to .75. This implies that the multiplier is equal to 4 since the multiplier is equal to $1/(1 - MPC) = 1/.25 = 4$. The relationship between a change in autonomous aggregate spending and the resultant change in real GDP can be expressed as change in real GDP = (multiplier)(change in autonomous aggregate spending). In this example, this equation would therefore be change in real GDP = 4 × ($100 million) = $400 million. Thus, if autonomous aggregate spending increases by $100 million and the $MPS$ is .25, then the change in real GDP will be predicted to equal $400 million, holding everything else constant.

# Answers to Module Review Questions

**1.   Answer a.** Both answers (b) and (c) are assumptions in our model of the multiplier process in this module. This model allows the level of aggregate output to vary in the short run (answer d). Answer (a) is not true.

2. **Answer a.** The multiplier in the simple model presented in this chapter is equal to $1/(1 - MPC)$. In addition, the sum of the MPC and the MPS is equal to one. Thus, a given level of the MPC implies a particular MPS (for example, if the MPC is equal to 0.8, then the MPS is equal to 0.2). Using this information, the greater the MPC, the larger the multiplier: the intuition for this is straightforward since a large MPC implies that consumers spend a greater proportion of an increase in their income, and this spending leads to the multiplier process. Hence, the multiplier is larger when the MPS is low, and smaller when the MPS is high.

3. **Answer c.** If the MPC is equal to 0.5, then the multiplier is equal to 2. In the first round of spending, expenditure will increase by the $100 of additional investment spending. But this spending is income for people in the economy and in the second round (0.5)($100) or $50 will be spent. In the third round (0.5)($50) will be spent. This process will continue until the total amount of new spending converges to $200 or the change in real GDP is equal to $[1/(1 - MPC)] \times$ (the initial change in investment spending).

4. **Answer g.** Answers (b) and (d) are the definition of the MPC with one expressed verbally and the other expressed as a mathematical relationship. Answer (c) is incorrect since the MPC must always be a number that is greater than zero but less than one since people cannot consume more than 100% of their disposable income.

5. **Answer e.** To calculate Joe's MPC, look at the ratio of the change in consumer spending divided by the change in disposable income: $400/$500 = 0.8. If Joe's MPC is equal to 0.8, then his MPS is equal to 0.2. When Joe's MPS is 0.2, this implies that he saves 20% of any increase in his disposable income, since 0.2 is equal to 20% when expressed as a percentage rather than a decimal.

6. **Answer a.** The multiplier process describes the effect of a change in autonomous aggregate expenditure on the level of aggregate income. When there is a change in autonomous aggregate expenditure, this leads to an increase in aggregate income: part of this increase in aggregate income is spent and part is saved. The increase in aggregate income leads to more spending and more saving. Each successive round of increases in income is smaller than the preceding round since individuals save a portion of the increase in income.

# Consumption and Investment

## Summary

This module develops the concept of the aggregate consumption function: this function illustrates the relationship between current disposable income and consumer spending. It also explores how expected future income and aggregate wealth affect the level of consumer spending. Also described are the determinants of investment spending in the aggregate economy. The module discusses why investment spending is a leading indicator of the future state of the aggregate economy.

## Module Objectives

**Objective #1.** The consumption function is an equation that shows the relationship between a household's current disposable income and its level of consumer spending. We can write a simple version of the consumption function for an individual household as $c = a + MPC \times yd$, where $c$ is individual household consumer spending, $a$ is individual autonomous consumer spending or the level of consumer spending a household would do if its disposable income equaled zero, and $yd$ is individual household current disposable income. In this equation individual autonomous consumption and $yd$ are assumed to be constant. A graph of the individual household consumption function with disposable income on the horizontal axis and consumer spending on the vertical axis would have a slope equal to the $MPC$ and a y-intercept equal to $a$. Figure 25.1 on the next page illustrates an example of an individual household consumption function. Consumer spending and disposable income are positively related to each other: as disposable income increases, consumer spending increases.

**Figure 25.1**

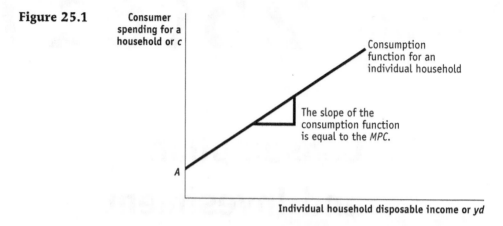

Consumer spending for a household or c

Consumption function for an individual household

The slope of the consumption function is equal to the *MPC*.

A

Individual household disposable income or *yd*

**Objective #2.**   The aggregate consumption function illustrates the relationship between the aggregate disposable income in an economy and the level of aggregate consumer spending. This relationship is similar to the one depicted in the individual household consumption function. The aggregate consumption function is written as $C = A + MPC \times YD$, where $C$ is aggregate consumer spending, $A$ is aggregate autonomous consumer spending, and $YD$ is aggregate disposable income. The aggregate consumption function, $C$, indicates a positive relationship between the level of aggregate consumer spending and the level of aggregate disposable income. Figure 25.2 provides an example of an aggregate consumption function.

**Figure 25.2**

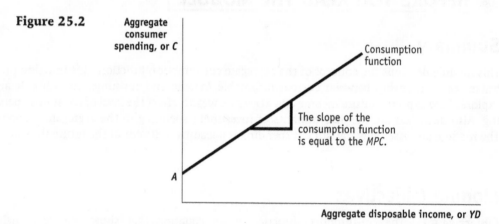

Aggregate consumer spending, or *C*

Consumption function

The slope of the consumption function is equal to the *MPC*.

A

Aggregate disposable income, or *YD*

**Objective #3.**   The two principal causes of shifts in the aggregate consumption function are changes in expected future disposable income and changes in aggregate wealth. The life-cycle hypothesis theorizes that consumers plan their spending over a lifetime, and as a result try to smooth, or even out, their consumption spending over the course of their entire lives.

- An increase in expected future disposable income or wealth causes the vertical intercept $A$, aggregate autonomous consumer spending, to increase, and this results in an upward shift of the aggregate consumption function. Similarly, a decrease in expected future disposable income or aggregate wealth causes the aggregate consumption function to shift down.

**Objective #4.**   The level of investment spending is a critical determinant of economic performance: most recessions result from a decrease in investment spending. In addition, declines in consumer spending are usually the result of a reaction to a fall in investment spending and the accompanying multiplier process.

- The three most important factors determining the level of investment spending are interest rates, expected future real GDP, and the current level of productive capacity.

- The level of investment spending that businesses actually engage in is not always the level of investment spending that they have planned.

  - Planned investment spending refers to the investment spending firms plan to make during a given time period and is dependent primarily on the interest rate, the expected future level of real GDP, and the current level of productive capacity.

  - The level of interest rates determines whether or not a firm will undertake a particular investment project. Investment projects with a rate of return equal to or greater than the equilibrium interest rate will be funded, while those investment projects with a rate of return less than the equilibrium interest rate will not be funded.

- Retained earnings refer to past profits that are used to finance investment spending. Even if the firm finances its investment spending using retained earnings, the firm still compares the rate of return for the investment project to the equilibrium interest rate. This interest rate reflects the opportunity cost of using the firm's retained earnings to fund the investment project rather than lending out the retained earnings and earning interest.

- An increase in the market interest rate makes any given investment project less profitable, while a decrease in the market interest rate makes any given investment project more profitable. Therefore, planned investment spending is inversely related to the interest rate.

**Objective #5.**   The accelerator principle is the idea that a higher rate of growth in real GDP leads to higher planned investment spending. The higher rate of growth in real GDP typically indicates rapid growth in sales, leading businesses to quickly use up any excess productive capacity and resulting in higher planned investment spending.

**Objective #6.**   Inventories are the stock of goods that firms hold in anticipation of future sales and the stock of inputs firms hold in order to have a reliable, and at hand, supply of raw materials and spare parts. Inventory investment refers to the change in total inventories held in the economy during a given period of time. Inventory investment may be positive, negative, or equal to zero. Positive inventory investment indicates that the economy has added to its stock of inventories, while negative inventory investment indicates that the level of inventories in the economy has decreased.

- Inventories fluctuate over time. Unintended changes in inventories, due to unpredicted fluctuations in sales, are referred to as unplanned inventory investment.

- Thus, actual investment spending in an economy in any given period of time is comprised of two parts: planned investment spending, $I_{Planned}$, and unplanned inventory investment, $I_{Unplanned}$. Positive unplanned inventory investment typically occurs in a slowing economy where actual expenditure on goods and services is less than forecasted expenditure. Negative unplanned inventory investment occurs in a growing economy where actual expenditure exceeds forecasted expenditure on goods and services.

- Inventories play a key role in short-run macroeconomic models, and the behavior of firms' inventories often signals the future state of the economy.

# Key Terms

**consumption function** an equation showing how an individual *household's consumer spending* varies with the household's current *disposable income.*

**aggregate consumption function** the relationship for the *economy* as a whole between aggregate current *disposable income* and aggregate *consumer spending.*

## Key Terms *(continued)*

**planned investment spending** the *investment spending* that *firms* intend to undertake during a given period. Planned investment spending may differ from actual investment spending due to *unplanned inventory investment*.

**accelerator principle** the proposition that a higher rate of growth in *real GDP* results in a higher level of planned *investment spending*, and a lower growth rate in real GDP leads to lower planned investment spending.

**inventories** stocks of goods and raw materials held to satisfy future sales.

**inventory investment** the value of the change in total *inventories* held in the *economy* during a given period. Unlike other types of *investment spending*, inventory investment can be negative, if inventories fall.

**unplanned inventory investment** unplanned changes in *inventories*, which occur when actual sales are more or less than businesses expected.

**actual investment spending** the sum of *planned investment spending* and *unplanned inventory investment*.

## ■ AFTER YOU READ THE MODULE

## Tips

**Tip #1.** The model being developed in Modules 24, 25, and 26 relies heavily on the consumption function. It is important that you have a thorough understanding of this function. The slope of the consumption function is given by the marginal propensity to consume (MPC), and the y-intercept of this consumption function is autonomous spending or that level of spending that consumers in an economy will do when their disposable income is equal to zero. Remember that increases in expected future income or aggregate wealth will cause the consumption function to shift up while decreases in expected future income or aggregate wealth will cause the consumption function to shift down.

**Tip #2.** An understanding of investment spending and its components is a critical aspect of this module. The level of investment spending depends upon the interest rate in the aggregate economy, and the level of production capacity in the aggregate economy expected future GDP.

1.  You are told that the consumption function in an economy is a linear relationship. Furthermore, you are told that when disposable income is equal to $200, consumption spending is equal to $184 and when disposable income is equal to $500, consumption spending is equal to $385. You are asked to compute autonomous consumer spending for this economy, the value of the marginal propensity to consume, the consumption function, and finally the impact on real GDP in this economy if autonomous consumption increases by $50 from its initial level. Assume that in this economy there is no government sector, no taxes, no transfers, and that the aggregate price level and the interest rate are fixed.

**STEP 1:** Use the given information to find the marginal propensity to consume (*MPC*) for this economy.

In the information we are provided, there are two relationships between disposable income and consumption spending: (disposable income, consumption spending) = (200, 184) and (500, 385). From this information we can calculate the change in consumer spending as 385 – 184, or 201, and the change in disposable income as 500 – 200 = 300. Using this information and recalling that the marginal propensity to consume is defined as the change in consumer spending divided by the change in disposable income, the $MPC = 201/300 = 0.67$.

**STEP 2:** Use the *MPC* and one of the given consumption points to find the value of autonomous consumer spending for this economy.

From the discussion in the text, we know that a linear consumption function can be written as $C = A + MPC \times$ (disposable income). From Step 1, we know that the *MPC* has a value of 0.67. Thus, $C = A + 0.67 \times$ (disposable income). Replacing $C$ and disposable income with one of the given points, we can find the value of autonomous consumer spending. Thus, $385 = A + 0.67(500)$, or $184 = A + 0.67(200)$. Using either of these equations, we find that the value of $A$ is 50.

**STEP 3:** Write the equation for the consumption function for this economy.

The consumption function for this economy can be written in general as $C = A + MPC \times$ (disposable income), or given the values we calculated in Steps 1 and 2, as $C = 50 + 0.67$(disposable income).

**STEP 4:** Calculate the value of the multiplier for this economy.

Recall that the multiplier in this model is defined as $1/(1 - MPC)$. From Step 1, we know that the *MPC* is equal to 0.67. Using this information, we can calculate the value of the multiplier as 3.03.

2. Glenda has been presented with the following table showing different levels of disposable income, YD, and consumption, C, in the economy of Oz. Both C and YD are measured in dollars in the table, below. She needs to provide an equation that expresses the consumption function in Oz given this data. She knows that the consumption function is linear and she also knows there are no taxes in Oz. But, she is perplexed about how to find this function. She seeks your help.

| Level of disposable income, YD | Level of consumption, C |
|---|---|
| 20 | 20 |
| 50 | 35 |
| 90 | 55 |
| 200 | 110 |

**STEP 1:** To answer this question start with a brief review of the consumption function and its components.

The consumption function expresses the relationship between the level of disposable income and the level of consumption spending. Its general form is $C = A + MPC \times YD$, where C is consumption spending, A is the level of autonomous spending, MPC is the marginal propensity to consume, and YD is disposable income. Close inspection of this general form quickly reveals that you will need to figure out both the value of A as well as the value of the MPC.

**STEP 2:** Review the definition of the MPC and then use this definition and the provided data to calculate the value of the MPC in Oz.

The MPC is defined as the ratio of the change in consumption spending to the change in disposable income. That is, MPC = (change in consumption spending)/(change in disposable income). Unfortunately, that information is not in the table! But we can use the information in the table to calculate this: for example, the change in disposable income going from 20 to 50 is a change of 30; and the change in consumption from going from 20 to 35 is a change of 15. Using the numbers from this example implies that the $MPC = 15/30 = 0.5$.

But might we get a different number using different data from the table? Let's repeat the exercise. When disposable income changes from 90 to 200 this represents a change of 110; and the change in consumption spending at these levels of disposable income is from 55 to 110 or a change of 55. Using the numbers from this second example implies that the $MPC = 55/110 = 0.5$. We get the same MPC and that is good since we generally assume that the MPC is constant in the ideas being developed in this section of the text.

**STEP 3:** Use the MPC value you calculated in Step 2, and one of the consumption spending and disposable income pairs from the table to calculate the value of autonomous consumption spending or A.

From Step 2 we can rewrite the consumption function as $C = A + 0.5YD$. We can find A by substituting in one of the (YD, C) points from the table. For example, suppose we choose the point (50, 35): we get $35 = A + 0.5(50)$ or $A = 10$. To be certain that this method works, try another point. For example, suppose we choose the point (200, 110): we get $110 = A + 0.5(200)$ or $A = 10$.

**STEP 4:** State the consumption function once you have found it.

The consumption function based on this information is $C = 10 + 0.5YD$. You can check this by verifying that any level of $YD$ you put into this equation from the table will result in the value of $C$ in the table for this level of disposable income. For example, if disposable income is 90 the table tells us that $C$ should be 55. If we put 90 into the equation in place of $YD$ we get $C = 10 + 0.5(90)$ or $C = 55$.

# Problems and Exercises

1.  Econoland analyzes its aggregate consumer spending and aggregate disposable income and finds the following data. All numbers in the table are dollar amounts.

| YD | C |
|------|------|
| $ 0 | $100 |
| 100 | 180 |
| 200 | 260 |
| 300 | 340 |
| 500 | 500 |

Assume Econoland is a closed economy with no government spending, no taxes, and no transfers. Furthermore, assume the aggregate price level and interest rate are fixed in Econoland.

**a.** What does autonomous consumer spending equal in this economy?

**b.** What is the value of the *MPC* for Econoland?

**c.** Use the following graph to graph the data given in the previous table. Use the label *C* for the consumption function you construct.

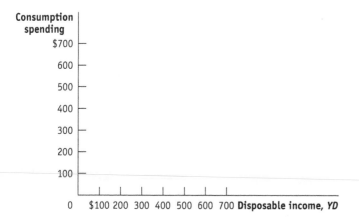

**d.** What is the slope of the consumption function you graphed in part (c)?

**e.** What is the relationship between the slope of the consumption function and the *MPC*? Explain your answer.

**f.** Suppose future expected disposable income increases in Econoland. How will this affect autonomous consumer spending, the *MPC*, and the consumption function?

2.  Acme Groceries would like to keep $100,000 in inventoried goods in order to meet customer demands for its products. However, a recent snowstorm in Acme's market area has resulted in the value of Acme's inventories falling to $20,000. Suppose the total level of planned investment in the economy is $2 million and the change in Acme's inventories is the only change in investment that you must take into account.

**a.** Given the above information what is the level of unplanned inventory investment in this economy?

**b.** What is the level of actual investment in this economy?

3.  Suppose that in Germantown the consumption function is assumed to be linear but that Germantown government officials are still trying to provide an equation for this consumption function. These officials know that when disposable income is $1,000, consumption is equal to $800; and that when disposable income is $10,000, consumption is equal to $7,100. Given this information provide an equation for the consumption function using $C$ as the symbol for consumption and $YD$ as the symbol for disposable income.

4. Josie is trying to understand the concept of planned investment and actual investment and she has several questions she needs you to address.

   **a.** What are the primary determinants of planned investment?

   **b.** How would you explain the relationship between the interest rate and the level of planned investment?

   **c.** Why is planned investment inversely related to the level of current productive capacity?

   **d.** How is planned investment different from actual investment?

   **e.** What do rising inventories tell you about an economy?

## ▮ BEFORE YOU TAKE THE TEST

## Module Review Questions

1. Which of the following statements is true?
   a. Investment spending during the Great Depression fell by more than 80%.
   b. Automatic stabilizers, like taxes and some government programs, reduce the size of the multiplier.
   c. The marginal propensity to consume in an economy is a positive number.
   d. Statements (a), (b), and (c) are all true.
   e. Statements (a) and (b) are both true.

2. Consumer spending is affected by changes in
   a. current disposable income.
   b. expected future disposable income.
   c. wealth.
   d. All of these factors affect consumer spending.

Use the following information to answer the next two questions.

Suppose aggregate consumer spending equals $5,000 when aggregate disposable income is zero. Furthermore, suppose that when disposable income increases from $300 to $400, consumer spending increases by $70 and that this relationship between a change in disposable income and its affect on consumer spending is predictable and constant.

3. What is the equation for the aggregate consumption function, given the previous information?
   a. $C = 5,000 + 70YD$
   b. $C = 500 + 0.7YD$
   c. $C = 5,000 + 0.7YD$
   d. $C = 5,000 + 7YD$

4. If aggregate disposable income equals $2,000, then what is the value of aggregate consumer spending?
   a. $7,000
   b. $19,000
   c. $6,400
   d. $5,140

5. An increase in the market interest rate
   a. will make any given investment project less profitable.
   b. will cause companies to rely more heavily on financing their investment projects through retained earnings rather than borrowing.
   c. will reduce the rate of return for any given investment project.
   d. Answers (a), (b), and (c) are all correct.

6. The accelerator principle
   a. helps to explain investment booms.
   b. refers to an increase in planned investment spending due to a higher rate of growth in real GDP.
   c. refers to an increase in government spending intended to stimulate the economy.
   d. Answers (a), (b), and (c) are all correct.
   e. Answers (a) and (b) are both correct.

7. The relationship between consumer spending and current disposable income is a
   a. positive relationship.
   b. negative relationship.

8. Suppose when Sue's disposable income is $10,000 she spends $8,000 and when her disposable income is $20,000 she spends $14,000. Sue's autonomous consumer spending is equal to _____ and her MPS is equal to _____.
   a. $0; 0.2
   b. $2,000; 0.2
   c. $0; 0.4
   d. $2,000; 0.4

9. Which of the following statements is true?
   a. The slope of the consumption function is the change in consumption divided by the change in disposable income.
   b. The slope of the consumption function is equal to $(1 - MPS)$.
   c. A change in autonomous consumer spending will cause the slope of the consumption function to change.
   d. Statements (a), (b), and (c) are all true.
   e. Statements (a) and (b) are both true.

10. The argument that consumers smooth their spending over a lifetime rather than adjusting their consumer spending in response to their current disposable income is referred to as the
    a. life-cycle hypothesis.
    b. permanent wealth effect.

11. Planned investment spending depends on the
    a. interest rate.
    b. expected future level of real GDP.
    c. current level of production capacity.
    d. Answers (a), (b), and (c) are all correct.
    e. Answers (a) and (c) are both correct.

12. Holding everything else constant, when interest rates rise, this
    a. does not affect the profitability of investment projects financed through retained earnings.
    b. makes any given investment project less profitable.
    c. does not affect the opportunity cost of an investment project financed through retained earnings.
    d. leads to a lower level of planned investment spending, holding everything else constant.

13. Suppose an economy expects its future growth rate of real GDP to be high. This will
    a. have no effect on investment spending, but will lead to an increase in the growth rate of real GDP due to the accelerator principle.
    b. cause investment spending to increase in the economy, which will lead to an increase in the growth rate of real GDP due to the accelerator principle.
    c. cause investment spending to slow in anticipation of the increase in the future growth rate of real GDP, which will lead to a decrease in the current growth rate of real GDP due to the accelerator principle.
    d. cause investment spending to increase in anticipation of the increase in the future growth rate of real GDP, which will lead to a decrease in the current growth rate of real GDP due to the accelerator principle.

## ▮ ANSWER KEY

# Answers to Problems and Exercises

1.  **a.** Autonomous consumer spending refers to the level of consumer spending that occurs when disposable income equals zero. In the data given, when disposable income equals zero, consumer spending equals 100: autonomous consumer spending therefore equals 100.

    **b.** The MPC equals the change in consumption divided by the change in disposable income. For any two data points (consumption and disposable income combinations), the MPC = 0.8.

    **c.**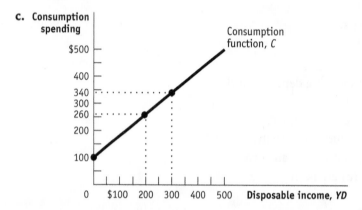

    **d.** The slope of the consumption function equals the MPC, or 0.8.

    **e.** They are equal. It indicates there is a positive relationship between changes in disposable income and changes in consumption. The MPC tells us the change in consumer spending for a dollar increase in disposable income. In this problem, the MPC equals 0.8, so we know that when disposable income increases by $1, then consumer spending will increase by $0.80.

    **f.** An increase in future expected disposable income will increase autonomous consumption, according to the life-cycle hypothesis. This will cause the consumption function to shift upward by the amount of the change in autonomous consumer spending. There will be no change in the MPC.

2.  **a.** The level of unplanned inventory investment in this economy is –$80,000 since inventories have fallen by $80,000 due to the effects of the snowstorm.

    **b.** The level of actual investment in this economy is equal to the sum of unplanned inventory investment plus planned investment. Thus the level of actual investment in this economy is equal to –$80,000 plus $2 million, or $1.8.

3.  From the provided information you have two points of the consumption function: $(YD, C)$ = ($1,000, $800) and ($10,000, $7,100). From this you can write an equation for the consumption function. First, remember that the equation will take the general form of $C = mYD + b$ where "m" is the slope of the consumption function and "b" is the y-intercept of the consumption function. To find the slope recall that we measure slope as the rise/run, or in this example, $(7,100 – 800)/(10,000 – 1,000) = 6,300/9,000 = 0.7$. Rewrite the equation with this slope measure: $C = 0.7YD + b$ and then substitute one of the known $(YD, C)$ points into this equation to solve for "b." Thus, $800 = 0.7(1,000) + b$ or $b = 100$. The consumption function for Germantown can be expressed as $C = 0.7YD + 100$.

4.  **a.** The primary determinants of planned investment are the level of the interest rate, the expected future level of real GDP, and the current productive capacity.

**b.** When interest rates rise, other things being held constant, this leads to less planned investment since the cost of any potential investment will be greater when the interest rate increases. Thus, the relationship between the level of planned investment and the interest rate is an inverse one: as interest rates rise, planned investment falls and as interest rates fall, planned investment rises.

**c.** When a firm has a substantial amount of capacity relative to their current production levels they have less need to engage in expansion of their productive plant. This suggests that as current productive capacity increases, holding everything else constant, this will lead to less planned investment. Planned investment and current productive capacity are inversely related to one another.

**d.** Actual investment includes planned investment plus unplanned inventory changes.

**e.** When inventories are rising this tells us that unplanned inventory changes are occurring and resulting in an increase in inventories. This suggests that the economy is slowing and that there are fewer sales of this good.

# Answers to Module Review Questions

1.  **Answer d.** Statements (a) and (c) are factual. Automatic stabilizers, like taxes and some government programs, reduce the size of the multiplier. For example, in a recession as people's incomes fall, their tax obligations also decrease: this decrease in taxes moderates or lessens the overall fall in aggregate income from the recession.

2.  **Answer d.** All three of these variables affect the level of consumer spending.

3.  **Answer c.** The basic equation for the aggregate consumption function is $C = A + MPC \times YD$, and from the information we know, $A$, the aggregate autonomous consumer spending, equals $5,000 and the $MPC$ can be calculated as the change in consumer spending divided by the change in aggregate disposable income, or 70/100, which equals 0.7. So, $C = 5,000 + 0.7YD$.

4.  **Answer c.** Using the equation from question 3, substitute $2,000 for $YD$ and solve for $C$. In this case, $C$ equals $5,000 + 0.7($2,000), or $6,400.

5.  **Answer a.** A change in the market interest rate does not affect the rate of return for any given investment project. It does, however, affect the opportunity cost of borrowing and as the market interest rate increases, this makes any given investment project less profitable due to the relationship between the market interest rate and the project's rate of return. Firms, whether they use retained earnings or borrow, recognize that the market interest rate reflects the opportunity cost of using or acquiring funds.

6.  **Answer e.** The accelerator principle states that a higher rate of growth in real GDP leads to higher planned investment spending. This results in a boom in investment spending. Government spending intended to stimulate the economy is expansionary fiscal policy.

7.  **Answer a.** As the level of current disposable income increases, this leads to a higher level of consumer spending: the two variables are positively related to one another.

8.  **Answer d.** To find Sue's autonomous consumer spending, it is helpful to write Sue's consumption function, $C = MPC \times YD + A$. You know two points on Sue's consumption function are ($10,000, $8,000) and ($20,000, $14,000) where the variable measured on the x-axis is disposable income and the variable measured on the y-axis is consumer spending. The $MPC$ can be calculated as (the change in consumer spending)/(the change in disposable income) or ($6,000)/($10,000) = 0.6. Thus, the $MPS$ is equal to 0.4. Using this information, Sue's consumption function can be written as $C = 0.6 \times YD + A$. Using one of the two known points from Sue's consumption function you can solve for the value of $A$, Sue's autonomous consumer spending, as $2,000.

9. **Answer e.** The slope of the consumption function is given by the *MPC*, which is equal to the change in consumer spending divided by the change in disposable income. When autonomous consumer spending changes, this causes the consumption function to shift: it shifts up if there is an increase in autonomous consumer spending, and it shifts down if there is a decrease in autonomous consumer spending.

10. **Answer a.** The life-cycle hypothesis emphasizes the effect of wealth on spending and hypothesizes that consumers plan their spending over their lifetime rather than planning their consumer spending on the basis of their current income.

11. **Answer d.** Investment spending primarily depends on these three factors.

12. **Answer d.** When interest rates rise, this makes any given investment project less profitable since the firm is either going to find that borrowed funds are now more expensive or that retained earnings used to finance the project will not be available to be invested in order to earn the higher rate of interest. When a firm finances an investment project through retained earnings, there is still an opportunity cost to using these funds for the project since the firm cannot invest the funds and earn the higher interest rate. Interest rates and the level of investment are inversely related to each other.

13. **Answer b.** The accelerator principle is a proposition about the relationship between the future growth rate of real GDP and the level of investment spending: when the future growth rate of real GDP is expected to be high, this leads to an increase in investment spending and this increase in investment spending leads to a higher growth rate of real GDP. Conversely, when the future growth rate of real GDP is expected to be low, this leads to lower planned investment spending; this, in turn, does affect the growth rate of future real GDP.

# module 26(62)

# The Income–Expenditure Model

## Summary

This module discusses how aggregate expenditure determines the income–expenditure equilibrium. It also explores how the inventory adjustment process moves the economy to a new equilibrium after there is a change in the level of planned aggregate spending.

## Module Objectives

**Objective #1.** In a closed economy with no government and a fixed aggregate price level, there are only two sources of aggregate demand (*AD*): consumer spending and investment spending. In this type of economy, aggregate disposable income, *YD*, equals GDP. Figure 26.1 illustrates a simple economy and the following points about that simple economy.

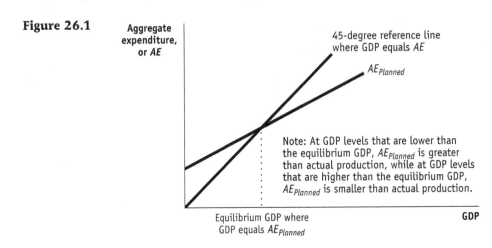

Figure 26.1

Aggregate expenditure, or *AE*

45-degree reference line where GDP equals *AE*

$AE_{Planned}$

Note: At GDP levels that are lower than the equilibrium GDP, $AE_{Planned}$ is greater than actual production, while at GDP levels that are higher than the equilibrium GDP, $AE_{Planned}$ is smaller than actual production.

Equilibrium GDP where GDP equals $AE_{Planned}$

GDP

- In this economy planned aggregate spending, $AE_{Planned}$, or the total amount of planned spending in the economy, is comprised of consumption spending, $C$, and planned investment, $I_{Planned}$.

- The slope of the $AE_{Planned}$ line equals the $MPC$.

- $AE_{Planned}$ may differ from GDP because of the influence of unplanned aggregate spending in the form of unplanned inventory investment, $I_{Unplanned}$.

- Over time the economy moves to that point where $AE_{Planned}$ equals GDP, or the income-expenditure equilibrium.

**Objective #2.**   The ideas in Objective #1 can be expressed using equations. In this simple economy with no government sector, a fixed aggregate price level, and a given interest rate, $GDP = C + I$. Furthermore, investment spending, $I$, can be written as the sum of planned investment plus unplanned inventory investment or $I = I_{Planned} + I_{Unplanned}$. Thus, $GDP = C + I_{Planned} + I_{Unplanned}$. Planned aggregate spending, $AE_{Planned}$, is the sum of consumption spending plus planned investment or $AE_{Planned} = C + I_{Planned}$. Thus, $GDP = AE + I_{Unplanned}$.

- When GDP is greater than $AE_{Planned}$, this implies that $I_{Unplanned}$ is positive: the inventories of firms increase, and this acts as a signal to firms to decrease their production. Over time the economy moves back to the income-expenditure equilibrium.

- When GDP is less than $AE_{Planned}$, this implies that $I_{Unplanned}$ is negative: the inventories of firms decrease, and this acts as a signal to firms to increase their production. Over time the economy moves back to the income-expenditure equilibrium.

- When GDP equals $AE_{Planned}$, then the economy is at the income-expenditure equilibrium. At this equilibrium, $I_{Unplanned}$ equals zero and firms have no incentive to change their levels of production in the next period. We refer to this level of GDP as the income-expenditure equilibrium GDP. A 45-degree reference line helps identify the income-expenditure equilibrium GDP. When $AE_{Planned}$ is graphed on the vertical axis and GDP is graphed on the horizontal axis, the income-expenditure equilibrium GDP is that level of GDP where the $AE$ line intersects the 45-degree line. This diagram identifying the income-expenditure equilibrium GDP where $AE_{Planned}$ equals GDP is called the Keynesian cross diagram. Figure 26.1 illustrates the Keynesian cross diagram.

- When GDP is not equal to $AE_{Planned}$, the macroeconomy self-corrects through inventory adjustment.

**Objective #3.**   The $AE$ line, or $AE_{Planned}$, shifts in this simple model if there is a change in planned investment spending, $I_{Planned}$, or if there is a shift in the consumption function, $C$. Either shift triggers the multiplier process, so for a change in either variable there will be an even bigger change in the equilibrium level of GDP. This idea can be expressed as the change in the income-expenditure equilibrium GDP equals the multiplier times the change in planned aggregate spending. Recall that the multiplier in this simple model equals $1/(1 - MPC)$.

**Objective #4.**   The paradox of thrift refers to how individuals concerned about a potential economic downturn may worsen that economic downturn when they choose to act prudently and increase their level of saving. It is a paradox, since what is "good," households saving their money, produces a "bad," an economy with a more severe recession.

## Key Terms

**planned aggregate spending** the total amount of planned spending in the *economy*; includes *consumer spending* and *planned investment spending.*

**income–expenditure equilibrium** a situation in which *aggregate output*, measured by *real GDP*, is equal to *planned aggregate spending* and *firms* have no incentive to change output.

**income–expenditure equilibrium GDP** the level of *real GDP* at which real GDP equals *planned aggregate spending.*

**Keynesian cross** a diagram that identifies *income-expenditure equilibrium* as the point where the *planned aggregate spending* line crosses the 45-degree line.

# AFTER YOU READ THE MODULE

## Tips

**Tip #1.** A thorough understanding of the aggregate consumption function and the variables that shift the aggregate consumption function is essential. Make sure you review the aggregate consumption function and understand the relationship between consumer spending and autonomous consumer spending, the marginal propensity to consume, and disposable income. The consumption function will shift upward with increases in wealth or expected future disposable income. Figure 26.2 is a representation of an aggregate consumption function: the slope of this function equals the *MPC*, and the *y*-intercept equals autonomous consumption spending, or *A*.

**Figure 26.2**

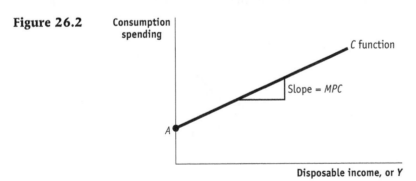

**Tip #2.** The 45-degree line in the Keynesian cross diagram provides a helpful visual tool for identifying the income–expenditure equilibrium GDP. The Keynesian cross diagram illustrates the relationship between $AE_{Planned}$ and GDP: to the left of the point of intersection in the Keynesian cross, we know that AE is greater than GDP, inventories are falling, and firms will respond by increasing their production; to the right of the point of intersection in the Keynesian cross, we know that *AE* is less than GDP, inventories are rising, and firms will respond by decreasing their production. Figure 26.3, which follows, illustrates these points.

**Figure 26.3**

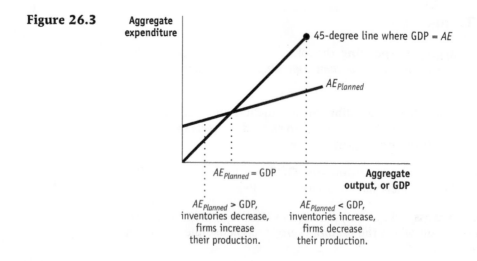

**Tip #3.** An understanding of investment spending and its components is a critical aspect of this module. Make sure you can distinguish between planned investment spending and unplanned inventory investment. In the macroeconomic model presented in this module, the mechanism that ensures the attainment of equilibrium is unplanned inventory adjustment. This concept is essential for understanding how this short-run model of the economy works. Figure 26.3 illustrates this inventory adjustment.

**Tip #4.** This module develops the concept of the multiplier and it considers the impact of the multiplier on the macroeconomic model presented in this module. The text starts with a relatively simple economic model to develop important economic concepts like the multiplier. Review the definition of the multiplier, its calculation, and then practice using this concept in questions provided in the text and the study guide. Figure 26.4 illustrates this multiplier effect. The economy is initially producing $Y_1$. When there is an increase in autonomous spending, this causes $AE_{Planned}$ to shift up by an amount equal to this change in spending. This leads to a higher equilibrium level of output, $Y_2$. The multiplier equals the ratio of this change in aggregate output divided by the change in autonomous spending.

**Figure 26.4**

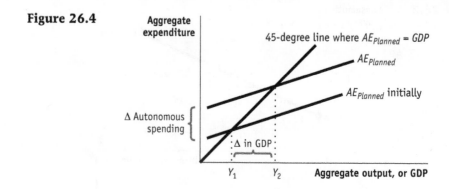

1. Consider a simple economy in which there is only consumption spending by households and investment spending by businesses. Furthermore, assume that the consumption function in this economy is linear and that the level of taxes in this economy is equal to zero. You are told that when consumption spending is equal to $150, disposable income is equal to $100 and that when consumption spending is equal to $350, disposable income is equal to $500. Planned investment spending in this economy is equal to $100 no matter what the level of disposable income. You are asked to find the consumption function, to identify the equilibrium level of real GDP in this economy, to depict the equilibrium level of real GDP as well as the aggregate expenditure function and consumption function in a graph, and to describe what is happening in this economy when real GDP is equal to $200. Assume that in this economy there is no government sector, no taxes, no transfers, and that the aggregate price level and the interest rate are fixed.

**STEP 1:** Find the value of the marginal propensity to consume (*MPC*) for this economy from the given information.

Recall that the multiplier is equal to the change in consumer spending divided by the change in disposable income. From the given information, we know two points on the consumption function: (disposable income, consumption) = (100, 150) and (500, 350). Thus, the change in consumption spending is equal to 350 – 150, or 200, while the change in disposable income is equal to 500 – 100, or 400. Thus, the *MPC* is equal to 200/400, or 0.5.

**STEP 2:** Find the consumption function for this economy given the above information.

From Step 1, we know that the *MPC* is equal to 0.5. We also know that the consumption function can be written as $C = A + MPC \times$ (disposable income). Using one of the points that we are given from the consumption function, we can solve this equation for the value of *A*, the autonomous consumer spending. Thus, $150 = A + 0.5(100)$, or $A = 100$, or $350 = A + 0.5(500)$, or $A = 100$. The consumption function can be written as $C = 100 + 0.5 \times$ (disposable income).

**STEP 3:** Calculate the equilibrium value of real GDP for this economy.

In this simple economy, planned aggregate expenditure is equal to consumption spending plus investment spending. Thus, $AE_{Planned} = C + I$. Or, $AE_{Planned} = 100 + 0.5 \times$ (disposable income) $+ 100$. Simplifying this we get $AE_{Planned} = 200 + 0.5 \times$ (disposable income). In equilibrium the level of real GDP produced is equal to $AE_{Planned}$. Thus, $Y = 200 + 0.5 \times Y$, since there are no taxes and that implies that disposable income is equal to real GDP or *Y*. We can solve for the equilibrium value of *Y* and we will find that equilibrium *Y*, or equilibrium real GDP, is 400. When this economy's real GDP is equal to $400, then planned aggregate expenditure is equal to this level of production.

**STEP 4:** Provide a graph illustrating the equilibrium level of real GDP for this economy as well as the aggregate expenditure function.

**STEP 5:** Describe what is happening in this economy when the level of real GDP is equal to $200. Illustrate this idea by referencing the graph you created in Step 4.

When real GDP is equal to 200, consumption is equal to 200, and planned aggregate expenditure is equal to 300 (since C is equal to 200 and planned investment spending is equal to 100, for a total planned expenditure of 300). That implies that the level of production (200) is less than the level of expenditure (300) and therefore, holding everything else constant, that there are unplanned changes in inventories of 100. That is, since spending is greater than production, there is unplanned investment in the form of inventory changes in order to meet the demand for goods and services. As unplanned inventories fall, this decrease acts as a signal for producers to produce a higher level of output, and the economy will naturally move toward the equilibrium level of real GDP that we found to be equal to 400 in Step 4.

2.  Morty is confused. This week he went to hear a lecture about macroeconomics and came home with a graph that the speaker said would help him understand the economy better. But Morty is having trouble interpreting the graph and has sought your help. Here is the graph that Morty is worried about:

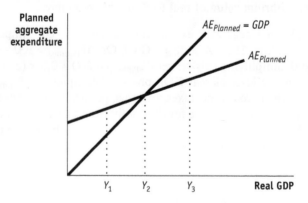

The speaker said this graph could help Morty understand the critical role of inventories in the economy, what the income-expenditure equilibrium is, and how the economy moves toward equilibrium. Morty needs you to help him see these ideas and he knows he will only understand this if you give him a really complete description.

**STEP 1:** A good place to start is with a description of what you see in the graph. In particular it would be helpful for you to identify what the graph is measuring and the significance of the two lines in the graph.

This graph is the Keynesian cross. In the graph the vertical axis measures planned aggregate expenditure: in an earlier module the text discussed aggregate expenditure and defined this as the sum of all the spending that occurs in an economy in a given time period on final goods and services. Along the horizontal axis real GDP is measured: recall that real GDP is the constant dollar value of the final goods and services produced in an economy in a given time period. Both the vertical and horizontal axes are measured in constant dollar terms since this model assumes that the price level is fixed and there is therefore no inflation. This is an important point since the equivalency of the units of measurement on these two axes allows us to draw a 45-degree reference line such that the numeric value of real GDP on the horizontal axis is equivalent to the numeric value of planned aggregate expenditure on the vertical axis.

The other line in the diagram depicts planned aggregate expenditure ($AE_{Planned}$): this line tells us for every specific level of real GDP what the level of planned expenditure is.

**STEP 2:** It would also be helpful to briefly discuss what $Y_1$, $Y_2$, and $Y_3$ are in the graph.

$Y_1$, $Y_2$, and $Y_3$ all represent different levels of real GDP in the diagram. $Y_1$ represents a lower level of real GDP than $Y_2$ because $Y_1$ is further to the left than $Y_2$. Similarly $Y_2$ represents a lower level of real GDP than $Y_3$ because $Y_2$ is further to the left than $Y_3$.

It is also important to realize that $Y_1$, $Y_2$, and $Y_3$ are related to specific, but different, levels of planned aggregate expenditure in the diagram. To find the specific level of planned aggregate expenditure for a level of real GDP requires that you move vertically up from the horizontal axis to the planned aggregate expenditure line. Since the planned aggregate expenditure line is upward sloping we can easily see that the level of planned aggregate expenditure when real GDP is at $Y_1$ is lower than the level of planned aggregate expenditure when real GDP is at $Y_2$. Similarly we can see that the level of planned aggregate expenditure when real GDP is at $Y_2$ is lower than the level of planned aggregate expenditure when real GDP is at $Y_3$.

**STEP 3:** Given the three levels of real GDP depicted in the diagram—$Y_1$, $Y_2$, and $Y_3$—explain which one represents the income-expenditure equilibrium.

The income-expenditure equilibrium occurs when planned aggregate expenditure equals real GDP. Or, in other words, it occurs at that level of real GDP where the $AE_{Planned}$ line intersects the 45-degree reference line. In the diagram Morty has provided this occurs at $Y_2$. At $Y_2$, the level of real GDP, or the aggregate level of production in the economy, is equal to the aggregate expenditure in the economy.

At $Y_1$, $AE_{Planned}$ is greater than real GDP. That implies that inventories are falling, since spending in the economy is greater than the current level of production. As inventories fall, this acts as a signal to producers to expand their production from $Y_1$ toward $Y_2$.

At $Y_3$, $AE_{Planned}$ is less than real GDP. That implies that inventories are rising, since spending in the economy is less than the current level of production. As inventories increase, this acts as a signal to producers to contract their production from $Y_3$ toward $Y_2$.

**STEP 4:** Morty needs you to provide a restatement of how the economy moves toward equilibrium.

The critical determinant of this adjustment toward equilibrium is the role played by unplanned inventory changes. When unplanned inventories increase this is a signal that the economy is producing more than the amount that people want to purchase. As inventories increase, producers recognize that they are overproducing and they adjust their production to a lower level. This adjustment brings the level of production closer to the equilibrium level.

When unplanned inventories decrease this is a signal that the economy is not producing enough: $AE_{Planned}$ exceeds the current level of production. As inventories decrease producers recognize that they need to adjust their production by increasing it. This adjustment brings the level of production closer to the equilibrium level.

Whether the economy is producing too much ($Y_3$) or too little ($Y_1$), the important idea here is that unplanned inventory changes will occur and producers will adjust their production in response to these unplanned inventory changes. This adjustment will result in the economy naturally moving toward the income-expenditure equilibrium.

# Problems and Exercises

1. Use the following data to answer this question for Funland, a closed economy with no government sector, a fixed aggregate price level, and a fixed interest rate. All numbers in the table are dollar amounts.

| GDP | YD | C | $I_{Planned}$ | $AE_{Planned}$ | $I_{Unplanned}$ |
|-----|-----|-----|-----|-----|-----|
|  | $20 | $22 | $20 |  |  |
|  | 50 |  | 20 |  | −$10 |
| $ 80 |  |  | 20 |  | 2 |
| 100 |  | 70 | 20 |  |  |

a. Fill in the missing values in the table.

b. What is the value of autonomous consumer spending?

c. What is the *MPC* for Funland?

**d.** Graph the above information using a Keynesian cross diagram. Label the income-expenditure equilibrium GDP.

**e.** What is the income–expenditure equilibrium real GDP for Funland? (*Hint:* The table does not include the income–expenditure equilibrium GDP, but the table does provide the information necessary to find this equilibrium.)

**f.** Suppose $I_{Planned}$ increases by 20, holding everything else constant. Fill in the table given this change.

| GDP′ | YD′ | C′ | $I'_{Planned}$ | $AE'_{Planned}$ | $I'_{Unplanned}$ |
|------|-----|-----|-----------|------------|-------------|
|      | $20 | $22 | $40 |     |     |
|      | 50  |     | 40  | $80 |     |
| $ 80 |     |     | 40  | 98  |     |
| 100  |     | 70  | 20  |     |     |

**g.** Given the change in part (f), what is the new equilibrium level of real GDP for Funland?

**h.** Explain the relationship between the multiplier and the answer you gave for part (f).

**2.** Outlandia's planned aggregate expenditure line is depicted in the following graph, where the vertical axis measures planned aggregate expenditure and the horizontal axis measures real GDP.

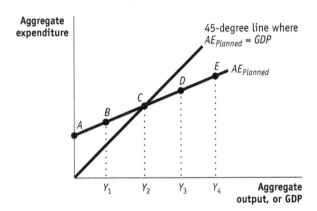

**a.** The graph is referred to as a Keynesian cross diagram. Interpret the information provided in the graph.

*Suppose Outlandia's economy currently is operating at point B.*

**b.** Is this an income–expenditure equilibrium for Outlandia? Explain your answer.

**c.** At point B, describe what is happening to inventories and production in Outlandia.

**d.** What level of GDP will this economy produce once it is at an income–expenditure equilibrium?

**e.** At what levels of labeled GDP on the graph is unplanned inventory investment positive? Explain your answer.

**f.** At what levels of labeled GDP on the graph is planned aggregate expenditure greater than income? Explain your answer.

**g.** Explain the significance of point C in the graph.

**3.** Suppose Inlandia's autonomous consumer spending equals 500 and that consumer spending increases by $50 for every $100 increase in aggregate disposable income. Assume Inlandia is a closed economy with no government sector, a fixed aggregate price level, and fixed interest rates.

**a.** Use the following graph to plot Inlandia's consumption function.

**b.** Suppose you are told that planned investment spending equals $100, no matter what the level of income in the economy. Graph this information in the graph and label the line you draw $I_{Planned}$.

**c.** On the graph, graph the $AE_{Planned}$ line and label it $AE_{Planned}$.

**d.** What is the income-expenditure equilibrium real GDP for Inlandia?

**e.** Sketch a diagram showing the relationship between $AE_{Planned}$, $I_{Planned}$, the consumption function, and the 45-degree line.

**f.** What is the value of the multiplier for this economy?

**g.** What will be the change in the income-expenditure equilibrium level of real GDP if autonomous consumption decreases by $50?

**4.** In Mainland, a small closed economy with no government sector, when disposable income is equal to $800, consumer spending is equal to $800 and when disposable income is equal to $1,800, consumer spending is equal to $1,600. Assume that the aggregate price level and the interest rate are fixed in Mainland.

**a.** What is the value of autonomous consumer spending in Mainland?

**b.** What is the value of the *MPC* in Mainland?

**c.** What is the consumption function in Mainland?

**d.** Suppose that planned investment spending is equal to $500 in Mainland and this level of planned investment spending does not change, no matter what the level of income is in Mainland. Suppose the current level of aggregate expenditure is equal to $3,000. Describe how this economy will respond to this level of aggregate expenditure given the model developed in this module. In your answer, comment on what is happening to unplanned investment spending, inventories, and the level of real GDP. Explain your answer fully.

**e.** Suppose that planned investment spending is equal to $500 in Mainland and this level of planned investment spending does not change, no matter what the level of income is in Mainland. Suppose the current level of aggregate expenditure is equal to $4,000. Describe how this economy will respond to this level of aggregate expenditure given the model developed in this module. In your answer, comment on what is happening to unplanned investment spending, inventories, and the level of real GDP. Explain your answer fully.

**f.** What is the income–expenditure equilibrium in Mainland if planned investment spending is equal to $500 and this level of planned investment spending does not change, no matter what the level of income is in Mainland?

**5.** Suppose the economy described in problem 4 is currently in income–expenditure equilibrium. For each of the following situations, describe the effect of the described change on the consumption function and the planned aggregate expenditure function, and then identify the new income–expenditure equilibrium given the consumption function and the initial level of planned investment identified in problem 4.

**a.** The level of autonomous consumer spending increases by $200.

**b.** The level of planned investment spending falls to $400.

**c.** The level of planned investment spending increases to $700.

**d.** The level of wealth in the economy increases, which leads to an increase in autonomous consumer spending of $100.

## BEFORE YOU TAKE THE TEST

# Module Review Questions

1.  Consumer spending
    a. usually accounts for two-thirds of total spending on final goods and services in the U.S. economy.
    b. holding everything else constant, will cause the *AE* function to shift if there is a change in consumer spending.
    c. has a powerful impact on the economy's aggregate output and aggregate price level according to the simple model developed in this module.
    d. Answers (a), (b), and (c) are all correct.
    e. Answers (a) and (b) are both correct.

2.  Suppose aggregate wealth decreases in the economy due to the bursting of a housing price bubble. This will, holding everything else constant,
    a. reduce wealth and result in a decrease in autonomous consumer spending.
    b. cause the aggregate expenditure function to shift down.
    c. result in a lower level of consumer spending for any given level of disposable income.
    d. Answers (a), (b), and (c) are all correct.
    e. Answers (a) and (b) are both correct.

3.  Which of the following statements is true?
    a. Holding everything else constant, an increase in planned investment spending shifts the *AE* function downward, leading to a higher level of GDP.
    b. Most recessions start with a decrease in investment spending.
    c. Economists think that decreases in consumer spending often follow decreases in investment spending.
    d. Answers (a), (b), and (c) are all true.
    e. Answers (b) and (c) are both true.

Use the following information to answer the next five questions.

Suppose Macroland is a closed economy with no government sector and therefore no government expenditure, taxes, or transfers. Furthermore, assume the aggregate price level and interest rate in Macroland is fixed. You are also told that the MPC in Macroland is constant. You are provided the following information about Macroland. (All numbers in the table are dollar amounts.)

| GDP | YD | C | $I_{Planned}$ | $I_{Unplanned}$ |
|---|---|---|---|---|
| $100 | $100 | $150 | $50 | −$100 |
| 200 | | | 50 | |
| 400 | | 300 | 50 | |

4.  What is the consumption function for this economy?
    a.  $C = 150 + 0.5YD$
    b.  $C = 250 + 0.5YD$
    c.  $C = 100 + 0.5YD$
    d.  $C = 50 + 0.5YD$

5.  When GDP equals 400, which of the following statements is true?
    a.  Unplanned inventory investment is negative.
    b.  Planned aggregate expenditure equals 400.
    c.  Unplanned inventory investment is positive.
    d.  The economy is in income-expenditure equilibrium when GDP equals 400.

6.  What is the income-expenditure equilibrium GDP for Macroland?
    a.  200
    b.  300
    c.  500
    d.  600

7.  Holding everything else constant, suppose aggregate wealth in an economy increases by $100. Which of the following statements is true?
    a.  The AE curve shifts upward.
    b.  The income-expenditure equilibrium real GDP increases by more than $100.
    c.  The multiplier effect on real GDP is a positive number that is greater than $0 and less than $100.
    d.  Statements (a), (b), and (c) are all true.
    e.  Statements (a) and (b) are both true.

8.  Given the change in wealth in question 7, the equilibrium level of GDP
    a.  increases relative to its initial level.
    b.  decreases relative to its initial level.
    c.  is unaffected.
    d.  may increase, decrease, or stay the same relative to its initial level.

9.  Suppose the level of planned aggregate expenditure in an economy is $500 while the level of real GDP is $600. According to the simple model developed in this module, where the aggregate price level is assumed to be constant, we can expect

    a. inventories will increase.

    b. inventories will decrease.

    c. inventories will be unaffected and will remain at the planned inventory level.

    d. this situation of excess production to continue since there is no mechanism to restore the level of production to the level of spending.

10. In the model presented in this module, the role of inventories is to

    a. ensure that aggregate expenditure is equal to aggregate production.

    b. provide a signal to producers to increase or decrease their prices.

■ **ANSWER KEY**

## Answers to Problems and Exercises

1. **a.**

| GDP | YD | C | $I_{Planned}$ | $AE_{Planned}$ | $I_{Unplanned}$ |
|---|---|---|---|---|---|
| $ 20 | $ 20 | $22 | $20 | $42 | −$22 |
| 50 | 50 | 40 | 20 | 60 | −10 |
| 80 | 80 | 58 | 20 | 78 | 2 |
| 100 | 100 | 70 | 20 | 90 | 10 |

**b.** We know $C = A + MPC \times YD$. We can calculate the $MPC$ as the change in consumer spending divided by the change in disposable income: for example, the $MPC$ equals $(40 − 22)/(50 − 20) = 0.6$. Plugging this value for the $MPC$ back into our equation for the consumption function yields $C = A + 0.6YD$. We can choose a consumption spending and disposable income level like (22, 20), substitute these values into this equation, and solve for $A$. Doing this, we find $A$ equals 10.

**c.** The $MPC$ equals the change in consumption divided by the change in disposable income, or in this case, 0.6. See explanation in part (b).

**d.**

**e.** To find the income-expenditure equilibrium real GDP in Funland, set $AE_{Planned}$ equal to GDP, since at the income-expenditure equilibrium these two variables are equal. $AE_{Planned}$ equals consumption spending plus planned investment spending. So, GDP = $C + I_{Planned}$ or GDP = $10 + 0.6YD + 20$. Recall that GDP equals $YD$ in this simple model with no government sector, so we can rewrite this equation as GDP = $10 + 0.6$GDP + 20 and then solve for GDP to get 75 for our equilibrium real GDP.

**f.**

| GDP′ | YD′ | C′ | $I'_{Planned}$ | $AE'_{Planned}$ | $I'_{Unplanned}$ |
|---|---|---|---|---|---|
| $ 20 | $ 20 | $22 | $40 | $ 62 | −$42 |
| 50 | 50 | 40 | 40 | 80 | −30 |
| 80 | 80 | 58 | 40 | 98 | −18 |
| 100 | 100 | 70 | 40 | 110 | −10 |

**g.** The old equilibrium level of real GDP from part (d) was 75. We have a change in investment spending of 20, and this change will be magnified by the multiplier process. The multiplier in this example equals 2.5, so the change in real GDP equals 2.5 times the $20 change in investment spending. The new equilibrium is the original

75 plus the 2.5(20) or 50, for a total new equilibrium of 125. We could also find the equilibrium by equating $GDP' = AE'_{Planned}$ where $AE'_{Planned} = 10 + 0.6YD + 40$. Recalling that GDP equals YD in this simple model, we can rewrite this relationship as $GDP = 50 + 0.6GDP$. Solving for GDP, we get 125 as the new equilibrium GDP. The graph illustrates this.

**h.** We can use the multiplier to see the effect of a change in investment spending on the change in the equilibrium level of real GDP.

**2.  a.** This is a graph of the Keynesian cross, which depicts the planned aggregate expenditure line: this line illustrates the positive relationship between GDP and the level of planned expenditure in the economy. The cross is made by this line and the 45-degree reference line. The point of intersection of these two lines identifies the income–expenditure equilibrium where GDP equals $AE_{Planned}$. When Y is less than $Y_2$, planned aggregate expenditure is greater than GDP, inventories are falling, and this change in inventories acts as a signal to producers to increase their production. When Y is greater than $Y_2$, planned aggregate expenditure is less than GDP, inventories are rising, and this change in inventories acts as a signal to producers to decrease their production.

**b.** No, the income–expenditure equilibrium is at point C on the graph. At point B, $AE_{Planned}$ is greater than GDP, or income. This causes inventories to fall, and firms view this as a signal that they should increase their production from $Y_1$ toward $Y_2$, the income-expenditure equilibrium real GDP.

**c.** See the answer in part (b).

**d.** This economy, holding everything else constant, will produce GDP equal to $Y_2$ when it is in income-expenditure equilibrium.

**e.** Unplanned inventory investment is positive wherever GDP is greater than $AE_{Planned}$: GDP output levels $Y_3$ and $Y_4$ represent two output levels where unplanned inventory investment is positive. So, at any output level greater than $Y_2$, unplanned inventory investment is positive.

**f.** This is true for any level of GDP less than $Y_2$. For example, at points A and B, $AE_{Planned}$ exceeds GDP.

**g.** Point C represents the income-expenditure equilibrium level of real GDP where $AE_{Planned}$ equals GDP.

**3.  a.** See answer at part (c).

**b.** See answer at part (c).

**c.**

**d.** Solving for the income-expenditure requires us to know the consumption function ($C$ = 500 + 0.5$YD$) and the level of planned investment spending (100). We know $AE_{Planned}$ equals GDP in equilibrium and that $AE_{Planned}$ is the sum of consumption spending plus planned investment spending. So, GDP = $AE_{Planned}$ = $C$ + $I_{Planned}$ = 500 + 0.5$YD$ + 100. We also know in our simple model that GDP equals $YD$. So, GDP = 600 + 0.5GDP, and solving for GDP we find it is equal to 1,200.

**e.**

**f.** We calculate the multiplier as 1/(1 − $MPC$): if the $MPC$ equals 0.5, then the multiplier equals 2.

**g.** The change in equilibrium real GDP equals the multiplier times the change in autonomous consumption or (2)(−50) or −100. Equilibrium real GDP will fall by 100 with this change in autonomous consumption.

**4. a.** The value of autonomous consumer spending in Mainland is equal to $160. To find this value first recall that the consumption function can be written as $C = A + MPC \times YD$. Then find the $MPC$, which is the change in consumer spending divided by the change in disposable income, or 800/1,000 = 0.8. Then substitute one of the consumer spending and disposable income combinations into the consumption function to find the value of autonomous consumer spending: thus, $C = A + 0.8 \times YD$ and 800 = $A$ + (0.8) × (800) or $A$ = $160.

**b.** The $MPC$ is equal to 0.8. See the explanation in part (a) of this problem.

**c.** The consumption function is $C = 160 + 0.8 \times YD$. See the explanation in part (a) of this problem.

**d.** When the level of planned aggregate expenditure is $3,000, the level of real GDP is equal to $2,925: this economy is not in equilibrium since the level of planned aggregate expenditure is greater than the level of real GDP. To find the level of real GDP, start with the aggregate expenditure function, $AE = 160 + 0.8 \times YD + 500$ and substitute $3,000 for $AE$. Then solve for $YD$. When $AE$ is equal to $3,000, $YD$ is equal to $2,925. When spending exceeds production, this causes a change in unplanned investment as inventories fall due to the fact that spending is greater than production. Firms increase their level of production in response to their falling inventories, moving the economy toward the income–expenditure equilibrium.

**e.** When the level of planned aggregate expenditure is $4,000, the level of real GDP is equal to $4,175: this economy is not in equilibrium since the level of planned aggregate expenditure is less than the level of real GDP. To find the level of real GDP, start with the aggregate expenditure function, $AE = 160 + 0.8 \times YD + 500$ and substitute $4,000 for $AE$. Then solve for $YD$. When $AE$ is equal to $4,000, $YD$ is equal to $4,175. When spending is less than production, this causes a change in unplanned investment as inventories rise due to the fact that spending is less than production. Firms decrease their level of production in response to their rising inventories, moving the economy toward the income–expenditure equilibrium.

**f.** The income-expenditure equilibrium in Mainland is $3,300. To find this equilibrium recall that, in equilibrium, planned aggregate expenditure is equal to real GDP. Or, in the model presented in this module, $YD = AE$ since disposable income and real GDP are equal to one another when there is no government sector. $AE$ is equal to $660 + 0.8 \times YD$. So, $YD = 660 + 0.8 \times YD$, or $YD$ is equal to $3,300.

5. **a.** The consumption function will change to $C = 360 + 0.8 \times YD$, the planned aggregate expenditure function will shift upward and the new income-expenditure equilibrium will be $4,300.

**b.** The level of investment spending will now equal $400, so the planned aggregate expenditure function will be $AE = 160 + 0.8 \times YD + 400$. There will be no change in the consumption function, but the planned aggregate expenditure function will shift down. This will lead to a decrease in the income-expenditure equilibrium: the new income-expenditure equilibrium will be $4,300.

**c.** The level of investment spending will now equal $700, so the planned aggregate expenditure function will be $AE = 160 + 0.8 \times YD + 700$. There will be no change in the consumption function, but the planned aggregate expenditure function will shift up. This will lead to an increase in the income-expenditure equilibrium: the new income-expenditure equilibrium will be $4,300.

**d.** The consumption function will change to $C = 260 + 0.8 \times YD$, the planned aggregate expenditure function will shift upward, and the new income-expenditure equilibrium will be $3,800.

## Answers to Module Review Questions

1. **Answer e.** Answer (a) is a factual answer. Consumer spending affects the level of $AE$ on goods and services and will therefore cause the $AE$ function to shift if there is a change in the level of consumer spending. Consumer spending in the model developed in this module has a powerful impact on the level of aggregate output, but it does not affect the aggregate price level since the model assumes that the aggregate price level is fixed.

2. **Answer d.** When the housing price bubble bursts, households' wealth is reduced, which causes them to reduce their level of consumption spending, including autonomous

consumption spending, at every level of disposable income. This downward shift in the consumption function results in a downward shift of the aggregate expenditure function and a decrease in the value of autonomous consumer spending.

3.  **Answer e.** An increase in planned investment spending increases $AE$ for goods and services and causes the $AE$ function to shift upward (and not downward), leading to a higher level of GDP. Studies of recessions indicate that most recessions follow a drop in investment spending, and this drop in that spending results in a fall in consumer spending.

4.  **Answer c.** We know the general equation for the consumption function is $C = A + MPC \times YD$. We need to find the values for $A$ and the $MPC$. From both the table and the assumptions underlying Macroland's economy, we know $GDP$ equals $YD$. The $MPC$ is the change in consumption divided by the change in disposable income: from the table, we can calculate that the change in consumption from 150 to 300 equals 150 and that the change in $YD$ from 100 to 400 equals 300: thus, the $MPC$ equals 0.5. We can now write $C = A + 0.5YD$ and use one of the combinations of consumption and disposable income from the table to solve for $A$; for example, when consumption equals 150, $YD$ equals 100 and $A$ can be computed as 100.

5.  **Answer c.** When GDP equals 400, we can calculate $AE_{Planned}$ by summing $C$ plus $I_{Planned}$. $AE_{Planned}$ equals 350, so income (GDP) is greater than expenditure, and therefore unplanned inventory investment is positive.

6.  **Answer b.** To find the income-expenditure equilibrium level of real GDP, we need to identify where $AE_{Planned}$ equals GDP. Recall that $AE_{Planned} = C + I_{Planned} = 100 + 0.5YD + 50 = 150 + 0.5YD$. Since GDP equals $YD$ for Macroland, this gives us GDP $= 150 + 0.5YD = 150 + 0.5GDP$. Solving for GDP we get 300. When $YD$ equals GDP at 300, $AE_{Planned}$ also equals 300.

7.  **Answer e.** An increase in wealth, holding everything else constant, leads to an increase in consumption spending, which causes the $AE$ curve to shift upward. When the $AE$ curve shifts upward, this leads to a higher income-expenditure equilibrium and, because of the multiplier effect, the increase in the income-expenditure equilibrium will be greater than the initial change in wealth: real GDP will increase by more than $100.

8.  **Answer a.** A change in wealth of 100 will cause the equilibrium level of real GDP to increase, since the increase in wealth causes the planned aggregate expenditure line to shift up.

9.  **Answer a.** When real GDP exceeds the level of planned aggregate expenditure, this implies that the level of spending in the economy is too low to absorb all the goods and services being produced. This situation will lead to an increase in inventories if the aggregate price level is assumed to be constant since the level of spending is less than the level of aggregate production.

10. **Answer a.** In the model presented in this module, the prices of goods and services are assumed to be constant. The role of inventories is to adjust the level of output to the level of aggregate expenditure: when aggregate expenditure exceeds aggregate production, the level of inventories fall; and when aggregate expenditure is less than aggregate production, the level of inventories rises.

# Aggregate Demand

## BEFORE YOU READ THE MODULE

## Summary

The module develops the concept of aggregate demand, which describes the relationship between the aggregate price level and the level of aggregate output demanded at each price level. The module discusses the wealth effect and the interest rate effect and how these two effects explain the aggregate demand curve's negative slope. It also explains how the aggregate demand (*AD*) curve can be derived from the income–expenditure model, and it includes a discussion of those factors that shift the aggregate demand curve.

## Module Objectives

**Objective #1.** The *AD* curve depicts the inverse relationship between the aggregate price level (*P*) and the total quantity of aggregate output demanded by households, businesses, government, and the foreign sector. A higher aggregate price level, other things equal, reduces the quantity of aggregate output demanded; a lower aggregate price level, other things equal, increases the quantity of aggregate output demanded.

- A movement up or down the *AD* curve is due to changes in the prices of all final goods and services. In contrast, a movement up and down the demand curve for any individual good is due to a change in the price of that good while all other prices are held constant.

- *AD* curves are downward sloping because of the wealth effect and the interest rate effect.

  - When the aggregate price level changes, this affects the purchasing power of consumers' assets and hence consumers' wealth. This effect on purchasing power is called the wealth effect. For example, a decrease in the aggregate price level increases the purchasing power of many assets and therefore leads to an increase in the quantity of aggregate output demanded.

  - When the aggregate price level changes, this affects the purchasing power of a given amount of money; for example, as the price level increases, people find they need more money to purchase the same basket of goods and services. Consumers bid up interest rates with their increased demand for money. As interest rates increase, this results in less investment spending and therefore a reduction in the quantity of aggregate output demanded. This effect is referred to as the interest rate effect.

**Objective #2.** When the aggregate price level decreases, this increases the level of planned spending at every level of real GDP. When the aggregate price level increases, this decreases the level of planned spending at every level of real GDP. Thus, as the aggregate price level increases, the level of spending, or aggregate demand, will decrease: the *AD* curve is thus downward sloping, indicating an inverse relationship between the level of real GDP and the aggregate price level. Figure 27.1 illustrates this relationship.

**Figure 27.1**

**Objective #3.** The *AD* curve shifts, holding everything else constant, when there are changes in expectations, wealth, or physical capital, or when there are changes in government fiscal or monetary policy.

- When consumers and firms become more optimistic, spending increases and the *AD* curve shifts to the right. A negative change in consumer or firm expectations shifts the *AD* curve to the left.

- When the value of household assets increases, consumer spending increases. *AD* shifts to the right with an increase in household wealth and to the left with a decrease in household wealth, other things held constant.

- Firms' incentives to engage in investment spending depend on many things, including how much physical capital they already have. If firms already have a high level of physical capital, the incentive to engage in investment spending is low: *AD*, holding everything else constant, shifts to the left when firms experience higher levels of physical capital. If firms have a low level of physical capital, the incentive to engage in investment spending is high: *AD*, holding everything else constant, shifts to the right when firms experience low levels of physical capital.

- Fiscal policy, or government spending and taxing policy, can cause the *AD* curve to shift to the right or to the left. An increase in government spending or a decrease in taxes, holding everything else constant, shifts *AD* to the right. A decrease in government spending or an increase in taxes, holding everything else constant, shifts *AD* to the left.

- Monetary policy, or the use of changes in the quantity of money or the interest rate, can cause the *AD* curve to shift to the right or to the left. When the Federal Reserve increases the supply of money (effectively decreasing the interest rate), this causes the *AD* curve to shift to the right, holding everything else constant. When the Federal Reserve decreases the supply of money (effectively increasing the interest rate), this causes the *AD* curve to shift to the left, holding everything else constant.

## Key Terms

**aggregate demand curve** a graphical representation that shows the relationship between the *aggregate price level* and the quantity of *aggregate output* demanded by *households, firms,* the government, and the rest of the world. The aggregate demand curve has a negative slope due to the *wealth effect of a change in the aggregate price level* and the *interest rate effect of a change in the aggregate price level.*

**wealth effect of a change in the aggregate price level** the effect on *consumer spending* caused by the change in the purchasing power of consumers' assets when the *aggregate price level* changes. A rise in the aggregate price level decreases the purchasing power of consumers' assets, so consumers decrease their consumption; a fall in the aggregate price level increases the purchasing power of consumers' assets, so consumers increase their consumption.

**interest rate effect of a change in the aggregate price level** the effect on *consumer spending* and *investment spending* caused by a change in the purchasing power of consumers' money holdings when the *aggregate price level* changes. A rise (fall) in the aggregate price level decreases (increases) the purchasing power of consumers' money holdings. In response, consumers try to increase (decrease) their money holdings, which drives up (down) interest rates, thereby decreasing (increasing) consumption and investment.

## AFTER YOU READ THE MODULE

## Tips

**Tip #1.** It is important to distinguish between a movement along the *AD* curve and a shift of the *AD* curve. Holding everything else constant, a change in the aggregate price level causes a movement along the *AD* curve (see Figure 27.2). A change in expectations, wealth, physical capital, fiscal policy, or monetary policy shifts the *AD* curve (see Figure 27.3).

**Figure 27.2**

**Figure 27.3**

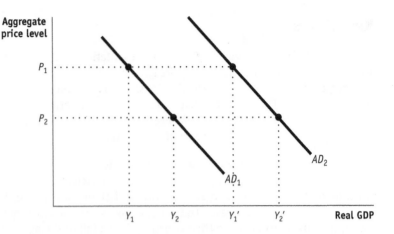

**Tip #2.** It is important to know the variables that shift *AD* curves. The text provides a list and an explanation for the variables that cause *AD* curves to shift. It is crucial that you know these variables and that you understand the direction the curves shift with changes in these variables. (See the previous tip for a quick review of these variables.)

**Tip #3.** It is important to understand why the *AD* curve is downward sloping. Note that the negative relationship between the aggregate price level and aggregate output are explained by the wealth and interest rate effects.

# WORKED PROBLEMS

1.  Today on a radio talk show you heard the commentator say that aggregate demand expresses an inverse relationship between the level of aggregate production and the aggregate price level. The commentator said this was due to the wealth effect and the interest rate effect. A friend listening to the show with you doesn't understand what this means, and she has asked you to explain the ideas behind these two effects and how they are related to the inverse relationship between the aggregate price level and the aggregate level of production.

**STEP 1:** Review the definitions of the wealth effect and the interest rate effect.

The wealth effect focuses on the effect of a change in the aggregate price level on the purchasing power or real income of consumers. When the aggregate price level increases, this reduces the real income that consumers have: for any given level of nominal income, a rise in the aggregate price level will lower consumers' ability to purchase goods and services. As the aggregate price level rises, consumption spending will therefore fall. Thus, as the aggregate price level increases, the level of aggregate output demanded will fall.

The interest rate effect focuses on the effect of a change in the aggregate price level on the interest rate in the economy. When the aggregate price level increases, people will demand more money since they will need more money in order to purchase the same basket of goods and services. As the demand for money increases, this causes the interest rate to rise, and this rise in interest rates means that it will cost more for businesses to borrow to finance their investment spending. Thus, as the interest rate rises, investment spending falls. This fall in investment spending results in a decrease in aggregate demand as the aggregate price level rises.

**STEP 2:** Explain why these two effects suggest that there is an inverse relationship between the aggregate price level and the aggregate level of production.

Both effects, the wealth effect and the interest rate effect, indicate that when the aggregate price level rises, this will cause aggregate demand to decrease. The aggregate demand curve is downward sloping: there is an inverse relationship between the level of real GDP and the aggregate price level.

**2.** For each of the following changes, determine the effect on the aggregate demand curve.

| Description of change | Impact of change on the aggregate demand curve |
|---|---|
| The aggregate price level increases in an economy | |
| Consumer confidence decreases | |
| Consumer wealth increases | |
| The government increases its level of spending while not changing its level of taxation | |
| The government increases the level of taxes that must be paid | |

**STEP 1:** Review the factors that shift the aggregate demand curve. In addition, think about sketching a graph that will help guide your answer to this question.

Before you try to answer this question you will find it helpful to review the factors that shift the aggregate demand curve.

**STEP 2:** Fill in the table.

| Description of change | Impact of change on the aggregate demand curve |
|---|---|
| The aggregate price level increases in an economy | There is a movement upward along the aggregate demand curve |
| Consumer confidence decreases | The aggregate demand curve shifts to the left |
| Consumer wealth increases | The aggregate demand curve shifts to the right |
| The government increases its level of spending while not changing its level of taxation | The aggregate demand curve shifts to the right |
| The government increases the level of taxes that must be paid | The aggregate demand curve shifts to the left |

# Problems and Exercises

1. Suppose the aggregate price level increases by 20% in an economy.

   a. What is the wealth effect of this increase in the aggregate price level? In your answer make sure to explain how the wealth effect impacts aggregate demand in this economy.

   b. What is the interest rate effect of this increase in the aggregate price level? In your answer make sure to explain how the interest rate effect impacts aggregate demand in this economy.

2. Suppose the central bank in an economy decreases the amount of money in circulation.

   a. Holding everything else constant, how will this monetary policy affect the interest rate in this economy?

   b. Given the change in the interest rate in part (a), what do you predict will happen to the level of consumer spending and the level of investment spending in this economy at a given aggregate price level?

   c. How will this monetary policy affect the aggregate demand curve for this economy?

3. For each of the following scenarios describe what happens to the aggregate demand curve.

   a. The government increases the level of government spending.

   b. The government decreases the level of taxation in the economy.

   c. People anticipate that the economy will improve in the next twelve months.

   d. An economy has a financial crisis and there is much uncertainty about what government policy will be to address the financial crisis.

**e.** An economy has a financial crisis and this financial crisis results in people's wealth decreasing by 25%.

**f.** An economy experiences an increase in the aggregate price level.

## ■ BEFORE YOU TAKE THE TEST

# Module Review Questions

1.  *AD*
    a. depicts the relationship between the aggregate price level and the quantity of aggregate output demanded.
    b. is a positive relationship between the aggregate price level and the quantity of aggregate output demanded.
    c. is always equal to potential output, no matter what the aggregate price level is.
    d. increases, other things equal, as the aggregate price level increases.

2.  As the aggregate price level increases, holding everything else constant,
    a. this reduces the purchasing power of many assets.
    b. this reduces the purchasing power of a given amount of money.
    c. the wealth and interest rate effects lead to a reduction in the quantity of aggregate output demanded.
    d. Answers (a), (b), and (c) are all correct.

3.  Holding everything else constant, the *AD* curve will shift to the right when
    a. the central bank decreases the money supply.
    b. household wealth increases.
    c. the government increases taxes paid by households.
    d. Answers (a), (b), and (c) are all correct.
    e. Answers (a) and (b) are both correct.
    f. Answers (b) and (c) are both correct.

4. Which of the following statements is true?
   I. One reason the aggregate demand curve slopes downward is the wealth effect, which states that as the aggregate price level increases, holding everything else constant, the purchasing power of people's assets decline, leading people to reduce their aggregate demand for goods and services.
   II. One reason the aggregate demand curve slopes downward is the interest rate effect, which states that as the aggregate price level increases, holding everything else constant, people demand more money and this causes interest rates to rise. This increase in interest rates causes the level of investment spending in the economy to decline.
   III. One reason the aggregate demand curve slopes downward is that as the aggregate price level decreases, people decide to buy more units of relatively inexpensive goods and fewer units of relatively expensive goods.
   a. Statements (a), (b), and (c) are all true.
   b. Statements (a) and (b) are both true.
   c. Statements (a) and (c) are both true.
   d. Statements (b) and (c) are both true.

5. An increase in the interest rate, holding everything else constant,
   a. reduces investment spending since the cost of borrowing is now higher.
   b. reduces consumer spending since households will respond to the higher interest rate by saving more.
   c. leads to a reduction in the level of aggregate demand for final goods and services.
   d. Answers (a), (b), and (c) are all correct.

6. Which of the following will *not* cause a shift in the *AD* curve?
   a. an increase in the level of wealth in the economy
   b. a reduction in government spending
   c. the decision by the central bank in an economy to expand the money supply
   d. the increase in the price of a commodity

7. Suppose the aggregate price level in the economy falls. Holding everything else constant, this will result in the wealth effect,
   a. which will cause the *AD* curve to shift to the right.
   b. since the fall in the aggregate price level increases consumers' purchasing power and this increase in purchasing power will result in a downward movement along the *AD* curve.
   c. which will cause the *AD* curve to shift to the left.
   d. since the fall in the aggregate price level increases consumers' purchasing power and this increase in purchasing power will result in an upward movement along the *AD* curve.

8. Suppose that the aggregate price level increases. Holding everything else constant, this will cause the level of aggregate real GDP demanded to
   a. increase.          b. decrease.

9. A change in the aggregate price level in an economy, holding everything else constant, will cause
   a. the aggregate demand curve to shift.
   b. a movement along the aggregate demand curve.

**10.** Suppose that over the past five years there has been an exceptional amount of new residential building in an economy; this building boom has led to an excess supply of new houses in the economy. Holding everything else constant, what do you predict will happen to aggregate demand in this economy?

a. There will be a movement along the aggregate demand curve and real GDP will increase as the aggregate price level decreases.

b. There will be a shift of the aggregate demand curve to the left as firms decrease their level of spending in the economy.

c. There will be a shift of the aggregate demand curve to the right as firms increase their level of spending in the economy.

d. There will be no change in the level of aggregate demand in this economy.

## ▮ ANSWER KEY

# Answers to Problems and Exercises

1.  **a.** The wealth effect refers to the effect on consumer spending of a change in the aggregate price level. In this case since the aggregate price level has risen this reduces consumers' real purchasing power and their level of consumer spending decreases when the aggregate price level rises. As the level of consumer spending decreases this results in a movement along the aggregate demand curve so that as the aggregate price level increases the level of real GDP falls.

    **b.** The interest rate effect refers to the effect of a change in the aggregate price level on the value of money holdings by consumers. When the aggregate price level increases this reduces the purchasing power of the money people hold: as the aggregate price level increases, consumers will now need to hold more money. As consumers either borrow more or sell assets in order to increase their money holding, the interest rate will rise. As the interest rate increases this reduces the level of investment spending as well as consumer spending: there is a movement along the aggregate demand curve so that as the aggregate price level increases the level of real GDP decreases.

2.  **a.** When the central bank decreases the amount of money in circulation it reduces the amount of money available for consumers and firms to borrow. This reduction in available funds will cause the interest rate to increase in the economy at any given aggregate price level.

    **b.** When the interest rate increases at any given aggregate price level this causes consumers and firms to decrease their level of consumer spending and investment spending, respectively.

    **c.** As consumer spending and investment spending decrease at any given aggregate price level this causes the aggregate demand curve to shift to the left.

3.  **a.** When the government increases the level of government spending, holding everything else constant, this will cause the aggregate demand curve to shift to the right.

    **b.** A decrease in the level of taxation in the economy will result in an increase in the level of disposable income in the economy. As disposable income rises this will result in an increase in the level of aggregate demand at every aggregate price level: the aggregate demand curve will shift to the right.

    **c.** People's positive expectations about the future leads to increases in both consumer spending and investment spending at every aggregate price level. The aggregate demand curve will shift to the right as a result of this increase in consumer and investment spending.

    **d.** When people are uncertain about the future there are decreases in both consumer spending and investment spending at every aggregate price level. The aggregate demand curve will shift to the left as a result of this decrease in consumer and investment spending.

    **e.** A decrease in wealth will cause people to reduce their consumer spending as the value of household assets falls in value. This decrease in consumer spending will cause the level of aggregate demand to fall at every aggregate price level: the aggregate demand curve will shift to the left.

    **f.** A change in the aggregate price level will cause a movement along the aggregate demand curve: when the aggregate price level increases there is a reduction in the level of aggregate demand.

# Answers to Module Review Questions

1. **Answer a.** The aggregate price level and the quantity of aggregate output demanded is the relationship captured by the *AD* curve. It is an inverse relationship: as the aggregate price level increases, other things equal, there is a decrease in the quantity of aggregate output demanded.

2. **Answer d.** An increase in the aggregate price level, holding everything else constant, leads to a reduction in demand for aggregate output. This is due to the wealth effect and the interest rate effect. Answer (a) expresses how an increase in the aggregate price level affects people's wealth, while answer (b) expresses how this price change affects their purchasing power (via the interest rate effect).

3. **Answer b.** The *AD* curve will shift to the left if the central bank decreases the money supply, since this policy action will increase interest rates, reduce investment spending, and therefore lead to lower *AD* at every aggregate price level. An increase in taxes reduces the disposable income households have and will therefore lead to lower *AD* at every aggregate price level (the *AD* curve will shift left). An increase in household wealth will shift the *AD* curve to the right, since households will increase their spending due to their increased wealth.

4. **Answer b.** The aggregate demand curve slopes downward due to the wealth and interest rate effects. Answer (c) is true for the demand for a particular good or service, but is not true for the aggregate demand for all final goods and services.

5. **Answer d.** When the interest rate rises, this makes borrowing more expensive for firms and leads firms to reduce their level of investment spending. At the same time, a higher interest rate will provide households with an incentive to save more. Both of these effects will lead aggregate demand to fall when there is a rise in the interest rate: this is referred to as the interest rate effect on aggregate demand.

6. **Answer d.** An increase in the price of a commodity will shift the *AS* curve to the left, which will result in a movement along the *AD* curve. Changes in wealth, the level of government spending, or the money supply will shift the *AD* curve.

7. **Answer b.** A fall in the aggregate price level changes the purchasing power of consumers' existing wealth and this wealth effect, due to the fall in the aggregate price level, will result in a movement down the *AD* curve. At the new lower aggregate price level, the quantity of aggregate demand for the economy increases.

8. **Answer b.** The aggregate demand curve is downward sloping due to the wealth effect and the interest rate effect. If the aggregate price level increases, this results in a reduction in wealth and therefore a reduction in the level of consumer spending in the economy: this reduction in consumer spending causes the level of aggregate real GDP demanded in the economy to decrease as the aggregate price level increases. If the aggregate price level increases, this results in a loss of value of money holdings and consumers will respond to this decrease in the value of their money holdings by reducing their level of consumer spending in the economy: this reduction in consumer spending causes the level of aggregate real GDP demanded in the economy to decrease as the aggregate price level increases.

9. **Answer b.** When there is a change in the aggregate price level there is a movement along the aggregate demand curve due to the wealth and interest rate effects. These two effects explain why aggregate demand curves are downward sloping: real GDP and the aggregate price level are inversely related to one another.

10. **Answer b.** If the existing stock of physical capital, in this case new residential building, is relatively large, then the level of investment spending will decrease. This decrease in investment spending will cause the aggregate demand curve to shift to the left at every aggregate price level.

# module 28(64)

# Aggregate Supply

## Summary

This module discusses the aggregate supply curve and how this curve illustrates the relationship between the aggregate price level and the aggregate level of production in the economy. The module also discusses the factors that shift the aggregate supply curve and provides a description of both the short-run and long-run aggregate supply curve.

## Module Objectives

**Objective #1.** The aggregate supply (*AS*) curve illustrates the relationship between the aggregate price level and the total quantity of final goods and services, or aggregate output, producers are willing to supply. In the short run there is a positive relationship between the amount of aggregate output or real GDP producers are willing to supply and the aggregate price level. That is, holding everything else constant, in the short run as the aggregate price level increases, the level of aggregate production increases. Figure 28.1 illustrates a short-run *AS* curve (*SRAS*): notice the positive relationship between the aggregate price level and the level of aggregate output or real GDP.

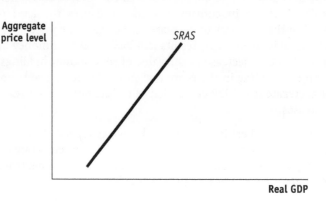

**Figure 28.1**

Aggregate price level

*SRAS*

Real GDP

- In the short run, producers decide on their level of production by comparing the price they receive from selling a unit of output to their costs of producing that unit of output. Since some production costs are fixed in the short run, an increase in the aggregate price level increases profit per unit and therefore leads producers to increase their level of production. Hence, the short-run AS curve is upward sloping.

- In the short run, nominal wages are sticky due to the existence of both formal and informal agreements. This means that nominal wages decrease slowly even in the presence of high unemployment and increase slowly in the presence of low unemployment. In the long run, nominal wages are completely flexible.

- The short-run AS curve shifts due to changes in commodity prices, nominal wages, and productivity. An increase in commodity prices or nominal wages results in a shift to the left of the short-run AS curve, while a decrease in commodity prices or nominal wages results in a shift to the right of the short-run AS curve. An increase in productivity shifts the short-run AS curve to the right. There will be a movement along the AS curve with a change in the aggregate price level.

**Objective #2.** In the long run, nominal wages and prices are flexible and therefore in the long run, the aggregate price level has no effect on the quantity of aggregate output supplied. The AS curve in the long run is vertical, where the level of aggregate output equals potential output, or the level of real GDP the economy would produce if all prices and wages were completely flexible. Figure 28.2 illustrates a long-run AS curve (LRAS): notice that this curve is vertical and that no matter what the aggregate price level, the level of real GDP is constant and equal to potential GDP.

**Figure 28.2**

- Over time if the level of potential output for an economy increases, the implication is that the long-run AS curve is shifting to the right. These shifts represent economic growth and are due to increases in the labor force and increases in the productivity of labor.

**Objective #3.** The economy is always in only one of two states with respect to the short-run and long-run AS curves: (1) it can be on both curves simultaneously by being at a point where the two curves cross; or (2) it can be on the short-run AS curve but not on the long-run AS curve. Figure 28.3 illustrates these two possibilities. In the graph on the left, the SRAS and the LRAS curves intersect at the potential output level $Y_P$ and the aggregate price level $P$. In the graph on the right, the economy is producing at $Y_1$ with the aggregate price level $P$: this level of production is not equal to potential output. In the short run, the economy can produce at a level of aggregate output that is less than potential output (as illustrated in the right graph in Figure 28.3), or it can produce at a level of aggregate output that is greater than potential output (you might want to practice drawing this situation).

**Figure 28.3**

- When the level of aggregate production is less than potential output, the implication is that unemployment is high. Jobs are scarce and workers are abundant, which causes nominal wages to fall over time; the short-run *AS* curve will shift to the right, moving the short-run level of aggregate production closer to potential output. Figure 28.4 illustrates this situation.

**Figure 28.4**

- When the level of aggregate production is greater than potential output, this implies that unemployment is low. Jobs are abundant and workers are scarce, which causes nominal wages to rise over time; the short-run *AS* curve will shift to the left, moving the short-run level of aggregate production closer to potential output. Figure 28.5 illustrates this situation.

**Figure 28.5**

## Key Terms

*Notes*

**aggregate supply curve** a graphical representation that shows the relationship between the *aggregate price level* and the total quantity of *aggregate output* supplied.

**nominal wage** the dollar amount of any given wage paid.

**sticky wages** *nominal wages* that are slow to fall even in the face of high *unemployment* and slow to rise even in the face of labor shortages.

**short-run aggregate supply curve** a graphical representation that shows the positive relationship between the *aggregate price level* and the quantity of *aggregate output* supplied that exists in the short run, the time period when many production costs, particularly *nominal wages*, can be taken as fixed. The short-run aggregate supply curve has a positive slope because a rise in the aggregate price level leads to a rise in profits, and therefore output, when production costs are fixed.

**long-run aggregate supply curve** a graphical representation that shows the relationship between the *aggregate price level* and the quantity of *aggregate output* supplied that would exist if all prices, including *nominal wages*, were fully flexible. The long-run aggregate supply curve is vertical because the aggregate price level has no effect on aggregate output in the long run; in the long run, aggregate output is determined by the *economy's potential output*.

**potential output** the level of *real GDP* the *economy* would produce if all prices, including *nominal wages*, were fully flexible.

## AFTER YOU READ THE MODULE

## Tips

**Tip #1.** It is important to distinguish between short-run and long-run *AS*. In the short run, wages are sticky: this stickiness results in a short-run *AS* curve (*SRAS*) that is upward sloping. In the long run, wages are fully flexible, leading the economy to always produce its long-run equilibrium at the potential output level of real GDP. This is the output level the economy produces when all wages and prices are fully flexible. In Figure 28.6, the short-run aggregate supply curve is *SRAS*, the aggregate demand curve is *AD*, the long-run aggregate supply curve is *LRAS*, and the potential output level, which represents the long-run equilibrium level of output, is $Y_P$. The economy in the short run may produce an aggregate output level that is greater than or less than the potential level of output $Y_P$. Figure 28.6 represents an economy where the short-run level of aggregate output $Y_1$ is less than the long-run level of output, labeled $Y_P$.

**Figure 28.6**

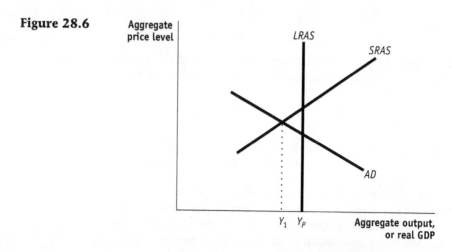

**Tip #2.** It is important to distinguish between a movement along the SRAS curve and a shift of the SRAS curve. Holding everything else constant, a change in the aggregate price level causes a movement along the SRAS curve (see Figure 28.7). A change in commodity prices, nominal wages, or productivity shifts the SRAS curve (see Figure 28.8).

**Figure 28.7**

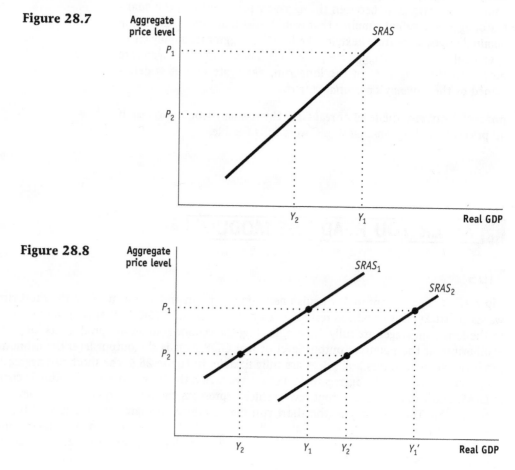

**Tip #3.** Changes in commodity prices have large impacts on production costs. It is important to understand the impact of commodity prices on the SRAS curve.

**Tip #4.** The long-run *AS* curve (*LRAS*) is vertical, and its position represents the economy's potential output when all resources are fully employed. It is important to understand why the *LRAS* curve is vertical as well as the relevance of its position on the horizontal axis. Over time if an economy experiences economic growth the *LRAS* curve shifts to the right, indicating the economy's potential output has increased.

## WORKED PROBLEMS

1. For each of the following changes, determine the effect on the short-run aggregate supply curve and the effect on the long-run aggregate supply curve.

| Description of change | Impact of change on short-run aggregate supply | Impact of change on long-run aggregate supply |
|---|---|---|
| The aggregate price level increases in an economy | | |
| There is an increase in the price of petroleum | | |
| There is an increase in nominal wages | | |
| The economy's potential level of output increases | | |
| Labor becomes less productive | | |

**STEP 1:** Review the factors that shift the short-run aggregate supply curve and the long-run aggregate supply curve. In addition, think about sketching a graph that will help guide your answer to this question.

Before you try to answer this question you will find it helpful to review the factors that shift the short-run aggregate supply curve. You will also find it helpful to review what determines the location of the long-run aggregate supply curve.

**STEP 2:** Fill in the table.

| Description of change | Impact of change on short-run aggregate supply | Impact of change on long-run aggregate supply |
|---|---|---|
| The aggregate price level increases in an economy | There will be a movement along the short-run aggregate supply curve | There will be no change in the long-run aggregate supply curve |
| There is an increase in the price of petroleum | The short-run aggregate supply curve shifts to the left | There will be no change in the long-run aggregate supply curve |
| There is an increase in nominal wages | The short-run aggregate supply curve shifts to the left | There will be no change in the long-run aggregate supply curve |
| The economy's potential level of output increases | There will be no change in the short-run aggregate supply curve | The long-run aggregate supply curve will shift to the right |
| Labor becomes less productive | The short-run aggregate supply curve shifts to the left | There will be no change in the long-run aggregate supply curve |

2.  Polly reads in the newspaper that her country's potential level of output is $500 billion and its current level of output is $450 billion. She has asked you to comment on this information and to guide her in understanding what this information says about the current level of unemployment in her country, your predictions about what will happen to nominal wages, and is if she can say whether this economy is operating with a recessionary gap or an inflationary gap.

**STEP 1:** **Examine the data and explain the relationship between the data and the economy's short-run aggregate supply curve and its long-run aggregate supply curve.**

Current production in this economy is lower than the potential level of output for this economy. This tells us that the economy has the capability and capacity to produce a higher dollar value of final goods and services than it is currently producing. This information implies that the economy is currently producing at some point on its short-run aggregate supply curve, but that it is not currently producing on its long-run aggregate supply curve.

**STEP 2:** **Explain what this information tells you about the current level of unemployment in this economy. In your explanation identify whether the economy is operating with a recessionary gap or an inflationary gap.**

When an economy produces at a level of production that is lower than its potential level of production this tells us that the economy is operating with a recessionary gap. This implies that the economy's unemployment rate is higher than normal and that jobs are scarce.

**STEP 3:** **Make a prediction about what will happen to nominal wages and then explain your prediction.**

Since this economy is operating on its short-run aggregate supply curve with a recessionary gap, we can expect nominal wages to fall over time so that the short-run aggregate supply curve will shift to the right and return this economy to its long-run aggregate supply curve, where the economy is producing at its potential level of output. With unemployment initially high and many people looking for work we can expect this to exert downward pressure on nominal wages.

# Problems and Exercises

1.  For each of the following scenarios, describe the effect on the *SRAS* curve and the *LRAS* curve. Identify whether the effect causes a shift of the curve or a movement along the curve and identify the direction of the shift if one has occurred.

    a.  The price of commodities increases by 10% this year.

    b.  The price of oil falls.

**c.** Labor unions successfully negotiate an increase in nominal wages for their workers.

**d.** There is an increase in labor productivity due to increases in human capital.

**2.** In the short run nominal wages are often thought of as sticky wages. What does this term mean and why do economists believe that these wages in the short run are sticky?

**3.** Suppose an economy is booming and firms find that they are having trouble keeping their workers at the current nominal wages they are paying. How do you think firms will respond to this situation and what will be the impact of their response on the *SRAS* curve?

**4.** Why is the *LRAS* curve vertical? What is the meaning of potential output for an economy?

5. Suppose the potential output level for an economy is $400 billion but the economy is currently producing $350 billion in the short run.

   a. What do you predict will happen to the SRAS curve given the above information?

   b. Given your prediction in part (a), what will cause this change in the SRAS curve? In your answer be specific and make sure you comment on what is happening to the level of nominal wages in this economy.

## ▮ BEFORE YOU TAKE THE TEST

## Module Review Questions

1. Nominal wages
   a. are often determined by contracts that were signed at some previous point in time.
   b. are slow to decrease in times of high unemployment, since employers may be reluctant to alter wages as a response to economic conditions.
   c. are fully flexible in both the short run and the long run.
   d. Answers (a) and (b) are both correct.

2. Which of the following statements is true? In the short run, holding everything else constant,
   a. as production costs increase, profit per unit decreases, and this causes suppliers to increase their production.
   b. as production costs increase, profit per unit decreases, and this causes suppliers to reduce their production.
   c. as production costs decrease, profit per unit increases, and this causes suppliers to reduce their production.
   d. the AS curve is unaffected by changes in production costs.

3. Suppose there is an increase in the price of a commodity, holding everything else constant. In the short run,
   a. the producer will increase production since commodity prices have risen.
   b. the producer's profit per unit of output will decrease.
   c. the producer's price per unit of output will decrease.
   d. there will be a movement along the AS curve.
   e. Answers (a) and (b) are both correct.

4.  Which of the following will *not* make the AS curve shift to the left?
    a.  an increase in the aggregate price level
    b.  a decrease in commodity prices
    c.  an increase in nominal wages
    d.  None of the above cause the AS curve to shift to the left.
    e.  Answers (a) and (c) are both correct.
    f.  Answers (b) and (c) are both correct.

5.  An increase in the aggregate price level, holding everything else constant, causes
    a.  movement along the AS curve.
    b.  a shift to the right of the AD curve due to the wealth effect and the interest rate effect.
    c.  a shift to the left of the AD curve due to the wealth effect and the interest rate effect.
    d.  a shift to the right of the AS curve since producers will be willing to supply more goods and services at every price than they were initially.
    e.  a shift to the left of the AS curve since producers will supply fewer goods and services at every price than they did initially.

6.  Between 1929 and 1933 the U.S. economy
    a.  experienced a rightward shift in its SRAS curve.
    b.  experienced a leftward shift in its SRAS curve.
    c.  experienced a downward movement along its SRAS curve.
    d.  Answers (a), (b), and (c) are all false statements.

7.  Profit per unit of output is equal to the price per unit of output minus the production cost per unit of output. So, if nominal wages increase and everything else is held constant, then
    a.  profit per unit of output is unaffected.
    b.  profit per unit of output will increase.
    c.  profit per unit of output will decrease.
    d.  since nominal wages are sticky, this increase in nominal wages will not affect the level of profit per unit of output.

8.  Suppose the aggregate price level in the economy increases. Given this change and holding everything else constant, which of the following statements is true?
    a.  Since many labor contracts fix nominal wages for some period of time, this increase in the aggregate price level will result in an increase in profitability for some firms in the economy.
    b.  When the aggregate price level in the economy increases, nominal wages in the economy rise immediately so that the purchasing power for consumers is unaffected by the change in the aggregate price level.
    c.  When the aggregate price level in the economy increases, firms increase their level of production, and this higher level of production results in greater production costs and therefore lower profits for firms.
    d.  Since many labor contracts are informally made, firms will adjust nominal wages as the aggregate price level increases and firm profitability will be unaffected.

9.  An economy experiences decrease in labor productivity. This will
    a.  cause the SRAS curve to shift to the right.
    b.  cause the SRAS curve to shift to the left.

## ANSWER KEY

# Answers to Problems and Exercises

1. **a.** When the price of commodities increases, the *SRAS* curve shifts to the left. There will be a movement upward along the *AD* curve and no change in the *LRAS* curve.

   **b.** When the price of oil decreases, this causes the *SRAS* curve to shift to the right and results in a downward movement along the *AD* curve. There is no change in the *LRAS* curve.

   **c.** The result of the successful labor union negotiation is higher wages, which leads to a leftward shift in the *SRAS* curve and an upward movement along the *AD* curve. There is no change in the *LRAS* curve.

   **d.** When labor productivity increases, this causes the *SRAS* curve to shift to the right, but it also causes the *LRAS* curve to shift to the right since the economy can now produce at a higher potential output level. There is a downward movement along the *AD* curve.

2. Sticky wages are nominal wages that are slow to adjust. When there is high unemployment nominal wages should fall but with sticky wages this fall in nominal wages is slow to occur; or when there is low unemployment nominal wages should increase but with sticky wages this increase in nominal wages is slow to occur. Nominal wages are thought to be sticky because these wages are often determined by formal contracts that set nominal wages at a particular level for a period of time, or because of informal agreements between management and workers that make companies reluctant to change wages in response to economic conditions.

3. If firms find that they are having trouble keeping their workers at the prevailing nominal wage then they will conclude that they need to pay a higher nominal wage. But, when nominal wages increase this causes the *SRAS* curve to shift to the left at every aggregate price level.

4. The *LRAS* curve is vertical and touches the horizontal axis at the potential output level for the economy. The *LRAS* curve illustrates the relationship between the aggregate price level and the quantity of aggregate output supplied that would exist if all prices, including nominal wages, were fully flexible. Potential output is an important benchmark for an economy since it indicates that level of aggregate output that the economy can produce when all prices are flexible.

5. **a.** The *SRAS* curve will shift to the right.

   **b.** Since the short-run level of output in this economy is less than the potential output level in the economy, we can conclude that the economy has a high level of unemployment. This high level of unemployment will eventually lead to a decrease in the nominal wage rate and a rightward shift of the *SRAS* curve.

# Answers to Module Review Questions

1. **Answer d.** In the short run, nominal wages are sticky and take time to adjust to changes in economic conditions due to pre-existing contracts and employer reluctance to frequently alter wages. In the long run, nominal wages are fully flexible.

2. **Answer b.** Production costs affect the level of aggregate production: as production costs increase, holding everything else constant, profit per unit decreases. Producers respond to this decrease in profit per unit by decreasing the quantity of goods and services they are willing to supply.

3. **Answer b.** An increase in the price of a commodity, holding everything else constant, will cause the *AS* curve to shift to the left as aggregate production decreases at any given aggregate price level. Aggregate production decreases due to the decrease in producers' profit per unit, arising from the higher commodity price they must now pay.

4. **Answer e.** An increase in the aggregate price level results in a movement along the *AS* curve and not a shift of the curve. A decrease in commodity prices results in a rightward shift of the *AS* curve. An increase in nominal wages causes the *AS* curve to shift to the left.

5. **Answer a.** A change in the aggregate price level, holding everything else constant, causes a movement along the *AS* curve. It is important to realize that a change in the aggregate price level, holding everything else constant, causes a movement along the *AD* and the *AS* curves. For instance, suppose the aggregate price level is currently greater than the equilibrium aggregate price level. In the *AD-AS* model this will result in a situation of excess aggregate supply and over time as the aggregate price level falls the level of *AD* will increase while the level of *AS* will decrease until the aggregate price level falls to that level where *AD* equals *AS*.

6. **Answer c.** During the years 1929 through 1933 the aggregate price level in the United States fell and this led to decreases in the level of aggregate real GDP supplied in the economy. As the aggregate price level fell there was a movement along the *SRAS* curve.

7. **Answer c.** Since nominal wages increase, the cost of producing a unit of output has risen. If output prices do not change, then the profit per unit of output must decrease. Answer (d) is not true since the information tells you that nominal wages have increased, nominal wages since they are changing cannot be considered sticky in this example.

8. **Answer a.** Nominal wages are slow to adjust in the aggregate economy due to the use of formal contracts to set wages for extended periods of time. When the aggregate price level increases, on average, firms will receive a greater price per unit of output while their production costs are unaffected due to the stickiness of nominal wages. This will lead to a higher level of profit per unit of output. Answer (b) is incorrect since some nominal wages in the economy will be slow to rise due to the stickiness of those wages. Answer (c) is incorrect since as firms increase their level of production their production costs do not increase at as fast a rate due to the stickiness of nominal wages in the short run. Answer (d) is incorrect since nominal wages are slow to adjust to changes in economic conditions in the short run.

9. **Answer a.** This fall in labor productivity causes the *SRAS* curve to shift to the right since a fall in labor productivity implies that a worker can produce fewer units of output with the same quantity of inputs. A decrease in labor productivity reduces producers' profits and shifts the *SRAS* curve to the right.

# The *AD–AS* Model

---

## ▮ BEFORE YOU READ THE MODULE

### Summary

This module considers equilibrium in the aggregate demand–aggregate supply model. It examines both short-run and long-run equilibrium in this model. The module also discusses the causes and effects of demand shocks and supply shocks. It defines recessionary gaps and inflationary gaps and then indicates how to measure the output gaps that occur when the economy is operating with either a recessionary gap or an inflationary gap. This module also considers how monetary and fiscal policy can be used to stabilize the economy.

### Module Objectives

**Objective #1.**  The model of aggregate supply (*AS*) and aggregate demand (*AD*) can help us understand economic fluctuations and the use of macroeconomic policy to reduce these fluctuations.

**Objective #2.**  The *AD–AS* model is the basic model we use to understand economic fluctuations. In this model there are two states of equilibrium: (1) the economy can be in short-run equilibrium where *AD* equals short-run *AS*; or (2) the economy can be in long-run equilibrium where *AD* equals long-run *AS* (as well as short-run *AS*) and aggregate output equals potential output. If the economy is in the first state, over time the short-run *AS* curve will shift eventually, bringing the economy into long-run equilibrium.

- In short-run equilibrium, aggregate output may be less than, equal to, or greater than potential output. If aggregate output is less than potential output, this implies that unemployment is relatively high: since jobs are scarce and workers are abundant, nominal wages will respond by falling over time and this will shift the short-run *AS* to the right, leading output to expand toward the level of potential output. Figure 29.1 illustrates this situation. The economy moves from the short-run equilibrium where real GDP equals $Y_1$ and the aggregate price level equals $P_1$, to the long-run equilibrium where real GDP equals $Y_2$ or the potential output level $Y_P$ and the aggregate price level equals $P_2$.

**Figure 29.1**

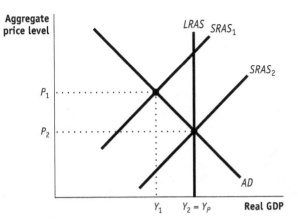

- If aggregate output is greater than potential output, this implies unemployment is relatively low. Since jobs are plentiful and workers are scarce, nominal wages will respond by rising over time and this will shift the short-run *AS* to the left, leading output to contract toward the level of potential output. Figure 29.2 illustrates this situation. The economy moves from the short-run equilibrium where real GDP equals $Y_1$ and the aggregate price level equals $P_1$, to the long-run equilibrium where real GDP equals $Y_2$ or the potential output level $Y_P$ and the aggregate price level equals $P_2$.

**Figure 29.2**

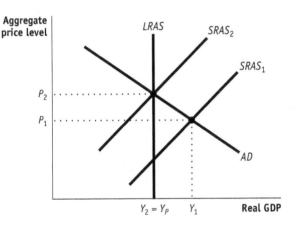

**Objective #3.** In the *AD–AS* model, the short-run macroeconomic equilibrium occurs at the intersection of the *AD* curve with the short-run *AS* curve.

- An event that shifts the short-run *AS* curve is called a supply shock. Negative supply shocks shift the short-run *AS* curve to the left, while positive supply shocks shift the short-run *AS* curve to the right.

  - A negative supply shock leads to stagflation, where falling aggregate output and rising unemployment combine with an increasing price level.

  - A positive supply shock leads to rising aggregate output, falling unemployment, and a decrease in the aggregate price level.

  - Supply shocks cause aggregate output and the aggregate price level to move in opposite directions.

- An event that shifts the *AD* curve is called a demand shock.

  - A positive demand shock shifts the *AD* curve to the right, resulting in higher aggregate output and a higher aggregate price level.

- A negative demand shock shifts the *AD* curve to the left, resulting in lower aggregate output and a lower aggregate price level.

- Demand shocks cause aggregate output and the aggregate price level to move in the same direction.

- Short-run macroeconomic equilibrium aggregate output may be less than, equal to, or greater than potential output. Thus, the short-run macroeconomic equilibrium can represent an economy in an economic recession or an economy in an economic expansion.

**Objective #4.** Long-run macroeconomic equilibrium occurs when the short-run macroeconomic equilibrium is also a point on the long-run *AS* curve. Long-run macroeconomic equilibrium aggregate output is always equal to potential output.

- A recessionary gap occurs when the short-run macroeconomic equilibrium is below potential output. Recessionary gaps are hurtful due to the high levels of unemployment and low levels of production associated with them. Eventually, high unemployment causes nominal wages to fall, which shifts the short-run *AS* to the right, leading to higher levels of production and lower unemployment as the economy reaches long-run macroeconomic equilibrium. Figure 29.1 represents a recessionary gap since the equilibrium level of short-run production ($Y_1$) is less than the long-run equilibrium level of production ($Y_2$ or $Y_P$); the recessionary gap is the difference between potential output and actual short-run output, or $Y_P - Y_1$.

- An inflationary gap occurs when the short-run macroeconomic equilibrium is above potential output. In an inflationary gap, unemployment is low, which leads to increases in nominal wages that shift the short-run *AS* to the left, leading to lower levels of production and higher unemployment as the economy reaches long-run macroeconomic equilibrium. Figure 29.2 represents an inflationary gap since the equilibrium level of short-run production ($Y_1$) is greater than the long-run equilibrium level of production ($Y_2$ or $Y_P$); the inflationary gap is the difference between actual short-run output and potential output, or $Y_1 - Y_P$.

- In both the recessionary gap and inflationary gap, the economy is self-correcting. Given enough time the economy will adjust to economic shocks so that these shocks affect aggregate output in the short run but have no effect on aggregate output in the long run, provided the government does not intervene with activist policy.

- The output gap provides a measure of how the economy responds to recessionary and inflationary gaps. The output gap is equal to [(Actual aggregate output – Potential output)/(Potential output)] × 100. Our analysis of recessionary and inflationary gaps indicates that the output gap always tends toward zero, since the economy is self-correcting.

# Key Terms

**AD–AS model** the basic model used to understand fluctuations in *aggregate output* and the *aggregate price level*. It uses the *aggregate supply curve* and the *aggregate demand curve* together to analyze the behavior of the *economy* in response to shocks or government policy.

**short-run macroeconomic equilibrium** the point at which the quantity of *aggregate output* supplied is equal to the *quantity demanded*.

**short-run equilibrium aggregate price level** the *aggregate price level* in *short-run macroeconomic equilibrium*.

## Key Terms *(continued)*

**short-run equilibrium aggregate output** the quantity of *aggregate output* produced in *short-run macroeconomic equilibrium*.

**demand shock** an event that shifts the *aggregate demand curve*. A positive demand shock is associated with higher demand for *aggregate output* at any price level and shifts the curve to the right. A negative demand shock is associated with lower demand for aggregate output at any price level and shifts the curve to the left.

**supply shock** an event that shifts the *short-run aggregate supply curve*. A negative supply shock raises production costs and reduces the *quantity supplied* at any *aggregate price level*, shifting the curve leftward. A positive supply shock decreases production costs and increases the quantity supplied at any aggregate price level, shifting the curve rightward.

**stagflation** the combination of *inflation* and falling *aggregate output*.

**long-run macroeconomic equilibrium** the point at which the *short-run macroeconomic equilibrium* is on the *long-run aggregate supply curve*; so *short-run equilibrium aggregate output* is equal to *potential output*.

**recessionary gap** exists when *aggregate output* is below *potential output*.

**inflationary gap** exists when *aggregate output* is above *potential output*.

**output gap** the percentage difference between the actual level of *real GDP* and *potential output*.

**self-correcting** describes an *economy* in which shocks to aggregate demand affect *actual aggregate output* in the short run but not in the long run.

**stabilization policy** the use of government policy to reduce the severity of recessions and rein in excessively strong expansions.

## AFTER YOU READ THE MODULE

# Tips

**Tip #1.** It is important to understand the difference between short-run and long-run macroeconomic equilibria and the relationship between these equilibria. In long-run macroeconomic equilibrium, aggregate output equals potential output and the economy's *AD* equals both its short-run and long-run *AS* (see Figure 29.3). In short-run macroeconomic equilibrium aggregate output, need not equal potential output, but the economy's *AD* must equal the short–run *AS*. Figure 29.4 illustrates a short-run equilibrium for an economy that is operating with an inflationary gap. Figure 29.5 illustrates a short-run equilibrium for an economy that is operating with a recessionary gap.

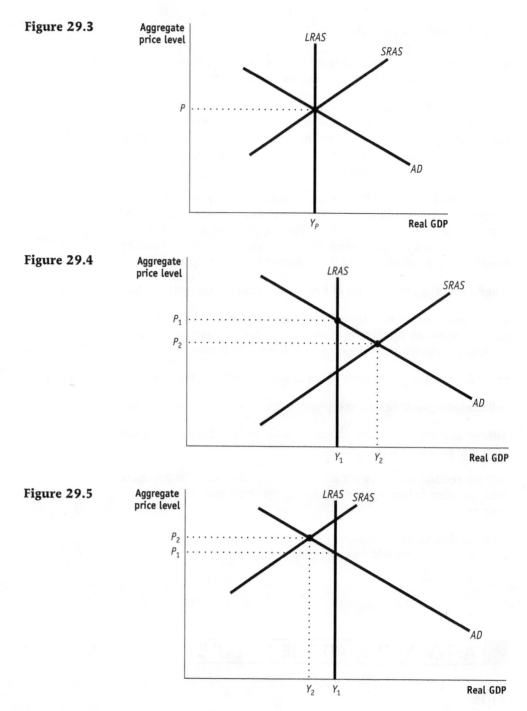

**Figure 29.3**

**Figure 29.4**

**Figure 29.5**

**Tip #2.** It is important to practice the analysis in moving from short-run equilibrium in the *AD-AS* model to long-run equilibrium in the *AD-AS* model. You will find it helpful to remember that this model always returns to long-run equilibrium through adjustment of nominal wages. If the economy has an inflationary gap in the short run, this indicates that nominal wages are too low, and in the long-run you can expect a leftward shift of the *SRAS* supply curve to restore the economy to its long-run equilibrium. If the economy has a recessionary gap in the short run the indication is that nominal wages are too high, and in the long-run you can expect a rightward shift of the *SRAS* supply curve to restore the economy to its long-run equilibrium.

**Tip #3.** The output gap tends to zero because in the long-run the aggregate economy is self-correcting. That is, both inflationary and recessionary gaps are eliminated in the long run as nominal wages adjust to return the aggregate economy to long-run equilibrium.

# WORKED PROBLEMS

1. For each of the following changes, determine the effect on the aggregate demand curve and the short-run aggregate supply curve, as well as the effect on the aggregate price level and aggregate level of output.

| Description of change | Effect on aggregate demand | Effect on short-run aggregate supply | Effect on the aggregate price level | Effect on the aggregate level of production |
|---|---|---|---|---|
| World oil prices increase | | | | |
| The central bank increases the money supply | | | | |
| The government reduces taxes | | | | |
| The government reduces taxes at the same time that nominal wages increase | | | | |
| The country goes to war at the same time that world oil prices increase | | | | |
| People's real wealth decreases | | | | |

**STEP 1:** **Review the factors that shift the aggregate demand curve and the aggregate supply curve. In addition, think about sketching a graph that will help guide your answer to this question.**

Before you can begin to answer this question, you must have a firm grasp of the factors that shift the aggregate demand curve and the factors that shift the short-run aggregate supply curve. Then, for each description determine which curve or curves are shifting and sketch a diagram to guide your thinking.

**STEP 2:** **There is a challenge in this question when both the aggregate demand curve and the short-run aggregate supply curve shift simultaneously.**

When both curves shift and there is no quantitative information about the size of the shift, this results in either the change in the equilibrium aggregate price level or the change in the equilibrium aggregate output level being ambiguous. Be particularly careful in your analysis when you see that both curves are shifting.

**STEP 3:** Fill in the table.

| Description of change | Effect on aggregate demand | Effect on short-run aggregate supply | Effect on the aggregate price level | Effect on the aggregate level of production |
|---|---|---|---|---|
| World oil prices increase | This event causes a movement along the *AD* curve. | This event causes the *SRAS* curve to shift to the left. | The aggregate price level increases. | The aggregate level of production decreases. |
| The central bank increases the money supply | This event causes the *AD* curve to shift to the right. | This event causes a movement along the *SRAS* curve. | The aggregate price level increases. | The aggregate level of production increases. |
| The government reduces taxes | This event causes the *AD* curve to shift to the right. | This event causes a movement along the *SRAS* curve. | The aggregate price level increases. | The aggregate level of production increases. |
| The government reduces taxes at the same time that nominal wages increase | The reduction in taxes causes the *AD* curve to shift to the right. | The increase in nominal wages causes the *SRAS* curve to shift to the left. | The aggregate price level will increase. | The aggregate level of production may increase, decrease, or remain the same. |
| The country goes to war at the same time that world oil prices increase | The country's entry into war causes the *AD* curve to shift to the right. | The rise in world oil prices causes the *SRAS* curve to shift to the left. | The aggregate price level will increase. | The aggregate level of production may increase, decrease, or remain the same. |
| People's real wealth decreases | This event causes the *AD* curve to shift to the left. | This event causes a movement along the *SRAS* curve. | The aggregate price level will decrease. | The aggregate level of production will decrease. |

2.  Suppose that you know the following information about an economy.

Long-run aggregate supply:    $Y = 8$
Short-run aggregate supply:    $P = 100Y$
Aggregate demand:    $P = 1,000 - 100Y$

As shown here, $P$ refers to aggregate prices and $Y$ refers to the aggregate level of production. You are asked to determine the short-run equilibrium aggregate price level and aggregate output level. You are also asked to identify if there is a short-run recessionary gap or a short-run inflationary gap. Comment on the implications of this gap on the level of unemployment in this economy in the short run. In addition, you are asked to provide a graph that depicts this short-run equilibrium as well as the long-run aggregate supply curve for this economy. Finally, you are asked to propose several policy options for the government of this country if it wishes to return to the long-run equilibrium. You are also asked to discuss the implications of not implementing any active policy to return the economy to long-run equilibrium.

**STEP 1:** Use the short-run aggregate supply curve and aggregate demand curve to determine the short-run equilibrium level of aggregate prices and the short-run equilibrium level of aggregate output.

Since you are given equations for the three curves, you can solve for the equilibrium values of $P$ and $Y$. To find the short-run equilibrium aggregate price level and the short-run equilibrium aggregate output level, use the short-run aggregate supply curve and the aggregate demand curve. Thus, $100Y = 1,000 - 100Y$, and therefore $P = 500$ and $Y = 5$.

**STEP 2:** Determine whether there is a recessionary gap or an inflationary gap by comparing the short-run equilibrium level of aggregate output to the long-run level of aggregate output. Then consider the implications of this gap on this economy's unemployment rate.

A recessionary gap occurs when the short-run level of aggregate output is less than the long-run level of aggregate output. An inflationary gap occurs when the short-run level of aggregate output is greater than the long-run level of aggregate output. In this case, the short-run level of aggregate output is equal to 5 and the long-run level of aggregate output is equal to 8: this economy has a recessionary gap. It is currently producing a level of aggregate output that is lower than its potential or long-run level of output; the economy is in a recession and unemployment is relatively high.

**STEP 3:** Draw a graph that depicts the short-run aggregate supply curve, the long-run aggregate supply curve, and the aggregate demand curve. On your graph, mark the short-run equilibrium aggregate price level and the short-run equilibrium level of aggregate output. Also, mark the long-run level of aggregate output.

Here is the graph of this economy's short-run equilibrium as well as its long-run level of aggregate output.

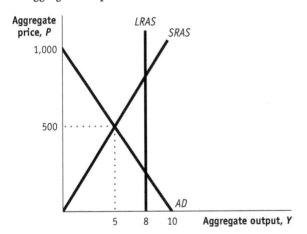

**STEP 4:** Determine what type of activist policy, monetary or fiscal, will move this economy to the long-run level of aggregate output.

Since short-run aggregate output is less than long-run aggregate output, activist policy should stimulate the economy. The government could implement activist fiscal policy, which could involve an increase in government spending, a decrease in taxes, or a combination of these two policies. The effect of this government intervention in the economy would be to shift the aggregate demand curve to the right, restoring the economy to its long-run equilibrium level of aggregate output. This policy would also raise the aggregate price level.

Alternatively, the government could pursue activist monetary policy: the central bank could increase the money supply in order to shift the aggregate demand curve to the right. As with fiscal policy, activist monetary policy in this example will cause aggregate output to increase to the long-run level while also causing the aggregate price level to rise.

**STEP 5:** **Discuss what would happen in this economy if no activist policy is implemented.**

If there is no activist policy implemented, this economy will return to the long-run level of aggregate output eventually. With the recessionary gap, the economy finds that its unemployment rate is relatively high; over time this will cause nominal wages to decrease. As nominal wages decrease, this will cause the short-run aggregate supply curve to shift to the right. The short-run aggregate supply curve will shift to the right until the economy's production returns to the potential or long-run level of aggregate output. Notice that this adjustment to the long-run equilibrium results in a higher level of aggregate output than was present in the short run and a lower aggregate price level than the short-run aggregate price level.

3.  For this question, continue with the information you were given in Worked Problem 2 about the economy's short-run aggregate supply curve, the economy's long-run aggregate supply curve, and the economy's aggregate demand curve. You are told that simultaneously this economy experiences three shocks. These three shocks are as follows:

    - The price of every unit produced in this economy increases by $100 due to a change in the price of inputs. This shock only affects the short-run aggregate supply curve.

    - There is an increase in the wealth of individuals that increases the y-intercept of the aggregate demand curve by 30%. This change in wealth does not alter the slope of the aggregate demand curve.

    - A hurricane destroys a significant amount of capital in this economy, and the long-run aggregate supply curve is now $Y = 5$.

Given these three shocks to the economy you are asked to determine the short-run equilibrium aggregate price level and the short-run equilibrium level of aggregate output. You are also asked to identify if there is a short-run recessionary gap or a short-run inflationary gap. Comment on the implications of this gap on the level of unemployment in this economy in the short run. In addition, you are asked to provide a graph that depicts this short-run equilibrium as well as the long-run aggregate supply curve for this economy. Finally, you are asked to propose several policy options for the government of this country if it wishes to return to the long-run equilibrium. You are also asked to discuss the implications of not implementing any active policy to return the economy to long-run equilibrium.

**STEP 1:** **Determine what the new short-run aggregate supply curve is, given the above information. Then determine what the aggregate demand curve is, given this information. Finally, determine what the long-run aggregate supply curve is, given the above information.**

To answer this set of questions, you will first need to determine how these three shocks affect the three equations that you have been given.

We know that the short-run aggregate supply curve has shifted to the left due to the increase in the price of inputs. The y-intercept of the short-run aggregate supply curve has shifted up by $100. We can write this as $P = 100 + 100Y$.

The aggregate demand curve has shifted to the right due to the increase in wealth. The y-intercept of the aggregate demand curve is initially 1,000 and now it will be

30% greater. 30% of 1,000 is 300, so the new *y*-intercept for the aggregate demand curve is 1,300. Since the slope of the aggregate demand curve is unaffected, we can write the new aggregate demand curve as $P = 1,300 - 100Y$.

The long-run aggregate supply curve has shifted to the left due to the loss in the capital stock. The new long-run aggregate supply curve can be written as $Y = 5$.

**STEP 2:** Use the short-run aggregate supply curve and aggregate demand curve to determine the short-run equilibrium level of aggregate prices and the short-run equilibrium level of aggregate output.

From the short-run aggregate supply, we have $P = 100 + 100Y$ and from the aggregate demand, we have $P = 1,300 - 100Y$. Setting these two equations equal to one another, we find that $Y = 6$ and that $P = 700$.

**STEP 3:** Determine whether there is a recessionary gap or an inflationary gap by comparing the short-run equilibrium level of aggregate output to the long-run level of aggregate output. Then consider the implications of this gap on this economy's unemployment rate.

A recessionary gap occurs when the short-run level of aggregate output is less than the long-run level of aggregate output. An inflationary gap occurs when the short-run level of aggregate output is greater than the long-run level of aggregate output. In this case, the short-run level of aggregate output is equal to 6 and the long-run level of aggregate output is equal to 5: this economy has an inflationary gap. It is currently producing a level of aggregate output that is greater than its potential or long-run level of output: the economy currently has an unemployment rate that is lower than its natural rate of unemployment.

**STEP 4:** Draw a graph that depicts the short-run aggregate supply curve, the long-run aggregate supply curve, and the aggregate demand curve. On your graph, mark the short-run equilibrium aggregate price level and the short-run equilibrium level of aggregate output. Also, mark the long-run level of aggregate output.

Here is the graph of this economy's short-run equilibrium as well as its long-run level of aggregate output.

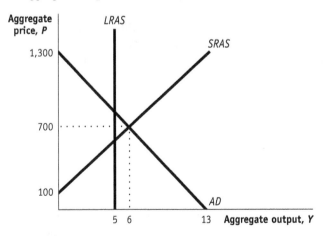

**STEP 5:** Determine what type of activist policy, monetary or fiscal, will move this economy to the long-run level of aggregate output.

Since short-run aggregate output is greater than long-run aggregate output, activist policy should contract the economy. The government could implement activist fiscal policy: this could involve a decrease in government spending, an increase in taxes, or a combination of these two policies. The effect of this government intervention in the economy would be to shift the aggregate demand curve to the left, restoring the economy to its long-run equilibrium level of aggregate output. This policy would also decrease the aggregate price level.

Alternatively, the government could pursue activist monetary policy: the central bank could decrease the money supply in order to shift the aggregate demand curve to the left. As with fiscal policy, activist monetary policy in this example will cause aggregate output to decrease to the long-run level while causing the aggregate price level to fall.

**STEP 6:** Discuss what will happen in this economy if no activist policy is implemented.

If no activist policy is implemented, this economy will eventually return to the long-run level of aggregate output. With the inflationary gap, the economy finds that its unemployment rate is relatively low, and over time this will cause nominal wages to increase. As nominal wages increase, this will cause the short-run aggregate supply curve to shift to the left. The short-run aggregate supply curve will shift to the left until the economy's production returns to the potential or long-run level of aggregate output. Notice that this adjustment to the long-run equilibrium results in a lower level of aggregate output than was present in the short run and a higher aggregate price level than the short-run aggregate price level.

4. Suppose that an economy is initially in long-run equilibrium and is producing a level of aggregate output that is equal to its potential output level. What will the short-run consequences be in this economy if there is an increase in the price of oil? Make sure that your answer addresses the effect of this price increase on both the level of aggregate output and the aggregate price level. In the short run, will this economy experience an inflationary gap or a recessionary gap?

**STEP 1:** Analyze the short-run effect of a change in the price of oil on the short-run aggregate supply curve and the aggregate demand curve.

When the price of oil rises, this is a change in a commodity price or an input price, which will cause the short-run aggregate supply curve to shift to the left. The change in the oil price will not cause a shift in the aggregate demand curve.

**STEP 2:** Having determined in Step 1 what the impact of this change in the price of oil was on the short-run curves in the aggregate demand and aggregate supply model, now predict the impact of this change on the aggregate price level and the aggregate output level.

If the short-run aggregate supply curve shifts to the left, this will cause a movement along the aggregate demand curve: the aggregate price level will increase while the aggregate output level will decrease.

**STEP 3:** Determine whether this economy experiences an inflationary gap or a recessionary gap in the short run.

Since the level of aggregate output has decreased, which implies that the economy is now producing at a level of output that is lower than the potential or full employment level of output. The economy is experiencing a recessionary gap. Notice that this economy has both higher prices and lower output: this is an example of stagflation.

# Problems and Exercises

1.  Consider an economy that is initially in long-run equilibrium as drawn in the following graph, where *LRAS* is the long-run *AS* curve, $AD_1$ is the aggregate demand curve, $SRAS_1$ is the short-run *AS* curve, $Y_1$ is potential output, and $P_1$ is the equilibrium aggregate price level.

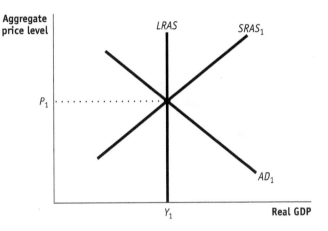

a.  Draw a graph using the *AD–AS* model to illustrate the effect of each of the following separate changes to the model in the short run.

(1) The economy's central bank decreases the money supply.

(2) Productivity decreases in the economy.

**Aggregate price level**

**Real GDP**

(3) Consumer confidence in the economy increases.

(4) Commodity prices fall dramatically.

**b.** Identify verbally what happens to aggregate output and the aggregate price level relative to the initial long-run equilibrium for each of the scenarios.

**c.** For each of the scenarios determine whether the economy faces a short-run recessionary gap or an inflationary gap.

**d.** For each of the scenarios determine if there is an active stabilization policy that will offset the particular shock. If so, discuss what this active stabilization policy is. You may find it helpful to draw a graph illustrating the effects of your active policy prescription on the aggregate economy.

e. For each of the scenarios identify what happens in the long run to the aggregate price level and the aggregate output level if there is no active stabilization policy.

2. Consider an economy operating with an inflationary gap in the short run. Briefly describe what this short-run equilibrium looks like, making specific reference to potential output, and then describe the process by which this economy moves from short-run to long-run macroeconomic equilibrium. Use a graph to illustrate your description.

**Aggregate price level**

**Real GDP**

3. Consider an economy operating with a recessionary gap in the short run.

a. Why does this represent a problem for this economy? Draw a graph illustrating your answer.

**Aggregate price level**

**Real GDP**

b. What policies are available to policy makers to address this problem? Draw graphs illustrating possible policies.

**Aggregate price level**

**Real GDP**

c. If policymakers do nothing, describe the mechanism by which this economy will return to long-run macroeconomic equilibrium. Draw a graph illustrating this long-run adjustment.

4. The *AD–AS* model is said to have a self-correcting mechanism. Explain what this means and how this mechanism works. Use a graph to illustrate your answer.

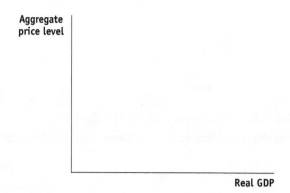

5. Use a graph of the *AD–AS* model to illustrate long-run economic growth in an economy. Explain your graph and how it illustrates economic growth. Assume in your answer that *AD* does *not* change over time.

**6.** For each of the following scenarios, describe the effect on the *AD* curve, the *SRAS* curve, and the *LRAS* curve. Identify whether the effect causes a shift of the curve or a movement along the curve and identify the direction of the shift or the movement.

    **a.** An increase in the money supply causes interest rates to fall.

    **b.** The supply of unsold houses in an economy increases by 20%.

    **c.** The government increases spending in order to finance the war against terrorists.

## ■ BEFORE YOU TAKE THE TEST

## Module Review Questions

**1.** In the short run, a situation where the aggregate price level increases while the aggregate output level decreases is
a. best explained as the result of a positive demand shock.
b. stagflation.
c. best explained as the result of a negative demand shock.
d. Answers (a) and (b) are both correct.
e. Answers (b) and (c) are both correct.

**2.** In the short run, an increase in the aggregate price level due to a shift in *AD* first results in
a. a rightward shift in the *SRAS* curve.
b. a movement along the *SRAS* curve.
c. no change in the level of aggregate production.
d. a leftward shift in the *SRAS* curve.

**3.** Suppose the *AD-AS* model is initially in long-run equilibrium. Suppose there is an increase in wealth, holding everything else constant. Then, in the short run,
a. there will be a movement along the *AD* curve.
b. the economy will produce at its potential level of output.
c. there will be a rightward shift in the *AD* curve.
d. the aggregate level of production will increase while the aggregate price level will fall.

4. In comparing the short run with the long run, which of the following statements is true?
   a. In both the short run and the long run, the aggregate price level and the aggregate output level are positively related.
   b. In the short run, the economy never produces at the potential output level, while in the long run, the economy always produces at the potential output level.
   c. In the short run, nominal wages are slow to fully adjust to economic changes, while in the long run, nominal wages are completely flexible and make full adjustment to economic changes.
   d. All the above are correct.
   e. Answers (a) and (c) are both true.
   f. Answers (b) and (c) are both true.

5. In the long run, the aggregate price level increases. This
   a. is due to the short-run *AS* curve shifting to the right and the economy producing a level of aggregate output that is not equal to its potential output.
   b. is due to the *AD* curve shifting to the right.
   c. has no effect on the level of aggregate production in the economy.
   d. results in the economy moving to the level of production where aggregate output exceeds potential output.
   e. Answers (a) and (c) are both correct.
   f. Answers (b) and (c) are both correct.
   g. Answers (c) and (d) are both correct.

6. Suppose the economy is in short-run equilibrium and the level of aggregate output is less than potential output. Then it must be true that
   a. unemployment in this economy is relatively low.
   b. over time the short-run *AS* curve will shift to the left.
   c. over time nominal wages will fall.
   d. the economy is also in long-run equilibrium.

7. Which of the following statements is true?
   a. Stagflation refers to the economic situation where aggregate output is falling and the aggregate price level is rising.
   b. Stagflation is most easily explained as the economic outcome that occurs due to a negative supply shock.
   c. Stagflation is most easily explained as the economic outcome that occurs due to a negative demand shock.
   d. Stagflation is most easily explained as the economic outcome that occurs due to either a negative supply shock or a negative demand shock.
   e. Answers (a) and (b) are both true.
   f. Answers (a) and (c) are both true.
   g. Answers (a) and (d) are both true.

8. Which of the following statements is true?

   a. In a recessionary gap, aggregate output exceeds potential output.

   b. In an inflationary gap, aggregate output exceeds potential output.

   c. A recessionary gap is a long-run phenomenon that requires government policy action to eliminate.

   d. Recessionary gaps and inflationary gaps, if they exist, will be eliminated in the short run by the natural workings of the economy.

9. Suppose an economy is currently in short-run equilibrium at which the level of real GDP is less than potential output. Which of the following statements is true?

   a. In the long run, nominal wages will fall and the *SRAS* curve will shift to the left, restoring the economy to potential output.

   b. In the long run, nominal wages will fall and the *SRAS* curve will shift to the right, restoring the economy to potential output.

   c. In the long run, nominal wages will fall and the *AD* curve will shift to the left, restoring the economy to potential output.

   d. In the long run, nominal wages will fall and the *AD* curve will shift to the right, restoring the economy to potential output.

10. In the *AD-AS* model a key feature that distinguishes the long run from the short run is

    a. wages and prices are sticky in the long run.

    b. wages and prices are sticky in the short run.

11. Suppose that short-run equilibrium real GDP for an economy is currently greater than potential output. This implies that

    a. nominal wages will need to adjust upward as the economy moves from the short run to the long run.

    b. the level of unemployment is very low for this economy.

    c. jobs are plentiful in this economy.

    d. to reach long-run equilibrium, the *SRAS* curve will shift to the left, resulting in a higher aggregate price level.

    e. Answers (a), (b), (c), and (d) are all correct.

    f. Answers (a), (b), and (c) are correct.

    g. Answers (a) and (d) are both correct.

12. A positive demand shock

    a. shifts *AD* to the right and results in a higher aggregate price level and a higher level of real GDP in the short run, holding everything else constant.

    b. shifts *AD* to the left and results in a higher aggregate price level and a higher level of real GDP in the short run, holding everything else constant.

Answer the next two questions using the following information:

Suppose Macroland is initially in long-run equilibrium. Then, suppose the central bank of Macroland increases the money supply.

13. In the short run, we know that this policy action
    a. will reduce interest rates and therefore stimulate investment spending.
    b. will lead to a reduction in unemployment and an increase in aggregate production.
    c. will lead to the short-run *AS* curve shifting to the right.
    d. Answers (a), (b), and (c) are all correct.
    e. Answers (a) and (b) are both correct.
    f. Answers (b) and (c) are both correct.
    g. Answers (a) and (c) are both correct.

14. In the long-run, Macroland will produce at
    a. the potential output level.
    b. a level of aggregate output greater than potential output.
    c. a level of aggregate output less than potential output.
    d. the same level of aggregate output as it did initially before the central bank increased the money supply, but with a lower aggregate price level than its initial level.

15. Suppose Funland is initially in long-run macroeconomic equilibrium. Then, there is a supply shock due to a severe increase in commodity prices. If Funland's policy makers use active stabilization policy to offset this supply shock
    a. they can effectively eliminate the economic effects of the supply shock.
    b. they can either reduce the aggregate price level down to its initial equilibrium level, or they can increase aggregate output to its initial level.
    c. they can either increase the aggregate price level to its initial equilibrium level, or they can decrease aggregate output to its initial level.
    d. this will greatly reduce the economic fluctuations Funland experiences from this supply shock.

# ANSWER KEY

# Answers to Problems and Exercises

1.  a.

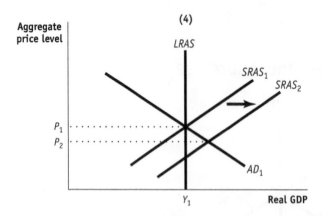

**b.** In scenario (1), the aggregate price level and the aggregate level of output both decrease relative to their initial levels. In scenario (2), the aggregate price level increases, while the aggregate level of output decreases relative to their initial levels. In scenario (3), the aggregate price level and the aggregate level of output both increase relative to their initial levels. In scenario (4), the aggregate price level falls, while the aggregate level of output increases relative to their initial levels.

**c.** A *short-run recessionary gap* is defined as a situation in which the economy produces at a level of output that is less than potential output: scenarios (1) and (2) illustrate this situation. Scenarios (3) and (4) represent inflationary gaps since the level of aggregate output is greater than potential output.

**d.** For scenario (1), active stabilization policy can be used to bring the economy back to its initial aggregate price level and aggregate output level. This policy would need to shift *AD* to the right (back to its initial position) and could be accomplished by increasing government spending, decreasing taxes, or increasing the money supply.

For scenario (2), active stabilization policy cannot restore the economy to its initial equilibrium. A policy that shifts *AD* to the right would result in an increase in the aggregate price level relative to its initial level ($P_3$ versus $P_1$), and a return to the initial level of production, $Y_1$, for aggregate output. The following graph illustrates the implementation of an active stabilization policy that shifts *AD* to the right.

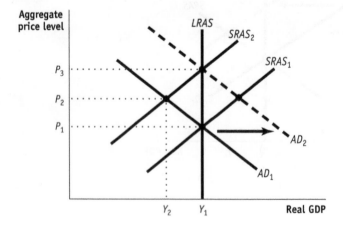

A policy that shifts *AD* to the left would result in a return to the initial aggregate price level of $P_1$, and a decrease in the level of aggregate output relative to its initial position ($Y_3$ versus $Y_1$). The following graph illustrates this.

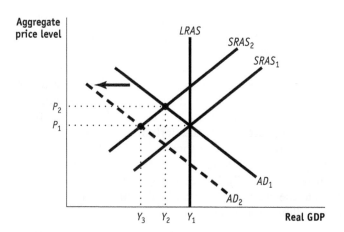

In scenario (3), active stabilization policy can be used to bring the economy back to its initial equilibrium. This policy would shift *AD* to the left and could be accomplished by decreasing government spending, increasing taxes, or decreasing the money supply.

In scenario (4), active stabilization policy cannot restore the economy to its initial equilibrium: shifting *AD* to the right restores the original price level to $P_1$, but increases the level of output above the initial level ($Y_3$ versus $Y_1$), thus creating an inflationary gap. The following graph illustrates this.

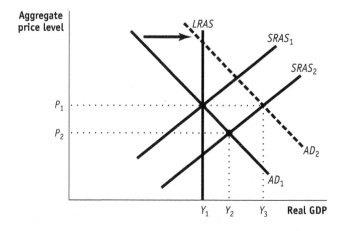

Shifting *AD* to the left restores output to its initial level $Y_1$, but the aggregate price level falls relative to its initial level ($P_3$ versus $P_1$). The following graph illustrates this.

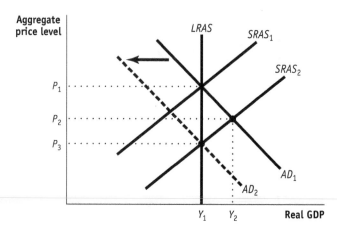

**e.** If there is no active stabilization policy implemented, then in scenario (1) the short-run *AS* curve will shift to the right as the nominal wage decreases in response to the recessionary gap. As the short-run *AS* curve shifts out, the economy will eventually reach long-run equilibrium where the aggregate output level returns to potential output, $Y_1$, while the aggregate price level falls to a lower long-run aggregate price level than the initial long-run $P_1$. In scenario (2), if there is no active stabilization policy implemented, the short-run *AS* curve will shift to the right, returning the economy back to its initial long-run macroeconomic equilibrium. In scenario (3), if there is no active stabilization policy implemented, the short-run *AS* curve will shift to the left, restoring the economy to the original level of aggregate output but a higher aggregate price level than the initial long-run $P_1$. In scenario (4), if there is no active stabilization policy implemented, the short-run *AS* curve will shift to the left, returning the economy to its initial equilibrium position.

**2.** An economy operating in the short run with an inflationary gap is producing a level of aggregate output, $Y_1$, that is greater than potential output, Y. This is illustrated in the following diagram.

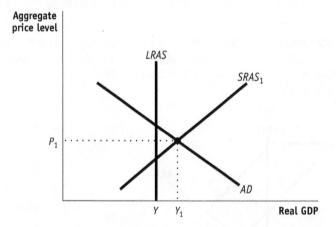

This implies that unemployment is relatively low and, therefore, workers are scarce and jobs are abundant. Over time this situation puts pressure on nominal wages to rise and this causes the short-run *AS* curve to shift to the left. As *AS* shifts to the left ($SRAS_2$), the level of aggregate production in the economy falls, which brings aggregate output closer to potential output. The nominal wage will continue to adjust until the short-run *AS* curve intersects the *AD* curve and the long-run *AS* curve at the same point. Then the economy will be in long-run macroeconomic equilibrium, where aggregate output equals potential output while the aggregate price level has risen to $P_2$ from $P_1$. This is illustrated in the following diagram.

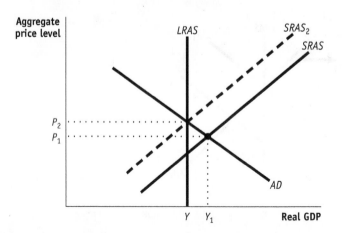

**3.**  **a.** A recessionary gap for an economy is problematic, since it indicates that the economy is producing a lower level of aggregate output ($Y_1$) than its potential ($Y$): this lower output also signals that the economy faces higher unemployment than necessary. This is illustrated in the following graph.

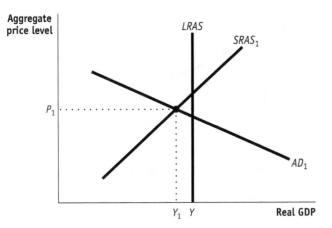

**b.** To offset a recessionary gap, active stabilization policy can be implemented that will return the economy to potential output. A recessionary gap caused by a leftward shift in *AD* is easily offset by using fiscal policy or monetary policy to shift *AD* to the right and returning the aggregate output to the level of potential output ($Y$). A recessionary gap caused by a leftward shift in *AS* is a more difficult problem: active stabilization policy that shifts *AD* to the right can bring the aggregate level of production back to potential output but only by raising the aggregate price level to a higher level ($P_2$ versus $P_0$). This is illustrated in the following diagram.

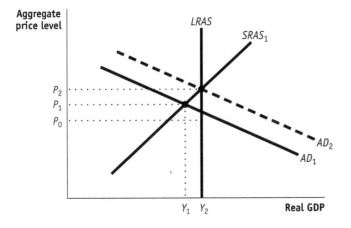

**c.** If policymakers do nothing, the economy will return to a long-run macroeconomic equilibrium over time through changes in the nominal wage and accompanying shifts in the short-run *AS* curve. If the recessionary gap is due to a leftward shift in *AD*, over time we can expect short-run *AS* to shift to the right, bringing the economy back to potential output and a lower aggregate price level than experienced during the recessionary gap. If the recessionary gap is due to a leftward shift in *AS*, over time we can expect short-run *AS* to shift back to the right, returning the economy to its potential output and a lower aggregate price level than it experienced during the recessionary gap. Both of these possibilities are illustrated in the following diagram.

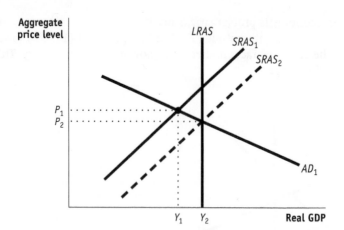

4.  The *AD-AS* model is self-correcting, since it will always return to long-run macroeco-
    nomic equilibrium if given a sufficient amount of time for the short-run *AS* curve to
    adjust to economic changes through changes in the nominal wage. This adjustment
    process has been reviewed in several earlier problems: essentially, it is the idea that the
    short-run *AS* curve shifts due to changes in the nominal wage until that point where *AD*
    intersects both the short-run and the long-run *AS* curves at potential output. If this is
    still unclear to you, review questions 1 and 2 and the diagrams illustrating their answers.

5.  Long-run economic growth is depicted in the *AD-AS* model as the long-run *AS* shifting
    to the right. Thus, your graph should depict several vertical *AS* curves, with each one far-
    ther to the right on the horizontal axis representing the ability of the economy to reach
    even higher levels of potential output. For a given *AD* curve, the level of aggregate out-
    put increases as the *LRAS* curve shifts to the right. The following graph illustrates this
    idea.

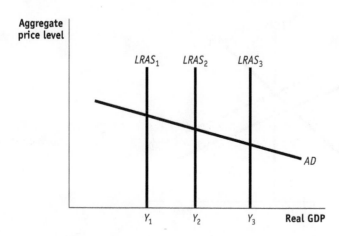

6.  a. An increase in the money supply is an example of monetary policy: the *AD* curve will
       shift to the right.

    b. When the inventory of unsold houses increases in an economy, this implies that the
       level of investment is high and, therefore, there is less incentive for firms to invest in
       this economy. As investment spending falls, this causes the *AD* curve to shift to the
       left.

    c. When the government increases spending to finance a war, this causes the *AD* curve
       to shift to the right.

# Answers to Module Review Questions

1.  **Answer b.** Stagflation refers to the combination of rising inflation and decreasing aggregate production. When the *AS* curve shifts to the left (a negative supply shock), this causes the aggregate price level to increase and the aggregate level of output to decrease.

2.  **Answer b.** A change in the aggregate price level due to a shift in *AD* results in a movement along the *AS* curve. In the short run the *AS* curve is upward sloping, so an increase in the aggregate price level results in a higher level of aggregate production.

3.  **Answer c.** The economy produces at its potential level of output if it is at a long-run equilibrium. The increase in wealth will cause the *AD* curve to shift to the right, causing a movement along the *AS* curve, and an increase in aggregate production and the aggregate price level.

4.  **Answer c.** In the long run, the *AS* is vertical and not upward sloping as it is in the short run. It is possible for an economy to be in both long-run and short-run equilibrium simultaneously so that the economy is producing its potential level of output. In the short run, we assume nominal wages are constrained from full adjustment and are therefore sticky, while in the long run, nominal wages are assumed to be fully flexible.

5.  **Answer f.** In the long run, the economy, by definition, is already producing at the level of aggregate output we refer to as potential output. An increase in the aggregate price level in the long run can only be explained by a shift in the *AD* curve, and this shift will not affect aggregate output since the long-run *AS* curve is vertical.

6.  **Answer c.** Since the economy is producing at a level of aggregate output smaller than the level of potential output, the economy cannot be in long-run equilibrium. Since output is below potential output, we know that not all workers are being fully utilized: if all workers were fully employed this would result in higher levels of production. Therefore, unemployment must be relatively high, and this will lead to decreases in the nominal wage over time since jobs are scarce and workers are abundant.

7.  **Answer e.** Stagflation refers to a falling aggregate output level accompanied by a rising aggregate price level. In the *AD–AS* model this is most easily explained as a negative supply shock since this shift in the short-run *AS* curve causes economic output to fall while the aggregate price level increases.

8.  **Answer b.** A recessionary gap is a situation in the short run where aggregate output is less than potential output. A recessionary gap is eliminated in the long run as the short-run *AS* curve adjusts to return the economy to potential output and long-run equilibrium. An inflationary gap is a situation in the short run where aggregate output is greater than potential output. As the economy moves to a long-run equilibrium, this inflationary gap will be eliminated and aggregate output will return to potential output.

9.  **Answer b.** In the short run this economy is producing a level of real GDP that is less than potential GDP. This implies that jobs are scarce and unemployment high: over time workers will accept lower nominal wages in order to find employment. As the level of nominal wages falls, this causes the *SRAS* curve to shift to the right, causing the level of real GDP to increase toward the potential output level.

10. **Answer b.** In the short run wages and prices are not perfectly flexible because of informal and formal agreements that limit the short-run flexibility of wages and prices. Ultimately, formal contracts and informal agreements can be renegotiated to take into account changed economic circumstances. In the long run, wages and prices are fully flexible.

11. **Answer e.** When the economy in the short run produces a level of real GDP that is greater than potential output, this implies that unemployment is very low (since output is greater than the long-run potential level of output) and jobs very plentiful. In order to reach long-run equilibrium at the potential output, this economy's *SRAS* curve must shift

to the left, which will cause the aggregate price level to rise. This shift of the *SRAS* curve will be due to the increase in nominal wages that occurs over time due to the tension between very low levels of unemployment and the abundance of jobs.

12. **Answer a.** A positive demand shock implies that the quantity of goods and services demanded at any given aggregate price level has increased: *AD* shifts to the right. As *AD* shifts to the right for a given *SRAS* curve, the aggregate price level and the aggregate level of real GDP increases.

13. **Answer e.** Since the economy is initially in long-run macroeconomic equilibrium, we know aggregate output is initially equal to potential output. The central bank's policy action will cause interest rates to fall and investment spending to increase. This will cause the *AD* curve to shift to the right, resulting in short-run aggregate output exceeding potential output. This increase in output will result in a decrease in unemployment. Over time, this will lead nominal wages to increase, which will result in the short-run *AS* curve shifting to the left.

14. **Answer a.** In the long run, macroeconomic equilibrium requires that the economy produce at that point at which *AD* equals long-run *AS*, as well as short-run *AS*. Short-run *AS* adjusts through changes in nominal wages to bring the equilibrium to this long-run equilibrium. When the central bank increases the money supply, this shifts the *AD* curve to the right. For a given long-run *AS* curve and this central bank action, it is possible to return to long-run macroeconomic equilibrium only if the short-run *AS* curve shifts to the left, resulting in a higher aggregate price level.

15. **Answer b.** Policy makers face a difficult trade-off when they try to offset a supply shock. In this case, the supply shock reduces aggregate output and increases the aggregate price level. Active stabilization policy can shift *AD* to the right or to the left: if *AD* shifts to the right, this will stimulate aggregate output while simultaneously increasing the aggregate price level to even higher levels; and if *AD* shifts to the left, this will reduce the aggregate price level while simultaneously decreasing the aggregate output level to even lower levels.

# Fiscal Policy Basics

## BEFORE YOU READ THE MODULE

## Summary

This module defines fiscal policy, and then discusses how fiscal policy can be used to eliminate a recessionary gap or an inflationary gap.

## Module Objectives

**Objective #1.** Government collects funds in the form of taxes and government borrowing and then uses these funds to make government purchases of goods and services and government transfers to individuals. Total government spending includes government expenditure on goods and services as well as expenditure on transfer payments.

- The three most expensive transfer programs in the United States are Social Security, Medicare, and Medicaid.

- Social insurance refers to government programs aimed at protecting families against economic hardship.

**Objective #2.** From the circular flow diagram of income and spending, recall that funds flow into government in the form of taxes and borrowing, and funds flow out of government in the form of government purchases of goods and services and government transfers to households.

**Objective #3.** In the United States taxes at the federal level are primarily income taxes on personal income and corporate profits, and social insurance taxes; at the state and local level of government, governments rely on a mix of sales taxes, property taxes, income taxes, and different kinds of fees for their revenue sources.

**Objective #4.** The basic equation of national income accounting, $GDP = C + I + G + X - IM$, reminds us that government purchases of goods and services ($G$) has a direct impact on total spending in the economy. The government also affects GDP through changes in taxes and transfers, and it may affect $I$ through government policy.

- Increases in taxes, holding everything else constant, reduce disposable income and consumer spending. Decreases in taxes, holding everything else constant, increase disposable income and consumer spending.

- Increases in government transfer payments, holding everything else constant, increase disposable income and consumer spending. Decreases in government transfer payments, holding everything else constant, decrease disposable income and consumer spending.

- Government can impact the incentives to engage in investment spending through changes in tax policy.

- The government can use changes in taxes or government spending to shift the *AD* curve. Holding everything else constant, *AD* shifts to the right with increases in government spending, decreases in taxes, or increases in government transfers; *AD* shifts to the left with decreases in government spending, increases in taxes, or decreases in government transfers.

- When the country faces a recessionary gap, aggregate output is less than potential output: use of expansionary fiscal policy will shift *AD* to the right to help eliminate the gap between actual and potential GDP.

- When an economy faces an inflationary gap, aggregate output is greater than potential output: use of contractionary fiscal policy will shift *AD* to the left to help eliminate the gap between actual and potential GDP.

**Objective #5.** Important lags exist in the use of fiscal or monetary policy. These lags include the time necessary for the government to realize the need for policy intervention, the time necessary for the government to develop policy, and the time necessary for the government to implement the policy and have the policy take effect. The existence of lags makes the use of fiscal policy and monetary policy to correct economic fluctuations more challenging than our simple analysis suggests.

**Objective #6.** The use of expansionary fiscal policy is often controversial. Critics of the use of expansionary fiscal policy argue that (1) government spending always crowds out private spending, (2) government borrowing always crowds out private investment spending, and (3) government budget deficits lead to reduced private spending. The text reviews these criticisms and explains that the first argument is wrong in principle, the second argument is valid under some circumstances, and the third argument, although it raises some important issues, does not justify the position that expansionary fiscal policy is ineffective in stimulating the economy.

# Key Terms

**social insurance** government programs—like Social Security, Medicare, unemployment insurance, and food stamps—intended to protect families against economic hardship.

**expansionary fiscal policy** fiscal policy that increases aggregate demand by increasing government purchases, decreasing taxes, or increasing transfers.

**contractionary fiscal policy** fiscal policy that reduces aggregate demand by decreasing government purchases, increasing taxes, or decreasing transfers.

*Notes*

## AFTER YOU READ THE MODULE

# Tips

**Tip #1.**   Expansionary fiscal policy can be used to help return the economy to full employment if the economy is operating with a recessionary gap. When the economy operates with a recessionary gap, the level of real GDP being produced is lower than the potential level of real GDP for the economy. Expansionary fiscal policy can shift the $AD$ curve to the right, resulting in a higher level of real GDP than is currently being produced. Figure 30.1 illustrates this idea. Initially the economy is producing at $Y_1$ which is a level of real GDP that is less than the potential level of real GDP, $Y_P$. Expansionary fiscal policy in the form of increased government spending, decreased taxes, or a mix of spending and taxation changes can shift the $AD$ curve from $AD_1$ to $AD_2$, thus returning the economy to $Y_P$.

**Figure 30.1**

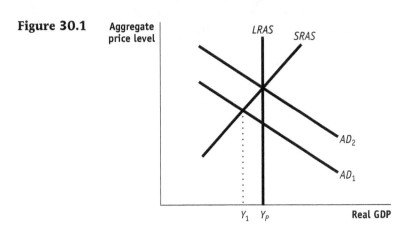

**Tip #2.**   Contractionary fiscal policy can be used to help return the economy to full employment if the economy is operating with an inflationary gap. When the economy operates with an inflationary gap, the level of real GDP being produced is greater than the potential level of real GDP for the economy. Contractionary fiscal policy can shift the $AD$ curve to the left resulting in a lower level of real GDP than is currently being produced. Figure 30.2 illustrates this idea. Initially the economy is producing at $Y_1$, which is a level of real GDP that is greater than the potential level of real GDP, $Y_0$. Contractionary fiscal policy in the form of decreased government spending, increased taxes, or a mix of spending and taxation changes can shift the $AD$ curve from $AD_1$ to $AD_2$, thus returning the economy to $Y_P$.

**Figure 30.2**

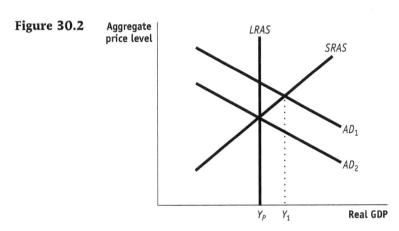

**Tip #3.**   There are two forms of government spending: spending on purchases of goods and services and spending on government transfers, which are payments by the government to households for which no good or service is provided in return.

**Tip #4.** Contractionary fiscal policy is government spending policy that contracts the economy. Contractionary fiscal policy includes reductions in government spending on goods and services, reductions in government spending on transfers, and increases in taxes.

**Tip #5.** Expansionary fiscal policy is government spending policy that expands the economy. Expansionary fiscal policy includes increases in government spending on goods and services, increases in government spending on transfers, and decreases in taxes.

# WORKED PROBLEMS

1. Suppose you are an economic advisor for a country with a closed economy. You estimate that this country's potential level of output is $1,000 in year 1 and that this level of potential output will grow 10% a year for the next four years. Your government employers ask you to complete the following table for them based on this information.

| Year | Potential output |
|---|---|
| Year 1 | $1,000 |
| Year 2 | |
| Year 3 | |
| Year 4 | |
| Year 5 | |

You are also given the following information (all numbers in the table are in dollars) about projected spending over the next five years and are asked to provide the government with an equation that expresses this country's consumption function based on the information you have received. In the table, $T$ is net taxes (taxes – transfers), $YD$ is disposable income, $C$ is consumption spending, $I$ is investment spending, and $G$ is government spending. Besides providing an equation for the country's consumption function, you are also asked to fill in the missing information in the table.

| Year | Potential output | Actual output | $T$ | $YD$ | $C$ | $I$ | $G$ |
|---|---|---|---|---|---|---|---|
| Year 1 | $1,000 | | $50 | $950 | $770 | $200 | $30 |
| Year 2 | | $1,200 | 50 | | | 200 | 110 |
| Year 3 | | 1,300 | 50 | | | 200 | 150 |
| Year 4 | | | 50 | 1,100 | | 200 | 90 |
| Year 5 | | | 50 | 1,200 | 920 | 200 | 80 |

You are also asked to provide this country with guidance about the projected state of its economy in each of the next five years. From your previous work, fill in the following table for this economy.

| Year | Recessionary gap | Inflationary gap | Actual output equals potential output |
|------|------------------|------------------|---------------------------------------|
| Year 1 | | | |
| Year 2 | | | |
| Year 3 | | | |
| Year 4 | | | |
| Year 5 | | | |

Finally, suppose this economy wishes to pursue fiscal policy that will ensure that actual output equals potential output every year. For each year, describe whether the government should pursue contractionary fiscal policy, expansionary fiscal policy, or no fiscal policy. Summarize your findings in the following table.

| Year | Fiscal policy |
|------|---------------|
| Year 1 | |
| Year 2 | |
| Year 3 | |
| Year 4 | |
| Year 5 | |

**STEP 1:** Start by calculating potential output, or GDP, based on an annual growth rate of 10%.

You will want to enter your calculations in the summary table. To find year 2's potential GDP, multiply year 1's GDP by 1.10 since year 2's GDP will be 10% greater than year 1's GDP. Continue the same calculation for the next three years.

| Year | Potential output |
|------|------------------|
| Year 1 | $1,000 |
| Year 2 | 1,100 |
| Year 3 | 1,210 |
| Year 4 | 1,331 |
| Year 5 | 1,464 |

**STEP 2:** From the information that you have been given, find this economy's consumption equation.

Inspecting the table, you see that there are two rows that provide you with information about consumption and disposable income: in year 1, when disposable income is $950, consumption is $770; and in year 5, when disposable income is $1,200, consumption is $920. You know that in general the relationship between consumption and disposable income can be written as $C = a + b(Y - T)$, where $a$ is autonomous consumption, $b$ is the marginal propensity to consume, and $(Y - T)$ is disposable income. From the information in the table, you can write two consumption relationships: $770 = a + b(950)$ and $920 = a + b(1,200)$. Use these two equations to find the values for autonomous consumption and the marginal propensity to consume. The consumption equation for this economy can be written as $C = 200 + 0.6(Y - T)$.

Now, you are ready to complete the table. Recall that actual output is equal to the sum of spending in the economy: thus, actual output = $C + I + G$. In year 1, actual output = $770 + 200 + 30 = 1,000$. In year 2 and year 3, you need first to calculate disposable income and then to use this disposable income and the consumption equation to find consumption. In year 4 and year 5, you are given disposable income and net taxes, and with this information you can find actual output.

The following table summarizes this work.

| Year | Potential output | Actual output | T | YD | C | I | G |
|------|------|------|------|------|------|------|------|
| Year 1 | $1,000 | $1,000 | $50 | $ 950 | $770 | $200 | $30 |
| Year 2 | 1,100 | 1,200 | 50 | 1,150 | 890 | 200 | 110 |
| Year 3 | 1,210 | 1,300 | 50 | 1,250 | 950 | 200 | 150 |
| Year 4 | 1,331 | 1,150 | 50 | 1,100 | 860 | 200 | 90 |
| Year 5 | 1,464 | 1,250 | 50 | 1,200 | 920 | 200 | 80 |

**STEP 3:** From the information you are given and the work you did in Steps 1 and 2, determine whether this economy is projected to operate with a recessionary gap, an inflationary gap, or at potential output for each of the five years.

Remember that when actual output is less than potential output, the economy is operating with a recessionary gap; when actual output is greater than potential output, the economy is operating with an inflationary gap. Use this information and the table you completed in Step 2 to ascertain the projected state of the economy for the next five years. The following table summarizes this work.

| Year | Recessionary gap | Inflationary gap | Actual output equals potential output |
|------|------|------|------|
| Year 1 | No | No | Yes |
| Year 2 | No | Yes | No |
| Year 3 | No | Yes | No |
| Year 4 | Yes | No | No |
| Year 5 | Yes | No | No |

**STEP 4:** Determine the type of activist fiscal policy the government of this economy will need to implement in each of the five years if the economy is going to produce at the level of aggregate output at which actual output equals potential output. Base your advice on the projections you have calculated in the previous steps of this problem.

Expansionary fiscal policy acts to increase the level of actual output: activist expansionary fiscal policy is the appropriate fiscal policy response if the desire of the government is to increase the level of actual output. Contractionary fiscal policy acts to decrease the level of actual output: activist contractionary fiscal policy can slow the economy and bring actual output down to the level of potential output.

| Year | Fiscal policy |
|------|---------------|
| Year 1 | None needed since actual output equals potential output |
| Year 2 | Contractionary fiscal policy needed since actual output exceeds potential output |
| Year 3 | Contractionary fiscal policy needed since actual output exceeds potential output |
| Year 4 | Discretionary fiscal policy needed since actual output is less than potential output |
| Year 5 | Discretionary fiscal policy needed since actual output is less than potential output |

2.  The current short-run economic situation in Urbana is depicted in the following graph: *SRAS* is the short-run aggregate supply curve, *LRAS* is the long-run aggregate supply curve, and *AD* is the aggregate demand curve. You are asked to describe the current short-run economic situation with regard to the relationship between current production and potential production. In addition, you are asked to compare the current level of unemployment to the natural rate of unemployment. Is Urbana operating with a recessionary gap or an inflationary gap? Finally, you are asked to comment on the effect of three possible government policies on both the short-run and the long-run economy in Urbana. The first government policy is a policy that would provide incentives to increase private investment spending. The second government policy is a decision to attack a neighboring country and engage in a large-scale war effort. The third government policy is a decision to increase the level of taxes in this economy. Consider each of these policy choices as independent of one another: that is, assume the government in Urbana will only implement one of these policies at a time.

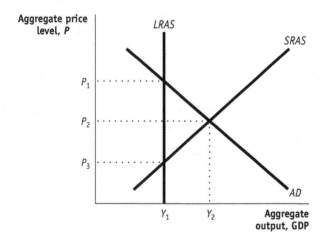

**STEP 1:** Describe the current state of the economy in Urbana, making sure to identify whether the economy is operating with a recessionary gap or an inflationary gap. In your description, describe the state of the labor market as well as the relationship between actual output and potential output.

In the previous graph, you can see that the long-run level of aggregate output, or the potential output level, is at $Y_1$. Since the economy is currently operating at the short-run equilibrium where SRAS intersects AD, we know that actual output is at $Y_2$. Thus, actual output is greater than potential output, and therefore this economy is operating with an inflationary gap. Since actual output exceeds potential output, this tells us that unemployment is relatively low and is below the natural rate of unemployment.

**STEP 2:** Evaluate the short-run and long-run implications of the government of Urbana implementing a policy to encourage greater private investment spending.

If the government implements a policy that encourages increased private investment spending, this will cause the aggregate demand curve to shift to the right. Holding everything else constant, in the short run this will cause the level of actual output to increase to an even higher level and the aggregate price level to increase as well. In the long run, the low unemployment rate will cause nominal wages to increase, and this will shift the SRAS curve to the left. In the long-run equilibrium, aggregate output will return to potential output, while the aggregate price level may increase, decrease, or remain unchanged. To see why the aggregate price level in the long run is ambiguous, consider the effect of increased private investment spending on the level of capital in this economy. Increases in private investment spending will increase the capital stock in this economy, leading to greater economic growth. This, in turn, will shift the long-run aggregate supply curve to the right. Since we do not know how big this shift is, we cannot with certainty predict what will happen to the aggregate price level in the long run.

**STEP 3:** Evaluate the short-run and long-run implications of the government of Urbana implementing a policy to go to war.

A decision to go to war will shift the aggregate demand curve to the right, as the government increases its spending in order to fight the war. In the short run, this will cause the level of aggregate output to increase, which will lead to an even greater inflationary gap. In the short run, there will be an increase in the aggregate price level as well. In the long run, the very low levels of unemployment will cause nominal wages to rise. As these nominal wages rise, the short-run aggregate supply curve will shift back to the left, returning the economy to potential output but at a higher level of aggregate prices.

**STEP 4:** Evaluate the short-run and long-run implications of the government of Urbana increasing the level of taxes in the economy.

A decision to increase the level of taxes will shift the aggregate demand curve to the left, since the increase in taxes will reduce disposable income and therefore lead to decreases in consumption spending. In the short run, this will cause the level of aggregate output to fall relative to its initial short-run level. The aggregate price level will also fall. In the long run, the economy will return to potential output as the short-run aggregate supply curve adjusts. Since we do not know the magnitude of the tax increase, it is impossible to tell whether the short-run aggregate supply curve will need to shift to the left or to the right to bring the economy back to the natural level of output.

# Problems and Exercises

1.  Macroland is a small, closed economy that is currently operating at the long-run equilibrium level of output. It is therefore producing $Y_P$ where $Y_P$ is potential output. Its aggregate price level is $P_1$.

    a.  Draw a graph of this long-run equilibrium for Macroland depicting the *AD* curve, the *SRAS* curve, and the *LRAS* curve. Label both axes and identify $Y_P$ and $P_1$ on your graph.

    b.  Suppose that Macroland experiences a negative demand shock. Draw a new graph depicting the short-run changes in the original equilibrium that will occur because of this demand shock. On your graph identify the new short-run equilibrium level of output $Y_2$ and the new short-run equilibrium aggregate price level $P_2$. Label any shifts in *AD* or *AS* clearly.

    Aggregate
    price level

    Real GDP

c. Given the change in part (b), draw a third graph illustrating the long-run adjustment to the negative demand shock. Label any shifting curves clearly and identify the new long-run equilibrium level of aggregate output $Y_3$ and the new long-run aggregate price level $P_3$.

**Aggregate price level**

**Real GDP**

d. Given the change in part (b), suppose the government wishes to engage in fiscal policy in order to restore the economy to its initial equilibrium. Provide two fiscal policies that would enable this economy to return to its initial equilibrium.

2. Suppose the economy is initially in long-run equilibrium. The economy experiences a financial crisis that reduces the value of people's assets.

   a. What is the short-run effect of the financial crisis on the aggregate price level and the level of real GDP? Use the *AD–AS* model to explain your answer. If any curves shift in your analysis, provide an explanation for why the curve shifts. Also, explain whether the economy experiences a recessionary or inflationary gap in the short run.

   b. What is the long-run effect of the financial crisis on the aggregate price level and the level of real GDP? Use the *AD–AS* model to explain your answer. If any curves shift in your analysis, provide an explanation for why the curve shifts.

   c. Suppose that policy makers in this economy were unhappy with the short-run effects of the financial crisis. If policy makers wanted to engage in fiscal policy to return the economy to its potential output level, what policy might they suggest given the financial crisis?

**3.** Suppose the economy is initially in long-run equilibrium. The economy experiences a 25% increase in the price of petroleum and petroleum-based products.

    **a.** What is the short-run effect of this increase in the price of petroleum and petroleum-related products on the aggregate price level and the level of real GDP? Use the *AD–AS* model to explain your answer. If any curves shift in your analysis, provide an explanation for why the curve shifts. Also, explain whether the economy experiences a recessionary or inflationary gap in the short run.

    **b.** What is the long-run effect of this change in petroleum prices on the aggregate price level and the level of real GDP? Use the *AD–AS* model to explain your answer. If any curves shift in your analysis, provide an explanation for why the curve shifts.

    **c.** Can fiscal policy successfully address the short-run economic effects of this increase in petroleum prices? Explain your answer completely.

**4.** The following graph depicts the economy of Macroland's short-run aggregate supply curve (*SRAS*), its long-run aggregate supply curve (*LRAS*), and its aggregate demand curve (*AD*). Macroland is currently producing at point *E*.

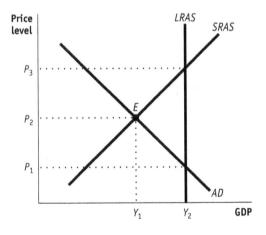

    **a.** Is potential GDP for Macroland equal to $Y_1$ or $Y_2$? Describe Macroland's current production relative to its potential production.

**b.** Does Macroland have a recessionary gap or an inflationary gap? Explain your answer.

**c.** Suppose Macroland wishes to produce at its potential output level. Holding everything else constant, identify which of the following policy initiatives might help it reach this goal and how these policy initiatives would help.

i. The government initiates policies that encourage private investment spending.

ii. The government increases the amount of money it borrows in the loanable funds market in order to increase its level of government spending in the economy.

iii. The government increases taxes on consumers and corporations.

iv. The government authorizes new spending programs.

**d.** What is the current price level in Macroland? If Macroland successfully engages in expansionary fiscal policy so that *AD* shifts and actual output equals potential output, what will happen to the price level?

**5.** Funlandia's economists estimate that its potential level of output is $100 in year 1, and that this level of potential output grows 5% per year. Assume Funlandia is a closed economy.

**a.** Fill in the following table for Funlandia given the information.

| Year | Potential output |
|--------|------------------|
| Year 1 | $100 |
| Year 2 | |
| Year 3 | |
| Year 4 | |

Suppose Funlandia's economists provide you with the following table of data. All numbers in the table are in dollars.

| Year | Potential output | Actual output | T | YD | C | I | G |
|---|---|---|---|---|---|---|---|
| Year 1 | $100 | | $10 | $ 90 | $55 | $30 | $15 |
| Year 2 | | $104 | 10 | | | 30 | 17 |
| Year 3 | | 115 | 10 | | | 30 | 22.5 |
| Year 4 | | | 10 | 108 | 64 | 30 | 24 |

**b.** What is the consumption function for this economy?

**c.** Fill in the missing values for the same table using the information you have been given or that you computed in parts (a) and (b).

**d.** Fill in the following table for Funlandia.

| Year | Recessionary gap | Inflationary gap | Actual output equals potential output |
|---|---|---|---|
| Year 1 | No | No | Yes |
| Year 2 | | | |
| Year 3 | | | |
| Year 4 | | | |

**e.** Suppose Funlandia maintains a policy of using discretionary fiscal policy to ensure that actual output equals potential output. Summarize the recommended discretionary fiscal policy necessary to achieve this goal in the following table.

| Year | Discretionary fiscal policy |
|---|---|
| Year 1 | |
| Year 2 | |
| Year 3 | |
| Year 4 | |

## ▌ BEFORE YOU TAKE THE TEST

# Module Review Questions

1. Which of the following statements is true?
   a. Personal income taxes, corporate profits taxes, and social insurance taxes are the primary taxes at the federal level of government in the United States.
   b. State and local governments in the United States rely on sales taxes, property taxes, income taxes, and fees for their sources of revenue.
   c. In 2007, 48% of government revenue in the United States came from taxes on personal income and corporate profits.
   d. All of the above statements are true statements.
   e. Statements (a) and (b) are both true.
   f. Statements (b) and (c) are both true.

2. Total government spending differs from government expenditure because it
   a. refers to the purchase of goods and services and does not include transfers since this represents a transfer of income from one individual to another.
   b. refers to the purchase of goods and services as well as expenditures on transfers.
   c. includes, in the United States, transfers such as Social Security, Medicare, and Medicaid spending.
   d. Answers (a) and (c) are both correct.
   e. Answers (b) and (c) are both correct.

3. Contractionary fiscal policy
   a. is most helpful for restoring an economy to the potential output level of production when there is a recessionary gap.
   b. shifts the *AD* curve to the right, restoring the equilibrium level of output to the potential output level for the economy.
   c. often causes inflation or an increase in the aggregate price level.
   d. if effective, shifts *AD* to the left, resulting in a reduction in the aggregate output and the aggregate price level for a given short-run aggregate supply curve (*SRAS*).

4. Which of the following statements is true? Holding everything else constant,
   a. an economy can eliminate an inflationary gap by increasing government spending.
   b. expansionary fiscal policy refers to an increase in taxes.
   c. when potential output is greater than actual aggregate output, the economy faces a recessionary gap.
   d. when *SRAS* intersects *AD* to the right of the long-run aggregate supply (*LRAS*) curve, the economy faces a recessionary gap.

5. Fiscal policy
   a. affects the economy in predictable ways and with relatively short time lags.
   b. involves significant time lags with regard to their implementation and effect on the economy.
   c. takes so long to implement in the economy that it proves to be useless policy.
   d. when implemented always worsens economic fluctuations because of the lags involved in its implementation.

6. Revenue for the operation of state and local governments comes primarily from
   a. personal income taxes.
   b. corporate taxes.
   c. a mix of sales taxes, property taxes, income taxes, and fees of various kinds.
   d. payroll taxes.

7. Government transfers are payments from the government
   a. to households as compensation for taxes that the household has paid.
   b. to households for which no good or service is provided in return.
   c. that redistribute purchasing power from one group of households to another group of households.
   d. Answers (a) and (c) are both correct.
   e. Answers (b) and (c) are both correct.

8. Government programs that are designed to protect individuals or families from economic hardship are described as
   a. fiscal policy.
   b. discretionary fiscal policy.
   c. monetary policy.
   d. social insurance.

9. Which of the following will cause the *AD* curve to shift to the left?
   a. Government increases the amount of transfer payments it makes.
   b. Government increases the amount of taxes it collects from households.
   c. Government increases its level of defense spending after declaring war on a nearby country.
   d. Government institutes an investment tax credit that effectively reduces the cost of investment purchases made by firms.

10. Suppose an economy currently is operating with an inflationary gap. If the government wishes to return the economy to potential output, which of the following initiatives is most likely to achieve this goal?
    a. The government implements an investment tax credit.
    b. The government passes more generous social insurance programs for the retired and disabled in the economy.
    c. The government increases taxes.
    d. The government increases spending on national defense.

11. Which of the following situations describes the use of contractionary fiscal policy?
    a. Recovery Rebate and Stimulus for the American People Act of 2008
    b. Investment Tax Credit of 2002
    c. Argentina's reductions in government spending and increases in taxes during the period 1997 to 2001
    d. President Lyndon Johnson's surcharge on income taxes in 1968
    e. Answers (c) and (d) are both examples of contractionary fiscal policy.

**12.** Which of the following policies will shift the *AD* curve to the right?
a. The government increases its level of taxation in the economy.
b. The government decreases the money supply in the economy.
c. The government decreases its level of taxation in the economy.
d. The government decreases its level of spending in the economy.
e. Answers (a) and (d) will both shift the *AD* curve to the right.
f. Answers (c) and (d) will both shift the *AD* curve to the right.

## ANSWER KEY

# Answers to Problems and Exercises

1. **a.**

**b.**

**c.**

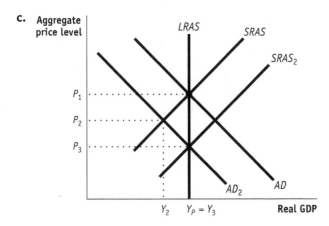

**d.** To offset a negative demand shock, the government needs to shift the *AD* curve to the right. Fiscal policy offers two approaches to shifting the *AD* curve to the right: the government can increase the level of government spending or it can decrease the level of taxes.

2. **a.** In the short run, the financial crisis will cause the *AD* curve to shift to the left at every aggregate price level since both households and firms will reduce their spending due to the decrease in asset values. The economy will move away from potential output: the economy will produce a lower level of real GDP and the aggregate price level will fall. The economy will have a recessionary gap in the short run since real GDP will be less than potential GDP.

**b.** In the long run, the economy will return to potential output. The *SRAS* curve will shift to the right because, with a recessionary gap, that implies that unemployment is high and that nominal wages need to adjust downward. As nominal wages fall, this decrease in nominal wages will cause production costs to fall and the *SRAS* curve to shift to the left. The economy will return to potential output and its *LRAS* curve, but at a lower aggregate price level than the initial aggregate price level.

**c.** Policymakers could offset the leftward shift of the *AD* curve by engaging in either fiscal or monetary policy. With both types of policies, the goal would be to shift the *AD* curve back to the right to restore the economy to its initial position. An increase in government spending or a decrease in taxes would be examples of expansionary fiscal policy; an increase in the money supply or a decision to lower interest rates by the central bank would be an example of expansionary monetary policy.

**3. a.** The economy is initially in long-run equilibrium, which tells us that *LRAS, SRAS* and *AD* all intersect one another to determine the level of aggregate price level and the level of real GDP. Furthermore, since the economy is in long-run equilibrium, we know that real GDP is equal to potential output. When petroleum prices increase, this causes the *SRAS* supply curve to shift to the left as production costs for firms in the economy increase when the price of petroleum increases. In the short run, this results in a decrease in real GDP and an increase in the aggregate price level. Since real GDP is now less than potential GDP, the economy has a recessionary gap.

**b.** In the long run, we know that the economy must produce at its potential output level. Since the economy is operating with a recessionary gap, we can expect that nominal wages will fall over time due to the unemployment rate being relatively high. As nominal wages decrease, the *SRAS* curve will shift back to the right restoring the economy to its potential output level and to a lower aggregate price level relative to the short-run level of the aggregate price level.

**c.** Fiscal policy cannot successfully address the economic challenges of reduced production (a decrease in real GDP) accompanied by increases in the aggregate price level. For example, expansionary fiscal policy will shift the *AD* curve to the right and that will cause real GDP to increase, but it will also result in a higher aggregate price level. Contractionary fiscal policy, in contrast, will shift the *AD* curve to the left and that will cause real GDP to fall even lower while bringing the aggregate price level down. Policy makers will find it impossible to simultaneously increase real GDP while lowering the aggregate price level when there is a negative supply shock.

**4. a.** The potential output level for Macroland is $Y_2$ where *LRAS* equals *SRAS* equals *AD*. Currently, Macroland is producing $Y_1$ at price level $P_2$: this represents a recessionary situation, or a recessionary gap, since Macroland has the potential to produce a higher level of output than it is currently producing.

**b.** Macroland has a recessionary gap since their current level of production, $Y_1$, is less than their potential level of production, $Y_2$.

**c.** Any policy initiative that shifts *AD* to the right will help Macroland move toward its potential output level. Items (i) and (iv) will both shift *AD* to the right: government policies that stimulate private investment spending lead to higher levels of aggregate spending and a rightward shift in *AD*; and new spending by government will also lead to higher levels of aggregate spending and a rightward shift in *AD*. Item (ii) will cause the *AD* to shift to the right unless the increase in government borrowing crowds out private investment to that point where private investment decreases by an amount equal to the increase in government spending. In that case item (ii) would result in no shift in the *AD* curve. Item (iii) will reduce disposable income and lead to lower levels of aggregate spending: *AD* may shift to the left if the decrease in spending is greater than the increase in government spending, or *AD* may shift to the right if the increase in government spending is greater than the decrease in spending.

**d.** The current price level in Macroland is $P_2$. If the government engages in fiscal policy that results in the economy's returning to the potential level of output, this will lead to increases in the price level from $P_2$ to $P_3$.

**5.  a.**

| Year | Potential output |
|------|------------------|
| Year 1 | $100 |
| Year 2 | 105 |
| Year 3 | 110.25 |
| Year 4 | 115.76 |

**b.** The consumption function can be written as $C = A + MPC(Y - T)$. From the table we can compute the $MPC$ as the change in consumption divided by the change in disposable income, or 9/18, which equals 0.5. To find $A$, we need to use one of the consumption and disposable income combinations from the table. For example, when disposable income equals 90, consumption equals 55. So, $C = A + 0.5(Y - T)$ can be rewritten as $55 = A + 0.5(90)$ and solving for $A$, we find $A$ equals 10. Thus, the consumption function for this economy is $C = 10 + 0.5(Y - T)$.

**c.**

| Year | Potential output | Actual output | T | YD | C | I | G |
|------|------------------|---------------|---|----|----|---|---|
| Year 1 | 100 | 100 | 10 | 90 | 55 | 30 | 15 |
| Year 2 | 105 | 104 | 10 | 94 | 57 | 30 | 17 |
| Year 3 | 110.25 | 115 | 10 | 105 | 62.5 | 30 | 22.5 |
| Year 4 | 115.76 | 118 | 10 | 108 | 64 | 30 | 24 |

**d.**

| Year | Recessionary gap | Inflationary gap | Actual output equals potential output |
|------|------------------|------------------|----------------------------------------|
| Year 1 | No | No | Yes |
| Year 2 | Yes | No | No |
| Year 3 | No | Yes | No |
| Year 4 | No | Yes | No |

**e.**

| Year | Discretionary fiscal policy |
|------|------------------------------|
| Year 1 | No policy necessary |
| Year 2 | Increase government spending or decrease taxation |
| Year 3 | Decrease government spending or increase taxation |
| Year 4 | Decrease government spending or increase taxation |

# Answers to Module Review Questions

1.  **Answer d.** This question is a review of facts presented in the module. Each statement is factual.

2.  **Answer e.** Total government spending includes the government's purchases of goods and services as well as the expenditures the government makes in the form of transfer payments. The three primary transfer programs in terms of dollar cost in the United States are Social Security, Medicare, and Medicaid.

3. **Answer d.** Contractionary fiscal policy is a reduction in government spending or an increase in taxes aimed at shifting *AD* to the left. For a given *SRAS*, this leftward shift in *AD* will lead to a lower level of equilibrium aggregate output and a reduction in the aggregate price level. Contractionary fiscal policy is implemented when the economy produces a level of output in excess of potential output: contractionary fiscal policy is used to offset an inflationary gap.

4. **Answer c.** When *SRAS* intersects *AD* to the right of *LRAS*, the economy faces an inflationary gap. This inflationary gap can be eliminated through a decrease in government spending or an increase in taxes, since either policy will cause *AD* to shift to the left holding everything else equal. A decrease in government spending and an increase in taxes are examples of contractionary fiscal policy. By definition, when potential output is greater than actual aggregate output, the economy is operating with a recessionary gap.

5. **Answer b.** There are significant lags involved in the implementation of fiscal and monetary policy. These lags can result in a situation where the implemented policy actually worsens the economic situation (for example, using expansionary fiscal policy to counteract a recessionary gap that has turned into an inflationary gap by the time the fiscal policy takes effect).

6. **Answer c.** State and local governments rely on revenue that comes from sales taxes, property taxes, income taxes, and various fees.

7. **Answer e.** Government transfers are payments that the government makes to households even though the government has not received a good or a service from the household. These transfer payments effectively redistribute purchasing power in the economy: the household receiving the transfer payment can now command more goods and services than they could before the transfer.

8. **Answer d.** This is just a definitional question. See the text for a description of these programs. For example, social insurance programs include Social Security, Medicare, and Medicaid.

9. **Answer b.** When the government increases the amount of taxes it collects from households, disposable income is reduced and households reduce their level of consumption spending. This decrease in consumption spending leads to further reductions in spending in the economy due to the multiplier effect: the *AD* curve shifts to the left. Answers (a), (c), and (d) would all shift the *AD* curve to the right.

10. **Answer c.** If the economy is currently operating with an inflationary gap, the implication is that the level of actual output in this economy is greater than potential output. To return the economy to its potential output level, the government will need to shift the *AD* curve to the left. Only answer (c) causes a leftward shift in *AD*; the other answers all cause the *AD* curve to shift to the right.

11. **Answer e.** Argentina's reduction in government spending and increase in taxes in the period 1997–2001 were designed to contract the economy as was the Lyndon Johnson surcharge on income taxes enacted in 1968. This was a temporary increase of 10% on income taxes designed to reduce consumer spending and thereby contract the economy. Answers (a) and (b) are both examples of expansionary fiscal policy; in each example, the policy was enacted with the hope that it would spur greater spending and hence higher levels of aggregate output.

12. **Answer c.** When the *AD* curve shifts to the right, this implies that the level of aggregate demand is greater at any given aggregate price level than it was initially. When the government increases government spending, decreases taxes, or increases the money supply, this results in greater aggregate demand at every price level. When the government decreases government spending, increases taxes, or decreases the money supply, this results in less aggregate demand at every price level.

# Fiscal Policy and the Multiplier

## Summary

This module focuses on fiscal policy—government spending and taxation—and its use as an economic tool for managing economic fluctuations. In addition, the module explores the multiplier effect of fiscal policy as well as the effect of automatic stabilizers on the size of the multiplier.

## Module Objectives

**Objective #1.**  Discretionary fiscal policy refers to the use of government spending or tax policy to manage aggregate demand (*AD*). Discretionary fiscal policy may be used to stimulate or contract *AD*.

**Objective #2.**  A change in government spending is an example of an autonomous change in aggregate spending. Holding the price level constant, this change in autonomous aggregate spending will change GDP by an amount equal to the multiplier times the change in autonomous aggregate spending. Recall that the multiplier in our simple model equals $1/(1 - MPC)$.

**Objective #3.**  A change in taxes or government transfers of a given size shifts the *AD* curve by less than an equal-sized change in government purchases. A decrease in taxes or increase in transfers will increase GDP by $MPC/(1 - MPC)$ times the change in taxes (measured in absolute value terms) or the change in transfers; an increase in taxes or a decrease in transfers will decrease GDP by $MPC/(1 - MPC)$ times the change in taxes or the change in transfers (measured in absolute value terms).

**Objective #4.**  Holding everything else constant, when GDP increases, government tax revenue automatically increases. The effect of this automatic increase in government tax revenue when GDP rises is to reduce the size of the multiplier.

- When the economy slows down and GDP falls, the automatic fall in government tax revenue acts like an automatic expansionary fiscal policy implemented in the face of the recession.

- When the economy expands, the automatic increase in government tax revenue acts like an automatic contractionary fiscal policy implemented in the face of the expansion.

- Government spending and taxation rules that cause fiscal policy to be automatically expansionary when the economy contracts and automatically contractionary when the economy expands are referred to as automatic stabilizers, since they act to automatically stabilize the economy.

- Examples of automatic stabilizers include taxes, unemployment insurance benefits, Medicaid, and food stamps. Transfer programs as well as taxes can act as automatic stabilizers.

**Objective #5.** Discretionary fiscal policy refers to fiscal policy that is the direct result of policy action by policy makers. It does not refer to automatic adjustment in the economy that occurs because of automatic stabilizers.

**Objective #6.** Taxing income at a tax rate $t$ allows us to model a macroeconomy where taxes increase as the level of aggregate output increases. The inclusion of this tax rate alters the multiplier for a change in autonomous spending from $1/(1 - MPC)$ to $1/[1 - MPC(1 - t)]$. This new multiplier will have a smaller value than the original multiplier for a given $MPC$.

## Key Terms

**lump-sum taxes** taxes that don't depend on the taxpayer's income.

**automatic stabilizers** government spending and taxation rules that cause *fiscal policy* to be automatically expansionary when the *economy* contracts and automatically contractionary when the economy expands.

**discretionary fiscal policy** *fiscal policy* that is the deliberate result of deliberate actions by policymakers rather than automatic adjustments.

*Notes*

## AFTER YOU READ THE MODULE

## Tips

**Tip #1.** The multiplier for changes in government spending is equal to $[1/(1 - MPC)]$. To find the change in aggregate production from a change in government spending use the following formula:

Change in aggregate production $= [1/(1 - MPC)][$change in government spending$]$

**Tip #2.** The effect of a tax cut on aggregate production is smaller than the effect of an equal-sized increase in government purchases of goods and services. With a tax cut the change in the increase in autonomous spending is smaller because households save part of the amount of the tax cut.

**Tip #3.**  Automatic stabilizers reduce the size of the multiplier.

**Tip #4.**  Two multipliers are presented and used in this module: the multiplier for a change in government spending and the multiplier for a change in taxes. The multiplier for a change in government spending equals $1/(1 - MPC)$, while the multiplier for a change in taxes equals $[-MPC/(1 - MPC)]$. For example, if the $MPC$ equals 0.8, then the multiplier for a change in government spending is equal to 5, while the multiplier for a change in taxes is equal to –4. A \$1 increase in government spending will increase aggregate output by \$5, holding everything else constant, while a \$1 increase in taxes will decrease aggregate output by \$4, holding everything else constant. Make sure you work some problems using these multipliers and that you understand why they do not have equivalent values. Also, spend time thinking about why the multiplier for government spending is positive while the multiplier for a change in taxes is negative. An increase in government spending represents an increase in the level of spending in the economy and will stimulate aggregate production, while an increase in taxes reduces the level of spending in the economy and will therefore contract aggregate production.

**Tip #5.**  The use of the multiplier thus far in our models presumes a horizontal $SRAS$. If the $SRAS$ is upward sloping, then the impact on aggregate output will be smaller than that predicted by the multiplier. Essentially this tip should remind you that a horizontal $SRAS$ implies a fixed price level, while an upward-sloping $SRAS$ implies that the aggregate price level is not fixed. A shift in $AD$ due to a change in autonomous spending or taxes will cause a larger change in aggregate output (and a change equal to the amount predicted by the multiplier effect) if the aggregate price level is constant than if the aggregate price level is allowed to change. Let's look at a diagram of this represented in Figure 31.1.

**Figure 31.1**

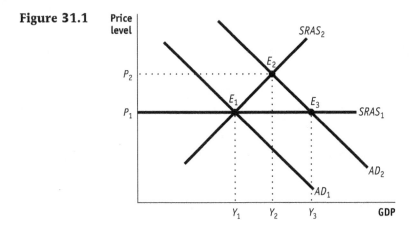

$AD_1$ is our initial $AD$ curve; $SRAS_1$ is the short-run aggregate supply curve if the aggregate price level is held constant, and $SRAS_2$ is the short-run aggregate supply curve if the aggregate price level is allowed to vary in the short run. Initially the economy is at point $E_1$, producing $Y_1$ at an aggregate price level $P_1$. When autonomous aggregate spending increases, this shifts $AD_1$ to $AD_2$, and the horizontal distance $Y_1$ to $Y_3$ measures the multiplier effect on aggregate output (moving from the initial equilibrium $E_1$ to the new equilibrium $E_3$). However, a rightward shift in $AD$ from $AD_1$ to $AD_2$ increases output from $Y_1$ to $Y_2$ while simultaneously increasing the aggregate price level from $P_1$ to $P_2$ (moving from the initial equilibrium $E_1$ to the new equilibrium $E_2$).

# WORKED PROBLEMS

1. Suppose you are told that in Moravia taxes are set at a constant level of $20 million. You also know that Moravia has investment spending that is constant and equal to $40 million, government spending that is constant and equal to $20 million, and net exports that are constant and equal to $20 million. In Moravia the level of autonomous consumer spending—the spending that does not depend upon the level of disposable income—is equal to $20 million. In Moravia every time disposable income increases by $1, the level of consumption spending in the economy increases by $0.80. You have been asked by the King of Moravia to provide him with an equation that generally describes the consumption function; to determine the level of current equilibrium real GDP for Moravia, as well as the level of current consumption in Moravia; and to provide an estimate of the effect on real GDP of either raising government spending by $10 million while holding everything else constant, or decreasing taxes by $10 million while holding everything else constant. In this problem assume that the aggregate price level in Moravia is constant.

**STEP 1:** Begin by finding the consumption function for the economy of Moravia.

Recall from your reading that in general the consumption function can be written as $C = A + MPC(Y - T)$ where $C$ is consumption spending, $A$ is autonomous consumption, $MPC$ is the marginal propensity to consume, $Y$ is real GDP, and $T$ is the level of lump-sum taxes. From the given information you know the value of $A$ is $20 million, the value of the $MPC$ is 0.8 (since consumers spend 80% of any increase in their disposable income), and the value of $T$ is $20 million. Thus, the general consumption function can be written as $C = 20 + 0.8(Y - T)$ or, more specifically, $C = 20 + 0.8(Y - 20)$ which can be simplified to $C = 4 + 0.8Y$.

**STEP 2:** Determine the current equilibrium level of real GDP for Moravia and its current level of consumption.

To find the current equilibrium level of real GDP for Moravia we start by remembering that $GDP = C + I + G + (X - M)$. In this problem real GDP is symbolized by $Y$ so let's rewrite this equation as $Y = C + I + G + (X - M)$. From the information given at the beginning of the problem we know the values of $I$, $G$ and $(X - M)$, and from Step 1 we have an equation for $C$. Thus, $Y = (4 + 0.8Y) + 40 + 20 + 20$. Solving this equation we find that $0.2Y = 84$ or $Y = $420$ million. The current equilibrium level of real GDP for Moravia is $420 million. Using this value and the consumption function we can calculate the current level of consumption in Moravia as $C = 4 + 0.8(420)$, or $C = $340$ million.

**STEP 3:** Analyze the impact of a change in government spending to $30 million, while holding everything else constant, on the level of real GDP in Moravia.

The impact of a change in government spending to $30 million can be analyzed using two different methods. The first method would simply entail repeating Step 2's process but using $G = $30$ million rather than $G = $20$ million. Thus, $Y = (4 + 0.8Y) + 40 + 30 + 20$ or $0.2Y = 94$ and thus, real GDP = $470 million. If we compare our two answers (Step 1 versus Step 2), we see that increasing government spending by $10 million while holding everything else constant, results in real GDP increasing by $50 million.

The second method for finding the impact of increasing government spending to $30 million would approach the problem by using the multiplier. In general we know from the text the multiplier for a change in government spending, holding everything else constant, is $(1/(1 - MPC))$. We can use this multiplier in this situation by recognizing the following relationship:

Change in real GDP = (multiplier)(change in government spending)

Since everything else is being held constant in Moravia's economy, it is only the change in government spending that will affect the level of real GDP. So, using this equation, we have (change in real GDP) = [1/(1 − 0.8)]($10 million) = $50 million. Thus, if government spending increases by $10 million in Moravia this will result in real GDP increasing by $50 million, or, in other words, GDP will increase from $420 million to $470 million.

**STEP 4:** Analyze the impact of a change in taxes to $10 million, while holding everything else constant, on the economy of Moravia.

The impact of a change in lump-sum taxes to $10 million can be analyzed using two different methods. The first method would simply entail repeating Step 2's process but using $T = \$10$ million rather than $T = \$20$ million. This change would alter the consumption function in Moravia to $C = 12 + 0.8Y$. Using this new consumption function and the general method we employed in Step 2 we have: $Y = (12 + 0.8Y) + 40 + 20 + 20$ or $0.2Y = 92$ and thus, real GDP = $460 million. If we compare our two answers (Step 1 versus Step 2), we see that decreasing lump-sum taxes by $10 million while holding everything else constant, results in real GDP increasing by $40 million.

The second method for finding the impact of decreasing lump-sum taxes by $10 million would approach the problem by using the multiplier. In general we know from the text the multiplier for a change in lump-sum taxes, holding everything else constant, is $(-MPC/(1 - MPC))$. We can use this multiplier in this situation by recognizing the following relationship:

Change in real GDP = (lump-sum tax multiplier)(change in lump-sum taxes)

Since everything else is being held constant in Moravia's economy, it is only the change in lump-sum taxes that will affect the level of real GDP. So, using this equation we have (change in real GDP) = [−0.8/(1 − 0.8)](−$10 million) = $40 million. Thus, if lump-sum taxes decrease by $10 million in Moravia the result will be real GDP increasing by $40 million, or, in other words, GDP will increase from $420 million to $460 million.

2. This module presents a simple multiplier and then illustrates how this multiplier can be used to make predictions about how changes in government spending or changes in taxes will affect the level of real GDP. In the real world, macroeconomic models of a specific economy are typically very complex mathematical models with many equations describing the economic activity that occurs in an economy. This complexity suggests that there are an infinite number of possible multipliers, wherein each multiplier depends on the underlying equations of the model describing an economy's economic activity. In this worked problem let's review finding the simple multipliers presented in the module for a situation in which there are lump-sum taxes; a situation in which the lump-sum tax is replaced by a tax on income, where the tax rate on income is given as $t$, a constant value between 0 and 1 (here we are assuming that we cannot tax income at a rate less than 0% of that income nor can we tax income at a rate more than 100% of that income). With this new income tax, disposable income can be written as $(Y - tY)$.

**STEP 1:** Let's begin this process by first writing the underlying consumption equation for the situation when taxes are at constant level, that is, when taxes are lump-sum.

The consumption function when taxes are assumed to be a constant, lump-sum amount can be written as $C = A + MPC(Y - T)$ where $C$ is the level of consumption spending, $A$ is the level of consumption spending that is autonomous or independent of the level of income in the economy, $MPC$ is the marginal propensity to consume, $Y$ is real GDP or real income, and $T$ is the level of the lump-sum tax.

**STEP 2:** Using the consumption function from Step 1, derive an expression for the multiplier.

Recall from our study of the circular flow diagram that we can write $Y = C + I + G + (X - M)$. From Step 1 we know that $C = A + MPC(Y - T)$ so we can rewrite the equation from the circular flow diagram as $Y = A + MPC(Y - T) + I + G + (X - M)$. Recall that GDP is the same as $Y$, both measure real GDP or real income (remember real GDP is equal to real income). Rearranging this equation we can rewrite it as $(1 - MPC)Y = A - MPC \times T + I + G + (X - M)$ or $Y = [1/(1 - MPC)][A - MPC \times T + I + G + (X - M)]$. The multiplier provides us with a number that expresses the relationship between a change in one of the variables on the right-hand side of this equation to its impact on the value of $Y$, or real GDP. For example, if the only variable that changes on the right-hand side is $A$, autonomous consumption, then this equation tells us the (change in $Y$) $= [1/(1 - MPC)][$change in $A]$. The multiplier for changes in $A$, changes in $I$, changes in $G$, or changes in $(X - M)$ is $[1/(1 - MPC)]$. Notice that the multiplier for changes in $T$ will be different! If the level of lump-sum taxes changes, then the equation we derived tells us that the (change in $Y$) $= [-MPC/(1 - MPC)][$change in $A]$. The multiplier for a change in $T$ is $[-MPC/(1 - MPC)]$.

**STEP 3:** Now, rewrite the consumption equation for the situation when taxes are given as a tax on income where the tax rate is $t$.

The consumption function when taxes are assumed to be dependent on the level of real income can be written as $C = A + MPC(Y - tY)$, where $C$ is the level of consumption spending, $A$ is the level of consumption spending that is autonomous or independent of the level of income in the economy, $MPC$ is the marginal propensity to consume, $Y$ is real GDP or real income, and $tY$ is the amount of income taxes.

**STEP 4:** Using the consumption function from Step 3, derive an expression for the new multiplier.

Now, we just need to repeat Step 2 while using our new consumption function that models taxes as income taxes rather than lump-sum taxes. We can rewrite the equation from the circular flow diagram as $Y = A + MPC(Y - tY) + I + G + (X - M)$. Recall that GDP is the same as $Y$, both measure real GDP or real income (remember real GDP is equal to real income). Rearranging this equation we can rewrite it as $(1 - MPC - t \times MPC)Y = A + I + G + (X - M)$ or $Y = [1/(1 - MPC - t \times MPC)][A + I + G + (X - M)]$. The multiplier provides us with a number that expresses the relationship between a change in one of the variables on the right-hand side of this equation to its impact on the value of $Y$, or real GDP. For example, if the only variable that changes on the right-hand side is $A$, autonomous consumption, then this equation tells us the (change in $Y$) $= [1/(1 - MPC - t \times MPC)][$change in $A]$. Thus, the multiplier for changes in $A$, changes in $I$, changes in $G$, or changes in $(X - M)$ is $[1/(1 - MPC - t \times MPC)]$.

# Problems and Exercises

1. For each of the following scenarios, consider the described change while holding everything else constant and describe the first-round effect of the change on consumer spending, government spending, and real GDP.

   a. The government increases the level of transfer payments in the economy.

   b. The government reduces the tax rate on income in the economy.

   c. The government increases its expenditures.

   d. The country goes to war and increases its military by 40%.

2. For each of the following situations identify whether it is an example of expansionary discretionary fiscal policy, contractionary discretionary fiscal policy, or fiscal policy in the form of an automatic stabilizer.

   a. During 2009, tax revenue for Macrovia falls as the economy enters a recession.

   b. During 2009, in light of projected deficiencies in *AD*, Macrovia's legislature authorizes an expenditure of $200 million to build a new hydroelectric dam.

   c. In 2012, fearing a too rapidly expanding economy, Macrovia adopts a budget that calls for 10% spending cuts in all government departments for the following fiscal year.

   d. In 2011, unemployment benefits rise 5% in response to rising unemployment in Macrovia.

3. Explain why automatic stabilizers reduce the size of the multiplier. Provide several examples of automatic stabilizers and their effect on the economy during economic fluctuations.

4. Suppose you are given the following set of equations to describe the closed economy of Fantasia.

$C = A + MPC\ (Y - T)$

$T = tY$, where $t$ is the tax rate

Furthermore, suppose the price level in Fantasia is fixed in the short run.

a. Using the information provided, derive an expression for the multiplier for this economy.

You are given some additional information about Fantasia's economy. You are told

$C = 10 + 0.5\ (Y - T)$

$T = 0.1Y$

$I_{Planned} = \$50$ million

$G = \$50$ million

b. What is the income–expenditure equilibrium in Fantasia?

c. What is the value of the multiplier for changes in autonomous spending in Fantasia?

Suppose you are told that the potential output level in Fantasia is $180 million.

d. Given your answer in part (b), is Fantasia operating with a recessionary or an inflationary gap?

**e.** The government in Fantasia decides to engage in discretionary fiscal policy to make Fantasia's level of aggregate output equal to its potential output. As Fantasia's chief economist, can you say what change in the level of government spending is necessary to restore the economy to potential output?

5. Use the following table to compare the effects of a $20 million decrease in government spending on goods and services to a $20 million dollar decrease in transfer payments. Assume for this example that the *MPC* for this economy is equal to 0.8.

| Round | Effect on real GDP of a $20 million decrease in government spending | Effect on real GDP of a $20 million decrease in transfer payments |
|---|---|---|
| Round 1 | –$20 million | –$16 million |
| Round 2 | | |
| Round 3 | | |
| Round 4 | | |
| .... | | |
| Eventual effect | | |

## ■ BEFORE YOU TAKE THE TEST

# Module Review Questions

1. Holding everything else constant, the multiplier effect for taxes or transfers
   a. is the same as the multiplier effect for changes in autonomous aggregate spending.
   b. is smaller than the multiplier effect for changes in autonomous aggregate spending.
   c. is larger than the multiplier effect for changes in autonomous aggregate spending.
   d. may be smaller than, larger than, or equal to the multiplier effect for changes in autonomous aggregate spending.

2. Which of the following statements is true?
   a. Automatic stabilizers act like automatic expansionary fiscal policy when the economy is in a recession.
   b. Automatic stabilizers refer to government spending and taxation rules that cause fiscal policy to be expansionary when the economy expands and contractionary when the economy contracts.
   c. Automatic stabilizers reduce the size of the multiplier.
   d. Statements (a), (b), and (c) are all true.
   e. Statements (a) and (c) are both true.

3. Discretionary fiscal policy refers to
   a. the effect of automatic stabilizers on the economy.
   b. a situation in which citizens can choose to participate or not participate in government programs.
   c. fiscal policy that is the direct result of deliberate decisions made by policy makers.
   d. fiscal policy that is either the direct result of deliberate decisions made by policy makers or the result of the impact of automatic stabilizers on the economy.

4. Assume an economy is initially in long-run income–expenditure equilibrium. In addition, assume that this economy's short-run aggregate supply curve is upward sloping. Holding everything else constant, an increase in government spending causes the planned aggregate expenditure line to shift up, the *AD* curve to shift to the
   a. right, the aggregate price level to increase, and the total change in output to equal the multiplier effect.
   b. left, the aggregate price level to increase, and the total change in output to be less than the amount calculated as the multiplier effect.
   c. right, the aggregate price level to increase, and the total change in output to be less than the amount calculated as the multiplier effect.

5. The government is considering two proposals: one would increase government spending by $100 while the other would decrease the level of taxes collected by the government by $100. Suppose the government's goal is to stimulate the economy as much as possible for a given level of expenditure. Which of the following statements is true?
   a. The government will stimulate the economy more when it increases government spending.
   b. The government will stimulate the economy more when it decreases taxes.
   c. The stimulus to the economy from these two proposals is the same: it does not matter which proposal the government implements.

6. Which of the following statements is true?
   I. The *MPC* for unemployed people is usually higher than the *MPC* for people who own stocks.
   II. The macroeconomic effects of an increase in unemployment benefits will be greater than the macroeconomic effects of a decrease in taxes on profits distributed as dividends to shareholders.
   III. Automatic stabilizers reduce the size of the multiplier.
   a. Statement I is true.
   b. Statement II is true.
   c. Statement III is true.
   d. Statements I and II are both true.
   e. Statements I and III are both true.
   f. Statements II and III are both true.
   g. Statements I, II, and III are all true.

7. Suppose the *MPC* equals 0.5 and the tax rate is 0.1 for an economy. Holding everything else constant, when government spending increases by $10 billion, what is the total change in aggregate output?
   a. $10 billion
   b. $20 billion
   c. $18.2 billion
   d. $10.5 billion

8.  When an economy is operating with a recessionary gap, the decision to increase govern-ment spending in order to stimulate the economy is an example of

a.  discretionary fiscal policy.

b.  monetary policy, since it will lead to everyone having more money than they did prior to the increase in government spending.

c.  automatic stabilizers acting to stabilize the economy.

d.  Answers (a) and (c) are both correct.

9.  Economists caution that

a.  recessionary gaps are so threatening that the government ought to be always ready to enact discretionary fiscal policy to counteract the recessionary gap.

b.  there are important time lags in the use of fiscal policy and that discretionary fiscal policy must be carefully employed if it is to result in less economic fluctuation rather than more economic fluctuation.

c.  recessionary gaps are often over before discretionary fiscal policy has any impact and, thus, the discretionary policy has no impact on the economy.

d.  the existence of lags makes the implementation of fiscal policy easier than it would be without the lags.

10.  Which of the following statements is true?

a.  When the government "captures" a fraction $t$ of any increase in GDP in the form of taxes, this produces a larger multiplier effect.

b.  If the tax rate is 0.05 and the $MPC$ is 0.4, then the multiplier for a change in autonomous spending equals 1.61.

c.  If the tax rate is 0.1 and GDP increases by $1.2 billion, then the government will collect an additional $0.12 billion during the given time period.

d.  Statements (a), (b), and (c) are all true.

e.  Statements (b) and (c) are both true.

11.  Which of the following statements is a true statement?

I.  Lyndon Johnson's tax surcharge is an example of expansionary fiscal policy.

II.  The American Recovery and Reinvestment Act is a legislative act that shifted the $AD$ curve to the left.

III.  There is no multiplier effect to expansionary fiscal policy.

a.  Statement I is true.

b.  Statement II is true.

c.  Statement III is true.

d.  Statements I and II are true.

e.  Statements I and III are true.

f.  Statements II and III are true.

g.  None of the statements is true.

**12.** When the government increases the level of transfer payments
  a. the households receiving this increased transfer payment amount typically will spend all of the increase in the transfer payment.
  b. the households receiving this increased transfer payment amount will typically spend only a portion of the increase in the transfer payment.
  c. the multiplier effect from this increase in transfer payments is typically smaller than the multiplier effect from an equal-size increase in the level of government spending on goods and services.
  d. the multiplier effect from this increase in transfer payments is typically larger than the multiplier effect from an equal-size increase in the level of government spending on goods and services.
  e. Answers (a) and (c) are both correct.
  f. Answers (a) and (d) are both correct.
  g. Answers (b) and (c) are both correct.
  h. Answers (b) and (d) are both correct.

**13.** A lump-sum tax is a tax that
  a. varies in monetary value depending upon the income of the taxpayer.
  b. is the same monetary amount irrespective of taxpayer income.
  c. is a tax that is collected by the government on the first of every month.
  d. is another name for the income tax.

## ■ ANSWER KEY

# Answers to Problems and Exercises

1.  **a.** When the level of transfer payments increases, this causes disposable income to increase. When disposable income increases, this increase causes consumer spending to increase and therefore real GDP to increase. An increase in transfer payments does not change government spending.

    **b.** When the government reduces the tax rate on income in the economy, this reduction in the tax rate causes disposable income to increase; therefore, consumer spending increases. An increase in consumer spending, holding everything else constant, will cause real GDP to increase. A decrease in the tax rate on income in the economy does not change government spending.

    **c.** Holding everything else constant, if the government increases its spending, this will cause real GDP to increase. There will be no change in consumer spending in the first round, but in the second round, consumer spending will increase because real GDP has risen.

    **d.** Holding everything else constant, if the country goes to war, government spending will increase. As government spending increases, real GDP will increase. There will be no change in consumer spending in the first round, but in the second round, consumer spending will increase because real GDP has risen.

2.  **a.** This is an example of an automatic stabilizer: as GDP in Macrovia falls, this leads automatically to smaller tax collections for a given tax rate.

    **b.** This is an example of expansionary discretionary fiscal policy: the additional government expenditure will stimulate *AD*.

    **c.** This is an example of contractionary discretionary fiscal policy: Macrovia moves to cut government spending, which will reduce *AD* and slow down the economic expansion.

    **d.** This is an example of an automatic stabilizer: as unemployment rises, this leads to less *AD*. But the payment of unemployment benefits lessens this fall in aggregate spending and results in a smaller overall impact on *AD*.

3.  Automatic stabilizers act to moderate the effects of economic recessions or economic expansions. In the case of economic recessions, the automatic stabilizers provide a source of additional spending that occurs as the economy goes into the recession. For example, as production and spending slow in the economy, the amount of taxes people pay naturally decrease as their income levels decrease, and this moderates the fall in consumer spending. Or, as unemployment rates increase, the number of people receiving unemployment compensation rises, and this enables people to spend more than they would otherwise be able to spend. In the case of economic expansions, the automatic stabilizers slow down spending: as people's incomes rise, their taxes also rise reducing the overall increase in consumer income, and this moderates the economic expansion. (Students may provide different examples of automatic stabilizers.)

4.  **a.** To find the multiplier, start by recalling the equilibrium condition where aggregate expenditure equals aggregate income. We can write this as $Y = C + I + G$ for the closed economy of Fantasia. We can substitute $A$ for $C$ and get $Y = A + MPC(Y - T) + I + G$. We can also substitute $tY$ for $T$ and have $Y = A + MPC(Y - tY) + I + G$. Rearranging terms we have $Y - MPC(1 - t)Y = A + I + G$ or $Y[1 - MPC(1 - t)] = A + I + G$. We can solve this equation for $Y$ and have $Y = \{1/[1 - MPC(1 - t)]\}(A + I + G)$. The multiplier is $\{1/[1 - MPC(1 - t)]\}$.

b. Use the equation $Y = C + I + G$ and substitute in the data you have to get $Y = 10 + 0.5$ $(Y - 0.1Y) + 100$. Solving for $Y$, the income–expenditure equilibrium equals $200.

c. The value of the multiplier, $\{1/[1 - MPC(1 - t)]\}$, equals 1.818, or approximately 1.82.

d. Fantasia is operating with an inflationary gap, since actual output of $200 million exceeds potential output of $180 million.

e. Since aggregate output needs to fall by $20 million and the multiplier equals 1.82, that implies that government spending must decrease by $10.99 million.

5.

| Round | Effect on real GDP of a $20 million decrease in government spending | Effect on real GDP of a $20 million decrease in transfer payments |
|---|---|---|
| Round 1 | –$20 million | –$16 million |
| Round 2 | –$16 million | –$12.8 |
| Round 3 | –$12.8 million | –$10.24 |
| Round 4 | –$10.24 | –$8.19 |
| .... | ..... | ..... |
| Eventual effect | –$100 million | –$80 million |

# Answers to Module Review Questions

1. **Answer b.** In our simple model, the multiplier effect for changes in taxes or transfers equals (in absolute value) $MPC/(1 - MPC)$, while the multiplier effect for changes in autonomous aggregate spending equals $1/(1 - MPC)$. The multiplier effect of changes in taxes and transfers is smaller than the multiplier effect of changes in autonomous aggregate spending.

2. **Answer e.** Automatic stabilizers act to automatically lessen the economic consequences of recessions and expansions. They do this by providing an automatic fiscal policy response that stimulates a contractionary economy and slows down, or contracts, an expansionary economy. This activity effectively lessens the multiplier process and therefore reduces the size of the multiplier.

3. **Answer c.** Discretionary fiscal policy refers to fiscal policy that is implemented at the discretion of policy makers. It is therefore the direct result of deliberate actions taken by policy makers.

4. **Answer c.** With an upward-sloping aggregate supply curve, an increase in government spending will cause the $AD$ curve to shift to the right (as the planned aggregate expenditure line shifts up) while causing a movement along the short-run aggregate supply curve. In the short run, the level of real GDP will increase in this economy but by an amount less than that predicted by the multiplier, while the aggregate price level increases.

5. **Answer a.** The multiplier effect for a change in government spending is greater than the multiplier effect for a change in taxes: the government will stimulate the economy more if it increases government spending.

6. **Answer g.** Unemployed people tend to be less wealthy than people who own stocks: this leads them to spend more of their disposable income. Since unemployed people tend to have a higher $MPC$ than people who own stocks, this leads to a larger multiplier effect on the level of aggregate output from an increase in unemployment benefits than from a decrease in taxes on profits. The effect of automatic stabilizers is to reduce economic fluctuations. For example, when income increases, this causes tax revenue to increase

automatically, and this increase in tax revenue results in the increase in aggregate output being less than it would have been had there been no taxes. Thus, automatic stabilizers reduce the size of the multiplier.

7.  **Answer c.** To find this answer we need to use the multiplier: $1/[1 - MPC(1 - t)]$. In this example, this multiplier equals 1.82, so the $10 billion increase in government spending leads to aggregate output increasing by (1.82)($10 billion), or $18.2 billion.

8.  **Answer a.** A change in government spending is an example of fiscal policy. An increase in government spending, holding everything else constant, will stimulate the economy in the short run while a decrease in government spending, holding everything else constant, will contract the economy in the short run.

9.  **Answer b.** Discretionary fiscal policy is difficult to use due to significant time lags: there is the lag in recognizing that there is an economic problem, there is a legislative lag, and there is an implementation lag. These lags result in a situation where the discretionary fiscal policy may not actually be felt in an economy until after the recessionary gap is eliminated; in this case, the discretionary fiscal policy may cause economic fluctuations to be greater than they would have been without the discretionary fiscal policy.

10. **Answer e.** We know that the inclusion of a tax rate in our model, holding everything else constant, reduces the size of the multiplier. Using the formula for this multiplier, $1/[1 - MPC(1 - t)]$, and substituting in the given information, we find that answer (b) is correct. Answer (c) is a simple, and an accurate, mathematical computation and also a correct answer.

11. **Answer g.** The tax surcharge passed during Lyndon Johnson's presidency is an example of contractionary fiscal policy: this policy pushed the *AD* curve to the left. The American Recovery and Reinvestment Act is an example of an expansionary fiscal policy that shifted the *AD* curve to the right. Expansionary fiscal policy, for example, an increase government spending or a decrease in taxes, will have a multiplier effect on the level of real GDP.

12. **Answer g.** The multiplier effect of an increase in transfer payments is typically smaller than the multiplier effect from an equal-size increase in government spending since households will save a portion of the increase in transfer payments, provided that their *MPC* is less than one. This nonspent portion of the increase in transfer payments will result in real GDP growing but by a smaller amount than would be true from an increase in government spending of the same amount.

13. **Answer b.** A lump-sum tax by definition is a tax that does not depend upon the taxpayer's income. A lump-sum tax is the same monetary value for all taxpayers.

# module 32 (68)

# Budget Deficits
# and Public Debt

## BEFORE YOU READ THE MODULE

## Summary

This module explores why governments calculate the cyclically adjusted budget balance. In addition, the module examines why a large public debt may be a cause for concern. The module also considers implicit liabilities and why these implicit liabilities may present challenges for an economy.

## Module Objectives

**Objective #1.**  Recall that the budget balance equals tax revenue minus government spending on both goods and services as well as government transfers. We can write the budget balance, $S_{Government}$, symbolically as $S_{Government} = T - G - TR$.

- A positive budget balance indicates a budget surplus, while a negative budget balance indicates a budget deficit.

- Holding everything else constant, discretionary expansionary fiscal policy reduces the budget balance, while discretionary contractionary policy increases the budget balance.

- Equal-sized changes in government spending or taxes impact the budget balance equally, but have very different impacts on aggregate demand (AD) due to the multiplier effect of a change in government spending being greater than the multiplier effect of an equal-sized change in government taxes or transfers.

- Changes in the budget balance often are the result of economic fluctuations.

**Objective #2.**  The cyclically adjusted budget balance estimates the size of the budget balance if real GDP was exactly equal to potential output. It effectively eliminates the impact of recessionary or inflationary gaps on tax revenue and government transfers.

**Objective #3.**  Most economists do not endorse legislation requiring that the government maintain a balanced budget, since this type of rule would undermine the role of taxes and transfers as automatic stabilizers.

**Objective #4.**   When governments spend more than their tax revenue, they usually borrow the extra funds needed. Governments that run persistent deficits find that they have a rising government debt.

- A government deficit is the difference between the amount of money a government spends and the amount of money the government receives in taxes over a given period of time.

- A government debt is the sum of money a government owes at a particular point in time.

- The public debt refers to the government debt held by individuals and institutions outside the government at a particular point in time.

- When the government runs persistent budget deficits, it competes with firms that plan to borrow funds for investment spending. The government borrowing may crowd out private investment spending and lead to a reduction in the economy's long-run growth rate.

- When the government runs persistent budget deficits, this leads to financial pressure on future budgets due to the increasing size of the interest payments on the accumulated debt. Holding everything else constant, a government that owes large amounts in interest must raise more revenue from taxes or spend less.

- Governments that print money to pay their bills find that this leads to inflation.

- The long-run effects of persistent budget deficits suggest that governments should run a budget that is approximately balanced over time.

**Objective #5.**   In the United States, government budget totals are kept for the fiscal year that starts on October 1 and runs through September 30. For example, fiscal 2015 began on October 1, 2014, and ended on September 30, 2015.

**Objective #6.**   The debt–GDP ratio is a measure used to assess the ability of governments to pay their debt. The debt–GDP ratio measures government debt as a percentage of GDP. This measure recognizes that the size of the economy as a whole, as measured by GDP, provides information about the amount of potential taxes a government can collect. When GDP grows at a faster rate than the rate of growth of the government's debt, then the burden of paying the debt is falling relative to the government's ability to collect tax revenue.

- The debt–GDP ratio can fall even when debt is rising provided that GDP grows faster than debt.

- The debt–GDP ratio will rise when debt is rising if GDP grows more slowly than debt.

**Objective #7.**   Implicit liabilities are promises made by governments that represent debt not included in the government's debt statistics. In the United States, the largest implicit liabilities are Social Security, Medicare, and Medicaid.

- Spending on Social Security is projected to rise dramatically over the next few decades due to demographic issues related to the retirement of the baby boomer generation.

- Spending on Medicare and Medicaid is also projected to rise dramatically, primarily because long-run health care spending increases faster than overall spending.

- Both Social Security and Medicare are funded from dedicated taxes, a special tax levied on wages. At the time of this writing, there is a surplus of tax revenue from these dedicated taxes. For example, the surplus funds of Social Security are held in a Social Security trust fund. The funds in these trust funds are owed to the Social Security system and other trust funds by another part of the government; this debt is referred to as the United States government debt held by Social Security and other trust funds. The gross debt for the U.S. government thus consists of two parts: first, the public debt, and second, the United States government debt held by Social Security and other trust funds.

## Key Terms

**cyclically adjusted budget balance** an estimate of what the *budget balance* would be if *real GDP* were exactly equal to *potential output.*

**fiscal year** the time period used for much of government accounting, running from October 1 to September 30. Fiscal years are labeled by the calendar year in which they end.

**public debt** government debt held by individuals and institutions outside the government.

**debt–GDP ratio** government debt as a percentage of GDP, frequently used as a measure of a government's ability to pay its debts.

**implicit liabilities** spending promises made by governments that are effectively a debt despite the fact that they are not included in the usual debt statistics. In the United States, the largest implicit liabilities arise from Social Security and Medicare, which promise transfer payments to current and future retirees (Social Security) and to the elderly (Medicare).

## ▮ AFTER YOU READ THE MODULE

## Tips

**Tip #1.**  This module contains some new vocabulary. You need to be familiar with these concepts, including the government deficit, government debt, implicit liabilities, and the debt–GDP ratio. As in the other modules it is essential that you learn and understand any new terms that are introduced. Many of the terms in this module represent complicated concepts or relationships.

**Tip #2.**  You will want to understand what the cyclically adjusted budget balance is and how it relates to the budget balance and to potential GDP. The cyclically adjusted budget balance is an estimate of what the budget balance would be if real GDP were exactly equal to potential GDP. This measure takes into account the extra tax revenue the government would receive and the smaller level of transfer payments the government would make if the recessionary gap were eliminated, or the tax revenue the government would lose and the extra transfer payments the government would make if the inflationary gap were eliminated. The cyclically adjusted budget balance fluctuates less than the actual budget deficit, because years with a large budget deficit are typically associated with large recessionary gaps.

1. Grandview is a closed economy where the level of planned investment spending is constant and equal to $50. In Grandview, people always spend 80% of any increase in disposable income, and their autonomous consumption is equal to $10. Grandview currently has a zero budget balance and the level of net taxes is equal to $20. Grandview also is assumed to have fixed prices in the short run. Long-run potential output in Grandview is equal to $400. You are asked to find the short-run level of production in Grandview and determine whether Grandview is currently operating with a recessionary gap or an inflationary gap. In addition, you are asked to provide three possible fiscal policies for returning Grandview to its long-run potential output: a tax policy using lump-sum taxes, a government spending policy, and a tax and government-spending policy that requires that the government budget balance remain zero (continue to assume that the tax change is a change in lump-sum taxes). For each of these three policies, you are asked to provide numerical values for the size of the policy to be implemented. In addition, you should calculate what happens to the government budget balance if there are no other changes.

**STEP 1:** Before you can find the short-run equilibrium level of output in Grandview, you will first need to find the consumption function for this economy.

Recall that the consumption function is written as $C = a + b(Y - T)$, where $a$ is autonomous consumption and $b$ is the marginal propensity to consume. In the provided information, we are told the value of autonomous consumption, and we are also told that consumers spend 80% of any increase in disposable income. The marginal propensity to consume is defined as the change in consumption divided by the change in disposable income: in this example, the marginal propensity to consume would equal 0.8. Thus, the consumption function is $C = 10 + 0.8(Y - T)$.

**STEP 2:** Recall that actual output is equal to the sum of expenditure in the economy. Use this information to find the short-run equilibrium level of output in Grandview.

Since Grandview is a closed economy, spending will only come from three sectors: households, businesses, and the government. We can find total expenditure by summing $C + I + G$. In equilibrium, total expenditure will equal production, $Y$. Thus, $Y = C + I + G$. By substituting the consumption function into this equation along with the given values for $I$ and $G$, we can solve for the short-run equilibrium level of output. $Y = 10 + 0.8(Y - T) + 50 + 20$, or the short-run equilibrium level of output, $Y$, is equal to $320.

**STEP 3:** Compare the short-run equilibrium level of output with the long-run potential level of output to decide whether Grandview is currently operating with a recessionary gap or an inflationary gap.

The short-run equilibrium level of output is $320, which is smaller than the long-run or potential level of output. Grandview is currently operating with a recessionary gap since its actual level of output is less than its potential level of output.

**STEP 4:** Grandview wishes to use activist fiscal policy to restore the economy to the potential level of aggregate output. Calculate the change in lump-sum taxes that would be necessary for Grandview to achieve this goal by changing current tax policy. Once you have calculated the change in lump-sum taxes, then calculate the change in the government budget balance.

The government of Grandview wishes to stimulate the economy through a change in lump-sum taxes so that output in the economy increases from $320 to $400. The tax expenditure multiplier is equal to $[(-b)/(1-b)]$, and in this case the value of this multiplier is $-4$. In order to increase output by $80, lump-sum taxes will need to be reduced by $20 since $(-4)(-20)$ is equal to $80, the desired increase in aggregate production. If government spending is constant at $20 and taxes decrease by $20, then the government budget balance will become negative since the government will be spending more than the amount of tax revenue that it is collecting.

**STEP 5:** Grandview wishes to use activist fiscal policy to restore the economy to the potential level of aggregate output. Calculate the change in government spending that would be necessary for Grandview to achieve this goal by changing current government spending. Once you have calculated the change in government spending, then calculate the change in the government budget balance.

The government of Grandview wishes to stimulate the economy through a change in government spending so that output in the economy increases from $320 to $400. The multiplier for a change in government spending is equal to $[1/(1-b)]$, and in this case the value of the multiplier is 5. In order to increase output by $80, government spending would need to be increased by $16 since $(5)(16)$ is equal to $80, the desired increase in aggregate production. If taxes are constant and equal to $20, then this increase in government spending will result in total government spending of $36. The government budget balance will be negative and equal to $-$16, since the government is spending more than it is collecting in tax revenue.

**STEP 6:** Grandview wishes to use activist fiscal policy to restore the economy to the potential level of aggregate output while at the same time maintaining a government budget balance of zero. Calculate what the change in government spending and lump-sum taxes must be to achieve this goal.

We know that the desired increase in aggregate output is $80, and the government of Grandview would like to achieve this level of output by increasing government spending and lump-sum taxes by an equivalent amount so that the government budget balance will remain equal to zero. This implies that the change in government spending should be exactly equal to the change in lump-sum taxes. The change in output will equal the government spending multiplier times the change in government spending, plus the tax expenditure multiplier times the change in lump-sum taxes. Symbolically we can write this as $\Delta Y = [1/(1-b)]\Delta G + [(-b)/(1-b)]\Delta T$. Since $\Delta G = \Delta T$, we can rewrite this equation as $\Delta Y = [1/(1-b)]\Delta G + [(-b)/(1-b)]\Delta G$, or $\Delta Y = \Delta G$. This means that if the government of Grandview wishes to increase output by $80 while maintaining a budget balance of zero, it will need to increase government spending and lump-sum taxes by $80.

2.  Zinfindel is a closed economy that is concerned about its debt–GDP ratio and the projections about this ratio for the next five years. The government of Zinfindel anticipates that real GDP will grow by 10% a year over the next five years, while the level of government deficit is expected to grow by 5% a year over the next five years. The following table provides information about Zinfindel this year. You are asked to complete the table, giving Zinfindel some projections about what it can expect over the next five years. For this problem assume that government debt in the next year is equal to the debt from the year before plus the deficit for that year: for example, in year 2, the debt would be equal to $25 million plus the additional $10 million in deficit spending, for a total debt of $35 million. Round all numbers to the nearest hundredth.

| Year | Real GDP (millions of dollars) | Debt (millions of dollars) | Budget deficit (millions of dollars) | Debt (percentage of real GDP) | Budget deficit (percentage of real GDP) |
|------|-------------------------------|---------------------------|--------------------------------------|-------------------------------|-----------------------------------------|
| Year 1 | $100 | $25 | $10 | 25% | 10% |
| Year 2 | | | | | |
| Year 3 | | | | | |
| Year 4 | | | | | |
| Year 5 | | | | | |

**STEP 1:** Start by calculating the value of real GDP for each of the next four years given the assumption that real GDP is growing by 10% a year.

To find real GDP for year 2, you will multiply real GDP in year 1 by 1.1. To find real GDP for year 3, you will multiply real GDP in year 2 by 1.1. The results of these calculations are provided in the table at the end of this problem.

**STEP 2:** Calculate the value of the government deficit for each year given the assumption that this deficit will grow by 5% a year.

To find the government deficit for year 2, you will multiply the government deficit for year 1 by 1.05. To find the government deficit for year 3, you will multiply the government deficit for year 2 by 1.05. The results of these calculations are provided in the table at the end of this problem.

**STEP 3:** Calculate the value of the debt using the budget deficit figures that you calculated in step 2.

Remember that the value of the debt in a particular year is equal to the sum of the debt and the budget deficit from the previous year. The results of these calculations are provided in the table at the end of this problem.

**STEP 4:** Calculate the debt as a percentage of GDP and the budget deficit as a percentage of GDP.

To find the debt as a percentage of GDP, divide the debt by real GDP and then multiply your answer by 100 to make it a percentage.

To find the budget deficit as a percentage of GDP, divide the budget deficit by real GDP and then multiply your answer by 100 to make it a percentage. The results of these calculations are provided in the table.

| Year | Real GDP (millions of dollars) | Debt (millions of dollars) | Budget deficit (millions of dollars) | Debt (percentage of real GDP) | Budget deficit (percentage of real GDP) |
|---|---|---|---|---|---|
| Year 1 | $100 | $25 | $10 | 25% | 10% |
| Year 2 | 110 | 35 | 10.5 | 31.82 | 9.55 |
| Year 3 | 121 | 45.5 | 11.03 | 37.60 | 9.12 |
| Year 4 | 133.1 | 56.53 | 11.58 | 42.47 | 8.70 |
| Year 5 | 146.41 | 68.10 | 12.16 | 46.51 | 8.31 |

# Problems and Exercises

1. Suppose Uplandia is a closed economy where the level of planned investment spending equals $100 and is unaffected by the level of aggregate spending. Furthermore, suppose consumers consume 60% of any increase in their disposable income and autonomous consumer spending equals $20. Uplandia currently has a zero budget balance, with taxes equal to $50, transfers equal to $0, and government spending on goods and services equal to $50. Furthermore, assume the price level is fixed in Uplandia in the short run.

   a. What is Uplandia's consumption function?

   b. What is the income–expenditure equilibrium for Uplandia?

   c. Suppose Uplandia wants output to equal $400, the potential level of output. Does Uplandia have an inflationary gap or a recessionary gap? Explain your answer.

   d. What is the change in government spending needed to enable this economy to reach its potential output, holding everything else constant?

**e.** Instead of a change in government spending, Uplandia decides to pursue a change in taxes in order to reach its potential output. Holding everything else constant, what is the change in taxes needed to enable this economy to reach its potential output?

**f.** Suppose the government decides it wants to maintain a zero budget balance. This implies that any increase in government spending, G, must be accompanied by an equivalent increase in taxes, T. Suppose Uplandia chooses to reach its potential output level while maintaining a zero budget balance. What will the change in G and T need to be in order to accomplish this goal?

**g.** In your answers to parts (d), (e) and (f), you use different multipliers to reach potential output in Uplandia. If your only criterion for choosing policy is getting the most "bang for the buck" or, in other words, getting the largest change in aggregate output for a given dollar change in government spending or taxation, which is the best policy? Explain your answer.

**h.** Relate your answer in part (g) to the debate over the wisdom of a balanced-budget rule for the federal government.

2. Uplandia is concerned about its debt–GDP ratio and the projections about this ratio over the next five years. The following table gives data about Uplandia's real GDP for this year (year 1) and its projected real GDP for the next five years. Real GDP is projected to grow 3% per year over the next five years as is the government deficit.

   **a.** Fill in the missing cells in the table.

| Year | Real GDP (millions of dollars) | Debt (millions of dollars) | Budget deficit (millions of dollars) | Debt (percentage of real GDP) | Budget deficit (percentage of real GDP) |
|------|--------|--------|--------|--------|--------|
| Year 1 | $800 | $200 | $20 | 25% | 2.5% |
| Year 2 | | | | | |
| Year 3 | | | | | |
| Year 4 | | | | | |
| Year 5 | | | | | |
| Year 6 | | | | | |

   **b.** Describe in words what is happening to the government's debt–GDP ratio and deficit–GDP ratio when real GDP and the government deficit grow at the same rate.

Suppose Uplandia decides to reduce government spending over the next five years. This results in the government deficit growing 1% per year over the next five years while real GDP continues to grow 3% per year.

c. Fill in the table based on these projections.

| Year | Real GDP (millions of dollars) | Debt (millions of dollars) | Budget deficit (millions of dollars) | Debt (percentage of real GDP) | Budget deficit (percentage of real GDP) |
|---|---|---|---|---|---|
| Year 1 | $800 | $200 | $20 | 25% | 2.5% |
| Year 2 | | | | | |
| Year 3 | | | | | |
| Year 4 | | | | | |
| Year 5 | | | | | |
| Year 6 | | | | | |

d. Describe in words what is happening to the government's debt–GDP ratio and deficit–GDP ratio when real GDP grows at 3% per year while the deficit grows at 1% per year.

Suppose Uplandia, buoyed by its projected real GDP growth rate, passes legislation reducing its taxes while simultaneously deciding to go to war. Its economists project real GDP will continue to grow at 3% per year but now, due to these policy decisions, the government deficit is projected to grow at 10% per year. The results of these changes are shown in the following table.

| Year | Real GDP (millions of dollars) | Debt (millions of dollars) | Budget deficit (millions of dollars) | Debt (percentage of real GDP) | Budget deficit (percentage of real GDP) |
|---|---|---|---|---|---|
| Year 1 | $800 | $200 | $20 | 25% | 2.5% |
| Year 2 | 824 | 222 | 22 | 26.94 | 2.67 |
| Year 3 | 848.72 | 246.2 | 24.2 | 29.01 | 2.85 |
| Year 4 | 874.18 | 272.82 | 26.62 | 31.21 | 3.05 |
| Year 5 | 900.41 | 302.10 | 29.38 | 33.55 | 3.25 |
| Year 6 | 927.42 | 334.30 | 32.2 | 36.05 | 3.47 |

e. Describe in words what is happening to the government's debt–GDP ratio and deficit–GDP ratio when real GDP grows at 3% per year while the deficit grows at 10% per year.

**f.** Can you generalize your findings from this exercise? What general principles does this exercise present?

**3.** Suppose that the government currently operates with a deficit and that this deficit grows by 4% a year. Furthermore, suppose that this economy initially had zero debt until the government started operating with a deficit. The economy's annual economic growth rate is 5% a year. What will happen to this economy's debt–GDP ratio over time given this information? Explain your answer fully.

## ▌ BEFORE YOU TAKE THE TEST

# Module Review Questions

**1.** Holding everything else constant, the government's budget balance
   a. tends to increase during a recession.
   b. tends to increase during an expansion.
   c. will increase if the government pursues expansionary fiscal policy.
   d. Answers (a) and (c) are both correct.
   e. Answers (b) and (c) are both correct.

**2.** Which of the following statements is true?
   a. Two different changes in fiscal policy that have equal effects on the budget balance will always have equal effects on *AD*.
   b. A change in taxes or transfers will have a larger effect on *AD* than an equal-sized change in government purchases of goods and services.
   c. The budget deficit almost always falls when unemployment rises.
   d. The cyclically adjusted budget balance provides an estimate of the budget balance, assuming real GDP is equal to potential output.

**3.** When a government decides to spend more than it collects in tax revenue,
   a. it usually borrows the necessary funds.
   b. the budget balance increases.
   c. it runs a budget deficit but reduces its overall level of government debt.
   d. it is forced to sell valuable assets to finance its spending.

4. Which of the following statements is true?
   a. The fiscal year 2001 runs from October 1, 2001 through September 30, 2002.
   b. Public debt is that amount of government debt held by individuals and institutions outside the government.
   c. The government's total debt includes the public debt as well as the debt owed by one part of the government to another part of the government (for example, the Social Security trust funds).
   d. Statements (a), (b), and (c) are all true.
   e. Statements (b) and (c) are both true.

5. In the United States, at the end of fiscal year 2013, the
   a. total federal government debt equaled 37% of GDP.
   b. federal government's public debt at the federal level equaled 71% of GDP.
   c. federal government's public debt equaled $7.4 trillion.
   d. Answers (a) and (c) are both true.

6. The government debt is
   a. an alternative but equivalent term for the government deficit.
   b. the difference between the amount of money government spends and the amount of tax revenue the government collects during a given period of time.
   c. the amount of money the government owes at a particular point in time.
   d. best measured over a given period of time.

7. Suppose the government of Macroland repeatedly finds itself running a deficit. This may
   a. result in less private investment spending as government borrowing crowds out this spending.
   b. result in lower long-run economic growth if the deficit reduces private investment spending.
   c. cause the government of Macroland to have less budgetary flexibility in the future due to the diversion of tax revenue to pay interest on the debt.
   d. Answers (a), (b), and (c) are all possible effects of repeatedly running a deficit.

8. The debt–GDP ratio
   a. provides a measure of government debt as a percentage of GDP.
   b. provides a measure of government debt relative to the potential ability of the government to collect taxes to cover that debt.
   c. can fall, even if the level of government debt is rising, provided that GDP grows faster than the debt.
   d. Answers (a), (b), and (c) are all correct.

9. Implicit liabilities
   a. are not included in the calculation of the debt–GDP ratio in the United States.
   b. are promises made by the government that represent a debt that must be paid by the government at some future point in time.
   c. are usually included in debt statistics.
   d. Answers (a), (b), and (c) are all correct.
   e. Answers (a) and (b) are both correct.

**10.** Which of the following statements is true?

  a. The demographic issues underlying Social Security will lessen with the passage of time in the United States as the baby boom generation moves into retirement.

  b. Health costs tend to rise at approximately the same rate as other costs in wealthy economies like the United States.

  c. Social Security and Medicare are funded by dedicated taxes: any excess funds collected from these dedicated taxes accumulate in trust funds that other parts of the government may borrow from to fund other spending. When this type of borrowing occurs an implicit liability is created.

  d. The sum of public debt and the United States government debt held by Social Security and other trust funds overstates the seriousness of the government's fiscal health.

**11.** The Social Security program in the United States

  a. is a "pay-as-you-go" system where current workers pay payroll taxes that fund the benefits of current retirees.

  b. had 35 retirees receiving benefits for every 10 workers in 2012, while projections suggest that in 2030 there will be 46 retirees receiving benefits for every 100 workers.

  c. had accumulated a Social Security trust fund of $2.9 trillion at the end of fiscal 2011.

  d. Answers (a), (b) and (c) are all correct.

**12.** Suppose the government spends $500 billion during the fiscal year 2007 on goods and services. In addition, the government collects tax revenues of $480 billion and makes transfer payments equal to $150 billion. Assume the economy is producing at the potential output level. The budget balance for this economy is equal to _____ and the government is running a _____.

  a. $170 billion; surplus

  b. −$170 billion; deficit

  c. $130 billion; surplus

  d. −$130 billion; deficit

**13.** Economists generally do not believe that the government should balance its budget every year. Instead, economists advocate that governments run a surplus during economic

  a. recessions and a deficit during economic expansions.

  b. expansions and a deficit during economic recessions.

**14.** When a government runs a deficit persistently year after year, this may

  a. place financial pressure on future budgets.

  b. result in higher taxes over time since the government will need to collect tax revenue to cover its interest payments on the government debt.

  c. reduce the level of private investment spending as the government's borrowing crowds out over investment spending.

  d. Answers (a), (b), and (c) are all correct.

  e. Answers (a) and (b) are both correct.

## ANSWER KEY

# Answers to Problems and Exercises

1.  **a.** To find the consumption function first recall the general form: $C = A + MPC$ $(Y - T)$. From the given information we know $A$ equals \$20 and the $MPC$ equals 0.6. Thus, $C = 20 + 0.6(Y - T)$.

    **b.** To find the income–expenditure equilibrium, solve the equation $Y = C + I + G$. We know $C$ can be written as $20 + 0.6(Y - T)$; $I$ equals \$100; and $G$ equals \$50. We also know $T$, taxes, equals \$50. So, $Y = 20 + 0.6(Y - 50) + 100 + 50$, or $Y$ equals \$350.

    **c.** Uplandia is currently producing with a recessionary gap, since its current output of \$350 is less than its potential output of \$400.

    **d.** The multiplier for a change in aggregate spending equals $1/(1 - MPC)$. We know that the change in aggregate production equals the multiplier times the change (in this case) in government spending. In this problem, we want output to increase by \$50, our multiplier value is 2.5, and thus government spending must increase by \$20 in order for this economy to produce its potential output of \$400.

    **e.** The multiplier for a change in taxes equals $-MPC/(1 - MPC)$, or in this case $-1.5$, since the $MPC$ equals 0.6. Recall that the change in aggregate output equals the multiplier times the change in the level of taxes. We want output to increase by \$50, the multiplier's value is $-1.5$, and, thus, taxes must decrease by \$33.33. Here you need to remember that aggregate output increases as taxes fall, holding everything else constant, and aggregate output decreases as taxes increase, holding everything else constant.

    **f.** We can find our answer by recognizing that we have two multiplier effects occurring simultaneously if the government chooses to maintain a zero budget balance. We could write this as the change in aggregate output equals the multiplier effect from the change in government spending plus the multiplier effect from the change in taxes. Note, though, that the change in government spending equals the change in taxes. Thus, the change in aggregate output equals $1/(1 - MPC)$ times the change in government spending plus $[-MPC/(1 - MPC)]$ times the change in government spending. Since the desired change in aggregate output equals \$50, we can solve this equation and find that the change in government spending and in taxes must both equal \$50.

    **g.** The most "bang for the buck" comes from a change in government spending since the multiplier has a value of 2.5. A change in taxes is multiplied by the smaller (in absolute value) multiplier of 1.5 and the balanced budget scenario has an even smaller multiplier value of 1.

    **h.** A balanced budget rule for the federal government would restrict the government's ability to engage in discretionary fiscal policy in times of economic need. It would also prove costly, since for any given change in aggregate output, a balanced-budget rule forces the federal government to spend more than it would if the government were free to pursue discretionary fiscal policy without regard to its budgetary consequences.

**2.  a.**

| Year | Real GDP (millions of dollars) | Debt (millions of dollars) | Budget deficit (millions of dollars) | Debt (percentage of real GDP) | Budget deficit (percentage of real GDP) |
|---|---|---|---|---|---|
| Year 1 | $800.00 | $200.00 | $20.00 | 25% | 2.5% |
| Year 2 | 824.00 | 220.60 | 20.60 | 26.77 | 2.5 |
| Year 3 | 848.72 | 241.82 | 21.22 | 28.49 | 2.5 |
| Year 4 | 874.18 | 263.68 | 21.85 | 30.16 | 2.5 |
| Year 5 | 900.41 | 286.18 | 22.51 | 31.79 | 2.5 |
| Year 6 | 927.42 | 309.37 | 23.19 | 33.36 | 2.5 |

**b.** When the real GDP and the government deficit grow at the same rate, the deficit–GDP ratio stays constant at 2.5%, while the debt–GDP ratio increases from 25% to 33.36% in five years.

**c.**

| Year | Real GDP (millions of dollars) | Debt (millions of dollars) | Budget deficit (millions of dollars) | Debt (percentage of real GDP) | Budget deficit (percentage of real GDP) |
|---|---|---|---|---|---|
| Year 1 | $800.00 | $200.00 | $20.00 | 25% | 2.5% |
| Year 2 | 824.00 | 220.20 | 20.20 | 26.72 | 2.45 |
| Year 3 | 848.72 | 240.60 | 20.40 | 28.35 | 2.40 |
| Year 4 | 874.18 | 261.21 | 20.61 | 29.88 | 2.36 |
| Year 5 | 900.41 | 282.02 | 20.81 | 31.32 | 2.31 |
| Year 6 | 927.42 | 303.04 | 21.02 | 32.67 | 2.27 |

**d.** When the real GDP grows at 3% per year and the government deficit grows at 1% per year, the deficit–GDP ratio falls from 2.5% to 2.27% in five years, while the debt–GDP ratio increases from 25% to 32.68% in five years.

**e.** When real GDP grows at 3% per year and the deficit grows at 10% per year, the deficit–GDP ratio increases from 2.5% to 3.47% over five years while the debt–GDP ratio increases from 25% to 36.05% over five years.

**f.** The rate of growth of both real GDP and the deficit each year are important when considering what happens to the debt–GDP ratio and the deficit–GDP ratio. If GDP grows at a faster rate than the deficit, the deficit–GDP ratio will decline while the debt–GDP ratio may continue to increase, but at a slower rate than would occur if the deficit and GDP grew at the same rate.

**3.**  The government will operate with a deficit each year and, therefore, the government debt will grow over time. But, because the economy is growing at a faster rate than the growth rate of the deficit, this means that the debt–GDP ratio will fall over time.

## Answers to Module Review Questions

1. **Answer b.** The budget balance, $S_{Government}$, is defined by the equation $S_{Government} = T - G - TR$. In an expansion, tax revenue increases and transfers decrease (both of these changes are the result of automatic stabilizers): for a given level of government spending, the budget balance increases. If the government pursues expansionary fiscal policy while holding everything else constant, this will decrease the budget balance.

2. **Answer d.** Answers (a), (b), and (c) are all incorrect. The multiplier effect from a change in taxes and transfers is smaller than the multiplier effect from a change in government spending and therefore the effect of a change in taxes and transfers on $AD$ will be smaller than an equal change in government spending. When unemployment rises, this leads to lower tax revenue (as income falls in the economy, tax revenue also decreases) and higher expenditures on transfer programs like unemployment compensation: thus, the budget deficit almost always rises when unemployment rises. Answer (d) provides a straightforward definition of the cyclically adjusted budget balance.

3. **Answer a.** When the government spends more than it collects in tax revenue, the government runs a deficit and must acquire additional funds: typically it does this by borrowing the necessary funds. When the government's deficit increases, this adds to the value of the government debt. It is unusual for governments to sell valuable assets to finance their spending programs. When the government spends more than it collects in tax revenue, this causes the budget balance to decrease (recall the budget balance is defined in equation form as $S_{Government} = T - G - TR$).

4. **Answer e.** The fiscal year runs from October 1st through September 30th: so, for example, if the fiscal year runs from October 1, 2001 through September 30, 2002, it is considered fiscal year 2002 (and *not* fiscal year 2001). Public debt is defined as given in answer (b), and the total government debt includes not only the public debt but also the debt that one part of government owes to another part of government.

5. **Answer b.** At the end of fiscal year 2013, the United States' total government debt equaled $16.7 trillion. The public debt for fiscal year 2013 equaled $12.0 trillion, which represented 71% of GDP.

6. **Answer c.** The government debt is not the same as the government deficit. The government deficit is the difference between the amount of money a government spends and the amount of money it collects in tax revenue during a given period of time. The government debt, in contrast, is the total amount of money a government owes at a particular point in time.

7. **Answer d.** Answers (a), (b), and (c) are all possibilities. When the government runs a deficit, it will typically borrow funds. When the government borrows funds, it competes with firms in the financial markets for those funds. This competition may crowd out private investment spending and therefore lead to lower long-run rates of economic growth. In addition, as the deficits persist, the government will find that increasing amounts of its tax revenue must be dedicated to paying the interest expense of the debt, and this means the government must either reduce its spending in other areas or raise more revenue from taxes.

8. **Answer d.** The debt–GDP ratio provides a measure of the size of the government debt relative to the size of the economy: this is a helpful comparison, since the size of the economy provides a measure of the potential tax revenue that can be raised by the government. If the government debt is increasing at the same time that GDP is also increasing, it is possible that the debt–GDP ratio is actually falling, provided that GDP is growing at a faster rate than debt.

9. **Answer e.** Implicit liabilities are promises made by governments that represent future payments that must be made by the governments. Examples in the United States would include transfer programs like Social Security and Medicare. Implicit liabilities are not included in debt statistics typically, nor are they included in the calculation of the debt–GDP ratio.

10. **Answer c.** The demographic issues of the retirement of the baby boom generation will only worsen as this group reaches retirement age and begins drawing on Social Security and Medicare. In addition to these demographic issues related to an aging population, we also need to recognize that health care costs rise faster than other costs in wealthy economies. This will place additional financial pressures on the cost of Medicare and Medicaid. Social Security and Medicare are funded by dedicated taxes: when the taxes generated exceed the level of spending, the excess funds are set aside in trust funds. These funds may then be borrowed by other parts of the government: this borrowing creates an implicit liability where the borrowing by one part of the government reflects a responsibility to repay these dollars back to the trust funds from which they originated. Often the focus is just on the United States debt owed to the public; such a focus understates the true nature of the government debt, since it does not include the implicit liabilities that represent borrowing within the government. Including both public debt and the United States government debt held by trust funds gives a full accounting of the level of debt the government faces.

11. **Answer d.** Answers (a), (b), and (c) are all factual statements about the Social Security program in the United States. These statements are all discussed in the text.

12. **Answer b.** To find the budget balance, recall that this is the same as government saving, or $S_{Government}$, which can be written as $S_{Government} = T - G - TR$. In this example, the budget balance is therefore equal to −$170 billion. When the budget balance is negative, this indicates that the government is running a deficit since the sum of spending plus transfer payments exceed the value of tax revenue.

13. **Answer b.** The government should run a deficit during a recession: in a recession there is too little spending and the government can augment the level of spending by operating with a deficit during the recession. The government should run a surplus during an expansion: in an expansion there is the potential for too much spending and the government can moderate this tendency toward overspending by operating with a surplus during the expansion.

14. **Answer d.** All of the answers are correct. See the text for the discussion of how persistent deficit spending can place financial pressure on future budgets, crowd out investment spending due to government borrowing, and result in the need for higher taxes in order to pay the interest payments on the government debt.

# Defining and Measuring Money

## BEFORE YOU READ THE MODULE

### Summary

This module explores the topic of money. It considers the role of money and the function of money in an economy as well as the different forms of money. The module also examines how to measure the amount of money in the economy.

### Module Objectives

**Objective #1.**   Money is an asset that can easily be used to make purchases of goods and services. Money includes cash, which is liquid, plus other assets that are highly liquid.

- Currency in circulation consists of cash in the hands of the public. Checkable bank deposits are bank accounts that provide check-writing privileges to the owners of these accounts.

- The money supply is the total value of financial assets in the economy that are considered money. There are multiple definitions of the money supply based on the degree of liquidity of the assets included in the particular measure of the money supply.

- Debit cards automatically transfer funds from the buyer's bank account, while credit cards access funds that can be borrowed by the user of the credit card. Debit cards allow the user to access part of the money supply while credit cards create a liability for the user and therefore are not part of the money supply.

**Objective #2.**   Money enhances gains from trade by making indirect exchange possible. In a barter economy, exchange can only occur when there is a double coincidence of wants: you must want the good or service I offer and I must want the good or service you offer. Money, by increasing gains from trade, increases welfare.

**Objective #3.**   Money acts as a medium of exchange, a store of value, and a unit of account.

- An asset that is used to make purchases of goods and services serves as a medium of exchange. Over time many different kinds of assets have served in this role.

- Money acts as a store of value due to its ability to maintain its purchasing power over time, provided there is little inflation.

- Money is a measure people use to set prices and make economic calculations. We refer to this role for money as the unit of account.

**Objective #4.**   The types of money fall into three broad categories.

- Commodity money refers to the use of an asset as a medium of exchange that has useful value independent of its role as a medium of exchange.

- Commodity-backed money refers to items used as a medium of exchange that have no intrinsic value (for example, paper currency) but whose ultimate value rests on the promise that they could be exchanged for valuable goods.

- Fiat money refers to money whose value derives strictly from the government's decree that it be accepted as a means of payment.

**Objective #5.**   The Federal Reserve (the Fed) provides two measures of the money supply. These monetary aggregates—M1 and M2—measure the money supply using different definitions. M1 defines money most narrowly as the sum of currency in circulation, traveler's checks, and checkable bank deposits. M2 is comprised of M1 plus other near-monies, which are financial assets that are easily converted into cash or checkable bank deposits. M1 measures the money supply from a liquidity perspective: all items included in M1 are highly liquid. M2 includes the liquid assets of M1 as well as a group of less liquid assets.

# Key Terms

**money** any asset that can easily be used to purchase goods and services.

**currency in circulation** actual cash held by the public.

**checkable bank deposits** *bank* accounts on which people can write checks.

**money supply** the total value of *financial assets* in the *economy* that are considered *money.*

**medium of exchange** an asset that individuals acquire for the purpose of trading for goods and services rather than for their own consumption.

**store of value** an asset that is a means of holding purchasing power over time.

**unit of account** a measure used to set prices and make economic calculations.

**commodity money** a *medium of exchange* that is a good, normally gold or silver, that has intrinsic value in other uses.

## Key Terms *(continued)*

**commodity-backed money** a *medium of exchange* that has no intrinsic value whose ultimate value is guaranteed by a promise that it can be converted into valuable goods on demand.

**fiat money** a *medium of exchange* whose value derives entirely from its official status as a means of payment.

**monetary aggregate** an overall measure of the *money supply*. The most common monetary aggregates in the United States are M1, which includes *currency in circulation*, travelers' checks, and *checkable bank deposits*, and M2, which includes M1 as well as *near-monies*.

**near-money** a *financial asset* that cannot be directly used as a *medium of exchange* but can be readily converted into cash or *checkable bank deposits*.

## ▮ AFTER YOU READ THE MODULE

## Tip

It is important to understand the distinction between the monetary aggregates, M1 and M2. M1 defines money *narrowly*. It defines money as the sum of currency in circulation, traveler's checks, and checkable bank deposits. M2 defines money more broadly. It takes M1 and adds other near-monies (financial assets or checkable bank deposits).

# WORKED PROBLEMS

1.  In a barter-based economy that does not have a monetary system, any trade typically involves two people who have both identified something they produce as desired or wanted by the other person. This is referred to as a *double coincidence of wants*. You have been asked to provide at least one example of a double coincidence of wants. How does the use of money solve the issue of two people needing to have a double coincidence of wants in order for a transaction to take place between these two people?

**STEP 1:** First review the meaning of *double coincidence of wants*. Provide an example that illustrates this idea.

A *double coincidence of wants* refers to the idea that in order for trade to occur a person must not only produce some kind of good or service that is valuable to others, but she must also find a person who produces some other kind of good or service that is valuable to her. For example, suppose the economy has no monetary system and your economic professor needs a new pair of shoes. She goes to the local cobbler and tells him she needs a pair of shoes. No problem for the cobbler since the cobbler makes shoes. But, the cobbler asks the professor what she can provide in exchange for the pair of shoes. When the professor replies that she has a great lecture on the definition and measurement of money, the cobbler is likely to reply that he has no interest in making the trade. Both parties must want what the other party can provide or else trade does not occur. This is referred to as the *double coincidence of wants*. In this case, there is no double coincidence of wants, so the trade does not occur.

**STEP 2:** Examine how the use of money solves the issue of finding someone who desires what you produce and who produces something you desire.

Let's return to the example provided in Step 1. With a monetary system the economics professor can be compensated with dollars for the lectures and education she provides. She can then use these dollars to purchase the needed shoes: no need to find a cobbler who also wants economics lectures. The cobbler, upon selling the shoes to the economics professor, receives dollars that he can now exchange for other goods and services he desires.

2.   Sally is still a bit confused about the idea that money has certain roles to play in the economy. She has asked you to help her more fully understand the three roles of money in the economy.

**STEP 1:** Identify the three roles of money in the economy.

The text identifies three roles of money in the economy: money as a medium of exchange; money as a store of value; and money as a unit of account.

**STEP 2:** Briefly discuss the role of money as a medium of exchange.

The role of money as a medium of exchange highlights money's use as a way to facilitate transactions. An individual can trade money for a good or service that they desire: money makes this transaction far easier than it would be if the individual were trading goods and services for other goods and services.

**STEP 3:** Briefly discuss the role of money as a store of value.

In order for money to be used as a medium of exchange it must be able to hold its purchasing power over time. Joe will accept money from Larry as payment for a good or service that Joe provides to Larry, provided that Joe has confidence that the money he receives will be able to be used in the future to purchase a similarly valued good or service.

**STEP 4:** Briefly discuss the role of money as a unit of account.

Money also has a role as a unit of account for an economy. Money provides a handy, commonly accepted measure of the value of one good relative to another. One can simply compare the prices of different goods to have a sense of their relative value to one another.

# Problems and Exercises

1. Explain how the use of money increases the gains from trade.

2. For each of the following situations, determine what kind of money—commodity money, commodity-backed money, or fiat money—is being described.

   **a.** Prisoners of war use cigarettes as the monetary unit.

   **b.** When they babysit for other families, young families in Anytown receive paper coupons that can be redeemed for babysitting services. These coupons serve as a monetary unit for these transactions.

   **c.** Two tribes use corn as the monetary unit when trading with one another.

   **d.** In Midtown, the central bank issues paper currency that is fully redeemable in gold or silver.

   **e.** In Uptown, the central bank issues paper currency that the government of Uptown accepts as payment for taxes.

3. Currently in the United States the money supply is large enough that people on average hold over $2,500 in their wallets. Yet, clearly most individuals do not carry that large an amount of money in their wallets. Explain how the money supply could be so large and yet we do not on average hold this amount of dollars per person.

## BEFORE YOU TAKE THE TEST

# Module Review Questions

1. Which of the following statements is true?
   a. The definition of money includes all forms of wealth.
   b. Money is an asset that can be easily used to purchase goods and services.
   c. Money consists of cash, which is liquid, plus other assets that are relatively illiquid.
   d. All of the above are true.
   e. Statements (a) and (b) are both true.
   f. Statements (b) and (c) are both true.

2. Money
   a. increases welfare since it increases gains from trade.
   b. eliminates the need for a "double coincidence of wants" between trading partners.
   c. includes currency in circulation plus checkable deposits.
   d. Answers (a), (b), and (c) are all correct.
   e. Answers (b) and (c) are both correct.

3. Use the following statements to answer the question.
   I. The price of bananas is quoted in dollars rather than in units of apples, and the price of apples is quoted in dollars rather than in units of bananas.
   II. The $100 Sue saved this year will have $100 worth of purchasing power five years from now, provided there is no inflation.
   III. The building contractor said the new roof for our house would cost $6,000.

   Money has three roles in an economy. Statement _____ illustrates the use of money as a medium of exchange; statement _____ illustrates the use of money as a unit of account; and statement _____ illustrates the use of money as a store of value.
   a. III; I; II          c. III; II; I
   b. I; III; II          d. II; III; I

4. Which of the following statements is true?
   a. Fiat money is paper currency issued by the government and redeemable in a valuable asset like gold.
   b. Fiat money is money issued by a ruler and thus is found only in countries with a monarchy.
   c. Commodity money is poor type of money, since it cannot be used in trade even though it is a valuable commodity.
   d. None of the statements is correct.

5. M1 includes
   a. currency in circulation, savings account deposits, and checkable bank deposits.
   b. currency in circulation, traveler's checks, other near-monies, and checkable bank deposits.
   c. currency in circulation, traveler's checks, and checkable bank deposits.
   d. currency in circulation, traveler's checks, checkable bank deposits, and saving account deposits.

6. Which of the following statements is true?
   I. Provided that no one knows that counterfeit dollars are being used, the use of these counterfeit dollars does not hurt anyone in an economy.
   II. The use of counterfeit dollars in an economy reduces the revenues available to pay for the operations of that economy's government.
   III. Counterfeit money is not an issue when the government uses fiat money and not commodity-backed money.
   a. Statement I is true.
   b. Statement II is true.
   c. Statement III is true.
   d. Statements I, II, and III are all true.
   e. Statements II and III are true.

7. To be included in the measure of M1, the asset must be
   a. a near-money.
   b. highly liquid.
   c. money.
   d. either money or some form of wealth.

8. Commodity-backed money
   a. restricts the use of fewer resources than does commodity money.
   b. is money that has no intrinsic value but whose value is guaranteed by a promise that the commodity-backed money can be converted into valuable goods on demand.
   c. is a way for society to provide the functions of money without tying up valuable resources.
   d. Answers (a), (b), and (c) are all correct.

9. Stocks and bonds are
   a. part of M1.
   b. part of M2, but not M1.
   c. not part of M1 or M2 because they are not sufficiently liquid.

## ANSWER KEY

## Answers to Problems and Exercises

1.  Money makes indirect exchange possible, which enhances the possible gains from trade since it eliminates the need for a double coincidence of wants between two trading individuals. Money enables people to trade for what they have to offer and then use the money they receive from selling these goods and services to then purchase the goods and services they want.

2.  **a.** Cigarettes are an example of commodity money since the unit of exchange is a commodity that has intrinsic value in other uses.

    **b.** The paper coupons are an example of commodity-backed money since these paper coupons can be redeemed for a particular commodity: a certain number of hours of babysitting.

    **c.** Corn is an example of commodity money since the unit of exchange is a commodity that has intrinsic value in other uses.

    **d.** This is an example of commodity-backed money since the paper currency can be exchanged for a commodity: gold or silver.

    **e.** This is an example of fiat money since it is not backed by anything other than the government's guarantee: if the government were no longer willing to accept this currency in payment for taxes, it would lose its value as a monetary unit.

3.  Although the money supply divided by the U.S. population suggests that individuals on average hold a very high level of dollars, the reality is that most people carry a considerably smaller amount of dollars. The other dollars are held in business cash registers, and by people not living in the United States since dollars are used by many foreigners, particularly in places where the stability of the national currency is questionable over time.

## Answers to Module Review Questions

1.  **Answer b.** Statement (b) provides a straightforward definition of money. Money includes cash plus other assets that are highly liquid like checking accounts. Money does not include all forms of wealth since some forms of wealth are highly illiquid.

2.  **Answer d.** Statements (a), (b), and (c) are factual statements about money that are all discussed in the text.

3.  **Answer a.** Statement I is an example of money used as a unit of account since it provides a standard measure for the prices of all goods and services in an economy. Statement II is an example of money's role as a store of value: we value money because of its ability to represent purchasing power over time. Statement III provides an example of money as a medium of exchange: the building contractor gives us a price for a particular item.

4.  **Answer d.** Each of these statements is incorrect. Fiat money is money whose value derives entirely from its official status as a means of exchange: this is not limited to countries with monarchies. Fiat money is not redeemable in some other commodity. Commodity money is a more limited form of money than commodity-backed money or fiat money, since it ties up more of an economy's resources to facilitate making transactions rather than using those resources for more productive uses.

5.  **Answer c.** M1 is the narrowest definition of money and includes only currency in circulation, traveler's checks, and checkable bank deposits.

6. **Answer b.** The use of counterfeit money in an economy hurts the ability of that economy's government to generate revenues to pay for government services even if no one in the economy recognizes that counterfeit dollars are being used to make exchanges. Governments cover a small amount of their expenses by issuing new currency to meet the growing demand for this currency. Counterfeit money exacts this cost of the government no matter if the government endorses fiat money or commodity-backed money.

7. **Answer b.** To be included in the measure of M1, the asset must be highly liquid since M1 is defined very narrowly to include only currency in circulation, traveler's checks, and checkable bank deposits. M2, a more broadly defined monetary aggregate, includes near-monies. Wealth is not the same as money and may include assets that are highly illiquid.

8. **Answer d.** Commodity-backed money is something that is used as a medium of exchange that has no intrinsic worth itself (e.g., paper money) but that can be converted into a valuable good on demand. Commodity-backed money reduces the amount of resources used to provide the functions of money since it does not require the circulation and direct use of the commodity in order to serve its various monetary roles. So, for example, if the commodity-backed money is backed by gold and silver, only enough gold and silver must be kept on hand in order to satisfy the demands for those individuals wishing to redeem their commodity-backed money.

9. **Answer c.** M1 is just checkable deposits, traveler's checks, and currency in circulation. M2 includes all of M1 plus other near-monies. Near-monies do not include stocks or bonds because neither of these two types of financial assets are sufficiently liquid.

# module 34(70)

# Banking and Money Creation

## ■ BEFORE YOU READ THE MODULE

## Summary

This module discusses the role of banks in the economy. It explores the reasons for banking regulation as well as the various types of banking regulation. The module also examines how banks create money.

## Module Objectives

**Objective #1.** A T-account is a type of financial spreadsheet that displays an institution's financial position. On the left-hand side of the T-account, the institution's assets and their values are listed; on the right-hand side, the institution's liabilities and their values are listed. Banks hold reserves in order to meet the demand for funds from their depositors. Bank reserves are composed of the currency in the banks' vaults and the bank deposits held by the Federal Reserve (the Fed) in each bank's own account. The reserve ratio is the fraction of bank deposits a bank holds as reserves: in the United States the reserve ratio is regulated by the Fed.

**Objective #2.** Banks receive deposits of funds from their customers and then use these funds to make interest-earning financial transactions. For example, banks make loans to customers and purchase Treasury bills: both financial transactions provide income in the form of interest to the bank.

**Objective #3.** Bank runs occur when many depositors at a bank, fearing a bank failure, simultaneously decide to withdraw their funds. Banks can find themselves in a situation in which they lack the liquidity to satisfy these depositor demands since many of the deposited funds are used to finance relatively illiquid bank loans.

**Objective #4.**  Bank regulation reduces the probability of bank runs.

- The Federal Deposit Insurance Corporation (FDIC) provides deposit insurance, a guarantee by the federal government that depositors will be paid up to a designated maximum amount per account (currently $250,000 per depositor at any given bank) even if the bank fails. When there is deposit insurance, depositors have no incentive to remove their funds from a bank, even if there are rumors that the bank is in financial trouble.

- The existence of deposit insurance creates an incentive problem: banks, knowing they are insured, are apt to engage in overly risky behavior while depositors, knowing they are insured, are inclined to not monitor bank behavior. Capital requirements address this incentive problem by requiring owners of banks to hold more assets than the value of their bank deposits. Should some loans prove bad, the bank will still have assets larger than their deposits: the bank owners, rather than the government, can absorb the loss from the bad loans.

- Bank runs are also prevented by requiring banks to hold a higher reserve ratio than the banks would otherwise choose to hold.

- Banks that are in financial trouble can borrow money from the Fed through an arrangement referred to as the discount window. This enables banks to get funds instead of being forced to sell their assets at prices below their value when confronted by a sudden demand for funds from depositors.

**Objective #5.**  Banks affect the money supply in two ways. First, they remove some money out of circulation by holding currency in their bank vaults and in their reserve accounts at the Fed. Second, banks create money when they accept deposits and make loans.

**Objective #6.**  Excess reserves are those reserves held by a bank that exceed the level of reserves required by the Fed.

- In a simplified model where banks lend out all their excess reserves and borrowers hold their loans as bank deposits and not currency, the increase in bank deposits from lending out the excess reserves equals the excess reserves divided by the required reserve ratio. We can write this money multiplier as $1/rr$, where $rr$ is the required reserve ratio.

- In the real world the money multiplier is smaller than the money multiplier in our simplified model. The monetary base equals the sum of currency in circulation and reserves held by the bank. The monetary base is controlled by the monetary authorities. The money supply equals currency in circulation plus bank deposits. The money multiplier is the ratio of the money supply to the monetary base. The actual money multiplier is smaller than our simple model predicted because a dollar of currency in circulation, unlike a dollar in reserves, does not support multiple dollars of the money supply.

## Key Terms

*Notes*

**bank reserves** currency held by *banks* in their vaults plus their deposits at the Federal Reserve.

**T-account** a simple tool that summarizes a business's financial position by showing, in a single table, the business's assets and liabilities, with assets on the left and liabilities on the right.

## Key Terms *(continued)*

**reserve ratio** the fraction of *bank deposits* that a *bank* holds as reserves. In the United States, the minimum required reserve ratio is set by the Federal Reserve.

**required reserve ratio** the smallest fraction of deposits that the Federal Reserve allows banks to hold.

**bank run** a phenomenon in which many of a *bank*'s depositors try to withdraw their funds due to fears of a bank failure.

**deposit insurance** a guarantee that a *bank*'s depositors will be paid even if the bank can't come up with the funds, up to a maximum amount per account.

**reserve requirements** rules set by the Federal Reserve that set the minimum *reserve ratio* for banks. For *checkable bank deposits* in the United States, the minimum reserve ratio is set at 10%.

**discount window** a protection against *bank runs* in which the Federal Reserve stands ready to lend money to *banks* in trouble.

**excess reserves** a *bank*'s *reserves* over and above the reserves required by law or regulation.

**monetary base** the sum of *currency in circulation* and *bank reserves*.

**money multiplier** the ratio of the *money supply* to the *monetary base*.

## █ AFTER YOU READ THE MODULE

## Tips

**Tip #1.** It is important to understand the definitions of and the distinctions among the monetary base, the money supply, and reserves. The money supply is the value of financial assets in the economy that are considered money: this would include cash in the hands of the public, checkable bank deposits, and traveler's checks, using the narrow definition of the money supply given by the monetary aggregate M1. Bank reserves are composed of the currency that banks hold in their vaults plus their deposits at the Federal Reserve. The monetary base is the sum of currency in circulation and bank reserves. The monetary base is not equal to the money supply: the money supply is larger than the monetary base.

**Tip #2.** It is important to understand the distinction between assets and liabilities. Make sure you clearly understand what an asset and a liability are and then recognize that any financial instrument represents both an asset and a liability. For example, a mortgage represents a liability for the borrower and an asset for the lender; a checking account deposit represents a liability for the bank providing the check service and an asset to the individual depositing the funds.

**Tip #3.**  For any T-account, clearly identify whose perspective is represented in the T-account. T-accounts represent the assets and liabilities of an institution or an individual. When making a T-account, consider whose T-account it represents: this will help you more clearly identify whether the financial instruments you include are assets or liabilities. For example, bank reserves are a liability in the Fed's T-account and an asset in a bank's T-account.

**Tip #4.**  Each T-account must always balance: that is, total assets must equal total liabilities where the total liabilities include capital. If your T-account does not balance, check your entries to find your error.

# WORKED PROBLEMS

1.  Your professor instructs you to create a T-account of your financial situation. In this T-account, you should list your assets and your liabilities and then you should compute your net worth. Your professor explains that net worth is simply total assets minus total liabilities. Your professor also instructs you to interview someone who is at least 20 years older than you are and create a T-account that lists this person's assets, liabilities, and net worth. How might your T-account differ from the T-account of this older person? Why do you anticipate this difference?

**STEP 1:** Review the definition of a T-account as well as the definitions of *assets, liabilities,* and *net worth.* Create a T-account form that you will be able to use both for yourself and when you interview the other person.

A T-account provides a summary of the financial position of an individual or firm. On the left side, assets are listed: these are all the items that the individual or firm owns that are valuable. The value of these assets is listed along with the name of the asset. On the right side, liabilities are listed: these are all the items that the individual or firm owes. The value of these liabilities is listed along with the name of the liability. Net worth, the difference between assets and liabilities, is listed on the right side of the T-account: the sum of the value of total liabilities and net worth always equals the value of total assets.

Here is a T-account form that you can use when constructing your own T-account or the T-account of the individual you have chosen to interview.

| Assets | Liabilities |
|---|---|
|  | Net worth |
|  | Value of total liabilities |
| Value of total assets | Value of total liabilities + net worth |

**STEP 2:** Make a list of all of those items, both physical and financial, that you own that are valuable. Make a list of all of those items, both physical and financial, that you owe to others or that represent a debt.

Enter the items that you own on the left side of your T-account along with their value. Sum the values together to get the value of total assets.

Enter the items that you owe or the debt that you have on the right-hand side of your T-account along with their value. Sum the values together to get the value of total liabilities.

Now compare the value of your total assets to the value of your total liabilities to get a measure of your net worth. It is possible that you have a negative net worth: if you have not had a chance to work full-time and you have taken out student loans, your liabilities may well exceed your assets.

Here is an example of a possible T-account for a mythical student, Joe. Joe is 20 years old and is a full-time student. He owns a car that is worth $2,000, he has $500 in a checking account, and he has student loans equal to $10,000. This is his T-account:

| Assets | | Liabilities | |
| --- | --- | --- | --- |
| Car | $2,000 | Student loan | $10,000 |
| Checking account | $500 | | |
| | | Net worth | −$7,500 |
| Total value of assets | $2,500 | Total liabilities + net worth | $2,500 |

**STEP 3:** Find a person to interview who will be comfortable discussing his or her financial position.

Make a list of the person's assets and liabilities and the dollar value of each item. Construct the person's T-account and calculate his or her net worth.

Answers in Step 3 will vary for each person since each person's financial situation is unique to him or her.

**STEP 4:** Compare and contrast the two T-accounts.

It is likely that the older individual has a positive and greater net worth than does the student. This is due to the fact that older people have had more time to accumulate assets, have likely saved for retirement, have had a full-time job for a longer period of time than the student, and have likely had time to pay off some of their debt, particularly educational debt.

2.    Suppose that there is only one bank, First National Bank, in your economy. First National Bank maintains its required reserves but never holds excess reserves. The required reserve ratio in this economy is 10% of checkable deposits. Furthermore, suppose that everyone in this community banks at this bank and that all of their transactions are made using checks or their debit cards. No one carries currency in this economy. The following tables provide the initial T-accounts of the central bank of this economy as well as of First National Bank. Suppose that the central bank in this economy purchases $50,000 worth of Treasury bills from First National Bank. How will this affect the money supply in this economy? Make sure you indicate what the initial money supply is before the central bank makes this purchase and what the final money supply is once all adjustments to this purchase have occurred. What is the value of the money multiplier in this economy? For this example, assume that the difference between First National Bank's assets and its liabilities stays constant.

Initial situation at the central bank:

| Assets | | Liabilities | |
| --- | --- | --- | --- |
| Treasury bills | $20,000 | Reserves of First National Bank | $20,000 |
| | | | |
| | | | |

Initial situation at First National Bank:

| Assets | | Liabilities | |
|---|---|---|---|
| Reserves at the central bank | $20,000 | Checkable deposits | $200,000 |
| Treasury bills and other loans | $180,000 | | |
| | | | |

**STEP 1:** Start by thinking about how the T-accounts for the central bank and First National Bank will change when the central bank purchases $50,000 worth of Treasury bills. Do not try to analyze more than just the initial change in the T-accounts.

When the central bank purchases Treasury bills, its assets will increase. But the central bank must pay for these new assets, and the simplest way to do this is for the central bank to simply credit the reserve account of First National Bank with the value of the purchase. The central bank's T-account looks like the following:

| Assets | | Liabilities | |
|---|---|---|---|
| Treasury bills | $70,000 | Reserves of First National Bank | $70,000 |
| | | | |
| | | | |

Notice that the central bank's purchase of Treasury bills alters both the asset and the liability entries for its T-account.

First National Bank's T-account is also altered by this transaction. First National Bank has $50,000 less in Treasury bills but $50,000 more in its reserve account. The T-account for First National bank follows.

| Assets | | Liabilities | |
|---|---|---|---|
| Reserves at the central bank | $70,000 | Checkable deposits | $200,000 |
| Treasury bills and other loans | $130,000 | | |
| | | | |

Notice that First National Bank now has excess reserves. First National Bank has $70,000 in reserves, but it needs only $20,000 to meet its required reserve. First National Bank will want to lend out these excess reserves in order to earn interest.

**STEP 2:** Calculate the level of checkable deposits that First National Bank can support if it holds $70,000 in reserves. Once you have calculated this, provide a new T-account showing First National Bank's financial position once all adjustments to the central bank's purchase have occurred.

A simple way to think about this is to realize that required reserves equal the product of the required reserve ratio and the level of checkable deposits. In this example, you know the level of reserves and the required reserve ratio, but you do not know the level of checkable deposits. Thus, $70,000 = (0.10)(checkable deposits), or checkable deposits equal $700,000.

| Assets | | Liabilities | |
|---|---|---|---|
| Reserves at the central bank | $70,000 | Checkable deposits | $700,000 |
| Treasury bills and other loans | $630,000 | | |
| | | | |

**STEP 3:** Compare the level of the initial money supply to the level of the money supply after all adjustments to the central bank's purchase of $50,000 in Treasury bills have occurred.

The money supply is defined as currency in circulation plus checkable deposits. In this example, there is no currency in circulation since all transactions are made with checks or with debit cards. The money supply initially is $200,000, and the money supply after the full adjustment to the central bank's purchase is $700,000. The money supply increases by $500,000.

**STEP 4:** Calculate the value of the money multiplier in this example.

The money multiplier is equal to [1/(required reserve ratio)], or in this example, 1/0.1, which is equal to 10. In this example, the central bank increased the amount of reserves in the banking system by $50,000 when it purchased the Treasury bills. This led to the money supply increasing by $500,000: the change in the money supply equals the product of the money multiplier and the change in reserves. That is, $500,000 = (10)($50,000).

3.  The government's provision of deposit insurance for checkable deposits is often cited as an example of government intervention that helps stabilize the financial system by eliminating or at least vastly reducing the probability of bank runs. Is there any incentive problem associated with the provision of deposit insurance? Discuss how deposit insurance reduces the risk of bank runs but creates a different kind of problem. How does regulation address the incentive problem created by deposit insurance?

**STEP 1:** Discuss what a bank run is and why provision of deposit insurance by the government eliminates bank runs.

A bank run is when bank depositors try to withdraw their funds due to fears that the bank may fail. If a sufficient number of depositors seek their funds, the bank will fail, since the bank will not have adequate funds on hand to meet all of these demands. In addition, the failure of one bank may lead to other banks failing as depositors at these other banks lose faith in their own bank's solvency.

   When the government provides deposit insurance this means that even if the bank fails, the depositor will not lose his or her deposit. Deposit insurance thus protects the banking system from bank runs.

**STEP 2:** Discuss the incentive problem that is created by banks once deposit insurance is in effect. In your answer, provide one method used by regulators to deal with this incentive problem.

Deposit insurance creates an incentive problem, since once people's deposits are insured, they have little incentive to actually monitor what their bank does. Banks will often take riskier positions than would be considered optimal from the perspective of the taxpayers who will have to cover the deposits should the bank fail. One way to reduce this incentive problem is to require banks to provide a minimum level of capital that provides a buffer against bad loans.

**4.** The Federal Reserve has three monetary policy tools: the required reserve ratio, the discount rate, and open-market operations. Briefly describe each of these tools and then comment on each tool's usefulness in controlling the money supply in the economy.

**STEP 1:** Review what the required reserve ratio is and how it can affect the money supply. Then explain why the Federal Reserve does not rely on this monetary policy tool to change the money supply.

The required reserve ratio refers to the percentage of checkable deposits that a bank must hold in its reserve account. The higher the required reserve ratio, the smaller will be the money multiplier. If the Federal Reserve wanted to alter the money supply using the required reserve ratio, it could either raise this ratio to reduce the money supply or lower this ratio to increase the money supply. However, changing the required reserve ratio is administratively costly to banks because they must adjust their balance sheets to meet the new required reserve levels. The Federal Reserve rarely changes the required reserve ratio.

**STEP 2:** Review what the discount rate is and how it can affect the money supply. Then explain why the Federal Reserve does not rely on this monetary policy tool to change the money supply.

The discount rate refers to the interest rate that the Federal Reserve charges banks that borrow funds from the Federal Reserve. Typically the Federal Reserve sets the discount rate above the federal funds rate: banks will find it cheaper to borrow funds from other banks than to borrow funds from the Federal Reserve at the discount window. If the Federal Reserve wanted to change the money supply via the discount rate, it could lower the spread between the discount rate and the federal funds rate: this would effectively reduce the cost of being short on reserves, and banks would therefore increase their borrowing. This action by banks to the reduced spread will cause the money supply to increase. In contrast, an increase in the spread between the discount rate and the federal funds rate will cause the money supply to decrease. The Federal Reserve does not try to manage the level of the money supply via the discount rate, however, because this method is not very flexible, nor is it easy to fine-tune this method to ensure that the appropriate level of the money supply is achieved.

**STEP 3:** Review what open-market operations are and how they can affect the money supply. Then explain why the Federal Reserve relies on this monetary policy tool to change the money supply.

Open-market operations refer to the buying and selling of Treasury bills by the Federal Reserve in the open market. This is the Federal Reserve's primary monetary policy tool because it is flexible, can easily be fine-tuned to get precisely the effect the Federal Reserve desires, and can be implemented at relatively low administrative cost. When the Federal Reserve purchases Treasury bills it injects new reserves into the financial system, and via the money multiplier process these new reserves lead to a higher level of the money supply. When the Federal Reserve sells Treasury bills it removes reserves from the financial system, and via the money multiplier process this reduction in reserves leads to an even greater reduction in the money supply.

# Problems and Exercises

1. Suppose Fantasia has a single bank that initially has $10,000 of deposits, reserves of $2,000, and loans of $8,000. To simplify our example, we will assume that bank capital equals zero. Furthermore, Fantasia's central bank has a required reserve of 10% of deposits. All monetary transactions are made by check: no one in Fantasia uses currency.

   a. Construct a T-account depicting the initial situation in Fantasia. In your T-account, make sure you differentiate between required and excess reserves and that your T-account's assets equal its liabilities.

   b. Explain how you calculated the level of excess reserves in Fantasia.

   c. Suppose the bank in Fantasia lends these excess reserves [the amount of excess reserves you calculated in part (b)] until it reaches the point where its excess reserves equal zero. How does this change the T-account?

   d. Did the money supply in Fantasia change when the bank loaned out the excess reserves? Explain your answer.

   e. What is the value of the money multiplier in Fantasia? Using the money multiplier, compute the change in deposits.

2. Bank deposit insurance provides insurance for depositors so that they do not have to worry about losing money they have deposited into insured banks. This seems like a really good protection to have. Is there a downside to this protection? Explain your answer fully.

3.  How does a requirement that banks hold more assets than liabilities help to reduce the banks' tendency to engage in riskier investment behavior than is optimal from the government's point of view?

## BEFORE YOU TAKE THE TEST

## Module Review Questions

1.  In a bank's T-account, which of the following is true?
    a. Joe's checking account deposit is treated as an asset.
    b. Ellen's car loan is counted as a liability.
    c. bank deposits at the Fed are an asset for the bank.
    d. assets exactly equal liabilities when there are positive capital requirements.

    Use the following T-account for a bank to answer the next two questions.

    | Assets | | Liabilities | |
    |---|---|---|---|
    | Required reserves | $100 | Deposits | $1,000 |
    | Loans | $400 | | |
    | Treasury bills | $800 | | |

2.  Given this T-account and assuming the bank holds no excess reserves, what is the required reserve ratio?
    a. 10%
    b. 40%
    c. 80%
    d. 1%

3.  Given this T-account, how much capital does this bank currently hold?
    a. zero
    b. $300
    c. $400
    d. $500
    e. $1,300

4. Bank runs
   a. can be reduced by providing deposit insurance, requiring banks to hold significant amounts of capital, and mandating required reserves.
   b. are often caused by rumor and the fear that other people will withdraw their funds.
   c. when rumored, may significantly impact the prices banks receive when they sell assets to increase their liquidity.
   d. Answers (a), (b), and (c) are all correct.

5. Banks affect the money supply
   a. when they take deposited currency out of circulation and deposit it into their bank vaults.
   b. when they lend their excess reserves to their customers.
   c. when a customer from one bank writes a check to a customer of another bank who deposits that check into his or her checking account.
   d. All of the above answers are true.
   e. Answers (a) and (b) are correct.

6. The monetary base consists of
   a. currency in circulation plus bank deposits.
   b. bank deposits plus bank reserves.
   c. bank deposits, bank reserves, and currency in circulation.
   d. currency in circulation plus bank reserves.

7. In a simple banking system in which banks hold no excess reserves and all funds are kept as bank deposits, then
   a. the money multiplier equals 1 divided by the required reserve ratio.
   b. total deposits will equal reserves multiplied by the reciprocal of the required reserve ratio.
   c. $1 increase in excess reserves will increase deposits by an amount equal to 1 divided by the required reserve ratio.
   d. Answers (a), (b), and (c) are all correct.

8. Bank regulation is helpful in reducing bank runs since bank regulation typically
   a. requires banks to keep a minimum required reserve ratio.
   b. provides deposit insurance so that depositors have little incentive to remove their money from a bank even when there are rumors about the bank's soundness.
   c. sets capital requirements to help align the incentive problem for banks so that they will have a lower tendency to engage in overly risky investment behavior.
   d. Answers (a), (b), and (c) are all correct.
   e. Answers (a) and (b) are both correct.
   f. Answers (a) and (c) are both correct.
   g. Answers (b) and (c) are both correct.

9. Suppose the required reserve ratio initially is 10% of bank deposits and is increased by the Fed to 20% of bank deposits. Holding everything else constant, this will
   a. reduce the size of the money multiplier.
   b. cause the banking system to contract the level of bank deposits in the banking system.
   c. change the value of the money multiplier from 10 to 5.
   d. Answers (a), (b), and (c) are all correct.

10. Bank reserves include
    a. the currency banks hold in their vaults.
    b. bank deposits held at the Federal Reserve.
    c. outstanding loans that the bank has made to borrowers.
    d. the bank capital that the owners of the bank provide.
    e. Answers (a), (b), (c), and (d) are all correct.
    f. Answers (a) and (b) are both correct.
    g. Answers (a), (b), and (d) are correct.

11. Which of the following statements is true?
    I. Banks decrease the money supply because they remove some currency from circulation when they place currency in their bank vaults or deposit currency at the Federal Reserve.
    II. Banks increase the money supply when they accept deposits and then make loans with some of the money that has been deposited.
    a. Statement I is true.
    b. Statement II is true.
    c. Statements I and II are true.
    d. Neither statement I nor II is true.

## ◼ ANSWER KEY

# Answers to Problems and Exercises

**1. a.**

| Assets | | Liabilities | |
|---|---|---|---|
| Required reserves | $1,000 | Deposits | $10,000 |
| Excess reserves | $1,000 | | |
| Loans | $8,000 | | |
| Total assets | $10,000 | Total liabilities | $10,000 |

**b.** Excess reserves are equal to total reserves minus required reserves, or $1,000. To find required reserves, multiply deposits by the required reserve ratio [($10,000)(0.1) = $1,000].

**c.**

| Assets | | Liabilities | |
|---|---|---|---|
| Required reserves | $2,000 | Deposits | $20,000 |
| Excess reserves | $0 | | |
| Loans | $18,000 | | |
| Total assets | $20,000 | Total liabilities | $20,000 |

**d.** Yes, since the money supply is defined as bank deposits plus currency in circulation. Since Fantasia has no currency in circulation, we need only consider what happens to bank deposits. Initially, bank deposits equaled $10,000 and after the lending out of all the excess reserves, bank deposits equal $20,000. Thus, the money supply increased by $10,000.

**e.** The money multiplier equals $1/rr$, or 10, in this example, since no one holds currency and the bank does not hold excess reserves. The change in deposits equals the money multiplier times the change in reserves or, in this case, the change in deposits equals $(1/0.1)($1,000)$, or $10,000.

**2.** Although deposit insurance protects individual depositors so that they do not have to fear losing the dollars they deposit in insured institutions, it does create a situation in which banks may engage in riskier business practices than is optimal from the taxpayers' perspective. Depositors, once they are insured, do not need to monitor the actions their banking institution engages in, which may lead to a situation in which the institutions engage in riskier investment activities than is optimal. The banks have an incentive to engage in risky investments since the owners of the bank will benefit if the investment proves profitable and can pass on the loss to the government if the investment proves unprofitable.

**3.** When a bank holds more assets than liabilities, this means that the bank faces a potential loss for any investment that proves unprofitable. Another way of thinking about this is to realize that if some of the banks' loans prove to be bad and the banks take a loss, the banks will still have assets larger than their deposits. This reduces the probability that the government will need to step in and provide funds to cover depositors' funds.

# Answers to Module Review Questions

1. **Answer c.** Joe's checking account balance is an asset from Joe's perspective but a liability from the bank's perspective since the bank is liable, or owes money, to Joe. Ellen's car loan is a liability for Ellen since it represents something she owes to someone else, while it represents an asset to the bank since it represents a promise to pay the bank a certain amount of money. When the bank deposits funds at the Federal Reserve, this deposit is an asset for the bank and a liability for the Federal Reserve. If there are positive capital requirements, then assets are greater than liabilities.

2. **Answer a.** The required reserve ratio is equal to required reserves divided by checkable deposits: in this example, this bank holds 10% of its checkable deposits as required reserves.

3. **Answer b.** The bank's capital is the difference between its total assets and total liabilities. In this case, the bank's assets sum to $1,300 while the liabilities total $1,000. The difference, $300, is the bank's capital.

4. **Answer d.** Even the rumor of a potential bank run can result in dramatic decreases in the value of a bank's assets. Rumor and fear can combine to create a self-fulfilling prophecy: depositors fear that the behavior of other depositors will drive even a financially stable bank into instability. The potential for bank runs can be eliminated through effective regulation that provides deposit insurance while mandating bank capital requirements and a designated reserve ratio.

5. **Answer e.** Banks affect the money supply, or the sum of currency in circulation plus bank deposits, when they hold currency in their bank vaults, thus reducing the total amount of currency in circulation. Banks also affect the money supply when they lend out their excess reserves and create additional bank deposits. Check-writing and check-cashing do not affect the money supply since they do not change the overall level of currency in circulation plus bank deposits.

6. **Answer d.** The monetary base consists of currency in circulation and bank reserves, while the money supply equals currency in circulation plus bank deposits.

7. **Answer d.** All of the statements restate the relationship between excess reserves and the required reserve ratio and their impact on the level of bank deposits. We can write this relationship as the change in bank deposits equals excess reserves times ($1/rr$). Recall that $1/rr$ is simply the reciprocal of the required reserve ratio.

8. **Answer d.** The text provides a description of these three components of bank regulation: deposit insurance, capital requirements, and reserve requirements. All three of these aspects of bank regulation help to reduce the probability of a bank run.

9. **Answer d.** When the required reserve ratio increases, the money multiplier, defined as $1/rr$, must necessarily decrease. If the required reserve ratio equals 10%, the money multiplier equals 10; and if the required reserve ratio equals 20%, the money multiplier equals 5. When the reserve requirement increases, banks find that their reserves' ability to support bank deposits decreases, which leads banks to contract the level of bank deposits in the banking system.

10. **Answer f.** Bank reserves are composed of the currency in bank vaults and the bank deposits held at the Federal Reserve. Bank reserves are not part of currency in circulation.

11. **Answer c.** Both of these statements are true. On the one hand, banks decrease the money supply when they remove currency from circulation and place that currency in their vaults or deposit it at the Federal Reserve; on the other hand, banks increase the money supply by accepting deposits and then lending out a portion of these deposited dollars to borrowers.

# The Federal Reserve System

## ■ BEFORE YOU READ THE MODULE

## Summary

This module discusses the history and structure of the Federal Reserve System. In addition, the module examines how the Federal Reserve has responded to major financial crises.

## Module Objectives

**Objective #1.** Central banks oversee and regulate the banking system and they control the monetary base. In the United States the central bank is the Federal Reserve. The Federal Reserve consists of a Board of Governors and 12 regional Federal Reserve Banks. The Board of Governors has seven members including the Chairman of the Federal Reserve.

- The Federal Reserve Bank of New York carries out open-market operations in which the Fed buys or sells some of the existing stock of U.S. Treasury bills.

- Monetary policy decisions are made by the Federal Open Market Committee (FOMC), whose members include the Board of Governors and five of the regional bank presidents. The president of the Federal Reserve Bank of New York is always a member of the FOMC while the other 11 presidents rotate on and off the FOMC.

- The Fed's organizational structure creates an organization that is accountable to the voting public while simultaneously insulated from short-term political pressures.

**Objective #2.** There are many different central banks in the world today. For example, the European Central Bank is the central bank for the members of the European Union. Like the Federal Reserve, the European Central Bank is answerable to voters while protected from short-term political pressures.

**Objective #3.** Financial crises over the course of U.S. history have resulted in legislation as well as awareness of policy issues with regard to financial markets and institutions.

- After the financial crisis of 1907, legislation was passed creating the Federal Reserve (the Fed). The Fed was given responsibility for centralizing the holding of reserves, inspecting banks, and providing a sufficiently elastic money supply in response to changing economic conditions.

- During the Great Depression in the early 1930s, bank runs were a problem and legislation was passed creating federal deposit insurance to help eliminate these bank runs. In addition, during this time period the federal government recapitalized banks by lending to them and purchasing shares of the banks. In 1933, banks were separated into two classes of banks: commercial banks and investment banks.

- In the 1980s, the S&L Crisis revealed tendencies for banking institutions to engage in overly speculative transactions and pointed out the need not only for federal deposit insurance, but also regulation with regard to capital requirements and reserve requirements.

- In the 1990s, some firms—using huge amounts of leverage—speculated in global markets, and this speculation led to financial crises in Asia and Russia. During these crises there were particular problems associated with deleveraging wherein large firms (in particular LTCM) sold their assets to cover their losses; this selling of assets created balance sheet problems for other firms around the world. These problems in turn led to the failure of various credit markets and required intervention by the New York Fed to get these world credit markets functioning.

- In the mid-2000s, the housing bubble in the United States—accompanied by the securitization of subprime lending—led to massive losses by banks and other nonbank financial institutions once the housing bubble burst. This financial crisis required intervention by the U.S. government to expand its lending to bank and nonbank institutions as well as the provision of bank capital through government purchase of bank shares. By 2008, it was clear that this latest financial crisis would result in the creation of a wider safety net and broader regulation of the financial sector.

## Key Terms

**central bank** an institution that oversees and regulates the banking system and controls the *monetary base*.

**commercial bank** a *bank* that accepts deposits and is covered by *deposit insurance*.

**investment bank** a *bank* that trades in *financial assets* and is not covered by *deposit insurance*.

**savings and loans (thrifts)** deposit-taking *banks*, usually specialized in issuing home loans.

**leverage** the degree to which a financial institution is financing its investments with borrowed funds.

**balance sheet effects** the reduction in a firm's net worth from falling asset prices.

**vicious cycle of deleveraging** the sequence of events that takes place when a *firm's* asset sales to cover losses produce negative *balance sheet effects* on other firms and force creditors to call in their *loans*, thus forcing sales of more assets and causing further declines in asset prices.

## Key Terms *(continued)*

**subprime lending** lending to home buyers who don't meet the usual criteria for borrowing.

**securitization** the pooling of loans and mortgages made by a financial institution and the sale of shares in such a pool to other investors.

## AFTER YOU READ THE MODULE

## Tips

**Tip #1.** It is important to realize that financial crises do occur in the economy. A brief review of the history of financial crises in the United States should help reinforce this idea.

**Tip #2.** The creation of a central bank with power to regulate the financial system in the economy can reduce the occurrence of financial crises. Review the structure and history of the Federal Reserve System in order to appreciate its role in managing the financial system.

## WORKED PROBLEMS

1. The structure of the Federal Reserve Bank is a complicated one that is purposefully designed to be both accountable to the voting public as well as insulated from short-term political pressure. Briefly discuss how the structure of the Federal Reserve Bank is able to accomplish these two goals.

**STEP 1:** Discuss the aspects of the Federal Reserve Bank's structure that makes it accountable to the voting public.

The Federal Reserve consists of 12 district Federal Reserve Banks, which are geographically dispersed throughout the United States, and the Board of Governors, located in Washington, DC. The Board of Governors has seven members that are appointed by the President and confirmed by the Senate. It is felt that the Board of Governors is accountable to the voting public since the President and Senate are elected by the public and, therefore, subject to public approval.

**STEP 2:** Discuss the aspects of the Federal Reserve Bank's structure that insulates it from short-term political pressure.

The seven members of the Board of Governors are appointed for long terms (four years for the Chair of the Federal Reserve and 14 years for the rest of the Governors). The length of these terms is thought to protect the Board of Governors from short-term political pressure since Congress and the President cannot alter the make-up of the Board of Governors over a short period, but must instead work with the Board of Governors as it exists.

**2.** You have been asked to identify common characteristics of the Financial Crisis of 1907, the S&L Crisis of the 1980s, and the Financial Crisis of 2008.

**STEP 1:** Review your textbook's description of these three financial crises.

**STEP 2:** Identify any common characteristics to these three crises.

All three of these financial crises involved financial institutions that were less heavily regulated than deposit-taking financial institutions. The three financial crises also involved excess speculation. In addition, in each instance the federal government was reluctant to take action to address the financial crisis until substantial damage had been done to the economy.

## Problems and Exercises

**1.** Financial panics have been a relatively common occurrence in U.S. history. Based upon the information provided in the text on financial crises, answer the following questions.

    **a.** During the panic of 1907, why did the failure of Knickerbocker Trust lead to bank runs among other trusts?

    **b.** As a result of the panic of 1907, the Federal Reserve Act was passed in 1913 creating the Federal Reserve. What did the legislature hope to accomplish with the creation of the Federal Reserve?

    **c.** Why were there more bank runs during the Great Depression?

    **d.** The text includes a discussion of the S&L Crisis of the 1980s and, in this discussion, the text mentions "new freedom did not bring with it increased oversight." Explain what the text meant by this statement and then explain how this statement helps us understand the S&L Crisis of the 1980s.

    **e.** How was the Financial Crisis of 2008 similar to other financial crises experienced in the United States?

## ◼ BEFORE YOU TAKE THE TEST

# Module Review Questions

**1.** Which of the following statements is true?

    a. Americans increased their holdings of currency between 1929 and 1933.

    b. As Americans withdrew currency from the banking system between 1929 and 1933, there was an increase in bank deposits as banks lent funds to customers who lacked adequate funding.

    c. M1 fell sharply between 1929 and 1933, as the decline in currency holding by the public was much greater than the decline in bank deposits.

    d. All of the answers are correct.

    e. Answers (a) and (b) are both true.

    f. Answers (a) and (c) are both true.

**2.** Which of the following statements is true?

    I. With respect to the United States and its economic history, the Financial Crisis of 2008 is an event that is unlike any other event in U.S. history.

    II. The U.S. economy is never subject to financial crisis.

    III. Financial crisis in a country usually results in legislation providing for greater financial regulation.

    a. Statement I is true.

    b. Statement II is true.

    c. Statement III is true.

    d. Statements I and II are true.

**3.** The Financial Crisis of 2008 can be characterized as a financial crisis with

    a. excessive speculation particularly in the housing market.

    b. a failure to regulate some of the involved institutions.

    c. inadequate intervention by the government when the crisis first appeared.

    d. excessive amounts of leverage in use by some of the involved firms.

    e. Answers (a), (b), (c), and (d) are all correct.

**4.** Holding everything else constant, in our simple banking model, the greater the required reserve ratio, the

    a. greater the effect on the monetary base.

    b. greater the effect on the money supply for any given change in the monetary base.

    c. greater the money multiplier.

    d. smaller the money multiplier.

    e. Answers (a) and (c) are both correct.

    f. Answers (a) and (d) are both correct.

    g. Answers (b) and (c) are both correct.

    h. Answers (b) and (d) are both correct.

## ANSWER KEY

## Answers to Problems and Exercises

1.  **a.** The failure of Knickerbocker Trust led to bank runs among other trusts because of rumors about these other institutions. Trusts, which were less regulated at the time, also opted not to join the New York Clearinghouse. Over time the trusts speculated in real estate and the stock market until 1907 when Knickerbocker Trust was the first trust to suffer massive losses due to unsuccessful stock market speculation.

    **b.** The Federal Reserve was meant to create a financial system in which all deposit-taking institutions would be forced to hold adequate reserves. In addition, the legislative act that created it made provision for all deposit-taking institutions covered by the Federal Reserve to undergo inspection by regulators.

    **c.** Even with the creation of the Federal Reserve, there were still problems with bank runs since it was possible for banks to hold fewer reserves than the value of their total deposits. The Glass-Steagall Act of 1932 created federal deposit insurance and increased the ability of banks to borrow from the Federal Reserve. The creation of federal deposit insurance effectively ended the problem of bank runs since depositors no longer had to fear losing their deposits.

    **d.** Prior to the S&L Crisis of the 1980s, the S&Ls were covered by federal deposit insurance and tightly regulated. During the 1970s, high inflation meant that S&Ls found it increasingly difficult to maintain the level of deposits they needed in order to make long-term mortgages. In addition, the high inflation rates eroded the value of the S&L assets. Congress passed legislation designed to help S&Ls respond to the problem of insufficient deposits and eroding asset values: this legislation, however, enabled S&Ls to undertake riskier investments. Unfortunately, the legislation gave the S&Ls greater investment freedom but it failed to consider what the appropriate level of oversight would be for this increased freedom. Thus some S&Ls engaged in riskier investments than was optimal from the government's point of view since the government ultimately had to cover any losses to depositors.

    **e.** The financial crisis of 2008 shared many commonalities with other financial crises from other periods of time. Like the Panic of 1907, the financial crisis of 2008 involved excessive speculation as well as institutions that were not as strictly regulated as depository institutions. As in the Great Depression, the financial crisis of 2008 involved a federal government that was reluctant to take action until the level of financial loss was very large.

## Answers to Module Review Questions

1.  **Answer a.** As banks failed in the period 1929 to 1933, many Americans withdrew their bank deposits from the banking system due to their fear that more banks would fail. As bank deposits were withdrawn, bank reserves were lowered, which reduced the capacity of the banking system to support bank deposits: bank deposits fell sharply. M1 did fall during this period due to the decrease in bank deposits being much greater than the increase in currency in circulation.

2.  **Answer c.** Over the course of its history, the United States has experienced numerous financial crises, with each crisis typically resulting in a mandate for greater regulation of the financial market.

3.  **Answer e.** All of these statements are true, and they are discussed in the text. As you read this section, notice the similarities and comparisons that the authors make among various financial crises.

4.  **Answer d.** Since the money multiplier is defined as $1/rr$, when the required reserve ratio increases, the money multiplier decreases, holding everything else constant. The required reserve ratio does not affect the monetary base, but, for a given change in the monetary base, the larger the required reserve ratio the smaller the effect of the change in the monetary base on the money supply.

# 36 (72)

# The Federal Reserve and Monetary Policy

## BEFORE YOU READ THE MODULE

## Summary

In this module there is a discussion of the functions of the Federal Reserve System as well as a description of the monetary policy tools available to the system. The module discusses these monetary policy tools and then examines how these monetary policy tools affect the money supply.

## Module Objectives

**Objective #1.** There are four primary functions of the Federal Reserve: provide financial services to depository institutions, supervise and regulate banks and other financial institutions, maintain the stability of the financial system, and conduct monetary policy.

**Objective #2.** The Federal Reserve (the Fed) possesses three monetary policy tools: the reserve requirement, the discount rate, and open-market operations.

- The reserve requirement sets the minimum level of reserves each bank must hold. Penalties are assessed on banks that fail to meet the required reserve ratio on average over a two-week period. The Fed seldom changes the required reserve ratio.

- The discount rate is the interest rate banks must pay the Fed if they borrow additional reserves from the Fed. Banks that are in need of additional reserves usually borrow these reserves from other banks in the federal funds market. The federal funds market interest rate, the federal funds rate, is determined by supply and demand. The Fed typically sets the discount rate above the federal funds rate to discourage bank borrowing from the Fed. Normally the discount rate is set one percentage point above the federal funds rate, but starting in the fall of 2008 the Fed, in response to the financial crisis, reduced the spread between the discount rate and the federal funds rate.

- Open-market operations are the Fed's most important monetary policy tool. The Fed possesses both assets and liabilities: its liabilities consist of bank reserves, both deposited at the Fed and in bank vaults, and currency in circulation. In other words, the Fed's liabilities are equal to the monetary base.

- When the FOMC directs the Federal Reserve Bank of New York to purchase Treasury bills, it effectively increases the amount of reserves in the banking system by crediting the commercial banks that sell the Treasury bills with additional reserves. These additional reserves start the money multiplier process, which leads the additional reserves to support a higher level of bank deposits. The money supply increases.

- When the FOMC directs the Federal Reserve Bank of New York to sell Treasury bills, it effectively decreases the amount of reserves in the banking system: commercial banks that purchase these Treasury bills pay for them when the Fed debits their reserve accounts at the Fed. This reduction in reserves starts the money multiplier process, which results in these reduced reserves supporting a lower level of bank deposits. The money supply decreases.

- The Fed can create the funds it needs to purchase Treasury bills. Thus, the Fed can create a monetary base at its own discretion. In addition, the Fed earns interest from the Treasury bills it holds: this interest is returned to the Treasury and provides a source of revenue to the Treasury.

## Key Terms

**federal funds market** the *financial market* that allows *banks* that fall short of *reserve requirements* to borrow funds from banks with *excess reserves*.

**federal funds rate** the *interest rate* at which funds are borrowed and lent in the *federal funds market*.

**discount rate** the rate of interest the Federal Reserve charges on loans to *banks* that fall short of *reserve requirements*.

**open-market operation** a purchase or sale of U.S. Treasury bills by the Federal Reserve, normally through a transaction with a *commercial bank*.

*Notes*

## ■ AFTER YOU READ THE MODULE

## Tip

Remember that when the Fed purchases Treasury bills it injects reserves into the banking system and this increases the money supply. When the Fed sells Treasury bills, it removes reserves from the banking system and this decreases the money supply.

1. Marty knows you have been studying macroeconomics during this semester and he keeps reading about the Federal Reserve in the business section of his newspaper. He is not quite sure what the Federal Reserve System is and he has asked you to clarify this for him. In particular, he is interested in hearing about the functions of the Federal Reserve Bank. Marty wants more than a list: he seeks to understand more fully the implied responsibilities of each function of the Federal Reserve Bank.

**STEP 1: Review the four functions of the Federal Reserve Bank as they are outlined in your text.**

The Federal Reserve System refers to the central bank of the United States. The Federal Reserve System is composed of a Board of Governors, a part of the United States government, and 12 regional Federal Reserve Banks that are privately owned. The Federal Reserve Bank has the responsibility to (1) provide financial services, (2) supervise and regulate banking institutions, (3) maintain the stability of the financial system; and (4) conduct monetary policy.

**STEP 2: Discuss the significance of the first function: the role of the Federal Reserve Bank as a provider of financial services.**

The Federal Reserve Bank provides numerous financial services: it holds reserves for commercial banks, clears checks issued by commercial banks, provides cash and transfers funds for commercial banks, and acts as a banker and fiscal agent for the federal government. In addition, the U.S Treasury has a checking account at the Federal Reserve: any check issued by the U.S. Treasury is a check written on this checking account.

**STEP 3: Discuss the significance of the second function: the role of the Federal Reserve Bank as a regulator and supervisor of banking institutions.**

The Federal Reserve Bank also has a responsibility to insure the safety and soundness of the banking system. It fulfills this role by regulating and supervising banking institutions.

**STEP 4: Discuss the significance of the third function: the role of the Federal Reserve Bank in maintaining the stability of the financial system.**

A third function of the Federal Reserve Bank is that of maintaining the stability of the financial system. The Fed acts to provide a stable financial system: if necessary, the Fed steps in to provide needed liquidity to banking institutions in order to maintain this stability.

**STEP 5: Discuss the significance of the fourth function: the role of the Federal Reserve Bank in conducting monetary policy.**

Finally, the Federal Reserve Bank also has a responsibility to conduct monetary policy to prevent or address extreme macroeconomic fluctuations in the economy. When the Federal Reserve Bank engages in monetary policy it alters the amount of money in the economy and thus affects the interest rate in the economy. The Federal Reserve pursues this monetary policy to change the level of spending in the aggregate economy: if the level of spending is deemed too low, the Federal Reserve acts to stimulate spending; and if the level of spending is deemed too high, the Federal Reserve acts to contract spending.

**2.** Suppose that the Federal Reserve Bank engages in an open-market purchase of $25 million worth of Treasury bills. How will this immediately affect the T-accounts for the Federal Reserve and for commercial banks? If the required reserve ratio is 10%, what will the money multiplier be? What will the change in the money supply from this open-market purchase of Treasury bills be?

**STEP 1:** Start by first constructing the T-accounts for the Federal Reserve and for commercial banks based on the given information.

When the Federal Reserve engages in an open-market purchase it is buying Treasury bills. The Federal Reserve receives these Treasury bills from commercial banks and in exchange the Federal Reserve credits the reserve accounts of these commercial banks with the value of the Treasury bills it has purchased. In the context of T-accounts, we would expect the value of Treasury bills held by the Federal Reserve to increase by the amount of the open-market purchase, while the value of Treasury bills held by commercial banks will decrease by the amount of the open-market purchase. We would also expect the level of reserves held by commercial banks to increase by the value of the Treasury bills they have sold to the Federal Reserve, while the monetary base liability of the Federal Reserve will increase by the value of the Treasury bills that have been purchased by the Federal Reserve. Here are the T-accounts showing these changes:

| Federal Reserve | | | |
|---|---|---|---|
| **Assets** | | **Liabilities** | |
| Treasury bills | +$25 million | Monetary base | +$25 million |
| **Commercial Banks** | | | |
| **Assets** | | **Liabilities** | |
| Treasury bills | −$25 million | No change | |
| Reserves | +$25 million | | |

Note: Both the Federal Reserve and the commercial banks' T-accounts balance: that is, the assets equal the liabilities for each separate T-account.

**STEP 2:** Identify what the money multiplier will be, given the required reserve ratio.

Earlier the relationship between the money multiplier and the required reserve ratio was discussed. Recall that the money multiplier is equal to one divided by the required reserve ratio. In this example, the money multiplier is therefore equal to 1/0.10 or 10.

**STEP 3:** Calculate the change in the money supply given the money multiplier and the described open-market operation.

The change in the money supply can be calculated using the formula: (Change in the money supply) = (Money multiplier)(Change in reserves). In this example, the money multiplier has a value of 10, the change in reserves is $25 million, and therefore the change in the money supply is $250 million.

# Problems and Exercises

1.  You are provided the following T-accounts for the central bank of Economia and the only commercial bank in Economia. In this country, all financial transactions occur within the banking system: no one holds currency. The required reserve ratio imposed by the central bank is 20% of deposits.

**Central bank of Economia**

| Assets | | Liabilities | |
|---|---|---|---|
| Treasury bills | $20,000 | Reserves | $20,000 |
| Total assets | $20,000 | Total liabilities | $20,000 |

**Commercial bank of Economia**

| Assets | | Liabilities | |
|---|---|---|---|
| Required reserves | $20,000 | Deposits | $100,000 |
| Loans | $70,000 | Capital | $20,000 |
| Treasury bills | $30,000 | | |
| Total assets | $120,000 | Total liabilities and capital | $120,000 |

Suppose the central bank in Economia purchases $2,000 of Treasury bills from the commercial bank.

a.  Provide a T-account for both the central bank and the commercial bank showing the immediate effect of this transaction. Be sure to differentiate between required and excess reserves for the commercial bank.

b.  Provide a T-account for the commercial bank once the commercial bank lends out its excess reserves and all adjustments have been made through the money multiplier process.

c.  What happens to the money supply when the central bank purchases $2,000 of Treasury bills from the commercial bank?

d.  Relate the change in the money supply to the money multiplier.

e.  What was the monetary base initially?

**f.** What is the monetary base after all adjustments to the central bank's monetary policy have taken effect?

**2.** The following T-accounts are for the central bank of Macropedia and its sole commercial bank. In Macropedia, citizens always hold $1,000 in currency and the reserve requirement equals 10%. The commercial bank adheres to a strict policy of always lending out its excess reserves.

**Central bank of Macropedia**

| Assets | | Liabilities | |
|---|---|---|---|
| Treasury bills | $11,000 | Reserves | $10,000 |
| | | Currency in circulation | $1,000 |
| Total assets | $11,000 | Total liabilities | $11,000 |

**Commercial bank of Macropedia**

| Assets | | Liabilities | |
|---|---|---|---|
| Reserves | $10,000 | Deposits | $100,000 |
| Loans | $80,000 | Capital | $0 |
| Treasury bills | $10,000 | | |
| Total assets | $100,000 | Total liabilities and capital | $100,000 |

**a.** Does the commercial bank initially satisfy the required reserve? Explain your answer.

**b.** Suppose the central bank sells $5,000 in Treasury bills to the commercial bank. Provide T-accounts for both the central bank and the commercial bank showing the immediate effect of this transaction.

**c.** Given your answer in part (b), describe the commercial bank's problem. Be specific in your answer and identify what options the commercial bank has for resolving its problem.

**d.** Provide a T-account for the commercial bank after it fully adjusts to the central bank's selling of $5,000 in Treasury bills.

**e.** What happens to the monetary base in this problem?

**f.** What happens to the money supply?

**3.** Use the following information about Macroland to answer this question.

| Bank deposits at the central bank | $100 million |
|---|---|
| Currency in bank vaults | $ 50 million |
| Currency held by the public | 75 million |
| Checkable deposits | 600 million |
| Traveler's checks | 5 million |

**a.** What are bank reserves equal to in Macroland?

**b.** Suppose banks hold no excess reserves in Macroland. What is the required reserve ratio given the information in the table?

**c.** If the public does not change its currency holdings, what will happen to the level of checkable deposits in Macroland, relative to their initial level, if the central bank of Macroland purchases $10 million worth of Treasury bills in the open market? Explain your answer and provide a numerical answer.

**d.** If the public does not change its currency holdings, what will happen to the level of checkable deposits in Macroland, relative to their initial level, if the central bank of Macroland sells $5 million in Treasury bills in the open market? Explain your answer and provide a numerical answer.

## ▮ BEFORE YOU TAKE THE TEST

## Module Review Questions

1. Suppose there is only one bank in the banking system. Furthermore, suppose all money is held in this bank and the bank holds no excess reserves. If the Fed makes an open-market sale of $50 worth of T-bills to this bank, what will happen to the money supply after all adjustments are made?
   a. The money supply will increase by $50.
   b. The money supply will decrease by $50.
   c. The money supply will increase by $500.
   d. The money supply will decrease by $500.

2. When banks find that they must borrow money, and they can borrow only from the Federal Reserve, this is referred to as using the
   a. open-market operations.
   b. discount window.
   c. FDIC.
   d. required reserve ratio.

3. The three primary policy tools available to the Federal Reserve include
   a. reserve requirements, the ability to tax banks, and the discount rate.
   b. reserve requirements, the discount rate, and open-market operations.
   c. reserve requirements, the ability to tax banks, and open-market operations.
   d. the ability to tax banks, the discount rate, and open-market operations.

4. When banks borrow from one another, the rate of interest they pay for this loan is called the
   a. discount rate.
   b. federal funds rate.

5. Suppose a hypothetical economy that uses a checkable-deposits-only monetary system has a required reserve ratio of 20%. When the central bank in this economy purchases $100 million worth of Treasury bills, this will
   a. increase the money supply by 20%.
   b. increase the money supply by $100 million.
   c. increase the money supply by $500 million.
   d. increase the money supply by $5 million.

6. Suppose a hypothetical economy that uses a checkable-deposits-only monetary system has a required reserve ratio of 10%. When the central bank in this economy sells $10 million worth of Treasury bills, this will
   a. decrease the money supply by 10%.
   b. decrease the money supply by $10 million.
   c. decrease the money supply by $100 million.
   d. decrease the money supply by $1 million.

# ANSWER KEY

## Answers to Problems and Exercises

**1.  a.**

**Central bank of Economia**

| Assets | | Liabilities | |
|---|---|---|---|
| Treasury bills | $22,000 | Reserves | $22,000 |
| | | | |
| Total assets | $22,000 | Total liabilities | $22,000 |

**Commercial bank of Economia**

| Assets | | Liabilities | |
|---|---|---|---|
| Required reserves | $20,000 | Deposits | $100,000 |
| | | Capital | $20,000 |
| Excess reserves | $2,000 | | |
| Loans | $70,000 | | |
| Treasury bills | $28,000 | | |
| Total assets | $120,000 | Total liabilities and capital | $120,000 |

**b.**

**Commercial bank of Economia**

| Assets | | Liabilities | |
|---|---|---|---|
| Required reserves | $22,000 | Deposits | $110,000 |
| Loans | $80,000 | Capital | $20,000 |
| Treasury bills | $28,000 | | |
| | | | |
| Total assets | $130,000 | Total liabilities and capital | $130,000 |

**c.** The money supply increases from $100,000 to $110,000. Recall that the money supply equals checkable deposits plus currency in circulation: since Economia has no currency in circulation, the money supply equals the level of deposits.

**d.** The change in the money supply equals the money multiplier times the change in the monetary base. In this problem, the money multiplier equals 5, and the change in the monetary base is the $2,000 increase in reserves that occurs when the central bank purchases the Treasury bills.

**e.** The monetary base equals reserves plus currency in circulation. In Economia, currency in circulation equals zero, so the monetary base is equivalent to reserves. Initially the monetary base is $20,000.

**f.** The monetary base increases to $22,000.

**2.  a.** Yes, the commercial bank has reserves of $10,000 and deposits of $100,000: reserves equal 10% of deposits, which satisfies the required reserve ratio.

**b.**

| Central bank of Macropedia | | | | Commercial bank of Macropedia | | | |
|---|---|---|---|---|---|---|---|

| Assets | | Liabilities | | Assets | | Liabilities | |
|---|---|---|---|---|---|---|---|
| Treasury bills | $6,000 | Reserves | $5,000 | Reserves | $5,000 | Deposits | $100,000 |
| | | Currency in circulation | $1,000 | Loans | $80,000 | Capital | $0 |
| | | | | Treasury bills | $15,000 | | |
| Total assets | $6,000 | Total liabilities and capital | $6,000 | Total assets | $100,000 | Total liabilities and capital | $100,000 |

**c.** The commercial bank has insufficient reserves to meet the required reserve ratio: when its deposits equal $100,000, it needs $10,000 in required reserves. With reserves of $5,000, it can only support $50,000 of deposits. In the short term, it can borrow reserves from the central bank of Macropedia. Since there is only one commercial bank in Macropedia, it cannot borrow from the federal funds market since there is no federal funds market. Over time the commercial bank will find it needs to decrease its outstanding loans and therefore deposits until its reserves are sufficient to meet the required reserve ratio.

**d.**

**Commercial bank of Macropedia**

| Assets | | Liabilities | |
|---|---|---|---|
| Reserves | $5,000 | Deposits | $50,000 |
| Loans | $30,000 | Capital | $0 |
| Treasury bills | $15,000 | | |
| Total assets | $50,000 | Total liabilities and capital | $50,000 |

**e.** The monetary base is initially equal to $11,000 ($10,000 in reserves plus $1,000 in currency in circulation). After the central bank's activity, the monetary base is $6,000 ($5,000 in reserves plus $1,000 in currency in circulation).

**f.** The money supply is initially $101,000 ($100,000 in checkable bank deposits plus $1,000 in currency in circulation). After the central bank's actions and full adjustment, the money supply is $51,000 ($50,000 in checkable bank deposits plus $1,000 in currency in circulation). The money supply decreases by $50,000, or the amount predicted by the money multiplier process.

**3. a.** Bank reserves equal currency in bank vaults plus bank deposits at the central bank, or $150 million.

**b.** We can calculate the required reserve ratio, $rr$, as the ratio of required reserves to checkable deposits. Since there are no excess reserves in Macroland, the bank reserves that are calculated in part (a) equal the required reserves: thus, $150 million/$600 million equals a required reserve ratio of 0.25.

**c.** When the central bank of Macroland purchases $10 million in Treasury bills, this increases the level of reserves in the banking system by $10 million. This increase in reserves starts the multiplier process: the change in the money supply is calculated as the increase in reserves times the money multiplier or ($10 million)(4) = $40 million. Thus, the money supply increases by $40 million when the Central Bank purchases Treasury bills on the open market.

**d.** Using the concept explained in part (c), this sale of Treasury bills by the central bank will decrease the money supply by $20 million. We can see this by recalling that the change in the money supply equals the change in reserves times the money multiplier or (–$5 million)(4), or –$20 million.

## Answers to Module Review Questions

1.  **Answer d.** When the Fed sells $50 worth of T-bills, it debits the reserve account of the bank that sells the T-bills to the Fed. This results in the bank having insufficient reserves to support their current level of deposits. The bank will contract the loans it holds until the deposits in the bank are the amount that can be supported by the new level of reserves. The new reserves in this problem equal $50 (the initial $100 minus the $50 spent on the T-bills): $50 in reserves can support $500 in deposits when the required reserve ratio equals 10. So the money supply will decrease from $1,000 to $500, or a decrease of $500.

2.  **Answer b.** Banks borrowing from the Federal Reserve is referred to as using the discount window. The FDIC is the Federal Deposit Insurance Corporation, and it refers to the group that provides and oversees deposit insurance for the banking industry. Open-market operations refers to the buying and selling of Treasury bills by the Federal Open Market Committee (FOMC). The required reserve ratio is set by the Federal Reserve and is the percentage of deposits that the Fed requires banks to hold either in their vaults or in their account at the Federal Reserve.

3.  **Answer b.** The Federal Reserve can affect the money supply by engaging in open-market operations in which the Federal Reserve either purchases Treasury bills or sells Treasury bills. The Fed can also affect the money supply by changing the reserve requirements: when the reserve requirement increases, this reduces the money supply, and when the Fed reduces the reserve requirement, this increases the money supply. Finally, the Fed can affect the money supply by changing the discount rate. When the discount rate falls relative to the federal funds rate, this means that it is now relatively cheaper to borrow from the Fed, which leads to increases in the money supply.

4.  **Answer b.** The interest rate charged for loans from one bank to another is called the federal funds rate. The interest rate charged for a loan to a bank from the Fed is called the discount rate.

5.  **Answer c.** In a checkable-deposits-only monetary system, the money multiplier is equal to $1/rr$, where $rr$ is the required reserve ratio. Thus, for this economy the money multiplier is equal to 5 and a $100 million purchase of Treasury bills by the central bank will result in an increase in the money supply of $500 million.

6.  **Answer c.** When the required reserve ratio is 10%, this implies that the money multiplier is equal to 10 in a checkable-deposits-only monetary system. Thus, an open-market sale of $10 million worth of Treasury bills will result in a $100 million decrease in the money supply.

# module 37(73)

# The Money Market

## BEFORE YOU READ THE MODULE

## Summary

This module explains money demand and then uses this concept to develop the liquidity preference model of short-run interest rate determination.

## Module Objectives

**Objective #1.** Money is held by individuals and firms in order to facilitate making transactions. There is an opportunity cost to holding money: money normally yields a lower rate of return than nonmonetary assets. The opportunity cost of holding money is the difference between the interest rate on assets that are not money and the interest rate on assets that are money. The higher the short-term interest rate, the higher the opportunity cost of holding money; people reduce their holding of money as the short-term interest rate increases. This implies that the demand curve for money slopes downward: as the interest rate decreases, the quantity of money demanded increases. Figure 37.1 illustrates the relationship between the quantity of money demanded and the interest rate.

**Figure 37.1**

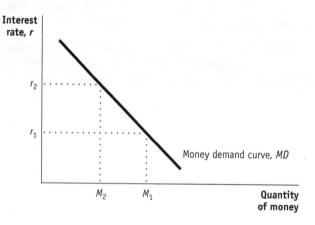

- Short-term interest rates are interest rates on financial assets that mature in less than a year. Short-term interest rates tend to move together since they are in effect competing for the same business. A short-term asset that offers a lower-than-average interest rate will be sold by investors. When these assets are sold, the interest rate on these assets is forced to increase, since new buyers must be rewarded with a higher rate in order to be willing to buy the asset. This reasoning implies that short-term interest rates will tend to equalize across the financial assets found in the short-term interest rate market.

- Long-term interest rates are interest rates paid on financial assets that mature a number of years into the future. Long-term interest rates may differ from short-term interest rates. In this module's discussion of interest rates, we will simplify our discussion and assume that there is only one interest rate.

**Objective #2.**   The money demand curve illustrates the relationship between the nominal quantity of money demanded and the interest rate. It is a downward-sloping curve. For a given interest rate, an increase in the aggregate price level causes the demand curve for money to shift to the right, while a decrease in the aggregate price level causes the demand curve for money to shift to the left. Figure 37.2 illustrates the effect of a change in the aggregate price level on the demand for money.

**Figure 37.2**

- The quantity of money, M, is proportional to the aggregate price level. Holding everything else constant, if the aggregate price level doubles, then the nominal quantity of money will double. In other words, holding everything else constant, the real quantity of money demanded after an aggregate price level change ($M_2/P_2$) is the same as the real quantity of money demanded before the aggregate price level change ($M_1/P_1$).

- There are a number of factors that shift the real money demand curve, including changes in the level of real aggregate spending, changes in banking technology, and changes in banking institutions that alter people's real demand for money.

  - Holding everything else constant, an increase in real aggregate spending will shift the real money demand curve to the right, while a decrease in real aggregate spending will shift the real money demand curve to the left.

  - Holding everything else constant, advances in information technology tend to shift the real money demand curve to the left since these advances make it easier for the public to make transactions while holding smaller amounts of money.

  - Changes in institutions can increase or decrease the demand for money by changing the opportunity cost of holding money.

**Objective #3.** In the United States, the Federal Open Market Committee (FOMC) sets a target interest rate for the federal funds rate and then uses open-market operations to achieve that target interest rate.

- The liquidity preference model of the interest rate illustrates how the Fed can control the interest rate through its open-market operations. The liquidity preference model says that the interest rate is determined by the intersection of the supply and demand for money in the market for money.

- In the liquidity preference model, the money supply is a vertical line whose location is controlled by the Fed through its open-market operations. The intersection of this vertical money supply curve with the downward-sloping money demand curve determines the equilibrium interest rate. Figure 37.3 illustrates this relationship.

**Figure 37.3**

- If the nominal interest rate is lower than the equilibrium level, then the quantity of money demanded will be greater than the quantity of money supplied. People will want to increase their money holdings, and they will sell other financial assets to achieve this goal: in order to sell these financial assets, they will have to offer a higher interest rate to attract buyers. This will lead the nominal interest rate in the market for money to increase, bringing about equilibrium between the demand and supply of money.

- If the nominal interest rate is higher than the equilibrium level, then the quantity of money demanded will be less than the quantity of money supplied. People will want to decrease their money holdings and they will do so by buying other financial assets. Due to the increased demand for these interest-bearing financial assets, sellers of these assets will find that they can offer them at a lower nominal interest rate and still find willing buyers. Thus, the nominal interest rate will decrease, thereby restoring the money market to equilibrium, where the supply of money equals the demand for money.

# Key Terms

**short-term interest rate** the *interest rate* on *financial assets* that mature within less than a year.

**long-term interest rate** the *interest rate* on *financial assets* that mature a number of years into the future.

**money demand curve** a graphical representation of the relationship between the *interest rate* and the quantity of money demanded. The money demand curve slopes downward because, other things equal, a higher interest rate increases the *opportunity cost* of holding money.

*Notes*

## Key Terms *(continued)*

**liquidity preference model of the interest rate** a model of the market for money in which the *interest rate* is determined by the supply and demand for money.

**money supply curve** a graphical representation of the relationship between the quantity of money supplied by the Federal Reserve and the *interest rate*.

*Notes*

## ■ AFTER YOU READ THE MODULE

## Tips

**Tip #1.** The interest rate is the price of money, because the interest rate provides a measure of the opportunity cost of holding money. As the interest rate increases, the quantity of money demanded decreases since the opportunity cost of holding money rises with increases in the interest rate. This relationship implies that the demand for money is downward sloping: the quantity of money demanded is negatively related to the interest rate. This relationship is illustrated in Figure 37.4: when the interest rate is $r_1$, the quantity of money demanded is $M_1$; when the interest rate rises to $r_2$, the quantity of money demanded decreases to $M_2$.

**Figure 37.4**

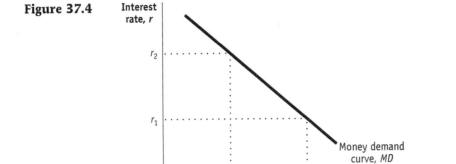

**Tip #2.** It is important to understand what causes a movement along the money demand curve and what factors cause a shift in the money demand curve. As with other demand curves, a change in the price of money—the interest rate—causes a movement along the demand curve (see Figure 37.4). A change in the aggregate price level shifts the nominal money demand curve: when the aggregate price level increases, the nominal money demand curve shifts to the right since people will now demand a greater amount of nominal money at every interest rate due to the higher aggregate price level. When the aggregate price level decreases, the nominal money demand curve shifts to the left since people will now demand a smaller amount of nominal money at every interest rate due to the lower aggregate price level. Money demand (real or nominal) also shifts with changes in real aggregate spending, changes in banking technology, and changes in banking institutions. We can summarize these changes in the following table.

| Change | Effect on money demand |
|---|---|
| Increase in interest rate | Movement along money demand curve and decrease in quantity of money demanded |
| Decrease in interest rate | Movement along money demand curve and increase in quantity of money demanded |
| Increase in aggregate price level | Money demand shifts to the right |
| Decrease in aggregate price level | Money demand shifts to the left |
| Increase in real aggregate spending | Money demand shifts to the right |
| Decrease in real aggregate spending | Money demand shifts to the left |
| Advance in bank technology | Money demand shifts to the left |
| Changes in institutions | Money demand shifts to the left or right, depending on the institutional change |

**Tip #3.** Equilibrium in the money market equates the quantity of money demanded with the quantity of money supplied at the equilibrium interest rate. Figure 37.5 illustrates the money market.

**Figure 37.5**

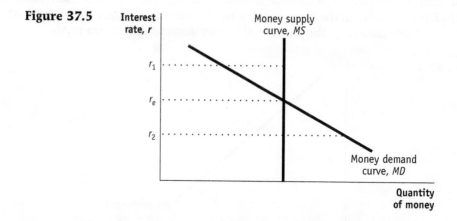

If the interest rate ($r_1$ in Figure 37.5) is greater than the equilibrium interest rate ($r_e$), the quantity of money supplied is greater than the quantity of money demanded at that interest rate. Investors will drive the interest rate down to the equilibrium level $r_e$ by shifting their assets out of money holdings and into nonmonetary interest-bearing financial assets. This will cause the interest rate to decrease toward $r_e$.

If the interest rate ($r_2$ in Figure 37.5) is less than the equilibrium interest rate ($r_e$), the quantity of money supplied is less than the quantity of money demanded at that interest rate. Investors will drive the interest rate up to the equilibrium level $r_e$ by shifting their assets out of nonmonetary interest-bearing financial assets and into money holdings. This will cause the interest rate to increase toward $r_e$.

1. Suppose there are two kinds of assets that an individual can choose between as a means of holding wealth: money, which does not provide any interest payment, and bonds, which provide the owner of the bond with an interest payment. Suppose that the money market is currently not in equilibrium and that the interest rate is lower than the equilibrium interest rate. First, describe the money market and whether there is a shortage or a surplus of money. Then, using these two types of assets, explain how the money market adjusts in order to ensure that the quantity of money demanded is equal to the quantity of money supplied.

**STEP 1:** Determine whether there is a shortage or a surplus of money when the interest rate is lower than the equilibrium interest rate in the market for money.

In general when price is lower than the equilibrium price this results in a situation of excess demand for the good. This is no different in the market for money: when the interest rate, the price of money, is lower than the equilibrium level, then we know that the quantity of money demanded will be greater than the quantity of money supplied.

**STEP 2:** Explain how the money market returns to equilibrium when the quantity of money demanded is greater than the quantity of money supplied.

When the quantity of money demanded exceeds the quantity of money supplied this means that people want to shift some of their wealth out of interest-bearing assets and into money. When there is excess quantity of money demanded this implies that there is excess supply of interest-bearing assets like bonds; to induce people to purchase bonds, the owners of these bonds will have to offer higher interest rates. Interest rates will rise until the bond market clears and the money market clears: when the interest rate rises sufficiently, then the quantity of money demanded will equal the quantity of money supplied.

2. Suppose there are two kinds of assets that an individual can choose between as a way of holding wealth: money, which does not provide any interest payment, and bonds, which provides the owner of the bond with an interest payment. Suppose that the money market is currently not in equilibrium and that the interest rate is higher than the equilibrium interest rate. First, describe the money market and whether there is a shortage or a surplus of money. Then, using these two types of assets, explain how the money market adjusts in order to ensure that the quantity of money demanded is equal to the quantity of money supplied.

**STEP 1:** Determine whether there is a shortage or a surplus of money when the interest rate is higher than the equilibrium interest rate in the market for money.

In general when price is higher than the equilibrium price this results in a situation of excess supply of the good. This is no different in the market for money: when the interest rate, the price of money, is higher than the equilibrium level, then we know that the quantity of money demanded will be less than the quantity of money supplied.

**STEP 2:** Explain how the money market returns to equilibrium when the quantity of money demanded is less than the quantity of money supplied.

When the quantity of money demanded is less than the quantity of money supplied this means that people want to shift some of their wealth into interest-bearing assets and out of money. When there is excess quantity of money supplied this implies that there is excess demand for interest-bearing assets like bonds: people desire bonds and the interest rate on bonds can fall since there is excess demand for these bonds. Interest rates will fall until the bond market clears and the money market clears. When the interest rate falls sufficiently, then the quantity of money demanded will equal the quantity of money supplied.

## Problems and Exercises

1. The following figure illustrates the relationship between the nominal quantity of money, $M$, and the interest rate, $r$.

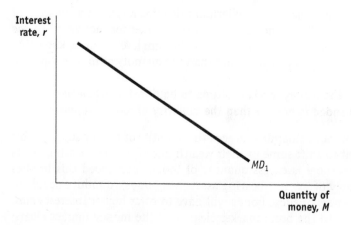

For each of the following situations, use the graph for reference.

   **a.** Holding everything else constant, the interest rate increases from $r_1$ to $r_2$. Graph this in the following figure.

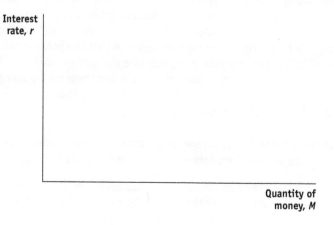

**b.** Holding everything else constant, the level of aggregate real income decreases. Graph this in the following figure.

Interest
rate, *r*

Quantity of
money, *M*

**c.** Holding everything else constant, there is an increase in the aggregate price level. Graph this in the following figure.

Interest
rate, *r*

Quantity of
money, *M*

**d.** Holding everything else constant, individuals in a community are now able to use Internet banking for their money and financial assets accounts. Graph this in the following figure.

Interest
rate, *r*

Quantity of
money, *M*

2. Consider two assets: both Asset A and Asset B are one-month bonds issued by different companies that have the same amount of risk. Asset A initially earns a higher interest rate for its holder than does Asset B. Explain why you would expect this interest rate differential to disappear. Explain the process that leads Assets A and B to have approximately the same interest rate.

3. Why is the quantity of money people want to hold negatively related to the interest rate? Explain your answer fully.

## BEFORE YOU TAKE THE TEST

## Module Review Questions

1. People choose to hold money because
   a. it has little or no opportunity cost since money does not earn interest.
   b. it facilitates making transactions.
   c. it yields a lower rate of return than nonmonetary assets.
   d. Answers (b) and (c) are both correct.

2. The opportunity cost of holding money is
   a. always greater than the short-term interest rate.
   b. equal to the difference between the interest rate on assets that are not money and the interest rate on assets that are money.
   c. equal to the long-term interest rate.
   d. always equal to zero since it costs you nothing to hold money.

3. Which of the following statements is true?
   a. The nominal demand for money is proportional to the real demand for money.
   b. All short-term interest rates tend to move together.
   c. The higher the short-term interest rate, the lower the opportunity cost of holding money.
   d. The quantity of money demanded is positively related to the interest rate.

**4.** Which of the following statements is true?

    a. The real quantity of money is equal to the nominal amount of money divided by the aggregate price level.

    b. The real quantity of money measures the purchasing power of the nominal quantity of money.

    c. The real quantity of money is proportional to the nominal quantity of money for any given interest rate.

    d. All of these statements are true.

    e. Statements (a) and (b) are both true.

    f. Statements (a) and (c) are both true.

    g. Statements (b) and (c) are both true.

**5.** If the price level doubles, holding everything else constant, we know that

    a. the nominal quantity of money demanded also doubles.

    b. the real quantity of money demanded also doubles.

    c. the interest rate also doubles.

    d. Answers (a) and (b) are both correct.

**6.** For a given interest rate, when the quantity of money demanded is greater than the quantity of money supplied, then

    a. interest rates will increase.

    b. interest rates will decrease.

    c. people will sell nonmonetary assets.

    d. people will buy nonmonetary assets.

    e. Answers (a) and (c) are both correct.

    f. Answers (b) and (d) are both correct.

    g. Answers (a) and (d) are both correct.

**7.** The Federal Open Market Committee sets a target interest rate and can achieve that interest rate through

    a. open-market purchases, if the federal funds rate is initially less than the target rate.

    b. open-market sales, if the federal funds rate is initially less than the target rate.

    c. legislative action by Congress that decrees the level of the discount rate and thus the federal funds rate.

    d. stimulating the demand for money, if the initial interest rate is less than the target rate.

**8.** The liquidity preference model of interest rate determination states that

    a. interest rates are determined solely by the Federal Open Market Committee.

    b. interest rates are determined by the supply of and demand for money.

    c. people always prefer liquidity and do not consider the opportunity cost of holding money when they decide how much money they wish to hold at any given point in time.

    d. interest rates are determined in the market for nonmonetary assets and not the market for money.

9. The money supply curve in the liquidity preference model is drawn as a vertical line, since
   a. there is only one level of money supply that will enable an economy to produce at the full employment level of output and the appropriate aggregate price level.
   b. Congress sets by law the level of the money supply in the economy.
   c. the Fed can control the level of the money supply through its open-market operations.
   d. the money supply curve is unimportant in determining the equilibrium level of interest rates in the liquidity preference model.

10. The money demand curve shifts to the right. The most likely cause for this shift among the following explanations is
    a. an increase in the interest rate.
    b. a decrease in the interest rate.
    c. a change in bank institutions that allows banks to pay even higher rates of interest on checking account funds.
    d. Answers (b) and (c) are both correct.

## ANSWER KEY

# Answers to Problems and Exercises

1.  **a.** An increase in the interest rate causes a movement along the money demand curve as illustrated in the following figure.

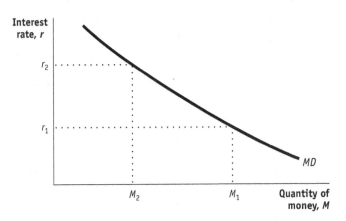

**b.** As the level of aggregate real income decreases, this causes the money demand curve to shift to the left as individuals demand less money at every interest rate. This is illustrated in the following figure.

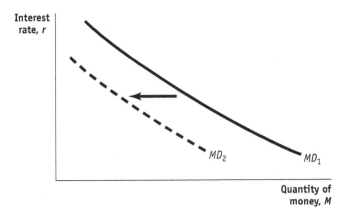

**c.** An increase in the aggregate price level causes the money demand curve to shift to the right, as individuals demand more money at every interest rate to facilitate making their transactions at the new higher price levels. This is illustrated in the following figure.

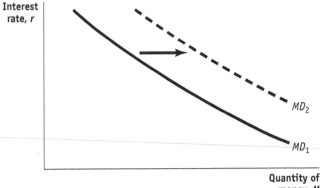

**d.** With new technology for managing money and financial assets, people will decrease their demand for money at every interest rate. This will cause money demand to shift to the left, as illustrated in the figure from part (b) of this answer.

2. Since both Asset A and Asset B are short-term financial assets, we anticipate that the interest rate paid on both assets should be roughly equivalent. If the returns differ, investors will sell the asset offering the lower return: to find a buyer for this asset, they must offer a higher rate on it. This buying and selling of assets will lead the returns on these short-term financial assets to move toward approximately the same return.

3. Holding money has an opportunity cost since the money could have been used to purchase a financial item that could have yielded the holder an interest return. Thus, when the interest rate increases, this implies that the opportunity cost of holding money has risen: people will want to hold less money as the opportunity cost of holding that money increases. Thus, the interest rate and the quantity of money that people want to hold (that is, the quantity of money they demand) are negatively related to one another.

## Answers to Module Review Questions

1. **Answer b.** Although money typically does yield a lower rate of return than nonmonetary assets, this is not the reason people choose to hold money. Rather, they choose to hold money because money facilitates making transactions. There is an opportunity cost of holding money: when holding money you forego the higher rate of return you could earn by holding nonmonetary assets.

2. **Answer b.** The opportunity cost of holding money is measured by what is lost when holding money: this is calculated as the difference between the rate of return you could earn by holding nonmonetary assets minus the rate of return on monetary assets.

3. **Answer b.** The nominal demand for money is proportional to the aggregate price level. The higher the short-term interest rate, the greater the opportunity cost of holding money since you could be earning this higher short-term interest rate if you chose to hold nonmonetary assets. The quantity of money demanded is inversely, or negatively, related to the interest rate: as the interest rate increases, the quantity of money demanded decreases. Short-term interest rates do move together since if there is a difference in the rate of return on short-term financial assets, there will be movement toward the asset that pays the higher return and away from the asset that pays the lower return. As the market adjusts to this movement, there will be a tendency for the rate of returns for both assets to move toward one another: short-term interest rates will therefore tend to move together.

4. **Answer e.** The first two statements are factual statements that are true by definition. The real quantity of money is not proportional to the nominal quantity of money. However, the nominal quantity of money demanded is proportional to the aggregate price level.

5. **Answer a.** To maintain the same level of purchasing power as was initially had, when the aggregate price level doubles, the nominal quantity of money demanded will also double. However, a doubling of prices will have no effect on the real quantity of money demanded since this real money demand is, by definition, the amount of money that holds purchasing power constant. Holding everything else constant assumes that a doubling of the price level will have no impact on the interest rate.

6. **Answer e.** When the quantity of money demanded is greater than the quantity of money supplied, people wish to increase their money holdings. This will cause them to sell their nonmonetary assets: as the supply of these nonmonetary assets increases, people will find they must offer higher interest rates on these assets in order to sell them. Thus, interest rates will increase.

7.  **Answer b.** If the target interest rate is greater than the federal funds rate, then the Fed needs to engage in monetary policy that will shift the money supply curve to the left, resulting in an increase in interest rates for a given money demand curve. The FOMC, therefore, will engage in open-market sales of Treasury bills. Congress does not set the discount rate, and the Fed's monetary policy affects the money supply curve and not the money demand curve.

8.  **Answer b.** The liquidity preference model uses the interaction between the quantity of money demanded and the quantity of money supplied to analyze the determination of interest rates. Interest rates are impacted by Federal Reserve policy and its effect on the money supply curve. People consider the opportunity cost of holding money when making their decisions about the level of money they wish to hold. One can model interest rate determination in either the framework of money demand and supply or the framework of demand and supply of loanable funds.

9.  **Answer c.** The Fed controls the money supply through open-market operations. We know that the determination of interest rates depends not only on the quantity of money demanded but also on the quantity of money supplied. Congress does not have the authority to determine the country's money supply. Different levels of money supply are compatible with the full-employment level of output, since interest rate determination depends on both the money supply and the money demand.

10. **Answer c.** A change in the interest rate, whether an increase or a decrease, causes a movement along the money demand curve. An increase in the amount of interest that banks can pay on checking account funds reduces the opportunity cost of holding funds in a checking account rather than in an interest-bearing asset: people will increase the quantity of money they demand at every interest rate with this change, which will result in the money demand curve shifting to the right.

# module 38(74)

# Monetary Policy and the Interest Rate

## ▮ BEFORE YOU READ THE MODULE

## Summary

This module considers the Federal Reserve's ability to move the interest rate and explores the effect of monetary policy on the level of aggregate output. The module also explores why monetary policy is the primary tool used by the central bank to stabilize the economy.

## Module Objectives

**Objective #1.** When the Federal Reserve (the Fed) purchases Treasury bills in the open market, this increases the money supply, causing the money supply curve to shift to the right. For a given money demand curve, this increase in the supply of money will result in interest rates decreasing. Thus, if the Federal Open Market Committee (FOMC) sets a target interest rate lower than the prevailing interest rate, it can reach this target by engaging in open-market purchases. Figure 38.1 illustrates an open-market purchase by the Fed.

**Figure 38.1**

**Objective #2.** When the Fed sells Treasury bills in the open market, this decreases the money supply, causing the money supply curve to shift to the left. For a given money demand curve, this decrease in the supply of money will result in interest rates increasing. Thus, if the FOMC sets a target interest rate higher than the prevailing interest rate, it can reach this target by engaging in open-market sales. Figure 38.2 illustrates an open-market sale.

**Figure 38.2**

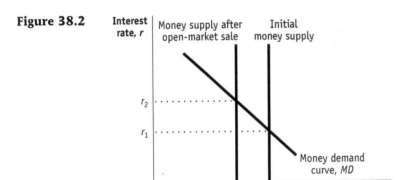

**Objective #3.** Changes in the money supply cause the short-run level of real GDP to change.

- Monetary expansion in the short run reduces the interest rate and leads to higher investment spending and higher consumer spending, holding everything else constant. This higher investment spending results in higher GDP through the multiplier process. Thus, an increase in the money supply causes the *AD* curve to shift to the right and is referred to as expansionary monetary policy. The Federal Reserve and other central banks tend to engage in expansionary monetary policy when real GDP is below potential real GDP.

- Monetary contraction in the short run increases the interest rate and leads to lower investment spending and lower consumer spending, holding everything else constant. This lower investment spending results in lower GDP through the multiplier process. Thus, a decrease in the money supply causes the *AD* curve to shift to the left and is referred to as contractionary monetary policy. The Federal Reserve and other central banks tend to engage in contractionary monetary policy when real GDP is above potential real GDP.

- The Taylor rule for monetary policy is a rule for setting the federal funds rate that takes into account both the inflation rate and the output gap. The Taylor rule for the period from 1988 to 2008 can be summarized as: Federal funds rate = 2.07 + (1.28 × inflation) − (1.95 × unemployment gap).

**Objective #4.** The Federal Reserve bank does not set an explicit inflation target, but pursues monetary policy that will keep inflation low but positive. Other central banks do set inflation targets: central banks with inflation targets announce the inflation rate that they are trying to achieve and then set policies in an attempt to hit the stated target. Inflation targeting is based on forecasts of future inflation while the Taylor rule adjusts monetary policy in response to past inflation: the former is forward looking while the latter is backward looking.

- Inflation targeting proponents argue that this type of policy is both transparent and accountable.

- Inflation targeting opponents argue that this type of policy is too restrictive.

## Key Terms

**target federal funds rate** the Federal Reserve's desired level for the *federal funds rate*. The Federal Reserve adjusts the *money supply* through the purchase and sale of Treasury bills until the actual rate equals the desired rate.

**expansionary monetary policy** *monetary policy* that, through the lowering of the *interest rate*, increases aggregate demand and therefore output.

**contractionary monetary policy** *monetary policy* that, through the raising of the *interest rate*, reduces aggregate demand and therefore output.

**Taylor rule for monetary policy** a rule for setting the *federal funds rate* that takes into account both the *inflation rate* and the *output gap*.

**inflation targeting** an approach to *monetary policy* that requires the *central bank* try to keep the *inflation rate* near a predetermined target rate.

**zero lower bound for interest rates** interest rates cannot fall below zero.

*Notes*

## ▮ AFTER YOU READ THE MODULE

## Tip

It is important to understand how the Federal Open Market Committee (FOMC) through its open-market operations effectively controls interest rates in the economy. Figure 38.3 illustrates the effect of an open-market purchase on the interest rate. When the FOMC purchases Treasury bills in the open market, this injects new reserves into the banking system and leads to an expansion in the money supply from $MS_1$ to $MS_2$. For a given money demand curve MD, this results in a decrease in the interest rate from $r_1$ to $r_2$.

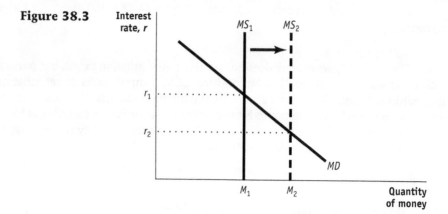

**Figure 38.3**

When the FOMC sells Treasury bills in the open market, this removes reserves from the banking system and effectively shifts the money supply curve to the left. For a given money demand curve, this action by the FOMC results in an increase in the interest rate.

1.   The following table provides different situations. For each situation, determine whether the money demand curve or the money supply curve shifts and, if so, the direction of the shift. Then, determine what happens to the equilibrium interest rate and the equilibrium quantity of money.

| Situation | Shift in the demand for money (provide direction of shift) | Shift in the supply of money (provide direction of shift) | Effect on the equilibrium interest rate | Effect on the equilibrium quantity of money |
|---|---|---|---|---|
| The information technology for making transactions improves | | | | |
| The Federal Reserve makes an open-market purchase of Treasury bills | | | | |
| Real GDP increases in the economy | | | | |
| Real GDP decreases in the economy, and the Federal Reserve makes an open-market purchase of Treasury bills | | | | |
| The aggregate price level increases | | | | |

**STEP 1:** Before you fill out the table, you will want to review the factors that shift the money demand curve. You may also find it helpful to review the effect of open-market operations by the Federal Reserve on the money supply curve.

The money demand curve will shift to the right with increases in the aggregate price level and increases in real income. The money demand curve will also shift with changes in institutions (the shift may be to the right or the left depending upon the nature of the change) or changes in technology (again, the shift can be to the right or the left depending upon the nature of the change).

The money supply curve will shift to the right when the Federal Reserve makes an open-market purchase of bonds, since the Federal Reserve will be injecting new reserves into the banking system with this purchase. The money supply curve will shift to the left when the Federal Reserve makes an open-market sale of bonds, since the Federal Reserve will be removing reserves from the banking system when it makes this sale.

**STEP 2:** Now that you have reviewed the factors that shift the two curves, you are ready to fill in the table.

Here is the completed table.

| Situation | Shift in the demand for money (provide direction of shift) | Shift in the supply of money (provide direction of shift) | Effect on the equilibrium interest rate | Effect on the equilibrium quantity of money |
|---|---|---|---|---|
| The information technology for making transactions improves | Demand for money shifts left, since at every interest rate people will wish to hold less money | There is a movement along the supply of money curve due to the shift in the demand for money | The equilibrium interest rate will decrease | The equilibrium quantity of money will be unchanged |
| The Federal Reserve makes an open-market purchase of Treasury bills | There is a movement along the demand for money curve due to the shift in the supply of money | Supply of money will shift to the right, as the Federal Reserve injects new reserves into the banking system | The equilibrium interest rate will decrease | The equilibrium quantity of money will increase |
| Real GDP increases in the economy | Demand for money will shift to the right when real GDP increases | There is a movement along the supply of money curve due to the shift in the demand for money | The equilibrium interest rate will increase | The equilibrium quantity of money will be unchanged |
| Real GDP decreases in the economy, and the Federal Reserve makes an open-market purchase of Treasury bills | Demand for money will shift to the left when real GDP decreases | Supply of money will shift to the right when the Federal Reserve makes an open-market purchase | The equilibrium interest rate will decrease | The equilibrium quantity of money will increase |
| The aggregate price level increases | Demand for money shifts to the right when the aggregate price level increases | There will be a movement along the supply of money curve due to the shift in the demand for money | The equilibrium interest rate will increase | The equilibrium quantity of money will be unchanged |

2. Morey read in the newspaper that the Federal Reserve engaged in open-market operations that expanded the money supply. He is trying to understand how this action on the part of the Federal Reserve will stimulate the economy. He has heard of the aggregate demand/aggregate supply model, but he does not understand the connection between monetary policy conducted by the Federal Reserve and this model. He has asked you to educate him in these matters.

**STEP 1:** Briefly review the impact of open-market operations on the money supply curve and the interest rate in the economy.

When the Federal Reserve engages in open-market operations it acts to either expand the money supply through open-market purchases of Treasury bills or contract the money supply through open-market sales of Treasury bills. When the Federal Reserve performs an open-market purchase this effectively shifts the money supply curve to the right: for any given money demand curve, the equilibrium interest rate will fall. When the Federal Reserve performs an open-market sale this effectively shifts the money supply curve to the left: for any given money demand curve, the equilibrium interest rate will increase.

**STEP 2:** Describe how changes in monetary policy can impact the level of aggregate demand in the economy.

When the Federal Reserve performs an open-market purchase of Treasury bills, this is expansionary monetary policy: the impact of this monetary policy is a decrease in the interest rate. When the interest rate decreases, this lowers the opportunity cost of money, which acts to spur on higher levels of consumption spending and investment spending. We can model this impact on the macroeconomy using the *AD-AS* model: expansionary monetary policy will shift the *AD* curve to the right resulting in a higher level of real GDP.

When the Federal Reserve performs an open-market sale of Treasury bills, this is contractionary monetary policy: the impact of this monetary policy is an increase in the interest rate. An increase in the interest rate raises the opportunity cost of money: this acts to slow down consumption spending and investment spending. We can model this impact on the macroeconomy using the *AD-AS* model: contractionary monetary policy will shift the *AD* curve to the left, resulting in a lower level of real GDP.

**STEP 3:** Explain to Morey the reasoning behind using expansionary monetary policy to alter the performance of the macroeconomy.

If the Federal Reserve perceives through the economic data it analyzes that the economy is underperforming, it can act via its open-market operations to stimulate the economy to a higher level of production and employment. Effectively the Federal Reserve engages in open-market purchases to steer the economy out of recession and back to full employment.

**STEP 4:** While you are discussing this with Morey take the time to explain the reasoning behind using contractionary monetary policy to alter the performance of the macroeconomy.

If the Federal Reserve analyzes economic data and concludes that the economy is overheating and in a boom, it can use its open-market operations to contract the economy to a lower level of production and employment. The Federal Reserve engages in open-market sales to steer the economy away from an inflationary gap and back to full employment.

# Problems and Exercises

1.  Use the following figure of the money demand and money supply curves to answer this question. Assume this market is initially in equilibrium with the quantity of money equal to $M_1$ and the interest rate equal to $r_1$.

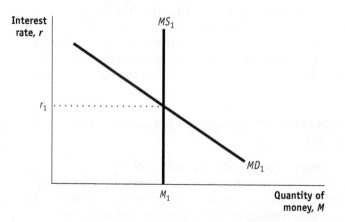

a.  Suppose the FOMC engages in an open-market purchase of Treasury bills. Holding everything else constant, what happens to the equilibrium quantity of money and the equilibrium interest rate? Sketch a graph illustrating these changes.

b.  Suppose the FOMC engages in an open-market sale of Treasury bills. Holding everything else constant, what happens to the equilibrium quantity of money and the equilibrium interest rate? Sketch a graph illustrating these changes.

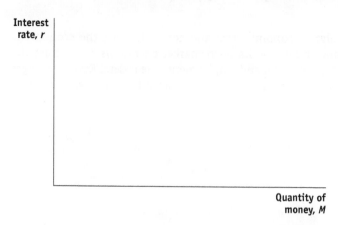

**c.** Suppose the aggregate price level increases. Holding everything else constant, what happens to the equilibrium quantity of money and the equilibrium interest rate? Sketch a graph illustrating these changes.

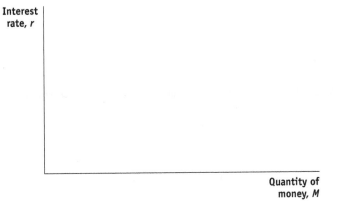

**2.** In your own words, explain how the Fed's actions can affect the economy. Be sure to include an explanation about how the Fed can affect the economy when the economy is in recession or when the economy is producing at an aggregate output level that is greater than the potential output level.

**3.** For each of the following situations, determine the appropriate central bank monetary response.

**a.** The central bank adopts an interest rate target of 5%. Currently the interest rate in the economy is at 8%.

**b.** The central bank adopts an inflation target of 3%. Currently the inflation rate is 4%.

**c.** The central bank adopts an inflation target of 4%. Current inflation is 4%. However, this quarter the central bank expects data to reveal that the economy is entering a recession and has a projected negative output gap.

**d.** Current unemployment is greater than the natural rate of unemployment.

## BEFORE YOU TAKE THE TEST

## Module Review Questions

1. When people offering to sell nonmonetary financial assets find that they must increase the interest rate these assets pay in order to sell them, this tells us that
   a. the quantity of money demanded is less than the quantity of money supplied.
   b. the quantity of money supplied equals the quantity of money demanded.
   c. the quantity of money demanded is greater than the quantity of money supplied.
   d. we cannot know anything about the relationship between the quantity of money demanded and the quantity of money supplied from this information.

2. Which of the following statements is true?
   a. Short-term interest rates tend to move independently of one another.
   b. Long-term interest rates tend to move together, and they tend to mimic short-term interest rates.
   c. Open-market purchases by the FOMC result in the interest rate decreasing.
   d. Open-market sales by the FOMC increase the money supply and cause a movement along the money demand curve.

Use the following graph to answer the next two questions.

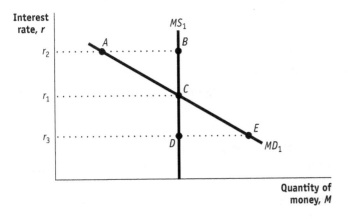

**3.** The economy is currently operating at its potential output level. Which point in the graph is most likely to represent this long-run situation in the money market? Point
a. *A,* since high interest rates encourage people to save more, leading to higher levels of investment
b. *B,* since the FOMC controls the money supply we know we must be on the money supply curve in the long run
c. *C,* since at this point the money market is in equilibrium
d. *D,* since low interest rates encourage business investment, which leads to higher economic growth
e. *E,* since low interest rates reduce inflationary pressures in the economy

**4.** In the graph, which point *most* likely represents a possible new short-run equilibrium if the FOMC conducts an open-market sale? Point
a. *A.*
b. *B.*
c. *C.*
d. *D.*
e. *E.*

**5.** The money supply curve shifts to the left. The most likely cause for this shift is the FOMC's open-market
a. purchase of Treasury bills.
b. sale of Treasury bills.

**6.** When the quantity of money demanded is greater than the quantity of money supplied, this implies that the interest rate is too low and people will decide to
a. sell interest-bearing assets, resulting in the price of these assets falling while the interest rate paid on these assets rises.
b. buy interest-bearing assets, resulting in the price of these assets rising while the interest rate paid on these assets rises.

**7.** When the Fed targets the federal funds rate, this means that the FOMC changes the money supply through open-market operations until the
a. rate of inflation in the economy matches their target.
b. actual federal funds rate equals the target rate.

8. The Taylor rule for monetary policy for the period from 1988 through 2008 provided guidance for setting the federal funds rate and stated that this rate should be set by considering
   a. both the inflation rate and the output gap.
   b. both the inflation rate and the unemployment gap.
   c. both the output gap and the unemployment gap.
   d. the inflation rate, the output gap, and the unemployment gap.

9. Inflation targeting means that
   a. the central bank adheres to maintaining a very strict interest rate target.
   b. the central bank announces the inflation rate that it is trying to achieve and then uses monetary policy to achieve this inflation rate.
   c. there may be a range of acceptable inflation rates or a specific inflation rate that the central bank hopes to achieve through monetary policy.
   d. Answers (a), (b), and (c) are all correct.
   e. Answers (b) and (c) are both correct.

10. After 2008, the Taylor rule
    a. resulted in a negative interest rate due to the combination of high unemployment and low inflation.
    b. did not predict Federal Reserve policy well since it is impossible to have a negative interest rate.

11. The zero lower bound refers to
    a. an upper limit for the interest rate where no matter what happens in the economy the interest rate cannot rise above this limit.
    b. the idea that interest rates cannot be less than zero since no one would be willing to accept a negative interest rate as the interest rate they would receive for lending out funds.

12. When an economy faces a zero lower bound, this implies that the central bank in this economy will be able to stimulate the economy
    a. by engaging in open-market purchases.
    b. by engaging in open-market sales.
    c. by engaging in open-market purchases since interest rates cannot fall any further than their current level.
    d. at very low cost since the interest rate is so low.

13. The Federal Reserve Bank engaged in "quantitative easing" in November of 2010 because
    a. the Fed no longer believed, no matter what the situation, in open-market operations as a monetary policy tool.
    b. the Fed recognized the zero lower bound problem and thought that "quantitative easing" might be a method of stimulating the economy given that open-market purchases were ineffective.
    c. the Fed hoped this would drive interest rates on long-term debt down and that this would lead to economic expansion.
    d. Answers (a), (b), and (c) are all correct.
    e. Answers (b) and (c) are both correct.
    f. Answers (a) and (c) are both correct.

## ANSWER KEY

# Answers to Problems and Exercises

**1.** **a.** When the Fed increases the money supply through an open-market purchase of Treasury bills, this shifts the money supply curve from $MS_1$ to $MS_2$ and results in a decrease in the equilibrium interest rate from $r_1$ to $r_2$ and an increase in the equilibrium quantity of money from $M_1$ to $M_2$. The following figure illustrates these changes.

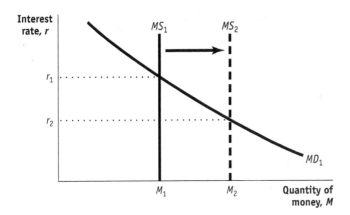

**b.** When the FOMC decreases the money supply through an open-market sale of Treasury bills, the money supply curve shifts from $MS_1$ to $MS_2$. This causes the equilibrium interest rate to increase from $r_1$ to $r_2$, while the equilibrium quantity of money decreases from $M_1$ to $M_2$. These changes are illustrated in the following figure.

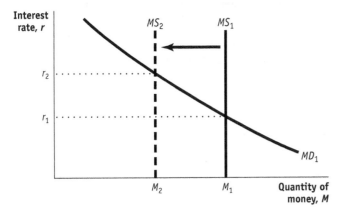

**c.** An increase in the aggregate price level shifts the money demand curve to the right from $MD_1$ to $MD_2$. This causes the equilibrium interest rate to increase from $r_1$ to $r_2$, while the equilibrium quantity of money is unchanged. The following figure illustrates this situation.

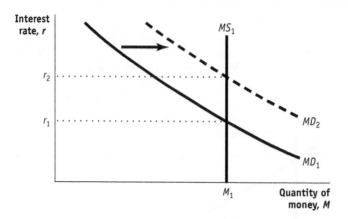

2. The Fed can affect the economy through its open-market operations. When the Fed expands the money supply by purchasing Treasury bills, this causes the interest rate to fall, holding everything else constant. As the interest rate declines, this acts as a stimulus to investment and consumer spending and, therefore, as a stimulus to aggregate demand. Thus, open-market purchases typically are used to stimulate the economy: when the economy is producing below the potential output level (i.e., the economy is in a recession), the Fed has the potential to alter this output level via active monetary policy. Conversely, when the economy is producing at a level greater than the potential output level, the Fed can engage in open-market sales that will effectively lead to higher interest rates and lower investment and consumer spending, thereby causing the level of aggregate demand to fall, holding everything else constant.

3. **a.** The central bank will want to decrease the interest rate. It can accomplish this goal by engaging in open-market purchases of Treasury bills.

   **b.** The central bank wants to reduce the inflation rate. It can do this by increasing the interest rate since this will slow the economy and result in a smaller output gap, which will help to pull the interest rate and, therefore, the rate of inflation down in the economy. The central bank should engage in open-market sales of Treasury bills.

   **c.** Since the central bank anticipates a slowdown in the economy, they also anticipate that there will be downward pressure on the aggregate price level as the level of spending in the economy falls. The central bank can stabilize the aggregate price level by engaging in expansionary monetary policy; the central bank should engage in open-market purchases of Treasury bills.

   **d.** Since the current rate of unemployment is greater than the potential rate of unemployment, the economy is in a recession. The central bank will want to engage in expansionary monetary policy unless it is actively seeking to reduce the targeted rate of inflation and the actual rate of inflation in the economy.

## Answers to Module Review Questions

1. **Answer c.** When interest rates must rise, this implies they are initially too low: in the money market, this would imply that the interest rate is initially below the equilibrium interest rate or where the quantity of money demanded is greater than the quantity of money supplied.

2.   **Answer c.** Short-term interest rates tend to move together, while long-term interest rates may or may not mimic short-term interest rates. When the FOMC makes an open-market purchase, this increases the level of reserves in the banking system, which leads to an expansion in the money supply and a decrease in the interest rate.

3.   **Answer c.** In the long run, the economy is in equilibrium, including the money market where the quantity of money demanded must equal the quantity of money supplied. This is only true at point C in the graph.

4.   **Answer a.** When the FOMC conducts an open-market sale, this causes the money supply to shift to the left and, for a given demand curve, results in the interest rate increasing. Only point A illustrates this scenario.

5.   **Answer b.** When the FOMC engages in open-market sales of Treasury bills, it sells Treasury bills to the public and receives dollars for those Treasury bills. The FOMC effectively removes reserves from the banking system with the sale of Treasury bills, which reduces the quantity of money supplied at every interest rate: the supply of money curve shifts to the left.

6.   **Answer a.** When quantity of money demanded is greater than quantity of money supplied, this implies that the interest rate is too low: the opportunity cost of holding money is relatively low and, therefore, people choose to hold more money. This causes people to sell interest-bearing assets (like bonds), and as the supply of these interest-bearing assets increases, this leads to a decrease in the price of these interest-bearing assets. As the price of these assets decreases, this implies that the interest rate paid on these assets is increasing.

7.   **Answer b.** Targeting the federal funds rate means that the Fed is using open-market operations to alter the interest rate banks charge one another for loans (the federal funds rate) so that it reaches a desired, or targeted, level.

8.   **Answer b.** The original Taylor rule for setting the Federal funds rate for the period 1988 through 2008 is given by the following equation: Federal funds rate = 2.07 + 1.28 × inflation − 1.95 × unemployment gap. Although there is a relationship between the level of output and the unemployment rate, the Taylor rule for this time period does not explicitly include the output gap.

9.   **Answer e.** Inflation targeting involves having the central bank announce the inflation rate or range for the inflation rate it is trying to achieve and then use its monetary policy to achieve this announced goal. Monetary policy to achieve a stated inflation goal will necessarily imply the loss of interest rate control since the interest rate will need to vary in order for the central bank to achieve its inflation target.

10.   **Answer b.** Application of the Taylor rule after 2008 predicted that interest rates would be negative. But it is impossible for interest rates to be negative, so the Taylor rule was not very insightful after 2008 due to the combination of high unemployment and low inflation creating a prediction that simply could not come true.

11.   **Answer b.** Interest rates must be positive or equal to zero because no one would willingly accept a negative return since they can always earn an interest rate of zero if they choose to hold cash. The zero lower bound refers to the idea that interest rates cannot fall below zero.

12.   **Answer c.** Open-market purchases are used by central banks to stimulate the economy because these open-market purchases typically result in the interest rate decreasing when the money supply increases. When an economy is operating at its zero lower bound, this implies that interest rates in the economy are as low as they can go and that any open-market purchase will have little impact since the interest rate will not drop any further.

13.   **Answer e.** In November 2010, the Fed wanted to pursue an expansionary economic policy due to the state of the economy. However, the interest rate at that time was at or near zero and open-market purchases would have been ineffective since the interest rate could not be lowered any further. The Fed engaged in "quantitative easing" so that it would lead to lower interest rates on long-term debt, which, the Fed hoped, would lead to an expansionary effect on the economy.

# Money, Output, and Prices in the Long Run

## BEFORE YOU READ THE MODULE

## Summary

This module examines the effects of an inappropriate monetary policy. In addition, the module discusses the concept of monetary neutrality, or the idea that monetary policy in the long run does not affect real aggregate output but does affect the aggregate price level. The module explores the relationship between monetary neutrality and its relationship to the long-term economic effects of monetary policy.

## Module Objectives

**Objective #1.** Monetary expansion in the short run can increase aggregate output beyond the potential output level. However, in the long run this monetary expansion does not result in an increase in aggregate output since aggregate output in the long run always equals potential output due to adjustments in the level of nominal wages. Thus, a monetary expansion in the long run raises the aggregate price level while having no effect on real GDP.

- A change in the money supply leads to a proportional change in the aggregate price level in the long run. That is, if an economy is initially in long-run equilibrium and the nominal money supply increases, long-run equilibrium can only be restored when all real values return to their original levels. Since the nominal money supply increased, the real money supply can only return to its initial level with a proportionate increase in the aggregate price level.

- Money neutrality refers to the idea that changes in the money supply have no real effects on the economy. An increase in the money supply results in the money supply curve shifting to the right. It also results in the money demand curve shifting to the right. In the long run, these two shifts result in the interest rate returning to its initial level and the money supply increasing from its initial level. Monetary policy, in the long run, has no effect on the interest rate.

- Monetary policy does have powerful real effects in the short run and can be used to ward off recessions or slow an expanding economy.

## Key Term

**monetary neutrality** the concept that changes in the *money supply* have no real effects on the *economy* in the long run and only result in a proportional change in the price level.

*Notes*

## AFTER YOU READ THE MODULE

## Tip

It is important to distinguish between the short-run and long-run effects of monetary policy. In the short run, monetary policy can be used to stimulate *AD* and shift it to the right, resulting in an increase in aggregate real output, or monetary policy can be used to contract *AD*, thereby shifting it to the left and leading to a decrease in the level of aggregate real output. In the long run, monetary policy has no effect on aggregate real output since aggregate real output in the long run will always equal potential output. Economists refer to this as monetary neutrality: money is neutral in its effect on aggregate real output in the long run, since it cannot affect the level of aggregate real output.

## WORKED PROBLEMS

1.  Suppose the economy in the short run is currently operating with an inflationary gap in which actual output is greater than potential output. If the government wishes to address this issue with activist monetary policy in order to restore the economy to potential output, what monetary policy should the central bank pursue? How will the implementation of this monetary policy work to return the economy to potential output?

**STEP 1:** First think about the implications of operating in the short run with an inflationary gap.

It is important that you can visualize this economic situation in terms of the *AD-AS* model. The following graph depicts the initial situation for this economy.

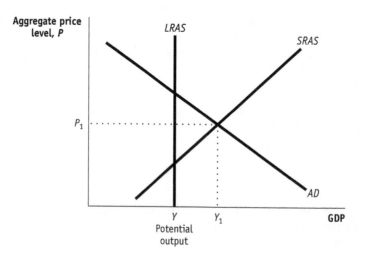

This economy is producing $Y_1$ in the short run: it is operating with an inflationary gap since actual output exceeds potential output. This implies that the economy has very low unemployment.

**STEP 2:** Consider the effect of a change in the money supply and how this will impact the level of aggregate production. Make a decision about the optimal activist monetary policy to pursue.

When the Federal Reserve engages in an open-market purchase, this increases the level of reserves in the banking system, expands the money supply through the money multiplier process, and reduces interest rates. These in turn cause aggregate demand to shift to the right at every aggregate price level.

When the Federal Reserve engages in open-market sales, this decreases the level of reserves in the banking system, reduces the money supply through the money multiplier process, and increases interest rates. These in turn cause aggregate demand to shift to the left at every aggregate price level.

If you examine the preceding graph, you can see that to return to the potential output level using an aggregate demand curve shift, the aggregate demand curve must shift to the left. The Federal Reserve will need to make open-market sales in order to shift the aggregate demand curve to the left.

**STEP 3:** Discuss how this activist monetary policy returns the economy to potential output.

When the Fed contracts the money supply this leads to a higher interest rate. The higher interest rate leads investment spending to fall, and therefore the level of aggregate expenditure will fall. As aggregate expenditure falls, this results in a decrease in real GDP. With the fall in the total quantity of goods and services demanded, the *AD* curve shifts to the left, restoring the economy to potential output $Y$.

2.  Suppose the economy is initially in long-run equilibrium as depicted in the *AD–AS* model. Suppose politicians view the current level of output as too low, and they encourage the central bank to engage in expansionary monetary policy. Describe the effects of this expansionary monetary policy on this economy in the short run, and then discuss what will happen in this economy in the long run if there are no further shocks to the economy. How does this example illustrate monetary neutrality?

**STEP 1:** Start by drawing a graph of this economy in long-run equilibrium using the *AD–AS* model.

In the *AD-AS* model, long-run equilibrium occurs at that output level at which *SRAS*, *AD*, and *LRAS* all intersect. This will occur at the potential output level of real GDP. The following figure illustrates this long-run equilibrium.

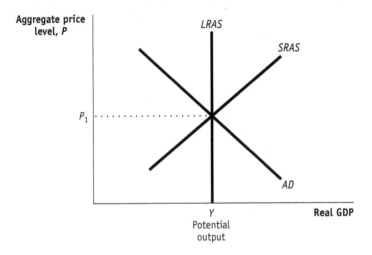

**STEP 2:** Alter your graph to illustrate the short-run effects of the expansionary monetary policy on this economy, making sure to note what happens to real GDP in the short run.

When the Fed engages in expansionary monetary policy this means that the Fed is purchasing Treasury bills in the open market. This will cause *AD* to shift to the right. The following graph illustrates the short-run effects of this policy: notice that real GDP increases to $Y_2$ and the aggregate price level increases to $P_2$. $Y_2$ is greater than potential output, which indicates that the economy is operating with an inflationary gap and that unemployment is unusually low.

**STEP 3:** Discuss the adjustment process in this economy to the long-run equilibrium, making sure to note what happens to real GDP in the long run.

Since unemployment is unusually low, this indicates that over time there will be pressure for nominal wages to increase. As nominal wages increase, this will cause the *SRAS* curve to shift to the left. This curve will continue to shift until it intersects $AD_2$ at the potential output level. The following figure represents this shift. Notice that the economy returns to a real GDP level that is equal to potential output and that the aggregate price level has increased to $P_3$.

**STEP 4:** Discuss monetary neutrality and how it relates to your findings in Step 3.

In the preceding graph, we see the economy return to long-run equilibrium after the full adjustment to the expansionary monetary policy. Although the expansionary monetary policy altered real GDP in the short run to $Y_2$, in the long run this expansionary monetary policy had no effect on real GDP. The expansionary monetary policy does have a long-run impact on our model: this policy causes the aggregate price level to increase.

This idea that changes in the money supply have no long-run impact on the level of real GDP is an illustration of the concept of monetary neutrality. Money is neutral in the long run since it does not impact the level of real GDP; the impact of money in the long run is to alter the aggregate price level.

# Problems and Exercises

1. Use the following table to answer this question.

| Change | Effect on nominal money demand | Effect on real money demand |
|---|---|---|
| Decrease in aggregate price level | | |
| Increase in interest rate | | |
| Change in regulation so that interest is now allowed on checking accounts | | |

   **a.** In the table, enter how each scenario will affect nominal money demand and real money demand.

   **b.** Explain why a change in the aggregate price level affects the nominal demand curve differently than it does the real money demand curve.

2. Use the *AD–AS* model to answer this question.
   (i) Scenario I

   The economy of Macroland is initially in long-run equilibrium. Then the FOMC of Macroland decides to reduce interest rates through an open-market operation.

   **a.** Draw a graph representing the initial situation in Macroland. In your graph, be sure to include the short-run aggregate supply curve (*SRAS*), the long-run aggregate supply curve (*LRAS*), and the aggregate demand curve (*AD*). On your graph mark the equilibrium aggregate price level and the aggregate output level as well as potential output.

   Aggregate
   price
   level, *P*

   Real GDP

**b.** Draw a graph of the money market depicting Macroland's initial situation before the FOMC engages in expansionary monetary policy as well as the effect of the FOMC's monetary policy actions. Be sure to label the *MS* and *MD* curves as well as the initial equilibrium and the equilibrium after the monetary policy action.

**c.** How does this monetary policy action affect the aggregate economy in the short run? Explain your answer verbally while also including a graph of the *AD–AS* model to illustrate your answer.

**d.** How does this monetary policy action affect the aggregate economy in the long run?

(ii) Scenario II

Econoland is currently operating with a recessionary gap.

e.  Draw a graph representing Econoland's economic situation using an *AD–AS* model. Be sure to indicate in your graph *SRAS*, *LRAS*, *AD*, the short-run equilibrium aggregate price level ($P_1$), the short-run equilibrium aggregate output level ($Y_1$), and the potential output level ($Y_E$).

Aggregate
price
level, *P*

Real GDP

f.  What monetary policy would you suggest the FOMC of Econoland pursue if its only goal is to restore production in Econoland to the potential output level? Explain how this monetary policy would achieve this goal.

g.  Is there a potential drawback to the implementation of this particular monetary policy? Explain your answer.

(iii) Scenario III

Upland is currently operating with an inflationary gap.

h.  Draw a graph representing Upland's economic situation using an *AD–AS* model. Be sure to indicate in your graph *SRAS*, *LRAS*, *AD*, the short-run equilibrium aggregate price level ($P_1$), the short-run equilibrium aggregate output level ($Y_1$), and the potential output level ($Y_E$).

Aggregate
price
level, *P*

Real GDP

**i.** What monetary policy would you suggest the FOMC of Upland pursue if its only goal is to restore production in Upland to the potential output level? Explain how this monetary policy would achieve this goal.

**j.** Is there a potential drawback to the implementation of this particular monetary policy? Explain your answer.

**3.** Suppose that when the FOMC reduces the interest rate by 1 percentage point it increases the level of investment spending by $500 million in Macroland. If the marginal propensity to save equals 0.25, what will be the total rise in real GDP, assuming the aggregate price level is held constant? Explain your answer.

**4.** Suppose the aggregate price level increases by 25%. What does this increase imply about the percentage increase in the quantity of money demanded in the long run? Explain your answer fully.

## BEFORE YOU TAKE THE TEST

# Module Review Questions

1.  Which of the following statements is true?
    a. In the long run, an increase in the nominal money supply increases the potential output level.
    b. In the long run, an increase in the nominal money supply will have no effect on real variables, including the aggregate price level.
    c. In the long run, an increase in the nominal money supply will lead to a proportionate increase in the aggregate price level.
    d. Statements (a) and (b) are both true.
    e. Statements (a), (b), and (c) are all true.

2.  Suppose that an economy experiences an increase in the aggregate output level. Assuming that the central bank does not engage in monetary policy, which of the following statements is true?
    a. The interest rate in this economy will increase.
    b. The interest rate in this economy will decrease.
    c. The interest rate in this economy will be unaffected by this change in aggregate output.
    d. This change in aggregate output will cause a movement along the money demand curve.

3.  Expansionary monetary policy will, holding everything else constant,
    a. lower the interest rate and cause *AD* to shift to the right.
    b. lower the interest rate and cause *AD* to shift to the left.
    c. raise the interest rate and cause *AD* to shift to the right.
    d. raise the interest rate and cause *AD* to shift to the left.

4.  Suppose in the short run the level of aggregate output in an economy decreases at the same time the aggregate price level decreases. This is most likely due to a
    a. leftward shift in the short-run aggregate supply curve, holding everything else constant.
    b. rightward shift in the short-run aggregate supply curve, holding everything else constant.
    c. leftward shift in the aggregate demand curve, holding everything else constant.
    d. rightward shift in the aggregate demand curve, holding everything else constant.

5.  When the economy is currently producing at a short-run level of aggregate output that is less than potential output, it is most likely that the Fed will engage in open-market
    a. purchases of Treasury bills.
    b. sales of Treasury bills.

6. Suppose the aggregate economy in the short run is operating at an aggregate output level that is greater than the potential output level. Holding everything else constant, what do you anticipate will happen to nominal wages in the long run given this information?

   a. Nominal wages will decrease.

   b. Nominal wages will remain constant.

   c. Nominal wages will increase.

7. In the short run, money is

   a. neutral since it can have no effect on real aggregate output.

   b. not neutral since changes in the money supply can cause real aggregate output to change.

## ANSWER KEY

# Answers to Problems and Exercises

1.  a.

| Change | Effect on nominal money demand | Effect on real money demand |
| --- | --- | --- |
| Decrease in aggregate price level | Shifts the nominal money demand curve to the left | Has no effect |
| Increase in interest rate | Causes a movement along the nominal money demand curve | Causes a movement along the real money demand curve |
| Change in regulation so that interest is now allowed on checking accounts | Shifts the nominal money demand curve to the right | Shifts the real money demand curve to the right |

b. When the aggregate price level changes, the nominal money demand curve does not automatically take into account the effect of this change in prices on the nominal demand for money. For example, as the aggregate price level rises, people will find that, due to the increase in the aggregate price level, they need to hold greater amounts of money in order to make their transactions. This causes the nominal money demand curve to shift to the right: people demand a greater quantity of nominal money at every interest rate. In contrast, the real money demand curve automatically takes into account any change in the aggregate price level: a change in the aggregate price level requires a proportionately equal change in the nominal quantity of money in order that the real quantity of money is unchanged.

2.  a.

b.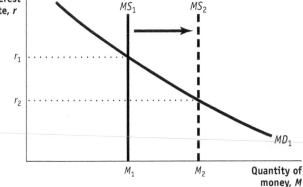

**c.** When the FOMC reduces interest rates through an open-market purchase of Treasury bills, this increases aggregate demand and causes the *AD* curve to shift to the right to $AD_2$. In the short run, this causes aggregate real output to increase to $Y_2$ and the aggregate price level to increase to $P_2$. This is illustrated in the following figure.

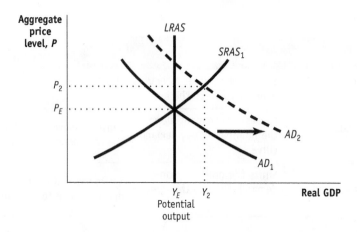

**d.** In the long run, the economy must return to producing its potential output, $Y_E$. This economic adjustment will occur as the *SRAS* curve shifts to the left as nominal wages rise. As the *SRAS* curve shifts back to $SRAS_3$, this will eliminate the inflationary gap, restore the economy to its potential output level, and lead to an even higher aggregate price level, $P_3$. The following figure illustrates this long-run adjustment.

**e.**

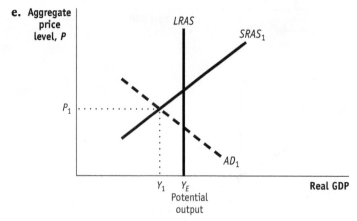

**f.** If the FOMC expands the money supply through open-market purchases, this will reduce interest rates and stimulate investment spending and, therefore, aggregate demand. As $AD$ shifts to the right from $AD_1$ to $AD_2$, this will cause real GDP to increase to $Y_E$ and prices to rise to $P_2$. The following figure illustrates this situation.

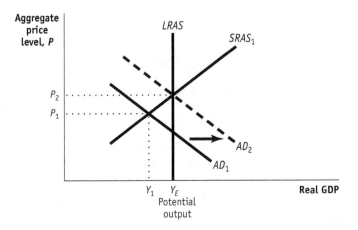

**g.** If the FOMC engages in activist monetary policy, this will cause the aggregate price level to increase. Alternatively, policymakers could do nothing and wait for the $SRAS$ to shift to the right as nominal wages fall. In the long run, aggregate output would return to $Y_E$ and the aggregate price level would fall below its initial level of $P_1$.

**h.**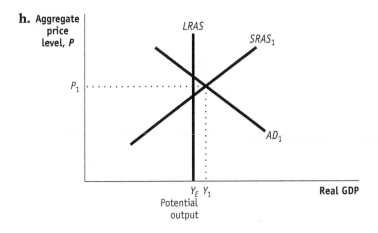

**i.** The FOMC should decrease the money supply and thereby increase the interest rate through open-market sales of Treasury bills. This action by the FOMC will cause the $AD$ to shift to the left, restoring the economy to its potential output level at a lower aggregate price level than $P_1$.

**j.** No, this policy restores the economy to its long-run position without raising the aggregate price level.

**3.** The action by the FOMC effectively creates a change in autonomous investment spending of $500 million. This change in autonomous investment spending will cause real GDP to increase by a larger, multiplied amount due to the multiplier process. Since the multiplier equals $1/(1 - MPC)$ or, in this case, 4, we can compute the total change in real GDP as 4($500 million), or $2 billion.

4.  When the aggregate price level increases by 25%, this means that, on average, prices in the economy have risen by 25%. This in turn implies that people will need 25% more money to make the same purchases; thus, the demand for money at any given interest rate will need to shift to the right and by an amount that is 25% greater than the original money demand. The idea here is that the demand for money will be proportional to the price level in the long run.

## Answers to Module Review Questions

1.  **Answer c.** In the long run, the economy will operate at the potential output level: any increase in the money supply will not affect the real value of aggregate output, but will lead to a proportionate increase in the aggregate price level.

2.  **Answer a.** When aggregate real output increases in an economy, this causes the demand for money to shift to the right. For a given money supply curve (remember the central bank is not engaging in monetary policy), this will cause the interest rate to increase.

3.  **Answer a.** Expansionary monetary policy is an increase in the money supply: when the money supply increases, this means that the supply of money curve shifts to the right causing the interest rate to fall. A fall in the interest rate results in higher investment spending and consumption spending: this causes the *AD* curve to shift to the right.

4.  **Answer c.** If there is only one shift in either the short-run *AS* curve or the *AD* curve, then a fall in both the aggregate output level and the aggregate price level is only possible with a leftward shift of the *AD* curve.

5.  **Answer a.** When the current level of aggregate output is less than potential output, the Fed will likely engage in expansionary monetary policy to stimulate the economy to return to the potential output level. Expansionary monetary policy implies that the Fed is increasing the money supply; hence, the Fed is purchasing Treasury bills in the open market.

6.  **Answer c.** When the economy operates in the short run at an aggregate output level greater than the potential level of output, this implies that unemployment is below the natural rate of unemployment. As the economy moves to the long run, nominal wages will increase due to labor market pressures arising from this lower-than-natural level of unemployment. The nominal wage will continue to increase until the short-run *AS* curve shifts far enough to the left to return this economy to its potential output level.

7.  **Answer b.** Money in the short run is not neutral: when the central bank changes the money supply, this causes the *AD* curve to shift and in the short run this shift will cause the economy to either contract or expand. In the long run, the short-run aggregate supply curve shifts, returning the aggregate economy to its potential output level: in the long run, money is neutral since it cannot alter the level of aggregate real output.

# Inflation, Disinflation, and Deflation

## ▮ BEFORE YOU READ THE MODULE

## Summary

This module analyzes the underlying causes of inflation by presenting the classical model of the price level. The module explores the relationship between the rate of growth of the money supply and the inflation rate: economies that collect an inflation tax by printing money find that this practice can lead to high rates of inflation.

## Module Objectives

**Objective #1.**   Economists define hyperinflation as a very high rate of inflation. Hyperinflation is always associated with rapid increases in the money supply.

**Objective #2.**   In the long run, any given percentage increase in the money supply does not change the level of real GDP, but it does result in an equal percentage rise in the overall price level. Thus, an increase in the nominal money supply, $M$, leads to a long-run increase in the aggregate price level, $P$, that leaves the real money supply, $M/P$, at its original level.

**Objective #3.**   The classical model of the price level is a simplified model that equates the short run as equivalent to the long run. In this model, the real quantity of money, $M/P$, is always at its long-run equilibrium level. This model assumes the neutrality of money in the long run: that is, in the long run, the level of the nominal money supply does not affect the level of real GDP. The classical model of the price level assumes that the economy moves from one long-run equilibrium to another because wages and prices are flexible: in this model, the economy always produces at a point on its *LRAS* curve. This assumption is a poor one during periods of low inflation, but it seems to work well as a model in periods of high inflation, since in periods of high inflation wage and price stickiness seem to disappear.

- In countries with high inflation, changes in the money supply are quickly translated into changes in the inflation rate.

- Fiat money is money that has no intrinsic value, and in modern economies this reliance on the use of fiat money means that governments can choose to pay for some of their expenditures by simply printing money and using this printed money to pay some of their bills. In the United States, the U.S. Treasury finances the government's spending; the Fed monetizes this debt by creating money when it buys the debt back from the public through open-market purchases of Treasury bills.

- Sources of revenue for the government include the right to print money, or seigniorage. When governments run large deficits and are unwilling to increase taxes or decrease spending, they often turn to printing money to finance their deficit and this leads to large increases in the aggregate price level. This action imposes an inflation tax on those people who currently hold money. When inflation is high, people will try to avoid holding money and will instead substitute real goods as well as interest-bearing assets for money.

- The revenue created by printing money in real terms is the real seigniorage. Real seigniorage, as calculated as the change in the money supply divided by the price level, is equal to the rate of growth of the money supply times the real money supply.

- Over time for a given amount of real seigniorage the government must impose an ever-higher rate of inflation. Thus, governments that pay for goods and services by printing money may end up creating higher and higher rates of inflation leading eventually to hyperinflation.

**Objective #4.** In the face of high inflation, the public will reduce the level of real money it holds. This reduction in real money holding forces the government to generate a higher rate of inflation in order to collect the same amount of real inflation tax: this action causes the inflation rate to accelerate and can easily lead to the inflation rate spiraling out of control.

**Objective #5.** Economies will experience moderate inflation if they pursue economic policies that target an unemployment rate that is below the natural rate of unemployment. Governments may purposefully pursue such targets prior to an election in order to achieve low rates of unemployment at the time of the election. A government may choose too low a target for the natural rate of unemployment, and the pursuit of this overly optimistic target will lead to moderate inflation.

**Objective #6.** In an economy, actual output fluctuates around potential output in the short run: a recessionary gap occurs when actual output is less than potential output, and an inflationary gap occurs when actual output is greater than potential output. The percentage difference between the actual level of real GDP and the potential output is called the output gap. A negative output gap is associated with an unusually high unemployment rate, while a positive output gap is associated with an unusually low unemployment rate.

**Objective #7.** A government may print money in order to pay some of its expenses rather than raising taxes or borrowing funds. This government is engaging in seigniorage. A government will engage in seigniorage if it finds itself running a large deficit and it lacks the political will to eliminate this deficit by either cutting spending or raising taxes, or it lacks the ability to borrow funds because potential lenders question that government's ability to repay its debts.

**Objective #8.** Inflation imposes a tax on those who hold money since inflation erodes the purchasing power of that money. The real inflation tax collected by a government, or the real seigniorage, is equal to the rate of growth of the money supply times the real money supply. This tells us that the real inflation tax will increase as the government allows the money supply to grow rapidly.

## Key Terms

**classical model of the price level** a simplified financial model of the price level in which the real quantity of money, *M/P*, is always at its long-run *equilibrium* level. This model ignores the distinction between the short run and the long run but is useful for analyzing the case of high *inflation*.

**inflation tax** the reduction in the value of money held by the public caused by *inflation*.

## ▰ AFTER YOU READ THE MODULE

# Tips

**Tip #1.** The module introduces new vocabulary that you will want to learn and understand. In particular, you will want to be able to define and distinguish between deflation and disinflation. Deflation refers to a fall in the aggregate price level and disinflation refers to a decrease in the inflation rate reflecting policymakers' decisions that the economy has built-in inflationary expectations that need to be reduced.

**Tip #2.** It is important to understand the distinction between inflation and hyperinflation and their causes. Inflation refers to an increase in the general price level in the economy and may be due to positive demand shocks or negative supply shocks. Figure 40.1 illustrates a positive demand shock while Figure 40.2 illustrates a negative supply shock; both types of shocks lead to higher aggregate price levels.

**Figure 40.1**

**Figure 40.2**

Hyperinflation refers to very high rates of inflation; in an economy it is caused by the government printing money to finance its government deficits.

**Tip #3.** If the money supply grows rapidly, this will lead to inflation: if there is inflation people will wish to hold smaller amounts of real money. This implies that if the government needs to print money in order to finance its deficit, the government will find that the increase in the money supply needed to finance these deficits will grow over time because of higher rates of inflation. As the government increases the growth of the money supply, the rate of inflation will continue to climb: the result is a spiral of ever-higher inflation.

**Tip #4.** Remember that real seigniorage can be calculated as

$$\text{Real seigniorage} = (\Delta M/M) \times (M/P)$$

where $\Delta M/M$ is the rate of growth of the money supply and $M/P$ is the real money supply. This equation tells you that the inflation tax imposed by the government is equal to the product of the growth rate of the money supply times the real money supply. With inflation, $M/P$ grows smaller since people will want to hold less money in times of inflation. As $M/P$ gets smaller this implies that the growth rate of the money supply will need to increase in order for the government to have sufficient funds to finance its deficit if it is unwilling to reduce the deficit by decreasing spending to pay for the deficit by raising taxes, or it is unable to finance the deficit through borrowing.

# WORKED PROBLEMS

1. In Zerbia, the aggregate price level has been changing quite rapidly. Your friend, Zorba, owns a restaurant where he charges a fixed price of $10 per dinner. He has come to you for advice on what price he should charge for dinner, given the changes in the aggregate price level. You tell him you will provide him guidance after you look into the situation. Upon consulting the available economic data, you find that the aggregate price level in Zerbia is increasing 50% per month. Using this information, provide Zorba with his menu prices for the next year using the following table to organize your response. Finally, calculate the percentage increase in the price of dinner from the beginning of the year to the end of the year.

| Month | Price of dinner |
|-----------|-----------------|
| January | $10.00 |
| February | |
| March | |
| April | |
| May | |
| June | |
| July | |
| August | |
| September | |
| October | |
| November | |
| December | |

**STEP 1:** Analyze the data you have been given and determine how to use that data to answer Zorba's question.

The aggregate price level in Zerbia is increasing by 50% per month. That means that if Zorba wants to price his dinners at a nominal price that maintains the real price of the dinner at $10, he will need to increase his dinner price by 50% each month. For February, the price of dinner will be equal to (the price of the dinner in January)(1 + the inflation rate as a decimal) or (the price of the dinner in January)(1 + 0.5). For March, we will use this basic formula but replace the price of the dinner in January with the price of the dinner in February. This process will continue for each of the months for which we want to compute the price of dinner.

**STEP 2:** Use the given monthly inflation rate to calculate the needed adjustment in the price of dinner. Fill in the table for Zorba.

| Month | Price of dinner |
|-----------|-----------------|
| January | $10.00 |
| February | 15.00 |
| March | 22.50 |
| April | 33.75 |
| May | 50.63 |
| June | 75.94 |
| July | 113.91 |
| August | 170.86 |
| September | 256.29 |
| October | 384.43 |
| November | 576.65 |
| December | 864.98 |

**STEP 3:** Finally, calculate the percentage increase in the price of dinner from the beginning of the year to the end of the year.

To find the percentage increase in the price of dinner from the beginning of the year to the end of the year, we use the prices in the preceding table and the simple percentage change formula. Thus, [($864.98 − $10.00)/($10.00)](100) = 8,549.80%.

**2.** Joe's Used Cars negotiates a loan from First Bank of $500,000 for its business operations for the coming year. Joe's Used Cars and First Bank agree on the terms of the loan: First Bank will loan Joe's Used Cars the $500,000 for the year, and Joe's Used Cars will repay the full amount of the loan at the end of the year plus $50,000. At the time the loan is made, both Joe's Used Cars and First Bank anticipate that the rate of inflation for the year will be 5%. The actual rate of inflation during the year is 2%. Given this information, identify the nominal interest rate on the loan, the expected real interest rate on the loan, and the actual real interest rate on the loan. In addition, determine who is made better off when the actual rate of inflation is less than the expected rate of inflation, and then explain your answer.

**STEP 1:** Calculate the nominal rate of interest given the information.

The nominal rate of interest on this loan is found by using the following formula:

Loan repayment = Principal (1 + nominal interest rate)

We know that the loan repayment is $550,000 and we know that the principal, or the amount borrowed, is $500,000. Thus, the given formula can be written as 550,000 = 500,000(1 + nominal interest rate). Simplifying this formula we get (50,000)/(500,000) = nominal interest rate or the nominal interest rate is equal to 10%. An alternative way to see this is to recognize that $50,000, the interest payment, is 10% of the total amount borrowed.

**STEP 2:** Calculate the expected real rate of interest.

The expected real rate of interest can be found by using the formula

Expected real interest rate = nominal interest rate − expected inflation rate

From Step 1 we know that the nominal interest rate is 10%, and from the given information we know that the expected inflation rate is 5%: thus, the expected real interest rate is 5%.

**STEP 3:** Calculate the actual real rate of interest.

The actual real rate of interest can be found by using the formula

Actual real interest rate = nominal interest rate − actual inflation rate

From Step 1 we know that the nominal interest rate is 10%, and from the given information we know that the actual rate of inflation was 2%: thus, the actual real interest rate is 8%.

**STEP 4:** Determine who benefits when the actual rate of inflation is greater than the expected rate of inflation.

First Bank benefits since it made the loan anticipating that it would earn a real rate of interest of 5%, and instead it actually earned a real rate of interest of 8%. Joe's Used Cars is hurt because it agreed to pay a real interest rate of 5% for the loan, and it is instead paying a real interest rate of 8% for this loan.

# Problems and Exercises

1. Use the following table to answer this question.

| Real inflation tax | Inflation rate | Real money supply |
|---|---|---|
| $ 5 million | 5% | $100 million |
|  | 5 | 120 million |
| 12.80 million |  | 160 million |
| 14 million | 7 |  |
| 20 million |  | 200 million |

   a. We know that the real inflation tax is equal to the inflation rate times the real money supply. Use this information to fill in the missing entries in the table.

   b. For a given level of the real money supply, what happens to the real inflation tax if the inflation rate increases?

   c. For a given level of the real money supply, if the real inflation tax is decreasing, what must be true about the inflation rate?

   d. For a given real inflation tax, what happens to the real money supply if the inflation rate increases?

2. Suppose you live in an economy that is currently experiencing hyperinflation. At the start of the year, the cost of a loaf of bread is $2.00.

   a. If the inflation rate is 100% a month, what will be the price of the loaf of bread in 12 months? You might find it helpful to organize your answer in a table giving the month of the year and the price of the bread for that month.

**b.** What is the total price increase in percentage terms for the year?

**3.** Use the following graph to answer this question.

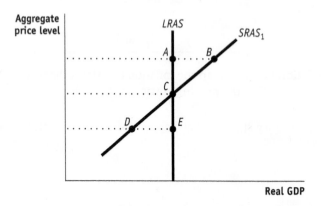

**a.** On the graph, which point best represents a recessionary gap for this economy in the short run? Explain your answer.

**b.** Given the graph, how would you explain this economy's recessionary gap? What are the consequences of a recessionary gap on a country's unemployment rate?

**c.** What is the level of actual unemployment relative to the natural rate of unemployment when this economy operates in the short run with a recessionary gap? Explain your answer and be sure to indicate what type of unemployment would cause these two rates to be different from one another.

**d.** At what point(s) on the graph is the actual unemployment rate equal to the natural rate of unemployment? Explain your answer.

**e.** On the graph, which point best represents an inflationary gap for this economy in the short run? Explain your answer.

**f.** Given the graph, how would you explain this economy's inflationary gap? What are the consequences of an inflationary gap on a country's unemployment rate?

**g.** What is the level of actual unemployment relative to the natural rate of unemployment when this economy operates in the short run with an inflationary gap? Explain your answer.

## BEFORE YOU TAKE THE TEST

# Module Review Questions

1. Which of the following statements is true?
   a. Hyperinflation refers to a very high rate of inflation.
   b. During periods of high inflation, people are eager to hold large sums of money since these sums of money grow in value the higher the inflation rate.
   c. In the long run, an increase in the money supply does not change real GDP.
   d. Statements (a), (b), and (c) are all true.
   e. Statements (a) and (b) are both true.
   f. Statements (a) and (c) are both true.

2. The classical model of the price level
   a. reflects the work of John Maynard Keynes.
   b. ignores the short-run movements of the economy in response to a change in the money supply.
   c. works well particularly for periods in which inflation is low.
   d. All of the above answers are correct.
   e. Answers (a) and (b) are both correct.
   f. Answers (a) and (c) are both correct.
   g. Answers (b) and (c) are both correct.

3. In periods of high inflation, the short-run *AS* curve
   a. adjusts quickly by shifting to the right.
   b. adjusts slowly, if at all, and will eventually shift to the left.
   c. is insensitive to the high inflation and is therefore unaffected by it.
   d. adjusts swiftly and shifts to the left due to rising nominal wages.
   e. None of the above answers is correct.

4. The Federal Reserve monetizes the government's debt when it
   a. sells U.S. Treasury bills on the open market.
   b. purchases U.S. Treasury bills on the open market.
   c. mandates the use of fiat money as a medium of exchange.
   d. Answers (a) and (c) are both correct.
   e. Answers (b) and (c) are both correct.

5. *Seigniorage* is the term
   a. used to describe open-market operations.
   b. that dates back to the Middle Ages and refers to the government's right to issue coins and to charge, and therefore, collect a fee for issuing these coins.
   c. that economists use to refer to the government's right to print money.
   d. Answers (a), (b), and (c) are all correct.
   e. Answers (a) and (b) are both correct.
   f. Answers (a) and (c) are both correct.
   g. Answers (b) and (c) are both correct.

6. An inflation tax
   a. is a tax that is levied on the Fed when it increases the money supply.
   b. is a tax on those who hold money that occurs when the inflation erodes the purchasing power of their money.
   c. occurs when the government prints money to cover its budget deficit.
   d. Answers (a), (b), and (c) are all correct.
   e. Answers (a) and (b) are both correct.
   f. Answers (a) and (c) are both correct.
   g. Answers (b) and (c) are both correct.

7. For a given inflation rate, an increase in the real money supply
   a. does not affect the real inflation tax.
   b. increases the real inflation tax.
   c. decreases the real inflation tax.
   d. may increase, decrease, or have no effect on the real inflation tax.

8. Which of the following statements is true?
   a. When actual output is equal to potential output, the natural rate of unemployment equals the actual rate of employment.
   b. During an inflationary gap, the unemployment rate is greater than the natural rate of unemployment.
   c. During a recessionary gap, the unemployment rate is greater than the natural rate of unemployment.
   d. Actual output fluctuates around potential output in the long run.

9. Which of the following statements is true?
   a. Moderate inflation may be the result of politicians pursuing too low an unemployment rate for the economy prior to an election.
   b. Moderate inflation may be the result of an aggregate supply shock to the economy.
   c. Moderate inflation is easily brought under control through a process called disinflation.
   d. Statements (a), (b), and (c) are all true.
   e. Statements (a) and (b) are both true.
   f. Statements (a) and (c) are both true.
   g. Statements (b) and (c) are both true.

10. Which of the following statements is true?
   a. Zimbabwe in June 2008 had the world's highest inflation rate.
   b. Zimbabwe's hyperinflation was due primarily to political instability, which led President Mugabe to finance government spending through the printing of money.
   c. During the hyperinflation in Zimbabwe, the government's ability to raise tax revenue was greatly restricted due to political instability.
   d. Statements (a), (b), and (c) are all true.
   e. Statements (a) and (c) are both true.
   f. Statements (b) and (c) are both true.

11. Which of the following statements is true?
   a. In the short run, an increase in the money supply will increase the aggregate price level but will not alter the level of real GDP.
   b. In the long run, an increase in the money supply will increase the aggregate price level but will have no effect on the level of real GDP.
   c. In the long run, an increase in the money supply will cause nominal prices and nominal wages to increase by the same percentage as the percentage increase in the money supply.
   d. Statements (a) and (c) are both true.
   e. Statements (b) and (c) are both true.

12. A negative supply shock will, holding everything else constant, cause the aggregate price level to
   a. increase and the aggregate level of real GDP to decrease in the short run.
   b. decrease and the aggregate level of real GDP to decrease in the short run.
   c. increase and the aggregate level of real GDP to increase in the short run.
   d. decrease and the aggregate level of real GDP to increase in the short run.

## ■ ANSWER KEY

# Answers to Problems and Exercises

**1. a.**

| Real inflation tax | Inflation rate | Real money supply |
|---|---|---|
| $ 5 million | 5% | $100 million |
| 6 million | 5 | 120 million |
| 12.80 million | 8 | 160 million |
| 14 million | 7 | 200 million |
| 20 million | 10 | 200 million |

**b.** The real inflation tax will increase. When the inflation rate increases, then the purchasing power of the money supply is reduced: this is equivalent to a tax on the value of all money held by the public. In the table shown here, in part (a) you can see this illustrated when the real money supply equals $200 million: when the inflation rate is 7%, the real inflation tax is $14 million, and when the inflation rate is 10%, the real inflation tax is $20 million.

**c.** If the real inflation rate is falling, this indicates that the purchasing power of the money supply is being eroded more slowly. This can only be true if the inflation rate is lower than its previous levels. Again, this is illustrated in the table.

**d.** There is a trade-off between the inflation rate and the money supply for a given constant level of real inflation tax: that tax can be constant with an increasing inflation rate only if the real money supply is decreasing.

**2. a.** To calculate the price of the bread in 12 months use the following table to organize your answer.

| Month of the year | Price of a loaf of bread |
|---|---|
| 1 | $   4.00 |
| 2 | 8.00 |
| 3 | 16.00 |
| 4 | 32.00 |
| 5 | 64.00 |
| 6 | 128.00 |
| 7 | 256.00 |
| 8 | 512.00 |
| 9 | 1,024.00 |
| 10 | 2,048.00 |
| 11 | 4,096.00 |
| 12 | 8,192.00 |

**b.** To calculate the total increase in price for the period, we use the following formula: percentage change in price equals (the current price − the base price) × 100/(the base price), or the percentage change in price equals ($8,192 − $2) × 100/2 equals 459,500%.

**3. a.** Point $D$ best represents a recessionary gap for this economy since at point $D$ actual real GDP is less than the potential level of real GDP.

**b.** The economy would produce at point *D* if there was a negative demand shock that caused the *AD* curve to shift to the left so that it intersected the *SRAS* at point *D*. This is illustrated in the following graph.

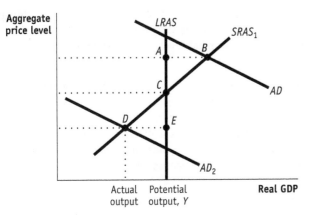

When a country produces a level of real GDP corresponding to a recessionary gap ($Y_1$ versus $Y$ in the above graph), this creates a negative output gap. This negative gap will increase the unemployment rate above the natural rate of unemployment.

**c.** The level of actual unemployment exceeds the natural rate of unemployment due to the existence of both structural and cyclical unemployment.

**d.** At points *A*, *C*, and *E* the natural rate of unemployment and the actual unemployment rate are equal. We know this because the economy is producing at its potential output level, which is the level of output at which the unemployment rate equals the natural rate.

**e.** Point *B* best represents an inflationary gap, since actual output at point *B* is greater than the potential output level of real GDP.

**f.** The economy would produce at point *B* in the short run given the *SRAS* if there was a positive *AD* shock that shifted the *AD* curve to the right so that it intersects the *SRAS* curve at point *B*. This is illustrated in the graph below.

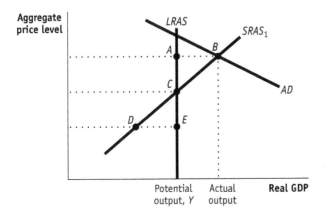

If the economy produces with an inflationary gap, a positive output gap is created. A positive output gap will decrease the actual unemployment rate below the natural rate of unemployment.

**g.** The rate of actual unemployment is less than the natural rate of unemployment since the economy will need to employ more workers in order to increase production beyond the potential output level of real GDP.

# Answers to Module Review Questions

1.  **Answer c.** High inflation is not the same as hyperinflation: economists distinguish between the two terms, calling any inflation rate in excess of 50% per month a hyper-inflation. During periods of high inflation, people reduce their money holdings since the purchasing power of their money holdings falls due to the inflation. In the long run, the economy will produce at its potential level of output no matter what the level of the money supply.

2.  **Answer b.** The classical model of the price level was used by the "classical" economists who wrote before the work of John Maynard Keynes. It is a model that ignores the short-run movements of the economy in response to a change in the money supply and instead focuses on the long-run adjustment process. It is a model that works particularly well when analyzing periods with high inflation, since these long-run adjustments are apt to be quicker than the economic adjustment that occurs when the inflation rate is relative-ly low.

3.  **Answer d.** In periods of high inflation, the short-run *AS* curve adjusts quickly through wage and price adjustment; this causes the short-run *AS* curve to shift to the left due to the higher nominal costs associated with the high inflation in order to move the econo-my toward its long-run equilibrium.

4.  **Answer b.** The Fed monetizes the government's debt when it purchases U.S. Treasury bills on the open market: this purchase has the effect of increasing the money supply in circulation in the economy. The adoption of fiat money by an economy does not lead to monetization of the debt: it is the actual use of this money issued by the government to purchase the debt that monetizes the debt.

5.  **Answer g.** This term is covered in the text: it dates from the Middle Ages and referred to the right to stamp gold and silver into coins and then charge a fee for making the coins and belonged to the medieval lords, or seigniors. Today the term is used by economists to describe the government's right to print money. The U.S. government, through the Fed, engages in seigniorage when the Fed makes an open-market purchase (which is a type of open-market operation) of Treasury bills.

6.  **Answer g.** An inflation tax is the reduction in purchasing power that occurs during inflation. This inflation tax occurs when the government spends more than its revenue coming in and turns to printing money to cover its deficit. This printing of money, by expanding the money supply, leads to inflation and a loss of purchasing power for peo-ple who hold money.

7.  **Answer b.** The real inflation tax is equal to the inflation rate multiplied by the real money supply. Thus, for a given inflation rate if the real money supply increases, this must necessarily result in an increase in the real inflation tax.

8.  **Answer c.** When actual output equals potential output, the unemployment rate equals the natural rate of unemployment and not the natural rate of employment. During an inflationary gap, the unemployment rate is less than the natural rate of unemployment, since, when the economy is producing an output level greater than its potential output level, it is temporarily using resources at more than the normal rate. Thus, during a reces-sionary gap, the unemployment rate will be greater than the natural rate of unemploy-ment, since there is a negative output gap and this is associated with unusually high unemployment. Actual output fluctuates around potential output in the short run: in the long run, actual output equals potential output due to full price adjustment.

9.  **Answer e.** Moderate inflation may be caused by politicians pursuing too low an unem-ployment rate due to using a target rate of unemployment that is lower than the natural rate of unemployment; or because of aggregate supply shocks to the economy. Eliminating moderate inflation through disinflation is a costly procedure, since it requires accepting a higher-than-normal unemployment rate in order to reduce inflationary expectations.

10. **Answer d.** These are all factual statements found in the text. The Zimbabwe inflation was due to the excessive printing of money in order to finance government spending. This printing of money to provide funds for government spending was necessary since the level of political instability in the country made it impossible to raise the needed revenue through taxes.

11. **Answer e.** In the short run, an increase in the money supply will cause the *AD* curve to shift to the right and for a given *SRAS* curve this will result in the aggregate price level and the level of real GDP increasing. But, in the long run, an increase in the money supply will result in nominal wages and prices rising in order to restore the economy to the long-run level of real GDP (that is, to potential GDP). This will require that the percentage change in nominal prices and nominal wages equal the percentage change in the money supply.

12. **Answer a.** A negative supply shock will cause the short-run *AS* curve to shift to the left. For a given *AD* curve this will cause the short-run aggregate price level to increase and the short-run aggregate level of real GDP to decrease.

# module 41 (34)

# The Phillips Curve

## ■ BEFORE YOU READ THE MODULE

### Summary

This module defines the Phillips curve and uses it to explain the short-run trade-off between inflation and unemployment. The module also discusses why there is no long-run trade-off between inflation and unemployment. The module considers expansionary policies and their efficacy: expansionary policies are limited in their impact due to the effects of expected inflation. The module also discusses why inflation, even when it is moderate, is difficult to stop in an economy. It also explores the effect of deflation in an economy and why policymakers seek to avoid deflation. The module examines why policy makers are inclined to favor policies that result in a low but positive inflation rate.

### Module Objectives

**Objective #1.** Economic data suggests that when the unemployment rate is high, the wage rate tends to fall, and when the unemployment rate is low, the wage rate tends to rise. There is a similar pattern between the unemployment rate and the rate of inflation: in the short run, the rate of inflation is negatively related to the unemployment rate. The short-run Phillips curve (SRPC) represents this negative relationship between the unemployment rate and the inflation rate. The SRPC says that at any given point in time, there is a trade-off between unemployment and inflation: lower unemployment is possible only with higher inflation.

- In the short run, an increase in the aggregate price level due to shifts in the AD result in increases in real GDP, which in turn lead to lower unemployment rates. Thus, aggregate price increases occur as unemployment decreases. That is, a low rate of unemployment corresponds to an economy in which there are shortages of labor and other resources, leading to rising prices.

- The most important factor affecting inflation rates other than the unemployment rate is the expected inflation rate. The expected inflation rate is that rate of inflation that employers and workers expect in the near future.

- The expected inflation rate affects the SRPC. When the expected inflation rate increases, this causes the SRPC to shift up by the amount of the expected inflation at every unemployment rate.

- In general people base their expectations about inflation on experience. If the inflation rate has been 5%, then people will expect the inflation rate to continue to be around 5%; if the inflation rate rises to 10%, then people will expect the inflation rate to be around 10%.

- The *SRPC* worked in the 1960s but seemed to break down in the 1970s as the economy experienced both high unemployment and high inflation. This stagflation is believed to be the result of supply shocks and a buildup of expectations about inflation.

- The long-run Phillips curve (*LRPC*) is a vertical line at an unemployment level high enough that the actual inflation rate equals the expected inflation rate. This unemployment rate is called the nonaccelerating inflation rate of unemployment, or the NAIRU, since it is the level of unemployment that equates the actual rate of inflation with the expected inflation rate. An economy operating at levels of unemployment below the NAIRU will experience accelerating inflation; that is, an unemployment rate below the NAIRU cannot be maintained in the long run. The NAIRU is just another name for the natural rate of unemployment, or the sum of frictional and structural unemployment.

**Objective #2.**   Deflation refers to a falling aggregate price level. Unexpected deflation benefits lenders who are owed money, because the real value of the payments they receive from borrowers increases during deflation; unexpected deflation hurts borrowers who owe money, because the real value of the payments they make to lenders increases during deflation.

- During a period of deflation, borrowers must cut their spending when the burden of their debt increases due to the deflation: this leads to a sharp decrease in aggregate demand that worsens the economic slump. The effect of deflation in reducing aggregate demand is known as debt deflation.

- During a period of deflation, people will expect inflation to fall, and these expectations will lead to a reduction in the aggregate price level. There is a limit, however, to how far the nominal interest rate can fall: this is called the zero bound, a situation in which the nominal interest rate cannot fall below 0%. This means that the central bank can find itself in a situation where it cannot effectively use monetary policy to stimulate the economy: if the nominal interest rate is already zero, the central bank cannot cut the nominal interest rate any further. This situation is called the liquidity trap where monetary policy is useless as a means of stimulating aggregate demand because the nominal interest rate simply cannot fall any further.

**Objective #3.**   Disinflation refers to the process of bringing down inflation when the inflation has become embedded in expectations. An economy trying to reduce inflation that is built into expectations will find this a difficult task: policy makers will need to keep the unemployment rate above the natural rate for an extended period of time in order to bring down this kind of inflation.

**Objective #4.**   Moderate inflation may also be the result of supply shocks to the economy. If the short-run *AS* curve shifts to the left, this brings a higher level of aggregate prices while reducing the level of real GDP. Policy makers find it difficult to pursue anti-inflationary policy when there is a negative supply shock, since this will produce even higher levels of unemployment. The great disinflation of the 1980s in the United States illustrates this problem: disinflation was achieved by pushing the economy into the worst recession since the Great Depression.

## Key Terms

**short-run Phillips curve (SRPC)** a graphical representation of the negative short-run relationship between the *unemployment rate* and the *inflation rate*.

**nonaccelerating inflation rate of unemployment (NAIRU)** the *unemployment rate* at which, other things equal, *inflation* does not change over time.

**long-run Phillips curve (LRPC)** a graphical representation of the relationship between *unemployment* and *inflation* in the long run after expectations of inflation have had time to adjust to experience.

**debt deflation** the reduction in aggregate demand arising from the increase in the real burden of outstanding debt caused by *deflation*; occurs because borrowers, whose real debt rises as a result of deflation, are likely to cut spending sharply, and lenders, whose real assets are now more valuable, are less likely to increase spending.

**zero bound** the lower bound of zero on the *nominal interest rate*.

**liquidity trap** a situation in which *monetary policy* is ineffective because *nominal interest rates* are up against the *zero bound*.

## AFTER YOU READ THE MODULE

## Tips

**Tip #1.** Debt deflation refers to a situation in which deflation makes existent loan contracts more costly for borrowers: as the real burden of their debt increases, borrowers will decrease their spending. This reduction in aggregate spending is referred to as debt deflation.

**Tip #2.** You will want to review the concept of the liquidity trap and the zero bound for nominal interest rates. The zero bound refers to the lower limit for the nominal interest rate: these interest rates cannot fall below zero percent. When an economy finds that its nominal interest rate has fallen to zero, it will no longer be able to use monetary policy to stimulate the economy: monetary policy will be unable to stimulate aggregate spending through decreases in the nominal interest rate. This situation is referred to as a liquidity trap: increasing the money supply, an increase in liquidity, does nothing for the economy since the economy is "trapped" by the inability of the nominal interest rate to fall further.

**Tip #3.** It is important to fully understand the concept of the natural rate of unemployment, or the NAIRU. The NAIRU provides a measure of the unemployment rate that corresponds to the economy operating at its potential output level without any inflationary pressures. Economies that adopt policies in order to reduce their unemployment rate below this natural rate will experience inflation: persistent adoption of these policies will generate accelerating inflation.

**Tip #4.** It is important to understand the short-run Phillips curve (*SRPC*) and how the expected inflation rate affects it as well as why the long-run Phillips curve (*LRPC*) is a vertical line at the NAIRU. The *SRPC* illustrates the negative relationship between the inflation rate and the unemployment rate. The *SRPC* is drawn with a given level of expected inflation. If expected inflation increases, this will shift the *SRPC* upward by the change in the expected inflation rate. In the long run, the economy—no matter what the expected inflation rate—will settle at an unemployment rate equal to the NAIRU. Figure 41.1 depicts three *SRPC*s: $SRPC_0$ is drawn with expected inflation equal to 0%; $SRPC_1$ is drawn with expected inflation equal to 1%; and $SRPC_2$ is drawn with expected inflation equal to 3%. On the graph we see that this economy operates at its natural rate of unemployment (point *A*) when the unemployment rate equals 4%, the inflation rate equals 0%, and the expected inflation rate equals 0%. If the expected inflation rate increases to 1%, then the natural rate of unemployment of 4% is only possible with an inflation rate of 1% (point *B* on the graph). If the expected inflation rate rises to 3%, this shifts the *SRPC* to $SRPC_2$ and the natural rate of unemployment of 4% is only possible with an inflation rate of 3% (point *C*). The economy in the long run will gravitate back to the vertical line representing the natural rate of unemployment and its independence in the long run from the inflation rate.

**Figure 41.1**

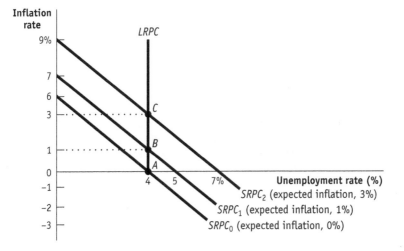

1. Pedro bought a house in 2004 and his monthly mortgage payments for this house are equal to $1,200 a month. In 2004, when he bought the house, Pedro's annual income was $57,600. Unfortunately, Pedro lost his job during the financial crisis of 2008. He was lucky to find new employment, but his employer is only willing to pay him $48,000 a year. This loss in income reflects an overall decrease in the aggregate price level that occurred as a result of the financial crisis of 2008. Pedro knows that he is earning a lower nominal income, but he is also recognizing that his debt on the house is creating additional stress. What was the ratio of annual mortgage payments to income when Pedro took out the loan, and what is this ratio now? Using these two ratios, calculate what the percentage change in Pedro's mortgage payment to income ratio has been. What do you anticipate Pedro will do if you assume that he continues to make his mortgage payment each month and if his income does not change? Finally, how will Pedro's behavior (along with the behavior of other homeowners in a similar position) affect the aggregate economy? In your answer be sure to incorporate the concept of debt deflation.

**WORKED PROBLEMS**

**STEP 1:** Calculate Pedro's yearly mortgage payments.

This is a simple mathematical calculation: Pedro pays $1,200 per month and there are 12 months in a year, so his yearly mortgage payment is equal to ($1,200/month)(12 months), or $14,400.

**STEP 2:** Calculate the ratio of Pedro's yearly mortgage payment to his initial income.

We know that Pedro's initial income is $57,600 and his yearly mortgage payment is $14,400. So the ratio of Pedro's yearly mortgage payment to his initial annual income is $14,400/$57,600, or 0.25. This ratio indicates that Pedro initially spent 25% of his annual income on his house payments.

**STEP 3:** Calculate the ratio of Pedro's yearly mortgage payment to his new income.

We know that Pedro's new income is $48,000 and his yearly mortgage payment is $14,400. So the ratio of Pedro's yearly mortgage payment to his new annual income is $14,400/$48,000, or 0.3. This ratio indicates that Pedro is now spending 30% of his annual income on his house payments.

**STEP 4:** Calculate the percentage change in Pedro's yearly mortgage payment to income ratio.

The percentage change in Pedro's yearly mortgage payment to income ratio is equal to [(0.3 – 0.25)/(0.25)](100), or 20%.

**STEP 5:** Comment on why this change in the ratio of yearly mortgage payment to income adversely affects Pedro and why this kind of change might also affect the aggregate economy if many homeowners were experiencing this kind of change in their incomes. In your answer include the concept of debt deflation and how it relates to this scenario.

Fisher, in discussing debt deflation, focused on how deflation would take away resources from borrowers and redistribute these resources to lenders, and as this happens it worsens the economic slump. In this story, Pedro has experienced a loss of income due to the economic slump and the accompanying decrease in the aggregate price level. This loss of income effectively means that a greater percentage of his income is now devoted to his house payments. As Pedro continues to make these house payments, he is apt to find that he is short of cash and must curtail other spending that he might otherwise undertake. If others are in a similar situation, the overall level of aggregate spending will fall, making the economic slump worse. This effect of deflation (in this case, a decrease in Pedro's annual income) in reducing aggregate demand is known as debt deflation.

2.   The following graph illustrates the short-run Phillips curve for an economy when expected inflation is 0%. You are asked to advise the leaders of the government of this economy as to what the natural rate of unemployment is in the economy. Currently, the economy is producing at 5% unemployment, and you are asked to explain to the government officials what the level of expected inflation is in this economy when unemployment is 5%, as well as discuss how this economy will adjust if unemployment is kept at 5%. You are also asked what will happen to expected inflation and the short-run Phillips curve if the government decides to pursue an unemployment rate of 2%. Finally, the government would like to know what the long-run Phillips curve looks like for this economy, given the graph that follows. The government officials hope that you will explain your findings with graphs as well as words. Assume that the short-run Phillips curve is linear for this question.

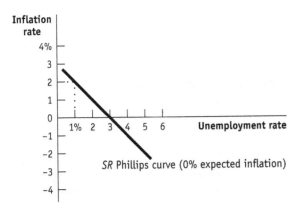

**STEP 1:** Identify the natural rate of unemployment.

The natural rate of unemployment for this economy is 3% because when the unemployment rate is at 3%, the actual rate of inflation (0%) is equal to the expected rate of inflation (0%). When the economy deviates from this unemployment rate the actual inflation rate will either rise (as the unemployment rate decreases), or the actual inflation rate will fall (as the unemployment rate increases). This deviation of actual inflation rate from expected inflation rate will cause the short-run Phillips curve to shift as these changes in actual inflation are incorporated into expectations about inflation.

**STEP 2:** Evaluate the effect of producing at 5% unemployment on this economy's expected inflation.

From the given graph, we can see that the unemployment rate and the inflation rate are negatively related to one another. When the unemployment rate is 5%, then the actual inflation rate is equal to −2% (deflation). This lower inflation rate will result in the short-run Phillips curve shifting downward as expectations about inflation get incorporated in this new short-run Phillips curve. If policy makers act to keep the unemployment rate at 5%, the result will be further revisions of the expected inflation rate with further downward shifts in the short-run Phillips curve. An unemployment rate above the natural rate of unemployment results in ever-accelerating deflation. The following graph illustrates the first shift in the short-run Phillips curve as people adjust to the deviation of the actual inflation rate from the expected inflation rate.

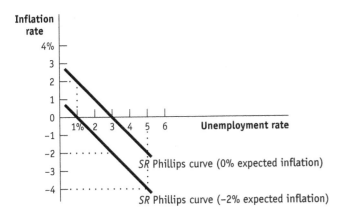

**STEP 3:** Discuss how the change in expected inflation alters the short-run Phillips Curve.

This is illustrated in the graph given in Step 2. When there is a change in expected inflation, the short-run Phillips curve shifts: it shifts upward if the change in expected inflation represents an increase in the expected rate of inflation, and it shifts downward if the change in expected inflation represents a decrease in the expected rate of inflation.

**STEP 4:** What happens to the expected inflation and the graph if the government decides to pursue policy that will result in an unemployment rate of 2%?

From the initial graph we can see that the rate of inflation associated with an unemployment rate of 2% is 1%. Since an actual inflation rate of 1% is different from the expected rate of inflation of 0%, this will cause the short-run Phillips curve to shift upward as people revised their inflationary expectations. If the government persists in pursuing policy that results in an unemployment rate of 2%, the short-run Phillips curve will continue to shift upward, resulting in ever-accelerating inflation. The following graph illustrates this idea.

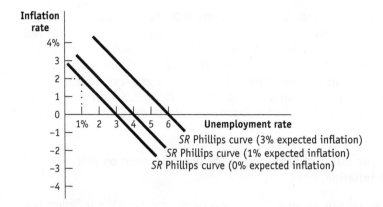

**STEP 5:** Identify the long-run Phillips curve given the initial graph.

The long-run Phillips curve is a vertical line at 3% unemployment. When unemployment is 3% and the expected inflation is 0%, the actual rate of inflation is equal to the expected rate of inflation. When the expected inflation increases to 1%, then the short-run Phillips curve shifts upward, and we see that at an unemployment rate of 3% the actual rate of inflation of 1% is equal to the expected inflation of 1%. As expectations of inflation change, the short-run Phillips curve shifts, but the long-run Phillips curve remains a vertical line at which unemployment is equal to 3%. The following graph illustrates this idea.

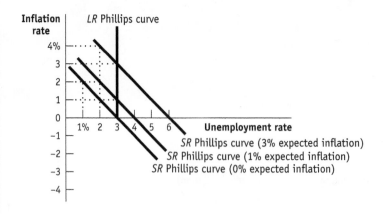

# Problems and Exercises

1. Joe lends Mary $1,000 for the year. They agree that Mary will repay the full $1,000 at the end of the year and in addition, they agree that Mary will pay Joe $50 in interest payments.

   **a.** What is the nominal interest rate that Mary and Joe have agreed to in this contract?

   **b.** If Joe and Mary both anticipate that inflation will be 3% for the year, what real interest rate are each of them trying to achieve in their loan contract?

   **c.** Suppose the actual inflation rate for the year is 2%. Who benefits more from this inflation rate, and why do you think he or she benefits more? Explain your answer.

   **d.** Suppose the actual inflation rate for the year is 4%. Who benefits more from this inflation rate, and why do you think he or she benefits more? Explain your answer.

   **e.** If the actual inflation rate equals the nominal interest rate, how does this affect the outcome of this loan contract?

   **f.** If you knew what the actual inflation rate was going to be, and it happened to equal the nominal interest rate, would you be willing to be a lender? Why or why not? Explain your answer.

2. Suppose that both borrowers and lenders anticipate correctly that the inflation rate will increase by 5 percentage points over the next year.

   **a.** What do you know will happen to the real interest rate?

   **b.** What do you know will happen to the nominal interest rate?

**c.** Describe the effects of this anticipated inflation on the demand for loanable funds curve and the supply of loanable funds curve. Use the following graph to illustrate your answer.

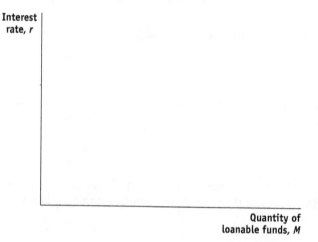

**3.** Modules 40 and 41 discuss both disinflation and deflation: write a brief essay contrasting and comparing these two terms. How are these terms similar and how are they dissimilar?

**4.** Expansionary monetary policy typically reduces the nominal interest rate, and this in turn acts as a stimulus for aggregate demand. Why does this not work in the case of a liquidity trap? In your answer, make sure you identify what a liquidity trap is and why it prevents monetary policy from stimulating the economy. Use the following graph to illustrate your answer.

Interest rate, *r*

Nominal quantity of money, *M*

5.  Explain why during a period of deflation the debt burden increases and how this relates to debt deflation.

6.  Suppose you are given the following information about the economy of Funland.

| Unemployment rate | Inflation rate | Expected inflation rate |
|:---:|:---:|:---:|
| 1% | 6% | 2% |
| 2 | 5 | 2 |
| 3 | 4 | 2 |
| 4 | 3 | 2 |

a.  Draw a graph with the unemployment rate on the horizontal axis and the inflation rate on the vertical axis. On this graph, represent the above short-run Phillips curve (SRPC) based on expected inflation of 2%. Label this $SRPC_1$. Assume this curve is linear.

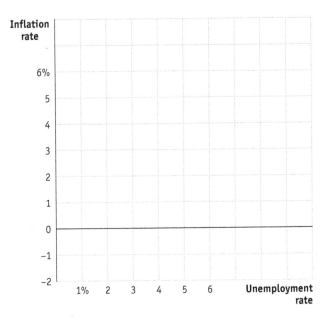

**b.** Given $SRPC_1$, at what rate of unemployment will inflation equal 0% for this economy? If expected inflation is 2%, then how will this economy adjust over time to this expected inflation rate? Illustrate this short-run adjustment on a graph and then explain your answer.

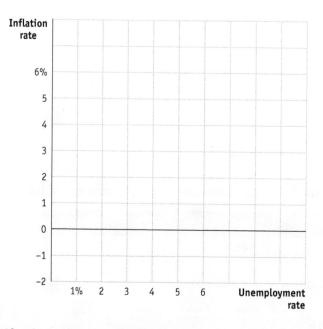

**c.** If policymakers could effectively change inflationary expectations to where people expected inflation to be 0%, then what would be this country's NAIRU? Illustrate this on a graph labeling all new information clearly on your graph. Explain your answer.

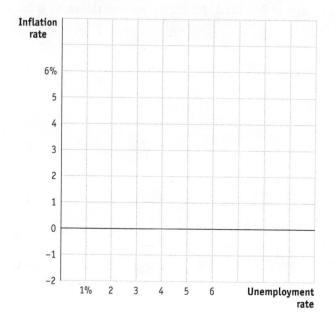

**d.** For the economy of Funland, what will the long-run Phillips curve (*LRPC*) look like and where will it be located? Explain your answer using a graph to illustrate.

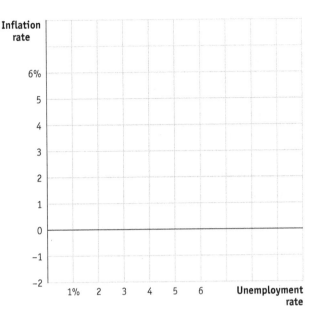

## BEFORE YOU TAKE THE TEST

## Module Review Questions

1. When there is unexpected inflation in an economy, then
   a. real GDP will decrease in the economy in the long run.
   b. real income will decrease in the economy in the long run.
   c. borrowers benefit while lenders lose.
   d. lenders benefit while borrowers lose.
   e. Answers (a), (b), and (c) are all correct.
   f. Answers (a), (b), and (d) are all correct.

2. According to the Fisher effect, changes in the expected inflation rate will
   a. have little or no effect on the nominal interest rate.
   b. cause both the demand and supply of loanable funds curves to shift in the same direction.
   c. cause both the demand and supply of loanable funds curves to shift, but in opposite directions.
   d. have no effect on the equilibrium quantity of loanable funds.
   e. Answers (a), (b), and (c) are all correct.
   f. Answers (a), (b), and (d) are all correct.
   g. Answers (c) and (d) are both correct.
   h. Answers (b) and (d) are both correct.

**3.** Which of the following statements is true?

a. The Fisher effect states that the expected real interest rate is unaffected by the change in expected inflation.

b. Borrowers and lenders should base their decisions on the real rate of interest and not the nominal rate of interest.

c. Anticipated inflation can impose real costs on the economy.

d. Statements (a), (b), and (c) are all true.

e. Statements (a) and (b) are both true.

f. Statements (a) and (c) are both true.

g. Statements (b) and (c) are both true.

**4.** Which of the following statements is true?

a. The short-run Phillips curve is a vertical line with the horizontal intercept equaling the NAIRU.

b. The short-run Phillips curve depicts the negative relationship between the unemployment rate and the inflation rate.

c. An economy with a low rate of unemployment is an economy that has a shortage of labor and other resources, which leads to falling prices.

d. Statements (a) and (c) are both true.

e. Statements (b) and (c) are both true.

**5.** Debt deflation

a. occurs when there is deflation, and the value of the borrower's debt is reduced due to the falling aggregate price level.

b. occurs when borrowers reduce their aggregate spending, because the deflation increases the debt burden that borrowers experience.

c. reduces the impact of the deflation on the level of aggregate demand, thus restoring the economy to its potential level of output in a timely manner.

d. affects only lenders and not borrowers.

**6.** An economy will experience a liquidity trap when the Fed

a. refuses to expand the money supply, even though there is an increased demand for money in the economy.

b. refuses to expand the money supply in order to raise nominal interest rates to an acceptable level.

c. finds that it cannot reduce nominal interest rates, even if it engages in open-market purchases of Treasury bills.

d. adopts a target inflation rate of 0%, and successfully achieves this target.

**7.** When the central bank finds that it cannot use monetary policy to reduce the nominal interest rate, it must be the case that

a. the economy is operating in a liquidity trap.

b. the central bank has reached the zero bound.

c. the money market is in disequilibrium.

d. Answers (a), (b), and (c) are all correct.

e. Answers (a) and (b) are both correct.

f. Answers (a) and (c) are both correct.

g. Answers (b) and (c) are both correct.

8.  Expected inflation
    a. does not impact the short-run or the long-run Phillips curve.
    b. is the rate of inflation that workers and employers expect in the near future.
    c. and the unemployment rate are the most significant factors affecting the rate of inflation in an economy.
    d. Answers (a), (b), and (c) are all correct.
    e. Answers (b) and (c) are both correct.

Use the following graph to answer the next three questions. In this graph $SRPC_1$ is the short-run Phillips curve for this economy when the expected inflation rate equals 0%.

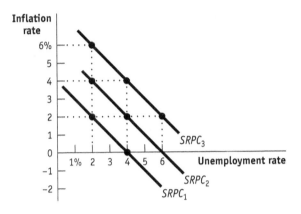

9.  Using the above graph, we know that the short-run Phillips curve ($SRPC$) equals $SRPC_2$ when the expected inflation rate equals
    a. 0%.
    b. 2%.
    c. 4%.
    d. 6%.

10. Suppose the inflation rate is 4% and this economy finds that its unemployment rate equals 3%. What is the NAIRU for this economy, given this information?
    a. 0%
    b. 2%
    c. 4%
    d. 6%

11. Suppose the policymakers for the economy depicted in the above graph decide to pursue an unemployment rate of 2%. This will
    a. cause accelerating inflation in the long run.
    b. lead to rightward shifts in the $SRPC$, with each shift reflecting the expected inflation rate.
    c. cause equilibrium wage rates to fall.
    d. Answers (a), (b), and (c) are all correct.
    e. Answers (a) and (b) are both correct.

**12.** Governments that run large deficits can
   a. reduce the size of the deficit by raising taxes.
   b. reduce the size of the deficit by reducing spending.
   c. finance the deficit by printing money.
   d. Answers (a), (b), and (c) are all correct.

**13.** A positive output gap implies an unemployment rate
   a. above the natural rate of unemployment.
   b. below the natural rate of unemployment.

**14.** Disinflation in an economy is
   a. easy to accomplish and relatively painless for people living and working in this economy.
   b. difficult to accomplish and typically results in reduced production of real GDP and high rates of unemployment.

■ **ANSWER KEY**

# Answers to Problems and Exercises

1.  **a.** The nominal interest rate that Mary and Joe have agreed to in this contract is 5%, since the $50 interest payment represents 5% of the $1,000 loan.

    **b.** We can calculate the real interest rate as the nominal interest rate minus the expected inflation rate: in this case, the nominal interest rate is 5% and the expected inflation rate is 3%, giving us a real interest rate of 2%.

    **c.** If the actual inflation rate is 2%, then the real rate of interest that is paid on the loan is 3%, which is higher than the real interest rate that Mary and Joe thought they were agreeing to when they signed their loan contract. For Joe, the lender, this means that he is earning more than he anticipated from the loan. For Mary, the borrower, this means that she is paying back more dollars in real terms than she planned on when she signed the contract.

    **d.** If the actual inflation rate is 4%, then the real rate of interest that is paid on the loan is 1%, which is lower than the real interest rate that Mary and Joe thought they were agreeing to when they signed their loan contract. For Joe, the lender, this means that he is earning less than he anticipated from the loan. For Mary, the borrower, this means that she is paying back fewer dollars in real terms than she planned on when she signed the contract.

    **e.** If the actual inflation rate equals the nominal rate of interest, then the real interest rate is zero. The real rate of interest equaling zero represents a situation in which the lender earns no real return on the money he or she has lent out, while the borrower is paying no real cost for the use of the money. The borrower wins, while the lender is hurt under this scenario.

    **f.** No, if you knew what the actual inflation rate was going to be and it equaled the nominal interest rate for the loan, you would refuse to be a lender since the real return you would earn on the loan would be zero. If you made the loan, you would be giving up the use of your funds for the period of the loan without receiving any real compensation for the use of those funds.

2.  **a.** The real interest rate will be unaffected by this anticipated inflation rate, since both demanders and suppliers in the loanable funds market will take this anticipated inflation into account.

    **b.** The nominal interest rate will increase by 5 percentage points due to the increase in the anticipated rate of inflation of 5 percentage points.

    **c.** Both the demand and the supply curves in the loanable funds market will shift upward (demand will shift to the right and supply will shift to the left) by the amount of the anticipated inflation rate: this will leave the equilibrium quantity of loanable funds unchanged in the market while increasing the nominal interest rate by the amount of the anticipated inflation. The following figure illustrates this.

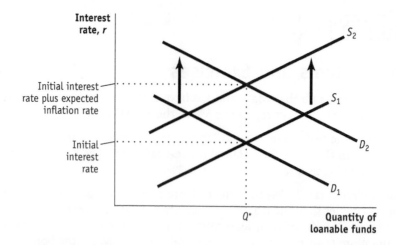

3.  Disinflation refers to the deliberate pursuit by policy makers to bring down inflation that has become embedded in expectations. Here, policy makers pursue policy aimed at reducing inflationary expectations in order to reduce the increase in the aggregate price level. Disinflation may be very expensive economically, since it may result in significant decreases in real GDP in order to remove inflationary expectations from the economy. Deflation, on the other hand, refers to a fall in the aggregate price level. This deflation is not the result of conscious policy-making activity, but may prove difficult to remedy through policy if the economy is operating in a liquidity trap where nominal interest rates are equal to zero. In such a situation, monetary policy cannot be used to stimulate aggregate demand through lower nominal interest rates. So, even though disinflation and deflation both are concerned with either slowing down inflation or a direct fall in the aggregate price level, they represent different challenges to the policy maker.

4.  In the case of a liquidity trap, the nominal interest rate initially is equal to zero and thus cannot fall any lower despite expansionary monetary policy. The following graph illustrates a liquidity trap, where $MS$ is the nominal money supply, $MD$ is the nominal money demand, and $r$ is the nominal interest rate.

In the graph, when the central bank pursues expansionary monetary policy to shift the $MS$ to the right, this will have no effect on the nominal interest rate since it is already at its minimal level of zero. Monetary policy cannot be used to stimulate the economy if the economy faces a liquidity trap.

5.  When there is a deflation, prices in an economy fall. The effect of this fall in prices is to increase the economic burden of any preexisting debt, since the borrower's payments are not adjusted downward to reflect the deflation. Borrowers lose from deflation due to the increased real burden of their debt; the increased debt burden may lead them to be short of cash and force them to cut their spending sharply when their debt burden rises. Thus, deflation reduces aggregate demand, which deepens the economic slump that may, in turn, lead to further deflation. This reduction in aggregate demand due to the effect of deflation is referred to as debt deflation.

6.  **a.**

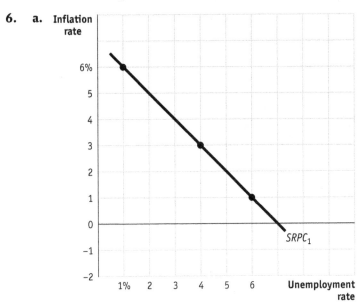

**b.** Given $SRPC_1$, inflation equals 0% when the unemployment rate equals 7%. Over time people will come to expect inflation of 2%, and this will cause the $SRPC$ to shift up by this amount and people's expectations of inflation to rise to 4%. The new $SRPC$ will be $SRPC_2$, as illustrated in the following graph.

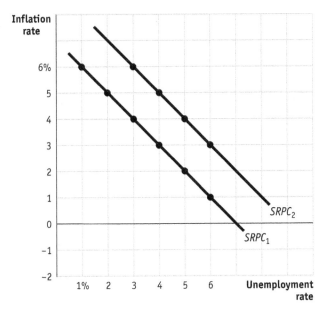

Of course, over time this will cause $SRPC_2$ to shift up, reflecting higher inflationary expectations.

**c.** This country's NAIRU would be 5%. Effectively, we are looking for the *SRPC* that has inflationary expectations of 0%, which we can illustrate as a downward shift of $SRPC_1$ where at any given unemployment rate, the inflation rate is reduced by 2%. We can illustrate this in the following figure as $SRPC_0$.

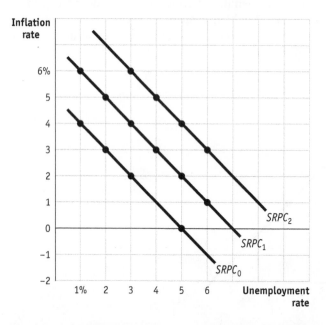

Remember that the expected inflation rate for $SRPC_2$ is 4%, the expected inflation rate for $SRPC_1$ is 2%, and the expected inflation rate for $SRPC_0$ is 0%.

**d.** For Funland the *LRPC* will be a vertical line at a 5% unemployment rate. This is illustrated in the following figure.

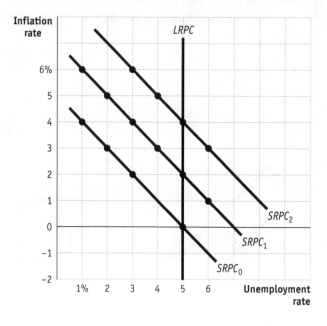

# Answers to Module Review Questions

1.  **Answer c.** Unexpected inflation has no effect on real GDP and real income in the economy in the long run: the economy will return to its potential output level. However, the unexpected inflation will hurt some people while benefiting other people: borrowers will find that they are paying back dollars with less purchasing power. Hence, borrowers will benefit from the unexpected inflation while lenders will be hurt.

2.  **Answer g.** When the expected inflation rate changes, this causes both the demand and supply curves for loanable funds to shift, but in opposite directions. For example, if demand shifts to the right then supply shifts to the left. The equilibrium quantity of loanable funds will be unaffected by this change, but the nominal interest rate will change by the amount of change in the amount of expected inflation rate.

3.  **Answer d.** All three statements are straightforward statements found in your text.

4.  **Answer b.** The short-run Phillips curve is downward sloping and depicts the relationship between the unemployment rate and the inflation rate. It is not vertical: the long-run Phillips curve is vertical and intersects the horizontal axis at the NAIRU. An economy that has a low unemployment rate will typically see rising prices in the short run due to shortages of labor and other resources.

5.  **Answer b.** Debt deflation is the reduction in aggregate demand caused by deflation. A borrower's existent debt is not reduced due to deflation: the borrower's real debt is increased during a period of deflation, since the deflation increases the real burden of the borrower's debt. Debt deflation reduces spending and therefore worsens the economic slump: the economy does not move quickly to its potential output level.

6.  **Answer c.** The liquidity trap is a situation in which monetary policy cannot be used because nominal interest rates must stay at zero or above. Monetary policy is ineffective when the economy operates in a liquidity trap, since the nominal interest rate cannot fall below zero. The Fed could adopt a target inflation rate of 0% and not necessarily run into the liquidity trap; however, the Fed would likely choose a higher inflation target, since it allows them more room to adjust nominal interest rates as a way of stimulating aggregate demand.

7.  **Answer e.** When the central bank cannot effectively use monetary policy to stimulate the economy, it must be at the zero bound, or the nominal interest rate must equal zero. When the nominal interest rate is at zero, then the economy is operating in a liquidity trap—a situation in which monetary policy is ineffective. The money market can still be in equilibrium, even though monetary policy cannot be used to stimulate the economy.

8.  **Answer e.** Expected inflation and the unemployment rate are the most significant factors affecting the inflation rate in an economy. Expected inflation is that rate of inflation that workers and employers expect in the near future. Changes in expected inflation cause the short-run Phillips curve to shift: increases in the expected inflation rate cause the short-run Phillips curve to shift up, while decreases in the expected inflation rate cause the short-run Phillips curve to shift down.

9.  **Answer b.** $SRPC_2$ reflects a short-run Phillips curve drawn with an expected inflation rate of 2%. We know this since this curve has shifted up by 2% at every unemployment rate from the short-run Phillips curve that is drawn with an expected inflation rate of 0% ($SRPC_1$).

10. **Answer d.** The NAIRU is the nonaccelerating inflation rate of unemployment for the economy, or that level of unemployment at which the inflation rate matches inflationary expectations. An unemployment rate below 4% requires ever-accelerating inflation.

11. **Answer e.** The unemployment rate of 2% is below the unemployment rate that this economy can maintain while still avoiding inflation. If this economy tries to pursue an unemployment rate of 2%, this unemployment rate will be initially accompanied by 2%

inflation. This inflation rate will then be built into inflationary expectations and the *SRPC* will shift to the right. But, again, if policy makers persist in trying to achieve 2% unemployment, this will cause even higher inflationary expectations to be built into the *SRPC*, shifting the *SRPC* further to the right. Thus, trying to achieve an unemployment level of 2% for this economy will lead to accelerating inflation in the long run, along with shifts in the *SRPC* in the short run. We can expect wages to rise with expectations of higher inflation and with higher actual inflation rates.

12. **Answer d.** Governments run deficits whenever their spending is greater than their revenue. They can reduce the size of the deficit by increasing the revenue they collect or by reducing the level of spending or by doing a combination of both of these options. When a government is unwilling to increase taxes or cut spending, they are forced to finance any deficit spending they incur by printing money to cover their budget deficit.

13. **Answer b.** When the output gap is positive, this implies that actual aggregate output is greater than potential output. When actual aggregate output exceeds potential output, this implies that the unemployment rate is below the natural rate since the level of production is greater than the potential output level.

14. **Answer b.** Disinflation involves eliminating inflation and inflationary expectations from an economy. Once an economy has developed inflationary expectations, the only way to reduce these expectations is to throw the economy into a major recession. Such a recession results in reductions in production as well as increases in the unemployment rate.

# Crises and Consequences

## BEFORE YOU READ THE MODULE

## Summary

This module discusses the difference between depository banks and shadow banks and how both types of banks are subject to bank runs. The module also discusses what happens during financial panics and bank crises and why these types of economic disruption result in severe and long-lasting impacts on the economy. The module also discusses the role of regulatory loopholes and the rise of shadow banking in the banking crisis of 2008 and how regulatory frameworks seek to avoid another banking crisis.

## Module Objectives

**Objective #1.** People face a trade-off between liquidity and the rate of return. Without banks people would be forced to hold large amounts of cash to meet their liquidity needs; as holdings of cash increase, the rate of return decreases. Banks allow depositors to have immediate access to their funds (addressing their liquidity needs) while simultaneously providing depositors interest on these deposited funds (addressing their desire for a return on their idle cash). Banks are able to do this through maturity transformation, where they transform short-term liabilities into long-term assets.

**Objective #2.** Shadow banks have grown since 1980. These banks provide a higher rate of return to savers than depository banks. Like depository banks, shadow banks engage in maturity transformation, using short-term borrowing to finance their investments in long-term assets. Until recently, these banks faced little regulation; due to their similarity to depository banks, however, they were vulnerable to bank runs.

**Objective #3.** Banking crises occur primarily due to two reasons: shared mistakes and financial contagion. Shared mistakes refer to financial institutions making the same mistake of investing in an asset bubble. Financial contagion spreads through bank runs or a vicious circle of deleveraging. Unregulated banking institutions, like the shadow bank sector, are highly vulnerable to contagion. The most recent financial crisis in the United States was a result of a real estate bubble, the rise of a very large shadow banking sector, and a vicious circle of deleveraging.

**Objective #4.** Banking crises are a frequent occurrence throughout the world. After a banking crisis or financial panic, there is usually a severe downturn in the economy. Bank crises typically result in bank reform that aims to reduce the frequency of future bank crises or financial panics.

**Objective #5.** A financial crisis typically results in a prolonged and severe drop in economic activity in an economy primarily because of the credit crunch, the debt overhang, and the ineffectiveness of monetary policy. The credit crunch refers to the increased difficulty that consumers and businesses have in getting needed credit: credit markets freeze up in the wake of financial crisis and do not operate properly. The debt overhang arises out of the vicious circle of deleveraging in which the value of assets falls, leaving individuals and businesses with greater debt but diminished assets. Monetary policy during a banking crisis is ineffective as a means to fight negative demand shocks caused by a fall in consumer and investment spending.

**Objective #6.** During a bank crisis, the government tries to limit the damage from the bank crisis by serving as a lender of last resort and by guaranteeing bank liabilities. The government may need to nationalize banks and then later reprivatize them in order to slow or halt the spread of the bank crisis.

**Objective #7.** The development of shadow banking eroded the bank regulatory system that was put into place in the 1930s. Particularly the repo market (short-term credit market), a primary feature of shadow banking that provides very short-term loans, was not regulated at the time of the financial crisis of 2008. The shadow bank sector was subject to bank runs due to the use of the repo, the lack of regulation, and the fact that this sector was not part of the lender-of-last resort system.

**Objective #8.** The financial crisis of 2008 started with a real estate bubble. The crisis was the most severe one since the Great Depression. Persistently high unemployment is likely to endure for many years as a result of this crisis.

**Objective #9.** The Dodd-Frank bill was passed by the United States Congress in hopes of preventing another financial crisis like that of 2008. This reform bill provides for consumer protection, greater regulation of derivatives, regulation of shadow banking, and resolution authority for a variety of financial institutions.

## Key Terms

*Notes*

**maturity transformation** the conversion of short-term liabilities into long-term assets.

**shadow bank** a nondepository financial institution that engages in maturity transformation.

**banking crisis** occurs when a large part of the depository banking sector or the shadow banking sector fails or threatens to fail.

## Key Terms *(continued)*

**asset bubble** when the price of an asset is pushed to an unreasonably high level due to expectations of further price gains.

**financial contagion** a vicious downward spiral among depository banks as well as shadow banks; each institution's failure increases the likelihood that another will fail.

**financial panic** a sudden and widespread disruption of the financial markets that occurs when people lose faith in the liquidity of financial institutions and markets.

**credit crunch** when potential borrowers either cannot get credit at all or must pay very high interest rates.

**debt overhang** occurs when a vicious circle of deleveraging leaves a borrower with high debt but diminished assets.

**lender of last resort** an institution, usually a country's central bank, that provides funds to financial institutions when they are unable to borrow from the private credit markets.

*Notes*

## ▌ AFTER YOU READ THE MODULE

# Tips

**Tip #1.** This module introduces new terms that you will want to spend time learning. The terms often are challenging for students, since they are related to the financial industry, and this industry may not be familiar to you. Mastery of these terms is important.

**Tip #2.** This module discusses the vicious cycle of deleveraging, and it is this concept that is essential for understanding why bank crises and financial panics can have such large and long-lasting impacts on the economy. This type of vicious cycle begins when financial institutions find that they need to reduce debt and raise cash. This need may force them into selling their assets quickly, which often means that these assets must sell at deeply discounted (lower) prices. As the institutions sell these assets at reduced prices, other financial institutions' positions are hurt as well. Thus, creditors may stop lending to more and more institutions. The vicious cycle of deleveraging leads to a downward spiral of asset prices, and this results in major impacts on consumer and business spending in the economy.

**Tip #3.** Students are used to thinking about the term *banking* as referring to financial institutions that provide checking and saving accounts. This module introduces and develops the idea of the shadow banking system. It is critical that students understand the concept of shadow banking: shadow banking and commercial banks are both in the business of maturity transformation, but the shadow bank—unlike commercial banks—does not take deposits.

Instead, the shadow bank uses short-term borrowing in markets to finance its lending. Shadow banking has grown in both size and impact on the financial system in recent years. Prior to the financial crisis of 2008, shadow banking was not regulated.

**Tip #4.** There is a tendency to think financial crises are rare and unusual events. This module provides historical evidence suggesting that these crises are not that rare, and that they do cause major economic disturbances, particularly with regard to unemployment and production. Recognizing that financial crises do occur and have some common causes can help policy makers design better policies aimed at reducing both the frequency and severity of financial crises.

**Tip #5.** It is important to understand the three reasons for why banking crises typically lead to recessions: (1) a credit crunch occurs, which reduces the availability of credit, (2) financial distress caused by a debt overhang occurs, and (3) there is a loss of monetary policy effectiveness. The loss of monetary policy effectiveness provides the primary explanation for why banking-crises recessions are so severe and why they last so long.

**Tip #6.** It is important for students to realize that financial regulation is a long-standing policy in most economies. However, regulation periodically lags financial innovation, and for regulation to be effective it must be continually updated in order to maintain pace with a changing world.

# WORKED PROBLEMS

1. The "Economics in Action" feature in this module details the demise of Lehman Brothers. Discuss how this story illustrates the vicious cycle of deleveraging and how this kind of vicious cycle can be destabilizing to otherwise financially sound institutions.

**STEP 1:** Review what the term the *vicious cycle of deleveraging* means before analyzing the Lehman Brothers story.

The *vicious cycle of deleveraging* refers to a phenomenon that occurs when a financial institution is under pressure to reduce debt and raise cash. Under these circumstances, the institution may be forced to sell assets quickly and at steeply discounted prices. This results in financial contagion, since other financial institutions that own similar assets will find that the values of these assets are negatively impacted by the decline in asset prices. As creditors reduce the amount of credit they are willing to provide, more financial institutions are forced to sell assets, reinforcing the downward spiral of asset prices.

**STEP 2:** Discuss Lehman's situation in September 2008, paying close attention to the assets it held and why these assets represented a potential problem for the firm.

In September of 2008, Lehman Brothers held a large number of subprime mortgages. These were mortgages made to individuals who had too little income or too few assets to quality for prime, or standard, mortgages. During the summer and heading into the fall of 2008, the real estate market in the United States saw housing prices decline. This decrease in prices lessened the value of the investments that Lehman Brothers had in the housing industry. The firm was rumored to have heavy exposure to housing price volatility, and this led it to have trouble getting short-term credit to finance its operations and trading. On September 15, 2008, Lehman Brothers declared bankruptcy. It was the largest bankruptcy in United States history.

**STEP 3:** Discuss the impact of Lehman's bankruptcy on the financial system.

Lehman's bankruptcy came as a big surprise to the financial system because the firm had hidden the magnitude of the problem it faced. Other financial firms holding securitized mortgages realized that their holdings of real estate loans were quickly falling in value, particularly as the default rates on these loans increased. In light of these troubles, credit markets froze as those with funds decided it was better to hold onto their funds rather than lend them, given the state of both the financial markets and the real estate market. This created a global credit crunch, and this inability to get credit resulted in dramatic declines in stock markets around the world. Lehman's collapse had triggered a financial panic and resulted in a severe recession.

2. For each of the following scenarios determine whether the scenario represents the concept of shared mistake, a credit crunch, financial contagion, debt over-hang, or the ineffectiveness of monetary policy. Explain your answers.

   a. Sarah and her husband Mario in the early 2000s built several houses as spec-ulation houses. They would borrow funds to build a house, then sell the house once the construction was finished. The real estate market was strong at the time, and they earned substantial returns on their investments. They continued to build these houses because they thought house prices would continue to rise. However, in 2007, they built a house and by the time it was finished they found that housing prices had fallen, and they were unable to sell the house for what they had put into building it. They also noticed that there were many similar houses on the market in similar subdivisions in their community.

   b. In the 1990s, tech stocks became very popular, and their prices rose dra-matically. At the end of the 1990s, tech stock prices fell dramatically.

   c. First State Bank finds that it has too much debt and needs cash. It is forced to sell some of its assets at a dramatic discount. This causes other firms hold-ing similar assets to find the values of their assets falling, and as the value of the assets fall, the firms find that they need to reduce their debt and raise cash quickly. This puts even greater downward pressure on the price of the assets.

   d. Rumor is circulating that Second Street Bank has substantial exposure in an asset that is losing value in the market. Second Street Bank needs short-term credit to insure its own operations and lending, and it finds that its credi-tors are no longer willing to lend funds. Second Street Bank is not the only financial institution facing this problem; in fact, it appears to be endemic to the entire banking system.

   e. Lucinda bought a house for $200,000 in 2005. She financed this purchase with a mortgage for 90% of the value of the house. However, house prices have fallen since 2005 by 25%. Lucinda is now substantially poorer than she was when she first bought the house.

   f. Since the financial crisis of 2008, the unemployment rate has been very high and the level of production has been low in the United States. In the period immediately after that financial crisis, the Federal Reserve pursued a policy of very low interest rates. But the economy at that time continued to have a high unemployment rate as well as aggregate production levels below the potential level of production.

**STEP 1:** Before characterizing each of the preceding scenarios, review the definitions of each of the given terms.

*Shared mistake* refers to the idea of many institutions (or individuals) making the same mistake of investing in an asset bubble. A *credit crunch* refers to a disruption in the availability of credit due to the disruption in the banking system. *Financial contagion* refers to a vicious downward spiral in which each institution's failure increases the odds that another institution will fail. Financial contagion is usually accompanied by a vicious cycle of *deleveraging*, in which institutions are under pressure to reduce debt and raise cash: this pressure results in assets being sold at a deep discount, and this discounting of asset values has an adverse impact on other institutions holding similar assets. *Debt overhang* refers to the situation where a vicious cycle of deleveraging leaves a borrower with high debt but diminished assets. *Ineffective monetary policy* refers to a situation where monetary policy is not effective at fighting negative demand shocks, often occurs during banking-crisis recessions.

**STEP 2:** Consider each of the scenarios and decide which of the preceding terms describes the scenario best.

a.    The house construction business of Sarah and Mario illustrates the idea of shared mistakes: they erroneously believed that housing prices could only continue to increase, and when housing prices fell they lost money on their houses built for speculation. The fact that there were many houses for sale in the subdivisions illustrates that they were not the only ones to believe that housing prices could only move in one direction.

b.    Tech stock prices were bid up beyond their worth in the tech stock bubble. This is another illustration of shared mistakes, whereby many people made the same mistake of investing in tech stocks, leading to a tech stock bubble.

c.    This scenario illustrates a vicious circle of deleveraging, which is one of the identifying characteristics of a financial contagion. One firm's need to reduce debt and raise cash quickly results in many firms having problems with falling asset prices and an inability to secure needed credit.

d.    Second Street Bank is suffering from a credit crunch. The bank is not able to get the needed credit, and as the credit situation tightens, more and more banks will need to reduce their lending. This will lead businesses and consumers to cut back on their spending, causing the economy to go into a recession.

e.    Lucinda's situation illustrates the concept of debt overhang, where a vicious circle of deleveraging leaves a borrower with high debt but diminished assets. Lucinda still owes most of her mortgage, but the value of the house has fallen. This has increased her level of debt even though the value of her house is lower.

f.    A key feature of banking-crisis recessions is that monetary policy is not very effective. Despite a very low interest rate, the monetary policy was not particularly effective in the aftermath of the financial crisis of 2008. Monetary policy tends to break down after a banking crisis due to a lack of confidence on the part of banking institutions and an unwillingness on the part of consumers and businesses to borrow.

3.    Your neighbor Sanjay exclaimed to you the other night, "I have lived through a number of recessions, but this recession is the worst I have ever seen!" Sanjay was speaking of the recession following the financial crisis of 2008. Sanjay knows that you have been studying macroeconomics this term, and he would

like you to help him understand why the recession following this crisis was so severe and why it has lasted so long.

**STEP 1:** Show how the financial crisis of 2008 illustrates both shared mistakes as well as financial contagion.

The financial crisis of 2008 was preceded by a real estate bubble, in which real estate prices rose by more than 60% in the period after 2000 before they fell back down to levels more in keeping with their historical levels. As real estate prices fell, many homeowners found that the value of their homes had fallen below their mortgage amounts: these homeowners were "underwater," owing more money than the value of the assets—their homes—were worth. Many of these homeowners went into default on their mortgages, and many homes went into foreclosure. Many of the loans to homeowners were subprime mortgages that were subsequently securitized with other mortgage loans. Shares in these securitized loans were sold to other investors who were highly exposed to losses from the bursting of the housing bubble. This led to financial contagion due to a vicious downward spiral of deleveraging, which worsened the recession and hindered economic recovery.

**STEP 2:** Identify the three main reasons that banking and financial crises lead to severe recessions.

There are three main reasons a banking and financial crisis can lead to a severe recession: (1) A credit crunch, whereby potential borrowers find they either cannot get credit or, if they can get credit, they must pay very high rates of interest for this credit; (2) debt overhang, whereby borrowers find that the pushing down of asset prices results in their having additional financial stress due to their continuing to have high amounts of debt, while the assets the borrowers hold have diminished in value; and (3) in the aftermath of a financial crisis, loss of monetary policy effectiveness as a means of restoring consumer and investment spending.

**STEP 3:** Discuss how the financial crisis of 2008 created a credit crunch.

When the real estate bubble burst, it left many homeowners with mortgages that were greater than the value of their homes. As the homeowners went into default and foreclosure, the financial institutions holding these mortgages found that they were highly exposed to losses from the bursting of the housing bubble. Financial institutions became concerned about the solvency of other financial institutions, and that led to a freezing up of the credit markets. This situation was a classic illustration of a credit crunch.

**STEP 4:** Discuss how the financial crisis of 2008 created a debt overhang.

After the housing bubble burst, many homeowners found that the amount they owed on their mortgages was greater than the value of their homes. These homeowners were "underwater," and their plight illustrated the debt overhang concept. Recall that debt overhang refers to a situation in which the individual or institution has high levels of debt but diminished assets. As housing prices fell, this diminished the value of the homes (the assets), while leaving the debt owed (the mortgages) at the same level.

**STEP 5:** Discuss how the financial crisis of 2008 created a scenario in which monetary policy was largely ineffective.

Even though the Federal Reserve kept interest rates at very low levels after the bursting of the housing bubble, this did little to stimulate the economy. Many households facing high debt levels and decreases in the value of their assets were not in a position to increase their spending levels. In addition, many households had been adversely affected by the recession and the accompanying loss of jobs in the economy. Businesses were equally reluctant to increase their spending despite very low interest rates: household demand was not strong, and there was excess capacity in the economy. Thus, monetary policy implemented to increase consumer and investment spending proved to be ineffective.

4.   Prime Bank has 500 customers who have each deposited $50,000. Prime Bank has kept 20% of these deposits as reserves to meet depositor demand for funds. The other 80% of deposits have been used to make mortgage loans to individuals who have not deposited funds at Prime Bank. Each mortgage loan has a value of $200,000. To make this problem simpler, we will assume that each mortgage represents a loan made to a customer to finance the purchase of a residence that is initially selling for $210,000. Suppose that there is a real estate bubble in the economy, and home prices fall by 10%. Prime Bank asks that you help it understand the effect of this drop in prices on the value of its assets relative to the value of its deposits. In your answer, provide an analysis of the total level of deposits at the bank, the total reserves, the total amount of funds the bank has loaned out as mortgages, and the new market value of these loans, given the fall in home prices should Prime Bank decide to sell some of these mortgages. Analyze the impact of this real estate price decrease on the assets and liabilities of Prime Bank. As a simplifying assumption, assume that there are no costs to running the bank.

**STEP 1:** Start by first calculating the level of deposits at First Bank, and use this information to then calculate the level of reserves and the dollar amount of mortgages financed at Prime Bank. Calculate how many mortgages Prime Bank will be able to make from this information.

This is a mathematical exercise: since there are 500 customers who each deposit $50,000 at the bank, this implies that total deposits at the bank are equal to 500($50,000), or $25,000,000. Since Prime Bank holds 20% of its deposits as reserves, this means that reserves at the bank are equal to $5,000,000. The remaining $20,000,000 is used by Prime Bank to finance mortgages. If each mortgage is worth $200,000, then the bank has funds to support 100 mortgages.

**STEP 2:** Analyze the effect of the fall in real estate prices on the value of the mortgages held by Prime Bank.

The homes that have been purchased with the mortgages issued by Prime Bank were initially valued at $210,000. So, at the time of purchase each home buyer provided $10,000 of the funds needed to buy the house, and the bank had loaned the home buyer the remaining balance of $200,000. Now that home prices have fallen by 10%, the value of the home can be computed as $210,000 − 0.1($210,000), or $189,000. Since Prime Bank holds 100 mortgages, this implies that the value of the mortgages according to the price that these homes are now selling for is equal to $18,900,000 instead of the original $20,000,000.

**STEP 3:** Analyze the effect of this real estate price decrease on the value of the assets and liabilities of Prime Bank.

Before the real estate price decrease, the value of assets at Prime Bank was equal to the sum of reserves plus loans or $25,000,000, while the value of liabilities at Prime Bank was equal to the value of deposits at the bank, or $25,000,000. After the real estate price decrease, the value of assets at Prime Bank is now equal to the sum of reserves plus the value of the mortgage loans following the price decrease, or $5,000,000 plus

$18,900,000 for a total of $23,900,000. The value of liabilities at Prime Bank is still equal to $25,000,000. The effect of the real estate price decrease on Prime Bank is to make its liabilities greater than its assets: Prime Bank is no longer solvent.

# Problems and Exercises

1.  Suppose First Bank has 1,000 customers who have each deposited $10,000 at the bank. First Bank has kept 20% of these deposits as reserves to meet depositor demand for funds. The other 80% of First Bank's deposits have been used to make mortgage loans to individuals who have not deposited funds at First Bank. Each mortgage loan has a value of $100,000. For simplicity sake, let's assume that each mortgage represents a loan made to a customer to finance the purchase of a residence that is initially selling for $120,000.

    a.  What is the total amount of deposits at First Bank, given the information provided?

    b.  What is the total amount of reserves at First Bank, given the information provided?

    c.  What is the total number of mortgages issued by First Bank, given the information provided?

    Suppose a rumor circulates that First Bank may be unable to meet its financial obligations, and 50% of First Bank depositors demand their funds.

    d.  Given its initial level of reserves, will First Bank have sufficient funds on hand to meet the demand by these depositors for their funds? Explain your answer and provide a numerical value of the surplus or shortage of funds that First Bank will have, given this scenario.

    e.  To meet the demand for funds, First Bank decides to sell some of the mortgages it holds. Since First Bank needs funds immediately, it must sell these mortgages for less than their face value. Suppose that it sells each $100,000 mortgage for $75,000 to raise the necessary funds to meet depositor demands. How many mortgages will First Bank need to sell to raise the needed funds?

f. Consider First Bank's financial position after the sale of the mortgages in part (e). First Bank has sold mortgages to cover the demand for depositor funds. How many deposits (liabilities for First Bank) are still in the bank? Suppose that the remaining mortgages held by First Bank are now also valued at $75,000, the price First Bank has been able to sell mortgages for in the market. What is the value of the mortgages still owned by First Bank? Finally, what do reserves at First Bank equal?

g. Given your answers in part (f), is First Bank solvent (that is, do the value of assets exceed the value of liabilities) after it meets the demand for depositor funds that arises from the rumor?

2. A bank accepts deposits and uses these deposits to finance 30-year mortgages. How do these transactions represent maturity transformation?

3. What is shadow banking and how is it similar to the banking represented by depository institutions? How is shadow banking different from the banking represented by depository institutions? Discuss how shadow banking can be subject to bank runs.

4. Consider a bank run that becomes a financial contagion. Who loses when this happens? Explain your answer.

5.  What kinds of bank regulation can policy makers impose to reduce the likelihood of banking and financial crises?

6.  Briefly discuss the four major elements of the Wall Street Reform and Consumer Protection Act, otherwise known as the Dodd-Frank bill. In your explanation, discuss why each of these elements is important.

## ▮ BEFORE YOU TAKE THE TEST

## Module Review Questions

1.  Which of the following statements is true?
    a.  Commercial banks and investment banks refer to identical financial institutions.
    b.  Commercial banks accept deposits from customers, while investment banks trade in financial assets but do not accept deposits from customers.
    c.  Investment banks accept deposits from customers, while commercial banks trade in financial assets but do not accept deposits from customers.
    d.  Commercial banks and investment banks both accept deposits from customers, but only investment banks trade in financial assets.

2.  A subprime mortgage is
    a.  a mortgage issued to a homebuyer who does not have sufficient income to qualify for a standard or prime mortgage.
    b.  a mortgage issued to a homebuyer who does have sufficient assets to qualify for a standard or prime mortgage.
    c.  less risky for the lender than a prime mortgage.
    d.  Answers (a), (b), and (c) are all correct.
    e.  Answers (a) and (b) are both correct.

**3.** A global credit crunch occurs when
   a. borrowers cannot find credit or they must pay very high interest rates for credit.
   b. lenders cannot loan money or they receive very low interest rates for any loans they do make.
   c. lenders are willing to loan money to borrowers, but borrowers refuse to take out loans.
   d. borrowers are willing to borrow money, but lenders do not have any money they can lend to borrowers.

**4.** *Shadow banking* refers to
   a. commercial banks that accept deposits and make loans.
   b. a wide variety of types of financial firms including investment banks, hedge funds, and money market funds.
   c. financial firms that, prior to the banking crisis of 2008, were not closely watched or effectively regulated.
   d. Answers (a), (b), and (c) are all correct.
   e. Answers (b) and (c) are both correct.

**5.** The existence of banks reduces the need to
   a. hold cash in the event of an unexpected financial need.
   b. balance the need for liquidity against the rate of return one can earn from interest-earning assets.
   c. have regulation of the financial industry.
   d. hold cash rather than using these funds to help pay for productive investment spending.
   e. Answers (a), (b), (c), and (d) are all correct.
   f. Answers (a), (b), and (d) are correct.

**6.** Depository banks
   a. borrow on a short-term basis from their depositors and lend these funds on a long-term basis to others.
   b. borrow on a long-term basis from their depositors and lend these funds on a short-term basis to others.

**7.** Maturity transformation is done by
   a. depository institutions when they borrow on a short-term basis and lend on a long-term basis.
   b. shadow bank institutions even though these institutions do not take deposits.
   c. Answers (a) and (b) are both correct.

**8.** Shadow banks prior to the banking crisis of 2008 were
   a. not regulated and therefore did not need to meet capital or reserve requirements.
   b. not regulated and could therefore offer their customers a higher rate of return on their funds.
   c. in the United States about 1.5 times larger, in terms of dollars, than the formal, deposit-taking banking sector.
   d. Answers (a), (b), and (c) are all correct.

**9.** A shadow bank is subject to a bank run if
   a. the shadow bank's lenders decide it is no longer safe to lend funds to the shadow bank, and the bank finds it is unable to fund its operations.
   b. bank regulators fail to adequately evaluate the safety and soundness of the shadow bank.
   c. the government issues a warning that shadow banks are inherently unstable.
   d. Answers (a), (b), and (c) are all correct.

**10.** Many banking institutions getting into trouble at the same time is due to
   a. government regulations that prevent banking institutions from pursuing profitable business opportunities.
   b. these institutions making similar mistakes that are often due to the existence of an asset bubble.
   c. these institutions suffering from financial contagion in which the problems and difficulties of one institution spread to and create trouble for other institutions.
   d. Answers (b) and (c) are both reasons for banking crises.
   e. Answers (a), (b), and (c) all provide reasons for banking crises.

**11.** Which of the following statements is true?
   a. A "vicious cycle of deleveraging" refers to the quick selling of assets that result in these assets being sold at a deep discount. This selling off of assets creates financial contagion, since other institutions holding similar assets will find that these assets have lost value.
   b. The shadow banking system is not prone to financial contagion.
   c. The shadow banking system, prior to 2007, was highly regulated.
   d. Lehman's was not affected by a "vicious cycle of deleveraging."

**12.** A financial panic
   a. is a sudden and widespread disruption of financial markets that arises when people lose faith in the liquidity of financial institutions and markets.
   b. is typically accompanied by a banking crisis.
   c. could be the result of an asset bubble and a vicious circle of deleveraging.
   d. Answers (a), (b), and (c) are all correct.
   e. Answers (a) and (b) are both correct.
   f. Answers (a) and (c) are both correct.

**13.** Banking crises are
   a. commonly associated with recessions.
   b. do not affect the overall health of the economy.
   c. typically not associated with long-running impacts on the aggregate economy.
   d. easily resolved within days of becoming apparent.

**14.** A severe banking crisis is characterized as
   a. a situation in which a large fraction of the banking system goes bankrupt or suffers a major loss of confidence.
   b. a situation requiring government intervention to bail out the banking system.
   c. a situation that always leads to deep recession followed by a slow economic recovery.
   d. Answers (a), (b), and (c) are all correct.
   e. Answers (a) and (b) are both correct.

**15.** Banking crises typically result in prolonged recessions because of
   a. the credit crunch that leads to a reduction in available credit due to the disruption of the banking system.
   b. the debt overhang that arises as a result of falling asset prices that lead to a vicious cycle of deleveraging; as this circle progresses, it leads to even greater decreases in asset prices. As asset prices fall, consumers and businesses cut back on their spending in order to reduce their debt and rebuild their assets.
   c. the loss of monetary effectiveness as a means to stimulate aggregate spending in the economy.
   d. Answers (a), (b), and (c) are all correct.
   e. Answers (a) and (b) are both correct.
   f. Answers (b) and (c) are both correct.
   g. Answers (a) and (c) are both correct.

**16.** After a banking crisis, when the central bank expands the money supply in order to reduce interest rates and stimulate the level of aggregate spending,
   a. banks tend to hold onto excess reserves rather than loaning out these reserves because the banks are worried about bank runs and/or a loss of confidence by their investors.
   b. consumers and businesses are unwilling to borrow because of the financial difficulties caused by a loss in the price of the financial assets they hold.
   c. even a very low interest rate may not be sufficient to encourage expanded economic activity.
   d. Answers (a), (b), and (c) are all correct.

**17.** When financial institutions find they are unable to borrow from private credit markets,
   a. the country's central bank may step in as a lender of last resort.
   b. they may have to sell their assets at steeply reduced prices unless the central bank steps in and provides credit to them.
   c. a vicious circle of deleveraging may begin.
   d. the government may step in to guarantee the liabilities of these financial institutions.
   e. All of the answers are correct.

**18.** When the government guarantees bank deposits via deposit insurance, this results in
   a. the risk that bank owners will engage in reckless behavior with these bank funds, since any loss is insured by the government.
   b. bank owners acting with greater caution, since they know that any adverse outcome of their decisions will cost taxpayers money due to the existence of deposit insurance.

**19.** Financial regulation broke down prior to the crisis of 2008 primarily because of the
   a. rise of shadow banking.
   b. expansion of the commercial banking system.
   c. rise of the shadow banking system as well as the expansion of the commercial banking system.

20. The shadow banking system in the 2000s
    a. had little safety net in the form of deposit insurance.
    b. did have capital requirements but these requirements were minimal compared to the capital requirements that conventional depository institutions had to meet.
    c. had no lender of last resort to turn to in the event of a bank run.
    d. Answers (a), (b), and (c) are all true statements.

21. A homeowner being "underwater," means that the
    a. value of the house is less than the amount owed on the homeowner's mortgage.
    b. value of the mortgage is less than the value of the house.
    c. institution providing the mortgage for the homeowner is insolvent; thus, the homeowner must find a new lender.
    d. homeowner has defaulted on their mortgage.
    e. home is in foreclosure in which the lending institution is in the process of reclaiming the house as the collateral on a loan that is not being paid back to the institution.

22. A subprime mortgage is a loan
    a. to people who would not qualify for a traditional, or "prime" mortgage.
    b. at a lower interest rate than a traditional, or "prime" mortgage.

23. After the banking crisis of 2008
    a. it was recognized that financial regulation was a continuing process that could require regulations to change over time to keep up with financial innovations.
    b. it was clear that the traditional scope of banking regulation was too wide and there was need to constrict the expansion of bank regulation.
    c. it was evident that shadow banking did not need to be regulated.
    d. Answers (a), (b), and (c) are all correct.
    e. Answers (a) and (b) are both correct.
    f. Answers (b) and (c) are both correct.
    g. Answers (a) and (c) are both correct.

24. The Wall Street Reform and Consumer Protection Act, often referred to as the Dodd-Frank bill, addresses which of the following four key elements?
    a. consumer protection, derivatives regulation, limits on interest rates, and regulation of shadow banks.
    b. consumer protection, derivatives regulation, subprime lending limits, and regulation of shadow banking.
    c. consumer protection, derivatives regulation, regulation of shadow banks, and resolution authority.
    d. consumer protection, derivatives regulation, subprime lending limits, and resolution authority.

## ■ ANSWER KEY

# Answers to Problems and Exercises

1. **a.** The total amount of deposits at First Bank is equal to the amount of each deposit ($10,000) times the number of depositors (1,000), or $10,000,000.

   **b.** The amount of reserves at First Bank is equal to 20% of $10,000,000, or $2,000,000.

   **c.** The total number of mortgages issued by First Bank is equal to the amount of money available for mortgages ($8,000,000) divided by the amount per mortgage ($100,000), or 80 mortgages.

   **d.** If 50% of First Bank's depositors demand their funds back, then First Bank will need 500($10,000), or $5,000,000 to meet this demand. Since First Bank only has $2,000,000 in reserve, the Bank will find that it has a shortage of $3,000,000.

   **e.** Since First Bank needs to raise $3,000,000 in funds to meet depositor demands, it will need to sell $3,000,000/$75,000 per mortgage, or 40 mortgages.

   **f.** Since 50% of depositors have withdrawn their funds from the bank, this implies that First Bank now has deposits of only $5,000,000. First Bank sold 40 mortgages to raise the needed funds to meet depositor demand, so it still owns 60 mortgages. If each mortgage is now valued at $75,000, this means that the value of First Bank's mortgages is now equal to 60($75,000), or $4,500,000. First Bank's reserves are now equal to $0, since the bank used the $2,000,000 it had in reserve plus the sale of 40 mortgages to raise the funds necessary to honor depositor demand for funds.

   **g.** First Bank's assets are now equal to $4,500,000 (the value of the mortgages it holds), while its liabilities are equal to $5,000,000 (the value of deposits at the bank). First Bank is not solvent.

2. The deposits made at the bank are short-term in nature: that is, the depositors place funds in the bank where these funds are available whenever the depositor demands them. These deposits represent liabilities to the bank, since the bank owes these funds to the depositors who made the deposits. The bank takes these funds and uses them to finance mortgages that have a maturity of 30 years: that is, the mortgage amount borrowed does not have to be repaid in full until 30 years have elapsed. These mortgages represent assets to the bank, since the bank owns these mortgages. The bank has transformed a short-term liability, the deposits, into a long-term asset, the 30-year mortgages. Maturity transformation is the conversion of short-term liabilities into long-term assets.

3. Shadow banking refers to a diverse group of financial firms including hedge funds, money market mutual funds, and investment banks. Like depository institutions, shadow banks borrow short-term funds and use these funds to create long-term assets. Shadow banks create long-term assets by borrowing funds in the short run and then lending or investing these funds over the longer term. This process is referred to as maturity transformation. Shadow banks are different from depository institutions in that shadow banks do not accept deposits. Shadow banks, like depository institutions, are subject to bank runs because both types of banking institutions perform the same economic task of allowing their customers to make a better trade-off between rate of return, or yield, and liquidity. If the shadow bank lenders decide that it is no longer safe to lend to the shadow bank, then this loss of credit means the shadow bank can no longer fund its operations. Unless the shadow bank is able to quickly sell its assets to immediately raise cash, it will fail. This failure to get funds to finance its operations is what happened to Lehman Brothers.

4. When a bank run occurs, many people are adversely impacted: the shareholders and the creditors of the bank, the depositors and loan customers at the bank, and the bank employees. A bank run that spreads like a contagion affects many more people: it can cause a loss of confidence among depositors at other banks, and this can lead to a cascade of events that creates more bank failures and even a bank crisis. In a bank crisis, a significant portion of the banking sector ceases to function. Often a banking crisis also precipitates a severe economic downturn that results in higher rates of unemployment and lower levels of aggregate production that persist for many years.

5. There are two broad types of regulation that governments can implement to reduce the likelihood of banking and financial crises. Government can act as a lender of last resort so that financial institutions have a source of funds or credit when they are unable to borrow from private credit markets. This lender of last resort protects solvent financial institutions from engaging in fire sales to raise needed funds when the private credit markets are not functioning well. The government can also provide guarantees to depositors and others with claims on banks. These guarantees effectively mean that when a financial institution becomes insolvent, the government will step in and take on the bank's risk. When the government does step in, it often demands the temporary ownership of the bank until the government can "reprivatize" the bank. This guarantee is a method for restoring depositor confidence in troubled financial institutions.

6. The Dodd-Frank bill called for consumer protection, derivatives regulation, regulation of shadow banks, and resolution authority. Consumer protection was deemed necessary after the financial crisis of 2008 because of the recognition that many borrowers prior to the crisis had accepted offers they did not understand. One of the goals of the Dodd-Frank bill was to reduce abusive financial industry practices while protecting borrowers.

   The bill called for regulation of derivatives because these complicated financial instruments were seen as a means of concealing risk. The new legislation calls for more transparent markets in derivatives. The Dodd-Frank bill also legislated regulation of shadow banks in recognition that these institutions, although they did not fit the traditional definition of a bank, played a major role in the banking crisis. Shadow banks will be regulated with regard to their levels of capital and their investments.

   The Dodd-Frank bill provided for resolution authority that empowered the government to seize control of financial institutions that require a bailout. This would be an extension of the government's resolution authority over not just depository institutions, but also over the shadow banking industry. Recognizing that government guarantees can lead institutions to take excessive risk, the provision for resolution authority allows the government to reduce its exposure to backing these overly risky institutions through the government's ability to seize these errant institutions if necessary. Knowing the government can do this will likely reduce risk taking on the part of financial institutions.

## Answers to Module Review Questions

1. **Answer b.** This is just a definitional question: commercial banks accept deposits from customers, while investment banks do not accept these deposits. In addition, investment banks trade in financial assets.

2. **Answer e.** A subprime mortgage is a mortgage issued to a homebuyer who lacks the level of income and/or assets that would allow him or her to qualify for a standard or prime mortgage. Because the borrower lacks the income and/or assets to qualify for a standard mortgage, he/she represents a greater threat of defaulting on, or not paying back, the loan.

3. **Answer a.** In a credit crunch, borrowers would like to borrow funds, but they find it either impossible to get credit because lenders are unwilling to lend, or it is very expensive to get credit because lenders are only willing to lend at very high interest rates. In a credit crunch, lenders have funds but are reluctant to make these funds available unless they receive unusually high interest rates on the loans they make.

4. **Answer e.** *Shadow banking* is a term coined by Paul McCulley to refer to a diverse group of financial firms including investment banks, hedge funds, and money market funds that prior to the crisis of 2008 were not closely watched or effectively regulated. Commercial banks are not considered shadow banks; the commercial banks are highly regulated.

5. **Answer f.** Banking reduces the need to hold cash in the event of a financial need because the existence of banks provides a means of borrowing funds if they are needed. In addition, the banking system provides liquidity for lenders while simultaneously providing a means for those individuals with surplus funds to make those funds available to those with productive opportunities but a deficit of funds. Thus, it is possible to have liquidity while earning an interest return on your assets because of the banking system. The system, however, does require regulation in order that asymmetric information issues like moral hazard and adverse selection can be addressed.

6. **Answer a.** Deposits at depository institutions are available at any time and are thus short term. These institutions lend out these funds to those seeking funds for productive purposes: the loans are due at some point in the future, but because they are not immediately due they are viewed as long term. This borrowing on a short-term basis and lending on a long-term basis is called maturity transformation.

7. **Answer c.** Maturity transformation refers to the conversion of short-term liabilities to long-term assets. Depository institutions as well as shadow bank institutions engage in maturity transformation.

8. **Answer d.** These are all definitional or descriptive statements that are covered in the text.

9. **Answer a.** Shadow banks are in the business of maturity transformation: they borrow on a short-term basis and lend or invest longer term. If lenders decide that the shadow bank is not a safe place for their funds, then this mismatch between short-term borrowing and long-term lending can result in a bank run when other lenders decide they also do not want to place their funds at the shadow bank. Shadow banking, prior to the banking crisis of 2008, was not regulated. The government does not issue warnings about the stability of the shadow bank institutions.

10. **Answer d.** Banking crises are typically the result of an asset bubble or financial contagion. With an asset bubble, financial institutions make a similar mistake in valuing an asset at a level greater than its true value. With financial contagion, the financial problems of one institution spread to other institutions and create problems for these other institutions. Government regulation is not a source of banking crises.

11. **Answer a.** Answer (a) describes what happens when a financial institution is forced to sell its assets quickly in order to reduce debt and raise cash. These quick sales drive the price of these assets down, and other institutions holding similar assets find that these assets are no longer as valuable. This causes the institutions to need to also sell assets to reduce their debt and raise cash. The data suggest that Lehman's did suffer from a downward spiral of asset prices. The shadow banking system prior to 2007 was not regulated; it is especially prone to fear- and rumor-driven contagion.

12. **Answer d.** These are all true statements and are discussed in the text.

13. **Answer a.** Banking crises typically are associated with recessions; severe banking crises often result in prolonged, and significant, economic slumps.

14. **Answer d.** These statements are from the text: a severe banking crisis results in many bank failures, a loss of confidence in the financial system, the need for government intervention, and a prolonged and deep recession that lasts for an extended period of time.

15. **Answer d.** The severity of recessions following banking crises is typically explained by the credit crunch, the debt overhang, and the loss of monetary effectiveness. Economic activity slows as credit becomes difficult to get, consumers and businesses slow their spending in order to reduce their debt and rebuild their assets, and monetary policy is not effective in stimulating the level of aggregate spending.

16. **Answer d.** These are all reasons for why monetary policy is ineffective following a banking crisis. Banks fearful of bank runs or a loss of confidence by their investors will want to hold excess reserves in order to have more of a cushion against a bank run or reluctance on the part of investors to provide funds. The vicious circle of deleveraging reduces the value of financial assets held relative to debt: consumers and businesses will be reluctant to increase their spending until they have reduced their debt levels relative to the value of their financial assets. Finally, a low interest rate when consumers and businesses are recovering from a vicious circle of deleveraging may not provide sufficient incentive to get these groups to borrow and spend.

17. **Answer e.** When financial institutions cannot borrow from private credit markets, they must find a source of credit. This source of credit can come from the sale of the institution's assets, but this sale typically is only possible if the financial institutions offer the assets at greatly reduced prices. This selling of assets at fire-sale prices starts the vicious circle of deleveraging and worsens the balance sheet for all the financial institutions. The central bank can prevent this from happening by stepping in as a lender of last resort and providing a means of credit for solvent, but credit-strapped, institutions. For a financial institution where the value of the assets is insufficient to cover its debts, the central bank's willingness to lend as a last resort will not be sufficient to restore the public's confidence in the financial institution; in this case, the government may choose to step in and guarantee the institution's liabilities.

18. **Answer a.** The existence of bank deposit insurance means that depositors no longer fear that their funds might not be safe at a banking institution: the deposit insurance effectively reduces the occurrence of bank runs because of the guaranteed protection of depositor savings. However, when these deposits are insured, it also creates an incentive for bank owners to engage in riskier behavior with regard to the use of these funds, since the bank owners know that the funds will be guaranteed by the government even if a speculative bet does not pay off. Bank owners know that the government, and therefore taxpayers, will cover the cost of any bad bet on their part.

19. **Answer a.** Financial regulation has traditionally been concerned with depository institutions. However, shadow banking also functions like depository banking because these banks engage in maturity transformation. It is the rise of shadow banking that has created the greatest problem in financial regulation.

20. **Answer d.** These are all descriptive statements about the shadow banking system in the 2000s prior to the financial crisis of 2008.

21. **Answer a.** A homeowner being "underwater" means that the value of the house is no longer worth as much as or more than the amount owed on the mortgage. This often results in the homeowner being in default: that is, the homeowner may not be making mortgage payments sometimes because he or she has chosen to walk away from the property, and sometimes because he or she could not keep up with mortgage payments and could not sell the home for enough to pay off the mortgage. When a homeowner is "underwater," the home may be foreclosed on: the lending institution may repossess the home as a result of the failure of the homeowner to make mortgage payments. With a housing bubble, lending institutions may fail, since the value of the mortgage-backed securities that they hold fall in value.

22. **Answer a.** This is just the definition of a subprime mortgage.

23. **Answer a.** Bank regulation had failed to keep up with financial innovation, and this became evident with the banking crisis of 2008, particularly with the recognition of the growth of shadow banking. In the aftermath of the banking crisis of 2008, it was recognized that bank regulation would need to be extended to cover more than traditional banking and that shadow banking also needed to be regulated.

24. **Answer c.** The four elements of the Wall Street Reform and Consumer Protection Act are delineated and discussed in the module.

# module 43(79)

# Capital Flows and the Balance of Payments

## BEFORE YOU READ THE MODULE

## Summary

This module introduces the balance of payments and explores the components that comprise the balance of payments accounts. In addition, the module considers the determinants of international capital flows.

## Module Objectives

**Objective #1.** The balance of payments accounts summarize a country's transactions with other countries.

- The balance of payments on financial account is the difference between a country's sales of assets to foreigners and the country's purchases of assets from foreigners during a given period of time. This is also referred to as the capital account. The financial account can be broken into subaccounts, including the private net purchases of assets by private individuals, and the official net purchases of assets, which represent transactions made by central banks.

- The balance of payments on current account is the difference between a country's exports and its imports plus net international transfer payments and factor income during a given period of time. Net international transfer payments is the difference between the payments foreigners send into the country and the payments that are sent out of the country to foreigners, while net international factor income is the difference between income payments received from foreigners and payments paid to foreigners.

- The sum of the balance of payments on current account ($CA$) and the balance of payments on financial account ($FA$) must equal zero. Thus, if $CA$ is a positive number, then $FA$ must be a negative number; conversely, if $CA$ is a negative number, then $FA$ must be a positive number of the same magnitude.

**Objective #2.** A modified circular-flow diagram can illustrate the flows between a country and the rest of the world.

- One flow represents the payments that are counted in the balance of payments on current account: here, the rest of the world sends payments into the country for goods and services (this would be payments for the country's exports), factor income, and transfers, and the rest of the world receives payments from the country for the goods and services (this would be payments for the country's imports), factor income, and transfers.

- A second flow represents payments that are counted in the balance of payments on financial account: here, the rest of the world sends the country payments for assets the world purchases from the country, while the country sends the rest of the world payments for assets it purchases. The country's balance of payments on financial account is a measure of the capital inflows or the amount of foreign savings that are available to finance domestic investment spending.

- Since the total flow into the country must be equal to the total flow out of the country, the implication is that the balance of payments on current account plus the balance of payments on financial account must equal zero.

**Objective #3.** The merchandise trade balance, or trade balance, is the difference between a country's exports and imports of goods. It does not include the value of services traded.

**Objective #4.** Countries can pay for their imports by selling assets that create liabilities, obligating the country to pay for these goods and services at some point in the future.

**Objective #5.** The loanable funds market can be used to illustrate capital flows between countries. Provided investors think that a foreign asset is as good as a domestic asset and a foreign liability is as good as a domestic one, funds will flow from a country with a low interest rate to a country with a high interest rate until the difference between the interest rates in the two locales is eliminated. That is, the capital flows will equalize the interest rate between the two countries.

- A country that has capital inflows must have a matching current account deficit, and a country that has capital outflows must have a matching current account surplus.

- The financial account reflects the movement of capital and the current account reflects the movement of goods and services: movements in the exchange rate ensure that the balance of payments, the difference between the current account and the financial account, equals zero. The exchange rate is the price at which one currency trades for another currency.

- International differences in the demand for funds reflect underlying differences in investment opportunities. International differences in the supply of funds reflect underlying differences in savings across countries.

# Key Terms

**balance of payments accounts** a summary of a country's transactions with other countries, including two main elements: the *balance of payments on current account* and the *balance of payments on financial account*.

**balance of payments on current account (current account)** transactions that do not create liabilities; a country's *balance of payments on goods and services* plus net international transfer payments and factor income.

*Notes*

## Key Terms *(continued)*

**balance of payments on goods and services** the difference between the value of *exports* and the value of *imports* during a given period.

**merchandise trade balance (trade balance)** the difference between a country's *exports* and *imports* of goods alone—not including services.

**balance of payments on financial account (financial account)** international transactions that involve the sale or purchase of assets and, therefore, create future liabilities.

## ■ AFTER YOU READ THE MODULE

## Tips

**Tip #1.** This module introduces new vocabulary. You will want to learn the definitions of these new terms and how to apply the definitions. You will need to study carefully the balance of payments accounts and all the new terms that are introduced with this new topic.

**Tip #2.** The balance of payments (illustrated in Figure 43-1 of your text) shows the flow of money between national economies. It illustrates why the balance of payments on current account must equal the balance of payments on financial account. It illustrates the relationship in a domestic economy between the payments from the rest of the world for goods and services, factor income, and transfers, and payments to the rest of the world for goods and services, factor income, and transfers.

## WORKED PROBLEMS

1. You have the following information about Macroland's transactions in 2014. Macroland exports $1,800,000 worth of goods and services to other countries while importing $675,000. Macroland makes payments of $525,000 to factors of production located outside of Macroland while receiving payments of $450,000 from foreigners for factors of production located inside of Macroland. The government of Macroland sells $350,000 worth of assets to foreigners while it buys $925,000 worth of assets from foreigners. Private citizens in Macroland purchase $405,000 worth of assets from foreigners, while private citizens sell $750,000 worth of assets to foreigners. Net transfers in Macroland for the year are –$280,000 and consist primarily of remittances sent from Macroland to other economies. You have been asked to calculate Macroland's balance of payments for 2014, including Macroland's current account and financial account. You have also been asked to calculate the net value of each category of payments

in Macroland's balance of payments. Finally, you are asked to summarize your findings by organizing this data in the following table.

| | Payments from foreigners | Payments to foreigners | Net |
|---|---|---|---|
| 1. Sales and purchases of goods and services | | | |
| 2. Factor incomes | | | |
| 3. Transfers | | | |
| Current account [(sum of (1) + (2) + (3)] | | | |
| 4. Official asset sales and purchases | | | |
| 5. Private sales and purchases of assets | | | |
| Financial account [sum of (4) + (5)] | | | |
| Total | | | |

**STEP 1:** Review the definitions of *current account* and *financial account*.

The current account is defined as the country's balance of payments on goods and services plus net international transfer payments and factor income during a given time period. The financial account is the difference between the country's sales of assets to foreigners and the country's purchases of assets from foreigners during a given time period.

**STEP 2:** Calculate the current account and explain your calculation.

To find the current account for Macroland in 2014, add together net exports plus net factor income plus transfers. That is, the current account is equal to (exports – imports) + (factor income paid by foreigners to factors in Macroland – factor income paid by Macroland to factors located outside of Macroland) + transfers. Remember that exports refer to the dollar value of goods and services sold to foreigners, while imports refer to the dollar value of goods and services produced outside of the country but sold to residents of the country. Thus, the current account for Macroland in 2014 is equal to ($1,800,000 – $675,000) + ($525,000 – $450,000) + (–$280,000), or $920,000.

**STEP 3:** Calculate the financial account and explain your calculation.

To find the financial account for Macroland in 2014, add together the sum of the official sales and purchases of assets and the private sales and purchases of assets. Official sales and purchases of assets are equal to the difference between payments from foreigners for these assets minus payments to foreigners for these assets. In this example, official sales and purchases of assets is equal to $350,000 – $925,000, or –$575,000. Private sales and purchases of assets are equal to the difference between payments from foreigners for these assets minus payments to foreigners for these assets. In our example, private sales and purchases of assets are equal to $405,000 –$750,000, or –$345,000. Summing these two figures together, we get that the financial account for Macroland for 2014 is equal to –$920,000.

**STEP 4:** Compare the current account and financial account and comment on why these two values should be quite similar to one another.

In the example, the value of the current account plus the value of the financial account sums to zero. That is, the current account is equal to the negative of the financial account. This is true since the flows of money into an economy must balance with the flows out of an economy. Macroland receives a flow of money into its economy as payments for goods and services sold abroad, as payments for the use of factors owned by people in Macroland, as transfer payments, and as payments to Macroland for assets bought by foreigners. Macroland has a flow of money going out of its economy as payments for goods and services produced outside of Macroland but consumed in Macroland, as payments to factors of production owned by people outside of Macroland, as transfer payments, and as payments to the rest of the world for assets. Review Figure 43-1 in your text on this topic.

**STEP 5:** Fill in the given table using the calculations you have made.

Here is the completed table based on the calculations done in Steps 2 and 3.

| | Payments from foreigners | Payments to foreigners | Net |
|---|---|---|---|
| 1. Sales and purchases of goods and services | $1,800,000 | $675,000 | $1,125,000 |
| 2. Factor incomes | 525,000 | 450,000 | 75,000 |
| 3. Transfers | | | −280,000 |
| Current account [(sum of (1) + (2) + (3)] | | | 920,000 |
| 4. Official asset sales and purchases | 350,000 | 925,000 | −575,000 |
| 5. Private sales and purchases of assets | 405,000 | 750,000 | −345,000 |
| Financial account [sum of (4) + (5)] | | | −920,000 |
| Total | | | $0 |

2.  Suppose there are two countries in the world, and each of these countries has its own loanable funds market. Initially, there are no capital flows between the two countries even though both countries view the two country's assets as being equally safe. The current loanable funds market for each country is provided in the following graphs, and you have been asked to comment on the current equilibrium interest rates in the two countries, given that there are no capital flows. You should provide a set of graphs illustrating the equilibrium interest rates in the two countries. Then, you are asked to comment on what will happen to interest rates in these two countries if capital flows are allowed. You are asked to provide the intuition behind your response.

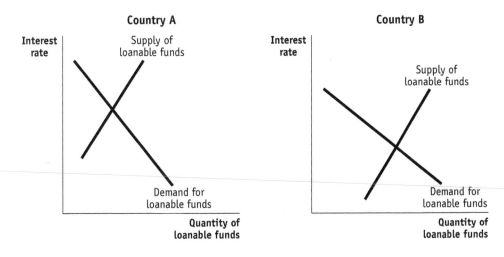

**STEP 1:** Identify the equilibrium interest rate in each country's loanable funds market.

If there are no capital flows between these two countries, then the equilibrium interest rate in each loanable funds market will be the interest rate that equates the quantity of loanable funds supplied to the quantity of loanable funds demanded. The equilibrium interest rate in country A is higher than the equilibrium interest rate in country B. The following graph illustrates these two equilibrium interest rates.

**STEP 2:** Explain the effect of allowing capital flows between countries.

If these two loanable funds markets open to capital flows, funds will flow out of country B, where the equilibrium interest rate is low, into country A, where the equilibrium interest rate is high. As funds flow into country A, we can anticipate that the interest rate in country A will decrease, since there will be more funds available at each interest rate, while, as funds flow out of country B, we can anticipate that the interest rate in country B will rise, since there will be fewer funds available at each interest rate.

**STEP 3:** Analyze the effect of allowing capital flows on the interest rate in the two countries.

As capital funds flow out of country B into country A, we see that both interest rates adjust. In country A, the interest rate decreases to $r_3$ (illustrated in the following graph). In country B, the interest rate increases to $r_3$. This adjustment continues until the interest rate reaches that level at which the total quantity of loans demanded by borrowers in the two countries is equal to the total quantity of loans supplied by lenders in the two countries. The following graph illustrates this concept.

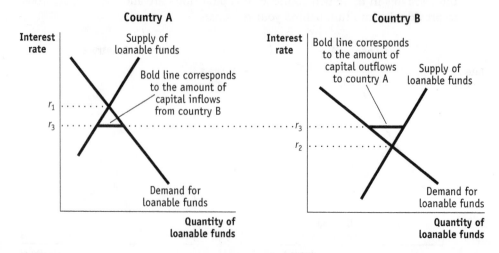

# Problems and Exercises

**1.** Use the following table of information to answer this question.

|  | Payments from foreigners (millions of dollars) | Payments to foreigners (millions of dollars) | Sales of assets to foreigners (millions of dollars) | Purchases of assets from foreigners (millions of dollars) |
|---|---|---|---|---|
| Goods | $200 | $80 | — | — |
| Services | 50 | 20 | — | — |
| Factor income | 70 | 10 | — | — |
| Transfer payments | 10 | 20 | — | — |
| Official sales and purchases | — | — | $100 | $300 |
| Private sales and purchases | — | — | 80 | 80 |

**a.** Provide a definition or an equation for each of the following items.

(i) Merchandise trade balance

(ii) Balance of payments on goods and services

(iii) Net international factor income

(iv) Net international transfer payments

(v) Balance of payments on current account

(vi) Balance of payments on financial account

**b.** Given the previous information, compute the value of each of the terms given in part (a).

    c. Explain why the sum of the balance of payments on current account and the balance of payments on financial account must equal zero.

**2.** The following graphs represent the loanable funds market in Macroland and Funland, the only two economies in the world.

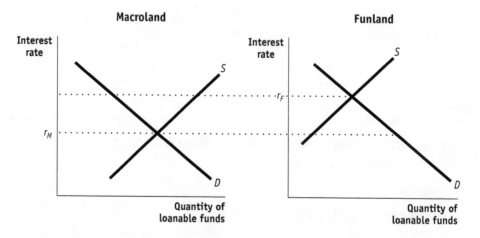

Residents in Macroland and Funland believe that foreign assets and liabilities are as good as domestic assets and liabilities.

    **a.** Given the two graphs, which country is likely to attract capital? Why?

    **b.** Given the Macroland graph, what do you predict will happen to the interest rate in Macroland over time? Explain your answer.

    **c.** Given the Funland graph, what do you predict will happen to the interest rate in Funland over time? Explain your answer.

    **d.** Briefly describe the capital flows between Macroland and Funland.

**3.** Suppose there are only two countries—Macrobia and Tacrobia—that investors view as being equally attractive for investment. Furthermore, suppose the loanable funds markets in these two countries can be described by the demand and supply equations given below:

Demand for loanable funds in Macrobia: $r = 10 - (1/100)LF$

Supply of loanable funds in Macrobia: $r = (1/100)LF$

Demand for loanable funds in Tacrobia: $r = 10 - (1/200)LF$

Supply of loanable funds in Tacrobia: $r = (1/300)LF$

In the above equations, $r$ is the interest rate expressed as a percentage (e.g., if the interest rate is 10%, then that would be expressed as 10 in the above equation) and $LF$ is the quantity of loanable funds measured in dollars. Currently the two countries do not allow capital inflows or capital outflows.

**a.** What is the equilibrium interest rate and quantity of loanable funds in Macrobia?

**b.** What is the equilibrium interest rate and quantity of loanable funds in Tacrobia?

**c.** If these two countries decide to allow capital flows, what do you predict will happen? Which country will provide capital outflows and which country will provide capital inflows? Explain your answer.

**d.** Suppose that at every interest rate, Tacrobia provides $200 of loanable funds to Macrobia. What will be the effect of this on the supply of loanable funds curve in Tacrobia? Write the new supply of loanable funds curve equation for Tacrobia.

**e.** Given the new supply of loanable funds curve you computed in part (d), what will be the new equilibrium interest rate and quantity of loanable funds in Tacrobia?

**f.** Suppose that at every interest rate, Tacrobia provides $200 of loanable funds to Macrobia. What will be the effect of this on the supply of loanable funds curve in Macrobia? Write the new supply of loanable funds curve equation for Macrobia.

**g.** Given the new supply of loanable funds curve you computed in part (f), what will be the new equilibrium interest rate and quantity of loanable funds in Macrobia?

**h.** Given your answers in parts (e) and (g), what do you predict about capital flows between these two countries?

**4.** Consider each of the following transactions and identify how the transaction would be categorized in the U.S. balance of payments accounts. For each transaction identify whether it would be counted as part of the balance of payments in the current account or the financial account. Lastly, identify whether the transaction will increase or decrease the relevant account.

**a.** An American company purchases machinery that is produced in Germany by a German company.

**b.** An American donates money to the foreign group organizing an international sporting event in another country.

**c.** A French citizen purchases cheese produced in the United States.

**d.** An American purchases 100 shares of a Swiss company.

## BEFORE YOU TAKE THE TEST

# Module Review Questions

1. Which of the following statements is true?
   a. The balance of payments on goods and services is the difference between the value of imports and the value of exports during a given period.
   b. The merchandise trade balance includes the sale of goods as well as financial assets.
   c. A country's international transactions are tracked by the balance of payments accounts.
   d. Statements (a), (b), and (c) are all true.
   e. Statements (a) and (c) are both true.
   f. Statements (b) and (c) are both true.

2. The balance of payments on goods and services plus net international transfer payments and net international factor income
   a. equals the merchandise trade balance.
   b. equals the balance on payments on current account.
   c. equals the balance on payments on financial account.
   d. plus the balance of payments on financial account equals zero.
   e. Answers (a) and (c) are both correct.
   f. Answers (b) and (c) are both correct.
   g. Answers (b) and (d) are both correct.

3. For a hypothetical economy if the balance of payments on financial account equals –$100 million, then the balance of payments on current account must
   a. equal –$100 million.
   b. be greater than –$100 million.
   c. be less than –$100 million.
   d. equal $100 million.

4. The balance of payments tracks the
   a. flow of payments into a country from the rest of the world as well as the flow of payments from the country to the rest of the world.
   b. flow of payments for goods and services, factor income, and transfers in the balance of payments on current account.
   c. flow of payments for assets in the balance of payments on financial account.
   d. Answers (a), (b), and (c) are all correct.

5.  Suppose that there are two countries with open economies. If the interest rate in the loanable funds market in the first country is higher than the interest rate in the loanable funds market in the second country, we can expect that

    a. this interest rate differential will continue if citizens in both countries view their domestic assets as comparable to foreign assets.

    b. this interest rate differential will be eliminated due to the movement of international capital flows.

    c. the supply of loanable funds in the first country will increase while the supply of loanable funds in the second country will decrease.

    d. the supply of loanable funds in the first country will decrease while the supply of loanable funds in the second country will increase.

    e. Answers (b) and (c) are both correct.

    f. Answers (b) and (d) are both correct.

6.  Which of the following statements is true?

    a. A country that receives capital inflows will have a matching financial account surplus.

    b. The exchange rate is always measured as the price of a dollar in terms of the foreign currency.

    c. The more euros it takes to buy a dollar, the fewer dollars Europeans will supply.

    d. When a country's currency appreciates, exports fall and imports rise.

7.  Which of the following represents a payment from foreigners to the hypothetical economy called Macropedia?

    a. the dollar value of corn Macropedia imports from Cornucopia

    b. the dollar value of bicycles Macropedia exports to Pedal Land

    c. the fees Macropedia engineering firms receive for bridge designs they provide to the foreign country of Islandville

    d. the fees Macropedia companies pay to Islandville in compensation for the financial services Islandville provides

    e. Answers (a), (b), (c), and (d) all represent payments from foreigners to Macropedia.

    f. Answers (b) and (c) represent payments from foreigners to Macropedia.

    g. Answers (a) and (d) represent payments from foreigners to Macropedia.

8.  In 2012, which of the following statements were true?

    I. The United States had a substantial current account deficit.

    II. The United States had a substantial financial account surplus.

    III. The value of the assets the United States sold to foreigners was greater than the value of the assets the United States bought from foreigners.

    a. Statements I, II, and III are all true.

    b. Statements I and II are both true.

    c. Statements I and III are both true.

    d. Statements II and III are both true.

9.  Suppose the loanable funds market in Macroland is currently in equilibrium. Holding everything else constant, if capital inflows increase to Macroland, this will cause the equilibrium interest rate

a.  to decrease while the equilibrium quantity of loanable funds will increase.

b.  to increase while the equilibrium quantity of loanable funds will decrease.

c.  and the equilibrium quantity of loanable funds to decrease.

d.  and the equilibrium quantity of loanable funds to increase.

10. Suppose the loanable funds market in Macroland is currently in equilibrium. Holding everything else constant, if businesses in Macroland increase the level of their investment spending that is financed by borrowing, this will cause a shift

a.  in the supply of loanable funds curve to the right and a movement along the demand for loanable funds curve.

b.  in the supply of loanable funds curve to the left and a movement along the demand for loanable funds curve.

c.  in the demand for loanable funds curve to the right and a movement along the supply of loanable funds curve.

d.  in the demand for loanable funds curve to the left and a movement along the supply of loanable funds curve.

11. Which of the following statements is true?

I.  Fast-growing economies often have greater demand for loanable funds than do slower-growing economies since these countries often have greater investment opportunities.

II. The supply of loanable funds in any particular country is impacted by the country's private savings rate: some countries have higher savings rates than do other countries.

III. In 2012, the United States ran a current account surplus and a financial account deficit.

a.  Statements I, II, and III are all true.

b.  Statements I and II are both true.

c.  Statements I and III are both true.

d.  Statements II and III are both true.

## ANSWER KEY

# Answers to Problems and Exercises

1.  **a.**  (i) Merchandise trade balance = (exports of goods) − (imports of goods) = (payments from foreigners for goods) − (payments to foreigners for goods)

    (ii) Balance of payments on goods and services = (exports of goods and services) − (imports of goods and services) = (payments from foreigners for goods and services) − (payments to foreigners for goods and services)

    (iii) Net international factor income = (factor income payments from foreigners) − (factor income payments to foreigners)

    (iv) Net international transfer payments = (transfer payments from foreigners) − (transfer payments to foreigners)

    (v) Balance of payments on current account = (balance of payments on goods and services) + (net international transfer payments) + (net international factor income)

    (vi) Balance of payments on financial account = (sales of assets to foreigners) − (purchases of assets from foreigners)

    **b.**  (i) Merchandise trade balance = $200 million − $80 million = $120 million

    (ii) Balance of payments on goods and services = $250 million − $100 million = $150 million

    (iii) Net international factor income = $70 million − $10 million = $60 million

    (iv) Net international transfer payments = $10 million − $20 million = −$10 million

    (v) Balance of payments on current account = $150 million + (−$10 million) + ($60 million) = $200 million

    (vi) Balance of payments on financial account = −$200 million

    **c.** This reflects a basic rule of balance of payments accounting for any country: the flow of money into a country must equal the flow of money out of the country.

2.  **a.** Funland will attract capital, because its equilibrium interest rate is higher than the equilibrium interest rate in Macroland.

    **b.** Over time the interest rate in Macroland will rise due to capital outflows. Since Macroland initially has a lower equilibrium interest rate than Funland, some Macroland lenders will decide to send their funds to Funland to take advantage of the higher interest rate. Over time this will cause the interest rates in the two countries to equalize.

    **c.** Over time the interest rate in Funland will fall due to capital inflows from Macroland. As funds from Macroland are attracted to Funland's loanable funds market, due to its initially higher equilibrium interest rate, the interest rate will fall in Funland. Eventually, the interest rates in the two countries will equalize.

    **d.** Capital will flow out of Macroland and into Funland. Thus, Macroland will experience capital outflows, while Funland will experience capital inflows.

3.  **a.** To find the equilibrium interest rate and quantity of loanable funds in Macrobia, you need to find the intersection of the demand and supply curves. Thus, the equilibrium interest rate is 5% and the equilibrium quantity of loanable funds is $500.

    **b.** To find the equilibrium interest rate and quantity of loanable funds in Tacrobia, you need to find the intersection of the demand and supply curves. Thus, the equilibrium interest rate is 4% and the equilibrium quantity of loanable funds is $1,200.

**c.** Since the interest rate is higher in Macrobia than in Tacrobia, you would expect loanable funds to be attracted to the higher interest rate: Tacrobia will have capital outflows and Macrobia will have capital inflows until the interest rates in the two countries are equalized.

**d.** If Tacrobia has capital outflows of $200 to Macrobia, this will cause the supply of loanable funds curve in Tacrobia to shift to the left by 200. This shift will be a parallel shift of the loanable funds supply curve since it is a constant amount of capital outflows irrespective of the interest rate. The new loanable funds curve is $r = (1/300)LF + (2/3)$.

**e.** With the new loanable funds supply curve and the original loanable funds demand curve, we can solve for the new equilibrium interest rate and quantity of loanable funds in Tacrobia. This new equilibrium is at an interest rate of 4.4% and a quantity of loanable funds equal to $1,120.

**f.** If Tacrobia provides Macrobia with $200 of capital inflows, this will cause the supply of loanable funds curve in Macrobia to shift to the right by 200. This shift will be a parallel shift of the loanable funds supply curve since it is a constant amount of capital inflows irrespective of the interest rate. The new loanable funds curve is $r = (1/100)LF - 2$.

**g.** With the new loanable funds supply curve and the original loanable funds demand curve, we can solve for the new equilibrium interest rate and quantity of loanable funds in Macrobia. This new equilibrium is at an interest rate of 4% and a quantity of loanable funds equal to $600.

**h.** Since the interest rates in the two countries are still different, you would expect capital flows to continue between the two countries until these interest rates are equalized. Thus, Tacrobia will increase its capital outflows and Macrobia will have higher capital inflows.

**4.** **a.** When the American company purchases machinery that is produced in Germany by a German company, the transaction enters the U.S. balance of payments current account as an import. This transaction will reduce the balance of payments on the U.S. current account.

**b.** When the American donates money to the foreign group organizing an international sporting event, this enters the current account as a transfer payment to a foreigner. This transaction will reduce the balance on the U.S. current account.

**c.** When a French citizen purchases cheese produced in the United States, the transaction enters the U.S. balance of payments on current account as an export. The transaction will increase the balance of payments on the U.S. current account.

**d.** When the American purchases 100 shares of a Swiss company, the transaction is categorized as part of the U.S. balance of payments on financial account. The balance of payments on the U.S. financial account will fall.

## Answers to Module Review Questions

**1.** **Answer c.** The balance of payments on goods and services is the difference between the value of exports and the value of imports during a given period. The merchandise trade balance does not include the sale of financial assets but does include the sale of goods. The balance of payments accounts provide a set of numbers that describe a country's international transactions.

**2.** **Answer g.** By definition, the balance of payments on goods and services plus net international transfer payments and net international factor income equals the balance of payments on current account. In addition, the sum of the balance of payments on current account plus the balance of payments on financial account equals zero.

3. **Answer d.** The sum of the balance of payments on current account and the balance of payments on financial account must sum to zero: thus, if the balance of payments on financial account equals –$100 million, then the balance of payments on current account must equal $100 million.

4. **Answer d.** Figure 43-2 in your text reviews this concept: the balance of payments tracks flows of goods and services, factor income, transfers, and assets between a country and the rest of the world. Transactions involving goods and services, factor income, and transfers are measured in the balance of payments on current account, while transactions involving assets are measured in the balance of payments on financial account.

5. **Answer e.** If two countries are open to trade and allow capital to flow freely between them, then an interest rate differential in their loanable funds market will disappear quickly due to capital flows between the two countries. Capital will tend to flow into the country with the relatively higher interest rate and out of the country with the relatively lower interest rate. Thus, the supply of loanable funds in the market with the higher interest rate will increase, while the supply of loanable funds in the market with the lower interest rate will decrease: this will cause the interest rate to fall in the first country and to rise in the second country until the interest rate differential is eliminated.

6. **Answer d.** A country that has capital inflows will have a matching current account deficit. The exchange rate may be measured as the price of a dollar in terms of the foreign currency, or it may be measured as the price of the foreign currency in terms of dollars. The more euros it takes to buy a dollar, the fewer dollars Europeans will demand in the foreign exchange market for dollars. When a country's currency appreciates, it means that the exchange rate for that currency in terms of the other currency has risen: this increase in the exchange rate makes goods and services produced in the country whose currency has appreciated more expensive relative to goods and services produced elsewhere. This will lead to a decrease in exports and an increase in imports for the country whose currency has appreciated.

7. **Answer f.** Payments to Macropedia from foreigners are represented by dollars that flow into Macropedia. For example, the farmers in Macropedia will receive compensation from abroad if they export their agricultural commodity to another country; or the providers of a service will receive compensation from abroad if they provide their service to people residing in another country. Thus, answers (b) and (d) both represent flows of funds into Macropedia, while answers (a) and (c) represent flows of funds out of Macropedia.

8. **Answer a.** The facts underlying this question are discussed in the module.

9. **Answer a.** An increase in capital inflows will cause the supply of loanable funds curve to shift to the right. This shift will cause a movement along the demand for loanable funds curve and result in a decrease in the equilibrium interest rate and an increase in the quantity of loanable funds.

10. **Answer c.** An increase in the level of investment spending that is financed through borrowing will cause the demand curve to shift to the right, since at every interest rate there is now greater demand for loanable funds. This shift will cause a movement along the supply of loanable funds curve as the interest rate rises in response to the increase in the demand for loanable funds.

11. **Answer b.** Fast-growing countries typically offer many attractive investment opportunities because of their rapid growth rates. The supply of loanable funds curve for any particular country is impacted by that country's private savings rate: some countries have much higher savings rates than other countries. In 2012, the United States ran a current account deficit and a financial account surplus.

# The Foreign Exchange Market

## Summary

This module discusses the role of the foreign exchange market. It also explains the distinction between the nominal exchange rate and real exchange rates and emphasizes the importance of the real exchange rate in the current account.

## Module Objectives

**Objective #1.** Currencies can be exchanged for one another in the foreign exchange market. This market determines the exchange rate, or the price for which two currencies exchange. When one currency becomes more valuable in terms of another currency, we say that the first currency has appreciated. When one currency becomes less valuable in terms of another currency, we say that the first currency has depreciated.

- The foreign exchange market brings together demanders and suppliers of currencies, and it is the interaction of this demand and supply that determines the equilibrium exchange rate. For instance, in the foreign exchange market for dollars, the demanders in this market are giving up foreign currency in order to acquire dollars. Their demand for dollars is influenced by the price they must pay for these dollars: this price is the exchange rate expressed as foreign currency per dollar. In the foreign exchange market for dollars, the suppliers of dollars provide dollars in exchange for the foreign currency; the supply of dollars they provide to this market depends on the price, or the exchange rate, they receive for those dollars. In the foreign exchange market for dollars, as the exchange rate increases, holding everything else constant, the quantity demanded of dollars will decrease, while the quantity of dollars supplied will increase. The equilibrium exchange rate is that exchange rate for which the quantity of dollars demanded equals the quantity of dollars supplied in the foreign exchange market.

- When there is an increase in capital inflows into a country, this increases the balance of payments on financial account. An increase in a country's exchange rate makes imports more attractive and exports less attractive for this country. This leads to a reduction in the balance of payments on current account for that country, which exactly offsets the increase in the balance of payments on financial account for that country. To generalize, a change in the balance of payments on financial account for a country must generate an equal and opposite reaction to that country's balance of payments on current account.

**Objective #2.** The real exchange rate is the exchange rate adjusted for international differences in aggregate price levels. The real exchange rate of country X's currency to country Y's currency equals the nominal exchange rate of country X's currency for country Y's currency times the ratio of the aggregate price level in country Y to the aggregate price level in country X. Equation 44-1 in your text provides an example of this calculation. The nominal exchange rate is the exchange rate unadjusted for inflation.

- The current account responds only to changes in the real exchange rate, and not to changes in the nominal exchange rate. A country's products become cheaper to foreigners only when that country's currency depreciates in real terms, and a country's products become more expensive to foreigners only when that country's currency appreciates in real terms.

**Objective #3.** Purchasing power parity refers to the nominal exchange rate between two countries at which a given basket of goods and services would cost the same in each country. Nominal exchange rates almost always differ from purchasing power parities. Sometimes this difference is due to systematic differences; for example, prices are lower in poor countries because services tend to be cheaper in poor countries than they are in rich countries.

**Objective #4.** The real exchange rate affects exports and imports. When a country's real exchange rate rises, or appreciates, that country's exports fall and its imports rise. When a country's real exchange rate falls, or depreciates, that country's exports rise and its imports fall.

## Key Terms

**foreign exchange market** the market in which currencies can be exchanged for each other.

**exchange rate** the price at which currencies trade, determined by the *foreign exchange market*.

**appreciation** a rise in the value of one currency in terms of other currencies.

**depreciation** a fall in the value of one currency in terms of other currencies.

**equilibrium exchange rate** the *exchange rate* at which the quantity of a currency demanded in the *foreign exchange market* is equal to the quantity supplied.

**real exchange rate** the *exchange rate* adjusted for international differences in *aggregate price levels*.

**purchasing power parity** (between two countries' currencies) the nominal *exchange rate* at which a given basket of goods and services would cost the same amount in each country.

*Notes*

## AFTER YOU READ THE MODULE

## Tips

**Tip #1.**  This module introduces new vocabulary. You will want to learn the definitions and be able to apply them. The module introduces an abundance of new terms. You will want to thoroughly understand concepts like the exchange rate, appreciation of a currency, depreciation of a currency, and how changes in a country's exchange rate affects its imports and exports. You might find the following table a helpful summary of these relationships.

Appreciation of country X's currency ⟶ Country X imports more, exports less

Depreciation of country X's currency ⟶ Country X imports less, exports more

**Tip #2.**  It is important to understand what an exchange rate is and how changes in the exchange rate affect the country's balance of payments. An exchange rate is the price of one currency in terms of another currency. When a country's exchange rate increases, or appreciates, this makes its domestically produced goods relatively more expensive than goods produced by other economies. This will decrease exports and increase imports for the domestic economy: the balance of payments on current account will decrease, while the balance of payments on financial account will increase.

# WORKED PROBLEMS

1.  The exchange rate between the United States and Mexico is initially 10 pesos per dollar. If the exchange rate changes to 12 pesos per dollar, how does that change the relative prices of goods in the two countries? Identify which currency has appreciated in value, and explain what this means. Identify which currency has depreciated in value, and explain what this means. Finally, a friend asks you, given the new exchange rate, whether this is a good time to visit Mexico or whether it would be better for her cousin in Mexico to visit her in the United States. Your friend wants a simple answer as well as an explanation for your answer.

**STEP 1:** Evaluate the effect of this change in the exchange rate on the United States dollar and on the Mexican peso, relative to the other currency.

Initially, someone holding pesos could trade 10 pesos for a dollar, while someone holding a dollar could trade this dollar for 10 pesos. After the exchange rate changes, the person holding pesos finds that it takes 12 pesos to get a dollar: from their perspective, the dollar has gotten more expensive. After the exchange rate changes, the person holding the dollar finds that the dollar buys 12 pesos instead of the initial 10 pesos: the dollar has greater purchasing power. From both perspectives, the dollar has gotten more valuable and the peso less valuable.

**STEP 2:** Review the definition of *appreciation* as it applies to currency, and then identify which currency has appreciated. Make sure you explain your choice of currency.

Appreciation of a currency refers to the currency becoming more valuable in terms of other currencies. In this example, the U.S. dollar has appreciated since originally it was worth only 10 Mexican pesos and now it is worth 12 Mexican pesos.

**STEP 3:** Review the definition of *depreciation* as it applies to currency and then identify which currency has depreciated. Make sure you explain your choice of currency.

Depreciation of a currency refers to the currency becoming less valuable in terms of other currencies. In this example, the Mexican peso has depreciated, since, originally, 10 pesos were worth a U.S. dollar and now 12 pesos are worth a U.S. dollar. It now takes more pesos to buy a U.S. dollar.

**STEP 4:** Decide whether your friend should travel to Mexico or stay home. Explain your answer.

Your friend should travel to Mexico, since the peso has depreciated. It is now cheaper to buy pesos, making the trip to Mexico relatively cheaper.

2.  Suppose that the currency market for Mexican pesos and U.S. dollars is initially in equilibrium, with 10 Mexican pesos trading for one U.S. dollar. Your friend reads that there has been a shift in demand for Mexican pesos due to a sudden increase in the capital inflow from the United States to Mexico. Using a graph, you are asked to evaluate how this increase in capital inflows will impact the exchange rate of Mexican pesos for U.S. dollars. You are also asked to comment on the effect of this change in the exchange rate on the Mexican and the U.S. economies. The following graph depicts the initial situation, where $S$ is the supply of U.S. dollars, $D$ is the demand for U.S. dollars, and $XR_1$ is the initial exchange rate of Mexican pesos per U.S. dollar.

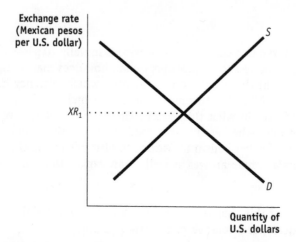

**STEP 1:** Identify the effect of increased capital inflows into Mexico from the United States on the demand for U.S. dollars curve.

Since the capital inflows are flowing into Mexico, this implies that there is reduced demand at every exchange rate for U.S. dollars because people will now want to hold Mexican pesos in order to fund their new investments in Mexico. The demand for U.S. dollars curve will therefore shift to the left, indicating that at every exchange rate fewer U.S. dollars are demanded. The following graph illustrates this idea: $D_2$ is the new demand for U.S. dollars as a result of the increase in capital inflows from the United States to Mexico.

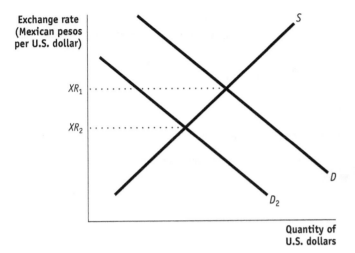

**STEP 2:** Identify the effect of increased capital inflows into Mexico from the United States on the supply of U.S. dollars curve.

As the demand for U.S. dollars shifts to the left there will be a movement along the supply of U.S. dollars curve resulting in a decrease in the exchange rate of Mexican pesos for U.S. dollars. As people want to exchange their U.S. dollars for Mexican pesos, they will find that each U.S. dollar purchases fewer Mexican pesos.

**STEP 3:** Identify the new exchange rate that is the result of this increased capital inflow into Mexico.

The new exchange rate is $XR_2$: since $XR_2$ is less than $XR_1$, this indicates that each dollar is now worth fewer Mexican pesos. The Mexican peso has appreciated against the dollar, while the U.S. dollar has depreciated against the Mexican peso.

**STEP 4:** Analyze what this new exchange rate means for both the U.S. economy as well as the Mexican economy.

As the exchange rate of Mexican pesos to U.S. dollars falls, this means that U.S.-produced goods and services are now relatively cheaper than Mexican-produced goods and services. This will lead to increases in U.S. exports and a decrease in Mexican exports. A fall in capital flows into the United States leads to a weaker dollar, and this decrease in the value of the dollar results in an increase in U.S. net exports. An increase in capital flows into Mexico leads to a stronger peso, and this increase in the value of the peso results in a decrease in Mexico's net exports.

## Problems and Exercises

1.  **a.** Calculate the missing values in the following table.

| | U.S. dollars | Funland dollars | Macroland dollars |
|---|---|---|---|
| 1 U.S. dollar exchanged for | | | 1.05 |
| 1 Funland dollar exchanged for | 0.005 | | |
| 1 Macroland dollar exchanged for | | | |

Suppose that the above exchange rates change as shown in the following table.

| | U.S. dollars | Funland dollars | Macroland dollars |
|---|---|---|---|
| 1 U.S. dollar exchanged for | 1 | 210 | |
| 1 Funland dollar exchanged for | | 1 | |
| 1 Macroland dollar exchanged for | 1.02 | | 1 |

   **b.** Fill in the missing values for this table.

   **c.** Which currencies appreciated against the U.S. dollar?

   **d.** Which currencies depreciated against the U.S. dollar?

   **e.** Holding everything else constant, what do you expect will happen to the level of U.S. exports to Funland?

   **f.** Holding everything else constant, what do you expect will happen to the level of U.S. exports to Macroland?

2.  Suppose you are shown the information in the following table. Assume net international transfers and factor income equal zero for this problem.

| | |
|---|---|
| Funland purchases of Macroland dollars in the foreign exchange market to buy Macroland goods and services | 3.0 million Macroland dollars |
| Funland total purchases in the foreign exchange market of Macroland dollars | 5.0 million Macroland dollars |
| Macroland sales of Macroland dollars in the foreign exchange market to buy Funland assets | 1.5 million Macroland dollars |
| Macroland sales of Macroland dollars in the foreign exchange market to buy Funland goods and services | 3.5 million Macroland dollars |

**a.** Given the information in this table, compute the values in the following table.

| | | |
|---|---|---|
| Funland purchases of Macroland dollars in the foreign exchange market to buy Macroland assets | = | _____ |
| Total sales of Macroland dollars in the foreign exchange market | = | _____ |
| Macroland balance of payments on current account | = | _____ |
| Macroland balance of payments on financial account | = | _____ |

Suppose capital flows to Macroland from Funland decrease and this causes Macroland's currency to depreciate against Funland's currency, holding everything else constant.

**b.** How will this affect the demand and supply of Macroland dollars in the foreign exchange market? Use the following graph to illustrate your answer.

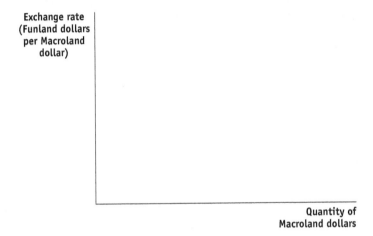

**Exchange rate (Funland dollars per Macroland dollar)**

**Quantity of Macroland dollars**

**c.** How will this depreciation affect Macroland's balance of payments on current account? Explain your answer.

**d.** How will this depreciation affect Macroland's balance of payments on financial account? Explain your answer.

**3.** Suppose initially the nominal exchange rate is 20 Macroland dollars per 1 Funland dollar, and the aggregate price index in both countries has a value of 100.

**a.** What is the real exchange rate expressed as Macroland dollars per Funland dollar?

**b.** Suppose the real exchange rate increases to 25 Macroland dollars per Funland dollar when the aggregate price index in Funland increases to 150. Assuming the nominal exchange rate is unchanged, what is the aggregate price index in Macroland?

   **c.** Suppose the aggregate price index in Funland is 150 and the aggregate price index in Macroland is 125. If the nominal exchange rate increases to 25 Macroland dollars per Funland dollar, what is the real exchange rate?

   **d.** If the real exchange rate measured as Macroland dollars per Funland dollar increases, holding everything else constant, what happens to the level of exports and imports in Macroland?

**4.** Suppose that currently the cost of a standardized market basket in Macroland is 300 Macroland dollars, while the same market basket in Funland costs 150 Funland dollars.

   **a.** If purchasing power parity holds for the two countries, what must the nominal exchange rate, expressed as Macroland dollars per Funland dollar, equal? Explain your answer.

   **b.** If the actual nominal exchange rate equals 4 Macroland dollars per 1 Funland dollar, what do you expect will happen to the nominal exchange rate over the long run, holding everything else constant? Explain your answer.

## ▐ BEFORE YOU TAKE THE TEST

# Module Review Questions

**1.** Suppose a U.S dollar trades for 0.9 euro. Which of the following statements is true?
   a. A euro trades for $1.11.
   b. If the exchange rate changes to 1 U.S. dollar in exchange for 0.95 euro, then the euro has appreciated.
   c. If the exchange rate changes to 1 U.S. dollar in exchange for 0.95 euro, then the dollar has appreciated.
   d. When the exchange rate changes to 0.95 euro per dollar, the United States will export more goods to European Union countries.
   e. Statements (a), (b), and (d) are all true.
   f. Statements (a), (c), and (d) are all true.
   g. Statements (a) and (b) are both true.
   h. Statements (a) and (c) are both true.

2.  An increase in capital inflows into a country, holding everything else constant, will
    a.  result in an increase in net exports for the country.
    b.  result in a decrease in net exports for the country.
    c.  result in an increase in the balance on financial account for the country and an equal and opposite reaction in the balance of payments on current account.
    d.  Answers (a) and (c) are both correct.
    e.  Answers (b) and (c) are both correct.

Answer the next two questions using the following information. Suppose the aggregate price level for a given market basket of goods in Macroland is 125, while the aggregate price level for the same market basket of goods in Funland is 150. Suppose that currently the exchange rate is 10 Macroland dollars for 1 Funland dollar.

3.  Given the previous information, what is the real exchange rate initially?
    a.  10 Macroland dollars for 1 Funland dollar
    b.  1 Macroland dollar for 10 Funland dollars
    c.  1 Macroland dollar for 1 Funland dollar
    d.  10 Macroland dollars for 10 Funland dollars
    e.  12 Macroland dollars for 1 Funland dollar

4.  If the aggregate price level of the market basket in Macroland increases to 150, what must the exchange rate be in order for the real exchange rate to be unchanged from its initial level?
    a.  10 Macroland dollars for 1 Funland dollar
    b.  1 Macroland dollar for 10 Funland dollars
    c.  1 Macroland dollar for 1 Funland dollar
    d.  10 Macroland dollars for 10 Funland dollars
    e.  12 Macroland dollars for 1 Funland dollar

5.  When the purchasing power parity rate is greater than the nominal exchange rate, then over time we can expect the
    a.  purchasing power parity to fall.
    b.  purchasing power parity to rise.
    c.  nominal exchange rate to rise.
    d.  nominal exchange rate to fall.

6.  Which of the following statements is true?
    a.  When a country's currency undergoes a real depreciation, this causes exports to fall and imports to rise.
    b.  Nominal exchange rates almost always equal the purchasing power parity rate.
    c.  The current account is affected by changes in the nominal exchange rate as well as the real exchange rate.
    d.  None of the above statements is true.

7.  Suppose that currently the exchange rate is 1 U.S. dollar to 5 Mexican pesos. If the exchange rate changes to 1 U.S. dollar for 10 Mexican pesos, then the peso has
    a.  appreciated against the dollar.
    b.  depreciated against the dollar.

8. Suppose there are only two currencies in the world: the U.S. dollar and the Mexican peso. Furthermore, suppose that the foreign exchange market for U.S. dollars is initially in equilibrium. If the demand for U.S. dollars increases, holding everything else constant, this will result in a movement along the supply of U.S. dollars curve and

   a. an increase in the peso–U.S. dollar exchange rate.

   b. a decrease in the peso–U.S. dollar exchange rate.

9. Holding everything else constant, if the U.S. dollar rises against the Mexican peso, then
   a. U.S. goods will look cheaper to Mexico.
   b. U.S. goods will look more expensive to Mexico.
   c. Mexico's goods will look cheaper to the United States.
   d. Mexico's goods will look more expensive to the United States.
   e. Answers (a) and (d) are both correct.
   f. Answers (b) and (c) are both correct.

## ANSWER KEY

# Answers to Problems and Exercises

1. **a.**

|  | U.S. dollars | Funland dollars | Macroland dollars |
|---|---|---|---|
| 1 U.S. dollar exchanged for | 1 | 200 | 1.05 |
| 1 Funland dollar exchanged for | 0.005 | 1 | 0.004762 |
| 1 Macroland dollar exchanged for | 0.952381 | 210 | 1 |

**b.**

|  | U.S. dollars | Funland dollars | Macroland dollars |
|---|---|---|---|
| 1 U.S. dollar exchanged for | 1 | 210 | 0.980392 |
| 1 Funland dollar exchanged for | 0.004762 | 1 | 0.004669 |
| 1 Macroland dollar exchanged for | 1.02 | 214.2 | 1 |

**c.** Macroland dollars appreciated against the U.S. dollar since in part (a), 1 Macroland dollar was worth 0.952381 U.S. dollar, and in part (b), 1 Macroland dollar was worth 1.02 U.S. dollars.

**d.** Funland dollars depreciated against the U.S. dollar since in part (a), 1 Funland dollar was worth 0.005 U.S. dollar, and in part (b), 1 Funland dollar was worth 0.004762 U.S. dollar.

**e.** U.S. exports to Funland, holding everything else constant, will fall because, as Funland's currency depreciates against the U.S. dollar, this makes U.S. products more expensive to the residents of Funland relative to Funland's products. Funland will export more to the United States and the United States will export less to Funland.

**f.** U.S. exports to Macroland, holding everything else constant, will increase since, as Macroland's currency appreciates against the U.S. dollar, this makes U.S. products cheaper to the residents of Macroland relative to Macroland's products. Macroland will export less to the United States and the United States will export more to Macroland.

2. **a.**

| | |
|---|---|
| Funland purchases of Macroland dollars in the foreign exchange market to buy Macroland assets | = 2 million Macroland dollars |
| Total sales of Macroland dollars in the foreign exchange market | = 5.0 million Macroland dollars |
| Macroland balance of payments on current account | = −0.5 million Macroland dollars |
| Macroland balance of payments on financial account | = 0.5 million Macroland dollars |

**b.** The depreciation of the Macroland currency against Funland's currency will cause the demand for Macroland dollars to decrease at every exchange rate (measured as

Funland dollars per Macroland dollars). This will, for a given supply of Macroland dollars, cause the exchange rate to decrease. This is illustrated in the following figure.

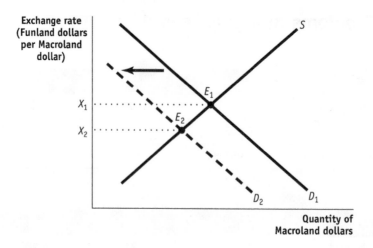

c. This depreciation of Macroland's currency against Funland's currency will cause Macroland's balance of payments on current account to increase, since Funland will now find Macroland goods and services relatively cheaper.

d. This depreciation of Macroland's currency against Funland's currency will cause Macroland's balance of payments on financial account to decrease, since any increase in Macroland's balance of payments on current account must be offset by an equal and opposite reaction in the balance of payments on financial account.

3.  a. Real exchange rate in Macroland dollars per Funland dollar = (20 Macroland dollars per Funland dollar)(100/100) = 20 Macroland dollars per Funland dollar

    b. To answer this question, we will want to use the equation:

    Real exchange rate = (nominal exchange rate)[(price index in Funland)/ (price index in Macroland)]

    Thus, 25 Macroland dollars per Funland dollar = (20 Macroland dollars per Funland dollar)[(150)/(price index in Macroland)], and solving for the price index in Macroland, we find that the price index in Macroland equals 120.

    c. To answer this question, we will want to use the equation given in part (b):

    Real exchange rate = (nominal exchange rate)[(price index in Funland)/ (price index in Macroland)]

    Thus, the real exchange rate = (25 Macroland dollars per Funland dollar) [(150)/(125)], and solving this equation for the real exchange rate yields a real exchange rate equal to 30 Macroland dollars per Funland dollar.

    d. An increase in real exchange rate is an appreciation of Macroland's currency, and this appreciation will make Macroland's products more expensive to foreigners: Macroland will export less and import more when the real exchange rate increases, holding everything else constant.

4.  a. If purchasing power parity holds in the two countries, then the price of the market basket in the two countries is 300 Macroland dollars equals 150 Funland dollars. This implies that the exchange rate must equal 2 Macroland dollars per Funland dollar or, equivalently, 1 Macroland dollar per 0.5 Funland dollar.

    b. If the actual exchange rate is greater than the purchasing power parity exchange rate, one would anticipate that the exchange rate will fall over time, since nominal exchange rates between countries at similar levels of economic development tend to fluctuate around levels that lead to similar costs for a given market basket.

# Answers to Module Review Questions

1. **Answer h.** If 1 U.S. dollar trades for 0.9 euro, this is the same as 1 euro trading for $1.11 (to see this, simply divide 1/0.9 to find how many dollars it takes to purchase 1 euro). If the exchange rate changes to 1 U.S. dollar in exchange for 0.95 euro, this means that dollars have appreciated and that euros have depreciated in value, since 1 dollar initially was worth only 0.9 euro and now is worth 0.95 euro. This means that a dollar has greater purchasing power in European Union markets and, therefore, imports of European goods to the United States will increase and exports of American goods to European Union countries will decrease.

2. **Answer e.** A country's increase in capital inflows causes the exchange rate to increase, leading to an appreciation of that country's currency. With this appreciation, the country will find that its goods and services become relatively more expensive and, therefore, its net exports will decrease. Furthermore, the increase in capital inflows will cause the balance on financial account to increase, and this increase will be met by an equal, but opposite, reaction in the balance of payments on current account.

3. **Answer e.** To find the real exchange rate, we need to know the nominal exchange rate (in this case, 10 Macroland dollars per 1 Funland dollar) and the aggregate price level in the two countries. Real exchange rate equals (10 Macroland dollars/Funland dollars)(150/125) = 12 Macroland dollars per 1 Funland dollar.

4. **Answer e.** To find the exchange rate, we need to know the real exchange rate (in this case, 12 Macroland dollars per 1 Funland dollar) and the aggregate price level in the two countries. Twelve Macroland dollars per 1 Funland dollar equals (the exchange rate)(150/150). Solving for the exchange rate yields an exchange rate of 12 Macroland dollars per 1 Funland dollar.

5. **Answer c.** Purchasing power parity between two countries' currencies is the nominal exchange rate at which a given basket of goods and services would cost the same amount in each country. When the purchasing power parity rate is greater than the nominal exchange rate, we would anticipate that the nominal exchange rate must increase over time in order for the two countries to have similar costs for a given market basket.

6. **Answer d.** When a country's currency undergoes a real depreciation, exports rise and imports fall, since the depreciation reduces the price of the country's goods and services relative to the prices for goods and services produced in other countries. Nominal exchange rates almost always differ from purchasing power parity rates: the nominal rate tends to fluctuate around the purchasing power parity rate. The current account responds only to changes in the real exchange rate, not the nominal exchange rate: it is a change in the real exchange rate that alters the relative cost of domestic goods and services in comparison to foreign-produced goods and services.

7. **Answer b.** Five pesos originally are worth 1 U.S. dollar, but when the exchange rate changes, five pesos are only worth $0.50 in U.S. dollars. The value of the peso in terms of U.S. dollars has fallen and, thus, the peso has depreciated against the U.S. dollar.

8. **Answer a.** When there is an increase in the demand for U.S. dollars, the demand curve for dollars shifts to the right. The subsequent move along the supply of U.S. dollars curve will cause the equilibrium exchange rate of pesos to U.S. dollars to increase.

9. **Answer f.** If the U.S. dollar rises against the Mexican peso, this means that it takes more pesos to buy a U.S. dollar: this then implies that U.S. goods are now relatively more expensive to Mexico than they were before the dollar rose against the peso. If U.S. goods are now relatively more expensive to Mexico, then Mexico's goods are now relatively cheaper to those of the United States.

# Exchange Rate Policy

---

■ **BEFORE YOU READ THE MODULE**

## Summary

The module discusses different exchange rate regimes as well as contrasts fixed exchange rate regimes with floating exchange rate regimes. The module also discusses why countries choose particular exchange rate regimes.

## Module Objectives

**Objective #1.**   Recall that money is not a good or service but is instead an asset whose quantity is controlled by government policy. Thus, government through its policies can influence the nominal exchange rate. There are a variety of exchange rate regimes that countries have adopted: these regimes represent different rules governing policy toward the exchange rate.

• When the government keeps the exchange rate against some other currency at or near a particular target, this is referred to as a fixed exchange rate.

• A country follows a floating exchange rate regime when it allows the exchange rate to fluctuate wherever the market takes it.

• There are other exchange rate regimes besides a fixed exchange rate and a floating exchange rate that lie somewhere between these two choices. For example, there are managed exchange rates where the government adjusts the fixed exchange rate often in order to avoid wide swings in its value; or there are exchange rates that float within a target zone but are prevented by the government from deviating from that zone.

**Objective #2.**   Under a fixed exchange rate regime, the government can affect the exchange rate through five primary activities.

• The government can affect its country's exchange rate by buying or selling currency in the foreign exchange market: this is an exchange market intervention. In order to engage in an exchange market intervention, a government must hold foreign exchange reserves, which are stocks of foreign currency that the government can use to buy its own currency when it needs to support its own currency's price. A large part of capital flows represent governmental transactions: these purchases and sales of foreign assets by governments and central banks support their currencies through exchange market intervention. When the government buys its currency, holding everything else constant, this will increase the value of its currency.

- The government can implement exchange rate intervention through its monetary policy. To support the exchange rate, the government can increase its interest rate, which will encourage increased capital flow into the economy and, therefore, an increased demand for that country's currency. Holding everything else constant, an increase in a country's interest rate will increase the value of its currency.

- The government can affect the exchange rate by reducing the supply of its currency in the foreign exchange market. Governments can achieve this reduction by limiting the right of their citizens to buy foreign currency through the imposition of foreign exchange controls. Holding everything else constant, imposition of foreign exchange controls increases the value of a country's currency.

- Thus, if the value of a country's currency in the foreign exchange market is lower than the target exchange rate, the government can prevent depreciation of its currency by buying the country's currency, by pursuing a higher interest rate via its monetary policy, or by imposing foreign exchange controls.

- If the value of a country's currency in the foreign exchange market is higher than the target exchange rate, the government can prevent appreciation of its currency by selling the country's currency, by pursuing a lower interest rate via its monetary policy, or by imposing foreign exchange controls that limit the ability of its citizens to sell their currency to foreigners. All of these actions, other things equal, will reduce the value of the country's currency.

**Objective #3.**   A fixed exchange rate provides certainty about the value of a currency. A commitment to a fixed exchange rate by a country is also a commitment to not engage in inflationary policies. Maintaining a fixed exchange rate requires the country to hold large quantities of foreign currency, and these holdings typically are a low-return investment. Use of monetary policy to help stabilize an exchange rate may also require a country to forego other goals like the stabilization of output or the control of the inflation rate. In addition, the use of exchange controls, like import quotas and tariffs, distort incentives for importing and exporting, and may lead to increased transaction costs due to bureaucratic red tape and increased corruption. In short, the pursuit of a fixed exchange rate eliminates uncertainty but limits monetary policy and may require the adoption of exchange rate controls, while the pursuit of a floating exchange rate leaves monetary policy available for stabilization but creates uncertainty for businesses.

## Key Terms

*Notes*

**exchange rate regime**  a rule governing policy toward the *exchange rate.*

**fixed exchange rate**  an *exchange rate regime* in which the government keeps the *exchange rate* against some other currency at or near a particular target.

**floating exchange rate**  an *exchange rate regime* in which the government lets the *exchange rate* go wherever the market takes it.

**exchange market intervention**  government purchases or sales of currency in the *foreign exchange market.*

**foreign exchange reserves**  *stocks* of foreign currency that governments can use to buy their own currency on the *foreign exchange market.*

**foreign exchange controls**  licensing systems that limit the right of individuals to buy foreign currency.

## AFTER YOU READ THE MODULE

### Tip

You will want to understand the distinction between fixed and floating exchange rate regimes, and the advantages and disadvantages associated with either type of exchange rate regime.

## WORKED PROBLEMS

1. In the text for Module 45, the authors write "The nominal exchange rate is a very important price for many countries: the exchange rate determines the price of imports; it determines the price of exports. . . ." Suppose that the nominal exchange rate in a country falls relative to other currencies, how does that affect this country's imports and exports, holding everything else constant?

**STEP 1:** First review the relationship between the level of the nominal exchange rate and a country's imports and exports.

The nominal exchange rate provides the price for which two currencies trade. If one country's currency is relatively cheaper than the other country's currency, we can expect the first country will have high levels of exports and low levels of imports.

**STEP 2:** Now, review the relationship between a change in the level of the exchange rate and the effect of this change on the level of imports and exports for this country.

If the nominal exchange rate decreases for a country the implication is that this country's currency buys less of the foreign currency. For example, if the nominal exchange rate is initially $1 for 10 pesos and then it changes to $1 for 12 pesos, the implication is that dollars have become more expensive relative to pesos. People in the country that uses pesos as its currency will find that goods from the other country are now relatively more expensive: this will cause the country with pesos as its currency to import less and export more.

**STEP 3:** Given that the described country had a fall in its nominal exchange rate relative to other currencies, predict the impact of this change on the country's imports and exports.

Given the fall in the nominal exchange rate we can anticipate that this country will increase its level of exports while decreasing its level of imports.

2. Suppose a country is committed to a fixed exchange rate policy but finds that the exchange rate in the foreign currency market is higher than the level of nominal exchange rate it is determined to maintain. Describe what this country can do to achieve the desired exchange rate.

**STEP 1:** Analyze the current situation and what must be true about the supply of this country's currency relative to the demand for its currency.

When a country pursues a fixed exchange rate policy, the policy means that the country wishes to maintain a particular exchange rate of its currency to some other currency (or currencies). If the country finds that the exchange rate in the exchange market is higher than the desired fixed rate the implication is that there is an excess demand for its currency at the fixed exchange rate. That is, at the desired fixed rate of exchange the quantity supplied of the country's currency is less than the quantity demanded.

**STEP 2:** Determine an appropriate policy response by the government of this country that will enable the government to fix the exchange rate at the desired level.

An appropriate policy response in this situation would be to address the excess demand for the country's currency. The government of this country can reduce its demand for its own currency and instead increase the supply of its currency by entering the exchange market and selling its currency in exchange for the other currency.

**STEP 3:** Explain how the policy response in Step 2 will affect the supply of this country's currency and the demand for the country's currency; then analyze the impact on the price of the currency in the foreign exchange market.

The impact of the country's increasing the amount of its own currency that it will sell at each exchange rate is a shift in the supply of this country's currency to the right. For a given demand curve for this currency, this shift in supply will result in a decrease in the exchange rate. The country's desire is to bring the exchange rate down to its desired fixed rate, and it can accomplish this goal by increasing the supply of its own currency in the exchange market: holding everything else constant, this increase in supply will result in a decrease in the price of the currency.

# Problems and Exercises

1.  Compare and contrast the advantages and disadvantages of a fixed exchange rate regime and a floating exchange rate regime.

2. Suppose that Breesia, a small country, has decided to follow a fixed exchange rate regime. Currently the demand and supply curves for pesetos, Breesia's currency, are given by the following equations, where $P$ is the price of one U.S. dollar for peseto and $Q$ is that quantity of pesetos.

Demand for pesetos: $P = 100 - 4Q$

Supply of pesetos: $P = 40 + 2Q$

a. If Breesia abandons their fixed exchange rate regime, what will be the exchange rate in Breesia?

b. Suppose Breesia decides to implement a target exchange rate of $75.00 per peseto. Describe the effect of this exchange rate target in the market for pesetos. What will Breesia's government need to do in order to maintain this target exchange rate?

c. Suppose Breesia decides to implement a a target exchange rate of $50.00 per peseto. Describe the effect of this exchange rate target in the market for pesetos. What will Breesia's government need to do in order to maintain this target exchange rate?

## BEFORE YOU TAKE THE TEST

## Module Review Questions

1. If a government wishes to fix the value of a currency above its equilibrium value in the foreign exchange market, it can
   a. engage in monetary policy to reduce interest rates, thereby increasing capital flows into its country.
   b. reduce the supply of its currency by limiting the right of its citizens to buy foreign currencies.
   c. engage in selling its currency through exchange market intervention.
   d. Answers (a), (b), and (c) will all help the government to reduce the exchange rate to its desired level.

2. Suppose that in the foreign exchange market there is a shortage at the target exchange rate. We know that
   a. the supply of the country's currency is less than the demand for that country's currency.
   b. it is impossible to maintain the target exchange rate unless the government engages in exchange market intervention, changes monetary policy, adjusts foreign exchange controls, or pursues some combination of these three policies.
   c. maintaining a fixed exchange rate will limit the ability of the government to pursue stabilization policy.
   d. Answers (a), (b), and (c) are all true.

**3.** A fixed rate regime
   a. reduces uncertainty for businesses about the value of a currency.
   b. exposes a country to a potential bias toward inflationary policies.
   c. reduces the amount of foreign currency a country must hold.
   d. creates an incentive to pursue monetary policy to help stabilize the country's economy.

**4.** Foreign exchange reserves are
   a. funds of one country's currency held by another country.
   b. funds of a country's currency that the government holds in case they need money unexpectedly.
   c. are sometimes used by a country to maintain a fixed exchange rate.
   d. Answers (a) and (c) are both correct.
   e. Answers (b) and (c) are both correct.

## ANSWER KEY

## Answers to Problems and Exercises

1. A fixed exchange rate regime provides certainty about the value of a country's currency: this certainty facilitates transactions between countries. In addition, adoption of a fixed exchange regime may help a country commit to not engage in inflationary policies. But, adherence to a fixed exchange rate presents challenges as well as benefits to the country. In order to fix the exchange rate, the country will find that it must hold large amounts of foreign currency: this is typically a low-return investment for the country. In addition, a country with a fixed exchange rate will find that it can no longer use monetary policy to pursue macroeconomic goals like output stabilization and control of the inflation rate. Finally, the adoption of a fixed exchange rate potentially distorts the incentives for importing and exporting goods and services.

   A floating exchange rate regime neither requires the country to hold large amounts of foreign currency, nor constrains the country with regard to monetary policy. It does, however, introduce uncertainty about the value of the country's currency, and that may hinder the level of international trade between it and other countries. A floating exchange rate does provide very clear price incentives for the determination of the level of exports and imports at any particular point in time.

2. **a.** The exchange rate with a floating exchange rate regime will be $60.00 per peseto.

   **b.** An exchange rate target of $75.00 per peseto will result in an excess supply of pesetos at that exchange rate since the supply of pesetos at that rate will equal 17.5 while the demand for pesetos at that rate will equal 6.25 pesetos. There will be an excess supply of 11.25 pesetos. In order to maintain this exchange rate target, the government of Breesia will need to buy pesetos and sell U.S. dollars.

   **c.** An exchange rate target of $50.00 per peseto will result in an excess demand for pesetos at that exchange rate: at that rate 12.5 pesetos will be demanded and 5 pesetos will be supplied. The excess demand for pesetos will equal 7.5. The government of Breesia will need to sell pesetos and buy U.S. dollars if they want to maintain this exchange rate target.

## Answers to Module Review Questions

1. **Answer b.** When the government wishes to fix the exchange rate to a rate that is above its equilibrium value in the foreign exchange market, it must deal with the fact that there is a surplus of its currency at that desired exchange rate. The government can eliminate this surplus by buying its currency through an exchange market intervention; by pursuing monetary policy that raises its interest rate relative to the interest rates of other economies, thus increasing capital flows into its country (and increasing the demand for its currency); or by reducing the supply of its currency to the foreign exchange market through the imposition of foreign exchange controls.

2. **Answer d.** When there is a shortage at the target exchange rate, the indication is that the demand for the country's currency is greater than the supply of its currency. A government will find that it can maintain the target exchange rate only if it is willing to give up its use of monetary policy for stabilization purposes and instead use monetary policy, exchange market intervention, and foreign exchange controls to pursue its target exchange rate.

3. **Answer a.** A fixed rate regime benefits businesses by eliminating uncertainty about the value of a currency while reducing the ability of the government to use monetary policy as a means of stabilizing the economy. A fixed rate regime reduces, in some cases, a country's bias toward inflationary policies, since it can send a signal to the foreign exchange market about the country's commitment to a stable exchange rate and decision to pursue noninflationary policies in the future.

4. **Answer d.** Foreign exchange reserves entail the holding of one country's currency by another country. For example, China and the major oil-exporting countries in 2007 held U.S. dollars. These dollars are sometimes used to help maintain a fixed exchange rate: for instance, if the exchange rate is depreciating, the country can buy some of its own currency using its foreign exchange reserves in order to keep the exchange rate from falling.

# Exchange Rates and Macroeconomic Policy

■ **BEFORE YOU READ THE MODULE**

## Summary

This module discusses the meaning and purpose of devaluation and revaluation of a country's currency under a fixed exchange rate regime. The module also considers the effect of open economies on macroeconomic policy when operating under a floating exchange rate regime.

## Module Objectives

**Objective #1.** A reduction in the value of a currency that previously had a fixed exchange rate is called a devaluation. A devaluation is a depreciation that is due to a revision in a fixed exchange rate target. An increase in the value of a currency that previously had a fixed exchange rate is called a revaluation.

- A devaluation makes domestic goods cheaper in terms of foreign currency; thus, a devaluation leads to higher exports and lower imports and, therefore, an increase in a country's balance of payments on current account. A devaluation acts as a stimulus to aggregate demand and can, therefore, be used to reduce or eliminate a recessionary gap.

- A revaluation makes domestic goods more expensive in terms of foreign currency; thus, a revaluation leads to lower exports and higher imports and, therefore, a decrease in a country's balance of payments on current account. A revaluation acts as a contractionary force on aggregate demand and can, therefore, be used to reduce or eliminate an inflationary gap.

**Objective #2.** Under a floating exchange rate regime, a country retains its ability to pursue independent monetary policy, but the use of monetary policy will affect the exchange rate, which in turn will affect the level of aggregate demand in the economy. Monetary policy in open economies has an effect beyond the effect we have described in closed economies.

- For example, a decision to use monetary policy to reduce the interest rate will lead to higher investment spending, but it will also provide less incentive for foreigners to move funds into the currency, which will then reduce the demand for the country's currency. There will also be an increase in the supply of currency as people exchange the domestic currency for foreign currency due to the incentive to move funds abroad, since the rate of return on loans at home has fallen relative to the rate of return on loans in other countries. Together these two effects cause the domestic currency to depreciate, and this depreciation leads to an increase in exports, a decrease in imports, and an overall positive impact on aggregate demand.

• Economic events in an economy also impact other economies. Changes in aggregate demand affect the demand for goods and services produced abroad as well as at home: holding everything else constant, a recession leads to a fall in imports and an expansion leads to a rise in imports. The link between aggregate demand in one country and aggregate demand in another country helps to explain why business cycles are often synchronized between different countries. A floating exchange rate regime is thought to limit the effect of aggregate demand in one country on aggregate demand in another country due to the behavior of the foreign exchange market: when there is a reduction in foreign demand for goods and services, what follows naturally is a depreciation of the domestic currency. This depreciation reduces the fall in the level of exports while simultaneously limiting the increase in imports. The overall impact of the movement in the exchange rate is to lessen the decline in the level of aggregate demand.

**Objective #3.**    Many European countries adopted the euro as their currency beginning in 1999. However, some countries chose not to adopt the euro, including Britain. Adoption of the euro increased international trade and led to more productive economies for those countries adopting the euro, but adoption of the euro also meant that these countries gave up their ability to have an independent monetary policy. Britain was unwilling to lose its independent monetary policy since this would limit its ability to use policy to correct macroeconomic problems.

## Key Terms

*Notes*

**devaluation** a reduction in the value of a currency that is set under a *fixed exchange rate regime.*

**revaluation** an increase in the value of a currency that is set under a *fixed exchange rate regime.*

### ■ AFTER YOU READ THE MODULE

## Tips

**Tip #1.**    This module introduces new vocabulary. You will want to learn the definitions and be able to apply these definitions. You will want to thoroughly understand devaluation of a currency and revaluation of a currency. You might find the following table a helpful summary of these relationships.

| | |
|---|---|
| Devaluation of country X's currency ⟶ | Country X imports less, exports more |
| Revaluation of country X's currency ⟶ | Country X imports more, exports less |

# WORKED PROBLEMS

1. Moheeb is the financial advisor for a small country that engages in trade. Moheeb recognizes that his country is in need of higher aggregate demand in order to provide higher levels of employment for the citizens who live in his small country. Moheeb knows that his country has a fixed exchange rate but he thinks that it might be possible to create higher aggregate demand by intervening in the exchange market for his country's currency. If this country wishes to attain its goal of higher aggregate demand, what policy would you suggest that Moheeb pursue with regard to the country's exchange rate, and how will this policy affect the level of aggregate demand?

**STEP 1:** Review the relationship between a change in the exchange rate and its impact on a country's imports and exports.

When a country has a fixed exchange rate it is still possible for the country to engage in a devaluation of its currency or a revaluation of its currency. When the country devalues its currency, it reduces the value of the currency relative to other currencies. The impact of currency devaluation is to make the devaluing country's goods and services relatively cheaper than the goods and services produced by other countries. When the country devalues its currency it will lead to increases in this country's exports and decreases in its country's imports.

**STEP 2:** Determine the direction of change in exports and imports needed to increase aggregate demand in this country.

Moheeb wishes to see an increase in aggregate demand. In order to accomplish this through a change in the value of the currency, Moheeb must pursue a policy that will increase the level of exports for his country while reducing the level of imports for his country.

**STEP 3:** Provide a policy recommendation with regard to the current fixed exchange rate.

Moheeb should advocate for currency devaluation since this policy will reduce the value of his country's currency relative to other currencies. This devaluation will result in greater demand for exports from his country and less demand for imports.

**STEP 4:** Explain how the policy recommendation in Step 3 will affect aggregate demand.

The currency devaluation advocated in Step 3 will result in more exports and fewer imports; the net effect of these changes in Moheeb's country is that the level of aggregate demand at every aggregate price level will be higher.

2. Muriel is reading about floating exchange rates in her economics textbook and she is a bit confused. She reads that if a country has a floating exchange rate an increase in the money supply will not only cause investment spending and consumption spending to increase, but it will also result in higher net exports, holding everything else constant. She wants you to help her understand these ideas. Provide Muriel with a logical step-by-step explanation of how an increase in the money supply will affect the level of aggregate demand in the economy if the economy has a floating exchange rate policy.

**STEP 1:** Begin by reminding Muriel what a floating exchange rate policy is.

A floating exchange rate policy refers to allowing a country's exchange rate to fluctuate to wherever the market takes it. That is, the exchange rate under a floating exchange rate policy is determined in the exchange market by the demand and supply of the currency.

**STEP 2:** Consider the effect of an increase in the money supply on the level of the interest rate and the level of investment spending and consumption spending in an economy.

Holding everything else constant, when the government increases the money supply, the money supply curve shifts to the right. As the money supply curve shifts to the right there is a movement along the money demand curve. The equilibrium interest rate in the market for money decreases relative to its initial equilibrium level. As the interest rate falls, greater investment spending and greater consumption spending follow.

**STEP 3:** Explain the impact of changes in the interest rate on the demand and supply of a currency.

If the interest rate decreases relative to the interest rate in other countries, we can expect that funds in this country will flow toward the higher interest rates and away from the relatively lower interest rate. This implies that in the exchange market people will exchange the less-desired currency for the more-desired currency. That is, the supply of the currency of the country whose interest rate is falling will decrease, while the demand for other currencies will increase. This desire to hold more of other currencies and less of the home country's currency means that the home country's currency will depreciate.

**STEP 4:** Examine the impact of an increase in the money supply on the level of the exchange rate for this economy. Remember that this economy has a floating exchange rate policy.

As the exchange rate depreciates, this depreciation will result in the home country's goods and services becoming relatively cheaper than the goods and services produced in other economies. We can expect that this country will export more and import less as its exchange rate depreciates.

**STEP 5:** Summarize the impact of an increase in the money supply on the level of aggregate demand in this economy.

Aggregate demand in this economy will shift to the right at every aggregate price level as a result of the increase in the money supply. That increase will affect investment spending, consumption spending, and the level of net exports in this economy. Investment spending, consumption spending, and net exports will all increase, and the increase will result in a higher level of aggregate demand for this economy.

# Problems and Exercises

1.  Suppose Macroland has adopted a fixed exchange rate regime and wishes to target the exchange rate to US$2.25 for each Macroland dollar.

    **a.** The following figure represents the current situation in Macroland.

    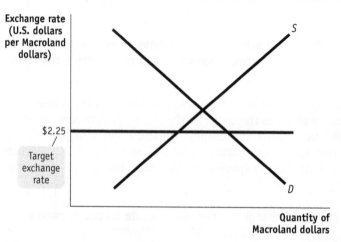

    Describe the situation depicted in this figure, given that Macroland would like to maintain a fixed exchange rate of US$2.25.

    **b.** Given the graph in part (a), what policies are available to Macroland if it is determined to maintain the exchange rate at US$2.25? Explain each option.

    **c.** The following figure represents the situation in Macroland six months later.

    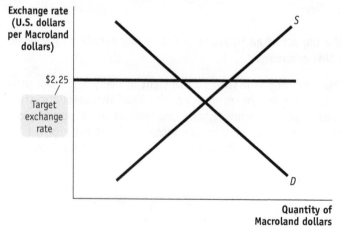

    Describe the situation depicted in this graph, given that Macroland would like to maintain a fixed exchange rate of US$2.25.

**d.** Given the graph in part (c), what policies are available to Macroland if it is determined to maintain the exchange rate at US$2.25? Explain each option.

**2.** Discuss the difference between a devaluation of a currency and a depreciation of a currency. How are these two concepts similar and what makes the two concepts different?

**3.** Suppose an economy operates under a floating exchange rate regime. Furthermore, suppose that this economy pursues expansionary monetary policy. Describe the effect of this expansionary monetary policy on the foreign exchange market.

## ▮ BEFORE YOU TAKE THE TEST

## Module Review Questions

**1.** A devaluation of a currency, holding everything else constant,
   a. makes foreign produced goods more attractive to purchase in the domestic economy and, therefore, leads to an increase in imports in the domestic economy.
   b. decreases the balance of payments on current account.
   c. may be used as a macroeconomic policy tool since a devaluation stimulates aggregate demand.
   d. Answers (a), (b), and (c) are all true.
   e. Answers (a) and (c) are both correct.
   f. Answers (b) and (c) are both correct.

**2.** Consider a country with a fixed exchange rate currently operating with an inflationary gap. Which of the following statements is true for this country?
   a. A revaluation of this country's currency will reduce its inflationary gap.
   b. A country with a fixed exchange rate regime has no macroeconomic policy tools available to it to combat an inflationary gap.
   c. A revaluation of this country's currency will increase exports and decrease imports, and this will help reduce the country's inflationary gap.
   d. Statements (a) and (c) are both correct.

**3.** A country pursuing an expansionary monetary policy will
   a. increase the level of investment spending.
   b. decrease the demand for that country's currency in the foreign exchange market.
   c. increase the supply of that country's currency in the foreign exchange market.
   d. Answers (a), (b), and (c) are all correct.

**4.** Which of the following statements is true?
   a. Demand shocks may originate from outside the domestic economy.
   b. Business cycles in different countries often seem to be synchronized, because changes in aggregate supply affect the demand for goods and services produced abroad as well as at home.
   c. A fixed exchange rate seems to lessen the impact of changes in aggregate demand in one country on the economic performance in other countries.
   d. Statements (a), (b), and (c) are all true.

**5.** A revaluation of a currency
   a. reflects an adjustment in the foreign exchange market due to changes in either the demand or the supply of the currency.
   b. is equivalent to an appreciation of the currency.
   c. results when a government operating under a fixed exchange rate regime decides to revise its exchange rate target to a higher level.
   d. results when foreign-produced goods get cheaper.

**6.** Which of the following statements is true?
   a. In 1944 the Bretton Woods Conference, held in Bretton Woods, New Hampshire, established a system of fixed exchange rates among major currencies.
   b. By 1971 the fixed exchange rates established at Bretton Woods had broken down.
   c. In 1991 countries in Europe agreed to establish a common European currency.
   d. All of these statements are true.

**7.** A country on a fixed exchange rate regime may devalue its currency in order to
   a. increase its level of imports while decreasing its level of exports.
   b. increase its level of exports while decreasing its level of imports.

## ANSWER KEY

# Answers to Problems and Exercises

1.  **a.** In the graph depicted in part (a), Macroland finds that there is a shortage of Macroland dollars at the target exchange rate of US$2.25 per Macroland dollar—that is, the quantity of Macroland dollars demanded exceeds the quantity of Macroland dollars supplied at the desired exchange rate.

    **b.** When there is a shortage of Macroland dollars, the government of Macroland can intervene in the foreign exchange market and sell Macroland dollars and acquire U.S. dollars to add to its foreign exchange reserves. In addition, the government can act to reduce interest rates in order to increase the supply of Macroland dollars while reducing the demand for Macroland dollars. By reducing the interest rate, the government of Macroland will decrease capital flows into Macroland, thus reducing the demand for Macroland dollars, and increase capital flows out of Macroland, thereby increasing the supply of Macroland dollars. Finally, the government of Macroland can impose foreign exchange controls that limit the ability of Macroland residents to sell currency to foreigners. Each of these policies will reduce the value of the Macroland dollar.

    **c.** In the graph depicted in part (c), Macroland finds that there is a surplus of Macroland dollars at the target exchange rate of US$2.25 per Macroland dollar. That is, the quantity of Macroland dollars demanded is less than the quantity of Macroland dollars supplied at the desired exchange rate.

    **d.** When there is a surplus of Macroland dollars, the government of Macroland can intervene in the foreign exchange market and buy Macroland dollars and sell U.S. dollars from its foreign exchange reserves. In addition, the government can act to increase interest rates in order to decrease the supply of Macroland dollars while increasing the demand for Macroland dollars. By increasing the interest rate, the government of Macroland will increase capital flows into Macroland, thus increasing the demand for Macroland dollars, and decrease capital flows out of Macroland, thereby decreasing the supply of Macroland dollars. Finally, the government of Macroland can impose foreign exchange controls that limit the ability of Macroland residents to buy foreign currency. Each of these policies will increase the value of the Macroland dollar.

2.  A depreciation of a currency is when that currency becomes less valuable in terms of another currency. A devaluation is a depreciation of the currency: when a currency is devalued it does become less valuable in terms of another currency. It occurs when a government operating under a fixed exchange rate regime decides to revise its fixed exchange rate target. A devaluation occurs because of direct government decision, while a depreciation may be the result of the normal operation of the currency market.

3.  Expansionary monetary policy will reduce the interest rate in this economy. As the interest rate falls there will be increases in investment spending and consumer spending in the economy. If will also affect the foreign exchange market. Since the interest rate has fallen, foreigners will have less incentive to move their funds into this economy; the demand for the country's currency will shift to the left. At the same time, the fall in the interest rate will create incentives for people in this economy to send their funds to other countries where the interest rate is higher: the supply of the country's currency will shift to the right. The demand for the currency shifts to the left and the supply of the currency shifts to the right; the combined impact of these shifts is to reduce the exchange rate.

## Answers to Module Review Questions

1. **Answer c.** A devaluation of a currency is a reduction in the value of a currency that previously had a fixed exchange rate. This devaluation makes domestic goods cheaper in terms of foreign currency and will, therefore, increase the level of exports and decrease the level of imports in the domestic economy. This in turn will stimulate aggregate demand in the domestic economy. The effect of these changes is to increase the balance of payments on current account.

2. **Answer a.** A revaluation of a country's currency will make domestic goods more expensive in terms of foreign currency and will, therefore, decrease exports while increasing imports. This will cause aggregate demand to decrease and, therefore, help the country reduce its inflationary gap.

3. **Answer d.** A country pursuing expansionary monetary policy causes the interest rate to decrease: this makes investment spending more attractive. In addition, the decrease in the interest rate also affects the foreign exchange market: the demand for the domestic currency will decrease since the domestic economy is now offering a relatively lower rate of return on their loans, and the supply of the domestic currency will increase because there is now a greater incentive to move funds abroad, since the rate of return on loans in the domestic economy has fallen.

4. **Answer a.** Business cycles in different countries often seem to be synchronized, because changes in aggregate demand in one country often have an effect on the level of aggregate demand in other countries. Adherence to a floating exchange rate regime helps insulate countries from recessions originating from outside their economies, since the movement in the exchange rate limits the level of change in aggregate demand.

5. **Answer c.** A revaluation is an appreciation of a currency but that appreciation is due to the government, under a fixed exchange rate rule, deciding to revise its exchange rate target to a higher level. This adjustment does not necessarily reflect any change in the demand or the supply of the currency.

6. **Answer d.** Page 480 of Module 46 covers this material in the article titled "From Bretton Woods to the Euro." All the provided statements are factual.

7. **Answer b.** When a country devalues its currency, its own goods are made cheaper to purchase by people outside of the country while making foreign-produced goods more expensive to import. A devaluation of the currency, holding everything else constant, will result in more exports for the country and fewer imports.

# History and Alternative Views of Macroeconomics

## Summary

This module discusses the limitations of the classical macroeconomics model and how it was not adequate for the economic problems posed by the Great Depression. The module also discusses how Keynes and the experience of the Great Depression led to the use of macroeconomic policy activism. The module continues with a discussion of monetarism and its views of the limitations of discretionary monetary policy. The module explores how challenges to Keynes's ideas led to a revision of these ideas and the emergence of the new classical macroeconomics.

## Module Objectives

**Objective #1.** The term *macroeconomy* was first used in 1933. Prior to the 1930s, the classical model of the price level dominated economic thinking about monetary policy. This model, based on the assumption of flexible prices, held that an increase in the money supply, holding other things constant, would lead to an equal proportional rise in the aggregate price level and no change in the level of real aggregate output. This model focused on long-run economic adjustments while regarding short-run economic adjustment as unimportant.

**Objective #2.** By the 1930s, the measurement of business cycles was well advanced even though there was no generally accepted theory of business cycles. The Great Depression served as a strong stimulus for economists to develop theories that could provide guidance for macroeconomic policies in the face of business cycle fluctuations.

**Objective #3.** Keynesian economics mainly reflects two innovations: first, it emphasized short-run effects of shifts in aggregate demand and their impact on aggregate output rather than the long-run determination of the aggregate price level; and second, it argued that changes in business confidence were the primary cause of business cycles.

Keynes's economic ideas have been accepted across a broad part of the political spectrum. The main practical consequence of Keynes's work was the justification of macroeconomic policy activism: Keynes's work indicated that monetary and fiscal policy could be used to smooth out business cycle fluctuations.

**Objective #4.**    Keynes's work suggested that economic recovery requires aggressive fiscal expansion: this deficit spending creates jobs. In the 1930s, the modest increases in deficit spending were inadequate to end the Great Depression; however, the massive expansionary fiscal policy that occurred as a result of World War II was sufficient to create jobs in the short run and to prove that aggressive fiscal policy could result in economic recovery.

**Objective #5.**    Keynes suggested that monetary policy would be ineffective in depression conditions due to the liquidity trap in which interest rates cannot fall below zero. Although this is true, Friedman and Schwartz persuaded many economists that the Great Depression could have been avoided if the Fed had acted to prevent a monetary contraction. Over time economists came to believe that monetary policy should play a key role in economic management.

- Economic management of the economy through monetary policy instead of fiscal policy makes macroeconomics a more technical and less political issue.

**Objective #6.**    Monetarism asserts that nominal GDP will grow steadily if the money supply grows steadily. Monetarists believed that a steady growth rate of the money supply would prove more effective in smoothing out business cycle fluctuations than active policy intervention, since active policy intervention encounters lags in its implementation and effectiveness. Friedman advocated the pursuit of a monetary policy rule, a formula that determines the Fed's actions, rather than discretionary monetary policy. This view used the velocity equation, $MV = PY$, to suggest that as long as the velocity of money, $V$, was relatively stable, then a steady rate of growth of the money supply, $M$, would lead to steady growth of nominal GDP, $PY$. The Fed's experience with monetarism proved less than successful: steady growth in the money supply in the late 1970s and early 1980s did not ensure steady growth in the economy. Data reveals that the velocity of money shifted around erratically starting around 1980, due probably to financial market innovations. Despite this experience, economists believe that too much or too little discretion in monetary policy is counterproductive.

**Objective #7.**    In 1968, Friedman and Phelps proposed the natural rate of unemployment of NAIRU. They claimed that the apparent trade-off between unemployment and inflation would not survive an extended period of time with increasing prices; that is, the existence of inflationary expectations would lead the economy to continue to experience inflation even with high levels of unemployment.

**Objective #8.**    The political business cycle results when politicians use macroeconomic policy to serve political ends. This can result in unnecessary economic instability.

**Objective #9.**    New classical macroeconomics returned to the classical view that shifts in the aggregate demand curve cause changes in the aggregate price level but not the aggregate output level. This approach challenged the Keynesian idea that the short-run aggregate supply curve is upward sloping and instead argued that the short-run aggregate supply curve was vertical. This position was based on two concepts: rational expectations and real business cycle theory.

- Rational expectations is the view that individuals and firms make decisions optimally using all the available information. If this is true, then people will form their expectations about inflation not only by considering historical data, but also by taking into account any available information about government intentions with regard to trading off higher inflation for lower unemployment. The implication of this logic is that monetary policy can change the level of unemployment only if it comes as a surprise to the public.

- Real business cycle theory argues that slowdowns in productivity growth are the primary causes of business cycle fluctuations in the economy. Further research in this area has resulted in wide acceptance that some of the correlation between total factor productivity and the business cycle is the result of the effect of the business cycle on productivity, rather than the effect of productivity on the business cycle.

## Key Terms

**macroeconomic policy activism** the use of *monetary policy* and *fiscal policy* to smooth out the *business cycle*.

**monetarism** a theory of *business cycles*, associated primarily with Milton Friedman, that asserts that GDP will grow steadily if the *money supply* grows steadily.

**discretionary monetary policy** policy actions, either changes in *interest rates* or changes in the *money supply*, undertaken by the *central bank* based on its assessment of the state of the *economy*.

**monetary policy rule** a formula that determines the *central bank's* actions.

**Quantity Theory of Money** a theory that emphasizes the positive relationship beween the price level and the money supply. It relies on the equation $(M \times V = P \times Y)$.

**velocity of money** the ratio of *nominal GDP* to the *money supply*.

**natural rate hypothesis** the hypothesis that because *inflation* is eventually embedded into expectations, to avoid accelerating inflation over time the *unemployment rate* equals the expected inflation rate.

**political business cycle** a *business cycle* that results from the use of macroeconomic policy to serve political ends.

**new classical macroeconomics** an approach to the *business cycle* that returns to the classical view that shifts in the *aggregate demand curve* affect only the *aggregate price level*, not *aggregate output*.

**rational expectations** a theory of expectation formation that holds that individuals and *firms* make decisions optimally, using all available information.

**new Keynesian economics** theory that argues that market imperfections can lead to price stickiness for the *economy* as a whole.

**real business cycle theory** a theory of *business cycles* that asserts that fluctuations in the growth rate of *total factor productivity* cause the business cycle.

## ▉ AFTER YOU READ THE MODULE

## Tips

**Tip #1.** This module requires you to be able to compare and contrast different macroeconomic theories. The following table provides a summary of these models. You will want to review each model and think about the focus of each, and how the models differ with regard to their underlying assumptions and their policy implications.

| | Classical macro | Keynesian macro | Monetarism | Modern consensus |
|---|---|---|---|---|
| Focus of model | Long-run determination of the aggregate price level | Short-run determination of the aggregate output level and the effects of shifts in *AD* on that level of aggregate output | Effect of money supply growth on the level of short-run aggregate output in the economy | Summarizing points of agreement among modern-day macroeconomists |
| Prices | Flexible in the short run and the long run | Flexible in the long run, but sticky in the short run | Flexible in the long run, but sticky in the short run | Flexible in the long run, but sticky in the short run |
| Unemployment | Model does not worry about unemployment: assumes that economy will produce at potential output level in both the short run and the long run, due to price flexibility | Unemployment possible in the short run due to leftward shifts in aggregate demand that lead to decreases in output and aggregate production less than the potential output level for the economy | Unemployment possible in the short run due to leftward shifts in aggregate demand that lead to decreases in output and aggregate production less than the potential output level for the economy | Unemployment possible in the short run due to leftward shifts in aggregate demand that lead to decreases in output and aggregate production less than the potential output level for the economy |
| Aggregate supply curve | Vertical in both the short run and long run, thus shifts in aggregate demand have no effect on the level of aggregate output | *SRAS* is upward sloping, so shifts in aggregate demand affect aggregate output and thus employment | *SRAS* is upward sloping, so shifts in aggregate demand affect aggregate output and thus employment | *SRAS* is upward sloping, so shifts in aggregate demand affect aggregate output and thus employment; *LRAS* is vertical at the potential output level for the economy |
| Shifts in aggregate demand | Focus on changes in money supply and how this shifts the aggregate demand curve and raises the aggregate price level | Changes in "animal spirits," or business confidence, cause shifts in aggregate demand; model emphasizes the importance of demand shocks | Shift in aggregate demand because of fiscal policy changes will have no effect on aggregate output due to crowding-out effect; shifts in aggregate demand affect aggregate output only if driven by changes in the money supply | Shift in aggregate demand possible because of changes in fiscal policy or the money supply |
| Effect of monetary policy | Increase in money supply leads to an equal and proportionate rise in the aggregate price level and no effect on aggregate output in the long run | Not particularly effective in depression conditions | Plays key role in economic management; GDP will grow steadily if the money supply grows steadily (a monetary policy rule) | Can be used to shift aggregate demand curve and to reduce economic instability |
| Policy ramifications | Economy in long run is at potential output: simply be patient for that result to occur | Legitimized macroeconomic policy activism: the use of monetary and fiscal policy to smooth out business cycles | Expansionary fiscal policy with a fixed money supply leads to crowding out: importance of monetary policy | Fiscal and monetary policy can shift the aggregate demand curve |

**Tip #2.**   A key issue underlying this module is the shape of the short-run aggregate supply curve. The classical macroeconomists thought the short-run aggregate supply curve was vertical; hence, shifts in aggregate demand curve could cause changes in the aggregate price level, but not changes in the level of aggregate output. Figure 47.1 illustrates this idea.

**Figure 47.1**

The Keynesian approach emphasized that the short-run aggregate supply curve is upward sloping and thus shifts in aggregate demand would cause both the aggregate price level as well as the aggregate output level to change. Figure 47.2 illustrates this idea.

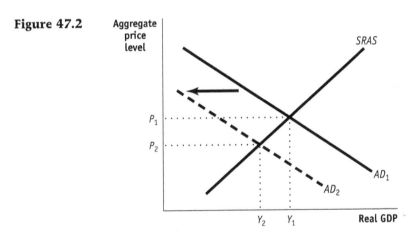

**Figure 47.2**

The monetarist approach concurred with the Keynesians that the short-run aggregate supply curve is upward sloping, but emphasized that fiscal policy would be relatively ineffective if the money supply was held constant due to the crowding-out effect. In addition, this approach favored the implementation of a monetary policy rule, thereby effectively reducing the scope of monetary policy.

The new classical macroeconomics returned briefly to the classical view that the short-run aggregate supply curve is vertical, but eventually found that economic data support an upward-sloping aggregate supply curve rather than a vertical aggregate supply curve.

**Tip #3.** The table below provides a summary and comparison of four different macroeconomic approaches. You will find it helpful to study this table until you fully understand each of these approaches and how they differ from one another.

| | Classical macroeconomics | Keynesian macroeconomics | Monetarism | New classical macroeconomics |
|---|---|---|---|---|
| Prices | Prices are completely flexible | Prices are sticky in the short run | Prices are sticky in the short run | Prices are completely flexible |
| AS curve | Vertical in the short run and the long run | Upward sloping in the short run | Upward sloping in the short run | Vertical in the short run and the long run based on rational expectations and real business theory |
| AD curve | Shifts in AD curve will cause changes in the aggregate price level but not the aggregate output level due to the AS curve being vertical: demand shocks do not affect the aggregate output level | Shifts in AD curve will cause changes in both the aggregate price level and the aggregate output level in the short run due to the AS curve being upward sloping; demand shocks affect aggregate output | Shifts in AD curve will cause changes in both the aggregate price level and the aggregate output level in the short run due to the AS curve being upward sloping: demand shocks affect aggregate output | Shifts in AD curve will cause changes in the aggregate price level but not the aggregate output level due to the AS curve being vertical: demand shocks do not affect the aggregate output level |
| Change in money supply | Shifts the AD curve and changes the aggregate price level but does not affect the aggregate output level; therefore, increases in the money supply lead to inflation | Shifts the AD curve and changes both the aggregate price level and the aggregate output level | Shifts the AD curve and changes the aggregate price level and the aggregate output level | Shifts the AD curve and changes the aggregate price level but does not change the aggregate output level; therefore, increases in the money supply lead to inflation |
| Emphasis | Aggregate output is determined by AS and aggregate price level is determined by AD | Aggregate output and aggregate price level determined by the interaction between AD and AS; therefore, demand shocks can cause fluctuations in output | Monetarists hold that GDP will grow steadily if the money supply grows steadily | Aggregate output determined by AS and the aggregate price level is determined by AD |
| Business cycles | No real theory of business cycles since this model emphasizes the long run: no role for fiscal or monetary policy to smooth out business cycle fluctuation | Business cycles caused by changes in business confidence; advocates the use of monetary and fiscal policy to smooth out business cycle fluctuations | Importance of the appropriate growth rate of the money supply to avoid business cycles; advocates monetary policy rule since too much discretionary monetary policy may destabilize the economy | Assumption of vertical AS curve rules out business cycles; economic fluctuations in aggregate output are due to shifts in the AS curve |
| Short run versus long run | Short run viewed as unimportant: focus on long run | Short-run emphasis | Short-run emphasis | Short run viewed as unimportant: focus on long run |

1. In agricultural economies, aggregate output and aggregate price level fluctuation in the short run are primarily due to shifts in aggregate supply because of weather. In contrast, modern, nonagricultural economies' aggregate output and aggregate price level fluctuations in the short run are due primarily to aggregate demand shocks. Use graphs to illustrate these business-cycle fluctuations in both agricultural economies and modern, nonagricultural economies.

**STEP 1:** Take time to reread the paragraph, paying particular attention to the idea that business-cycle fluctuations in aggregate output and the aggregate price level are driven by aggregate supply shocks in agricultural economies and, in contrast, these fluctuations are driven by aggregate demand shocks in more modern, nonagricultural economies.

In this step, you want to first realize that these are two very different perspectives on how fluctuations in output and the aggregate price level occur. This should suggest that separate graphs illustrating each of these perspectives would be helpful.

**STEP 2:** Draw a diagram illustrating short-run business cycle fluctuation in an agricultural economy in which business cycle fluctuation is due to shifts in the short-run aggregate supply curve due to weather.

On this graph, you will want to label the initial aggregate output level and the initial aggregate price level. Then, on your graph illustrate how a shift in the aggregate supply curve to the left due to weather adversely affecting the ability of farmers to get their product to market causes aggregate output to fall and the aggregate price level to rise. On your graph, you can also illustrate how a shift in the aggregate supply curve to the right due to weather positively affecting the ability of farmers to get their product to market causes aggregate output to rise and the aggregate output level to fall. The following diagram illustrates how short-run fluctuations in the aggregate supply curve can cause business-cycle fluctuations.

**STEP 3:** Draw a diagram illustrating short-run business cycle fluctuation in a modern, nonagricultural economy in which business-cycle fluctuation is due to shifts in the short-run aggregate demand curve.

On this graph, you will want to label the initial aggregate output level and the initial aggregate price level. Then, on your graph illustrate how a shift in the aggregate demand curve to the left due to a negative demand shock causes aggregate output to fall and the aggregate price level to decrease. On your graph, you can also illustrate how a shift in the aggregate demand curve to the right due to a positive demand shock causes aggregate output to rise and the aggregate output level to increase. The following diagram illustrates how short-run fluctuations in the aggregate demand curve can cause business-cycle fluctuations.

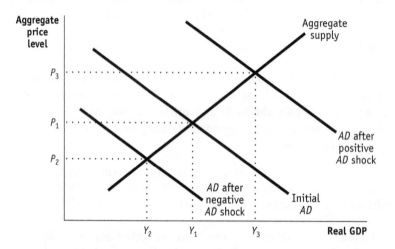

2. Milton Friedman and Anna Schwartz played a key role in convincing macroeconomists of the importance of monetary policy and the possibility that monetary policy rather than fiscal policy could be used to manage the economy. Fiscal policy involves economic management by politicians, while monetary policy theoretically allows for economic management that does not involve political choices. Explain why fiscal policy involves political choices and how monetary policy could be detached from the political process.

**STEP 1:** Review what fiscal policy is and then explain how fiscal policy necessarily involves political choices.

Fiscal policy is defined as changes in government spending or taxation designed to change the overall level of production in an economy. Anytime fiscal policy is contemplated or enacted it involves politicians making decisions about how the government should raise funds as well as how the government should expend its funds. These decisions are necessarily political: there will be disagreement about the right level of taxation as well as the right mix of goods and services for the government to provide. Due to the political nature of fiscal policy, this can make it difficult for the government to enact the economic management policy needed via fiscal policy.

**STEP 2:** Review what monetary policy is and then explain how monetary policy does not necessarily involve political choices.

Monetary policy is defined as changes in the quantity of money in circulation designed to change the interest rate and affect the overall level of spending. If the central bank engages in monetary policy, the change in the interest rate that occurs affects everyone. This implies that economic management via monetary policy can be more of a technical issue rather than a political issue.

# Problems and Exercises

1.  Why did Keynes respond to the classical viewpoint by claiming that in the long run, "we are all dead"? Explain how his economic thinking about the macroeconomy represented a departure from the prevailing economic thought of the day.

2.  How did the Great Depression provide an incentive for economists to develop new theories and new positions with regard to the efficacy of policy as a means of reducing business cycle fluctuations?

3.  Briefly describe the two primary innovations in Keynesian economics. How did Keynes's work legitimize macroeconomic policy activism? Use the following graph to help illustrate your answer, and be sure in your answer to compare the Keynesian viewpoint with the classical viewpoint.

Aggregate price level

Real GDP

4. The new classical macroeconomics, developed in the 1970s and 1980s, challenged the Keynesian macroeconomic view that the short-run aggregate supply curve is upward sloping. What did the new classical macroeconomists propose with regard to the short-run aggregate supply curve, and what reasons did they give for subscribing to this viewpoint?

5. Although most macroeconomists agree that fiscal policy can affect the level of aggregate output in the short run, many macroeconomists do not support the use of discretionary fiscal policy as a method for smoothing business cycle fluctuations. Why, if fiscal policy is potentially effective, do these macroeconomists reject it as a policy tool? Is there any time that these macroeconomists would advocate the use of discretionary fiscal policy?

6. Suppose the economy of Macroland reports a decline in output. The president of Macroland assembles a group of economic advisors to study this decline in output and to advise the government about appropriate policies to use to address this decline in output.

   a. The first advisor is a Keynesian macroeconomist. How would this advisor explain the decline in output, and what policy(ies) would she suggest to return the economy to its potential output level? Graph an aggregate demand and aggregate supply diagram to illustrate your answer.

   Aggregate
   price
   level

   Real GDP

**b.** The second advisor is a monetarist. How would this advisor explain the decline in output, and what policy(ies) would she suggest to return the economy to its potential output level? Use an aggregate demand and aggregate supply diagram to illustrate your answer.

**c.** The third advisor is an economist who accepts the viewpoints expressed by macroeconomists, in what the text terms the modern consensus. How would this advisor explain the decline in output, and what policy(ies) would he suggest to return the economy to its potential output level? Use an aggregate demand and aggregate supply diagram to illustrate your answer.

**7.** Use a diagram of the money market to explain why monetary policy is ineffective when there is a liquidity trap.

**Nominal interest rate**

**Quantity of money**

8. How does the assumption of rational expectations support the new classical macroeconomics position that shifts in the aggregate demand curve affect only the aggregate price level and not the aggregate output level?

## BEFORE YOU TAKE THE TEST

# Module Review Questions

1. Which of the following statements is true?
   a. Macroeconomists believe the use of expansionary monetary policy is always an ineffective method for reducing economic recessions.
   b. The classical model of the price level holds that prices are flexible, and therefore the long-run aggregate supply curve is horizontal.
   c. Statements (a) and (b) are both true.
   d. Statements (a) and (b) are both false.

2. The Great Depression
   a. reinforced prevailing economic views of the day that it was only long-run economic performance that was important.
   b. threatened both economic and political stability.
   c. illustrated that market economies produced consistently at the potential output level.
   d. Answers (a), (b), and (c) are all correct.
   e. Answers (b) and (c) are both correct.

3. Which of the following statements is true about Keynes's contributions to economic theory?
   a. In the long run, fluctuations in aggregate output are primarily due to fluctuations in aggregate demand.
   b. In the short run, the aggregate supply curve is upward sloping; therefore shifts in aggregate demand will cause fluctuations in aggregate output.
   c. Shifts in the aggregate demand curve in the short run are primarily due to changes in the money supply.
   d. "Animal spirits" primarily affect aggregate supply in the long run.

4. Macroeconomic policy activism refers to
   a. the use of expansionary monetary policy to fight economic expansions.
   b. the use of monetary and fiscal policy to smooth out business cycle fluctuations.
   c. the idea that running large government deficits is never an acceptable means of eliminating business cycle fluctuations.
   d. Answers (b) and (c) are both correct.

5. Which of the following statements is true?
   a. In a liquidity trap, expansionary monetary policy can effectively raise interest rates.
   b. Friedman and Schwartz's work helped to prove the effectiveness of fiscal policy as a way of managing the economy.
   c. Friedman and Schwartz's work helped make macroeconomics a more technical, and less political, issue.
   d. Keynes made other economists aware of the limitations of macroeconomic policy activism.

6. Monetarism
   a. states that there is no relationship between the rate of growth of the money supply and the level of aggregate output in an economy.
   b. has nothing in common with Keynesian ideas.
   c. includes a strong belief in the efficacy of discretionary fiscal policy.
   d. maintains that most efforts of policymakers to reduce economic fluctuation actually result in greater economic instability.

7. When the central bank pursues a formula that determines its actions, this is called
   a. monetarism.
   b. a monetary policy rule.
   c. discretionary monetary policy.
   d. discretionary fiscal policy.

8. The NAIRU
   a. is equivalent to the natural rate of unemployment.
   b. hypothesis states that inflation eventually gets built into expectations, so that any attempt to keep the unemployment rate above the natural rate will lead to an ever-rising inflation rate.
   c. states that once inflation is embedded in the public's expectations, it would continue even in the face of high unemployment.
   d. Answers (a), (b), and (c) are all correct.
   e. Answers (a) and (b) are both correct.
   f. Answers (a) and (c) are both correct.
   g. Answers (b) and (c) are both correct.

9. Which of the following statements is true?
   a. Activist macroeconomic policy lends itself to political manipulation.
   b. Adoption of a monetary policy rule by the central bank lends itself to political manipulation.
   c. Political business cycles reduce economic instability in an economy.
   d. Velocity, after 1980, was predictable and steady in the U.S. economy.

10. New classical macroeconomics
    a. holds that shifts in aggregate demand affect the aggregate output level and not the aggregate price level.
    b. incorporates rational expectations, the belief that individuals and firms make their decisions optimally using all available information.
    c. provides a logical argument that suggests monetary policy is ineffective as a method for stabilizing the economy.
    d. Answers (a), (b), and (c) are all correct.
    e. Answers (a) and (b) are both correct.
    f. Answers (a) and (c) are both correct.
    g. Answers (b) and (c) are both correct.

**11.** Real business cycle theory
   a. states that the correlation between total factor productivity and the business cycle is the result of the effect of the business cycle on productivity.
   b. states that fluctuations in the rate of growth of factor productivity cause the business cycle.
   c. states that fluctuations in the business cycle cause changes in the rate of growth of factor productivity.
   d. is a widely held view among macroeconomists today.

**12.** Expansionary monetary policy is helpful in fighting recessions, provided the economy is not operating in a liquidity trap, according to
   a. classical macroeconomics.
   b. monetarism.
   c. the modern consensus among macroeconomists.
   d. Answers (a), (b), and (c) are all correct.
   e. Answers (a) and (c) are both correct.
   f. Answers (b) and (c) are both correct.

**13.** Which of the following statements is true?
   a. According to the Keynesians, fiscal policy is ineffective in fighting recessions.
   b. According to the monetarists, fiscal policy is ineffective in fighting recessions.
   c. The modern consensus holds that discretionary fiscal policy is always acceptable.
   d. According to the classical macroeconomists, discretionary monetary policy is always acceptable.

**14.** True or false: "Aggressive monetary policy is effective in reducing the depth and extent of a recession."
   a. True          b. False

**15.** The classical model assumes prices are
   a. sticky and, therefore, both the short-run and long-run aggregate supply curves are vertical.
   b. flexible and, therefore, the short-run aggregate supply curve is upward sloping while the long-run aggregate supply curve is vertical.
   c. flexible and, therefore, both the short-run and long-run aggregate supply curves are vertical.
   d. sticky and, therefore, the short-run aggregate supply curve is upward sloping while the long-run aggregate supply curve is vertical.

**16.** If you were a classical macroeconomist, which of the following statements would you agree with?
   a. An increase in the money supply will result in an increase in the aggregate price level and will thus be inflationary.
   b. When the economy is in a recession, the government can reduce the recession by engaging in active monetary policy.
   c. The economy grows smoothly over time.
   d. Statements (a) and (c) are both correct.

**17.** Keynes argued that the focus of macroeconomists when there was a shift in aggregate demand should be on

a. the aggregate price level.      b. the aggregate output level.

**18.** "Animal spirits" refers to the

a. effect of monetary policy on investment decisions.

b. level of confidence that businesses have and how that confidence level effects spending decisions by firms and households.

c. inappropriate policies enacted by Congress during the political business cycle.

d. ability of the government through its spending policies to manage the economy and keep it from recession.

**19.** Mary and George, two economists, argue about the economic policy their government should pursue to help alleviate the current recession. Mary argues that the answer is for expansionary fiscal policy to provide a much-needed spending stimulus to the economy, while George argues that this spending will only result in the crowding out of private investment spending. Which of the following statements best describes the economic perspective of these two economists?

a. George adheres to the Keynesian model of the macroeconomy, while Mary favors the classical model.

b. George favors the classical model of the macroeconomy, while Mary favors the Keynesian model.

c. George favors the monetarist approach to the macroeconomy, while Mary favors the Keynesian approach.

d. George favors the Keynesian approach to the macroeconomy, while Mary favors the monetarist approach.

**20.** World War II demonstrated that

a. fiscal policy was unnecessary if the country went to war.

b. fiscal policy was ineffective if the country was at war.

c. fiscal policy that was expansionary had the capability of creating jobs in the short run.

d. the only way to get out of a deep depression was to go to war.

# ■ ANSWER KEY

## Answers to Problems and Exercises

1.  This classical model of the economy held that the economy, if it was in a recession, would self-correct and return to the natural rate of unemployment and the potential output level on its own. Keynes agreed with this assessment, but he recognized that it might take time for the economy to return to this point: during the time that the economy failed to produce at the potential level of aggregate output, some people would be without jobs. Keynes felt that waiting for the long run to arrive in a situation of recession was not the only option: active government intervention in the form of fiscal and monetary policy could help smooth out business cycles. Keynes, by his emphasis on the short run and his use of an upward-sloping aggregate supply curve, was able to provide a model of the economy that illustrated the importance of the short run as well as the potential efficacy of fiscal and monetary policy in addressing business cycle fluctuations.

2.  Prior to the Great Depression, the prevailing economic wisdom was that economies tended to full employment of their resources and that any change in the money supply would only result in changes to the aggregate price level, and not changes to the aggregate output level. The classical model of the price level based its analysis on a vertical aggregate supply curve for both the short run and the long run. With the onset of the Great Depression, economists found their conventional view of the macroeconomy tested: economists were forced to reconsider their model and to question the wisdom of using a model that emphasized only price level fluctuations, without regard to the possibility of aggregate output fluctuations. Thus, Keynes developed a model that considered the impact on the macroeconomy of a upward-sloping aggregate supply curve in the short run; such a model could model economic recessions and could also offer policy prescriptions for a depressed economy in the form of activist fiscal and monetary policy.

    After Keynes's work, other economists entered the discussion to question the limits of macroeconomic policy activism. In particular, Friedman revived interest in monetary policy, and his work led to a recognition that management of the economy could be shifted away from fiscal policy and toward monetary policy. His work meant that macroeconomics could be a more technical, less political, issue.

    The modern consensus reflects debate about and the study of macroeconomic issues. The modern consensus agrees that fiscal policy and monetary policy can each be effective in fighting recessions, but are unable to reduce unemployment in the long run. This consensus represents a melding of elements from both the classical model of the price level and Keynesian macroeconomics.

3.  Keynes emphasized (1) the short-run effects of shifts in aggregate demand on aggregate output, rather than the long-run determination of the aggregate price level; and (2) that shifts in the aggregate demand curve could be caused by factors other than a change in the money supply. These other factors were lumped together as "animal spirits," or business confidence. Keynes emphasized that changes in business confidence were the primary causes of business cycles in the economy. Therefore, Keynes modeled the economy as having an upward-sloping short-run aggregate supply curve with a shifting aggregate demand curve. Thus, if the aggregate demand curve shifted to the left, this would lead the economy in the short run to experience not only falling price levels but

also falling aggregate output and higher levels of unemployment. The following graph illustrates this idea.

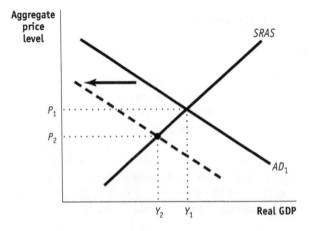

In contrast, the classical view held to a vertical aggregate supply curve (for both the short run and the long run) and thus, a shift in aggregate demand would alter the aggregate price level, but not the aggregate output level. The figure below illustrates this idea.

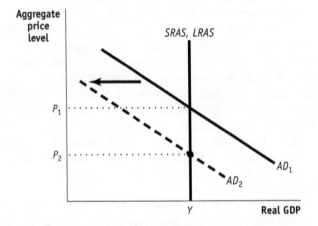

Keynes reasoned that activist fiscal and monetary policy could be used to offset these shifts in the aggregate demand curve, thus keeping the economy at its initial equilibrium. In fact, a failure to engage in activist policy could potentially cause the economy to operate in a recession or depression. Keynes provided a very strong justification for the role of government policy in reducing or eliminating business cycles.

4. The new classical macroeconomic model reverted to the classical view that the short-run aggregate supply curve was vertical: this implies that shifts in aggregate demand alter the aggregate price level, but do not affect the level of aggregate output. The new classical macroeconomic model based its conclusions on two arguments: rational expectations and real business cycle theory.

Rational expectations is the view that individuals and firms make their decisions based upon all available information, and people will therefore take into account not only historical information, but also government intentions with regard to future policy. Thus, any attempt by the government to trade off higher inflation in the short run in order to attain lower levels of unemployment will be noticed by individuals and firms, and this information will be included in the decision-making process. The new classical macroeconomics concludes that government policy to change the level of unemployment can only be effective if it is a surprise: this means that the government no longer can intentionally pursue policies to change the unemployment rate, since people will perceive its intent and act in a manner that eliminates the policy's effectiveness.

Real business cycle theory holds that fluctuations in the rate of growth of total factor productivity cause the business cycle. Rather than looking to shifts in aggregate demand as the cause of business cycle fluctuations (the Keynesian approach), the real business cycle theorists explained economic fluctuations as the result of variation in the rate of growth of total factor productivity. Subsequent research notes a strong correlation between growth rates of factor productivity and the business cycle, but does not identify the direction of causation.

5. Discretionary fiscal policy is rejected as a policy tool by many macroeconomists, because they view it as often counterproductive due to the existence of lags in the implementation and effectiveness of this policy. They argue that by the time the discretionary fiscal policy is implemented and takes effect, the economy is often no longer struggling with the particular economic conditions the fiscal policy was intended to address. In addition, there is concern that the use of discretionary fiscal policy may contribute to greater business cycle fluctuations due to the political business cycle. These economists view the use of discretionary fiscal policy as having a limited role: they advocate its use when monetary policy is ineffective (in the case of the liquidity trap).

6. **a.** The Keynesian macroeconomist would explain the recession using an *AD-AS* diagram like the one depicted in the following graph.

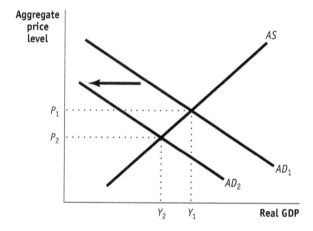

Output, Y, has fallen below its potential output level of $Y_1$ because of a shift in aggregate demand. The current level of production, $Y_2$, results in a higher level of unemployment. She explains the cause of this leftward shift in aggregate demand as a change in "animal spirits," or a decline in business confidence. To remedy the situation, she proposes macroeconomic policy activism: the use of monetary and fiscal policy. In this case this policy should be directed at shifting the aggregate demand curve back to the right so that aggregate output can return to its initial level of $Y_1$.

**b.** The monetarist advisor would utilize the same diagram as the Keynesian economist to depict the fall in aggregate output. However, she would caution that expansionary fiscal policy would not restore the economy to $Y_1$ if the money supply is held constant. She reasons that the increase in spending (or decrease in taxes) by the government while stimulating aggregate demand will also stimulate money demand. With no change in the money supply this increase in money demand will cause interest rates to rise: the rise in interest rates will crowd out investment spending so that the increase in spending due to the change in fiscal policy will be offset by an equal decrease in investment spending. The monetarist would therefore emphasize the inability of expansionary fiscal policy to address and correct the recession. She would advise steady growth of the money supply in order to generate steady growth of aggregate output.

**c.** This third advisor could also use the diagram in part (a) to explain the decline in aggregate output. This economist would assert that expansionary monetary policy could be used to shift the aggregate demand curve back to the right provided the economy was not operating in a liquidity trap. He would also advise that expansionary fiscal policy could also be used to shift the aggregate demand curve to the right.

7. The liquidity trap refers to a situation in which the nominal interest rate has fallen to zero and, therefore, cannot be lowered further through expansionary monetary policy. Therefore, the Fed cannot stimulate the economy by expanding the money supply and decreasing the interest rate since the interest rate cannot fall lower than zero. The figure below illustrates the liquidity trap.

Note that in this figure, if the Fed were to engage in expansionary monetary policy, this would cause the money supply to shift to the right; but the interest rate cannot fall any further than zero, so this expansionary monetary policy would not stimulate investment and consumption spending.

8. The assumption of rational expectations holds that people will take into account any available information about monetary and fiscal policy. By building in this information, people will already adjust the aggregate supply curve to whatever they perceive to be the policy intentions of the government; hence, the short-run as well as long-run aggregate supply curve will be vertical, which means that the new classical macroeconomics ends up with the same results as those of classical macroeconomics.

## Answers to Module Review Questions

1. **Answer d.** Both of these statements are false. There is general consensus among macroeconomists that expansionary monetary policy is effective in reducing recessions. In the classical model of the price level, prices are flexible and, hence, the aggregate supply curve is vertical and not horizontal.

2. **Answer b.** The Great Depression illustrated for economists that short-run economic fluctuations were important and that a theory to understand these fluctuations was needed. The Great Depression threatened economic stability due to the economic pain of extremely high levels of unemployment and the political instability that led to the rise of Hitler in Germany. Although some economists thought that a market-oriented economy was unstable, there were other economists that did not support this view.

3. **Answer b.** Keynes demonstrated that fluctuations in aggregate demand could cause short-run fluctuations in aggregate output. These fluctuations in short-run aggregate demand were primarily due to changes in "animal spirits," the term Keynes used to describe business confidence. Keynes focused on the short run and the effects of shifts in aggregate demand on a short-run upward-sloping aggregate supply curve.

4. **Answer b.** Macroeconomic policy activism is the use of monetary and fiscal policy to smooth out business cycle fluctuations. Expansionary monetary policy can be used effectively to reduce economic recessions. Large government deficits can be used to effectively fight economic recessions, but may worsen economic expansions.

5. **Answer c.** In a liquidity trap, expansionary monetary policy is ineffective, since interest rates can fall no further once they are equal to zero. Expansionary monetary policy, if effective, reduces interest rates. Friedman and Schwartz provided proof of the effectiveness of monetary policy as a way of managing the economy. Their work helped to shift macroeconomics from a reliance on fiscal policy to a reliance on monetary policy as a means of managing the economy. This shift meant that macroeconomics became a more technical issue instead of a political issue. Keynes proved there was a role for macroeconomic policy activism.

6. **Answer d.** Monetarism states that GDP will grow steadily if the money supply grows steadily. Monetarists, like Keynesians, believe that the short run is important and that short-run changes in aggregate demand can affect aggregate output as well as aggregate prices. Monetarism does not believe in the effectiveness of discretionary fiscal policy due to the fact that government perceptions about the economy often lag behind reality. Monetarists believe that the steady growth of the money supply will result in less economic instability and will prove better for smoothing out economic fluctuations than the pursuit of discretionary monetary or fiscal policy.

7. **Answer b.** A monetary policy rule describes the use of a formula by the central bank to determine its actions.

8. **Answer f.** The NAIRU is the same as the natural rate of unemployment, and the NAIRU hypothesis says that once inflation is built into expectations any attempt to keep the unemployment rate below the natural rate will lead to accelerating inflation. Thus, once inflation is embedded in the public's expectations, then that inflation will continue even if the unemployment rate is high.

9. **Answer a.** Activist macroeconomic policy does lend itself to political manipulation, since there is an obvious temptation for politicians to pump up the economy in an election year. One of the appeals of a monetary policy rule for a central bank is that it takes policy discretion away from politicians. Political business cycles increase economic instability in an economy. After 1980, velocity was highly unstable and therefore not predictable in the United States' economy.

10. **Answer g.** New classical macroeconomics returns to the classical model's vertical aggregate supply curve: a shift in aggregate demand, given this vertical aggregate supply curve, will cause the aggregate price level to change, but will have no effect on the level of aggregate output. Answer (b) is a straightforward definition of rational expectations, which is one of the underlying concepts in the new classical macroeconomics. If rational expectations is true (as is assumed in new classical macroeconomics), then individuals and firms will fully anticipate any planned monetary policy: thus, monetary policy is effective only when it is a surprise, and this implies that monetary policy no longer can be used to stabilize the economy.

11. **Answer b.** Real business cycle theory focuses on the rate of growth of factor productivity and how variations in this growth rate can cause business cycle fluctuations. Subsequent analysis suggests that there is a correlation between the rate of growth of factor productivity and business cycles, but the direction of causation between the two variables is difficult to fully determine. Today, this theory is felt to be limited in its explanatory value, despite its important contributions to our understanding of macroeconomics.

12. **Answer f.** Classical macroeconomics did not believe that expansionary monetary policy was effective in fighting recessions, while Keynesian macroeconomics believed it was of limited value. Monetarists do believe that expansionary monetary policy can be helpful in fighting recessions. The modern consensus is that expansionary monetary policy is useful,

except when the economy finds itself in a liquidity trap in which nominal interest rates equal zero and cannot fall any further.

13. **Answer b.** Keynesians upheld the efficacy of fiscal policy as a method for fighting recessions, while monetarists believed that fiscal policy was not effective in fighting recessions. The modern consensus believes that discretionary fiscal policy is useful only under restrictive circumstances. The classical macroeconomists did not believe in discretionary monetary policy.

14. **Answer a.** The broad consensus among macroeconomists today is that expansionary monetary policy can be effective in reducing the extent of a recession.

15. **Answer c.** The classical model holds that prices are flexible, which results in the aggregate supply curve being vertical in both the short run and long run. An increase in the money supply causes an equal proportionate increase in the aggregate price level with no change in the level of aggregate output.

16. **Answer a.** Classical macroeconomists realized that the economy did not grow smoothly over time despite their focus on the long run and their assumption that the aggregate supply curve is vertical. They did believe that increases in the money supply would ultimately only result in an increase in the aggregate price level without any long-run stimulus to aggregate output. Classical macroeconomists did not believe in activist government intervention because they held that the economy would self-correct with time.

17. **Answer b.** Keynes, writing at the time of the Great Depression, argued that the classical model's focus on the aggregate price level was misplaced during times of economic recession that were due to inadequate spending. Keynes thought that economists needed to focus on the impact of shifts in aggregate demand on the aggregate output level and, hence, the level of unemployment in the economy.

18. **Answer b.** "Animal spirits" refers to business confidence and the effect of this confidence level on the business cycle: when businesses are less confident, they spend less, which results in households also spending less as their income falls.

19. **Answer b.** The classical model of the macroeconomy holds that shifts in aggregate demand that are the result of fiscal policy will have no effect on aggregate output but will affect the aggregate price level; the Keynesian model of the macroeconomy holds that shifts in aggregate demand that are the result of fiscal policy can cause short-run changes in the level of aggregate demand. Mary believes that an increase in fiscal spending will act to stimulate the economy (i.e., shift the aggregate demand curve to the right) and help diminish the recessionary economic impact, while George believes such a change in government spending will only lead to less spending by the private sector.

20. **Answer c.** Fiscal policy can affect the aggregate demand curve in the short run: if fiscal policy is expansionary, it will shift the aggregate demand curve to the right, which will lead to a higher level of aggregate output and, therefore, a higher level of employment in the short run. Prior to World War II, it was not clear whether expansionary fiscal policy could increase the level of short-run employment, but with the war it became clear that this was possible.

# The Modern Macroeconomic Consensus

## Summary

This module addresses the main elements of modern macroeconomic consensus before addressing the main areas of dispute among macroeconomic theorists today. The module provides a broad generalization of the macroeconomic models discussed in this section while emphasizing where the models reach agreement as well as where there is still dissent among macroeconomic theorists.

## Module Objectives

**Objective #1.**   There is broad consensus among macroeconomists about how the economy works. Macroeconomists believe that recessions can be fought effectively through expansionary monetary policy.

**Objective #2.**   Among macroeconomists there is broad agreement that monetary policy is an effective policy tool for stabilizing the economy, but that it cannot successfully reduce the unemployment rate below the natural rate of unemployment. In addition, most macroeconomists agree that discretionary fiscal policy should be avoided except in exceptional cases that call for activist government intervention in the form of fiscal policy.

**Objective #3.**   Macroeconomics is a contentious field with much debate as to which policies are appropriate. There is broad agreement among macroeconomists that central banks should be politically independent, but they debate whether or not central banks should pursue formally stated inflation targets, what the level of formal inflation targets should be if the central bank adopts such a policy, and whether or not central banks should intervene to prevent extreme movements in asset prices.

723

## AFTER YOU READ THE MODULE

## Tip

You will want to closely review the description of the modern consensus and be able to explain what this term means and how the modern consensus answers the five questions found in text Table 48-1. The text provides a concise summary of these four approaches in the table. Review the table to reinforce the similarities and distinctions among these different approaches.

# WORKED PROBLEMS

1. Classical economists argued that shifts in the aggregate demand curve in the long run would result in changes in the aggregate price level but would not change the level of real GDP. Keynes emphasized the short-run effects of aggregate demand curve shifts and how these shifts would alter the level of real GDP. Using graphs, illustrate these two approaches and provide an explanation for each of these conclusions. In your explanation, identify two ways in which these two approaches differed from one another.

**STEP 1:** Review the classical macroeconomic model and the Keynesian macroeconomic model and provide a verbal explanation comparing these two different approaches. In your explanation, identify two ways in which these two models differed from one another.

One key difference between the classical macroeconomic model and the Keynesian was that the classical model emphasized the effects of shifts in aggregate demand in the long run on the aggregate price level, while the Keynesian model emphasized the effects of shifts in aggregate demand in the short run on the level of real GDP.

The classical macroeconomic model focused on the long run. Although many classical macroeconomists would have agreed with the Keynesians that the short-run aggregate supply curve was upward sloping, they did not feel that the short run was important. The classical view was that the economy would operate at the long-run level of production, and any shift in the aggregate demand curve would only cause changes in the aggregate price level and not the level of real GDP.

In contrast, the Keynesian view focused on the short run and the impact of aggregate demand shifts if the short-run aggregate supply curve was upward sloping. Such shifts in the aggregate demand curve would cause changes in both the level of aggregate output and the aggregate price level.

A second key difference in these two perspectives was the emphasis that the classical model placed on the role of changes in the money supply in shifting the aggregate demand curve. The classical model, for the most part, ignored other factors that would shift the aggregate demand curve. In contrast, the Keynesian model argued that there were other factors, including changes in "animal spirits" (i.e., business confidence), that could cause shifts in the aggregate demand curve.

**STEP 2:** Draw a diagram of the classical view and provide a verbal explanation for this diagram.

The classical view can be depicted as a vertical *SRAS*, since the classical perspective focused not on short-run fluctuations in aggregate output but rather on long-run attainment of full employment. Thus, if the aggregate demand curve shifted, this would only cause a change in the aggregate price level. The following diagram illustrates this idea.

**STEP 3:** Draw a diagram of the Keynesian view and provide a verbal explanation for this diagram.

The Keynesian view can be depicted as an upward sloping SRAS, since the Keynesian perspective focused on the possibility of short-run fluctuations on aggregate output due to shifts in the aggregate demand curve. Thus, if the aggregate demand curve shifted, this would cause a change in the level of real GDP as well as a change in the aggregate price level. The following diagram illustrates this idea.

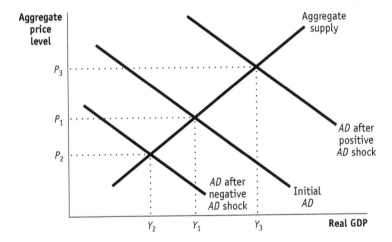

2.   Joe and Susie are just about finished with their study of Introductory Macroeconomics. But, Joe is a bit confused about the idea of macroeconomic consensus. He wants Susie to clarify when monetary policy is helpful in fighting recessions, and whether discretionary fiscal policy should ever be used. He hopes that Susie in her answer will help him separate the viewpoints held by classical macroeconomists, Keynesian economists, monetarists, and the modern consensus.

**STEP 1:** Review the general positions of the four different economic perspectives: represented by the classical macroeconomists, the Keynesian economists, the monetarists, and the modern consensus.

Classical macroeconomists believe that prices are completely flexible, that the *AS* curve is vertical, and that shifts in the *AD* curve result only in changes in the aggregate price level and not changes in the level of real GDP. Their position is that the *AS* curve determines the level of real GDP and that the *AD* curve determines the aggregate price level. Classical macroeconomists see no role for discretionary monetary or fiscal policy. Their perspective emphasizes the long run.

Keynesian economists hold that prices are sticky in the short run, that the *SRAS* curve is upward sloping, and that the *LRAS* curve is vertical and equal to the full employment level of real GDP. Keynesians believe that shifts in the *AD* curve can change both the level of real GDP and the aggregate price level. They believe there is a role for discretionary monetary and fiscal policy. Their perspective emphasizes the short run.

Monetarists believe that prices are sticky in the short run, that the *SRAS* curve is upward sloping, and that real GDP will grow steadily if the money supply grows steadily. Monetarists see no role for discretionary monetary or fiscal policy. Their perspective emphasizes the short run.

The modern consensus holds that expansionary monetary and fiscal policy can be helpful in fighting recessions, although there may be some recessions where the monetary policy is ineffective. The modern consensus is that the level of real GDP in the long run is determined by the full employment level of output. Proponents of this perspective have come to no firm conclusion with regard to the use of discretionary monetary policy, although it is possible under certain circumstances that discretionary fiscal policy might be helpful.

**STEP 2:** Consider the use and efficacy of monetary policy as a way to fight recessions.

Monetary policy has no impact on real GDP and unemployment according to Classical macroeconomists. If you are unhappy with the performance of the macroeconomy, this school of thought advocates being patient since the aggregate economy will return to full employment on its own accord.

Keynesians argue that monetary policy may be helpful in fighting recessions (particularly if the recession is not due to a financial crisis) since monetary policy can stimulate aggregate demand. As the *AD* curve shifts to the right with expansionary monetary policy, this shift will lead to a higher level of real GDP and an increase in employment.

Monetarists hold that monetary policy is important primarily in its role of economic management: when the money supply is allowed to grow steadily, it will lead to steady growth of real GDP and, hence, employment.

The modern consensus is that monetary policy can be used to shift the *AD* curve and to reduce economic instability.

**STEP 3:** Consider the use and efficacy of discretionary fiscal policy.

Classical macroeconomists see no role for discretionary fiscal policy since the economy naturally returns to the full employment level of real GDP in the long run. Shifts in *AD* curve due to discretionary fiscal policy will only cause price instability from the classical macroeconomist viewpoint.

Keynesian economists believe that discretionary fiscal policy can help an economy recover from a recession more swiftly than a policy of simply waiting for the economy to self-correct. In addition, if the recession is one due to a financial crisis, then discretionary fiscal policy may need to play a prominent role in helping the economy recover.

Monetarists are in general wary of discretionary fiscal policy since they hold that expansionary fiscal policy with a fixed money supply will lead to crowding out. Monetarists are very heavily invested in managing the macroeconomy through a monetary policy rule.

The modern consensus is that discretionary fiscal policy has the potential to shift the *AD* curve and therefore change the level of real GDP and the aggregate price level in the short run.

## Problems and Exercises

1.  Why is it essential that central banks be politically independent?

2.  Why are the time lags involved in implementing discretionary fiscal policy of importance? In your answer be sure to present the monetarist view of these lags.

3.  Some economists worry about the political business cycle and the use of activist macroeconomic policy for political gain. Why would economists worry about the use of macroeconomic policy for political gain?

# BEFORE YOU TAKE THE TEST

## Module Review Questions

1. Which of the following statements is true for the modern consensus in macroeconomics?
   I. Prices are flexible in the long run but likely to be sticky in the short run.
   II. Inadequate spending can cause short-run decreases in the aggregate output level.
   III. In the long run the macroeconomy will produce at the full employment level of output.
   a. Statements I, II, and III are all true.
   b. Statements I and II are both true.
   c. Statements II and III are both true.
   d. Statements I and III are both true.

2. Keynes argued that
   a. the Depression could be eliminated with expansionary monetary policy since this would reduce the interest rate, and this reduction would result in higher levels of investment and consumer spending.
   b. ending the Depression required a focus on spending and the need for government to ensure that the level of spending was adequate.
   c. the Depression would end with the passage of time: we just all need to be patient and wait for the economy to move back to long-run equilibrium.
   d. during the Depression the liquidity trap was luckily not an issue and, therefore, monetary and fiscal policies would both work to end the Depression.

3. Discretionary fiscal policy
   a. due to implementation lags often end up feeding a boom rather than fighting a recession.
   b. refers to the use of government spending and taxing policies used to smooth out the economy's ups and downs.
   c. without expansionary monetary policy will result in crowding out that limits the effect of the fiscal expansion, according to Friedman.
   d. Answers (a), (b), and (c) are all correct.
   e. Answers (a) and (b) are both correct.
   f. Answers (b) and (c) are both correct.

4. The president's economic advisors advocate that the president pursue economic policies that will result in an unemployment level of 4%. However, the NAIRU for this economy is estimated to be 5.5%. The president's implementation of these policies will
   a. lead to deflation.
   b. lead to inflation.
   c. lead to higher levels of unemployment than the NAIRU.
   d. move the economy to a higher long-run potential output level.

5. Monetary policy can
   a. change the level of aggregate output in the short run according to macroeconomists who support the classical model.
   b. have no impact on unemployment unless the monetary policy is unexpected according to models that assume rational expectations.
   c. lower the nominal interest rate even when there is a liquidity trap.
   d. Answers (a), (b), and (c) are all correct.
   e. Answers (a) and (b) are both correct.
   f. Answers (a) and (c) are both correct.

## ■ ANSWER KEY

## Answers to Problems and Exercises

1. Central banks, through monetary policy, exert strong influences on the macroeconomy. When a country's central bank is not politically independent, policymakers can adopt inflationary monetary policies that wreak economic havoc. Typically, this havoc is the result of excessive growth of the money supply. When a central bank is politically independent, it can maintain more appropriate money supply growth rates, thereby avoiding high levels of inflation and the resultant economic problems this inflation can cause.

2. Discretionary fiscal policy requires that the government first identify a macroeconomic problem and then pass the legislation to address this problem using discretionary fiscal policy. But it takes time for the government to recognize that there is a macroeconomic problem and then it takes more time for the government to write and pass legislation; meanwhile, the aggregate economy is dynamic and changing with this passage of time. Often discretionary fiscal policy is implemented after the economy has moved to a different part of the business cycle: the discretionary fiscal policy passed to combat recessionary concerns may actually be implemented during the boom part of the economic business cycle. Monetarists worry that these efforts by policy makers to smooth out the business cycle may actually make things worse due to the timing effects that occur because of implementation lags.

3. The political business cycle refers to the deliberate manipulation of the macroeconomy with the intent of reaching particular political outcomes. For example, the incumbent party in government may enact economic policies designed foremost to improve their chances at reelection: they attempt to manipulate macroeconomic policy to ensure that the economy is performing well at the time of the election. This manipulation for political gain may result in greater macroeconomic fluctuations than are optimal for the economy or for the individuals living and working in this economy.

## Answers to Module Review Questions

1. **Answer a.** All three of these statements are part of the modern macroeconomic consensus. The text discusses the consensus in detail.

2. **Answer b.** Keynes refuted the classical approach of relying upon the economy to move to long-run equilibrium: he reminded all that "in the long run we are all dead" and that, in the case of the Great Depression, it would be a very long time until the economy self-corrected and, in the interim, many people would be out of work and there would be substantial loss of production. Keynes instead argued for expansionary fiscal policy stimulus from the government; if the government could raise the level of spending to offset the decrease in spending by households and firms, then this would allow the economy to restore itself more quickly to full employment. During the Depression the liquidity trap was an issue: interest rates were so low that the central bank could not stimulate the economy through reductions in the nominal interest rate.

3. **Answer d.** Government perceptions about the state of the economy often lag behind reality, which results in timing issues with regard to discretionary fiscal policy; often the policy that is implemented is designed to address recession but it is not enacted and does not begin to affect the macroeconomy until after the recession has ended and the economy has moved toward an economic boom. Discretionary fiscal policy is designed to smooth out business cycle fluctuations but is less effective when not accompanied with expansionary monetary policy, since the increased spending by the government may crowd out spending by private firms and by households.

4. **Answer b.** If the NAIRU is 5.5% unemployment, then the attempt to lower the unemployment level below this amount will ultimately result in the raising of inflationary expectations: any attempt to keep the unemployment rate below the natural rate will lead to an ever-rising inflation rate.

5. **Answer b.** Statement (a) is false since the classical model holds that the aggregate supply curve is vertical: in the short run and the long run, the level of aggregate output is assumed to be constant. Statement (c) is false since the nominal interest rate cannot be lowered once the economy is in the liquidity trap with the nominal interest rate at the zero bound. Statement (b) is correct. The rational expectations assumption holds that the public takes into account all available information about monetary and fiscal policy: the only way that monetary policy can change unemployment is for that monetary policy to not be anticipated by the public.